W0374432

Context

Hessen

Vokabel Trainer

Cornelsen

Vokabeltrainer-App

Verfügbar für: iOS, Android und Windows Phone

Dieses Buch gibt es auch auf
www.scook.de

Es kann dort nach Bestätigung der Allgemeinen Geschäftsbedingungen genutzt werden.

Buchcode: g3bhz-h2et5

Cornelsen

Context · Ausgabe Hessen

Im Auftrag des Verlages herausgegeben von
Dr. Annette Leithner-Brauns, Dresden; Ingrid Becker-Ross, Krefeld; Prof. Hellmut Schwarz, Mannheim

Erarbeitet von
Irene Bartscherer, Bonn; Ingrid Becker-Ross, Krefeld; Friederike von Bremen, Hannover; Ulrike Elsäßer, Stuttgart; Gerit Fredrich, Meiningen; Prof. Dr. Britta Freitag-Hild, Potsdam; Veronika Gastpar, Mainburg; Dr. Peter Hohwiller, Landau; Markus Hözel, Köln; Ulrich Imig, Wildeshausen; Elke Jentsch, Reichenbach im Vogtland; Manuela Kistner, Gernsheim am Rhein; Bernd Koch, Marburg; Sylvia Loh, Esslingen; Dr. Paul Maloney, Hildesheim; Markus Marzinzik, Landau; Claudia Meixner, Erlangen; Neil Porter, Tel Aviv; Birgit Rietgraf, Backnang; Angela Ringel-Eichinger, Bietigheim-Bissingen; Victoria Schoeneberg, Köln; Dr. Andreas Sedlatschek, Esslingen; Claudia Spieler, Gießen; Marcel Sprunkel, Köln; Michael Thürwächter, Heidelberg; Inga Wittbrodt, Sankt Augustin

unter beratender Mitwirkung von
Martina Baasner, Berlin; Dr. Sabine Buchholz, Hürth; Jochen Lüders, München; Gunthild Porteous-Schwier, Moers; Sieglinde Spranger, Chemnitz

in Zusammenarbeit mit der Englischredaktion
Elke Lehmann *(Projektleitung)*; Dr. Marion Kiffe, Laura Morgenthal, Dr. Georg-Christian v. Raumer, Ingrid-Maria Sauer, Anna Schwarz, Hartmut Tschepe, Ralph Williams sowie Katrin Gütermann, Berlin, und Neil Porter, Tel Aviv

Layoutkonzept
zweiband.media, Berlin

Layout und technische Umsetzung
designcollective, Berlin

Umschlaggestaltung
axeptDESIGN, Berlin; Michaela Müller für agentur corngreen, Leipzig

Weitere Bestandteile des Lehrwerks

- E-Book zum Schülerbuch
- Workbook (978-3-06-031667-0)
- ABI to go · VOCABI (978-3-06-033490-2)
- ABI to go · SKILLS (978-3-06-033858-0)
- Vokabeltrainer-App
- Audio-CDs (+ MP3) (978-3-06-033487-2)
- Video-DVD (978-3-06-033488-9)
- Lehrerfassung des Schülerbuchs (978-3-06-031451-5)
- Handreichungen für den Unterricht (978-3-06-031487-4)
- Digitaler Unterrichtsmanager
- Vorschläge zur Leistungsmessung (978-3-06-033590-9)
- More Speaking Practice (Rollen- und Bildkarten) (978-3-06-031504-8)

Website zum Lehrwerk: **www.cornelsen.de/context**

Die Webseiten Dritter, deren Internetadressen in diesem Lehrwerk angegeben sind, wurden vor Drucklegung sorgfältig geprüft. Der Verlag übernimmt keine Gewähr für die Aktualität und den Inhalt dieser Seiten oder solcher, die mit ihnen verlinkt sind.

Alle Drucke dieser Auflage sind inhaltlich unverändert und können im Unterricht nebeneinander verwendet werden.

© 2016 Cornelsen Schulverlage GmbH, Berlin

Das Werk und seine Teile sind urheberrechtlich geschützt. Jede Nutzung in anderen als den gesetzlich zugelassenen Fällen bedarf der vorherigen schriftlichen Einwilligung des Verlages.
Hinweis zu den §§ 46, 52 a UrhG: Weder das Werk noch seine Teile dürfen ohne eine solche Einwilligung eingescannt und in ein Netzwerk eingestellt oder sonst öffentlich zugänglich gemacht werden.
Dies gilt auch für Intranets von Schulen und sonstigen Bildungseinrichtungen.

Druck: Mohn Media Mohndruck, Gütersloh

1. Auflage, 1. Druck 2016
broschiert
ISBN 978-3-06-031449-2

1. Auflage, 1. Druck 2016
gebunden
ISBN 978-3-06-031450-8

PEFC
PEFC/04-31-1033

PEFC zertifiziert
Dieses Produkt stammt aus nachhaltig bewirtschafteten Wäldern und kontrollierten Quellen.

www.pefc.de

Contents

Contents

Contents

Reference Section

Contents

Abbreviations and labels used in *Context*

adj	adjective
adv	adverb
AE/BE	American English / British English
ca. *(Latin)*	circa = about, approximately
cf.	confer (compare), see
derog	derogatory *(abfällig, geringschätzig)*
e.g. *(Latin)*	exempli gratia = for example
esp.	especially
et al. *(Latin)*	et alii = and other people/things
etc. *(Latin)*	et cetera = and so on
f./ff.	and the following page(s)/line(s)
fml/infml	formal/informal English
i.e. *(Latin)*	id est = that is, in other words
jdm./jdn.	jemandem/jemanden
l./ll.	line/lines
n	noun
pt(s)	point(s)
p./pp.	page/pages
pl	plural
sb./sth.	somebody/something
sing	singular
sl	slang
usu.	usually
v	verb
vs. *(Latin)*	versus *(gegen, im Gegensatz zu)*

CC	Communicating across Cultures
EE	Everyday English
EP	Exam Practice
LP	Language Practice
SF	Skills File
PREVIEW	refers to the advance organizer (chapter preview) in the Lead-in of each chapter.
LANGUAGE HELP	gives you ideas, words and phrases to get started on tasks.
TROUBLE SPOT	points out language difficulties and common mistakes.
CHALLENGE	marks a more difficult task.
SUPPORT	refers you to the Support Pages (pp. 266–287) where you can find more help to do the assignment.
YOU CHOOSE	lets you decide which of the two given assignments you would like to do.
BASIC	marks a task that tests language skills you should already be familiar with.
*metaphor	indicates that a word or expression (here: *metaphor*) is explained in the Glossary (pp. 393–409).
► SF 21	directs you to the Skills File (here: Skill 21).
► LP 7	directs you to the Language Practice section (here: Language task 7).
CD2 04	indicates that the sound file can be found on the accompanying audio CD (here: CD2, track 4).
DVD	indicates that the film or video clip can be found on the accompanying video DVD.
Webcode	can be entered at www.cornelsen.de/webcodes to connect you to a website with additional material or support.

About the photograph on the cover of this book

The cover photo, taken in April 2013 near the junction of St Mary Axe and Leadenhall Street in London, shows a number of well-known buildings in the City of London's 'Tower Cluster' zone:

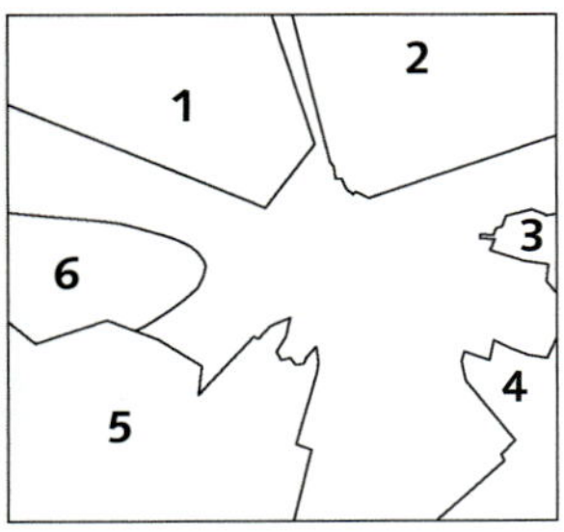

1 *St Helen's*, 1 Undershaft, Gollins Melvin Ward Partnership 1969, 28 storeys

2 *The Leadenhall Building (the Cheesegrater)*, 122 Leadenhall Street, Rogers Steark Harbour + Partners 2013, 48 storeys

3 *Lloyd's building*, 1 Lime Street, Richard Rogers 1986, 14 storeys

4 *Willis Building*, 51 Lime Street, Foster + Partners 2007, 26 storeys

5 *St Andrew Undershaft*, 1532

6 *30 St Mary Axe (the Gherkin)*, Foster + Partners 2003, 41 storeys

1 The USA – Still the Promised Land?

A

B

C

Download a list of chapter vocab here: **Webcode** context-18

Download a detailed timeline as well as further information and tasks based on the pictures: **Webcode** context-19

1 GROUP PUZZLE **The American experience**

a Form six groups. Give each group a letter A–F.
In your group, talk about the picture that matches your letter:
What situation does it show? What do you know about this episode in US history? Share your knowledge.

b Use the webcode to access further information on the story behind your picture. Share the new information in your group.

c Form new groups of at least six members each; all six letters must be represented in each group. Tell each other about your pictures. Discuss what makes them part of the American experience.

Timeline of American history

1607 – 1620 – 1775–1783 – 4 July 1776 – 1789 – 1803 – 1861–1865 – 1890

1989–1991
2001
2006
2008
1955
1954
1945

D

E

F

1941
1929

2 Putting yourself in the picture

a Choose one person from any of the six pictures. Write an *interior monologue for your person: How (or why) did you get into your present situation? How do you imagine your future?

b Form groups of 4–5. Read your monologues to each other. The listeners try to guess which person you have chosen.

c Discuss the different motives of the people you have talked about, and how they are connected with the idea of America as 'the Promised Land'.

TROUBLE SPOT

The term 'America' is often used to refer to the USA (rather than the entire American continent). Strictly speaking this is not correct. If you do use the term, make sure the meaning is made clear by the context.

1919
1917

PREVIEW

In this chapter you will examine the image of the USA at home and abroad and learn more about some of the challenges facing the United States today.

Main topics

A country like no other

CD2 04

Listen to an audio version of the text on the CD or download it here:
Webcode context-21

A nation founded on principle

Most nations are held together by a common history, language and culture. The USA is different: it is a nation united solely by the shared values of equality, democracy, and individual freedom. The Founding Fathers, inspired by the ideas of the Enlightenment, created a self-governing republic without social barriers. The crowned heads of Europe expected the young nation to collapse in chaos; instead, it grew and prospered, ultimately rising to the status of a world power.

'Remember, gentlemen, we aren't here just to draft a constitution. We're here to draft the best damned constitution in the world.'

Land of opportunity

While the promise of freedom from religious and political persecution played and continues to play a major role in attracting immigrants to America's shores, it became clearer as the United States expanded west-ward that the continent also held vast stores of natural resources. In the first half of the 19th century, it was mainly the availability of cheap farmland that drew millions to try their luck in the New World; later, huge supplies of coal and iron ore powered the growth of industry, attracting further waves of immigration. The economic vitality of the young nation gave rise to the material side of the American dream, expressed in slogans like 'from rags to riches' or 'the sky's the limit'. In a country so rich in opportunity, success was believed to lie in the hands of the individual. A culture arose that honoured personal material success; as long as upward mobility guaranteed equality of opportunity for all, the majority felt that the self-made millionaire had a right to his wealth.

The American century – and beyond

The 20th century saw the United States rise to a position of economic and military leadership in the world. America viewed itself as a beacon of democracy, which it strove to export to other countries. With the collapse of the Soviet Union and the end of the Cold War (1989), the USA was seemingly the only superpower left standing. Yet since the turn of the century, the USA has increasingly been forced to cope with doubts and difficulties. The attacks of 11 September 2001 left Americans with a deep-seated feeling of insecurity. The official response – two undeclared wars and an unprecedented expansion of surveillance operations – cost the USA sympathy abroad and contributed to the heavy debt burden. Economic turmoil, the massive loss of jobs in the manufacturing sector, a housing crisis that cost millions their home, and a widening gap between rich and poor that undermines the equality of opportunity – all of these factors cause Americans today to wonder if the American dream still holds true for their generation. It remains to be seen if this extraordinary nation, which has in the past so often demonstrated its ability to reinvent itself, will once more rise to the challenges of a new era.

TROUBLE SPOT

the USA (l. 32) + *singular verb*
The USA is/was/has …

► SF 2: Learning new words

1 Words in use

Replace the underlined words with highlighted expressions from the text:

1 In the 20th century the United States became the most powerful country in the world.
2 Americans believe in giving everyone the same chance in life.
3 We don't know yet if the USA will remain the leading world power.
4 The availability of cheap land was an important factor attracting Europe's rural poor to America's shores.
5 The growing difference between rich and poor is without parallel.

► LP 19: Collocations

2 Collocations with prepositions

a Complete the underlined collocations with the correct prepositions. If you need help, look at the text again:

1 By 1900, the USA had risen … the status of a major industrial country.
2 The United States of America became known as the land of promise, a country rich … opportunity.
3 Hundreds of different ethnic groups have all contributed … American culture.
4 Stories of successful immigrants gave rise … the saying that in America the streets were paved with gold.
5 For many European Jews, freedom … persecution made the USA the new Promised Land.
6 The American dream didn't hold true … everyone; African Americans and Native Americans, for example, were long excluded.

b Find four more collocations with prepositions in the text and write a quiz for your partner. Then do the quiz your partner gives you.

3 Connotation

Most people react positively to the word *freedom* and negatively to *slavery*. This emotional aspect of language is called *connotation.

a Sort the words in the list on the right into two groups (positive/negative connotation). Compare results with your partner.

b Together, find three more words from the text for each of the two groups.

values • persecution • doubts • prosper • opportunity • insecurity • undermine • equality

4 General terms ('Oberbegriffe')

a Find general terms to describe each of the five (groups of) examples. Choose the terms from the highlighted expressions in the text.

1 George Washington and Benjamin Franklin
→ **general term:** *the Founding Fathers*
2 coal, oil, water, farmland → **general term:** …
3 Free public schools are available to everyone. → …
4 A factory worker rises to become the director of a large firm. → …
5 Only landowners are allowed to vote. → …

b Choose three more general terms from the highlighted words in the text. Write an example illustrating each of them. Swap examples with a partner and find the correct terms from the text.

5 Your view

The USA – still 'a beacon of democracy' (ll. 30–31) for the rest of the world? State your opinion in a short text (ca. 200 words).

► LP 14: Linking words and phrases

The American dream

A1 ¡Viva América! *Liz Balmaseda*

Pulitzer Prize-winning journalist Liz Balmaseda

FACT FILE

Pulitzer Prize
The Pulitzer Prizes were established in 1917 by the US publisher Joseph Pulitzer. They are awarded annually in the fields of journalism, literature and musical composition.

Liz Balmaseda (born 1959) is a Cuban-American journalist who has worked for various Miami newspapers as well as for Newsweek and NBC News. She won Pulitzer Prizes for journalism in 1993 and 2001. Balmaseda contributed this text to an online collection of immigrant stories.

I grew up in America's most Cuban city – Hialeah, Florida. The municipality's tagline, 'The City of Progress', far more often was quoted in Spanish. The cheering section at local football games brought conga drums. The Catholic saint statues that often adorned front lawns concealed Afro-Cuban alter egos. And the 'fries' at fast-food drive-thru joints were made of yuca.

But the city was fiercely American, just as my parents were fiercely American. Having fled Cuba shortly after its Communist regime took hold of the island, they brought me to Florida when I was 10 months old and raised me to cherish the American dream. Cuba lingered only in the flavor notes of my mother's cooking, the rhythms on our stereo, and the bottomless sense of yearning for loved ones stranded on the island. The rest of it was all-American: The stray threads I pulled off my mother's clothes when she returned each night after a grueling day at her clothing factory job. The snazzy ties my dad wore to work as a car salesman. His religious attention to Election Day, when he'd leap out of bed to cast his vote. The pride I sensed in my parents after I brought home the miniature trophy that declared me the winner of the first-grade spelling bee, in the year I learned to speak English.

I could say it was by magic that a loving and supportive community emerged around our family. But that village force of good neighbors, church friends, American-born school teachers who took the initiative to visit our home and offer a word of praise and encouragement – that doesn't happen by magic. It happens in response to a life embraced, a life that is often turbulent, painful and imperfect. This is what I learned from my mother, may she rest in peace. This is what I continue to learn from my father. At 84, he is stricken with Parkinson's. Last Election Day, I sat with him at the polling place and, at his direction, filled out the ballot. I watched as he slipped the ballot into the box and gave the poll worker a smile of great accomplishment. It's an image I'll carry with me always.

My Cuba is now buried in a Miami cemetery. But my America resounds in all its glory, like a hundred conga drums playing beneath Friday night lights in Hialeah.

From: *The Huffington Post*, 19 July 2013

Hialeah City Hall

1 **municipality** [mjuːˌnɪsɪˈpæləti] town
tagline motto, slogan
3 **conga drum** kind of African drum
4 **adorn sth.** *etwas schmücken*
conceal sth. hide sth.
alter ego [ˌælter‿ˈiːgəʊ] alternate identity
5 **joint** *(infml)* small restaurant
yuca *(Spanish) Cassava (Wurzel der Maniokpflanze)*
6 **fiercely** passionately, intensely
8 **cherish sth.** love sth.
9 **linger** [ˈlɪŋgə] remain
10 **yearning** [ˈjɜːnɪŋ] *(fml)* feeling of wanting sth. badly
11 **stray threads** *einzelne Fäden*
12 **grueling** *(AE) = (BE)* **gruelling** very hard
13 **snazzy** *(infml)* showy
religious (here) taking sth. very seriously
14 **leap** *(v)* jump
16 **spelling bee** spelling contest
17 **supportive** offering support
emerge come into existence
21 **embrace sb.** take sb. into your arms
23 **be stricken with sth.** *an etwas erkrankt sein*
24 **polling place** place where voters can cast their vote in an election
25 **accomplishment** [əˈkʌmplɪʃmənt] feeling of having achieved sth.
27 **resound** [rɪˈzaʊnd] *ertönen*

COMPREHENSION

1 First reactions
Talk about your reactions to the text. Why do you think Balmaseda chose to submit her family's story to the immigrants website?

ANALYSIS

2 From Havana to Hialeah
Balmaseda uses many *images to describe life in Hialeah. Find some examples and explain why they are important to her.

LANGUAGE AWARENESS

3 Words that convey emotion

a Collect words from the text that express the author's (or someone else's) feelings (e.g., 'fiercely', l. 6). Examine how they influence the effect of the text.

b The following text sounds bland because it lacks words that convey feelings. Rewrite it to give it more emotional impact. ▶ LANGUAGE HELP
My father thought that his life would change for the worse if Castro came to power in Cuba. He applied to the US Embassy in Havana for an immigration permit. He waited three months. Then a letter arrived saying we could leave for the USA. My parents packed their belongings and said goodbye to their friends and relatives in Cuba. On March 11th, 1958, on board a small passenger ship bound for Miami, they had their first glimpse of the US mainland.
SUPPORT ▶ p. 266

LANGUAGE HELP
- anxious
- be ~ to do sth.
- excited
- fear *(n, v)*
- hope *(n, v)*
- nervous
- overjoyed
- relieved
- sad
- tearful
- thrilled
- with a feeling of ~
- with trembling hands

BEYOND THE TEXT

4 GROUP INTERVIEW One family's American dream

a Form groups of four. One of you is Liz Balmaseda, another is her father, and the third member is her mother. The fourth member of the group is a journalist who is interviewing the family on the subject 'Our American dream'. Prepare your roles using the role cards that your teacher will give you. Then carry out the interview.

b Summarize the aspects of the American dream that were named in your group and present them to the rest of the class.

▶ SF 26: Taking part in an interview

A2 Reinventing the American dream *June Sochen*

- Speculate on the title of the following text. Why might the author, a former professor of history, think that the American dream needs reinventing?

Certain parts of the text have been left out (cf. gap 1, etc.) – don't worry about them on your first reading.

Given the uncertain economic conditions, a contentious presidential campaign and the high cost of a college education, it is difficult to know how the traditional definition of the Dream can be applied for the younger generation. [1] Answering the question looking backward is easier than looking forward.

For the generation that fought to free the American colonies from Great Britain, it meant freedom of religion and speech and the liberty to pursue your own path. Contrary to the experience of most people across the Atlantic in the 1700s, Americans looked to a bright future. Children benefited from public school education, hardworking parents, and seemingly endless land to be purchased and cultivated.

1 **contentious** full of conflict
8 **benefit** ['benɪfɪt] *(v) profitieren*
9 **purchase sth.** ['pɜːtʃəs] *(fml)* buy sth.

Part A

If things were not favorable for you in Boston, you could pack your belongings, hitch your wagon, and take your family to the West. [...]

The popular press and penny novels heralded the 'rags to riches' stories of ordinary Americans. This country could fulfill both the ideals and the material aspirations of all newcomers, or so the rhetoric promised. For much of the 19th Century, upward mobility became a constant theme in all political pronouncements, sermons, and business proposals. If you worked hard, you could achieve the American Dream of more education than your parents, greater economic success than your parents, and a larger home than your parents.

There were enough measurable examples of success to make most Americans believe that the American Dream was attainable for them. [2] Though the Civil War surely set back the hopes and plans of a generation, the post-war generation looked forward to a brighter future.

The 20th Century, though promising much of the same, had more obstacles in its path. Two world wars, the worst depression in American history, the Cold War, Korea and Vietnam all slowed down the belief, and the actuality, of inevitable progress toward everyone's fulfillment of the American Dream. Indeed, the seeming certainty that each generation would do better than the last one, has been dashed in recent years.

The 21st Century started with a new threat: September 11, 2001 and the attack on the World Trade Center. [3] The dot.com bubble burst early in the century followed by the Great Recession of 2007; though the recession is formally over, it has left us five years later with high unemployment and great uncertainty about the future.

The divide between the generations is dramatic. [4] Recent college graduates find their career hopes unrealized in the current job market. Wages have stagnated in the last 30 years with manufacturing and service industries going overseas.

Only a small segment of the economy – the banks and insurance companies, for example – seem[s] to be thriving.

[5] This country remains a desirable destination for immigrants from all over the world. Just as new immigrants believe in the American Dream, most Americans, according to the polls, also appreciate the multiple benefits offered by this country and have no desire to live elsewhere. The current economic troubles are seen as challenges to overcome, not as insuperable obstacles. Home ownership remains a goal as does job security.

Despite our troubles, the original meaning of the Dream, the ideological portion, remains vibrant while the material promises are harder to obtain. The freedoms enjoyed in this country cannot be taken for granted as there are still many places on the globe where repression describes daily life for many people. Though surely the material aspect of the Dream continues to be a goal – a home [...], a yearly vacation, and a job that pays all the bills – preserving the ideals of the American Dream is more important than ever before.

From: *Naples Daily News*, 8 August 2012

10 **favorable** *(AE)* = *(BE)* **favourable** *günstig*
11 **hitch your wagon** (here) attach your wagon to horses
12 **herald sth.** ['herəld] *(v, fml)* call attention to sth.
14 **rhetoric** ['retərɪk] *(fml)* (here) speech-making
15 **pronouncement** public statement
16 **proposal** plan, idea
20 **attainable** within reach
21 **set sth. back** *etwas zurückwerfen*
23 **obstacle** ['ɒbstəkl] sth. that is in the way
26 **inevitable** [ɪn'evitəbl] *unvermeidlich*
28 **dash sth.** destroy sth.
30 **dot.com bubble** period from ca. 1997–2000, when the value of internet start-ups rose sharply and then collapsed
33 **divide** *(n)* gap
38 **desirable** [dɪ'zaɪərəbl] attractive
40 **appreciate sth.** [ə'pri:ʃieɪt] know the value of sth.
benefit *(n)* advantage
42 **insuperable** [ɪn'su:pərəbl] *(fml)* *unüberwindlich*
45 **vibrant** ['vaɪbrənt] alive
46 **take sth. for granted** *etwas als selbstverständlich ansehen*
47 **repression** *Unterdrückung*

COMPREHENSION

1 Filling in the gaps

► SF 10: Working with closed test formats

a Five sentences have been removed from the text; the gaps are marked and numbered. Choose the right sentence for each gap from sentences A–G below (there are two sentences that don't belong to the text):

A Workers over 50 who lost their jobs may never recover the earnings and positions they once had.

B But the American Dream continues to live.
C In particular, African Americans and many women felt excluded from the Dream.
D There was little government on any level to help or hinder individual accomplishment.
E Americans have always believed in the power of the individual to shape his or her own life.
F Indeed, all future generations may have to reinterpret the Dream.
G International terrorism became a new concern.

b Compare solutions with your partner and discuss points where you differ.

2 The main idea

Sum up the main reasons Sochen gives why the American dream needs to be reinvented. Compare her reasons with the ideas your class had before reading the text.

ANALYSIS

3 Exploring the American dream

a Form small groups. Each group will need a blank poster. Your task is to present the information on the American dream contained in the text in the form of a clearly structured mind map. Follow these steps:
1 Divide the subtopics from the list on the right among the members of your group. Each member makes notes on their subtopic.
2 Pool your results and create a mind map that presents your information in a clearly structured form.

b Display your posters on the walls of your classroom. Compare the minc maps created by your classmates and discuss their pros and cons.

Find a mindmapping tool here:
Webcode context-53

- *political ideals*
- *economic opportunity*
- *upward mobility*
- *threats to the dream*
- *state of the dream today*

BEYOND THE TEXT

4 YOU CHOOSE **Comparing interpretations**

a Reread **A1** (¡Viva América!) in the light of what you have learned about the American dream. Then write a comment of ca. 200 words on the topic: 'The Balmasedas – an American dream come true'.

OR

b Write a comment relating June Sochen's views on the American dream (**A2**) to the cartoon below.

▶ SF 34: Argumentative writing
▶ SF 13: Analysing cartoons
▶ SF 18: Analysing non-fiction

CULTURE SPOT

Flag *(1954)*

is a painting by the American artist Jasper Johns (born 1930). It is on display at the Museum of Modern Art in Manhattan, New York City.

► CC 1: Cultural awareness

1 Describe your reaction to the work of art above. Would you react the same way to a painting of the German flag in a German art museum? Explain.

CD2 05

2 Listen to a recording of two US teenagers talking about the picture. How do their views influence your reaction to the painting?

3 The photo on the right shows a small section of the painting in detail. Describe what you can recognize in the painting, and discuss why you think the artist chose this technique.

4 Jasper Johns's 'Flag': a statement on the American dream? Discuss.

For another work of art based on the Stars and Stripes, see p. 211.

Dealing with diversity

FACT FILE

Ethnic neighbourhoods

Because of its history, the USA is a racially and ethnically diverse nation. With immigrants pouring in from all over the world, it was only natural that newcomers to America's shores flocked to neighbourhoods where they could speak their own language and live their culture. They often had networks of friends and relatives from the Old World who helped them find work and a place to live. By 1900, Polish, Irish, Italian, German, Jewish and Asian quarters had arisen in virtually every city in the US.

Although **ghetto** is technically just another word for 'ethnic neighbourhood', in the USA it is used mainly for the – usually undesirable – quarters of a city in which African Americans formerly were forced to live. Black families wishing to move to a better part of town found that no landlord would rent them an apartment and no bank would give them credit to buy a house. White homeowners feared that the appearance of black faces in their street would send property values into a downward spiral. It was only after the Civil Rights Act of 1968 prohibited discrimination in housing that the situation of African American families slowly began to improve.

List the 'push and pull factors' that lead to the creation of ethnic neighbourhoods. Do they exist in Germany too?

B1 The new neighbours *Bruce Norris*

September 1959. *Karl comes to visit his neighbours Russ and Bev, who have just sold their inner-city house (where the scene takes place) and bought a new one in the suburbs. Jim is a young clergyman who has come to talk to Russ. Ted Driscoll is the real estate agent who has sold the house for Russ and his wife. Betsy is Karl's wife.*

- While you are reading the dialogue, form a mental image of the situation, i.e. the characters and what they may be doing while they are speaking.

Stuart McQuarrie (Russ) and Sophie Thompson (Bev) in a performance of Clybourne Park

KARL [...] I take it, Russ, you're aware that the Community Association meets the first Tuesday of each month? And as I'm sure you know, Don Skinner is part of the steering committee. And somehow it came to Don's attention at this late juncture that Ted Driscoll had found a buyer for this house and I have to say it *did* come as something of a shock when Don told us what sort of people they were.

RUSS What sort of people are they?

(Beat. Karl stares at Russ.)

KARL Well. *(Chuckles.)* Uhh ... Huh. I suppose I'm forced to consider the possibility that you actually don't *know.*

RUSS Don't know *what*?

KARL Well, I mean. That they're colored.

RUSS Who are?

KARL The family. It's a colored family.

(Pause.)

So: I contacted the family –

JIM Wait wait wait.

KARL *(To Russ.)*

You're saying Ted never bothered to tell you?

RUSS We, uhh ... sort of gave Ted free rein on the –

JIM I don't think you're right on this one, Karl.

KARL Oh, but I am. Oh, I've spoken with the family.

RUSS Bev?

JIM On the *telephone*?

real estate agent *Immobilienmakler/in*
1 **I take it** *(infml)* I assume
6 **steering committee** [kə'mɪti] *Steuerungskomitee*
9 **juncture** ['dʒʌŋktʃə] *(fml)* moment in time
16 **beat** *(n)* brief pause
17 **chuckle** laugh briefly and quietly
25 **colored** *(AE)* = *(BE)* **coloured** *(used for black people until the late 1950s, now an old-fashioned or offensive word)*
32 **bother to do sth.** ['bɒðə] think it necessary to do sth.
33 **give sb. free rein (on sth.)** [reɪn] *jdm. freie Hand geben (in einer Sache)*

45 **c'mere** = come here
65 **Negro** *(used for black people up until 1966, now an old-fashioned or offensive word)*
► CC 6: Talking about sensitive issues (Fact File: Political correctness)
69 **common courtesy** ['kɜ:təsi] standard politeness
70 **interchangeable** *austauschbar*
73 **conduct one's business** [kən'dʌkt] behave
78 **pull a stunt** *(infml)* play a trick
88 **one hundred percent** (here) pure African American
93 **unsavory** *(AE)* = *(BE)* **unsavoury** unpleasant looking
117 **love thy neighbor** *(AE)*/**neighbour** *(BE)* *allusion to the Bible *(„Liebe deinen Nächsten")*
119 **principled** basing our behaviour on moral principles

KARL Oh, no. As a matter of fact, Betsy and I've just come directly from ... *(Beat, for effect.)* well, from *Hamilton Park.*

BEV *(To Russ.)* What is it?

RUSS C'mere a second.

KARL Now, Russ. You know as well as I do that this is a progressive community.

BEV *(To Russ as she joins them.)* What's he talking about?

KARL If you take the case of Gelman's grocery: That's a fine example of how we've all embraced a different way of thinking –

RUSS Slow down a second. Bev, get Ted Driscoll on the phone.

BEV *(To Russ.)* What for?

RUSS Karl says. Karl is *claiming* –

KARL Russ, I have met *personally* with the family, and –

BEV What family?

RUSS He claims this family. The family to whom Ted sold the house.

KARL It's a colored family. *(Jim shakes his head.)*

JIM *(To Karl.)* Sorry, don't we say *Negro,* now?

KARL *(Irritated.)* I *say* Negro. –

JIM *(Overlapping.)* Well, it's only common courtesy, and I'm –

KARL *(Continuous.)* – I say them *interchangeably* –

JIM *(Overlapping.)* – not trying to tell you how to conduct your business.

KARL *(Continuous.)* – and of course I said *Negro* to them – No I think we both know what you're doing.

JIM And furthermore, I don't think Ted would pull a stunt like that.

KARL Yes. We all admire Ted. But I don't think any of us would accuse him of putting the community's interests ahead of his own. [...]

BEV Waitwaitwait. Karl, are you *sure*?

KARL I was sitting with them not two hours ago.

BEV But isn't it possible that they're ... I don't know, *Mediterranean,* or – ?

KARL Bev, they are *one hundred percent.* And I don't know how much time any of you have spent in Hamilton Park, but Betsy was waiting in the car and I can tell you, there are some *unsavory* characters. [...] Now, some would say change is inevitable. And I can support that, if it's change for the better. But I'll tell you what I *can't* support, and that's disregarding the needs of the people who *live* in a community.

BEV But don't they have needs, too?

KARL Don't who?

BEV The family.

KARL Which family?

BEV The ones who –

KARL The *purchasers*?

BEV I mean, in, in, in, in *principle,* don't we *all* deserve to – shouldn't we *all* have the opportunity to, to, to –

KARL *(Chuckles with amazement, shakes his head.)* Well, *Bev.*

JIM In *principle,* no question.

KARL But you can't *live* in a principle, can you? Gotta live in a *house.*

BEV And so do they.

KARL Not in *this* house, they don't.

JIM But here's the real question:

KARL And what happened to *love thy neighbor*? If we're being so principled.

BEV They would *become* our neighbors.

KARL And what about the neighbors you already *have,* Bev?

BEV I care about them, too!

KARL Well, I'm afraid you can't have it both ways.

RUSS Okay. Assuming –

BEV Wait. Why not? [...]

JIM But the key question is this:

BEV No. Why *not* have it both ways?

KARL Darling, I came to talk to Russ. [...]

BEV Why not, if it would *benefit* someone?

JIM But *would* they benefit?

BEV If we could make them our *neighbors.*

KARL But they won't be *your* neighbors, Bev. *You're* the ones moving *away*!

From: *Clybourne Park*, 2010 – Act One

COMPREHENSION

1 The topic
Sum up the main topic of the conversation in one sentence.

2 True or false?
Check each of the following statements. If you think the statement is true, point to evidence in the dialogue. If you think it is false, correct it.
1 A black family has bought Ted Driscoll's house.
2 Karl has just phoned the people who bought the house.
3 Russ didn't know that the house had been sold to African Americans.
4 Karl is upset about a black family moving into the neighbourhood.
5 Karl thinks that Hamilton Park is a progressive community.
6 Bev believes that everyone should be given a chance.

► SF 10: Working with closed test formats

ANALYSIS

3 Working with a *dramatic text
a In groups of four, each of you chooses one of the four roles in the scene. Listen to a recording of the text and concentrate on 'your' character while listening. Try and imagine what your character is doing, and where he/she is standing, etc.
b 'Playback': In your group, decide where you want to stand while you are playing your roles. Then practise playing your part in pantomime while the recording is on.

CD2 06
► SF 22: Listening

4 Examining the *characters
Copy and complete the table. For the second column, choose phrases from the box on the right, or make up your own. ► LANGUAGE HELP

	Behaviour/character traits	Evidence from text (line numbers)
Karl		
Russ		
Bev		
Jim		

LANGUAGE HELP
- naïve
- shocked
- angry
- hypocritical
- idealistic
- wants to appear liberal
- self-confident
- tries to mediate
- embarrassed
- bossy

5 The dramatic conflict
At the heart of every drama is a conflict that is usually embodied by two of the characters. Choose the two characters that you think most clearly embody conflict in this scene. Contrast their points of view in a text of 100–150 words.

► SF 20: Analysing drama

BEYOND THE TEXT

6 The other side of the coin SUPPORT ► p. 266
Form groups of four. Two of you are Bev and Russ, the other two are the African American couple who have bought the house in Clybourne Street. Imagine that after Karl has left, the black couple come to look at the house. How would Russ and Bev behave? How might the black couple explain their wish to move to an all-white neighbourhood? Discuss the issues at hand, then prepare role cards for your parts. Practise the scene, then perform it for your class.

► SF 37: Doing a creative writing task

Bill Clinton,
42nd President of the USA

2 **strengthen sth.** make sth. stronger
7 **ensure** make sure *(sicherstellen)*
8 **the brass ring** *(AE, infml)* the opportunity to be successful
14 **industrious** [ɪnˈdʌstriəs] hard-working
15 **heritage** [ˈherɪtɪdʒ] cultural tradition
26 **magnitude** *Größenordnung*
29 **unequivocally** [ˌʌnɪˈkwɪvəkli] *unmissverständlich*
30 **revitalize sth.** [ˌriːˈvaɪtəlaɪz] give sth. new life
32 **energize sth.** [ˈenədʒaɪz] give sth. energy
35 **descendant** [dɪˈsendənt] *Nachkomme*
36 **Ellis Island** N.Y. centre for new immigrants, 1892–1954
38 **faith** religion

New York doorbell nameplate

B2 The changing face of America *William J. Clinton*

*Looking back on history of the USA at the end of the 20th century, Clinton, President of the United States from 1993–2001, points out how the lessons of the past can help the United States cope with the challenges of the future. His message still sounds true in the second decade of the 21st century. Clinton made the *speech from which this excerpt is taken to graduating students at Portland State University.*

Today I want to talk to you about what may be the most important subject of all, how we can strengthen the bonds of our national community as we grow more racially and ethnically diverse. [...]

The driving force behind our increasing diversity is a new, large wave of immigration. It is changing the face of America. And while most of the changes are good, they do present challenges which demand more, both from new immigrants and from our citizens. Citizens share a responsibility to welcome new immigrants, to ensure that they strengthen our Nation, to give them their chance at the brass ring. In turn, new immigrants have a responsibility to learn, to work, to contribute to America. If both citizens and immigrants do their part, we will grow ever stronger in the new global information economy.

More than any other nation on Earth, America has constantly drawn strength and spirit from wave after wave of immigrants. In each generation, they have proved to be the most restless, the most adventurous, the most innovative, the most industrious of people. Bearing different memories, honoring different heritages, they have strengthened our economy, enriched our culture, renewed our promise of freedom and opportunity for all. [...]

But now we are being tested again by a new wave of immigration larger than any in a century, far more diverse than any in our history. Each year, nearly a million people come legally to America. Today, nearly one in ten people in America was born in another country; one in five schoolchildren are from immigrant families. Today, largely because of immigration, there is no majority race in Hawaii or Houston or New York City. Within five years, there will be no majority race in our largest State, California. In a little more than 50 years, there will be no majority race in the United States. No other nation in history has gone through demographic change of this magnitude in so short a time.

What do the changes mean? They can either strengthen and unite us, or they can weaken and divide us. We must decide.

Let me state my view unequivocally. I believe new immigrants are good for America. They are revitalizing our cities. They are building our new economy. They are strengthening our ties to the global economy, just as earlier waves of immigrants settled the new frontier and powered the Industrial Revolution. They are energizing our culture and broadening our vision of the world. They are renewing our most basic values and reminding us all of what it truly means to be an American. [...]

My fellow Americans, we descendants of those who passed through the portals of Ellis Island must not lock the door behind us. Americans whose parents were denied the rights of citizenship simply because of the color of their skin must not deny those rights to others because of the country of their birth or the nature of their faith.

We should treat new immigrants as we would have wanted our own grandparents to be treated. We should share our country with them, not shun them or shut them out. But mark my words, unless we handle this well, immigration of this sweep and scope could threaten the bonds of our Union.

Around the world, we see what can happen when people who live on the same land put race and ethnicity before country and humanity. If America is to remain the world's most diverse democracy, if immigration is to strengthen America as it has throughout our history, then we must say to one another: Whether your ancestors came here in slave ships or on the Mayflower, whether they landed on Ellis Island or at Los Angeles International Airport, or have been here for thousands of years, if you believe in the Declaration of Independence and the Constitution, if you accept the responsibilities as well as the rights embedded in them, then you are an American. Only that belief can keep us one America in the 21st century.

From: 'Commencement Address at Portland State University', 13 June 1998

TROUBLE SPOT

treat sb. (l. 40) = *jdn. behandeln (auch als Arzt/Ärztin)*
deal with a topic = *ein Thema behandeln*
handle a situation/problem (l. 41) = *mit einer Situation / einem Problem o. Ä. umgehen, zurechtkommen*

40 **shun sb.** avoid sb.
41 **sweep, scope** *Größenordnung*
44 **ethnicity** [eθ'nɪsəti] *ethnische Zugehörigkeit*

COMPREHENSION

1 Clinton's message

Summarize Clinton's position on diversity in no more than four sentences.

LANGUAGE AWARENESS

2 Political vocabulary

a Clinton's speech contains many words and phrases related to the idea of a country and the people who live in it, e.g. *our national community* (l. 2). Collect more examples from the text.

b Compare lists with a partner and add any words or phrases that are missing from your list.

c Examine the connotations of the words and phrases.

d YOU CHOOSE

Arrange the terms you have found in the form of a mind map.

OR

Use at least five of the terms you have found in sentences of your own.

Find a mindmapping tool here:
Webcode context-53

New York street sign

SPEAKING **FOCUS ON SKILLS**

Speaking in front of an audience

*Before you speak in front of an audience, you should consider how to make your speech more effective. Analysing a professional speech is a good way to examine *stylistic devices and their effect.*

Analysing a speech

1 Analysing the structure

a Identify the following parts of Clinton's speech (pp. 144–145) by putting them in the correct order and giving line numbers:
1 Statement of the main topic
2 Appeal to the audience to be fair in dealing with the consequences
3 Appeal to the audience to make a commitment
4 Description of historical developments
5 Statement of the challenge
6 Description of the present situation
7 Statement of opinion

b Examine how Clinton links the parts of his speech to make it easier for his listeners to follow his ideas. List the different ways of linking ideas for your own later use.

2 Analysing the *stylistic devices

a Examine the language of the speech. Point out passages where Clinton
- catches his listeners' attention
- emphasizes his message
- creates a feeling of unity with his audience
- reveals a positive or negative attitude to his topic
- appeals to his listeners' sense of fairness.

Make notes on your findings (including line numbers).

b Compare notes with your partner. Analyse your examples and explain the techniques used. The terms you may need are in the list on the left.

c Team up with another pair and give Clinton's speech an 'effectiveness rating' (on a scale from 1 to 6).

**alliteration • *anaphora [əˈnæfərə] • comparative/superlative • *connotation • *contrast • *direct address • *enumeration • *emphasis • *metaphor • *parallelism • personal pronoun • *repetition • *rhetorical question • *simile • *wordplay*

Preparing your own speech

1 Choosing a topic

Choose one of the following topics to prepare and deliver your own speech modelled on the one you have just analysed:
- *Living together in our multicultural school*
- *The world is changing – let's change with it!*
- *The challenges of freedom in a diverse society*

2 Collecting and organizing ideas

a Brainstorm what ideas/associations/aspects of your topic come into your head.

b Sort the ideas, keeping in mind that your speech will need a clear structure.

c Prepare an outline that includes suitable linking phrases and signpost words, e.g. 'for one thing ...', 'In addition ...', 'above all ...'.

► SF 8: Structuring ideas
► LP 14: Linking words and phrases

3 Writing a first draft

a Decide on a good opening sentence. Choose from the following list, or phrase your own:

- *Today I would like to talk to you about what we can do to make life easier for all of us at this school.*
- *Last night I went to a multicultural community event, and that gave me the idea of talking to you about how our world is changing and what we can do to change our attitudes.*
- *The other day I saw a sign that said 'Freedom is never free', and I started thinking about the price of freedom in our democracy. Today I would like to tell you my thoughts on this subject.*

► SF25: Giving a speech

b Remember to use stylistic devices like those you identified in Clinton's speech in order to

- catch your listeners' attention: *Do you know how many nations are represented by the students at our school?*
- emphasize your message: *Cheap air travel, the internet, the end of the Cold War – all of these developments have made our world smaller and more connected than it has ever been before.*
- create a feeling of unity with your audience: *Together, we can find a solution.*
- convey a positive or negative attitude: *Tolerance and respect lead to understanding and cooperation; intolerance and distrust to conflict and violence.*
- appeal to your listeners' sense of fairness: *Imagine how you would feel if this happened to you.*

► LP 13: Placing emphasis on key points

c Take special care with your closing sentence(s), because this is what will stick in your listeners' minds.

4 Revising your draft

Read your draft aloud to a partner to test its effect as a spoken text. Mark the passages that don't 'work' and note what changes you want to make. Then write a revised version, always keeping in mind that it is a speech with which you want to make an impact on your listeners.

Rehearsing and delivering your speech

1 Decide how you want to deliver your speech, and take the necessary precautions to ensure you don't get mixed up and can be seen and understood clearly:

Method	Position
Speaking freely from notes on index cards	Standing in front of the class
Reading aloud from a manuscript	Sitting at a desk in front of the class

2 Practise your speech until you feel comfortable with it. You can make a recording of the speech and then listen to yourself speaking to get an 'outside impression'. Practise speaking in front of a full-length mirror to monitor your eye contact and body language. Refer to the Skills File (p. 280) for additional tips on how to deliver a speech.

Find a tool to improve your speaking skills here:
Webcode context-51

Find a recording tool here:
Webcode context-55

▸ SF 22: Listening

Barack Obama, 44th President of the USA

CD2 07

premise ['premɪs] assumption *(cf. German Prämisse)*
land-grant college college funded with money from the sale of state-owned land
bust *(v)* break up
Medicare, Medicaid state-supported healthcare programs
New Deal, War on Poverty, Great Society slogans of social policy under (F. D.) Roosevelt and Johnson
prosperity [prɒ'sperəti] *Wohlstand*
confine sb. to sth. limit sb. to sth.
blue-collar job factory job
debt [det] money you owe sb.
consistently [kən'sɪstəntli] regularly
unravel [ʌn'rævl] fall apart
automate ['ɔːtəmeɪt] become automated
leverage *[AE:* 'levərɪdʒ, *BE:* 'liːvərɪdʒ] negotiating power
begrudge sth. *etwas missgönnen*
aspire to sth. strive to reach sth.
handsomely ['hænsəmli] generously
offend sb. upset sb.

Equality and inequality

C1 The danger to the dream *Barack Obama*

The extract you are about to hear is taken from a speech made by President Barack Obama on 4 December 2013.

COMPREHENSION

1 Listening for gist

After listening to the excerpt once, decide which of the following statements best summarizes the main idea:

1 America has always rewarded success.
2 The present imbalance between poor and rich threatens the American dream.
3 The task of the government is to ensure that everyone has a fair share of the United States' wealth.

2 Listening for detail

YOU CHOOSE Together with your partner, choose either task **a** or task **b** before listening to the speech a second time.

a Looking backward

1 Obama begins by pointing to four former presidents: Abraham Lincoln, Theodore ('Teddy') Roosevelt, Franklin D. Roosevelt ('FDR'), and Lyndon B. Johnson ('LBJ'). Take notes on each of them while listening.
2 Compare notes with your partner. Together, decide what these presidents had in common and why Obama mentions them.
3 Link up with a pair that chose task **b**. Tell each other what you have learned.

OR

b Then and now

1 Take notes on the following points:
- the American attitude to success
- upward mobility
- factors that limited upward mobility in the past
- the threat to upward mobility in the present.

2 Compare notes with your partner. Make any necessary additions or corrections.
3 Link up with a pair that chose task **a**. Tell each other what you have learned.

BEYOND THE TEXT

3 More success stories

Choose one American person who you regard as a success story. Research this person's *biography and report back to your class.

Steve Jobs *Steven Spielberg* *Henry Ford*

Bill Gates *Lady Gaga*

Oprah Winfrey *Hillary Clinton* *...*

C2 How to become homeless

You are going to watch an excerpt from the 2009 documentary Capitalism: A Love Story. *In it, film-maker Michael Moore explains how millions of Americans lost their homes following the financial crisis of 2008.*

FACT FILE

Home ownership
Since only few people can afford to pay cash for a house, the usual procedure is to borrow the money you need from a bank. The so-called **mortgage** ['mɔːɡɪdʒ] (a kind of loan) can have either a fixed **interest rate** (e.g., for a 10-year period) or a floating rate that varies with the money market. If the borrower cannot pay the monthly rate, the bank **forecloses**, meaning it cancels the mortgage and tries to sell the house to get its money back. In a **boom market**, this is usually no problem, but if housing prices fall, the bank can be left with a loss.

Make sure you understand the four terms ***in bold print****. Then shut your book. Together with your partner, take turns asking each other to explain each of the terms in bold.*

DVD

hunky-dory *(infml)* state in which everyone is happy
tap sth. *etwas anzapfen*
home equity ['ekwəti] net value of your house
refinance your home pay back old loans by taking out new ones
scam dishonest plan for making money
down payment *Anzahlung*
approved [ə'pruːvd] accepted (as customers)
demeanor *(AE)* = *(BE)* **demeanour** way sb. looks or behaves
pitch sales talk
subprime used to describe loans to people who are considered bad risks
on disability receiving disability payments *(Erwerbsunfähigkeitsrente)*
foreclosure notice letter stating that your mortgage has been cancelled

COMPREHENSION

1 Writing conference: first reactions (first viewing)
Form small groups. Write down your first reaction to the video. Then pass your paper to the right. Add comments to the papers you are given.

2 Understanding the background
Copy and complete the following text using words from the list on the right:

US *homeowners* were persuaded to … from banks to finance … The new … had a … interest rate. When the interest rate …, many … were unable to pay the … rates. They lost the … of their houses and were forced to … .

borrow money • consumer spending • floating • homeowners • monthly • mortgages • move out • owners • ownership • rose

ANALYSIS

3 Film technique (second viewing)
While watching the film for the second time, make notes on the effect it has on you. Fill in the missing information on the worksheet that your teacher will give you.

► SF 23: Analysing a film

BEYOND THE TEXT

4 Discuss how effective the film is at helping people to understand the housing crisis.

5 YOU CHOOSE **Michael Moore: an American institution**

a Research Moore's career and report back to your class.

OR

b Read a few online reviews of *Capitalism: A Love Story* and report back to your class: What did the critics praise or criticize about the film?

Film-maker Michael Moore

Anti-bank bailout protests on Wall Street in 2008

C3 A politics lesson *Todd Strasser*

In Todd Strasser's 2014 novel No Place, *the narrator Dan Halprin, a popular high-school athlete in his final year, is forced to move in with relatives when both his parents lose their jobs. For some weeks, a student activist has been trying to recruit him for a protest march on Washington.*

One day the following week I was leaving the cafeteria with Noah and some friends from the team, talking and laughing when the ratty-haired kid at the table in the hall called out, 'Hey, Dan, ready to sign up?'

I felt myself tense. All my friends, plus a couple of kids at the sign-up table, were watching and listening. 'Why do you ask?' 'Seems like a good time,' he said.

Had he heard that we'd lost our home? Did he think that would make me more sympathetic to his cause? 'Why's that?' I gave him a hard look.

Some kids will back down when you give them that look, but this kid kept his eyes steadily on mine. 'Just figured for once I had your undivided attention.'

It took a second to realize that for the past few weeks I'd been with Talia every time I'd passed him, and he probably remembered that time she'd pulled me away before he had a chance to lay out his spiel. But Talia wasn't feeling well and had stayed home that day. Still, it had to take guts to stand up in front of senior athletes and call one out. I looked at the posters on the wall behind him.

> **400 Americans have more than half the wealth in this country.**
>
> **Why is it easier to believe that 150,000,000 Americans are being LAZY rather than that 400 Americans are being GREEDY?**
>
> **STOP THE WAR ON THE POOR!**
>
> **Bail out schools, not banks!**

'People are suffering,' the kid said. 'They can't find work, or get a decent education. You think it's fair that someone dies because he can't pay for adequate medical care while someone else with the same disease lives because he can?'

My friends started to drift away. Meanwhile, I thought of Meg's family living in Dignityville because her mom and brother had to spend practically everything they earned on medicine for Mr. Fine. I used to think that life was like sports: Things were rarely fair. The other team cheated. Your best player got hurt. You threw a perfect strike and the ump called it a ball.

But that's a game, not life.

In sports people don't die because they can't afford medicine.

They don't become homeless because a company goes out of business or moves jobs overseas.

I gestured at the posters. 'You really think marching's gonna make a difference?'

The ratty-haired kid looked surprised. 'You don't think protests changed the war in Vietnam or segregation in the South?'

4 **tense** *(v)* become tense
7 **be sympathetic to sth.** [ˌsɪmpəˈθetɪk] *einer Sache gegenüber aufgeschlossen sein*
cause *Sache, Anliegen*
9 **figure** [*AE:* ˈfɪɡjər, *BE:* ˈfɪɡə] *(v) (infml)* think, believe
10 **Talia** Dan's girlfriend
12 **lay out a spiel** *(infml)* make a speech
13 **guts** *(infml)* courage
call sb. out *jdn. namentlich ansprechen*
21 **bail sb. out** rescue sb. from a difficult situation

TROUBLE SPOT

decent [ˈdiːsnt] (l. 22) = *anständig*
But: *dezent* =
1. subdued, soft *(colours, music, etc.);*
2. tactful, discreet *(behaviour)*

25 **Meg Fine** girl in Dan's class. Her father has cancer.
26 **Dignityville** name of tent city for the homeless in Dan's town
28 **You threw a perfect strike and the ump called it a ball.** The ball you threw was in the valid zone but the umpire *(Schiedsrichter/in)* said it wasn't.

I couldn't say. We may have studied those events in school, but those old protest movements were about as real to me as trigonometry. You learned what you needed to ace the test. And not for an instant did it feel like it had any actual meaning in your life.

'If we don't do something, it's only going to get worse,' the kid said. 'And it's not the kind of thing one person can do. Marches show strength. They tell politicians that we have the numbers and the votes to change elections.'

I was more than three years away from being able to drink legally, but only months from being able to vote. Sure, voting may have been way more important, but given the choice, I would have switched those two age requirements in a heartbeat.

The kid was still waiting for me to respond.

'Can I ask you something personal?' I said. 'Why do you care? You homeless or something?'

The kid gave me a long, curious look, then said, 'No, I care ... because I'm *not* homeless.'

From: *No Place*, 2014

39 **ace a test** get a good mark on a test

TROUBLE SPOT
actual ['æktʃuəl] (l. 39) = *real, concrete*
But: *aktuell* = ***current, topical***

COMPREHENSION

1 Mediation (English → German)
Tell your parents/little brother/sister at the dinner table in two German sentences what the novel extract is about.

► SF 41: Mediation of written and oral texts

2 Interviews
Write five interview questions for Dan Halprin based on the text you have just read. Ask your partner your questions, then answer your partner's questions. Discuss any points on which you differ.

► SF 26: Taking part in an interview

ANALYSIS

3 Dan's political development
Point to examples from the text that show how Dan's interest in politics and political action is changing. Examine the factors that influence him.

LANGUAGE AWARENESS

4 Uses of the progressive form

a Collect examples of the past progressive from the extract. Compare lists with your partner. Together, formulate a rule explaining when the past progressive is used.

b In the following text, no progressive forms have been used. Rewrite the text, deciding which verbs should be put in the past progressive:
When Mr Purcellen arrived home that evening, I sat next to Talia on the front porch. It was a warm evening; the moon shone behind the trees, and a soft wind blew. Mr Purcellen got out of the old pickup he always drove to work. He walked across the dark lawn and stopped about ten yards from the house. I think he watched us, but I couldn't guess what he thought.

c CHALLENGE Examine the text on the poster (in the middle of the opposite page). The second sentence uses a progressive form of the verb *be* twice. Explain how this form differs in meaning from the simple form of the verb.

► LP 1: Simple and progressive verb forms
► SF 4: Using a grammar book

BEYOND THE TEXT

5 YOU CHOOSE **Creative writing**

a Retell the episode described in the extract from the point of view of the student activist.

OR

b Write a continuation of the extract, in which Dan decides whether he wants to sign up for the protest march.

► SF 37: Doing a creative writing task

The United States' place in the world

D1 Facts and figures

	USA	China	Germany	Brazil	Russia	India
1 GDP	16,244,600	8,277,103	3,428,131	2,252,664	2,014,775	1,841,710
2 Military spending	682,478	166,107	45,785	43,576	90,749	46,125
3 Balance of trade	–784,775	155,142	219,938	19,169	198,760	–154,401

All figures are in millions of US dollars and are from 2012, except (3), which contains data from 2011.

FACT FILE

GDP (**Gross** [grəʊs] **Domestic Product**) is defined as the total value of goods and services produced in a country. The **balance of trade** is the difference between the total value of exports from a country and imports into the same country. A negative balance (**deficit** ['defɪsɪt]; opposite: **surplus** ['sɜːpləs]) means the country imports more than it exports.

COMPREHENSION

▸ SF 12: Analysing charts and graphs

1 Understanding the figures

a Write eight sentences comparing the figures in the table. SUPPORT ▸ p. 266

b Compare sentences with your partner. Check each other's information to make sure you have both got the facts right.

BEYOND THE TEXT

2 The facts behind the figures

Link up with another pair and discuss what influence the facts from the table above could have on the balance of power in the world.

D2 The German view *Michael Hochgeschwender*

CD2 08

▸ SF 41: Mediation of written and oral texts

In the podcast you are about to hear, historian Michael Hochgeschwender is asked if the USA is still the leading world power. When you mention this interview to your American e-pal, she wants to know what the professor says about the USA's status in the world. You will hear the interview twice.

COMPREHENSION

▸ SF 22: Listening

1 While listening

Listen to what Hochgeschwender says about the position of the USA in the world. Take notes on the following aspects:

- what the historian says about the world status of the United States,
- his reasons for his opinion,
- his views on the future development of the United States' role.

2 After listening

Compare notes with your partner.

BEYOND THE TEXT

▸ SF 41: Mediation of written and oral texts

▸ CC 6: Talking about sensitive issues

3 Mediation (German → English)

a Use your notes to write an email of about 150 words explaining Hochgeschwender's position to your e-pal.

b CHALLENGE ▸ Add a further paragraph to your email from **a** in which you comment on the historian's views and ask your American e-pal for her opinion.

D3 Better than its reputation *Anne Applebaum*

The 20th century is sometimes called 'the American century'. Collect reasons why this might be. How do you think historians will refer to the present century?

LONDON – In Beijing a few months ago, I met a young Filipina journalist who did video interviews for a Chinese website. She seemed clever and competent. She spoke perfect American English, which she learned growing up near a U.S. base. She was very pleased to be in China: Her job in Beijing was interesting, well-paid, and gave her a future. I asked whether she thought her career might take her to the United States. She shrugged. She would never get a visa, let alone a job. Not worth trying.

At the time, I thought this conversation rather ominous. It seemed another reminder that the American dream is looking rather tarnished these days, and not only to Americans. To much of the outside world, the United States appears unpromising and unwelcoming, especially compared with the largest economy in East Asia, the new land of opportunity. We are growing far more slowly than China. Our middle class is downwardly mobile. U.S. news organizations are not scouring the world for talent, whereas China's apparently are. [...]

Members of the US and Philippine army unload US aid as part of relief efforts after Typhoon Haiyan

And yet, when a disaster unfolds and resources have to be rapidly mobilized, it's as if nothing has changed. One of the largest typhoons on record hit the Philippines last week. The extent of the damage isn't yet known. But the American response is already larger – by a factor of hundreds – than that of the largest economy in East Asia. The United States is sending an aircraft carrier to the worst-hit regions and has promised $20 million in emergency aid. Millions more will be raised by U.S. charities. The British are sending a warship and $16 million. Even the Vatican has promised $4 million. And the government of China, the new land of opportunity? $100,000.

There are politics behind China's stinginess. China has recently made claims on Philippine territory, citing historical documents that date to the fifth century. The Philippine government has responded with anger, a lawsuit, and an invitation to the U.S. Navy to reopen some bases closed in the 1990s. There are also politics behind American generosity, which partly reflects the renewed warmth and military cooperation between Washington and Manila.

But these differing responses to the typhoon also signify a different set of attitudes to power, and not just to 'soft power': Americans, like Europeans, have long believed that strength and wealth entail responsibility. That's why two American ex-presidents voluntarily coordinated the international response to the 2004 tsunami, even though Indonesia was not the site of a U.S. naval base. That's why massive amounts of U.S. aid went to victims of the 2005 earthquake in Kashmir, even though relations between the United States and Pakistan were deteriorating at the time.

That's also why an American president who is actively uninterested in engaging with the Syrian conflict has pledged more than $1 billion in humanitarian aid to Syrian refugees, accounting for nearly 30 percent of all such aid; European contributions as a whole make up a good percentage of the rest. China's contribution, meanwhile, comes to $3 million, less than that of Luxembourg. China plays an enormous political role in Syria – the Chinese veto has helped keep the United Nations firmly

6 **let alone** *geschweige denn*
7 **ominous** ['ɒmɪnəs] suggesting that sth. bad is going to happen
8 **tarnished** (here) no longer attractive
12 **scour sth.** ['skaʊə] search sth. intensely
14 **unfold** (here) happen
16 **on record** [*BE:* 'rekɔːd, *AE:* 'rekərd] *seit Menschengedenken*
17 **extent** *Ausmaß*
21 **aircraft carrier** *Flugzeugträger*
24 **charity** organization that helps people in need
28 **stinginess** ['stɪndʒinəs] *Geiz*
31 **lawsuit** *(juristische) Klage*
37 **entail sth.** have sth. as a consequence
41 **deteriorate** [dɪ'tɪəriəreɪt] become worse
42 **engage with sth.** get involved in sth.
43 **pledge sth.** promise to give sth.
44 **account for sth.** *etwas ausmachen*

Part D

47 **sidelined** unable to take action
obligated ['ɒblɪgeɪtɪd] *verpflichtet*
50 **counter sth.** deal with the effects of sth.
facilitate sth. [fə'sɪlɪteɪt] *(fml)* make sth. easier
52 **for its own sake** *als Selbstzweck*
56 **elaborate** [ɪ'læbərət] long and complex
58 **wane** become less
59 **taper off** become less

sidelined there – but clearly does not feel obligated to help those affected by its decisions.

The Chinese do give development aid, but differently: not in response to tragedies, not to counter disaster, but to facilitate the export of raw materials to China. There is merit to some of China's efforts, especially in Africa. But the Chinese state is not, for the most part, interested in generosity for its own sake. Nor do many Chinese billionaires believe that new wealth brings new obligations. Several of them refused even to meet Bill Gates a few years ago, apparently because they were afraid he might ask them to give away some of their money.

All of which is not an elaborate excuse for messy American foreign policy, or the still-weak American economy, or the indecisive American president. It's just a little reminder: U.S. strength may be waning, U.S. status may be fading, and U.S. attraction for talented foreigners may soon taper off. But there will be reasons to be sorry if America isn't a superpower anymore, perhaps more than America's critics think.

From: 'Why America's critics will miss the U.S. superpower', *Slate* (magazine), 13 November 2013

COMPREHENSION

1 Summarizing the text
Summarize the *author's views on the United States' role in the world in no more than four sentences.

2 Collecting information
a Copy and complete the table with information from the text:

	China	USA
strong points		
weak points		

b Compare tables with your partner; add any missing information.

ANALYSIS

► SF 18: Analysing non-fiction
► LP 13: Placing emphasis on key points

3 The author's bias
a Examine the author's position: Whose side is she on? Give examples from the text that illustrate her position (selection of facts, word choice, use of emphasis, juxtaposition, sentence structure, etc.). SUPPORT ► p. 267
b Use your results from tasks 1–3 to analyse the author's strategy: How does she structure her arguments and what *stylistic devices does the use?

LANGUAGE AWARENESS

► LP 20: Word formation
► SF 3: Using a dictionary

Find an online dictionary here:
Webcode context-52

4 Word formation
a Form eight word pairs (either 'noun – adjective' or 'noun – verb') using words from the text. Example: *generosity – generous; contribution – contribute*. Consult a monolingual dictionary if necessary.
b Use the words that don't appear in the text in sentences of your own.

BEYOND THE TEXT

► LP 2: Present tense or future?

5 WRITING CONFERENCE **The next ten years**
Form small groups. Write down your ideas on the topic: Will the USA still play a major role in the world ten years from now? Share your ideas with your group, and discuss the reasons for your opinions.

Giving a speech on why you would like to visit the USA

Imagine you discover this advert on the internet:

The Chance of a Lifetime!

The German-American Friendship Organization is offering ten stipends for German teenagers aged 18 or older. Winners will spend three months in the United States, living with American families, visiting schools, businesses and places of interest, talking to politicians, business people, and just plain Americans of all ages.

To apply to our program, send us a video of not more than five minutes in which you make a speech on the subject: 'Why I want to learn more about the United States of America.'

Excited at the prospect of an all-expenses-paid stay in the USA, you decide to apply.

1 Getting started
Collect your ideas using a suitable method: What do you find fascinating, irritating, or intriguing about the USA and about Americans? What kinds of people would you like to talk to? What questions would you ask them?

► SF 25: Giving a speech

2 Writing your speech
- **a** Organize your ideas in the form of an outline. Use the outline to write a first draft.
- **b** Read your drafts aloud in small groups and discuss them, suggesting improvements where needed.
- **c** Prepare a revised version. Make sure it does not take longer than five minutes. Practise reading your speech in front of a friend or a mirror until you feel confident with it. Then make a video of yourself delivering your speech.

Find a tool to improve your speaking skills here: **Webcode** context-51

Find a tool to create your video here: **Webcode** context-54

3 Evaluation
Form small groups. In your group, let the others watch your video (or you can deliver it 'live'). The others give you feedback. They fill in assessment sheets given out by your teacher.

2 Americans – Finding Freedom

A

B

Download a list of chapter vocab here: **Webcode** context-61

1 Photos and captions

a THINK Look at the photos and describe the situation or topic they depict. Then read the captions below, choose one for each of the photos or create one of your own. Give reasons why you consider them suitable.
- Together we're strong.
- We are all equal.
- There must be more than this.
- Life means pushing your limits.
- Two is company, three's a crowd.
- We are not alone.
- Let's move forward!
- All men are created equal.
- *E pluribus unum* (out of many – one.)
- Give peace a chance.
- …

b PAIR Exchange information on the photos and discuss your matchings with a partner. Agree on the best solutions.

c SHARE Share your findings with the class.

C

D

2 Identities and values

a Collect ideas that you consider to be central to US identity. Arrange them in a mindmap.

b Find documents, historical events or contemporary examples that support your ideas from **2a**, differentiating them from simple clichés.

Find a mindmapping tool here:
Webcode context-53

PREVIEW

In this chapter you will look at examples of how Americans see themselves, their country and their political system.

CD2 02

Listen to an audio version of the text on the CD or download it here:
Webcode context-61

Common identity and individual liberty

A history of conflict

The history of the United States is a history of conflict: the Puritan Pilgrims escaped religious conflict in Europe, the expansion of the US to the west caused major conflict with Native Americans and almost their extinction. What's more, the conflict over slavery and the right of the southern states to leave the Union led to the American Civil War.

Immigrants to the US came from diverse backgrounds but were often united by the dream of using their freedom to be economically successful – the American Dream. This dream is deeply rooted in the religious doctrine of Calvinism, which believes in predestination and considers economic success as a sign of God's grace. Many see this protestant work ethic and self-reliance as the core of the common identity of Americans.

US Republican presidential candidate Jeb Bush at a town hall meeting (3 September 2015)

The political system

One result of the concept of self-reliance is a particular ideal of the role of the state: most Americans are in favour of the concept of 'small government', i.e. minimum intervention of politics and the state in everyday matters and the right of the individual to take chances. So the ideal of 'rugged individualism' provides opportunities and allows people to take risks.

In the political system this is mirrored by a mistrust of the federal government, of politicians and political parties (the Republicans and the Democrats), and a need to stress the separation of powers ('checks and balances') and the constitutional rights of the citizen (civil liberties), e.g. the right to bear arms. Often, Supreme Court decisions are necessary to settle long-fought arguments in Congress.

African Americans

The heritage of racism continues to divide the nation long after the end of slavery and half a century after the Civil Rights Movement. The election of Barack Obama as the first 'black' president in 2008 once again raised the question of equality. While de jure equal in political rights, there is still a big de facto disadvantage of African Americans in everyday life. Some people see this as a continuation of discrimination. Others blame the African-American community for their failure to succeed (high crime rates, single mothers, gang violence, gun crimes in inner cities). Again, the question is: are the individuals to blame or the conditions under which they live?

Main stream and counterculture

The chasm between conservative mainstream America and a more progressive counterculture remains. The questions of illegal/undocumented mass immigration from Mexico, affordable health care ('Obamacare'), same-sex marriage, abortion clinics and race relations continue to split the nation and the political parties. The struggle of ideas, between community rules and the search for individual freedom, the role of the state, cultural heritage, diversity, justice, and practical policies resulting from this, goes on.

1 Words in use

► SF 2: Learning new words

Find the highlighted words and expressions in the text to match the definitions:

1 a group of people sharing the same habits or culture
2 what we are given by our ancestors
3 a system of division of powers
4 the belief that everything has been decided in advance by God
5 independence of an individual

2 Compound nouns

In English there are many compound nouns consisting of two or more words. Find German terms for these expressions:

1 Civil Rights Movement
2 race relations
3 civil liberties
4 same-sex marriage

3 Word field

► SF 3: Using a dictionary

Find an online dictionary here:
Webcode context-52

Use a dictionary or an online dictionary to understand the difference between the terms *politics* and *policies*. What words with the same origin can you find?

4 Political and legal terms

Give the German translation or equivalent of the following terms. Use expressions like 'this is like the ... in Germany'.
Democrats – Republicans – Supreme Court – Congress

5 Abstract concepts

Translate these terms into German and try to define them, first in German, if necessary:

1 individualism
2 racism
3 identity
4 discrimination
5 diversity
6 Calvinism

6 Writing

Using the vocabulary and ideas from the text on p. 38, write a short text about the political system in Germany.

10 **plantation** (here) settlement
20 **scattered** *(adj)* spread apart over a great distance
21 **be incorporated into sth.** be a part of sth.
41 **dignity** *Würde*
42 **salvation** *Rettung, Erlösung*
immutable [ɪ'mjuːtəbl] *(adj)* *(fml)* unchangeable
43 **beneficence** [bɪ'nefɪsns] *(fml)* generosity
52 **compound** ['‒‒] *Mischung, Verbindung*
53 **precious** ['preʃəs] valuable
Corinthian brass valuable metal alloy (*Legierung*) in classical antiquity
55 **Cossacks** ['‒‒] *Kosaken (Volk im zaristischen Russland)*
57 **vigorous** ['vɪgərəs] strong, full of energy

American identities

A1 Defining America

Nations and people tend to search for their identity, for a fitting description of themselves. Often outside observers join in in this attempt.
Before reading the following quotations from the early 17th to the second half of the 20th century, ask yourselves how you would define 'an American' and how Americans of today may regard themselves and their country.

John Winthrop

We shall find that the God of Israel is among us, when ten of us shall be able to resist a thousand of our enemies; when He shall make us a praise and glory that men shall say of succeeding plantations, 'may the Lord make it like that of New England.' For we must consider that we shall be as a city upon a hill.

From John Winthrop's (1588–1649) sermon "A Model of Christian Charity", delivered to Puritans in 1630. Winthrop became governor of the Massachusetts Bay Colony.

J. Hector St. John de Crèvecœur

The Americans were once scattered all over Europe; here they are incorporated into one of the finest systems of population which has ever appeared, and which will hereafter become distinct by the power of the different climates they inhabit. [...] The American is a new man, who acts upon new principles. He must therefore entertain new ideas and form new opinions.

J. Hector St. John de Crèvecœur (1735–1813) was a French-American writer who had emigrated to North America in 1755. In his Letters from an American Farmer *(1782) he described life in America to Europeans. The quote is from the best-known of these letters, titled "What is an American?".*

All this will be our future history, to establish on earth the moral dignity and salvation of man – the immutable truth and beneficence of God. For this blessed mission to the nations of the world, which are shut out from the life-giving light of truth, has America been chosen.

From The Great Nation of Futurity *(1839) by John L. O'Sullivan (1813–1895). In 1845, O'Sullivan coined the term 'Manifest Destiny' to promote the westward movement, arguing that the USA had a divine mandate to expand.*

John L. O'Sullivan

Ralph Waldo Emerson

Well, as in the old burning of the Temple at Corinth, by the melting and intermixture of silver and gold and other metals a new compound more precious than any, called Corinthian brass, was formed; so in this continent, – asylum of all nations, – the energy of Irish, Germans, Swedes, Poles, and Cossacks, and all the European tribes, – of the Africans, and of the Polynesians, – will construct a new race, a new religion, a new state, a new literature, which will be as vigorous as the new Europe [...].

Ralph Waldo Emerson (1803–1882) was an American philosopher, essayist and poet. In his public lectures he warned of the pressures of society and advocated individuality and personal freedom.

Fortunately, the time has long passed when people liked to regard the United States as some kind of melting pot, taking men and women from every part of the world and converting them into standardized, homogenized Americans. We are, I think, much more mature and wise today. Just as we welcome a world of diversity, so we glory in an America of diversity – an America all the richer for the many different and distinctive strands of which it is woven.

Hubert H. Humphrey (1911–1978), a Democrat, was US vice president 1965–1969 and US senator.

Hubert H. Humphrey

55 **mature** *(adj)* grown up; sensible
56 **glory in sth.** enjoy sth.
58 **strand** *Komponente*

COMPREHENSION

1 Talking about the quotations

a THINK Find the key phrases in each quotation.

b PAIR Compare your key phrases with a partner. Discuss their meaning, also making use of the information in the pictures and in the annotations.

c SHARE Present your findings to the class.

ANALYSIS

2 America and Americans

Describe the image of America and 'the Americans' conveyed in each quotation and analyse how these images are created.

SUPPORT ▸ p. 268

▸ SF 17: Analysing stylistic devices

BEYOND THE TEXT

3 Research

Find out more about the people quoted. Report to the class.

A2 The legacy of the Puritans *Matthew Hutson*

In 1620 the Puritans on board the Mayflower *reached New England. The following year, they founded Plymouth Colony. Four centuries later, science writer Matthew Hutson looks for the legacy of the Puritans – and finds some surprising traces.*

'I think I can see the whole destiny of America contained in the first Puritan who landed on those shores,' the French political thinker Alexis de Tocqueville wrote after visiting the United States in the 1830s. Was he right? Do present-day Americans still exhibit, in their attitudes and behavior, traces of those austere English Protestants who started arriving in the country in the early 17th century?

It seems we do. Consider a series of experiments conducted by researchers led by the psychologist Eric Luis Uhlmann and published last year in the *Journal of Experimental Social Psychology*. In one study, they investigated whether the work habits of today's Americans reflected the so-called Protestant work ethic. Martin Luther and John Calvin argued that work was a calling from God. They also believed in predestination and viewed success as a sign of salvation. This led to belief in success as a path to salvation: hard work and good deeds would bring rewards, in life and after.

In the study, American and Canadian college students were asked to solve word puzzles involving anagrams. But first, some were subtly exposed to (or 'primed' with) salvation-related words like 'heaven' and 'redeem', while others were exposed to neutral words. The researchers found that the Americans – but not the Canadians – solved more anagrams with salvation on the mind. They worked harder.

FACT FILE

Alexis de Tocqueville (1805–1859) was a French politician and political thinker. In his works, he examined the social conditions of individuals and their relationship to society. He stressed the importance of the French Revolution of 1789 and was in favour of a parliamentary government. His book *Democracy in America* (1835) remains influential to this day.

2 **shore** *(n) Ufer*
4 **exhibit sth.** [ɪg'zɪbɪt] *(fml)* show sth. (a quality)
austere [ɒ'stɪə] *(adj)* *(fml)* serious, strict
10 **predestination** *Vorbestimmung*
11 **salvation** *Rettung, Erlösung*
14 **anagram** *Anagramm (Wort, das durch Umstellung der Buchstaben eines anderen Wortes entsteht)*
prime sb. with sth. (here) prepare sb. with sth.
15 **redeem sb./sth.** *jdn. erlösen*

Part A

19 **prudishness** quality of being easily shocked by things to do with sex; *Prüderie*
20 **promiscuous** [prə'mɪskjuəs] *(adj)* having many sexual partners
harshly *(adj)* in a cruel way
22 **prom** *(Schulabschluss-)Ball*
23 **revealing** *(adj)* *freizügig*
26 **approval** agreement to sth.
29 **intermingling** *(n)* mixing
30 **hinge on sth.** [hɪndʒ] be dependent on sth.
affiliation [əˌfɪli'eɪʃn] *Zugehörigkeit*
34 **uprightness** quality of being very moral and honest
36 **self-reliance** *Selbstständigkeit*
37 **hostility** *Feindseligkeit*
38 **obese** [əʊ'biːs] *(adj)* overweight
self-denigration *Selbstherabsetzung*
43 **squinting** *(n)* *Blinzeln, Zusammenkneifen der Augen*

THE PURITANS ENJOY A REAL GOOD LAUGH

Professor Uhlmann and his colleagues also conducted an experiment to see if Americans shared the prudishness of the Puritans. They found that American students judged promiscuous women more harshly than British students did.

In a third experiment, the researchers asked Asian-Americans to rate their support for a school principal who had canceled a prom because of sexually charged dancing and also to rate their support for a school that had banned revealing clothing. But first, the researchers primed the participants with thoughts of either their Asian or their American heritage, as well as with thoughts of work or another topic. They found that the participants showed increased approval of the prudish school officials when primed with thoughts of work – if they had *also* been primed with their American heritage, but not when primed with their Asian heritage. These results suggest a tight Puritanical intermingling of work, sex and morality in the American mind.

In none of these studies did the results hinge on the participants' religious affiliation or level of religious feeling. Whatever these Americans explicitly believed (or didn't believe) about God, something like Puritan values seemed to be guiding their moral judgments. [...]

Not all of the legacy of Puritanism suggests moral uprightness. Studies since the '70s have also found that Americans who score high on a Protestant Ethic Scale (emphasizing self-reliance and self-discipline) or similar metric show marked prejudice against racial minorities and the poor; hostility toward social welfare efforts; and, among obese women, self-denigration. [...]

It's hard to say for sure that any given element of the American psyche results from our Puritan founders. 'The direct lines are few,' stresses David D. Hall, a professor of New England church history, 'mostly because of industrialization and immigration' and other factors that have led to immense social change.

But were Tocqueville to land on our shores today, with a bit of squinting he would probably see some of the same evidence of our Puritan destiny as he did nearly two centuries ago.

From: *The New York Times*, 5 August 2012

COMPREHENSION

1 The Puritans and their legacy

a Name and explain the Puritan beliefs and principles mentioned in the article.

b Identify positive as well as negative consequences of the Puritan legacy.

ANALYSIS

2 Alexis de Tocqueville

The French thinker Alexis de Tocqueville is mentioned twice in the text. Explain the relevance and function of this in terms of both the content and structure of the article.

3 Target readers

Identify Hutson's possible target readership. Examine how he tries to lend credibility to his article.

BEYOND THE TEXT

4 YOU CHOOSE Your opinion

▶ SF 27: Having a discussion

a Discuss whether in Germany there are similar fundamental beliefs or doctrines, religious or otherwise.

OR

b Comment on the notion of the American as an austere, hard-working and prudish Protestant that is analysed in the text.

CULTURE SPOT

On 27 April 2006, five years after the terrorist attacks of 11 September 2001, construction started of One World Trade Center on Ground Zero, the site where the Twin Towers had once stood. The new building was to be a memorial to all the victims of the attacks. It was completed in July 2013 and opened on 3 November the following year. With its symbolic height of 1,776 feet (541 meters), it is even taller than the former buildings, making it the tallest building in the Western hemisphere.

One World Trade Center

On 11 September 2012, One World Trade Center was lit in blue, white and red. Two vertical columns of light were projected skywards in remembrance of the former Twin Towers. In the photo above, the Statue of Liberty can be seen in the foreground.

Ground zero after 9/11

Work with a partner.

1. Exchange what you know about the attacks of 9/11.
2. Describe One World Trade Center and the symbolic value it has for many people.
3. Talk about buildings that have a special significance either for a large number of people, for a particular group of people or for you personally.

Politics – does the system still work?

B1 Why the system no longer works *Mickey Edwards*

Mickey Edwards, a former Congressman from Oklahoma (1977–1993), explains what he thinks is wrong with the American political system.

Angry and frustrated, American voters went to the polls in November 2010 to 'take back' their country. Just as they had done in 2008. And 2006. And repeatedly for decades, whether it was Republicans or Democrats from whom they were taking the country back. No matter who was put in charge, things didn't get better. They won't this time, either; spending levels may go down, taxes may go up, budgets will change, but American government will go on the way it has, not as a collective enterprise but as a battle between warring tribes.

If we are truly a democracy – if voters get to size up candidates for a public office and choose the one they want – why don't the elections seem to change anything? Because we elect our leaders, and they then govern, in a system that makes cooperation almost impossible and incivility nearly inevitable, a system in which the campaign season never ends and the struggle for party advantage trumps all other considerations. When Democrat Nancy Pelosi became speaker of the House, the leader of the lawmaking branch of government, she said her priority was to ... elect more Democrats. After Republican victories in 2010, the Senate Republican leader Mitch McConnell said his goal was to ... prevent the Democratic president's reelection. With the country at war and the economy in recession, our government leaders' first thoughts have been of party advantage.

This is not an accident. Ours is a system focused not on collective problem-solving but on a struggle for power between two private organizations. Party activists control access to the ballot through closed party primaries and conventions; partisan leaders design congressional districts. Once elected to Congress, our representatives are divided into warring camps. Partisans decide what bills to take up, what witnesses to hear, what amendments to allow.

Many Americans assume that's just how democracy works, that this is how it's always been, that it's the system the Founders created. But what we have today is a far cry from what the Founders intended. George Washington and James Madison both warned of the dangers posed by political parties. Defenders of the party system argue that parties – including Madison's own – arose almost immediately after the nation was founded. But those were not parties in the modern sense: they were factions uniting on a few major issues, not marching in lockstep on every issue, large and small. And while some defend the party system as a necessary provider of cues to voters who otherwise might not know how to vote, the Internet and mass media now make it possible for voters to educate themselves about candidates for office.

1 **the polls** *(pl)* ['pəʊlz] voting at an election
7 **warring** ['wɔːrɪŋ] *(adj)* involved in a war
tribe *Volksstamm*
8 **size sb./sth. up** *(infml)* form an opinion about sb./sth.
12 **trump sb./sth.** beat sb./sth. by doing sth. even better than sb./sth. else
22 **ballot** ['bælət] *Wahl*
23 **primary** *(n)* *(in den USA) Vorwahl*
convention large meeting of the members of a political party
26 **partisan** *(adj)* [ˈpɑːtɪzæn] *parteiisch*
27 **amendment** change or improvement made to a law or to a document
31 **be a far cry from sth.** be very different from sth. else
37 **faction** *Fraktion, Gruppierung*
38 **in lockstep** *im Gleichschritt*
40 **cue** *(n)* hint, tip

FACT FILE

Political parties in the US
Traditionally the United States has had a two-party system, as the electoral rules – similar to those in the UK – make it difficult for third parties to gain a foothold. For the past 150 years, the Democratic Party (symbolized in political cartoons by the donkey, cf. cartoon on p. 161) and the Republican Party (symbolized by the elephant) have dominated American politics. The Democrats tend to be more liberal and to favour the working class and minorities, welfare programmes and government intervention, whereas the Republicans are traditionally sympathetic to the interests of big business (deregulation, tax cuts).

In the US, party candidates for public office are not chosen by party leaders, but by the voters, in so-called primary elections. Moreover, each candidate must win their own electoral district; the party has no 'seats' to distribute, as it does in Germany. Voter preferences are distributed unequally across the US. It has become fashionable in the media to distinguish between 'blue' (mainly Democratic) and 'red' (mainly Republican) states.

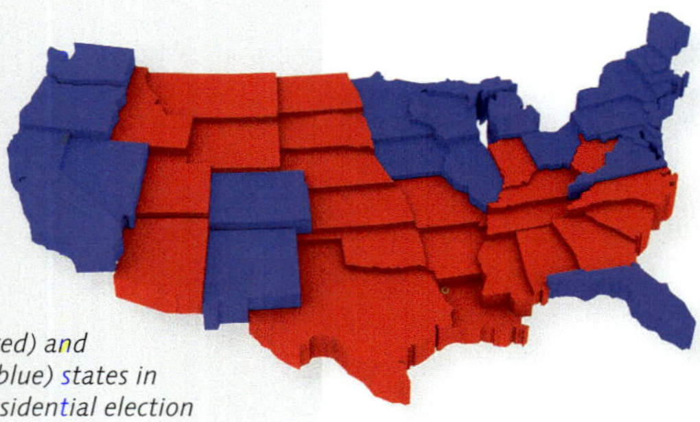

Republican (red) and Democratic (blue) states in the 2012 presidential election

What we have today is not a legacy of 1789 but an outdated relic of the late 1800s and early 1900s, when Progressives pushed for the adoption of primary elections. By 1916, all but a handful of states had instituted the 'direct primary' system, under which a party candidate was selected by a public vote, rather than by party leaders in backroom deals. But the primaries, and the nominating conventions, were open only to party members. This reform was supposed to give citizens a bigger role in the election process. Instead, the influence of party leaders has been supplanted by that of a subset of party activists who are often highly ideological and largely uninterested in finding common ground. In Delaware in 2010, a mere 30,000 of that state's nearly 1 million people kept Mike Castle, a popular congressman and former governor, off the general-election ballot. In Utah, 3,500 people meeting in a closed convention deprived the rest of the state's 3 million residents of an opportunity to consider reelecting their longtime senator Robert Bennett. For most of the voters who go to the polls in November, the names on the ballot have been reduced to only those candidates the political parties will allow them to choose between. Americans demand a multiplicity of options in almost every other aspect of our lives. And yet we allow small bands of activists to limit our choices of people to represent us in making the nation's laws.

I am not calling for a magical political 'center': many of the most important steps forward in our history have not come from the center at all, including women's suffrage and the civil-rights movement, and even our founding rebellion against the British crown. Nor am I pleading for consensus: consensus is not possible in a diverse nation of 300 million people (*compromise* is the essential ingredient in legislative decision-making). And I'm not pushing for harmony: democracy depends on vigorous debate among competing views. The problem is not division but partisanship – advantage-seeking by private clubs whose central goal is to win political power.

From: 'How to turn Republicans and Democrats into Americans', *The Atlantic*, July/August 2011

44 **legacy** ['legəsi] *Erbe, Hinterlassenschaft*
46 **all but** *alle außer*
50 **supplant sb./sth.** [sə'plɑːnt] replace sb./sth.
51 **subset** *Untergruppe*
55 **deprive sb. of sth.** *jdm. etw. vorenthalten*
65 **suffrage** *Wahlrecht*

'A system that makes cooperation almost impossible': donkey (i.e. Democrats) and elephant (i.e. Republicans)

COMPREHENSION

1 The main idea
Outline the writer's criticisms of the present state of US party politics.

ANALYSIS

2 Looking at language: political rhetoric

a Edwards frequently uses stylistic devices to underline his message, e.g. 'not as a collective enterprise but as a battle between warring tribes' (l. 6–7). Collect further examples; use the Glossary to label them.

b Compare lists with a partner and analyse the effect these devices have on the reader.

► Glossary, p. 393

3 Identifying key concepts
Evaluate the writer's notion of what makes a successful democracy by analysing the final paragraph of the text (ll. 63–73).

BEYOND THE TEXT

4 Writing
'[D]emocracy depends on vigorous debate among competing views.' (ll. 70–71) Comment on the role you believe political parties should play in a democracy.

WRITING **FOCUS ON SKILLS**

Writing a five-paragraph essay

Essays or compositions try to communicate a main idea which cannot be sufficiently developed in a single paragraph. The five-paragraph essay is a useful format that helps you to develop your composition skills.

Introductory paragraph
- Explain the meaning of the title and/or the importance of the question.
- Give your thesis statement.
- Add a 'hook' which moves the reader to the next paragraph.

Three body paragraphs
- Should all relate to the thesis.
- One idea = one paragraph
- Start with a topic sentence indicating the main idea of the paragraph.
- Support your ideas by giving examples, explanations, evidence, quotes, etc.

Concluding paragraph
- Restate your thesis.
- Review your main ideas by referring to the topic sentences.
- Close your essay with a final thought.

This is the topic of your essay:
"[D]emocracy depends on vigorous debate among competing views." (cf. **B1**, *p. 47, ll. 70–71) Comment on the role you believe political parties should play in a democracy.*
Together with a partner prepare your five-paragraph essay.

1 Writing an effective introduction
Discuss the following three introductory sentences with your partner. Explain which of them you find most effective and why.
1 In the following I am going to comment on the role political parties should play in a democracy.
2 Democracy was said to depend "on vigorous debate among competing views". For parties in working democracy this means …
3 Political parties are not exactly the darlings of public opinion, nevertheless democracy cannot do without them.
Write an introduction in which you explain the importance of your topic and briefly give a flavour of the conclusion you are going to reach (thesis).

2 Finding suitable arguments
From the following list, pick three arguments and use them as topic sentences of your body paragraphs. For each statement you choose, note down explanations, examples and quotes to provide support.
1 Political parties provide the connection between politics and society.
2 Political parties develop political ideas, programmes and positions.
3 Political parties discuss and evaluate conflicting demands and issues and shape them into policy alternatives.
4 Political parties are the main vehicles for recruiting and selecting people for government and legislative office.
5 Political parties supervise or control government.
6 Unfortunately, political parties often fail to perform these roles with sufficient credibility.

3 Writing a conclusive paragraph
Underline the thesis and the three topic sentences in the paragraphs you have written and use them to write your conclusion.

B2 The power of ordinary people

Stephen Collinson

In June 2015, things changed quickly with regard to two issues that had long been hotly debated in the US. One issue was settled by a Supreme Court decision, the other was greatly influenced by the killing of nine black churchgoers in Charleston, Georgia. Stephen Collinson reflects on this.

After a momentous week, same-sex couples can now marry in all 50 states, the Confederate flag's historic hold on the political institutions of the Deep South is fraying by the hour and Obamacare, after defying another attempt to dismantle it, is now reaffirmed as the law of the land. And as a capstone to these seismic events, the first black president of the United States spent Friday afternoon singing 'Amazing Grace' on live television in front of an African American congregation.

Political and social conventions on civil rights and race relations that for decades have seemed immovable are being swept away in a cascade of grass-roots change. Politicians have been left struggling to keep up. 'Progress on this journey often comes in small increments,' President Barack Obama said Friday, arguing that the task of each generation is to honor the Constitution's guarantee of equal rights as the times change. '(It's) sometimes two steps forward, one step back, compelled by the persistent effort of dedicated citizens,' he said, describing the process of transformational political change around which he has built his political career. 'And then sometimes there are days like this, when that slow, steady effort is rewarded with justice that arrives like a thunderbolt,' Obama said, moments after the Supreme Court delivered its historic decision legalizing same-sex marriage nationwide.

The pace of change is bewildering to some political figures, activists and candidates. In the case of the Confederate flag and gay rights, the shifts are happening despite politicians and not because of them: Federal and state leaders are simply being overtaken by the people on several key issues. [...]

Despite the forest of gay rights activists' rainbow flags that overwhelmed the marble plaza in front of the Supreme Court Friday, there are signs this battle in the culture wars will not be abandoned just yet – especially with possible Supreme Court cases on issues like abortion looming in the near future. [...]

Another example of people power outpacing politicians is unfolding in South Carolina following the massacre. Just over a week ago, Republican political leaders were arguing that the fate of the Confederate flag, which is revered by some white supremacist groups, was a matter for the states alone. But that position quickly became unsustainable. Within days, spurred by an outpouring of support for victims of the alleged hate crime, South Carolina Republican Gov. Nikki Haley joined other prominent local GOP leaders in calling on the legislature to remove the flag from state property. Similar calls came from leaders elsewhere in the South, as major corporations like Walmart announced they would stop selling Confederate Flag merchandise.

'What a vindication of the belief that ordinary people can do extraordinary things,' he [Obama] said after Friday's Supreme Court ruling, which came after years of campaigning by gay rights activists. 'What a reminder of what Bobby Kennedy once said, about how small actions can be like pebbles being thrown into a still lake, and ripples of hope cascade outwards and change the world.'

From: CNN, 28 June 2015

President Obama during the eulogy for the victims of the Charleston shooting of 17 June 2015

People rejoicing in front of the US Supreme Court (26 June 2015)

The Confederate flag in front of the South Carolina state Capitol building. It was taken down on 10 July 2015.

1 **momentous** [mə'mentəs] very important
3 **fray** *(v) ausfransen; schwächer werden*
Obamacare *(infml)* President Barack Obama's health-care reform program
defy sb./sth. resist sb./sth.
dismantle sth. take sth. apart
4 **seismic** ['saɪzmɪk] caused by an earthquake; having a great effect
10 **increment** ['– – –] *(n)* increase
12 **compel sb./sth.** drive sb./sth. forward
18 **pace** *(n)* speed
bewildering *(adj)* surprising, puzzling
28 **revere sb./sth.** [rɪ'vɪə] honour sb./sth.
white supremacist *(adj)* believing in the superiority of European ethnic groups
31 **alleged** *(adj) (fml) mutmaßlich, angeblich*
35 **vindication** proof
39 **ripple** small wave

Part B

COMPREHENSION

1 Issues
Outline the political and legal events mentioned in the text.

ANALYSIS

2 The context
Put the issues and events mentioned in the text into the context of US history and the political system. If necessary, find more information on the internet. SUPPORT p. 268

3 Politicians and the people
Analyse Collinson's view of politicians as compared to how he presents 'the people', either directly or by quoting others.

► SF 17: Analysing stylistic devices

4 Stylistic devices
CHALLENGE In l. 4, Collinson mentions 'seismic events'. Explain this metaphor. Examine the text and find more examples of this kind of imagery.

BEYOND THE TEXT

5 Current issues
Write an email to an American friend, in which you describe a current political issue in Germany. Discuss who the primary agents involved are: protest movements, the media, courts, parliaments, the government …

FACT FILE

The USA – a presidential democracy

The Founding Fathers created a federal government in which the power to 'rule' – i.e. to run the government on a day-to-day business – was given to a democratically elected president. The president is chosen by the people for a four-year term and may run for re-election once. He (or she) is authorized, among other things, to negotiate treaties, to appoint officials, and – as the executive branch of the government – to put laws into effect. The president may also propose laws to Congress. The president presides over the cabinet, consisting of the 'secretaries' (UK: ministers) responsible for the various 'departments' (UK: ministries). Furthermore, he or she is the official head of state and commander in chief of the armed forces.

Congress – the legislative branch – consists of two houses, the Senate and the House of Representatives. In the Senate, each of the 50 states is represented by two senators. The House has 435 members; the number for each state depends on the size of its population. The members of both houses are chosen by the people in general elections. Representatives are elected for a two-year term. The 100 Senators are divided into three so-called classes; one of the three classes comes up for re-election every two years. Senators serve a six-year term and, like the Representatives, can remain in office as long as they are re-elected. Congress makes laws, which then must be approved by the president to go into effect. As Congress has the power to levy taxes and authorize government spending, it has considerable political influence. Congress must also confirm presidential appointments.

The Supreme Court – the judicial branch – is the highest court of the land. It decides if laws made by Congress (or by state governments) are in keeping with the Constitution. New members of the Supreme Court are suggested by the president and must be approved by Congress. The so-called 'justices' are appointed for life. This system of mutual control is known as the system of checks and balances. It was created to make sure that no branch of government can abuse its power.

Make appointments with two students and compare the structures of the federal government in the USA and in Germany.

► The American System of Government, p. 413

African-American identities

C1 Der „Bloody Sunday“ in Selma *Sabrina Fritz*

CD4 03

The following text and the radio report commemorate an important day in the history of the Civil Rights Movement.

Der 7. März 1965 ging als „Blutiger Sonntag“ („Bloody Sunday“) in die US-Geschichte ein. Bürgerrechtsgruppen hatten in Selma damit begonnen, Schwarze zu registrieren, damit diese wählen konnten.

An dem Sonntag begannen 600 Menschen einen Marsch ins 86 Kilometer entfernte Montgomery. Dort wollten sie für ihre Rechte demonstrieren. Doch Polizisten drängten sie an der Stadtgrenze von Selma mit Tränengas und Schlagstöcken zurück. Dutzende wurden verletzt. Fernsehbilder des brutalen Einsatzes schockierten die Nation.

Es folgten zwei Märsche, von denen nur der von der Nationalgarde gesicherte dritte Zug ans Ziel kam. So konnte Martin Luther King am 25. März in Montgomery vor 25.000 Menschen sprechen. Im August unterschrieb Präsident Lyndon B. Johnson das neue Wahlrechtsgesetz. Danach konnten sich Millionen Schwarze erstmals als Wähler registrieren.

From: www.tagesschau.de, 7 March 2015

Commemorating 'Bloody Sunday'

Mediation (German → English)
Some American students ask you how the Civil Rights Movement is perceived in Germany. Tell them about the radio report you have listened to.

► SF 41: Mediation of written and oral texts

FACT FILE

Still struggling for justice and equality – African Americans today

On 9 August 2014, a police officer in Ferguson, Missouri, fatally shot Michael Brown, an 18-year-old African American suspected of robbery. The following days saw displays of mourning turn into protests, civil unrest, rioting and looting of local shops. The police in turn fired tear-gas and rubber bullets at protesters and reporters.

The conflict continued when, on 24 November the same year, a grand jury decided not to indict the police officer who had shot Brown. A number of further incidents made the debate concerning excessive use of police violence against African Americans more urgent. On 19 April, 2015, Freddie Gray, another African American, died in police custody in Baltimore, Maryland. Protests broke out, the National Guard was deployed and a state of emergency declared.

The Civil Rights Movement of the 1950s and 1960s successfully fought against de jure racial segregation and discrimination of African Americans. Half a century later, the situation of African Americans, notably their social and economic status, has certainly greatly improved. There is a solid black middle class, and African Americans are well represented on a political level.

At the same time, however, African Americans are still at a disadvantage. As a social group, they suffer disproportionately from poverty. They are still discriminated against in housing, education, criminal justice and employment and have inadequate access to health care.

'The whirlwinds of revolt will continue to shake the foundations of our nation until the bright day of justice emerges.' When civil rights leader Martin Luther King said these words in his famous 'I have a dream' speech in 1963, he envisaged a long struggle ahead. He was right. This struggle is still evident today.

THINK *Do some further research about the economic, educational and social situation of African Americans today.*
PAIR *Talk to a partner about the difference between de jure and de facto discrimination.*
SHARE *Exchange your findings with another pair.*

Ta-Nehisi Coates

C2 A letter to my son *Ta-Nehisi Coates*

In a letter to his teenage son, journalist Ta-Nehisi Coates reflects on growing up as a black teenager then and now.

Son,
Last Sunday the host of a popular news show asked me what it meant to lose my body. The host was broadcasting from Washington, D.C., and I was seated in a remote studio on the Far West Side of Manhattan. [...]

When the journalist asked me about my body, it was like she was asking me to awaken her from the most gorgeous dream. I have seen that dream all my life. It is perfect houses with nice lawns. [...] And for so long I have wanted to escape into the Dream, to fold my country over my head like a blanket. But this has never been an option, because the Dream rests on our backs, the bedding made from our bodies. And knowing this, knowing that the Dream persists by warring with the known world, I was sad for the host, I was sad for all those families, I was sad for my country, but above all, in that moment, I was sad for you. This is your country, this is your world, this is your body, and you must find some way to live within the all of it.

That was the week you learned that the killers of Michael Brown would go free. The men who had left his body in the street would never be punished. It was not my expectation that anyone would ever be punished. But you were young and still believed. You stayed up till 11 p.m. that night, waiting for the announcement of an indictment, and when instead it was announced that there was none you said, 'I've got to go,' and you went into your room, and I heard you crying. I came in five minutes after, and I didn't hug you, and I didn't comfort you, because I thought it would be wrong to comfort you. I did not tell you that it would be okay, because I have never believed it would be okay. What I told you is what your grandparents tried to tell me: that this is your country, that this is your world, that this is your body, and you must find some way to live within the all of it.

I write you in your 15th year. I am writing you because this was the year you saw Eric Garner choked to death for selling cigarettes; because you know now that Renisha McBride was shot for seeking help, that John Crawford was shot down for browsing in a department store. And you have seen men in uniform drive by and murder Tamir Rice, a 12-year-old child whom they were oath-bound to protect. And you know now, if you did not before, that the police departments of your country have been endowed with the authority to destroy your body. [...]

There is nothing uniquely evil in these destroyers or even in this moment. The destroyers are merely men enforcing the whims of our country, correctly interpreting its heritage and legacy. This legacy aspires to the shackling of black bodies. It is hard to face this. But all our phrasing – race relations, racial chasm, racial justice, racial profiling, white privilege, even white supremacy – serves to obscure that racism is a visceral experience, that it dislodges brains, blocks airways, rips muscle, extracts organs, cracks bones, breaks teeth. You must never look away from this. [...]

Never forget that we were enslaved in this country longer than we have been free. Never forget that for 250 years black people were born into chains – whole generations followed by more generations who knew nothing but chains.

From: Ta-Nehisi Coates, *Between the World and Me*, 2015

10 **persist** continue to exist
warring *(adj)* involved in a war
14 **Michael Brown** African-American teenager shot by a white police-officer in Ferguson, Missouri, on 9 August, 2014
17 **indictment** [ɪn'daɪtmənt] *Anklage(schrift)*
30 **endow sb. with sth.** [ɪn'daʊ] *(fml)* give sth. to sb.
33 **whim** sudden wish to do or have sth. *(Laune)*
34 **aspire to sth.** *(fml)* hope to achieve sth.
shackling *(n)* putting sb. in chains
35 **chasm** ['kæzəm] gap, difference
racial profiling targeting sb. because of their race, e.g. in a police search
36 **white supremacy** [suː'preməsi] racist concept of superiority of European ethnic groups
37 **visceral** ['vɪsərəl] deeply rooted, instinctive

COMPREHENSION

1 The dream
Describe the author's dream and what, according to him, has become of it.

ANALYSIS

2 No comfort
Explain why Coates did not comfort his son when he was sad (cf. ll. 19–21).

3 Racism – a visceral experience
Coates calls racism 'a visceral experience' (ll. 36–37). Explain what he means by this and why he makes this statement.

BEYOND THE TEXT

4 YOU CHOOSE Further research

a Find out more about the cases mentioned (Brown, Garner, McBride, Rice). Point out their similarities and differences.

OR

b Find out about Martin Luther King's "I have a dream" speech. Comment on King's view and compare it with Coates's dream.

C3 An interview with the president

CD 4 04

In June 2015, just days after a racist killing occurred in a church in Charleston, SC, stand-up comedian and podcast-host Marc Maron interviewed President Barack Obama. The president reflects on his time in office and discusses race relations during his lifetime.

Stand-up comedian and podcast host Marc Maron

1 Before listening
You are interviewing a politician towards the end of their time in office. What kind of questions will you ask them?

COMPREHENSION

2 Listening for gist
Listen carefully to an excerpt from the interview and find out whether the following topics are mentioned in the text. Put them in the order they appear in the text.

► SF 22: Listening

helping low-income communities • remembering 'Bloody Sunday' • training police officers • using racist language • improving the situation of elderly African Americans

3 Listening for detail
Listen again and take notes. What are Obama's suggestions for improving the lives of African Americans? Compare your findings with a partner.

BEYOND THE TEXT

4 After listening
Comment on Obama's statement that 'The march isn't over'.

Tea Party protester (2010)

Between community and rebellion

D1 A nation of rebels? *Claude Fischer*

'The land of the free', a place of few restrictions and boundless opportunities, a nation of individualists – is this a true description of the United States? Exchange ideas with a partner.
Now read what sociologist Claude Fischer has to say about the subject.

Americans like to see themselves as rugged individualists, a nation defined by the idea that people should set their own course through life. [...]

The idea that personal liberty defines America is deeply rooted, and shared across the political spectrum. The lifestyle radicals of the '60s saw themselves as heirs to this American tradition of self-expression; today, it energizes the Tea Party movement, marching to defend individual liberty from the smothering grasp of European-style collectivism.

But are Americans really so uniquely individualistic? Are we, for example, more committed individualists than people in those socialist-looking nations of Europe? The answer appears to be no. [...]

The image of America as the bastion of libertarianism is a long-established one. Our Founding Fathers stipulated a set of personal rights and freedoms in our key documents that was, by the standards of that day, radical. The quintessentially American philosopher Ralph Waldo Emerson, in *Self-Reliance*, extolled the person who does not defer to outside authority or compromise his principles for the sake of any collectivity – family, church, party, community, or nation.

This quality in the American character struck observers from overseas, including Alexis de Tocqueville, who in his 1830s book, *Democracy in America*, famously tied the relatively new word 'individualism' to what seemed so refreshingly new about the Americans. Popular culture today reinforces this image by making heroes of men (it's almost always men) who put principle above everything else, even if – perhaps especially if – that makes them loners.

But in modern America, when you look at real issues where individual rights conflict with group interests, Americans don't appear to see things this way at all. [...]

Americans are much likelier than Europeans to reject government or workers interfering with owners' authority to run their businesses. Americans are the most likely to choose freedom over equality, when equality is defined as a situation in which 'nobody is underprivileged and ... social class differences are not so strong.' Not surprisingly, Americans are the most hostile to having the government redress economic inequality.

Nonetheless, the libertarianism of Emerson does not characterize Americans' broader understandings of the role of the individual in society. In fact, Americans seem much more willing to submerge personal liberty to the group than Europeans are.

Yet, the notions of individualism and liberty have lost none of their rhetorical power in today's America – we clearly see ourselves as individualists, far more so than Europeans do. How do we explain this contradiction, between the celebration of America as the land of individual freedom and Americans' actual tendency to favor the group?

1 **rugged** ['rʌgɪd] *(adj)* determined, strong
4 **heir to sb./sth.** [eə(r)] sb. who has inherited sth. from sb.
5 **Tea Party movement** conservative movement in the USA and within the Republican Party
6 **smother sb.** suffocate sb.
grasp *(n)* grip
11 **libertarianism** political view that people should have the freedom to do whatever they want to do
12 **stipulate sth.** state and demand sth. clearly
13 **quintessentially** [ˌkwɪntɪ'senʃəli] *(adj) typisch, durch und durch*
14 **Ralph Waldo Emerson** (1803–1882) US philosopher, essayist and poet
extol sb./sth. [ɪk'stəʊl] praise sb./sth.
15 **defer to sb./sth.** [dɪ'fɜː(r)] *(fml)* accept what sb. else has said or decided
compromise sth. *etw. beeinträchtigen*
18 **Alexis de Tocqueville** (1805–1859) cf. Fact File, p. 41
29 **be hostile to sb./sth.** ['hɒstaɪl] be strongly opposed to sb./sth.
redress sth. *(fml)* correct sth. that is wrong or unfair
33 **submerge sth. to sth. else** (hier) *etw. etw. anderem unterordnen*

The answer, I think, is that Americans have historically adhered to a distinctive view of the individual's place in society, a view that can be called 'communal voluntarism'.

Americans insist on the reality and value of individual free choice, including, critically, free choice to join or leave groups, be they companies or countries. However, Americans also believe that, once individuals are members of the group, they must be loyal. You could think of this philosophy as 'love it or leave it' – with the understanding that you aren't forced to join and are genuinely free to leave. [...]

The Boston Tea Party – demonstrators dressed as Native Americans destroy a shipment of tea in Boston Harbour (1773).

We can see this impulse, too, in the very earliest days of American settlement. In 1630, John Winthrop, who would be the first governor of the Massachusetts Bay Colony, addressed his shipmates sailing to the New World. They were a mix of Puritan refugees and those simply traveling to seek their fortunes. He urged each one to submit to the group: 'We must be knit together in this work as one man. [...] We must delight in each other, make others' conditions our own, rejoice together, mourn together, labor, and suffer together, always having before our eyes ... our community as members of the same body.' [...]

There are several strands to what makes Americans a distinctive people. One strand is certainly the antigovernment impulse; and one is the embrace in the 19th century of laissez-faire ideas. But another, perhaps greater strand is the communalism that to celebrate Americanism, we can emphasize dumping taxed tea off the ship – or we can, with even more justification, emphasize that we are all in this boat together.

From: boston.com, 6 June, 2010

38 **adhere to sth.** [əd'hɪə(r)] *(fml)* believe sth., support sth.
39 **communal voluntarism** strong will to do sth. that is good for the community
61 **strand** *Komponente*
63 **laissez-faire** *(adj)* of or belonging to a policy that wants private business to develop without government control
64 **dumping taxed tea of the ship** reference to the so-called 'Boston Tea Party', when in 1773 American demonstrators destroyed a shipment of tea in Boston harbour, protesting against taxes imposed by the British parliament

COMPREHENSION

1 The topic
Summarize the two fundamentally different impressions that, according to Fischer, one may have of Americans.

ANALYSIS

2 No contradiction?
Explain why Fischer does not think that the two different views of Americans contradict each other and how he combines both views.

3 Style and register
a Identify the register of the article.
b Analyse the stylistic devices the writer uses to support his ideas.
SUPPORT p. 268

► S17: Analysing stylistic devices

BEYOND THE TEXT

4 Freedom or equality?
Interpret the following sentence: 'Americans are the most likely to choose freedom over equality, when equality is defined as a situation in which "nobody is underprivileged and [...] social class differences are not so strong".' (ll. 26–28).

■ FACT FILE

Communities, rebels, subcultures

Two elements can be seen throughout American social history: a strong spirit of community and a tradition of individualism and rebellion.

In the 20th century, several rebellious and innovative movements contributed to US culture. One of these was the **Beat Generation** in the 1950s, a group of authors who rejected materialism, advocated sexual liberation, experi-mented with psychedelic drugs and generally stood for non-conformity and creativity. Notable writers of this movement were Allen Ginsberg, William S. Burroughs and Jack Kerouac.

They were followed by the 1960s **hippie movement**. Hippies developed their own distinctive lifestyle (music, unconventional clothes, specific values) and played an important role in the protests against the Vietnam War ('Make love, not war'). The film *Easy Rider* (1969) captured the mood and values of the movement. Hippies had a strong and lasting influence on television, film, literature and the arts.

Scene from Easy Rider (1969)

Find out more about either the Beat Generation or the hippie movement. Then find a partner who researched the other movement and exchange your findings.

D2 Visiting Burning Man *Grover Norquist*

Have you ever been to any kind of festival? What were your expectations and what was your actual experience like?

Burning Man is a festival of experimental and interactive art that takes place in the Nevada desert. Based on principles like sharing things with others and leaving no traces behind, it draws tens of thousands of visitors every year. Grover Norquist, a conservative lobbyist, supporter of the Republican Party and member of the NRA (National Rifle Association), may seem to be an unlikely participant, but in 2014, he went to his first Burning Man. In his article, he describes his experience.

What is Burning Man? It is a larger version of ... what? Woodstock? That was a bunch of teenagers coming to watch artists perform. At Burning Man, everyone is expected to be a participant. Burners bring their art work, their art cars, their personal dress and/or undress: everyone is on stage. The story of Woodstock was thousands of young people, without the sense to bring their own food and water, being rescued by the state police and sensible bourgeois rural folks. The story of Burning Man is one of radical self-reliance.

It is a more intense than ... what? Not quite the Edinburgh Fringe Festival. Burning Man is an arts festival in the middle of the Nevada desert. It takes hours to get there, and you must bring what you eat or wear or need: you cannot buy anything there. Burning Man is more like Brigadoon – a western ghost town that springs to life. Dust storms. Cold nights. Black Rock City is completely built and then taken apart and disappeared each year, by 65,000 people.

Burning Man is greater than I had ever imagined. I have been to large demonstrations in favor of the environment, and the trash left behind is knee-deep. At Burning Man, you are hard-pressed to find a cigarette butt on the ground. There are no trash bins. Participants carry it in, and they carry it out. I have been to the Louvre. It is a very big

■ FACT FILE

The name **Woodstock** (cf. l. 1) refers to a three-day music and art festival that took place in New York State in the summer of 1969. With an audience of 400,000 people, the festival is seen as the climax of the hippie counterculture in the USA, celebrating freedom, individuality and peace.

The **Edinburgh Fringe Festival ('The Fringe')** (cf. l. 8) is a festival for the performing arts (and is, in fact, the largest arts festival in the world). It takes place in the capital of Scotland every August.

In the 1954 musical film **Brigadoon**, (cf. l. 11) which is set in Scotland, a fictional village miraculously appears every hundred years just for one day.

6 **bourgeois** ['buəʒwɑː] *(adj)* belonging to the middle class
7 **self-reliance** *Selbstständigkeit*

Giant wooden sculpture (Black Rock City, Nevada, 2001)

place with many nice paintings. I knew that. I was not disappointed. Burning Man is more like Petra, the lost city in Jordan, which I found more impressive than its advance billing or reputation. [...]

Some self-professed 'progressives' whined at the thought of my attending what they believed was a ghetto for liberal hippies. Yes, there was a gentleman who skateboarded without elbow or kneepads – or any knickers whatsoever. Yes, I rode in cars dressed-up as cats, bees and spiders; I watched trucks carrying pirate ships and 30 dancers. I drank absinthe. But anyone complaining about a Washington wonk like me at Burning Man is not a Burner himself: The first principle of Burning Man is 'radical inclusiveness', which pretty much rules out the nobody-here-but-us liberals 'gated community' nonsense. [...]

A community that comes together with a minimum of 'rules' demands self-reliance – that everyone clean up after themselves and help thy neighbor. Some day, I want to live 52 weeks a year in a state or city that acts like this. I want to attend a national political convention that advocates the wisdom of Burning Man. [...]

The demand for self-reliance at Burning Man toughens everyone up. There are few fools, and no malingerers. People give of themselves – small gifts like lip balm or tiny flashlights. [...]

On my last day of my first Burning Man, at the Reno airport, a shoeless man (he had lost his shoes in the desert) was accosted by another dust-covered Burner carrying sneakers: 'Take these,' he said. 'They are my Burning Man shoes.' The shoeless man accepted the gift with dignity.

From: *The Guardian*, 2 September 2014

Burning of the effigy 'Embrace' (Black Rock City, Nevada, 2014)

21 **self-professed** *(adj)* stating openly that one has a particular belief or feeling
whine *(v)* complain
23 **knickers** (here) underwear
25 **absinthe** ['æbsɪnθ] strong green alcoholic drink
wonk *(AE derog) Eierkopf*
27 **gated community** group of houses surrounded by a wall or fence
32 **advocate sth.** ['ædvəkeɪt] support sth. publicly
34 **malingerer** [mə'lɪŋgərə] *(infml) Drückeberger/in*
37 **accost sb.** *(fml) jdn. aufdringlich ansprechen*
39 **dignity** *Würde*

Part D

COMPREHENSION

1 True or false?

Decide whether the following statements about this text are true, false or whether the information is not given. Give line numbers to support your answer and correct the statement where necessary.

1 Burning Man draws as many visitors every year as Woodstock did.
2 People have to bring their own food and drink.
3 If you forget to bring something, the other participants will help you.
4 Black Rock City is a real village in the Nevada desert.
5 Most of the festival participants are eco-activists.
6 The writer's acquaintances did not want him to go to the festival.
7 There are parades at Burning Man.
8 None of the other Burning Man participants criticized Norquist for being politically conservative.

► SF15: Marking up a text / Making and taking notes

2 Norquist's experiences

Sum up the writer's experiences at Burning Man. Make notes.

ANALYSIS

3 Atmosphere

Analyse how Norquist gets the spirit and atmosphere of the festival across.

4 The final incident

Examine how Norquist finishes his article in ll. 36–39. Explain what significance the incident at Reno airport has for him.

BEYOND THE TEXT

► SF29: Writing a formal letter or email
► SF27: Having a discussion

5 YOU CHOOSE **Writing an email or holding a discussion**

a Imagine Norquist writing to his friends from the Republican Party about his plan to visit the festival again. Write his email, using your notes from 2.

OR

b In a small group, discuss whether you would be interested in visiting Burning Man. What would intrigue you, what makes you sceptical?

Participants at the Burning Man festival (Black Rock City, Nevada, 2014)

Writing an article for an online youth magazine

An international online youth magazine asks for contributions for the upcoming issue. The general topic is 'Freedom', but the individual articles should focus on more specific aspects.
Your article or essay should be a text of at least 250 words. You can include other forms of media, i.e. photos, illustrations, statistics, video clips etc.

1 Getting together
Organize editorial conferences by getting together in groups of four.

2 Brainstorming
Brainstorm the topic. Discuss different aspects and options, supporting each other with arguments, ideas, quotations or phrases. Refer back to the Focus on Skills page (cf. p. 46) for instructions on the five-paragraph essay. You could include historical, contemporary, political, national as well as international discussions, but also personal comments on aspects of individual freedom. Also consider creative writing, e.g. writing a short story.

3 Writing
Working on your own, write your individual contributions.

4 Revising
Work in your groups again – they now function as correction circles. Either focus on what you are especially good at (e.g. you may be an introduction specialist or an expert on grammar or spelling) or simply exchange your complete text with a partner. Use the assessment sheet that your teacher will give you to give feedback. Then, using the suggestions given by the correction process, try to improve your text.

5 GALLERY WALK **Comparing the texts**
Present your finished texts either in your classroom or on a website. Do a gallery walk and choose the five best contributions for your class magazine. Use the assessment sheet your teacher will give you.

3 The UK – a Kingdom United?

Download a list of chapter vocab here: **Webcode** context-12

1 Getting to know the British

a Choose four red words and four blue words from the flag. Explain them to a partner and say why you think they are part of 'Britishness'.

► SF 3: Using a dictionary

Find an online dictionary here: **Webcode** context-52

b Choose four words you do not know and look them up in a monolingual dictionary. Guess why these words are considered typically British.

c Find three words on the flag that you do not think are typically British. Compare your words with those chosen by a partner.

2 Looking at your own country

What's typically German? Collect your ideas and make up a German flag in the same way as the British flag above. Present your German flag to your partner. Explain your choices and discuss the words that are different.

PREVIEW

In this chapter you will gain an insight into British culture and learn about problems faced by people in Britain today.

Main topics

Focus on Skills: LISTENING

Chapter Task:

CD1 12

Listen to an audio version of the text on the CD or download it here:

Webcode context-13

Character of a country

A political state

The terms Great Britain, Britain, England and the UK are often mistakenly used as synonyms. Great Britain is the largest island of the British Isles (and also the largest island in Europe); England is a country on this island.
The United Kingdom (also called 'Britain') includes England, Scotland, Wales and Northern Ireland and is a state with a population of about 62 million people.
The Union Flag, also known as the Union Jack, has been the national flag of the United Kingdom since 1908 and represents the powerful community and strong individual identities of the different nations.
Characteristically, Scotland has always been seen as a separate nation and since the late 20th century, many Scots have wanted to be fully independent. However, in a 2014 referendum, 55% of the voting population voted to stay in the UK.
Even in the 21st century, the royal family remains a very important British institution. Events like the opening ceremony of the 2012 Olympic Games (in which one scene showed the Queen jumping out of a helicopter with James Bond), the Queen's Diamond Jubilee, Prince William's marriage to Kate Middleton and the birth of Prince George all saw the British population celebrate the fresh and modern image portrayed by their monarchy.

Multiculturalism

As head of the British Empire, the UK was once a colonial superpower with territories in many countries, like India, Australia, New Zealand and small island nations like the Seychelles, Mauritius and the Maldives. Today there is still a strong bond between many former states of the British Empire and most of these nations are members of the Commonwealth of Nations. Together, they work towards world peace, promotion of democracy worldwide, and ending racism, sexism, poverty, ignorance, and disease.
Partly due to its history, immigrants from all over the world have settled in the UK, shaping the culture and adding to the nation's diversity with their food, religions and music. The result is a very multicultural society with the aim that everyone, regardless of colour, race or culture, should feel at home.

An uncertain future

The UK plays a significant role in world politics as a member of the EU and has permanent representation on the UN Security Council and in NATO. Furthermore, the UK has one of the largest and most influential economies in the world.
However, the financial crisis of 2007–2008 did not leave the UK unaffected and has led to economic problems, increased unemployment, social inequality and poverty. Anti-immigration feeling has also increased in some parts of the population and politicians who oppose the EU and Britain's membership have become more and more popular.

► SF2: Learning new words

1 Using your own knowledge
For each of the three parts of the text, try to think of one piece of information which is not mentioned. Write them down and compare your findings with a partner.

2 Words in use

a Find a highlighted expression from the text that describes or names the following:
1. the name of the national flag of the UK
2. a person who joins a team, a union or an organization
3. relatives of the monarch of the United Kingdom
4. something that connects people or things, keeping them firmly together
5. a country that governs many other countries
6. an institution made up of countries that were once under the leadership or control of the British crown
7. having a strong effect on somebody or something

b Give definitions or use examples to explain the following terms from the text:

1. multicultural society
2. referendum
3. image
4. shape
5. former
6. diversity
7. crisis
8. social inequality

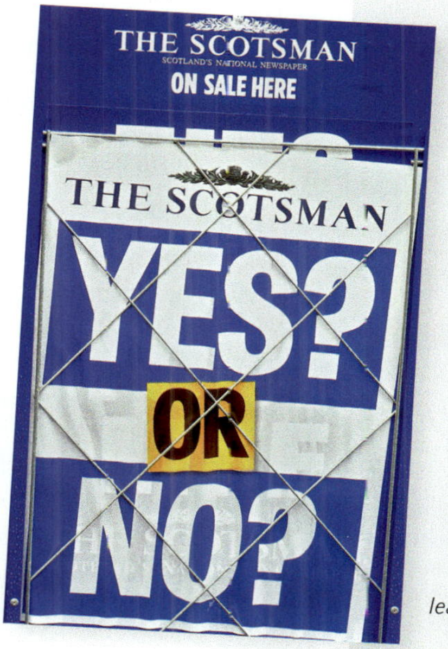

In the 2014 referendum, Scottish inhabitants voted either 'Yes' or 'No' over whether Scotland should leave the UK and become an independent country.

3 Phrases into English
In each of the following sentences, a useful phrase from the text is missing. Copy and complete the sentences. If you aren't sure how to translate the German words, look at the text again.
1. The royal family aims to *(ein frisches, modernes Erscheinungsbild vermitteln)*.
2. People with roots all over the world *(tragen zur Vielfalt der Nation bei)*.
3. Everyone should feel safe in the country they live in *(unabhängig von Hautfarbe, Rasse oder Kultur)*.
4. Events that began on Wall Street in New York *(haben das Vereinigte Königreich nicht unberührt gelassen)*.
5. Politicians *(die die EU ablehnen)* are gaining more popularity in some parts of the UK.

► LP16: Avoiding Germanisms

4 GALLERY WALK Writing
Create a slogan for an educational course on the UK's history and traditions, culture or politics. Write a short explanation for your slogan and use as many highlighted words from the text above as possible. Present your slogans in a gallery walk and decide on the best three.

FACT FILE
Slogans should be easy to understand and be memorable. Good slogans play with language (e.g. rhyme or rhythm and puns) to make you think.

A crowned nation

A1 Dangerous books *Alan Bennett*

- In three sentences, state why you think reading is or isn't important. Share your answers in class.
- Discuss whether you think reading plays a part in a typical day in the Queen's life. What other duties might be on her agenda?

In the following extract from the novel The Uncommon Reader, *the Queen has developed an intense passion for literature. This starts to affect the way she carries out her public duties and what people think of her.*

One of the Queen's recurrent royal responsibilities was to open Parliament, an obligation she had never previously found particularly burdensome and actually rather enjoyed: to be driven down the Mall on a bright autumn morning even after fifty years was something of a treat. But not any more. She was dreading the two hours the whole thing was due to take, though fortunately they were in the coach, not the open carriage, so she could take along her book. She'd got quite good at reading and waving, the trick being to keep the book below the level of the window and to keep focused on it and not on the crowds. The duke didn't like it one bit, of course, but goodness it helped.

The Queen and the Duke of Edinburgh making a journey in the royal carriage

Which was all very well, except it was only when she was actually in the coach, with the procession drawn up in the palace forecourt and ready for the off, that, as she put on her glasses, she realised she'd forgotten the book. And while the duke fumes in the corner and the postillions fidget, the horses shift and the harness clinks, Norman is rung on the mobile. The Guardsmen stand at ease and the procession waits. The officer in charge looks at his watch. Two minutes late. Knowing nothing displeases Her Majesty more and knowing nothing of the book, he does not look forward to the repercussions that must inevitably follow. But here is Norman, skittering across the gravel with the book thoughtfully hidden in a shawl, and off they go.

Still, it is an ill-tempered royal couple that is driven down the Mall, the duke waving viciously from his side, the Queen listlessly from hers, and at some speed, too, as the procession tries to pick up the two minutes that have been lost.

At Westminster she popped the offending book behind a cushion in the carriage ready for the journey back, mindful as she sat on the throne and embarked on her speech of how tedious was the twaddle she was called on to deliver and that this was actually the only occasion when she got to read aloud to the nation. 'My government will do this ... my government will do that.' It was so barbarously phrased and wholly devoid of style or interest that she felt it demeaned the very act of reading itself, with this year's performance even more garbled than usual as she, too, tried to pick up the missing couple of minutes.

It was with some relief that she got back into the coach and reached behind the cushion for her book. It was not there. Steadfastly waving as they rumbled along, she surreptitiously felt behind the other cushions.

2 **burdensome** implying hard work
3 **the Mall** [mæl] road leading to Buckingham Palace
14 **draw up** position yourself
ready for the off ready to go
16 **fume** be very angry
17 **postillion** [pɒ'stɪlɪən] driver of a coach with horses
fidget ['fɪdʒɪt] make nervous movements
Norman fictional character in *The Uncommon Reader* who works as the Queen's servant
18 **stand at ease** relax *(military)*
21 **repercussion** [ˌriːpə'kʌʃn] negative consequence
skitter run in a funny way
24 **vicious** ['vɪʃəs] angry
listless without energy or enthusiasm
28 **twaddle** ['twɒdl] *(infml)* silly speech
30 **barbarous** very unpleasant
31 **devoid of sth.** without sth.
demean sth. make people have less respect for sth.
36 **surreptitious** [ˌsʌrəp'tɪʃəs] subtle

'You're not sitting on it?'

'Sitting on what?'

'My book.'

'No, I am not. Some British Legion people here, and wheelchairs. Wave, for God's sake.'

When they arrived at the palace she had a word with Grant, the young footman in charge, who said that while ma'am had been in the Lords the sniffer dogs had been round and security had confiscated the book. He thought it had probably been exploded.

'Exploded?' said the Queen. 'But it was Anita Brookner.'

The young man, who seemed remarkably undeferential, said security may have thought it was a device.

The Queen said: 'Yes. That is exactly what it is. A book is a device to ignite the imagination.'

The footman said: 'Yes, ma'am.'

It was as if he was talking to his grandmother, and not for the first time the Queen was made unpleasantly aware of the hostility her reading seemed to arouse.

'Very well,' she said. 'Then you should inform security that I shall expect to find another copy of the same book, vetted and explosive free, waiting on my desk tomorrow morning. And another thing. The carriage cushions are filthy. Look at my gloves.' Her Majesty departed.

'Fuck,' said the footman, fishing out the book from where he had been told to hide it down the front of his breeches. But of the lateness of the procession, to everyone's surprise nothing was officially said.

From: *The Uncommon Reader*, 2008

40 **British Legion** ['li:dʒn] organization that helps ex-soldiers
44 **confiscate sth.** take sth. away
46 **Anita Brookner** (born 1928) British novelist and art historian
47 **undeferential** [ˌʌndɪfəˈrenʃl] showing no respect
49 **ignite sth.** *etwas entzünden*
55 **vet sth.** check sth.
59 **breeches** ['brɪtʃɪz] *(pl)* *Reiterhose*

COMPREHENSION

1 Identifying key points

a Point out how the Queen's reading habit interferes with her duties.

b Compare the Queen's day as shown in the passage to your initial ideas about a typical day in her life.

LANGUAGE AWARENESS

2 Analysing direct speech

Analyse the language used in direct speech by the Queen, the duke and the footman. Assess its effect on your impression of their characters.

ANALYSIS

3 Analysing humour

Analyse the *humour in this passage. Take into consideration how the *plot, certain aspects of the language and the *imagery contribute to the humorous effect.

► SF 19: Analysing narrative prose

► LP 21: Writing about texts

BEYOND THE TEXT

4 YOU CHOOSE Creative writing

a Imagine another situation (e.g. naming a ship / attending a pop-concert / being on a state visit) in which the Queen does not fulfil her duties because of her new hobby and write a similar passage. Try to include elements of *humour.

OR

b After the incident, the footman tells his wife about his encounter with the Queen. Write their dialogue and include the events that probably took place while the Queen was opening the Parliament.

SUPPORT p. 269

► SF 37: Doing a creative writing task

► EE 4: Talking about sensitive issues

Find out more about the British royal family here:
Webcode context-14

FACT FILE

The Palace of Westminster, London

The British system of government

The head of state is the king or queen, who has many ceremonial functions and social duties but no real power. The monarch's duties include opening Parliament and officially appointing the Prime Minister after his or her election.

The UK Parliament is known as the 'Mother of Parliaments' because it has served as a model for many governments all over the world. It dates back to the year 1215, when a group of noblemen forced King John of England to respect certain rights. Among these, set down in the Magna Carta, was their right to be consulted before the king could make them pay new taxes. Over the centuries, this group of noblemen evolved into today's Parliament.

Members of Parliament attending a session of Parliament in the House of Commons

The two houses of Parliament, the House of Lords and the House of Commons, meet in the Palace of Westminster. Thus journalists often refer to 'Westminster' when they mean Parliament, especially if they are talking about the House of Commons. There are currently over 700 members of the House of Lords, but their power is limited. Although both houses of Parliament must, in theory, approve laws before they are submitted to the king or queen, the Lords can only delay a bill that has passed in the House of Commons. Traditionally, a committee of the House of Lords was also the highest court in the land, but that function has been moved to the newly created Supreme Court.

Real power lies with the House of Commons, which is elected for up to five years (although the Prime Minister can call a general election any time before that). Each Member of Parliament (MP) represents one of 650 constituencies (electoral districts) in the UK. In each constituency, the candidate with the most votes wins, and that person then sits in the Commons. In the UK's so-called 'first-past-the-post' system, all other votes are worthless. This effectively prevents smaller parties being elected to Parliament and can potentially lead to a majority in Parliament that does not always reflect the total number of votes. For example, in the 2005 general election, the Labour party won 55% of the seats in the House of Commons with just 35% of the votes.

Her Majesty's Government consists of the Prime Minister (PM) and the Cabinet, which is made up of the MPs who run the different government departments. The most important ministers are the Chancellor of the Exchequer, who is in charge of finance, the Foreign Secretary and the Home Secretary, who is responsible for the country's internal affairs. In the press, the Prime Minister's office is often referred to as 'Number 10', after its address at 10 Downing Street, and the ministries are known as 'Whitehall', after the street in London where most of them are located.

1 *Describe the roles of the following people and groups to a partner using one sentence for each:*
Partner A: the Prime Minister • the Cabinet
Partner B: an MP • the monarch

2 *In a table, list what you now know about one of the houses of the UK Parliament. Present your list to your partner.*
Partner A: The House of Lords
Partner B: The House of Commons

3 *List differences and similarities to the German system of government.*

► The British System of Government, p. 412

LISTENING **FOCUS ON SKILLS**

Listening for gist and detail

Listening is the key to successful oral communication. It requires focus, preparation and practice.

What do the British think of the royal family?

1 Before listening
You are going to hear two short interviews about people's opinions of the British monarchy. What might people say? Write 2–3 sentences.

2 Dealing with different accents
When listening to native English speakers, you will often hear people speak with different accents. When somebody's accent is difficult to understand, you should focus on words you can understand and use the context to figure out the rest of the sentence. As you listen, you will probably get used to the accent.

a Listen to a short excerpt of an interview. The interviewer and the interviewee have different accents. Try to write down exactly what both men say, then compare your answers with a partner.
b Discuss which man was easier to understand and why.

FACT FILE

A regional accent is determined by where a speaker is from and where they live.
A social accent is often determined by a speaker's socio-economic status, i.e. their level of education, how wealthy their family is, and their family's level of education. People from the same region can have different accents if they are from different socio-economic groups.

CD1 13
► SF 22: Listening

3 First listening: listening for gist

CD1 14

a Skim through the task below and note down keywords that you can listen out for. Compare your notes with a partner.
b Listen to the extract, then choose the right answers.
1 The first interviewee …
… considers the institution of the monarchy a brilliant idea.
… isn't really sure what he thinks about the monarchy.
… completely rejects the monarchy.
2 The young couple …
… think the royal family should be abolished.
… have generally positive opinions about the royal family.
… think the royal family is mainly a bad thing for the UK.

4 Second listening: listening for detail
Again, skim through the questions to find out what specific information you will have to listen out for.

a Listen to the first interview again. Are the sentences below true or false? Correct the false answers.
1 The first interviewee understands why some people would like to have an elected president instead of a monarch.
2 The Queen is his favourite member of the royal family.
3 He was born during the Queen's reign.
4 He does not think that Charles will become King.

Buckingham Palace, home of the Queen in London

b Listen to the second interview and finish the sentences.
1. The young woman says that the royal family does a lot of good for …
2. The young man mentions … as two examples of the stereotypical English image.
3. The young man says that the … has been lost.
4. The young man's favourite member of the royal family is …
5. The young man thinks that Kate has …

c Compare and discuss your results with a partner.

5 Evaluating the listening procedure

a Compare your initial expectations which you wrote for Task 1 with what you actually heard.

b Discuss the listening procedure with a partner. To what extent were your anticipations useful? Which tip or strategy was most helpful to you?

A2 Does Britain still need the monarchy?

COMPREHENSION

CD1 15

► SF 22: Listening

► SF 10: Working with closed test formats

1 Listening for gist

Listen to part two of the podcast and decide which of the following statements best expresses the main ideas of the speakers.

a 1 The first interviewee would keep the monarchy, but doesn't like it very much.
2 The first interviewee thinks the media hate the royal family.

b 1 The second interviewee quite likes William and Harry.
2 The second interviewee thinks Australia should no longer be a member of the Commonwealth.

► SF 10: Working with closed test formats

2 Listening for detail

Listen to the first interview again. Match the arguments given in the list below to those of the interviewee. There are more arguments than needed.

do a lot of charity • *very expensive* • *outdated institution* • *symbol of Britain* • *attracts tourists* • *good role model* • *a tradition to keep* • *too many scandals* • *arrogant and snobby family* • *close to the people* • *loved by the media*

BEYOND THE TEXT

3 Preparing for a discussion

a Look again at the arguments put forward by all of the speakers in both parts of the podcast. Divide their arguments into two columns: 'in favour of' and 'against' the monarchy.

b Together with a partner, add further arguments to your list.

LANGUAGE HELP

Stating your opinion:
- In my opinion … / The way I see it …
- As far as I'm concerned / If you ask me …
- I'm absolutely convinced that …

Agreeing:
- I couldn't agree with you more.
- Exactly! / Precisely! / Certainly! / Definitely!

Disagreeing:
- I'm not so sure, really.
- I'm not convinced that …
- I strongly disagree / I don't agree with you at all.

4 Having a discussion

a In groups of 4–5, discuss whether the monarchy in Britain should be abolished. ► LANGUAGE HELP

b CHALLENGE Take notes of the different arguments raised during your discussion and present the three most convincing ones to the rest of the class.

► SF 27: Having a discussion

The multicultural face of the UK

FACT FILE

From Empire to Commonwealth

The British Empire was the largest colonial empire in the world covering nearly one fifth of the land worldwide during the late 19th and early 20th centuries.

Since the 16th century, Britain had established colonies all over the world including settlement colonies like Canada, Australia and New Zealand, trading colonies (e.g. India) as well as strategically important naval bases in the Mediterranean (e.g. Gibraltar). It was said that the sun never set on the Empire, so great was its power and territory. However, the effects of a decolonization movement and two world wars led to the decline of the British Empire and the foundation of the Commonwealth of Nations. The Commonwealth of Nations was founded in 1931 and is a voluntary association of 53 countries of the former British Empire.

Queen Victoria (1819–1901) ruled over almost a quarter of the world's population by the end of her reign.

The Head of the Commonwealth is the British monarch. The states are united by language (English), culture, history and in their values, such as democracy, economic development, the rule of law and the guarantee of human rights.

The Commonwealth includes about two billion people, or 30% of the world's population. Every four years, athletes from the member countries take part in the Commonwealth Games. These include classic Olympic sports as well as typical sports played in Commonwealth countries (e.g. netball). The three key values of the Commonwealth Games movement are humanity, equality and destiny.

Explain and comment on the quote 'The sun never sets on the British Empire'.

B1 The British Empire report

The video you are about to watch presents the rise, dominance and fall of the British Empire.

► SF23: Analysing a film

1 Before viewing

Before you watch the video, speculate about how the filmmaker might deal with the subject of colonialism. Take into consideration the Fact File 'From Empire to Commonwealth'.

DVD

peak highest point
leap big jump
shift sth. move sth.
spell trouble be a problem

ANALYSIS

2 Viewing for the first time

Watch the video and describe it with two adjectives which you find most suitable: e.g. funny, informative, exaggerated, annoying, innovative, childish, surprising, etc. Explain your choices.

3 Examining how material is presented

a Watch the video for a second time. Examine the different methods that are used to present information. Consider how the events are visualized and supported by film excerpts, still pictures, sound effects and music.

b Compare your findings and discuss their effect on the viewer. To what extent do the presenter and the different material that is shown support the viewer's understanding of the Empire's history?

Map of the world showing in red the extent of the British Empire in 1901

BEYOND THE TEXT

4 Beyond the video

a List five important dates and events in German history. With a partner compare your lists and decide on the four most important events.

b CHALLENGE Write the script for a video report aimed at an English audience in which you show and comment on important dates in German history. If you want to, you can use *irony and *humour or you can make it informative and objective.

▸ SF37: Doing a creative writing task

B2 Between two cultures *Mike Bartlett*

In the play Artefacts *by Mike Bartlett, Kelly is a teenage girl living in Great Britain with her mother Susan. Her father left the family when Kelly was little to live in his home country Iraq. In the following scenes, she meets her father Ibrahim for the first time since he left.*

- Read the two extracts and imagine what the scenes would look like on a stage.

Actor Peter Polycarpou played the role of Ibrahim in Artefacts *in 2008.*

Extract 1

IBRAHIM Do you think we look alike?
KELLY You and my uncle?
IBRAHIM You and me.
KELLY Uh ... No.
IBRAHIM You're passionate.
KELLY I'm English.
IBRAHIM You are half Iraqi. You can have an Iraqi passport now.
KELLY That's not much use.
IBRAHIM Would you prefer it if I had been an American?
KELLY No.
Well, yeah. That would be better though, wouldn't it? Cos an American passport's worth loads. I could go there and work and stuff. But I told you I'm not going to go to Iraq, am I?

After a short pause when Kelly's mother Susan enters, Kelly continues.

KELLY This afternoon when I was bored I looked in the mirror cos, apparently, I'm half Iraqi.
SUSAN Are you sure you're both all right?
KELLY But which bits?
SUSAN Up here?
KELLY Hips. Hands.
IBRAHIM Kelly?
KELLY I've got English legs. Iraqi breasts.
IBRAHIM I wish we could've met earlier.
KELLY But my stomach is slightly potted.
IBRAHIM Kelly? [...]
KELLY I have a little pot belly. Maybe this is the point they mix. The two countries. Where my genes got confused. This belly is not Iraqi or English. It's Engraqi. Iringlish. I like my belly. Yeah. [...]
Am I what you expected?
IBRAHIM I tried not to expect anything.

11 **cos** [kəz] *(infml)* because
24 **potted** (here) larger than usual

KELLY But you did.
IBRAHIM I imagined you might look like Kate Winslet.
KELLY This isn't going very well, is it?
IBRAHIM I don't know.
KELLY Bit of a fucking disappointment for you.
IBRAHIM No.
KELLY If you were after –
IBRAHIM You are better than Kate Winslet.
KELLY What do you want?
IBRAHIM You are you.
KELLY Why are you here? Now, what do you *want*?
IBRAHIM That we meet.
KELLY Just that.
IBRAHIM Yes.
KELLY You don't want money?
IBRAHIM I run the National Museum of Iraq. In Baghdad. A number of our artefacts were stolen. During the war. I was invited to come and give a lecture at the British Museum about the current state of our collection. That is where I have been today.
KELLY So I'm not actually sure why you came at all.
IBRAHIM It is expensive to fly here. I will probably never come back to Britain. So I thought it best we meet.

Actress Lizzie Watts performing in a production of Artefacts at the Bush Theatre in London

Extract 2

On her first visit to Iraq, Kelly meets her father's other family. One of Ibrahim's daughters has been kidnapped and Kelly asks her father about this incident.

IBRAHIM Why? Why are you asking? Why do you want to know?
KELLY I've got a right to know.
IBRAHIM A right? You have no right to know about my family.
KELLY She's my sister.
IBRAHIM And I'm your father.
KELLY Apparently.
IBRAHIM You should trust me that I will do the right thing. But you don't. Do you? You think you know better. You have not been here a day yet. What makes you think you will know better than me?
KELLY Maybe I don't trust you. Not hard to work out why, is it? [...]
IBRAHIM What makes you think what I am doing is a mistake?
KELLY You are that kind of man.
IBRAHIM Weak.
KELLY Careless.
IBRAHIM And why do you think I am *careless*? I will tell you.
KELLY Yeah, all right then, tell me what I think.
IBRAHIM You come here and you see this city and you see me and my normal house. You see how poor we are and we don't have things you have. And you see on your news how the country is fighting itself. And you think we are all careless. No, not just careless, you think we are stupid. So this is why you're asking what is going on, because you want to make sure that I am being civilised in what I am doing. That I am being intelligent – *reasonable* in how I am behaving. Because we Iraqis, you think, we tend to get things wrong all the time.

76 **tend to do sth.** do sth. regularly

78 **mess sth. up** do sth. very badly

We allow our girls to be kidnapped.
We tend to mess things up.
That is really why you do not trust me.

KELLY Cos I'm racist.

IBRAHIM Because you are English. And you don't know any better. When you are a child in England you are still taught underneath that you should rule the world. How in the end Britain has always made the world better.

KELLY You told me I'm half Iraqi.

IBRAHIM I hoped you were.

KELLY I am. Whether I like it or not. I can't choose.

IBRAHIM Yes, you can. You can choose where you belong.

From: *Artefacts*, 2008

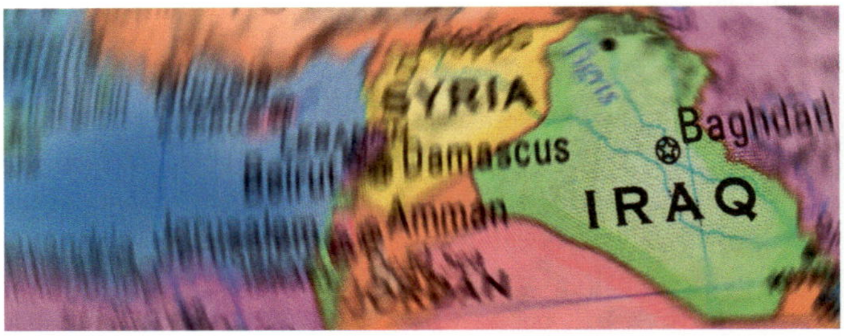

COMPREHENSION

1 Looking for the main idea

a Describe how Kelly tries to find out which culture she belongs to.
b Point out which prejudices towards the Iraqi and English cultures are discussed in the text.

ANALYSIS

► SF 20: Analysing drama
► LP 18: Writing about texts

2 Analysing character relationships

Analyse the relationship between Kelly and her father Ibrahim. Reflect on what they talk about and how they speak to each other.

SUPPORT p. 269

LANGUAGE AWARENESS

FACT FILE

In literature, **colloquialism** is the use of informal words and expressions in conversations to underline the speaker's social status, level of education, relationship with others, etc. The opposite of colloquialism is standard or formal English.
Examples:
wanna *want to*
gonna *going to*
go nuts *go insane*

3 Studying colloquial language

a Read the explanation of colloquialism on the left and find examples of colloquial language in the conversation between Kelly and Ibrahim.
b Rewrite the examples you found in the text in formal English.

BEYOND THE TEXT

► SF 37: Doing a creative writing task

4 YOU CHOOSE Creative writing

a Write an email Kelly sends to her best friend in Britain after she has met her father in Iraq.

OR

b Together with a partner, write a dialogue between Kelly's father Ibrahim and her mum Susan after the first meeting of father and daughter.

► SF 27: Having a discussion

5 Thinking about cultural identity

a Together with a partner, discuss whether 'You can choose where you belong' (l. 88). Who or what influences you in your choice? Think about family, culture, education and list concrete examples for and against the quote.

► LP 13: Placing emphasis on key points
► SF 34: Argumentative writing

b CHALLENGE Write a *comment on Ibrahim's idea that 'You can choose where you belong.' (l. 88)

B3 The British and their tea

The British are famous for their love of tea. In the following podcast, you will get to know more about this tradition.

- Before listening, brainstorm in class what you know about the British tradition of drinking tea.

COMPREHENSION

1 Listening for gist
In one sentence, summarize what the podcast is about.

► SF 22: Listening

CD1 16

rich (here) dark; strong

2 Listening for detail

a Complete the following statements about the history of tea.
 1 The British made their first cup of tea sometime in the middle of the … century.
 2 In the 19th century, tea became popular among … people.
 3 Tea drinking has a much longer history in …, where people have drunk tea for thousands of years.
 4 Nearly everyone in Britain puts … in their tea, and about a third of people add … to make the tea sweet.

b CHALLENGE While working on 2a, take notes on how to make a nice cup of tea the British way.

TROUBLE SPOT
drunk *(v) = getrunken*
drunk *(adj) = betrunken*
drunk *(n) = Betrunkene/r*

► EE 1: Eating in and out

3 Analysing style
How does the speaker of the podcast try to hold the audience's attention and entertain his listeners? SUPPORT p. 269

► SF 17: Analysing stylistic devices

CULTURE SPOT

The Fourth Plinth

The Fourth Plinth is one of four pillars in Trafalgar Square in London, which was built in 1840. As there wasn't enough money to make a statue for it, it stood empty for 150 years. In 1999 a commission decided to display contemporary artworks on it and in 2010 the artwork Nelson's Ship in a Bottle *by Anglo-Nigerian artist sculptor Yinka Shonibare was unveiled.*

Yinka Shonibare

1 Comment on the idea to use the fourth plinth as a display for art.

2 Research other artworks that have been featured on the Fourth Plinth. Present the one you like best to the class. Give reasons. ► S5: Doing research

B4 Halal food festival

'Britishness' is influenced by the many different cultures found in the UK. One such influence is Britain's large Muslim population.

Haloodies at the Halal Food Festival in London

The first ever to be held in the UK and the world's largest, the Halal Food Festival is a three-day consumer food show dedicated to foodies who eat halal, or haloodies as they have been coined by festival events director Norman Khawaja. [...]

Visitors can look forward to over 100 exhibitors from across the globe showcasing the most innovative and delicious halal food and drink products, restaurants and street-food stalls. In addition, there is a cooking school and live demonstration kitchen featuring top chefs. [...]

Halal is an Arabic word meaning lawful or permissible. It not only covers food and drink but also all matters of daily life. Followers of Islam (Muslims) must follow a dietary requirement that does not permit pork or pork products or alcohol and only allows meat slaughtered in accordance to strict guidelines in the Qur'an. Halal food is not a cuisine or a style of cooking in its own right. Therefore any cuisine or style can become halal provided it is cooked using halal ingredients and prepared in a halal manner.

With a growing UK Muslim population currently standing at 2.7 million (Census 2011) with a £20.5 billion a year spending power and expected to rise to 5.5 million people by 2030 (Pew Report, The Future of the Global Muslim Population 2011) access to delicious halal food in the UK is becoming increasingly important. [...]

Improving the range, availability and quality of halal foods and restaurants drives the Halal Food Festival's founder Imran Kausar, who comments: 'The growing British Muslim middle classes have greater needs and demands from food producers, retailers and restaurateurs, and command significant spending power.'

From: HalalFocus, 2013

TROUBLE SPOT

chef (l. 7) = *Koch / Köchin*
boss = *Chef / -in, Vorgesetzte/r*

2 **foodie** person who is interested in food culture
3 **coin sth.** name sth.
5 **innovative** ['----] using new ideas
10 **dietary** ['daɪətəri] related to what people eat
11 **slaughter sth.** kill sth. (an animal) for its meat
Qur'an [kə'rɑːn] *Koran*
27 **restaurateur** [ˌrestərə'tɜː] *(fml)* person who owns a restaurant
28 **command sth.** (here) have sth.

LANGUAGE HELP

- Halal food is delicious/interesting/exotic/important.
- Are YOU interested in / excited by trying new food?
- Come to the Halal Food Festival for ...
- Want to meet top chefs / taste good food / try cooking something new?
- Come and see us at ...

COMPREHENSION

1 Finding key points

a Explain the concept of halal.

b Create an electronic flyer for the halal festival in which you inform the public about the key details of the event. ▶ LANGUAGE HELP

BEYOND THE TEXT

2 YOU CHOOSE **Thinking about other food cultures**

a What other ideas for festivals to integrate different cultures can you think of? Choose one example and write an outline for an event similar to the text above.

OR

b Prepare a short oral presentation about similar food festivals in Germany.

▶ SF 8: Structuring ideas
▶ SF 24: Giving a presentation

Find a tool to design your flyer here:
Webcode context-50

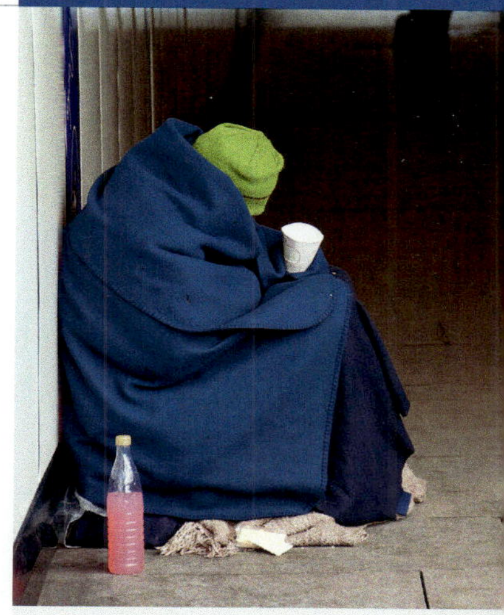

B5 Eastern Europeans in the UK *Amelia Gentleman*

Many Polish migrants want to work in the UK, but success is not guaranteed.

The UK remains a promised land in popular Polish mythology. When someone returns from a stint working there, they are expected to come home driving an expensive car, with a suitcase full of savings. For some, like Michal Novak, 30, the return was triumphant. He came back after 14 years in Britain with enough money to buy a smart flat in a good part of Warsaw, and the prospect of a good job in Poland, paying almost the same salary as he had received in London.

Even so, friends and colleagues were puzzled by his decision to return. 'People asked me "Why did you come back? It's so horrible here." As if it is a dogma that living in the UK is better. And it's not true,' he said.

Less triumphant will be the return of Lukasz Z, 24, and Adam B, 22, due to travel back by coach imminently, their fare paid for by the Polish charity Barka, that seeks out Poles sleeping rough in London, and encourages them to abandon their attempt to make it in the UK. It gives them tickets to get home and offers them somewhere to live once they arrive.

Adam has spent the past six months since he lost his factory job sleeping in parks, railway stations and squats, stealing food to survive. Lukasz has spent several chunks of the past year in Pentonville prison, sentenced for stealing and carrying a knife, after work as a painter and decorator dried up.

Neither man had been in trouble with the police at home, and neither has anything positive to say about their time here.

Their stories illustrate the successes and failures of UK-Polish migration, a phenomenon that exploded on an unexpected scale with Poland's accession to the EU in 2004. [...]

Whilst the vast majority have found work in the building industry, or as carers, cleaners or waitresses, not everyone has been happy. [...]

'I used to come across so many similar stories in London – of young Polish people with economics degrees working as waiters,' [Novak] said.

'Typically, they left Poland five years ago because they couldn't find any work here, but they fail to find anything proper there. So they got jobs much below what their education has prepared them for, and they spent four or five years of their lives, working in a bar, not getting any experience. What can you do here after four years as a waiter in the UK?'

From: *The Guardian*, 6 April 2011

FACT FILE

Since the end of World War II, there has been a continual flow of **migrants from Poland** to the UK. After the fall of Communism in 1989 and the relaxing of travel restrictions within Europe, Polish immigration increased sharply. The expansion of the EU to include Poland in 2004 also paved the way for more Polish workers to relocate to the UK, as citizens from EU member states could work there legally. However, after 2007, Polish migration to the UK began to decrease as economic growth and less unemployment in Poland made it more attractive for Poles to stay in there for work.

2 **stint** *Arbeitsperiode*
8 **dogma** unquestioned belief
11 **imminent** ['– – –] happening very soon
16 **squat** [skwɒt] *(n) besetztes Haus*
chunk large part

COMPREHENSION

1 Summarizing key parts of an article
Summarize the stories of Lukasz and Adam and present them to a partner.

► SF 31: Writing a summary

2 Mediation (English → German)
Write a blog entry in German about the successes and failures of immigrants in the UK, comparing the lives of the three Polish men portrayed in the article.

► SF 41: Mediation of written and oral texts
► LP 4: Present perfect and simple past

BEYOND THE TEXT

3 YOU CHOOSE **Writing**

a Write a *comment on the idea of Britain as 'a promised land' (l. 1) for migrants.

OR

b Write a letter from either Lukasz or Adam to friends or relatives in Poland, explaining what happened to them in the UK and why they are returning.

► SF 34: Argumentative writing
► LP 18: Writing about texts

Where do we go from here?

C1 A referendum on the EU

CD1 17

disillusionment [ˌdɪsɪˈluːʒnmənt] state of no longer feeling enthusiasm
ensure sth. [ɪnˈʃʊə] make sure that sth. happens

▶ SF 12: Analysing charts and graphs
▶ SF 22: Listening

- Before listening to a speech by British Prime Minister David Cameron about the UK's membership in the EU, describe the chart below left.

ON THE UK'S MEMBERSHIP OF THE EU

Thinking about the UK's membership of the European Union, would you say that this is generally a good thing or a bad thing?

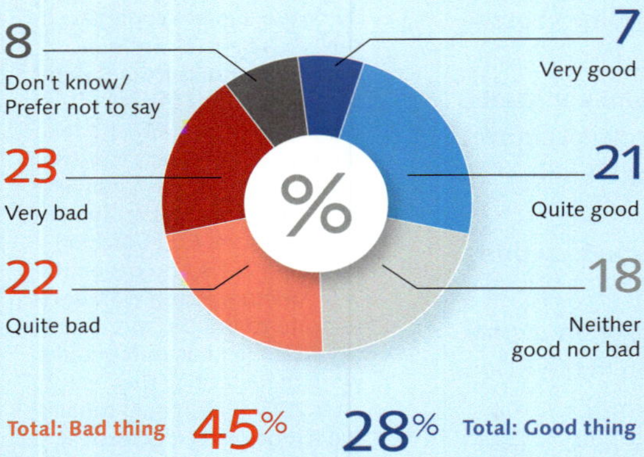

Opinion Research carried out an online survey of 1,957 GB adults aged 18+ from 13 to 15 November 2012. Results have been weighted to nationally representative criteria.

COMPREHENSION

1 Listening for gist
Which of these topics does David Cameron talk about?
1 reasons for the British to be sceptical about the EU
2 arguments why he wants a referendum right now
3 the right time for a referendum

2 Listening for detail
a Complete the sentences taken from Cameron's speech.
1 They resent the ... in our national life by what they see as unnecessary rules and ...
2 But I don't believe that to make a ... at this moment is the right way forward, either for Britain or for Europe as a ...
3 And when the referendum comes let me say now that if we can ... such an arrangement, I will ... for it with all my heart and ...

b CHALLENGE Explain the reasons for the anti-EU feeling mentioned by Cameron in your own words.

ANALYSIS

3 Analysing style
Listen again. Analyse how Cameron tries to convince his listeners of his views. Focus on language and content. Is he successful? SUPPORT p. 270

▶ SF 17: Analysing stylistic devices

C2 Merkel's speech in London

TROUBLE SPOT
eine Rede halten (l. 2) = *give / deliver / make a speech*
Not: ~~hold a speech~~

In February 2014, Angela Merkel gave a speech in London to both Houses of the British Parliament on the future of Europe. British expectations concerning her speech were high – perhaps too high, as Merkel said herself at the beginning of her address.

BERLIN – Es ist eine Geste besonderer Wertschätzung für die Bundeskanzlerin: Erst als dritte deutsche Politikerin nach Willy Brandt und Richard von Weizsäcker hielt Angela Merkel an diesem Donnerstag eine Rede vor beiden Kammern des britischen Parlaments. Die Regierungschefin selbst sprach zu Beginn ihres Auftritts von einer „großen Ehre", die ihr zuteil werde. Die Einladung sei „Ausdruck der engen Verbundenheit zwischen unseren Ländern".

Die Kanzlerin erinnerte an ihren ersten Besuch in London im Frühjahr 1990. Mit ihrem Mann sei sie durch den Hyde-Park zum dortigen Speakers Corner gegangen. Dies sei gerade für sie als Ostdeutsche ein „Symbol der freien Rede" gewesen. Merkel begann ihre Rede auf Englisch, wechselte erst nach einigen Minuten ins Deutsche.

Angela Merkel shakes David Cameron's hand in front of Number 10 Downing Street.

Die Kanzlerin wies selbst darauf hin, dass ihr Auftritt in der britischen Öffentlichkeit im Vorfeld mit hohen Erwartungen verbunden wurde. Die konservative Regierung um Premierminister David Cameron erhofft sich Schützenhilfe von Deutschland in der Europapolitik. Cameron will im Rahmen von Vertragsreformen unter anderem die Arbeitnehmerfreizügigkeit innerhalb der EU begrenzen und die Arbeitszeitrichtlinie beschneiden. Bis 2017 will er das Volk über den Verbleib in der EU abstimmen lassen.

„Einige erwarten, dass meine Rede den Weg für eine fundamentale Reform der europäischen Architektur ebnet, die alle angeblichen oder tatsächlichen britischen Wünsche zufriedenstellt", sagte Merkel. „Ich fürchte, ich muss Sie enttäuschen." Dies gelte aber auch für jene, die darauf setzten, dass sie den Briten in ihrer Rede klarmachen würde, dass man keinen Preis zahlen werde, um das Vereinigte Königreich in der EU zu halten. „Großbritannien braucht seine europäische Berufung nicht zu beweisen", sagte die CDU-Politikerin und zitierte damit aus der Rede von Weizsäckers an gleicher Stelle im Jahr 1986.

Merkel blieb in ihrer Rede beim Grundsätzlichen. „Wir brauchen den Mut zur Veränderung, um die Erfolgsgeschichte der europäischen Einigung fortzusetzen", sagte die Kanzlerin. „Wir brauchen starke europäische Institutionen und starke Nationalstaaten." Das Subsidiaritätsprinzip müsse in Europa wieder mehr Beachtung finden, mahnte sie.

Gerade letzteren Satz werden die Briten gerne gehört haben. Großbritannien will bei einer EU-Reform über eine Rückverlagerung von Kompetenzen von europäischer Ebene in die Nationalstaaten verhandeln. Merkel hatte zuletzt zwar ihre Bereitschaft dazu angedeutet – über das Ausmaß allerdings gehen die Vorstellungen weit auseinander. Das hatte Außenminister Frank-Walter Steinmeier (SPD) jüngst bei seinem Besuch in London klargemacht.

Merkel unterstrich denn auch die Grundwerte der EU, die nicht angetastet werden dürften: der freie Handel, die Arbeitnehmerfreizügigkeit und ein „Europa ohne Grenzen". Zugleich betonte sie, dass sie Großbritanniens Platz in der EU sieht. Die EU brauche „ein starkes Vereinigtes Königreich mit einer starken Stimme in der Europäischen Union". Hintergrund ist die anhaltende britische Debatte über eine Renationalisierung und sogar einen Austritt des Landes aus der EU. „Unsere Vorstellungen der künftigen Entwicklung der Europäischen Union mögen sich in Details immer wieder unterscheiden, aber wir, Deutschland und Großbritannien, teilen das Ziel einer starken, wettbewerbsfähigen Europäischen Union, die ihre Kräfte bündelt."

From: *Spiegel Online*, 27 February, 2014

1 Mediation (German → English)
A Spanish follower of your blog wants to find out about Merkel's speech. Summarize chancellor Merkel's future visions regarding the EU in general and the position of Great Britain in the EU in English for him.

- ► SF 41: Mediation of written and oral texts
- ► LP 4: Present perfect and simple past

2 YOU CHOOSE **Writing**

a Taking into account what you already know about Cameron's attitude towards the EU (from **C1**), write his reply to Merkel's speech.

OR

b Write a dialogue between a critical journalist and Merkel that takes place directly after the speech.

- ► SF 37: Doing a creative writing task
- ► SF 34: Argumentative writing
- ► CC 6: Talking about sensitive issues
- ► CC 2: The language of politeness

Bastian Schweinsteiger at the 2014 World Cup Final

1 **dip into sth.** examine or read sth. casually or superficially
blogosphere ['blɒɡəsfɪə] the blogs on the internet
musing *(usu. pl)* thought
twitterati frequent users of the social media website Twitter
5 **cloak sth.** cover sth., hide sth.
begrudging *(adj) missgünstig*
6 **ruthless** having no pity, merciless
7 **inanimate** [ɪn'ænɪmət] not living
8 **by implication** as a consequence / effect
9 **resentful** [rɪ'zentfl] having or showing a feeling of anger
13 **at sb.'s expense** *auf Kosten von jdm.*
15 **root for sb.** applaud for / encourage sb.
Messrs ['mesəz] plural of Mr
19 **bonnet** *Deckel, Haube*
21 **R&D** research and development

C3 It's OK to like the Germans *Stewart Wood*

Many Britons cheered for Germany in the 2014 World Cup final. But one journalist argues that there is a lot the Britons can learn from the Germans in the world outside the football stadiums.

Dip into the weekend papers, the blogosphere & the musings of the twitterati, and you'll see multiple variants on a similar sentiment: 'I can't quite believe it, and I never thought this would happen, but I find myself supporting Germany. Fancy that!'

Usually our praise for German football is similar to our praise for Germans in other spheres of life where they lead the world. We cloak it in begrudging virtues: 'efficient', 'clinical', 'ruthless'. Germans are applauded in the language we use to describe well-functioning inanimate objects, such as Mercedes cars, or Miele dishwashers. And characteristics of good cars and dishwashers are, by implication, characteristics of people that you admire in a slightly resentful way.

So we are impressed with Germany, but we don't have any particular affection for it or its people. We have respect for Germany, but we don't want to spend much time there. We applaud Germans' economic success, but we resent their dominance of the European Union. We make lots of jokes at their expense, but we say they have no sense of humour.

Maybe a day on which millions of Brits find themselves rooting for Messrs Müller, Hummels and Schweinsteiger is a good moment to challenge this approach to all things German. Because the truth is that there is much to like and admire about Germany. And – whisper it softly – there is a lot we can learn from them too. [...]

Take the state of Britain's economy. Underneath the bonnet of our recovery lies an economy characterised by low productivity, a poor record in technical skills, low levels of savings and investment and relatively weak performance in R&D. In the long run, we will simply not be able to compete internationally, or solve the cost of living crisis we face, without addressing these challenges. We cannot copy the German economy, or transplant the culture in which it is embedded. But we can learn much from the institutions and policies that have helped produce the most successful high-wage, high-skill economy of the modern era. [...]

Of course Germany has its share of problems, blind spots and policy failures too. And taking inspiration from German success does not mean wanting Britain to become Germany [...] But surely it is time for us as a country to take a collective deep breath, and tell ourselves: it's OK to like, admire and even learn lessons from Germany. And you never know: once we do, we may be on the long road to finally winning another World Cup.

From: *The Guardian*, 13 July 2014

COMPREHENSION

1 Summarizing
Summarize the writer's main points concerning Britons' relationship to Germany. SUPPORT p. 270

► SF 31: Writing a summary

ANALYSIS

2 Analysing key vocabulary
Analyse the three 'begrudging virtues' in ll. 5–6 and explain what they tell us about how some British view German people.

► SF 18: Analysing non-fiction

BEYOND THE TEXT

3 YOU CHOOSE Responding to the article

a Write an email to the *Guardian*'s editor in response to this article.

OR

b Write an article on what Germany can learn from Britain.

► SF 29: Writing a formal letter or email
► LP 11: Using the right register

A podcast on British culture

In this Chapter Task you will listen to a report on a British TV show and use what you learn to create your own podcast on an aspect of British culture.

FACT FILE

Downton Abbey is a well-known and popular British TV series that is broadcast by ITV in the UK and PBS in the USA. The period drama series, set in Yorkshire, England, follows the wealthy Crawley family through life's events as they are impacted by history. Some of the major historical events include the sinking of the Titanic, World War I and the Spanish influenza pandemic. Julian Fellowes is the creator, executive producer and writer of this series that is co-produced by Carnival Films and Masterpiece. *Downton Abbey* has won several awards, including a Golden Globe and a Primetime Emmy.

1 Understanding an example podcast

a Read the Fact File and look at the picture. Collect ideas about the setting and the characters of the series.

b Listen to the podcast and complete the sentence: In the interview …

1 … the executive producer summarizes the plot of *Downton Abbey* for those who do not know the series.

2 … *Downton Abbey's* success in the UK and worldwide is mentioned.

3 … the executive producer announces the final season of the series and gives hints about its ending.

c Listen again. Which statements are true? Correct the wrong statements.

1 *Downton Abbey* is set around the time of the Second World War.

2 *Downton Abbey* is a uniquely English *genre that cannot be produced anywhere other than in Great Britain.

3 *Downton Abbey* portrays the class system and shows how aristocrats lived in a very contemporary way.

4 The fourth series and the Christmas special have to be cancelled since many key stars are leaving the series for Hollywood.

CD1 18

expressly definitely
reverential [ˌrevəˈrenʃl] very serious
life blood sth. that is necessary for success and survival

► SF22: Listening

2 Thinking about podcasts

Collect ideas about what makes a podcast interesting.

3 Creating a podcast

Go back to the flag on the Lead-in pages (pp. 92–93). Choose a topic connected to the UK and discuss it in your own short podcast, between three and four minutes long. Organize your work, make an outline, write your script, practise and record it.

► SF6: Doing project work
► SF8: Structuring ideas
► LP13: Placing emphasis on key points

4 Evaluating a podcast

Present your podcast to the class. While listening to your classmates' podcasts, take notes on their content as well as their strengths and weaknesses. Give feedback, praising the aspects that you liked and giving clear, constructive advice for the aspects your classmates could improve. Your teacher will give you an assessment sheet.

Find a recording tool here:
Webcode context-55

4 Countries of the English-speaking world

Download a list of chapter vocab here: **Webcode** context-63

1 Comparing associations

a Your teacher will give you a card with one of these countries written on it: *Australia – Canada – New Zealand – Pakistan – South Africa*. Choose the words from the word cloud that you associate with this country and write them on your card.

b Find the other students who have been given the same country. Compare your word choices; discuss the reasons why you associate the chosen words with your country.

c As a group, choose the words that you think best describe your country.

d Present your results to your class, explaining the reasons for your choices.

2 Researching your country

In the course of this chapter, you will learn about each of the five countries named in **1a**. In addition, you and your group will become experts on the country you were given and present the information you have collected to the rest of the class. You can proceed like this:

a Divide the following aspects among the members of your group:

- **History:** How long have people been living in this region? When did settlement begin (and why)? When did the country achieve statehood/ independence?

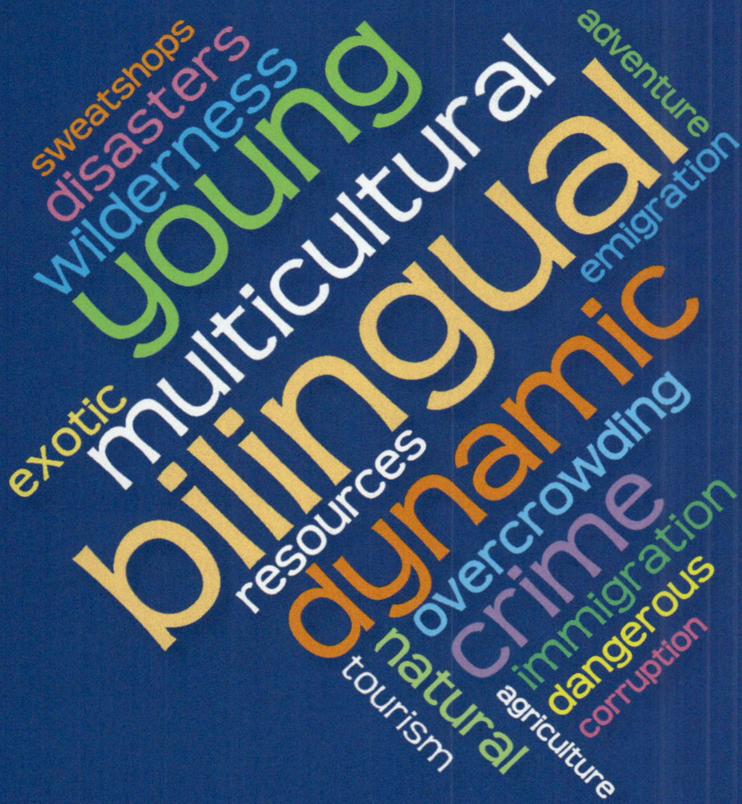

- **People:** What different groups of people live here? Where did they originally come from? Do they have a common language/religion/culture? What are the relations like between them?
- **Economy:** How do people earn a living in this country? What are the main sources of employment? Is poverty an issue? Does the country have significant natural resources? What are its main exports?
- **Government and politics:** How is the government organized (federal vs. central; branches of government)? How stable is the political system? What issues are especially urgent at the moment?

b Research your topic as you work with this chapter; make notes and copy charts, photos or other material you may want to use.

► SF5: Doing research

PREVIEW

In this chapter you will compare five countries linked by a common history and language and learn more about the challenges facing them today.

Main topics

CD4 05

Listen to an audio version of the text on the CD or download it here:

Webcode context-64

Post-colonial experiences

The legacy of the Empire

At its height, the British Empire comprised one fifth of the world's population and a quarter of its total land area. By 1947, virtually all of its members had achieved independence, and the Empire as such ceased to exist. Considering its former power and extent, it is not surprising that the Empire left its mark on many of the countries that once belonged to it. Several of the former dominions (e.g. Canada, Australia and New Zealand) have retained the British monarch as their official head of state. Almost all former British colonies are members of the Commonwealth of Nations. The post-colonial legacy also extends to the system of government, the legal system, education and culture (e.g. the love of cricket, the quintessential British sport).

► Fact File, p. 67

The shadows of colonialism

For many of the former colonies, history has left scars that have been slow to heal. The colonial regime imposed a strict division of society into a small class of white, English-speaking rulers and owners and a large underclass of disenfranchised, exploited workers. Oppression and harsh punishment were commonplace. This tradition of governmental tyranny has made it difficult for some newly created countries to establish a civil society based on the rule of law, equality and mutual respect. In other cases, the whims of colonial history threw peoples together in one nation who had little in common, leading to ethnic and sectarian violence following the end of British rule. Some former colonies have been confronted with the necessity of defining their national identity. What traits of character and culture distinguish them from their forefathers, the British settlers that first populated the region generations earlier? Language, too, may be closely connected with cultural identity. For former colonies with a high degree of ethnic diversity (e.g. South Africa and Pakistan), having a common lingua franca was a boon to communication and efficient administration. On the other hand, many citizens feel resentment at being forced to use the language of their colonial masters and regard the return to indigenous languages as a form of cultural emancipation.

TROUBLE SPOT

people *(pl)* (l. 20): *Leute, Menschen*

a people *(pl* ***peoples****): ein Volk*

► Chapter 6, Part C (pp. 137–138)

Aboriginal parade banner (Melbourne, Australia)

Indigenous peoples

In some cases, settlement took place at the expense of the people who had been living in the country long before the first white settlers arrived. Their nomadic lifestyle was an impediment to the use of the land for agriculture. As a result, they were often driven off their ancestral homelands or cheated out of the lands through dubious treaties. Large numbers died of European diseases against which they had no immunity. The survivors were forced to live in remote reserves where they could no longer practice their traditional lifestyles. Remarkably, Canada has taken steps to give back control of the land to its indigenous population (e.g. the creation of Nunavut as an autonomous Inuit province in 1999). And on National Sorry Day (26 May), Australians collectively apologize for the injustice suffered by the Aboriginal population.

1 Synonyms and antonyms
The words in the left-hand column below are all taken from the text.
Copy them and match them to their synonyms or antonyms on the right.
Use '=' or '↔' to show the relationship between the words.

autonomous	abolish
collectively	anger
commonplace	individually
diversity	native
establish	nearby
impediment	obstacle
indigenous	reward
punishment	self-governing
remote	uniformity
resentment	widespread

2 Nouns and verbs

a The table below contains eight words from the text. Copy the table and complete it with the missing words (use a dictionary if necessary).

► LP 20: Word formation

Noun	Verb
extent	*extend*
resentment	
oppression	
division	
	arrive
	exploit
	populate
	define

b Write eight sentences of your own, using the words you have added to the table.

3 Easily confused words
Choose the right word from the pair in brackets in each of the following sentences. Consult a dictionary if you need help.
1 Canada is (comprised/composed) of ten provinces and three territories.
2 Samantha has got a new job – she signed the (contract/treaty) yesterday.
3 The police threatened to use (force/violence) if the demonstrators didn't disperse.
4 I often find it difficult to (differ/distinguish) between Chinese and Koreans.
5 To me they all look (alike/equal).
6 Lucky Rob – he received a large (inheritance/legacy) when his uncle died.
7 Clarice sat at her desk, (considering/regarding) the photo thoughtfully.

4 Writing
The British Empire – a blessing or a curse for its former members? Write an essay of about 200 words in which you compare the positive and negative aspects of the colonial legacy.

► Chapter 5, Words in Context, pp. 104–105

► Fact File, p. 67

Down Under: Australia and New Zealand

A1 The making of an Aussie *Kevin Donnelly*

As part of a series on Australia Day, Australia's national holiday, the Australian Broadcasting Corporation (ABC) asked teacher and researcher Kevin Donnelly how he regards the Australian identity.

FACT FILE

Australia and New Zealand in numbers

	Australia	New Zealand
land area (sq km)	7,682,300	263,310
population	23,490,736	4,509,700
GDP (in millions US $)	1,453,770	188,384
median age	38.3	37.6

What are we celebrating on January 26 and what does it mean to be Australian? Traditionally, it's about celebrating the First Fleet's arrival in 1788 and recognising the early convicts and settlers, and the fact that our language, political and legal institutions are inherited from the British Isles. Not any more. The cultural left tells us that it's all about multiculturalism and celebrating diversity and difference, with some even arguing that Australia Day should be renamed Invasion Day.

It's now politically correct to argue that there is no such thing as an Australian because the nation, like the USA, is a melting pot made up of different ethnic, religious and national groups all deserving equal treatment and respect. Wrong. Australia is a Western, English-speaking nation and like other countries that share a common bond, like the USA and New Zealand, we are part of the Anglosphere.

Opera House and Harbour Bridge, Sydney, Australia

Anglosphere countries share a common history, culture, language, a Westminster form of government, and legal concepts like common law, habeas corpus and innocent until proven guilty. Even though religion is not as strong as it once was, we are also a Christian nation and it's no accident that parliaments around Australia at the state and Commonwealth level begin with the Lord's Prayer.

The fact that Australia is a Western, liberal democracy explains why so many millions of migrants have escaped war torn, oppressive regimes and migrated here searching for prosperity and peace. Unlike countries in Asia like China, Burma, Laos, Cambodia and Vietnam that are controlled by corrupt, self-serving regimes, Australia is a place where freedom is safeguarded, everyone has the right to vote, and nobody is above the law. Since federation in 1901, Australia has been a world leader in introducing universal franchise, votes for women, a fair day's pay for a fair day's work, and the old-age pension.

Australians are also unique. Forget old-world, English upper-class snobbery; Australians believe that every man is as good as his master, that ability and hard work lead to success, that mateship is paramount, that life shouldn't be taken too seriously, and that it's important to be optimistic.

Beginning with the convicts, early settlers, outback workers, and continuing with the First World War diggers and moving on to today's battlers fighting drought, fire and flood, the Aussie legend is about overcoming adversity, supporting loved ones and friends, and telling governments and bureaucrats where to go! [...]

3 **First Fleet** in 1788, fleet of British ships, commanded by Captain Arthur Phillip and transporting prisoners from England to found a permanent settlement at Sydney Harbour
11 **melting pot** *Schmelztiegel*
14 **Anglosphere** English-speaking countries with a historical and cultural link to England
16 **Westminster form of government parliamentary** form of government similar to that of the UK
18 **habeas corpus** *(Latin)* mediaeval law forbidding unlawful imprisonment
30 **safeguard sth.** *(fml)* protect sth.
32 **franchise** ['fræntʃaɪz] the right to vote
36 **mateship** *(infml)* friendship (cf. AusE **mate** *Kumpel*)
paramount *(adj) (fml)* more important than anything else
39 **drought** ['draʊt] *Dürre*
40 **adversity** difficulty
41 **tell sb. where to go** *(infml)* *jdm. die Meinung sagen*

Instead of adopting a cultural cringe, being politically correct and arguing there is nothing special about being Australian, let's celebrate our unique identity and the special history that binds us as a nation.

From: Kevin Donnelly, 'Don't deny our Australian identity', *ABC*, 22 January 2013

42 **cringe** ['krɪndʒ] *geduckte, übertrieben demütige Haltung*

COMPREHENSION

1 Summarizing the content

Summarize in no more than two sentences

- what the 'cultural left' (l. 6) says about Australian identity,
- Donnelly's position on this topic.

2 The Australian national character

Outline the qualities the writer ascribes to the Australian national character.

ANALYSIS

3 Examining stylistic devices

Point out stylistic devices that Donnelly uses to persuade his readers and to prove his point. SUPPORT ▸ p. 271

▸ SF 17: Analysing stylistic devices

4 Examining bias

In the process of defining his views on Australia, Donnelly takes issue with groups and countries he regards as his ideological opponents. Point out relevant passages in the text and analyse their function.

LANGUAGE AWARENESS

5 Using gerunds

a In a number of places in his text, the writer uses a gerund after a preposition, e.g. 'it's about celebrating the First Fleet's arrival in 1788' (ll. 2–3), 'Australia has been a world leader in introducing universal franchise' (ll. 31–32). Find two more examples in the text.

b Translate the four examples into German and examine the differences in sentence structure.

c Translate the following sentences into English, using a gerund wherever possible:

1. Seit seinem Austauschjahr spricht Tim davon, nach seinem Schulabschluss wieder nach Australien zu gehen.
2. Er hat sich bereits bei einer australischen Organisation beworben, die sehr aktiv darin ist, sozial benachteiligten (*disadvantaged*) Kindern zu helfen.
3. Die Organisation wollte wissen, ob Tim Erfahrung damit habe, mit Kindern aus armen Familien zu arbeiten.
4. Daraufhin interessierte sich Tim dafür, sich um Flüchtlingskinder in seiner Heimatstadt zu kümmern.

▸ LP 5: Infinitive or gerund after certain verbs

▸ LP 6: Infinitive or gerund after certain nouns

BEYOND THE TEXT

6 WRITING CONFERENCE **Thinking about national character**

Is there a 'German national character' or is this just a stereotype? Form groups of four or five. Each member takes a blank sheet of paper and writes their ideas on this question. After two minutes, pass the paper to the person on your right, who comments on what you have written (no talking permitted!). Continue until everyone in the group has got their own sheet back again. Present your most interesting findings to the class.

FACT FILE

Australia's indigenous people

When the first white settlers arrived, Aboriginal people were living throughout the continent in nomadic tribes that spoke hundreds of different languages. They lived as hunters and gatherers with very few tools or weapons, but with a highly developed culture. The white settlers drove them off the land or killed them; the official British doctrine of 'terra nullius' declared Australia to be an 'empty country' that belonged to no one. Unable to maintain their traditional lifestyle, Aborigines vegetated in slums or on reserves, often in abject poverty. For a number of decades in the 20th century, government and church authorities removed Aboriginal children from their families and placed them in institutions, allegedly for their own protection (the so-called 'Stolen Generations').
In 1998, 26 May was proclaimed National Sorry Day, a day on which Australians remember the injustice and suffering inflicted on the native population.

Research the status of Aborigines today and report to your class.

CD4 06

A2 Australia's boat people

COMPREHENSION

1 Mediation (German → English)

a In your class, you are discussing the issue of migration and how different countries deal with it. Listen to a podcast on Australia's boat people. Take notes on Australian attitudes and the explanations offered for them.

b Summarize the information you have collected in a short English text for a leaflet or a poster (ca. 150 words).

Find a tool to help you create your poster here:
Webcode context-50

BEYOND THE TEXT

2 Discussion

Compare the Australian and the German reactions to the influx of refugees. Discuss reasons for the differences.

DVD

stunning *(adj)* spectacular
stand in for sth. *(hier) als Ersatz für etwas dienen*
lure sb. [lʊə] *jdn. herbeilocken*
punt *(v)* ride in a punt (= a flat-bottomed boat moved using a long pole)
fly-fishing *Fliegenfischerei*
pristine ['prɪstin] *(fml)* unspoiled, not developed
humpback (whale) *Buckelwal*
destination *(Reise-)Ziel*

A3 Welcome to New Zealand

COMPREHENSION

1 Watching for gist

Watch the video, then decide which of the following statements best describes the content. Give reasons for your decision.

1 The film highlights New Zealand's geographic diversity.
2 The film concentrates on the possibilities for outdoor sports in New Zealand.
3 The film gives travellers to New Zealand practical tips on getting around.

2 Watching for detail

a While you are watching the film for the second time, make two lists of activities that can be done in New Zealand, one for the North Island and one for the South Island.

b Compare lists with your partner. Add any activities that are missing from your list.

BEYOND THE TEXT

3 Creative task

a Your pen friend in New Zealand has invited you to visit them and asks you what you would be interested in doing during your stay. Write an email in reply (ca. 200 words).

b CHALLENGE Create a text for a tourist brochure encouraging people interested in outdoors sports to visit New Zealand (ca. 150 words).

FACT FILE

Liberal New Zealand

New Zealanders take pride in a history based on compromise and consensus. In contrast to Australia, where the Aboriginal people were driven from the land, the European settlers in New Zealand concluded a peace treaty with the native Maori tribes (Treaty of Waitangi, 1840), and in 1893 New Zealand became the first nation in the world to give women (including native women) the right to vote.

SPEAKING **FOCUS ON SKILLS**

Presenting your ideas

The film 'Welcome to New Zealand' (A3, p. 84) presents its topic using certain presentation techniques. Which of the following are used?

still photos • video sequences • maps • charts • a presenter • voice-over • captions and labels • timelines • document • cartoons • background music • animation • infographics

Together with your group (cf. p. 78), you are going to report on one of the five countries dealt with in this chapter. Which techniques could you use for your presentation?

1 Preparing your presentation

a Organization

- First of all, compare your findings within your group. Look for overlap, obvious gaps, and internal contradictions. Make a note of any points that need further clarification.
- Structure your presentation by deciding in what order the topics should be presented. The first speaker has the additional task of introducing the topic and giving a brief overview of the presentation (cf. 2a).
- Check the material for words or names that will need explaining. Make sure you know the correct pronunciation of the words you intend to use.

► SF 5: Doing research
► SF 6: Doing Doing project work
► SF 8: Structuring ideas

b Media

- Decide whether visual media can be used to make your presentation easier to follow or more vivid (cf. the list at the top of this page).
- Does your group want to work with presentation software or with transparencies? Discuss the pros and cons of each before you make your decision.
- Decide whether you want to prepare a handout for the rest of the class, what the purpose of this handout should be, and whether the handout should be distributed before or after the presentation.

► SF 7: Making visual aids

c Notes

Prepare your part of the presentation in the form of notes using key words only. If you use index cards, be sure to number them.

2 Preparing your presentation

► SF 24: Giving a presentation

a Introduction

Begin by welcoming your audience before introducing your topic. Examine the sentences in the boxes below. Which of the alternatives is the best choice?

Hi guys. This is me, and these are my buddies …

Ladies and gentlemen! We are here today to …

Good morning everyone, and welcome to our presentation.

Have you ever wanted to go to Australia? Well, we're going to take you there today.

We want to tell you about a fascinating country – Australia.

Our topic is Australia, its history, its people, its economy and its political system.

I will begin by giving a brief overview of Australian history. After that, …

The structure of our presentation is: 1. History. 2. People. 3. Economy. 4. Politics and government.

OK, let's get started. First comes history. Then …

b Main part

Sort the following sentences into two lists:

Good presentation skills — Faulty presentation skills

In the cases of faulty behaviour, explain what you should do instead:

1. *You look at your notes while you are speaking.*
2. *You interrupt your talk to write a difficult word on the board.*
3. *You show your audience a schematic overview of your talk.*
4. *You read the information from the screen to your audience.*
5. *You give your audience time to study what is on the screen before you begin talking about it.*
6. *You keep talking while pointing to something on the screen.*
7. *You keep looking around the room to give the audience the feeling that you are really talking to them.*

c Conclusion

Use some of the phrases from the box below to put together a suitable conclusion:

Thank you for …	*We hope you …*	*If there are any …*
We appreciate …		*Would anyone care to …?*
… a very attentive audience.		*… your interest in our topic.*
If there are no further questions …		*Thanks again for …*

A4 Visiting the neighbours *Patricia Grace*

In the following excerpt from the short story 'A Way of Talking', the narrator, a young Maori woman named Hera, tells how she and her sister Rose, who has just come back from university, go to visit a neighbour, a dressmaker named Jane, who is to make a new dress for Rose.

Patricia Grace

Rose made a good impression with her kamakama ways and Jane's two nuisance kids took a liking to her straight away. They kept jumping up and down on the sofa to get Rose's attention and I kept thinking what a waste of a good sofa it was, what a waste of a good house for those two nuisance things. I hope when I have kids they won't be so hoha.

I was pleased about Jane and Rose. Jane was asking Rose all sorts of questions about her life in Auckland. About varsity and did Rose join in the marches and demonstrations. Then they went on to talking about fashions and social life in the city and Jane seemed deeply interested. Almost as though she was jealous of Rose and the way she lived, as though she felt Rose had something better than a lovely house and clothes and everything she needed to make life good for her. I was pleased to see that Jane liked my sister so much and proud of my sister and her entertaining and friendly ways.

Jane made a cup of coffee when she'd finished measuring Rose for the frock then packed the two kids outside with a piece of chocolate cake each. We were sitting

1 **kamakama** *(Maori)* clever
2 **nuisance** ['nju:sns] *(adj)* lively and troublesome
7 **hoha** *(Maori)* troublesome
10 **varsity** university
18 **frock** *(old-fashioned)* dress

having coffee when we heard a truck turn in at the bottom of Frazer's drive. Jane said, 'That's Alan. He's been down the road getting the Maoris for scrub cutting.'

I felt my face get hot. I was angry. At the same time I was hoping Rose would let the remark pass. I tried hard to think of something to say to cover Jane's words though I'd hardly said a thing all morning. But my tongue seemed to thicken and all I could think of was Rohe don't.

Rose was calm. Not all red and flustered like me. She took a big pull on the cigarette she had lit, squinted her eyes up and blew the smoke out gently. I knew something was coming.

'Don't they have names?'

'What. Who?' Jane was surprised and her face was getting pink.

'The people from down the road who your husband is employing to cut scrub.' Rose the stink thing, she was talking all Pakehafied.

'I don't know any of their names.'

I was glaring at Rose because I wanted her to stop but she was avoiding my looks and pretending to concentrate on her cigarette.

'Do they know yours?'

'Mine?'

'Your name.'

'Well, yes.'

'Yet you have never bothered to find out their names or to wonder whether or not they have any.'

The silence seemed to bang around in my head for ages and ages. Then I think Jane muttered something about difficulty, but that touchy sister of mine stood up and said, 'Come on Hera'. And I with my red face and shut mouth followed her out to the station wagon without a goodbye or anything.

From: 'A Way of Talking', *Landfall* 26/2 (1972)

21 **scrub** *Unterholz*
25 **Rohe** *(Maori) Rose*
26 **flustered** (adj) embarrassed
27 **squint** *(v) blinzeln*
32 **Pakehafied** ['pɑːkɪhɑːfaɪd] *(Maori)* acting like a Pakeha (= a white New Zealander)
34 **glare at sb.** stare angrily at sb.
43 **touchy** easily offended
45 **station wagon** *Kombi(wagen)*

COMPREHENSION

1 Summary
Write a summary of the plot. Use the present tense, a neutral point of view and indirect speech only.

► LP 31: Writing a summary

ANALYSIS

2 The language of discrimination
Explain in your own words why Rose takes offence at Jane's remark in ll. 29–41.

3 Examining the characters' behaviour
Compare the reactions of the two sisters to the situation. Point to evidence from the text to support your statements.

BEYOND THE TEXT

4 Dealing with discrimination
Discuss: Which reaction do you find better? Give reasons.

5 YOU CHOOSE **Creative task**

a Retell the incident from Rose's point of view (in the first person).

OR

b Write a continuation of the text after Rose and Hera have left Jane's house.

Pakistan: Rising star of the East?

B1 Colonized minds *Kanza Azeemi*

*In the following excerpt from a *blog entry, a young Pakistani woman writes about language in Pakistan and why it is important to her.*

FACT FILE

Pakistan in numbers

land area (sq km)	770,880
population	185,132,926
GDP (in millions US $)	246,876
median age	22.6

FACT FILE

Multilingual Pakistan
Pakistan has two official languages, English and Urdu; the latter is also the 'national language'. Although less than 8% of Pakistanis are native speakers of Urdu, it is understood throughout the country, especially in urban areas. In addition to Urdu and English half a dozen other languages are in common use. In 2015, the Pakistani government announced its intention to make Urdu the sole official language.

One of my friends, an American who has been living in Pakistan for seven years, does not know how to read Urdu. I was shocked when I first discovered this fact. Baffled, I asked:

'Why don't you know how to read Urdu? Why don't you learn?'

'Is there a need?' was the question I got in reply.

And although I hate to admit, I had to agree with her. Who needs to learn how to read Urdu? Even the people at the lowest level of the social hierarchy say 'thank you' instead of '*shukria*', and use numerous English words in daily speech. [...]

If asked to speak in Urdu without employing a single word from English, many students of some elite universities and schools will miserably fail. Even worse is the fact that they will 'laugh it off'. For them, apparently, speaking in English is related to having a higher self esteem.

How many times have people with fluent English not laughed at someone without the same proficiency level?

How many times have we not seen a person constantly struggling to converse in English?

How many of us have found ourselves talking to foreign visitors (British or American mainly) entirely in English instead of trying to teach them Urdu?

These behaviours denote much more than what we think they do.

They signify the 'colonization of the mind' – a concept many writers have talked about, in vain.

The 'colonization of the mind' theory was once more proved true by a friend [...] in Tokyo. I was called an 'English Pakistani' once he saw the wall posts on Facebook by my Pakistani friends, all of which were of course in English.

I hated to be called that. I was deeply ashamed that I, a Pakistani patriot, was not recognized for her true identity but had become accustomed to living in a borrowed one – English.

Why are we English Pakistanis?

I want to be a Pakistani. Just a Pakistani. We may know English, as the British may know French, but that shouldn't make us English Pakistanis just as it doesn't make the British French British.

From: *The Express Tribune*, 31 October 2011

3 **baffle sb.** confuse sb.
12 **laugh sth. off** *(infml)* treat sth. as unimportant
13 **self-esteem** *Selbstwertgefühl*
15 **proficiency level** *Kompetenzstufe*
27 **accustomed to sth.** used to sth.

COMPREHENSION

1 The main thesis
Summarize the writer's views on the relative status of English and Urdu in Pakistan in one sentence.

2 Collecting examples
Outline examples named by the writer that illustrate her point concerning the status of Urdu in Pakistan. Give line numbers as well.

ANALYSIS

3 Examining key concepts
Explain in your own words what the writer means when she refers to the 'colonization of the mind' (l. 21).

BEYOND THE TEXT

4 Patriot or parrot?
The decision of the Pakistani government to phase out English as an official language (see Fact File p. 88) can be related to the feelings of a younger generation of Pakistanis like Kanza Azeemi.
- **a** Write a comment (ca. 150 words) on Azeemi's blog.
- **b** CHALLENGE Discuss the pros and cons of replacing English with an indigenous language. Write about 200 words.

LISTENING **FOCUS ON SKILLS**

Working with closed test formats

► SF 10: Working with closed test formats

Listening comprehension is often tested using closed and half-open test formats. These can include multiple-choice tasks, sentence completion and short-answer questions.
The podcast you are about to hear deals with a spectacular project that could change the face of Pakistan dramatically – if it is realized.

1 Multiple-choice tasks
Don't forget: you only get points for an answer, so answer every question. If you aren't sure, make an intelligent guess.

a Read the task below carefully, then listen to the beginning of the podcast.

CD4 07

The topic of the programme is
A China's geopolitical situation.
B why China is interested in a Pakistani port.
C China's dream of becoming a major sea power.
D why Pakistan fears a Chinese invasion.

Which of the four answers is obviously wrong? Which words help you to choose the correct answer?

b Now listen to the continuation of the podcast and, on a separate sheet of paper, write down the letter of the correct answer next to the numbers 1–4.

CD4 08

1 Western journalists
  A are a common sight at Gwadar's airport.
  B are stopped from entering Gwadar by the police.
  C must wait a long time for permission to visit Gwadar.
  D must ask the Chinese government for permission to visit Gwadar.
2 The police accompany the journalists because
  A the region is dangerous.
  B they don't want them to talk to the separatists.
  C they are not allowed to see some of the facilities.
  D they are from the US.

Inauguration ceremony of Gwadar Port, Pakistan (12 May 2015)

3 Gwadar's location is of great strategic importance for China because
   A China has no deep-water port.
   B China is a major oil-exporting country.
   C Gwadar is close to China's industrial areas.
   D transporting goods via Gwadar would be faster than shipping them by sea.

4 China has agreed to
   A loan Pakistan 46 billion dollars.
   B import more fish from Gwadar.
   C invest 46 billion dollars in Gwadar.
   D take over the airport in Gwadar.

2 Sentence completion and short-answer questions

These two test formats are similar. In both cases, you are expected to identify specific information in the text and write it down in a few words (sometimes there is a word limit). Grammar and spelling do not count. The order of the test items corresponds to the order of the information in the text, so you can work from top to bottom while you are listening.

CD4 09

Prepare an answer sheet with the numbers as shown below. Listen to the third part of the podcast twice and write down the missing information. If you do not recognize the answer the first time, mark the number with a question mark and listen closely the second time.

Fishing boat being built on the seashore of Gwadar

1 The plans for Gwadar's development include

______ and ______.

2 The population of Gwadar is expected to rise from

______ and ______.

3 The native Baluch population is sceptical about the plans because

______ and ______.

4 Chairman Jamaldini of the Gwadar Port Authority has made

______ trips to China in ______ years.

5 The biggest obstacle to the plans according to Jamaldini is

______.

6 Nonetheless, some Pakistanis have already begun

______.

3 Three tips

Now write down what you think are the three most important tips for doing a closed or half-open test.

B2 Why we shouldn't underrate Pakistan *Daniel Runde*

Journalist Daniel Runde assesses Pakistan's potential in a report for a US economics magazine

The Pakistan of today is similar to that of Colombia in the late 1990s. Back then, words like 'drugs, gangs, and failed state' were freely associated with the Andean country. Today, Colombia has a free trade agreement with the United States, a stable 3.5 percent annual GDP growth, and security is vastly improved. Similarly, Western headlines on Pakistan today gloss over the progress on the security front, the increased political stability, and incremental progress on the economic front. In spite of this potential for Pakistan, it continues to suffer from a terrible country brand that has not caught up with realities on the ground.

Pakistan's improving security dynamic is the first change to note. It is hard to understate the before-and-after effects of the Taliban's horrendous December 2014 attack on a military-owned elementary school in Peshawar that killed 145 people, including 132 schoolchildren aged eight to eighteen. Almost immediately after the attack, the military responded in force by taking out 157 terrorists via air strikes and ground operations in the North Waziristan and Khyber tribal areas adjacent to Peshawar.

What has not sunk into international perceptions about the country is the tangible consensus among government, military, and Pakistani citizens against violent terrorists including the Pakistani Taliban and the alphabet soup of other terrorist groups in and around the country. Pakistan will continue to experience attacks by fringe groups, but policymakers and investors need to stop operating as if the Pakistani Taliban is at Islamabad's doorstep.

Prime Minister Nawaz Sharif is governing with a competent cabinet, a majority coalition, and is working in tandem with the military to deliver peace and security. Sharif was elected in Pakistan's transition of power between democratically elected governments in April 2013 and so far, he has demonstrated enough of a commitment to democracy. [...]

Chinese investment is another reason why the United States should reassess its Pakistan calculus. Since Xi Jinping first announced the $46 billion China-Pakistan Economic Corridor (CPEC) in 2014, the project has quickly become the centerpiece of diplomatic relations between the two countries. CPEC will include highways, railways, and oil and gas pipelines – all constructed via Chinese companies.

Even the possibility of the scheme's partial achievement has injected optimism in a country starved for infrastructure and energy investment. The deal has also greatly incentivized the government to clamp down on terrorist groups. Economic success is by no means guaranteed especially given China's checkered track record of investing in infrastructure projects abroad. Still, China's bet on Pakistan could overshadow US contributions unless we rethink our mix of engagement. [...]

Pakistan has a population of 182.1 million people and is the 6th largest country in the world. Sixty percent of the population is of working age. By 2050, Pakistan's total population will be nearly 300 million, making it roughly ten times the size of Afghanistan. Pakistan is also among the world's fastest urbanizing countries with half its people projected to live in cities by 2050. Twenty years ago, Islamabad, a planned city much like Brasilia, had a population of 400,000; today, it has a population of around 3 million including the peri-urban areas. Many Pakistani cities are

2 **failed state** state that is unable to fulfil its basic tasks
5 **gloss over sth.** treat sth. as unimportant
6 **incremental** gradual
12 **horrendous** very terrible
15 **take sb. out** (military jargon for) kill sb.
17 **adjacent to sth.** bordering on sth.
18 **perception** *Wahrnehmung*
tangible *greifbar*
20 **alphabet soup** allusion to use of abbreviations (TTP, SSP etc.)
21 **fringe group** *Randgruppe*
26 **transition** *Übergang*
34 **scheme** [skiːm] plan
35 **be starved for sth.** need sth. badly
36 **incentivize sb.** give sb. a reason for doing sth.
clamp down on sb./sth. *mit Härte gegen jdn./etwas vorgehen*
37 **checkered** *(adj) durchwachsen*
46 **peri-urban** *(adj)* surrounding a large city
undergo sth. experience sth.

undergoing a similar urbanization process, and this will create massive demands on food, energy, water, and consumer goods.

From: 'Pakistan, the next Colombia success story', *Forbes*, 3 August 2015

COMPREHENSION

1 Looking at the facts

Outline the reasons named in the text why Runde thinks Pakistan is better than its reputation.

ANALYSIS

2 Examining the writer's bias

Runde writes for the US magazine *Forbes*, which deals mainly with business and finance. Point to aspects of the text that make this bias evident.

LANGUAGE AWARENESS

3 Jargon

► SF 2: Learning new words

'Jargon' is the language used in a specialized field. It includes both technical terms (*download, transgenic*) and words taken from the general vocabulary that are used in a specific context with a different meaning. The list in the left-hand column below contains examples of economics jargon taken from the text. Match them with the more general meaning from the list on the right:

bet *(n)* (l. 38)	ensure sth., provide sth.
brand *(n)* (l. 8)	exceed sth.
calculus (l. 30)	expect sb./sth. to do sth.
deliver sth. (l. 25)	history
dynamic *(n)* (l. 10)	ignore sth.
gloss over sth. (l. 5)	in everyday life
on the ground (l. 9)	investment
on the ... front (ll. 5–7)	policy
overshadow sth. (l. 38)	reputation
project sb./sth. to do sth. (l. 44)	situation
track record (l. 37)	with regard to ...
via (ll. 15, 33)	with the help of sb./sth.

LANGUAGE HELP

- due to foreign investment
- improvements in the ... sector
- the benefits of political stability
- ... a young, well-educated workforce ...
- ... the prospect of continued economic growth
- ... crime and corruption
- ... the threat of terrorism
- ... regional unrest
- ... obstacles to economic progress

BEYOND THE TEXT

4 Looking into the futures

Based on what you have learned about Pakistan in this part of the chapter, do you agree with Runde that Pakistan can look forward to a brighter future? Name reasons for your opinion.

Technician inside the power station at the Tarbela dam, Pakistan

Rainbow nation: South Africa

C1 Soweto revisited *Thuso Khumalo*

South African writer Thuso Khumalo explains why the name Soweto (originally: 'SOuth WEstern TOwnships') is intimately connected with the history of the struggle for equal rights in South Africa.

Soweto is one of South Africa's oldest townships. Formerly home to Nelson Mandela and the center of anti-apartheid protests in 1976, it now attracts tourists from all over the world.

The township of Soweto was created for blacks by South Africa's oppressive apartheid government in 1963. Under apartheid, South Africans were classified as 'black', 'colored' (or mixed race), 'Asian' or 'white'. Today, seen from a distance, Soweto looks old and unremarkable. The old style houses and slum areas would in normal circumstances make it a no-go area for most people. However, the legacy left by apartheid has turned it into a tourist magnet.

Outside the township, on the road from Johannesburg of which Soweto is now officially a suburb, is the Apartheid Museum which was opened in 2001. Here visitors see the history of apartheid in all its brutality, presented through pictures, videos, audio installations and symbols portraying a system that equated blacks with dogs and massively curtailed their rights. Apartheid was introduced as an official policy in South Africa in 1948.

The permanent exhibition includes pictures and videos showing blacks being evicted from the towns and regions of their birth, others working like slaves on farms and in mines while white South Africans dined and partied.

Discriminatory signs like 'Europeans Only' and 'Dogs and Blacks Not Allowed' bring home to visitors the ugly face of South Africa during the apartheid era.

Deus Mwale, a Zambian national, recently attended a workshop in South Africa together with people from other African countries. Before they returned home, the group paid a visit to the Apartheid Museum and Soweto.

'We are excited that this evil system is now over. It is good that this history is preserved so that such a thing is not repeated,' Mwale told DW.

The group's first destination in Soweto was Vilakazi Street, formerly home to two Nobel Peace Prize laureates and apartheid struggle icons, Nelson Mandela and Archbishop Desmond Tutu. Tourists from all over the world regularly descend on this street to see Mandela's house which has now been turned into a museum. [...]

Not far from Vilakazi Street is the Hector Pieterson Memorial Museum. It is named in honor of a young boy who was killed at the age of 13 when police opened fire on unarmed protesting students during the Soweto uprising against apartheid in 1976. The museum was opened in 2002 close to the spot where Hector was killed. Alongside the museum is an arts and crafts market where many tourists purchase mementos of their visit. Katlego Mphuti, a guide at the Apartheid Museum, says for people interested in South Africa's history and the legacy of apartheid, visiting Soweto is a must.

Tourism researcher Gugu Dladla says the township's apartheid past has finally brought some benefits for residents. 'Soweto used to be known for a high rate of crime, but tourism has changed the face of the township. People are now getting jobs, and selling all sorts of things to make a living.'

From: DW Deutsche Welle, 22 April 2014

FACT FILE

Africa in numbers

land area (sq km)	1,213,090
population	54,001,953
GDF (in millions US $)	349,817
median age	25.7

4 **township** (under apartheid) living area set aside for non-whites
14 **curtail sth.** limit sth.
17 **evict sb.** force sb. to leave their home
27 **laureate** ['lɒriət] prizewinner
28 **descend on sth.** [dɪ'send] visit sth.
35 **memento** souvenir

COMPREHENSION

1 The ugly face of apartheid
Collect the facts about apartheid as they are presented in the text.

2 Soweto today
Outline the reasons presented in the text why the name Soweto is so closely connected with apartheid and the struggle for freedom and equality in South Africa.

ANALYSIS

3 Quotations
Name different people or groups of people quoted in the text and explain the function of the quotations in the context of the article.

BEYOND THE TEXT

► Fact File, p. 49

4 Racism as a way of life
Compare apartheid in South Africa with segregation in the southern states of the US before the Civil Rights Movement, pointing out parallels and differences.

FACT FILE

From apartheid to reconciliation
By the 1980s, the white racist government of South Africa's National Party was politically and economically isolated on the global level. At home, police brutality served only to generate new support for the ANC, the largest black protest organization. Seeing no alternative, President F. W. de Klerk (1989–1994) took radical steps by freeing Nelson Mandela (cf. Fact File, p. 112) and other black leaders from prison, legalizing the ANC, dismantling the apparatus of apartheid and paving the way for free, open and democratic elections. The first free elections in South African history were won by the ANC (62.6%), and Nelson Mandela became his country's first black president.
In a second unprecedented move, the new government created the Truth and Reconciliation Commission. Between 1996 and 2000, the TRC, led by Archbishop Desmond Tutu, heard the testimony of thousands of apartheid victims and those responsible for human rights violations.
From the outset, the purpose of the TRC was to bring about reconciliation between the races, not to punish the guilty. This model has since been adopted by other countries (e.g. Canada).

With a partner, find out more about the work of the TRC. Report to the class.

Archbishop Tutu hands over TRC report to South Africa's President Nelson Mandela (29 October 1998)

DVD

hub *Knotenpunkt*
in the rough in the natural state
ballpark figure rough estimate *(Schätzwert)*
cache [kæʃ] reserve, store
vibrant full of life
seize sth. [si:z] *von etwas Besitz ergreifen*

C2 One day in Johannesburg

The film you are going to watch conveys an impression of Johannesburg with the help of four residents who talk about their lives.

COMPREHENSION

1 Overall impression
The voice-over presents Johannesburg as a
A very wealthy city.
B city of stark contrasts.
C city of illiterates.
D multicultural city.

2 Who says what? (Multiple matching)
Match the names of the four people presented in the film (cf. left-hand column below) to the sentence completions (right-hand column) More than one statement can apply to the same person.

1 Thoko Sibeko 2 Ilan Kaplan 3 Didi Sole 4 Faith Mangope	A … works in Johannesburg's most important industry. B … is very proud of the place where she works. C … complains about the difficulty of travelling within Johannesburg. D … feels passionate about the future of Johannesburg. E … helps to bring culture to the poor. F … idolizes her father. G … works at a market. H … says she belongs to the 'Liberty Generation'. I … helps to create objects of beauty. J … explains how to give hand signals.

ANALYSIS

3 The language of film
Watch the film again and make notes of the way it uses the *juxtaposition of images. Describe the effect this has on the viewer.

BEYOND THE TEXT

4 A day in the life of …
You are offered the chance to accompany one of these four people in their daily life. Who is your first choice? Write a text of about 150 words in which you state and justify your decision.

C3 South Africa after Mandela *Milton Nkosi*

Nelson Mandela played a unique role in South African history. A year after his death, a South African journalist looks at the state of a nation that has lost its father figure.

People singing and dancing in celebration of the life of Nelson Mandela (11 December 2013)

It does not seem that it was a year ago that South Africans danced and sang in the streets all night to remember the life of Nelson Mandela, the man who liberated them from the scourge of racial oppression.

They did not mourn the 95-year-old's death – instead they rejoiced that Madiba (Mandela's clan name) had saved them from a potential racial bloodbath.

Yet despite this sense of unity, there were many, especially white South Africans, who were visibly worried that the man they regarded as the insurer of a peaceful future had gone too soon and had left them exposed.

They feared his departure opened up a door for the angry poor black masses to destroy their comfortable lives.

However, 12 months have passed since he died and life continues as normal.

In an attempt to try and understand how the Mandela dynasty is feeling one year on, I spoke to Madiba's first grandchild from his eldest son Thembekile.

We met Ndileka Mandela in Soweto at her grandfather's old home now turned a museum.

3 **scourge** [skɜːdʒ] *(fig)* sth. bad
4 **mourn sb./sth.** be sad because of sb./sth.
9 **insurer** *Garant*

As we walked around she told me that South Africa is at peace with itself. When I said many people had thought that when Mandela went South Africa would go up in flames, she replied with a smile: 'Even a year after he's gone peace still prevails. People are still upholding his legacy and what he stood for because he stood for peace and reconciliation.'

This, of course, does not mean that all is well in the land of Nelson Mandela. This week, a survey, appropriately named South African Reconciliation Barometer, showed that about 24% of those questioned felt apartheid was not a crime – with nearly half of white people surveyed agreeing with the statement. When the survey was first conducted in 2003, 86% of South Africans agreed that apartheid was a crime.

Kim Wale, the barometer's project leader, says this is an indication of how history is taught. 'The danger of forgetting is that it encourages denial. The implication is that we are doomed to repeat the past,' she told local media. [...]

As the nation enters its second year without Mandela, South Africa is coming of age. It is going to learn to face the joy and pain of being without a father figure. The rainbow nation, still celebrating 20 years of democracy, will have to rise to the occasion and follow his ideals of building rather than destroying – as we see the cancer of corruption eating away at the fabric of society. If it doesn't, then South Africans must face the consequences of not walking in his footsteps.

From: BBC, 5 December 2014

21 **prevail** *(fml) die Oberhand behalten*
uphold sth. *(fml)* respect sth.
29 **denial** statement that says that sth. is not true
implication conclusion that can be drawn from sth.
31 **come of age** *volljährig werden*
33 **rise to the occasion** *sich den Gegebenheiten stellen*

TROUBLE SPOT
fabric (l. 35): *Stoff, Tuch, Gewebe*
Fabrik: *factory*

COMPREHENSION

► SF 31: Writing a summary

1 Writing a summary

a Divide the text into sections based on content.
b Make notes on each of the sections you have chosen.
c Use your notes to write a summary of the text.

ANALYSIS

2 Examining the text type

a Nkosi's text is an example of a personal *essay. Point to one example of each of the following in the text: *personal remarks – generalizations – quotations.*
b Examine the text closely and point out other elements that Nkosi incorporates into his essay.

3 Imagery SUPPORT p. 271

Nkosi frequently uses metaphorical language in his essay, for example in ll. 10–11: 'They feared his departure opened up a door for the angry poor black masses to destroy their comfortable lives.'

a Analyse the *metaphor, explaining why it is appropriate in its context.
b Point out other examples of metaphorical language in the text and analyse their effect.

BEYOND THE TEXT

4 Writing a comment

'Every country needs a hero.' Do you agree? Comment on this saying in a personal essay of about 200–250 words.

Up North: Canada

D1 Why Canada works *Murtaza Hussain*

The author is a Toronto-based journalist who writes for Al Jazeera.

While I was born in Pakistan, I spent my formative years in Canada, and for the most part what I have observed is the seemingly effortless success of Canada's multicultural society. The 'otherness' of minorities in Europe is conspicuously absent in Canada, despite the fact that over one-fifth of Canadians themselves are foreign-born.

In major cities such as Toronto and Vancouver, roughly half the population consists of visible minorities, yet the type of social segregation and alienation prevalent in Europe is nonetheless conspicuously absent.

While immigrants tend to settle in the same neighbourhoods upon arrival, they also partake in Canadian society to a far greater degree than their European counter-parts. Immigrants to Canada tend to achieve economic success, high levels of education, and social integration at a level unseen in European societies. Correspondingly, Canadians also tend to have a much more positive opinion of immigration than Europeans. In a 2006 poll asking what made them 'proud to be Canadian', multiculturalism ranked second place, behind only the country's Charter of Rights and Freedoms. [...]

So why the discrepancy? What makes multiculturalism work in one place and fail in another? The easy answer is that different immigration policies attract different social classes of immigrants; but in reality this only tells part of the story. While Canada is home to many professional immigrants, it is also home to vast numbers of refugees from across the world. Despite this reality, they have still not encountered the difficulties and stagnation experienced by their European counterparts.

The real answer may be in something more deeply rooted in conceptions of national identity. European nation states were born with specific cultural criteria that defined the boundaries of inclusion in the community. Thus, there is an expectation that immigrants will conform to – but not in any meaningful sense change – the supposedly static 'national culture' of their new homes. [...]

Canada, in contrast, is a nation with a full awareness of the amorphous and fluid nature of its own culture. Canadians are bound together by a set of values and beliefs which are able to accommodate a broad range of cultural expressions and do not demand any strict homogeneity. All that is asked of immigrants is what is asked of any members of society: respect for the laws and institutions of the country, social amiability, and contribution to the maintenance and improvement of public works.

Given such an easygoing attitude, it is not surprising that many immigrant Canadians on their own tend to naturally adopt 'traditional' Canadian attitudes and mores. Today hockey games are often broadcast in Punjabi as well as French and English, and Canadians of every ethnicity and religion come together in enjoyment of the same foods, pastimes and holidays.

Further, polls have repeatedly shown that immigrants are in fact among the proudest of Canadians. All this is compelling evidence that 'integration' tends to work on its own when it is not being forcibly compelled, and when it is not a zero-sum game where newcomers are expected to conform but not create.

From: *Al Jazeera*, 16 September 2013

FACT FILE

Canada in numbers

land area (sq km)	9,093,510
population	35,540,419
GDP (in millions US $)	1,786,655
median age	41.7

1 **formative years** years in which you form your views
4 **conspicuous** [kən'spɪkjuəs] *auffällig*
8 **alienation** feeling of not belonging
prevalent ['prevələnt] widespread
10 **partake in sth.** *(fml)* take part in sth.
11 **counterpart** sb. who plays the same role as sb. else
13 **correspondingly** *dementsprechend*
17 **discrepancy** *Missverhältnis, Diskrepanz*
23 **conception** idea, notion
25 **inclusion** belonging
28 **amorphous** having no clearly defined shape
30 **accommodate sb./sth.** *jdn./etwas unterbringen*
33 **amiability** friendliness
maintenance ['meɪntənəns] *Aufrechterhaltung*
public works *öffentliche Dienstleistungen*
35 **mores** ['mɔːreɪz] *(Latin)* behaviour
40 **compelling** *(adj)* convincing, forceful
41 **zero-sum game** situation in which one person's gain is the other person's loss

COMPREHENSION

1 Canada vs. Europe

a Make notes on the differences between Canada and Europe in the way they treat newcomers, according to the writer.

b Summarize the reasons the writer names for this 'discrepancy' (l. 17).

ANALYSIS

2 Drawing conclusions

Examine the conclusion (or conclusions) Hussain draws from the Canadian experience. What evidence does he present to support his view?

BEYOND THE TEXT

3 Discussing the issue

Discuss Hussain's views on the integration of immigrants in European societies. Do you agree with his assessment with regard to Germany?

CD4 10

heritage tradition
head tax *Kopfsteuer*
curb sth. restrict sth.
requirement *Voraussetzung, Anforderung*
adhere to a criterion *ein Kriterium erfüllen*
outright completely, without exception
deem sb./sth. *(fml)* consider sb./sth.
narrative *(n) (here)* a generally accepted interpretation of events
the powers that be *(fml)* *die Machthabenden*
sporadic *gelegentlich, sporadisch*
overtures ['əʊvətʃʊəz] *(pl)* *Annäherungsversuche*
famine ['fæmɪn] *Hungersnot*
wrestle ['resl] with sth. *mit etwas ringen*
reconcile with sth. ['rekənsaɪl] come to terms with sth.

D2 The land of welcome?

The recording you are going to hear is an excerpt from a daily current affairs programme on Canadian radio.

1 Listening for gist

After listening to the recording for the first time, write down the main topic in one short sentence.

2 Listening for detail

While listening a second time, make notes on the following points:

- the image most Canadians have of Canada as a country of immigrants;
- what Rachel Décoste says about this image;
- why she calls Canada's self-image a 'myth';
- what advice Décoste would give her fellow Canadians.

FACT FILE

Making amends

The low population density in Canada meant that friction between newcomers and natives was less than in the United States, for example. Nevertheless, Canada's indigenous peoples (First Nations, Métis and Inuit) frequently saw their traditional way of life threatened as the nation expanded westward and northward. In the late 20th century, the Canadian government took unusual steps to make amends to its first peoples. The Canadian Constitution Act of 1982 specifically guaranteed the Aboriginal and treaty rights of all indigenous groups, including land use and cultural autonomy. The Nunavut Act of 1999 went a step further by creating the new autonomous territory of Nunavut, an area the size of Europe inhabited and administered mainly by its Inuit inhabitants. Despite such progress, Aboriginals continue to lag behind other Canadians in terms of income, employment, health and education.

Collect information on the work of the Truth and Reconciliation Commission of Canada and report to your class. What issue forms the main focus of the Commission's work?

Young Inuit boy on Ellesmere Island, Nanavut, Canada

D3 Rich land, poor land *Suzanne Goldenberg*

The oil-rich tar sands of northern Alberta have brought money and jobs to an arctic wilderness. But some Canadians wonder if the price isn't too high.

Amid the strip mines and steam plants sprawled across the northern Alberta wilderness, Fort McKay is just a tiny dot on the map. It is also one of the single biggest source sites of the carbon pollution that is choking the planet.

This tiny First Nations community grew rich on oil, and was wrecked by oil. Local Cece Fitzpatrick grabbed what she saw as a last chance for Fort McKay and decided to run for chief, promising to stand up to the industry which came here 50 years ago.

Within a 25-mile radius of Fort McKay, 21 projects with a capacity of up to 3.3m barrels a day have been approved or are in production. Another 20 with a combined capacity of about 1.6m barrels a day are in the planning stage, according to Fort McKay First Nation. Locals can hear, smell, feel and taste the evidence of extraction, even inside their homes. On bad days, it smells like cat piss, according to Cece Fitzpatrick. [...]

While oil made some people here rich, it is also poisoning the waters of the Athabasca River. Researchers last year confirmed high rates of cervical cancers and a rare bile duct cancer among First Nations communities who fish from the Athabasca and hunt off the land.

Which was why Cece decided to run for chief, challenging a leader in power almost continuously since 1986, and who long ago gave up trying to keep the industry out.

'The worst thing is my grandkids,' Cece said. 'Enough is enough. When do we stop and say: "Let's look at the future of our kids"? Because really I don't want people to have kids any more because our future here is so bleak. We don't want to live here anymore.'

Cece's opponent, Jim Boucher, a wise-cracking cynic, argued oil offered Fort McKay an escape from the poverty of other First Nations communities. The 400 permanent residents – Cree, Dene, and descendants of Scottish and French fur traders – claim a territory bigger than France. Another 400 live outside it.

Without oil, 'it would be like any other First Nation community in the north. We would essentially have no economy, no employment prospects, no business prospects,' Jim said in an interview at Fort McKay's administrative building.

The expansive wood and glass structure is by far the most impressive building in Fort McKay, which has no restaurants and a single shop which shares premises with a post office in a trailer. The shop does not sell vegetables or fruit.

Jim Boucher earned about CAD $644,000 (£350,000) last year. He makes no apology. 'I think it was a sign of the financial times of our First Nation,' he said. Some residents earn upwards of CAD $100,000 working for the oil companies, or for a handful of service companies operated by the Fort McKay First Nation.

Even Cece worked for a few years as a heavy equipment operator at Syncrude, though she said she always felt guilty. 'I used to feel like I was betraying myself and betraying my people because I was working at an industry that was destroying the land.' She now works as a dispatcher for a local contractor.

From: 'Fort McKay: The Canadian town that sold itself to tar sands', *The Guardian*, 28 May 2015

FACT FILE

Tar sands are a naturally occurring mixture of clay, sand, water and bitumen (a heavy, non-fluid kind of petroleum). Because bitumen can't be pumped from the ground, it has to be mined, usually in open pits. The bitumen has to be extracted and separated from the sand and clay before it can be refined and transported. This requires vast quantities of water and energy. The heavily polluted waste water is collected in so-called tailings ponds.
The high production costs make tar sands mining a risky business, and the environmental impact is enormous.

1 **amid** in the middle of
4 **First Nations** one of Canada's indigenous peoples (cf. Fact File, p. 98)
5 **run for sth.** be a candidate in an election for a public office
chief leader of a community
8 **barrel** unit of measurement in the oil industry (120–159 litres)
17 **cervical cancer** *Gebärmutterhalskrebs*
bile duct *Gallengang*
25 **bleak** unpleasant, not giving any reason for hope
27 **wise-cracking** *(adj)* in the habit of making clever remarks and jokes
cynic *Zyniker/in*
35 **premises** *(pl) Räumlichkeiten*
37 **CAD $** *(abbr)* Canadian dollar(s)
44 **dispatcher** *(AE) Mitarbeiter/in in einer Einsatz-/Taxizentrale*
contractor *Subunternehmer/in*

Part D

COMPREHENSION

1 Looking at both sides
Outline the arguments for and against exploiting the Alberta tar sands.

ANALYSIS

2 Presenting the candidates
Examine the way Cece Fitzpatrick and her opponent Jim Boucher are presented in the text. Analyze the means the writer uses to influence her readers. SUPPORT p. 271

BEYOND THE TEXT

3 Expressing your opinion
Write a comment on Goldenberg's text in which you make clear which you think is more important: economic development or an intact environment.

CULTURE SPOT

'We declare that we will take part in the Commonwealth Games in the spirit of true sportsmanship, recognising the rules which govern them and desirous of participating in them for the honour of our Commonwealth and for the glory of sport.'
(Oath spoken at the opening ceremony of the Games)

The Commonwealth Games

Cameroon delegation during the opening ceremony of the 2014 Commonwealth Games in Glasgow, Scotland

Every four years, the member states of the Commonwealth of Nations meet for an international sports competition rivalled only by the Olympics.

1 How do you explain the appeal of an event in which the former colonies of the British Empire compete with their former 'mother country'?

2 Does sport bring countries closer together or does it lead to increased rivalry? Discuss.

Taking part in a panel discussion

Your class is going to stage a panel discussion on the topic 'Children of the Commonwealth: hopes, dreams and fears'. One member from each of the five 'country groups' will play the role of a young person from 'their' country. In the panel discussion, you will be given the opportunity to show what you have learned about the present situation of your country, how it has come about, and what you hope for with regard to the future.

1 Preparation

- Each team sends one member to form a new group, the moderators' group.
- Each team chooses one member who will actively participate in the discussion.
- The teams prepare role cards with notes for their participant. These can include facts, ideas for statements or questions.
- The moderator's team must also prepare an introduction in which the topic and the guests are presented.

2 The discussion

► SF27: Having a discussion

The moderator ...

- opens the discussion,
- introduces the guests,
- asks the guests questions,
- makes comments,
- can change the subject,
- solicits questions from the audience,
- closes the discussion.

The guests ...

- make statements and answer questions.
- ask each other questions.

The audience ...

- can ask questions,
- make notes on the performance of 'their' participant.

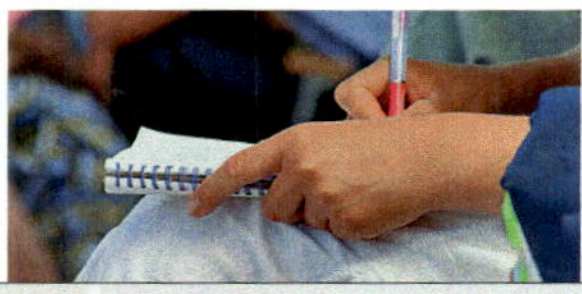

3 Evaluation

After the discussion, all participants return to their groups to get feedback from the other members. Use the assessment sheet that your teacher will give you.

The discussion can be repeated with different participants to give others a chance to actively take part.

5 India – a Kaleidoscope

A

- India is the largest democracy, the 2nd most populous country and the 9th largest economy in the world.
- Four world religions originated in the Indian subcontinent: Hinduism, Buddhism, Jainism and Sikhism.
- 50 % of all Indians are below the age of 25.

B

Download a list of chapter vocab here: **Webcode** context-15

► SF 11: Analysing pictures

1 A first glimpse of India: photos and facts
Work with a partner. Choose one picture and speculate about the people you see and where and when the photo might have been taken. Link your photo to the facts about India. Present your picture in class, saying what you find most interesting and surprising.

2 Presenting India
Form groups. Imagine you are going to produce a short video clip about India for a multicultural festival at your school. Brainstorm ideas about what your audience might want to know about India, and discuss how you would present them in your clip. Share your ideas in class. Use them when you work on the Chapter Task (cf. p. 121).

C

D

- The literacy rate in India is 65% among women and 82% among men.
- India is about 31% urban (as compared to 82.4% in the USA and 73% in Germany).
- Mumbai (21 million), Delhi (16 million) and Kolkata (14 million) are among the world's biggest metropolitan areas.

E

literacy ['lɪtərəsi] ability to read and write

PREVIEW

In this chapter you will learn about India as a modern society and about its history. You will gain an insight into India's development from a former British colony into an independent nation and learn about Indian communities abroad.

Main topics

Focus on Skills: LISTENING and VIEWING

CD2 02

Listen to an audio version of the text on the CD or download it here:
Webcode context-16

TROUBLE SPOT
***Hindi** = one of the official languages spoken in India*
***Hindu** (l. 27) = a person whose religion is Hinduism*

In 2001, Shahrukh Khan starred as Ashoka in the Bollywood blockbuster movie of the same name.

The 1982 biopic Gandhi retells Gandhi's life from his time in South Africa to his assassination. The movie won eight Oscars.

India then and now

India before the arrival of the Europeans

Mark Twain once referred to India as 'the cradle of the human race'. Indeed, India can look back on a long history. As early as 2500 BC large cities emerged along the Indus River. This civilization traded with Mesopotamia and Egypt and developed a distinctive culture, from which Hinduism emerged. The Mauryan Empire, the first and largest empire on the Indian subcontinent, reached its peak in the 3rd century BC. Under its ruler Ashoka, Buddhism spread throughout the region. Arts and science flourished again in the 4th century AD during the Golden Age of the Gupta emperors. The concepts of zero and infinity are believed to have been developed by Indian mathematicians during this era.
In the 12th century AD Islamic invaders conquered northern India. Islamic rule reached its zenith during the Mughal period, which began in 1526 and led to the unification of large parts of India. It was during the Mughal era that many magnificent buildings such as the Taj Mahal were built.

India and the British Empire

When European trading companies arrived in India in the early 17th century to gain access to the country's wealth, the decline of the Mughal empire was accelerated. A century later, the British East India Company had become the dominant force in the subcontinent. After a massive revolt against the British in 1857 the last Mughal emperor was deposed and the British Crown took over control, turning India into the largest and most profitable colony of its empire, its 'Jewel in the Crown'. British rule in India, also known as 'the Raj', lasted until 1947. During this era, the British modernized the country, but mismanagement, food shortages and diseases also led to the deaths of millions of people and resentment against the colonial power. The Indian struggle for independence, led by Gandhi and Nehru, culminated in 1947, when the former colony was divided into two separate countries, Hindu-dominated India and Muslim-dominated Pakistan. After Partition widespread displacement of Hindus and Muslims and sectarian violence between the two groups followed. To this day, the relationship between India and Pakistan remains tense.

India today

India is often described as a land of contrasts and paradoxes. It is home to ten percent of the world's millionaires, but also to one third of the world's poor. It is the world's largest democracy, but millions of its citizens are still illiterate. India is the largest country in southern Asia, yet it is densely populated with a population exceeding 1.2 billion people, half of them under the age of 25. India is also one of the world's most promising new markets, but the benefits of economic growth have not yet reached all Indians. In fact, India's growth poses many new challenges. India will need to feed, house and educate the next generation of Indians, who will both contribute to and benefit from the country's success. In the next two decades, India will see a massive migration from rural areas to the cities. The demand for energy will increase as future city dwellers will need electricity, water and mass transit. Today 400 million Indians are not connected to the electricity grid. The Indian government aims to increase power generation by 700% in the next 25 years. Will the new India manage to meet these challenges successfully?

► SF 2: Learning new words

1 Paraphrasing key terms

Paraphrase the following key terms, which are used frequently when talking about India:

1 Indian subcontinent
2 colonial power
3 the Jewel in the Crown
4 the Raj
5 Independence
6 Partition

2 Words in use

Find the highlighted words in the text to match the definitions:

1 the act of joining parts of a country together
2 a situation when people do not have enough to eat
3 the act of forcing people to leave the area where they live
4 a violent confrontation between different groups in society
5 increase in business activities
6 movement of a large number of people

► LP 19: Collocations

3 Prepositions

Complete the following sentences about India with the correct prepositions. Look at the text if necessary:

1 Gandhi united millions of Indians in their struggle … independence.
2 India is home … about 1.56 million millionaires.
3 There is great demand … highly-skilled IT professionals.
4 Indian citizens have started to show growing resentment … inequality.

► LP 19: Collocations

4 Verbs and nouns

a Many verbs in English have a tendency to form partnerships with nouns (as in *make a decision* or *find a solution*). These are called 'collocations'. Scan the text for the noun *challenge*: which verbs does *challenge* collocate with?

b Search for more examples of verbs collocating with *challenge* using a monolingual dictionary or a corpus, e.g. the British National Corpus (BNC). Illustrate each collocation with an example sentence.

c Do the same for the nouns *access* and *control*.

Find an online dictionary here:
Webcode context-52

► SF 38: Writing a well-structured text

5 Images of India

India has been described as 'the cradle of the human race' and as 'a land of contrasts and paradoxes'. Write two paragraphs in which you explain the two images. Choose appropriate vocabulary from the text and the tasks above.

India's past: echoes and reflections

A1 India's UNESCO World Heritage sites

The following WebQuest will take you on a virtual journey across India through time and space.

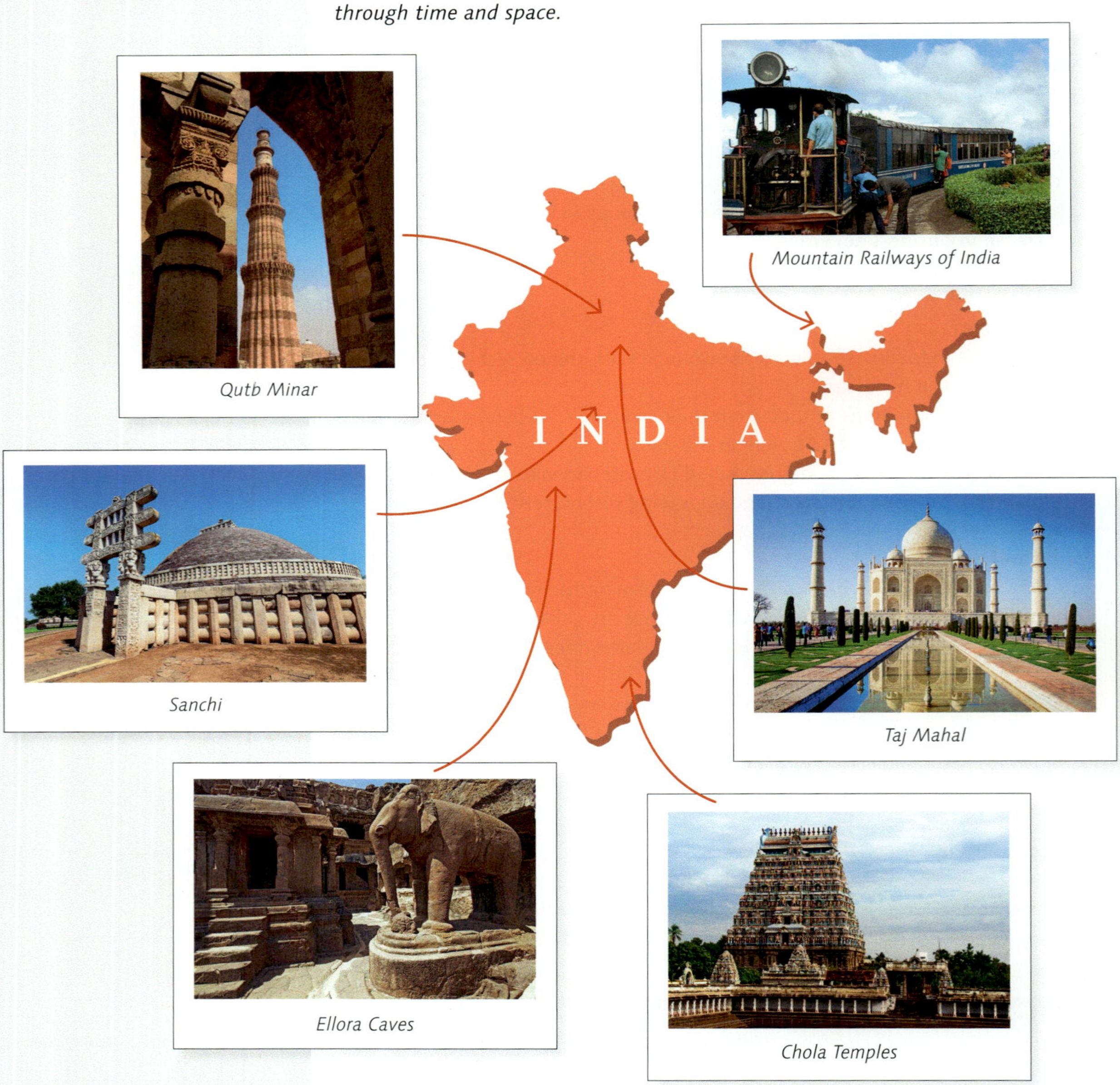

Qutb Minar

Mountain Railways of India

Sanchi

Taj Mahal

Ellora Caves

Chola Temples

► SF 5: Doing research
► SF 24: Giving a presentation

A WebQuest

a Form six groups. Each group works on one site. Go to the UNESCO World Heritage website and find information, videos, etc. there about the history and cultural significance of your site. Present your findings in class, explaining what makes them places of outstanding universal value.

b Together create a timeline of Indian history based on the information you have collected.

A2 Colonizers and colonized

To feel that somewhere among those millions you have left a little justice or happiness or prosperity, a sense of manliness or moral dignity, a spring of patriotism, a dawn of intellectual enlightenment or a stirring of duty where it did not before exist – that is enough, that is the Englishman's justification in India.

Lord Curzon, Viceroy of India from 1899 to 1905, in his farewell speech on leaving India

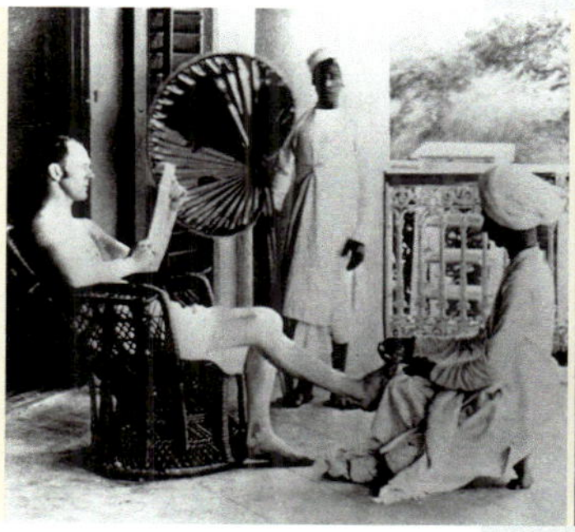

4 **dawn** time of day when light first appears
enlightenment process of understanding sth.
5 **stirring of sth.** ['stɜ:rɪŋ] beginning of sth.
viceroy ['vaɪsrɔɪ] person representing the British monarch in India

► SF 11: Analysing pictures

ANALYSIS

Comparing a quote and photos
Study the photos and the quote carefully. Then prepare an oral statement in which you explain what they tell you about the relationship between the British and the Indians during the British Raj. SUPPORT p. 272

A3 The British Empire from an Indian perspective

Gurcharan Das

In this text you will learn about the impact of the British Empire from an Indian perspective. Certain parts of the text have been left out (cf. gap A, etc.) – don't worry about them on your first reading.

[A] Britain gave us democracy, the rule of law, an independent judiciary and a free press. It built railways, canals, and harbors, but it could not bring about an industrial revolution. It could not raise economic growth or lift people out of poverty. It could not avert famines. The truth is the Raj was economically incompetent. It just did not know how to 'develop' a country. Had it known it, Britain could have gained much from having a larger market for its manufactures. It introduced modern education and helped create a small middle class, but it did not educate the mass of the people. This was its other failure and linked to the first, for development is not possible without mass literacy.

[B] Had India remained united, billions could have been saved in defense expenditures and invested instead in improving the lives of ordinary people in both countries. Whether an undivided India could have survived the Muslim-Hindu animosity is another counterfactual of history.

[C] Many Indians despair over the divisiveness of caste and would prefer to wish it away. However, the hold of the Indian way of life is also a bulwark against the onslaught of the global culture. The British gave us the English language, which allowed us to converse with our compatriots in a country with 16 official languages. However, English also divided us into two nations – the 10 percent elite who learned English and shut out the 90 percent who did not. Knowing English today, though, gives Indians a competitive advantage in the global economy and is an important factor in our nascent success in the information economy.

[D] In school we had learned that the Indian subcontinent was a triangle with the Himalayas, the Arabian Sea, and the Bay of Bengal as its sides. The Himalayas ran from east to west and cut off the cold winds from the north. This allowed agriculture

1 **judiciary** [dʒu'dɪʃəri] *Gerichtsbarkeit*
4 **avert sth.** [ə'vɜ:t] prevent sth.
famine ['fæmɪn] long period of time without food
6 **manufactures** (here) goods made in large numbers
10 **expenditure** [ɪk'spendɪtʃə] amount of money spent
12 **animosity** [ˌænɪ'mɒsəti] strong feeling of hatred
13 **counterfactual** sth. that has not happened but might have under different conditions
14 **divisiveness** [dɪ'vaɪsɪvnɪs] force that splits people into different groups
15 **bulwark** ['bʊlwək] *(fml)* person or thing that protects or defends sth.
17 **16 official languages** 23 languages are now recognized for official use at state level
21 **nascent** ['neɪsənt] beginning to exist

27 **Aryans** ['eəriənz] ancient race that moved into India from Central Asia around 1500 BC
Mughals ['mu:gɑ:lz] Muslim dynasty that conquered northern India in the 16th century
31 **infuriating** *(adj)* making you extremely angry

to prosper and created wealth, but it also attracted barbarian invaders from the north. It gave us a warm climate so that no one who came wanted to leave. First came the Aryans, then the Turks, the Afghans, and the Mughals. They came, they stayed, and they merged and became Indian. To accommodate them we merely created a new sub-caste each time and they became part of our diversity. The British did not. But now that they have been gone for more than fifty years, our confidence is restored, especially among the young. Our infuriating diversity may also be of some value. Because we have always learned to live with pluralism, it is possible that we might be better prepared to negotiate the diversity of the global economy.

From: *India Unbound*, 2001

COMPREHENSION

► SF 10: Working with closed test formats

1 Filling in the gaps

Four passages from the text above have been omitted. For each of the four gaps (A, B, C, D) select the most appropriate passage from the list below. Note that there are six passages to choose from. Compare with a partner.

1 Although Indians gloss over it, the British Raj was the most important event in the making of modern India – for better and for worse.
2 As a subdivisional officer, my father was an important official of the British Raj.
3 The British gave us a hundred years of peace – the so-called Pax Britannica – but they also consciously pursued a divide-and-rule policy which made Hindus and Muslims conscious of their separate identities. This led to a tragic division of the country.
4 The British were different from our other invaders. They did not merge with us and remained aloof* to the end. This shook our self-confidence.

*aloof distant, impersonal

5 The Raj gave us modern values and institutions, but it did not interfere with our ancient traditions and our religion. India has therefore preserved its spiritual heritage and the old way of life continues.
6 Western education provided the stimulus for the most dramatic change in the minds of Indians in a thousand years.

Statue of Queen Victoria in Kolkata

2 Aspects of British rule

List the positive and the negative aspects mentioned by Gurcharan Das about British rule in India.

► SF 41: Mediation of written and oral texts

3 Mediation (English → German)

In your History class, you are discussing the legacy of colonialism. You have read this text and offer to summarize the main points raised in the text in German. Make notes and practise your talk.

ANALYSIS

► SF 9: Paraphrasing

4 A critical view of British rule in India

Work with a partner. Explain the following quotes from the text and point out what they tell you about the legacy of the British Raj.

1 'The Raj was economically incompetent.' (l. 4)
2 'Had India remained united, billions could have been saved in defense expenditures.' (ll. 10–11)
3 'English ... divided us into two nations.' (l. 18)
4 'Our infuriating diversity may ... be of some value.' (l. 32)

BEYOND THE TEXT

5 CHALLENGE **The legacy of the Raj**
Discuss whether the British Raj was beneficial for India, both during the time of the Raj itself and following Independence. Justify your opinion by referring to the texts you have examined. SUPPORT p. 272

A4 Gandhi remembered *Chetan Bhagat*

- 3–2–1 BRAINSTORMING Write down three things you know about Mahatma Gandhi, two reasons why he is considered very important today, and one question you have about him. In class, share your ideas and create a mind map about Gandhi.

Find a mindmapping tool here:
Webcode context-53

FACT FILE

Gandhi and India's struggle for independence
Mohandas Karamchand Gandhi was born in Porbandar in Gujarat in 1869 to Hindu parents. At the age of 19, he was sent to London to become a barrister.

He returned to India in 1891 to practice law. Two years later, he moved to Durban, South Africa, where he accepted a job at an Indian law firm.

Gandhi was shocked at the way Indians were treated there. He became actively involved in fighting for their rights and developed his philosophy of non-violence, *satyagraha* ('devotion to truth'). After 20 years of fighting for the rights of Indians and Africans, Gandhi returned to India in 1915.

Gandhi continued his fight against colonial rule in India by organizing peaceful protests.

Millions of Indians followed him. His campaigns for independence ultimately led the British to withdraw from India in 1947.

But independence from British rule came at a price: the Partition of the subcontinent. In 1948 Gandhi, who had been opposed to Partition, was shot by a young Hindu fanatic who was angry at him for his tolerance towards Muslims.

Gandhi's philosophy of non-violent resistance has inspired millions of people around the world, and even today the Mahatma ('Great Soul') is admired for his courage, will-power, strength and determination in fighting for a just cause.

1 *Add more details to your mind map.*
2 *Use the mind map to give a one-minute speech about Gandhi.*

India celebrates Independence Day.

TROUBLE SPOT
fanatic (l. 16) = *noun (person who is extremely enthusiastic about sth.)*
fanatical = *adjective (enthusiastic)*

In 2012, Chetan Bhagat, one of the most popular Indian novelists writing in English today, wrote the following fictional letter to Gandhi.

Dear Gandhiji,
You left us more than sixty years ago. If you were still around, you would have been more than 140 years old. However, we have not forgotten you. You are on every banknote and most stamps. There are many statues of you. Prestigious roads in almost every city are named after you. Our politicians try to model themselves on you. They wear the fabric you promoted, they quote you at every instance, they've got a photograph of you in their offices and some even eat and live like you. There are books, TV programmes and movies about you. Seriously, you'd be impressed at how much we still adore you. However, there are things that won't make you feel proud. The India you spent all your life making free is far from free. True, the white guys are gone. But there are still millions of poor people. After sixty-plus years, we are still among the poorest nations on earth. This lack of money leads to a lot of problems in healthcare, infrastructure and education. Many children still don't go to a good school. Those who

1 **Gandhiji** in many Indian languages '-ji' can be added to names to show respect

TROUBLE SPOT
fabric ['fæbrɪk] (l. 6) = *material from which clothes are made*
Fabrik = *company, firm*

TROUBLE SPOT
programme (l. 8) = *sth. that people watch on TV or listen to on the radio*
Fernsehprogramm, -kanal = *TV channel*

Election campaign in India

do don't get into good colleges. And those who go to college don't get good jobs. We need to get rich, and fast. Not only to make more schools and colleges, but also because most Indian problems are linked to the lack of money. Yet, it is considered un-Indian to think that way. The young generation, which thinks like that, is considered materialistic and greedy. The older generation takes the moral high ground – slowness in work is termed patience, non-stop discussion and no action is called careful consideration and lack of improvement in standards of living is countered with claims about the need to live with austerity. And yes, in many cases, politicians who speak like this claim to be your fans.

The younger generation wishes you could come down for one day and clarify these points. Is progress un-Indian? Is change bad? Is a desire to see my country as rich as some other nations materialistic? Is getting things done fast impatience? If you blessed our purpose of building a developed India, the job would become so much easier.

The young generation needs you down here for something else, too. We have a new battle here just like the one you fought with the British. The enemy is not as clear as it was in your case – the white people. Our enemy is the old school of thought, or rather, the people who defend the old school of thought. They do this in the name of antique Indian policies, culture and values. You could help identify this enemy more clearly. Many people who are at the helm of affairs now have served India for decades, maybe with good intentions.

But obviously they don't want to accept they screwed up. We wish they would, though, and we'd have a national day of shame. It won't be easy, but from there we could make a new beginning. But they won't, for they are in power. And to defend themselves and their ways, they don't mind crushing the aspirations, ideas and talent of an entire generation.

Yes, there is a lot of talk of India being a young nation and about youth power. However, youth power is the biggest myth going around India right now. Of course, the youth has spending power – we can buy enough SIM cards, sneakers and fizzy drinks to keep many MNCs in business. But we do not have the power to change things. Can the youth get a new college set up? Can the youth ask the government to provide tax incentives to MNCs to relocate jobs to smaller towns? No way. We are wooed, used, but seldom heard. If you came down, you could unite us. You used religious festivals as social events and propagated your cause. You understood that people need entertainment to bind them. Perhaps we could integrate colleges in the same way, link all colleges maybe for their annual festivals and the message of change could be channelled through them. We have amazing technology such as the Internet now. You would use it so well. If the youth unites, there could actually be youth power.

With our purpose blessed, enemy identified and youth united, we could take the first steps towards the new Indian revolution. After all, China had one and only after that did they get on the path of true progress.

19 **lack of sth.** state of not having sth.
23 **greedy** wanting more money
take the moral high ground claim that your arguments are morally better than other people's arguments
29 **austerity** [ɒs'terəti] situation when people do not have a lot of money
42 **at the helm of sth.** in charge of sth.
44 **screw up** *(infml)* do sth. badly
52 **MNC** = **multinational company** company operating all over the world
53 **tax incentive** [ˌɪn'sentɪv] *Steueranreiz*
54 **woo sb.** try to get sb.'s support
56 **propagate your cause** ['prɒpəgeɪt] spread your ideas

But if it is not feasible for you to come back, we'll have to try to bring about change ourselves. If we can be inspired to do that, we can say we have not forgotten you and understand the meaning of your birthday. We hope you had a good one up there!
Lots of love, The Younger Generation

'Letter to Bapu from Generation Next on His Birthday', *What Young India Wants*, 2012

64 **feasible** that can be achieved

COMPREHENSION

1 True/false statements
Write six true/false statements on a piece of paper. Swap your statements with a partner. Check your partner's statements, correct the false ones and check each other's solutions.

► SF 10: Working with closed test formats

2 Finishing sentences
Finish the sentences with ideas from the text.
1 If Gandhi lived in India today, he would be shocked to hear that …
2 Young Indians need Gandhi to …
3 Gandhi's message to young Indians would be …

LANGUAGE AWARENESS

3 Informal style
Chetan Bhagat often uses informal language in his letter.
a Put the following examples of informal English into formal English:
1 'If you were still around.' (l. 1)
2 'True, the white guys are gone.' (l. 10)
3 'But obviously they don't want to accept they screwed up.' (l. 44)
4 'No way.' (l. 54)
b Scan the letter for at least three more examples of informal style and put them into formal style.
c Explain why Bhagat uses informal diction in this text.

► LP 11: Using the right register

BEYOND THE TEXT

4 YOU CHOOSE **Youth empowerment**
Choose one of the following writing tasks. ► LANGUAGE HELP

a An Indian newspaper has asked young people to write about their Indian dream and contribute a text for their online blog. Imagine you are a teenager growing up in India. Write a blog entry. Use ideas for your blog from Bhagat's letter. You could start like this: 'I dream of an India that …, a country that stands up to …, an India Mahatma Gandhi would be proud of …'

OR

b '[Young people] do not have the power to change things.' (l. 50) Comment on this statement with reference to the community *you* live in.

LANGUAGE HELP
- What I would like to see is …
- If we put all our efforts together …
- We have the potential to …
- One major obstacle is …
- If we want to see improvements, we have to …
- Our main contribution could be …

► SF 37: Doing a creative writing task
► SF 38: Writing a well-structured text

CD2 03

LISTENING FOCUS ON SKILLS

Listening to a radio interview

In this section you are going to focus on how to listen to a radio interview. Ela Gandhi, Mahatma Gandhi's granddaughter, is a peace activist and politician. She grew up in Durban, South Africa, and knew both Mahatma Gandhi and Nelson Mandela personally. You are going to listen to part of a radio interview with her.

Ela Gandhi

1 Before listening

Sometimes you may have an idea what a radio report or an interview you are about to listen to might be about. In this case it is useful to collect some words that you might expect to hear. This will make it easier to understand the interview.

Before you listen to the interview with Ela Gandhi, read the Fact File below left and brainstorm what an interview with someone who knew both Gandhi and Mandela might be about. Make a list of keywords you expect to hear.

► SF 22: Listening

2 Listening for gist

Listen to the interview for the first time to get the gist. Before you do, read the task below carefully so you know what information to listen out for.

What is Ela Gandhi speaking about? Choose the correct answers:
Ela Gandhi is speaking about:
1 Her childhood memories in South Africa.
2 Nelson Mandela's visit to India.
3 Similarities between Mahatma Gandhi and Nelson Mandela.
4 The situation in South Africa when Mandela was released from prison.
5 The political situation in South Africa after Nelson Mandela's death.

FACT FILE

Nelson Mandela (1918–2013) was a civil rights activist in South Africa who fought against apartheid. Inspired by Gandhi, he became a leader of the African National Congress (ANC) and was sent to prison after protesting against racial inequality. When he was released in 1990 after 27 years in prison, he continued his fight – and succeeded. In the 1994 presidential elections all races were finally allowed to vote, and Nelson Mandela won the election and became president. Like Gandhi, Mandela is regarded as a role model of tolerance and reconciliation around the world today.

3 Listening for detail

Listen to the interview again and pay attention to details. In the task below you will be asked to complete sentences while listening. When doing a task like this, you are usually not expected to write down exactly what you have heard. You may use your own words to show that you have understood that particular part of the text.

Listen again and complete the sentences:
1 Gandhi and Mandela were capable of inspiring people because …
2 Both Gandhi's and Mandela's ideal was to …
3 When Mandela visited Gandhi's home in India, he refused to … because …
4 The fact that Nelson Mandela invited the man who had demanded the death penalty for him symbolizes …
5 When Mandela was released from prison, South Africans hoped that … despite the fact that … .

Tales from modern India

B1 Urbanization in India: the big picture

net new employment *Nettoneubeschäftigung (= Differenz aus der Anzahl neu geschaffener Arbeitsplätze und der Anzahl beendeter Arbeitsverhältnisse)*
residential space area consisting of houses rather than offices

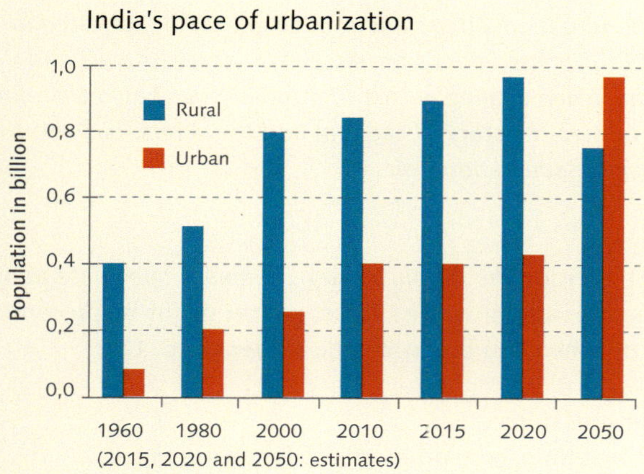

FACT FILE

India in 2030
- **590 million** people will live in cities, nearly twice the population of the USA today.
- **70%** of net new employment will be generated in cities.
- **91 million** urban households will be middle-class, up from **22 million** today.
- **68** cities will have a population of 1 million plus, up from **42** today; Europe has 35 today.
- **700–900 million m²** of commercial and residential space will be built – or a new Chicago every year.
- **2.5 billion m²** of roads will be built, 20 times the amount added in the past decade.
- **7,400 km** of metros and subways will be constructed – 20 times the capacity added in the past decade.

From: Equitymaster, 10 October 2012

COMPREHENSION

1 Indian urbanization
Use the bar chart above to describe the process of urbanization in India.
SUPPORT p. 272

► SF 12: Analysing charts and graphs

ANALYSIS

2 Key figures
Work with a partner and analyse the consequences of urbanization for the future of India. One partner focuses on the opportunities that urbanization provides, one on the dangers. Use the key figures provided in the Fact File as a starting point. Exchange your ideas with each other afterwards and discuss them.

B2 Life in a megacity

Kolkata is one of the fastest-growing megacities in the world. The poster on the right is of the documentary film The Revolutionary Optimists *(2013), which follows several young children growing up in Kolkata.*

ANALYSIS

1 The poster
Study the poster. Speculate about the girl: who is she, what may she be doing? Use the data and facts from **B1**.

BEYOND THE TEXT

2 Creative writing
Use your ideas to write down what the girl may be saying.

► SF 11: Analysing pictures
► SF 37: Doing a creative writing task

DVD

feature film main film with a story

▸ SF 23: Analysing a film

VIEWING **FOCUS ON SKILLS**

Watching a film trailer

In the previous section you examined a poster. Now you are going to watch the trailer for the documentary film The Revolutionary Optimists *(2013). A film trailer is a short film advertising a feature film or documentary. A trailer introduces audiences to the film it advertises and tries to get them interested in watching the whole film. Trailers use various techniques to create interest and grab the viewers' attention. When dealing with a film trailer you should therefore pay special attention not only to the story of the film and the actors, but also to camera work, visual elements, sound and music.*

1 Before viewing
Before you watch the trailer for *The Revolutionary Optimists*, speculate about what you expect to see in it and how the subject matter might be presented. Use the notes you made when you discussed the poster (cf. p. 113).

2 While viewing: first impressions
a While watching the first time, take notes on the following aspects:
- *characters and *setting (who do you see? where are they?)
- actions (what are people doing in the film?)

Share your findings.
b What would you say the documentary film is about?

3 While viewing: camera work
a Watch the trailer again, this time without sound so that you can concentrate on the camera work. Choose the correct answers:

1 The field size predominantly used in the trailer is			
a long shots	b full shots	c medium shots	d close-ups

2 The camera angle predominantly used in the trailer is		
a high angle	b low angle	c eye level

3 The type of camera movement predominantly used in the trailer is			
a zooming	b tilting	c tracking	d panning

b Explain the function of each of these techniques in this trailer.

4 Analysing the voice-over
Watch the trailer a third time, this time with sound. Concentrate on the intertitles and the voice-over. Make notes on the information they provide and explain how they contribute to the trailer.

5 Evaluating the trailer
Look through your findings in tasks 1–4 and discuss whether the trailer is successful in creating interest in the film.

B3 Celebrating Indian culture

Sanjeev Bhaskar is a well-known British comedian and broadcaster. In 2007 he made a four-part television series for the BBC, India with Sanjeev Bhaskar, *in which he travelled back to the country of his ancestors.*

BEFORE VIEWING

1 PLACEMAT **The importance of Holi**
On 15 March 2014, the President of India, Shri Pranab Mukherjee, published the following message on the occasion of one of the most important festivals celebrated in India, Holi:

On the happy occasion of Holi, I extend my greetings and good wishes to all my fellow citizens. As spring arrives, this festival of colours brings with it a joyous celebration of the rejuvenation of nature and ushers in renewed faith in peaceful co-existence. Holi not only brings joy and gaiety in our lives but also provides an opportunity to strengthen the bonds of friendship and brotherhood among people of all faiths. May this festival reinforce the multi-coloured hues of our extraordinary heritage and bring peace and prosperity to our Motherland.

From: the website of the President of India, 16 March 2014

Why are religious festivals important to people around the world? Generate ideas in a placemat activity. Include ideas from President Mukherjee's message to the Indian people.

► CC 1: Cultural awareness

COMPREHENSION

2 First viewing: no sound
You are going to watch a scene from *India with Sanjeev Bhaskar* showing Bhaskar celebrating Holi. Watch the clip without sound first and take notes on how Holi is celebrated.

DVD
► SF 23: Analysing a film

3 Second viewing: with sound
Watch the clip again, now with sound, and take notes on how Bhaskar explains the importance of Holi today.

ANALYSIS

4 Third viewing: analysing camera work and sound
Watch the clip for a third time and analyse how the camera work and the soundtrack contribute to creating Bhaskar's perspective of Holi.

BEYOND THE TEXT

5 The meaning of Holi
Research the religious side of Holi and explain its origins and meaning.

► SF 5: Doing research

6 Mediation (German → English)
Holi has become a global phenomenon in recent years. It is even celebrated in Germany today. An Indian friend of yours wants to know why. You have come across the following interview with Maxim Derenko (cf. p. 116), who started organizing Holi festivals in Germany in 2011. Based on this interview, write an email to your friend answering his question. SUPPORT p. 272

► SF 41: Mediation of written and oral texts

Wie kam die Idee, das indische Holi-Festival in Deutschland zu veranstalten?
Mein Kollege und Mitveranstalter, Jasper Hellmann, war 2011 in Indien auf Durchreise. Er war beim ursprünglichen Holi-Festival selbst vor Ort und war total begeistert davon. Bei seiner Rückkehr steckte er mich und Max Riedel, den dritten Mann im Bunde, mit der Idee an, ein Holi-Festival in Deutschland zu veranstalten.

In Indien ist das Holi-Fest ein hinduistisches Frühlingsfest. Wie kommt es, dass es trotz fehlenden traditionellen Hintergrunds in Deutschland so gut aufgenommen wird?
Die Reaktionen und Erfahrungen aus dem letzten Jahr haben gezeigt, dass die Kernelemente des Holi-Festes [...] bei den Leuten gut ankommen. Bei dieser Festlichkeit steht die Gleichheit aller Menschen im Vordergrund, denn in Indien werden die sogenannten Kasten aufgehoben. In Deutschland gibt es zwar keine Kasten, jedoch soziale Unterschiede. Des Weiteren wird Toleranz und gegenseitiger Respekt großgeschrieben. Die vielen bunten Farben spielen einen weiteren Faktor beim Festival. Die Symbolik für die Gleichheit und die Besonderheit dieses Festivals sind die Farben, diese sollen alle Menschen gleich (bunt) machen.

Habt ihr mit dem Erfolg der ersten Holi-Festivals im letzten Jahr gerechnet?
Wir haben natürlich nicht mit einem so durchschlagenden Erfolg gerechnet. Eigentlich war die Idee ein kleines Open-Air-Festival für einige Leute zu machen, in diesem Bereich haben wir auch schon Erfahrungen in Berlin gesammelt. Ein solches Festival gab es zuvor noch nie in Deutschland. [...]

Wird sich das Holi-Festival etablieren können oder handelt es um einen aktuellen Trend?
Die Resonanz des letzten Jahres hat gezeigt, dass der Hype ungebrochen ist und die Nachfrage immer noch sehr hoch ist. Wir haben unsere Tour für dieses Jahr durchgeplant und waren innerhalb weniger Stunden in fast allen Städten ausverkauft.

From: 'Holi Festivals – der neue Trend?!', *ARTikel*, 1 July 2013

CULTURE SPOT

Indian truck art

'[Indian truck art is] an art form that makes journeys through the dusty highways of India incredible in more ways than one. With a kaleidoscope of bright paints, motifs, typography and some unique couplets, these Indian trucks take you on a rather colourful journey of diverse cultures and beliefs of the country.'

From: the website of Horn Please, 2012

1 Describe the trucks in the photos.

2 Explain how Indian truck art relates to what you have learned about India in this chapter so far.

Indians abroad

C1 The Indian diaspora

1 BRAINSTORMING **Moving to foreign countries**
Work in pairs and brainstorm possible reasons why people move to foreign countries today.

2 Locating the Indian diaspora
The word *diaspora* describes communities of people who live outside their country of origin. India has the second largest diaspora comprising around 30 million ethnic Indians living in more than 100 countries.

a Work in pairs. Each pair focuses on one of the regions or countries on the right. Research the history, size and role of the Indian diaspora in the area you are dealing with and make a poster summarizing your findings.
SUPPORT ▶ p. 273

b GALLERY WALK Present your posters in a gallery walk activity.

Countries/regions
- United Kingdom
- United States
- Canada
- The Middle East (UAE, Saudi Arabia, Oman, Kuwait)
- South Africa
- East Africa (Tanzania, Kenya)
- South-East Asia (Malaysia, Singapore)
- South America and the Caribbean (Guyana, Suriname, Trinidad)
- Pacific Islands (Fiji)
- Indian Ocean Islands (Mauritius, Reunion)

Find a map showing the regions here:
Webcode context–17

Find a tool to make your poster here: **Webcode** context-50

C2 A taste of the Indian diaspora *Michelle Warwicker*

When it comes to food, the Indians of the diaspora have not only absorbed influences from the countries they live in but have also influenced the cuisine of their new countries.

Bunny chow has nothing to do with rabbits. [...] It is made with a half or a quarter loaf of bread, hollowed out and filled with steaming curry cooked with meat or beans. A traditional bunny chow (or simply 'bunny' if you are in Durban in South Africa where the dish originated) is made with mutton, chicken, mince, lamb or kidney beans. The loaf is crusty enough to hold the saucy filling in a parcel, and the bread from the centre is placed on top to keep the curry warm and provide diners with something to scoop with. Cheap, tasty and filling, bunny chow is one of the most popular takeaway meals in its home city. It is sold in small diners and takeaway kiosks and is rarely even served with a fork. [...]

Durban is home to a very large population of people of Indian ethnic origin, and the dish fuses Indian and African influences. Bunny chow may owe its origins to the Indian immigrants who arrived in South Africa in the second half of the 19th century to be put to work on sugar plantations. One theory is that they began to use a sturdy bread loaf so they could transport curry to the plantations to eat during the day. Today bunny chow has spread to other South African cities, but the original and for many people the best is still found in Durban.

From: 'What is bunny chow?', BBC, 20 January 2014

1 **chow** [tʃaʊ] *(sl)* food

Bunny chow

COMPREHENSION ◀

1 Thinking about food and culture
Outline how bunny chow reflects the Indian diaspora experience.

▶ EE 1: Eating in and out

BEYOND THE TEXT ◀

2 Fusion cuisine
Discuss to what extent fusion food is an integral part of modern society.

C3 English lessons *Shauna Singh Baldwin*

Shauna Singh Baldwin is an Indo-Canadian author. Born in Montreal, she grew up in Delhi and went to the USA to study. The following short story is about an Indian woman who has moved to the USA.

I told Tony – that is what he likes me to call him in America – I told Tony I will take English lessons till my green card comes. Valerie says there are English teachers who will teach me for free and she will find a good one who will come to the apartment so that I do not have to go outside. Tony says OK, and then he leaves for work at the cardboard factory.

I pick up the breakfast dishes and Suryavir's toys. No one can say his name here – I will tell them at the school to call him Johnny, like Tony's Johnny Walker whisky.

The phone rings and my heart starts to pound – *dharak dharak*. Our answering machine message has Valerie's voice, and I follow the words with her accent.

'We're naat here right naow, but if you leeev a mehsej, weell get right baak to you.' But it is only Valerie herself. 'Pick up the phone, Kanwaljit. I want to know if you're home so I can drop the kids off for the day.'

'Hello,' I say. 'I am here. You come.'

Valerie is a nice person, but you cannot be too careful. Tony says we cannot meet anyone from India till my green card comes, so Valerie is the only one who sees me. I call her Grocery Store Valerie to myself, because she answered my card in the grocery store, and now I babysit her two strong and unruly boys. What farmers they would have made in Punjab. My son is not so strong. More than two years of women's company. I spoilt him while we were waiting for Tony to get his citizenship, but what was I to do? If I had disciplined him, Tony's parents would have been angry – he is their only grandson.

Valerie's boys don't listen to love or scolding. But they go to school, and Valerie says it is the law. I have to send Suryavir to school. So I went there with her to register him and on the form I wrote the address I had memorized from Valerie's cheques, not ours. Still, Tony was worried in case anyone who might report us saw me. He makes me dress in pants so that I look Mexican, and says it is only a short while now. I hope so.

But first I will learn English. It's not that I don't understand it, but it has too many words. Get it. Put it. I am stuffed. Pick up your stuff. On the other hand. Hand it to you. I learned English in school, passed my matriculation examination, too. We learned whole passages of translation by heart – I had a good memory. Now Tony says I must speak English to pass my immigration interview and to memorize my amnesty story.

A knock. Someone is standing far away from the peephole – why are they doing that? Oh, it's Valerie; she was bending down to tie a shoelace for little Mark.

'Hello, hello. Come in. How are you?'

Valerie has found an English teacher who will come to the apartment and teach me for free. But Tony and I are afraid. This English teacher is from India and we didn't want to meet any people from India.

Valerie said she told the teacher I am Tony's girlfriend and that Suryavir is our son. She said the English teacher was surprised. Indian couples do not usually live together, she told Valerie. Tony says to tell Valerie we don't need this teacher. But I took her phone number to please Valerie. I may call her just to speak in Punjabi for a while.

I told Valerie I will change my name. I asked her to call me Kelly. No one here can say Kanwaljit. And Kanwaljit is left far away in Amritsar before the fire.

2 **green card** ['– –] document that allows sb. to work legally in the USA
7 **Johnny Walker whisky** US brand of whisky
18 **Punjab** [pʌn'dʒɑ:b] region in north-western India, largely populated by Sikhs
22 **scold sb.** speak angrily to sb. who has misbehaved
29 **stuffed** *(adj)* full from eating
30 **matriculation examination** exam taken in the final year of school

Some nights I lie next to Tony, here in America where I live like a worm avoiding the sunlight, and I wonder if he knows. And is it only because it was his brother that he does not sense that another man's body has come between us, or is it that he cannot remember the fire we felt in those early days? We only had three weeks in which Suryavir was made. Then he was gone.

If I had been able to return to my parents until he told me to come to America, I would not have been so weak. But to do so would have smelled of disgrace, and I am not shameless. Nor was it a matter of a month or two. Tony told me after six months, when I was becoming big with his son; it would take him two more years.

I tell myself it is not only another man's body that invades our bed, but another woman's too. And yet, that is different. I hear her tearful voice on our answering machine. Her anger follows us from city to city – Fremont, Dallas, Houston, Miami, New York, Chicago – threatening to report us to Immigration. He lived with her for two years, shared her bed, paid her our life savings for a marriage certificate. I will ask the English teacher how to say, 'Is not two years of our life enough? Is not my worm existence, my unacknowledged wifehood, enough for you? Enough that I call myself his girlfriend, my son his bastard?'

But she does not have form, no substance in our bed, I cannot imagine him with her black body – and if I can, what of it? Many men pay prostitutes. This one's price was higher and she lasted longer. And he got his green card after two years. Thus am I here.

The other man in bed with us – he has form. He looks like Tony, only younger. And he still laughs at me, waving pictures of Tony with her. Telling me Tony left me for an untouchable, a *hubshi*. Threatening to tell my parents if I would not open my legs to him.

I did. *Rubba-merey*, I did.

I thought some force would come upon us then and tear him from my flesh before the act was done. Save me, as the virtue of Dropadi was saved. And it did. Too late for virtue but soon enough for vengeance.

The police came looking for him. Oh, not for my protection – no. They were rounding up all Sikh boys between the ages of fifteen and twenty-five for 'questioning'. Tony's parents knew what was in store and they hid him in the servant's quarter, a concrete room on the flat roof of the house.

They told the police he was with Tony in America. That made them angry. One sinewy fellow with a whisky smell took a can of gasoline and slowly, as we marched from the rooms around, and as Suryavir's eyes grew larger, poured it in a steady dribble all round the centre courtyard. They all walked to the door and, almost as an afterthought, the sinewy policeman threw a lit match and the world exploded from silence into horror.

I took no chances. I gave Suryavir to Tony's mother and then climbed out of the back window. His father was blinded by tears and I pushed him after them. Then I ran up the narrow steep staircase to the servant's quarter on the roofs.

And I locked it.

And ran back through lung-searing smoke and purifying flame. I was given vengeance, and I took it as my due. But still he comes between us – the half-dead only half a world away.

I called the English teacher today. She speaks Punjabi with a city accent. I will have to ask Tony, but I think it will be, like Americans say, 'fine, fine' for her to come and teach me.

FACT FILE

The Sikhs
Since the formation of India, many Sikhs (l. 76) have demanded a separate Sikh state in Punjab. During the 1980s militancy reached a peak, leading to an attack by Indian forces on the Golden Temple of Amritsar, Punjab (l. 45) – the Sikhs' holiest temple – and the subsequent assassination of the prime minister, Indira Gandhi.

The Golden Temple of Amritsar

52 **disgrace** loss of respect
61 **unacknowledged** *(adj)* not publicly recognized
69 **hubshi** (here) black (originally Punjabi/Hindi for 'Ethiopian')
71 **rubba-merey** (Punjabi/Hindi) oh my God
73 **Dropadi** popular heroine in Hindu mythology who is regarded as a role model of virtue, bravery and resilience
74 **vengeance** ['vendʒəns] revenge
80 **sinewy** ['sɪnjuːi] having a thin body
89 **searing** *(adj)* so strong that it burns you
89 **purify sth.** make sth. pure

Her family on her father's side is from Rajasansi, just outside Amritsar. And she is married to a white guy so she is probably not part of the Gurdwara congregation; they have all heard of Tony's Green-Card Wife. (These matters travel faster than aeroplanes fly between cities.) I will tell Tony I will take English lessons, and that she will be my teacher.

Tony was finishing breakfast when Mrs Keogh, the English teacher, arrived. She knocked and I let her in. Then I asked her to sit down, offered her some tea and listened while she and Tony spoke English.

'Thank you very much. My girlfriend is just new from India. As soon as her green card comes we will be getting married, so till then I think English lessons will help her pass the time.'

The English teacher did not remark on 'my girlfriend'. Good. Not a prying woman. She said, 'I am glad to help you and your fiancée.'

Tony continued, 'I will not like it if you teach her more than I know. But just enough for her to get a good-paying job at Dunkin' Donuts or maybe the Holiday Inn. She will learn quickly but you must not teach her too many American ideas.'

The English teacher smiled at me.

Tomorrow, I will ask her where I can learn how to drive.

From: *English Lessons, and Other Stories*, 1996

96 **Gurdwara** building in which Sikhs worship
100 **Keogh** ['kiːəʊ]
106 **pry** try to find out things about other people's private lives
109 **Holiday Inn** US hotel chain

COMPREHENSION

1 Characters and plot

a Read up to l. 45 and collect facts about the narrator, her husband, her son and Valerie.

b Read on up to l. 91 and summarize what the narrator's dark secret is.

c Read the last part of the story and point out the meaning of the English lessons for the narrator and for her husband.

ANALYSIS

▶ SF 19: Analysing narrative prose

2 The protagonist's identity

a Work with a partner and examine the different facets of Kanwaljit's identity. Consider the following aspects: her personality, family, friends, relationships, cultural background, feelings and thoughts, language. Use visual aids to present your findings.

▶ SF 5: Doing research

b CHALLENGE Compare Kanwaljit's and Tony's migrant experiences. Consider their hopes for and expectations of living in the USA.

LANGUAGE AWARENESS

▶ LP 2: Present tense or future?
▶ LP 3: Simple present and present perfect
▶ LP 4: Present perfect and simple past

3 The use of tenses

Oral and written storytelling is traditionally done in the past tense. This story also uses the present tense and the future for narration. Analyse the use and functions of the different narrative tenses in the story.

SUPPORT p. 273

BEYOND THE TEXT

▶ SF 37: Doing a creative writing task

4 Writing a letter about your life

Imagine you are Kanwaljit in three years' time. Write a letter to your parents in which you tell them about your new life.

Presenting India

► SF 6: Doing project work
► SF 24: Giving a presentation

After working on this chapter, gather ideas for a multimedia presentation on the topic 'India – a kaleidoscope' for a multicultural festival at your school.

1 Form groups. Each group picks one topic. You could include some of the following aspects in your presentation:
Germans in India – the Indian diaspora in Germany – the global importance of India in the 21st century – Indian festivals – Indian foods – Indian classical and popular music – Indian literature – Indian movies – reasons to visit India – traces of India in your community (e.g. food, music, clothes) – ways to promote intercultural relations between India and Germany (e.g. exchange programmes, business cooperation, etc.)

2 Think about interesting ways of presenting *your* topic, e.g. interviews, slide shows, showing a film, making your own film, or reading out poetry or stories you like. Use ideas from this unit and choose at least one audio file (e.g. a radio interview or report) or video clip (e.g. an excerpt from a feature film or documentary, a trailer, song) for your presentation.

3 Prepare your presentation. Make sure work is distributed equally among the group and agree on a project schedule.

4 On the day of your presentation, come prepared and give your presentation.

5 With the use of an assessment sheet, which your teacher will give you, evaluate the work of the different groups.

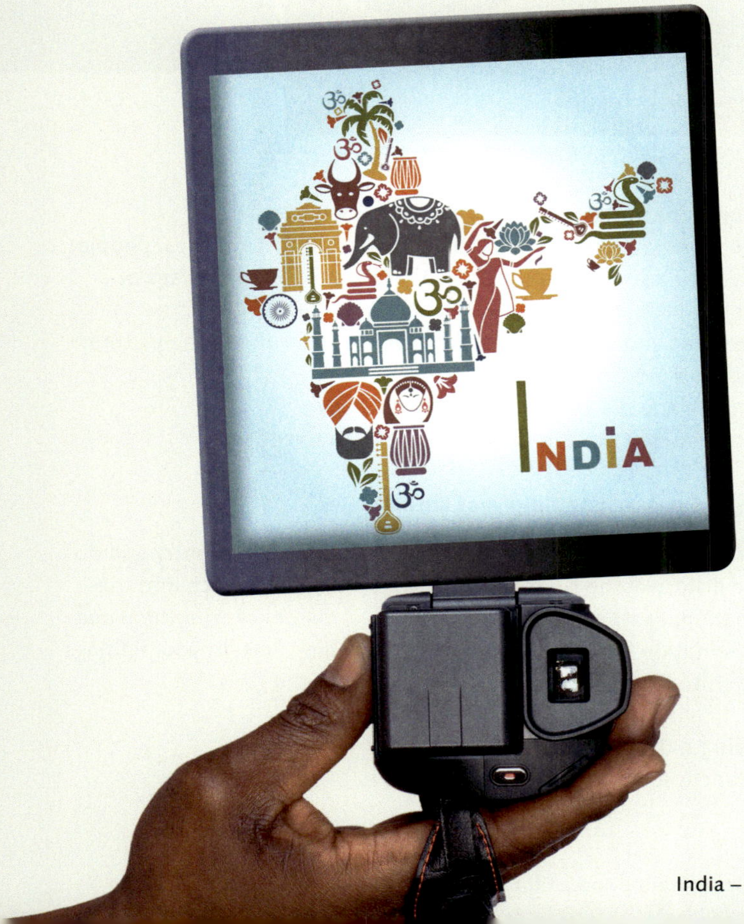

India

भारत

ଭାରତ

ভারত

6 Beyond the Nation – Europe and a Globalized World

A

B

C

Download a list of chapter vocab here: **Webcode** context-22

1 Displaying one's national identity
During great sports events, above all soccer world championships, people often display their national identity and patriotism by carrying flags or singing their national anthem.

▸ CC 1: Cultural awareness

- **a** THINK Describe your attitude to this behaviour, referring to the pictures above and your own experience.
- **b** PAIR Compare and discuss your ideas with a partner.
- **c** SHARE Present your most interesting findings to the class.

▸ SF 41: Mediation of written and oral texts
▸ SF 24: Giving a presentation

2 YOU CHOOSE **Researching flags and anthems**

- **a** Use German sources to find out about the history of the German flag and the national anthem. Prepare a short presentation for English-speaking visitors to your school.

OR

- **b** Choose a country and do some research into the history of its anthem and flag. Present your findings to the class.

3 Understanding national symbols
Define the function of national symbols such as flags and anthems.

D

E

4 Finding out about international institutions

a Find out about the roles of the following institutions: UN, UNESCO, WHO, Commonwealth, EU. Describe and explain their logos.

b Say why institutions that cut across national boundaries might be necessary.

5 Thinking about your sense of identity

a Complete this sentence: 'I rather see myself as (1) a German or other national citizen, (2) a European, (3) a cosmopolitan citizen, (4) none of the above.' Say why.

b Find out how the majority of your class see themselves and why.

PREVIEW

In this chapter you will learn what living in a globalized world means for the individual and the world.

Main topics

Focus on Skills: MEDIATION and READING

Chapter Task:

CD2 09

Listen to an audio version of the text on the CD or download it here:

Webcode context-23

TROUBLE SPOT

Preis = ***prize*** (award given to sb. for an achievement)
Preis = ***price*** (the money you have to pay for sth.)

Globalization: Europe, the world

European integration as a model?

Political experts say that the power of nation states has been declining and that today the most important decisions are taken on an international level. The European Union, which connects independent nation states, is a good example. The two principal purposes of the European Union (and of its predecessors) are to secure peace and promote economic growth. In 2012, the European Union was awarded the Nobel Peace Prize for overcoming the hostility among European countries after the Second World War and for advancing reconciliation and peace. At the moment of the award, however, Europe was and still is challenged by a monetary crisis, which forced many member states to make massive cuts in their budgets. As a result, unemployment rates increased and many young people, especially those from Spain or Greece were forced to leave their countries and find occupation elsewhere.

Chances and risks of globalization

Globalization can be described as a process in which barriers, especially trade barriers, between nations are removed. This process accelerated when modern communication technologies came into play and transport costs decreased. It made international collaboration and competition possible: Companies in the developed countries were able to outsource their production and services to countries whose labour force was prepared to work for significantly lower wages.

This international division of labour may have freed many people in the developing countries from extreme poverty; however, many of them have to work under poor working conditions with low safety standards. In the traditional industrialized countries, globalization has resulted in redundancies in the domestic workforce.

The threats and opportunities of globalization can be illustrated well through the example of international sports. Top soccer clubs pay enormous sums for the best players from all over the world, allowing for extraordinary labour mobility. Yet, only the richest clubs can participate in this 'leg-drain' and if players are frequently being bought and sold they may feel uprooted and unable to develop a sound sense of identity.

English as a global language

The cultural impact of globalization is illustrated most clearly by the role of English as a global language. Today, English is not only the native language of more than 360 million speakers worldwide, but it is also used as a lingua franca between non-native speakers of English in international business, science and technology, and popular culture. On the one hand, this makes international communication easier, but on the other hand, it threatens local languages and thus cultural and linguistic diversity.

▸ SF 2: Learning new words

Find an online thesaurus here:
Webcode context-52

1 Words in use: synonyms

Find a highlighted word or expression that means the same as …

1 the aim or function of something.
2 the percentage of people in a country without a job.
3 the readiness of people to work in different places.
4 not feel at home anywhere.
5 give a job to external workers, often in another country.
6 language spoken all over the world.

2 Word formation

For each gap in the sentences below choose a suitable word from the list on the right, turn it into the required word class (e.g. a verb into a noun) and adjust its grammatical form if necessary (e.g. the plural form).

1 Some European countries had an extremely … relationship for centuries.
2 With the Treaty of Friendship (1963) France and Germany were officially …
3 In our times of globalization, individuals world-wide have to … and …
4 Since the EU was …, lasting peace has been one of its aims.
5 Today, the EU is facing great …

collaboration • competition • challenge • foundation • hostility • reconciliation

▸ LP 20: Word formation

3 Activating your vocabulary

Translate the following passage. The underlined words and phrases are taken from the text, but you should try to translate them without looking at the text again. Paraphrase if you do not know the exact word or expression. Revise your version with the help of the text and a dictionary.

▸ SF 9: Paraphrasing
▸ SF 3: Using a dictionary

Find an online dictionary here:
Webcode context-52

> Globalisierung ist ein Prozess voller Chancen und Risiken. Kritiker befürchten, dass sie Arbeitsplätze in den traditionellen Industrieländern gefährdet und Arbeiter in den Entwicklungsländern ausbeutet, die oft unter sehr schlechten Arbeitsbedingungen arbeiten müssen. Befürworter der Globalisierung glauben, dass sie extreme Armut in vielen Ländern besiegen kann. Der Abbau von Handelsschranken sei von Vorteil für alle.

▸ LP 16: Avoiding Germanisms

4 Mediation (English → German)

You are asked to briefly inform your politics course in German on the future of nation states as described in this text. Prepare and give a short oral presentation. Make visual aids if necessary.

▸ SF 41: Mediation of written and oral texts
▸ SF 7: Making visual aids
▸ SF 24: Giving a presentation

European integration as a model?

A1 A great achievement of the past
Herman Van Rompuy

Since 1901 the Nobel Peace Prize has been awarded annually (with few exceptions) to individuals and institutions who have sought to establish or keep peace. During the award ceremony, the winner is required to give the Nobel Lecture, a lecture on a subject related to the topic of the prize. When in 2012 the European Union was awarded the prize, the Nobel Lecture was given by Herman Van Rompuy, President of the European Council, and José Manuel Barroso, President of the European Commission.

1 Before listening
Look at the picture below and describe the setting and the general atmosphere of the ceremony.

► SF 11: Analysing pictures
► SF 22: Listening
► SF 10: Working with closed test formats

CD2 10, 11, 12, 13

Herodotus [hə'rɒdətəs] (ca. 484–425 BC) Greek historian
Winston Churchill (1874–1965) British Prime Minister (1940–1945 and 1951–1955)
founder person who starts an institution or organization
ceasefire ['si:sfaɪə] time when enemies stop fighting
reconciliation [ˌrekənsɪli'eɪʃn] situation where two people or groups become friendly again after a disagreement
Konrad Adenauer (1876–1967) first post-war Chancellor of West Germany (1949–1963)
Treaty of Rome founding document of the European Economic Community from 1957
Willy Brandt (1913–1992) West German Chancellor (1969–1974)
Gdansk Danzig, Polish seaport
François Mitterand (1916–1996) French President (1981–1995)
Helmut Kohl (born 1930) West German Chancellor (1982–1998)
Tallin, Riga, Vilnius capitals of the Baltic states Estonia, Latvia and Lithuania, respectively
Jean Monnet (1888–1979) French diplomat, considered to be one of the founding fathers of the European Union
perpetual [pə'petʃuəl] continuing for a long period of time with no interruption
Srebrenica town in Bosnia, site of a massacre during the Balkan War (1995)
Abraham Lincoln ['lɪŋkən] (1809–1865) President of the United States (1861–1865)

COMPREHENSION

2 Listening for gist
Listen to the audio file, which contains Van Rompuy's part of the Nobel Lecture. From the following statements choose the one that best describes the speaker's message.
1 Peacekeeping is Europe's ongoing goal.
2 Lasting peace has been established in Europe.
3 Current challenges are threatening to seriously destabilize the EU.

3 Listening for detail: part 1
Listen to the first part of the speech, then decide whether the following statements are true or false according to the speaker.
1 The Nobel Prize belongs to Europe's political elite, who united Europe after World War II.
2 War used to be a constant feature of European history.
3 Van Rompuy still has wartime memories of his own.
4 Europe would not have gained peace without the European Union.
5 Konrad Adenauer was awarded a French medal in 1951.

4 Listening for detail: part 2

Say which historical events depicted in the photos are mentioned by Rompuy. Give the photos headings.

A

B

C

D

E

F

5 Listening for detail: part 3

Choose the correct statement.

a Rompuy mentions the example of Srebrenica to prove that …
 1 … there is no European post-war generation.
 2 … there was war in Europe not very long ago.
 3 … Soviet rule in Eastern Europe was responsible for massacres.

b According to the speaker, the economic crisis …
 1 … does not put the European Union to the test.
 2 … mainly affects young academics.
 3 … reduces the feeling of solidarity.

LANGUAGE AWARENESS

6 A non-native accent

a Listen to the speech once more and examine Van Rompuy's English. Identify elements that show that English is not his native tongue.
► LANGUAGE HELP

b Do you think it's a disadvantage to speak with an accent? Say why or why not.

LANGUAGE HELP
- pronounce … as … / say … instead of …
- not pronounce … properly
- use voiceless/voiced consonants
- long/short vowel / diphthong

BEYOND THE TEXT

7 YOU CHOOSE **Research on the EU**

Do some research on one of the topics below, then present your results:

a Describe the status of English in the European institutions. Discuss whether the use of other languages, e.g. German, should be promoted within European institutions.

OR

b Outline the events that led to European unification and describe their context and consequences. Add more 'historical moments' that helped to unite Europe.

► SF 24: Giving a presentation

A2 Young, educated – and leaving the country

Liz Alderman

The following extract from an article illustrates the consequences of the European financial crisis for individuals.

Soon after her 23rd birthday four years ago, Melissa Abadía made a wrenching decision: She would leave her close-knit family in Spain, where the grinding fallout from the 2008 financial crisis had made securing a good job impossible, and move to the Netherlands, where employers were still hiring.

'When I got on the plane, I was crying,' Ms. Abadía, a bright, ebullient woman, recalled. 'But I had to decide: Should I fight for something back home that makes no sense, or get out of there and make a life for myself?'

Despite five years of training in nursing in her hometown, Castellón de la Plana, in eastern Spain, she now works in a windowless stockroom in Amsterdam organizing purses, socks and other accessories at a clothing store.

It is a sign of the plight of her generation that simply having a job and a measure of independence makes her one of the lucky ones – never mind homesickness, dashed dreams of a very different career and a gradual acceptance that her life will probably never be the one she expected to live.

'Of course, I hate the fact that I have to do this,' she said, speaking in somber tones. 'Leaving your country should be a decision, not an obligation.'

Finding only unpaid nursing internships and a temporary nightclub job in Spain, Ms. Abadía scoured the Internet for work in Europe's more prosperous north. She quickly found employment as an au pair in Amsterdam.

For the first time, she experienced the shock of being an immigrant. Having arrived in Amsterdam as part of an influx of young Spanish, Greek, Italian and Portuguese men and women all searching for any employment, 'I now know what it's like to be seen as someone who's coming to steal jobs,' she said.

She soon found better-paying work at the clothing shop, near the Royal Palace. The store was crowded with at least 10 other young Spaniards who had migrated for employment.

She spent two years bouncing between short-term contracts, which employers have sharply increased during the crisis to cut costs and avoid the expensive labor protections granted to permanent employees.

In some countries, especially those with the highest youth unemployment rates, short-term contracts are nothing more than opportunities for employers to take advantage of the weak labor market.

But when used by employers as intended – to give experience to young people who otherwise could not get a start – they can lead to steady work. That was the case with Ms. Abadía, whose employer eventually turned her temporary job into a permanent contract with benefits overseeing the store's biggest stockroom.

On one level, having even that kind of employment is a victory in today's Europe. Her salary of €1,200 a month (about $1,600) was nearly twice what she could have expected to make in Spain.

'The day I signed a permanent contract was the best day of my life,' she said one recent weeknight, beaming as she sipped a Coke at a bustling pub.

'It is almost impossible to get one now in Spain,' she said. 'Here, they trust me, a Spanish girl, and give me responsibilities. I can pay my rent, save money and be independent. I'm even writing a book.'

Working in a clothes shop

1 **wrench** *(adj)* very difficult and painful
2 **grinding** ['graɪndɪŋ] *(adj)* never ending or improving
fallout ['– –] (here) long-term consequences of a disaster
5 **ebullient** [ɪ'bʌliənt] *(fml)* full of energy
9 **stockroom** room where goods are kept in a shop
11 **plight** difficult and sad situation
15 **somber** *(AE)* = *(BE)* **sombre** serious and a little sad
16 **obligation** *Pflicht*
17 **internship** ['– – –] temporary job, often for little or no pay, especially done by newcomers to a job
27 **bounce between jobs** move from one job to another
contract ['– –] formal document containing an agreement, e.g. between employer and employee
36 **benefits** ['benɪfɪts] advantages given to an employee in addition to their salary (e.g. sick pay, health insurance)
oversee sb./sth. (here) be the manager of sth.
41 **beam** *(v)* smile broadly

But because of her work hours, she still does not qualify for the Netherlands' monthly minimum wage of €1,477 (about $2,000), and her new career was a long way from where she had always hoped to end up.

Discussing the path that had brought her to this point, Ms. Abadía became suddenly pensive. Adjusting to a life far from home in a job beneath her skills has been harder than she imagined.

'I gave up the thought of working as a nurse long ago,' she said. 'With this job, I'm so tired sometimes that I can't move. I don't know what a weekend is anymore.'

Above all, Ms. Abadía still yearns for Spain. [...]

'Recently, I heard criticism that people like us are running away,' Ms. Abadía said. 'We didn't run away. We left because the economic situation and the politicians pushed us.'

'If they don't fix things, they are going to lose a couple generations of smart, young people,' Ms. Abadía added as her friends nodded in agreement. 'And then what will happen to the country that's left behind?'

That question is weighing on European leaders. An estimated 100,000 university graduates have left Spain, and hundreds of thousands more from Europe's crisis-hit countries have gone to Germany, Britain, and the Nordic states for jobs in engineering, science and medicine. Many others have gone farther afield to Australia, Canada and the United States.

The current migration 'is mostly the skilled part of the population,' said Massimiliano Mascherini, a research manager at Eurofound, a European Union research agency. 'It is alarming for the countries that young people are leaving, and it should be a big source of concern for their governments.'

From: *The New York Times*, 15 November 2013

TROUBLE SPOT

career (l. 46)
= *beruflicher Werdegang*
= *erfolgreiche Karriere*

49 **pensive** thinking deeply, worrying about sth.
49 **beneath sb./sth.** lower than sb./sth., not good enough for sb./sth.
60 **weigh on sb.** make sb. worried
63 **farther afield** far way from home

COMPREHENSION

1 Understanding Melissa Abadía's situation

Point out why Melissa Abadía left Spain, how her working life developed in Amsterdam and which consequences youth unemployment in Europe has in general.

► LP 4: Present perfect and simple past

LANGUAGE AWARENESS

2 Transforming direct into indirect speech

a Choose two quotations by Melissa Abadía and turn them into indirect speech.

b Explain what changes you have to make when turning direct into indirect speech. What role does the introductory verb play?

ANALYSIS

3 Examining the use of direct and indirect speech

► SF 18: Analysing non-fiction

a Go back to your results from task 2 and compare the effect of direct speech and indirect speech respectively.

b Analyse the effect the writer achieves by using many direct quotations.

c CHALLENGE Explain why direct statements are used frequently in reports and feature articles.

BEYOND THE TEXT

4 Creative writing SUPPORT p. 274

Form groups of four. Each select one important moment of Melissa Abadía's immigrant experience and write a diary entry. Read out your entries to your group and join your texts to form one coherent diary entry.

► SF 37: Doing a creative writing task

A3 Hunting for personnel *Sascha Schmierer*

▸ LP 6: Infinitive or gerund after certain nouns

In some European countries many young people face the problem of unemployment. In others, employers in some areas have great difficulty filling their job vacancies. Read this text from a German newspaper about a way to solve both problems.

Es steht nicht zu befürchten, dass die Krankenschwestern im Ludwigsburger Klinikum ihre Patienten beim Weckruf am Morgen künftig mit einem fröhlichen „Buenos Días“ begrüßen. Und das Küchenteam wird statt leckerer Tapas wohl auch weiterhin salzarm zubereitete Krankenhauskost servieren. Dennoch bricht für den Klinikenverbund Ludwigsburg-Bietigheim nächsten Mittwoch eine „spanische Ära“ an.

Pünktlich um 9.30 Uhr wird die Medizindirektorin Andrea Grebe im Konferenzraum an der Erlachhofstraße mehr als 30 neue Pflegekräfte von der Iberischen Halbinsel begrüßen. Nach einem ambitionierten Sprachkurs sollen die hoch qualifizierten neuen Mitarbeiter den eklatanten Personalmangel in der Intensivmedizin in den drei Häusern in Ludwigsburg, Bietigheim und Neuenbürg beheben – olé im OP sozusagen.

TROUBLE SPOT
jdn. / etwas pflegen
= (a sick person) ***nurse sb. / care for sb.***
= (an animal) ***look after sth.***
= (a garden, a plant) ***tend sth.***

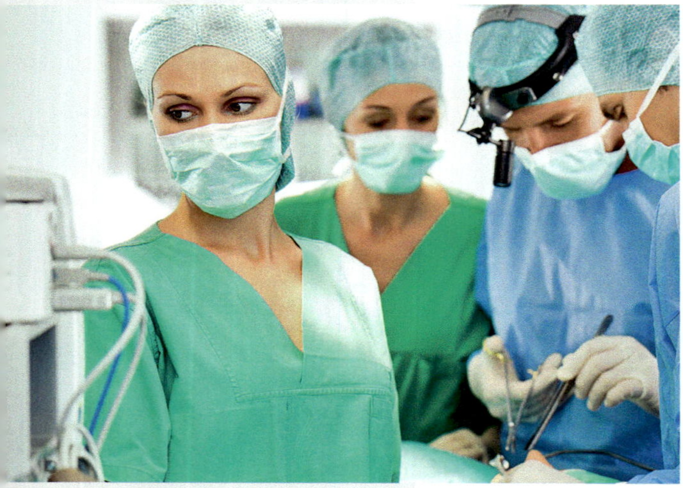

„Fachkräfte für Intensivstationen und den OP-Bereich sind in Deutschland fast nicht zu finden, der Markt ist leergefegt“, erklärt der Kliniken-Sprecher Alexander Tsongas den für ein schwäbisches Spital bisher noch eher ungewöhnlichen Schritt. Weil bei der Suche nach qualifiziertem Personal allerdings weder regionale Berufsmessen noch die Werbeaktionen in angrenzenden Bundesländern erfolgreich waren, wichen die Stellenbesetzer des Kliniken-Verbunds nach Südeuropa aus.

Auf die in Spanien geschalteten Anzeigen für OP-Pflegekräfte meldeten sich binnen weniger Tage zahlreiche Bewerber, mit 60 Kandidaten führten die Personalchefs ein Vorstellungsgespräch.

Ergebnis ist, dass bereits nächste Woche mehr als 30 spanische Pflegekräfte ihren Dienst in Ludwigsburg antreten. Bevor die neuen Mitarbeiter – bis auf wenige Ausnahmen handelt es sich um junge Frauen – auf die Tochterkliniken verteilt werden, steht ein je nach Vorkenntnissen zwischen vier und sechs Monaten dauernder Intensivsprachkurs auf dem Lehrplan. Parallel zum Deutschlernen sind Arbeitspraktika in den Krankenhäusern vorgesehen. Für das erste halbe Jahr sind die neuen Pflegekräfte mit einem Praktikantenvertrag ausgestattet. Nach der Probezeit winkt ein unbefristeter Arbeitsvertrag – schließlich hofft die Chefetage des Kliniken-Verbunds, dass die neuen Mitarbeiter aus dem Süden im kalten Deutschland nicht gleich das Weite suchen.

From: *Stuttgarter Nachrichten*, 12 October 2012

Comparing situations

Compare the information presented in the article with Melissa Abadía's situation (cf. p. 128).

MEDIATION FOCUS ON SKILLS

Mediating texts in oral communication

Imagine the following situation: On a trip to Amsterdam you meet Melissa Abadía (cf. A2, p. 128) in a pub and she tells you her story in English. You remember the article about job vacancies in Germany (cf. A3, p. 130) and decide to tell her about it.

▸ SF 41: Mediation of written and oral texts

1 Choosing the relevant information

a Examine the situation closely, then look at the following keywords from text A3. Which of them do you think would be relevant to Abadía?

TROUBLE SPOT
information *(sing)*
Not: ~~informations~~

1 Um 9.30 werden die neuen Pflegekräfte in Ludwigsburg begrüßt. 2 Auf Messen und durch Werbeaktionen konnte kein zusätzliches Pflegepersonal gewonnen werden. 3 Pflegekräfte müssen einen Sprachkurs absolvieren.	4 In Deutschland gibt es nicht genügend Pflegekräfte für Intensivstationen. 5 Die neuen spanischen Pflegekräfte sind vor allem Frauen. 6 Sie sind zunächst als Praktikant/innen angestellt.

b Note down any other information you consider useful to Abadía.

2 Explaining specific terms

When mediating information from German into English, you will have to paraphrase or explain words, either because you (or the person you are talking to) don't know their English equivalents or because your partner has a different cultural background.

a Imagine you knew the translations for the words below. Which of them would you explain to Melissa Abadía all the same? Say why.

▸ LP 16: Avoiding Germanisms

1 *Intensivstation*	4 *Praktikantenvertrag*
2 *Arbeitspraktikum*	5 *unbefristeter Arbeitsvertrag*
3 *Sprachkurs*	6 *Probezeit*

LANGUAGE HELP
- continue/conclude/cancel/end a contract
- a contract expires after …
- dismiss sb.

b Paraphrase or explain the words from **a**. ▸ LANGUAGE HELP

▸ SF 9: Paraphrasing

3 Choosing the correct register

The place where a conversation takes place and your relationship to the addressee influence the way you speak to them. Read the two beginnings of the conversation with Melissa Abadía and decide which of them would be more appropriate in the given situation. Say why.

▸ LP 11: Using the right register

'Well, actually, I read an article just a few days ago and I think it might interest you. Basically it was all about how Germany really needs nurses and …'	'Bearing in mind the situation you have been telling me about I would like to inform you about the opportunities that have opened in Germany for qualified nurses.'

4 Speaking to the addressee

a Structure your ideas and prepare your side of the conversation, bearing in mind your results from tasks **1–3**.

▸ CC 4: Meeting and greeting

b Work with a partner to role-play the conversation. Answer their questions and pay attention to their facial expression or gestures to find out whether they have understood you. Rephrase your statements if necessary. Then swap roles.

▸ LP 12: Avoiding German-sounding sentence patterns

Find a recording tool here:
Webcode context-55

Chances and risks of globalization

B1 How big is the impact?

Globalization is a complex process that affects various aspects of life. The video you are going to watch explains how it works.

1 Identifying the players in globalization

► LP 7: The passive

Describe the aspects of globalization that are presented in the picture below. Based on what you already know about globalization try to say how they are connected.

COMPREHENSION ◀

DVD

► SF 15: Marking up a text / Making and taking notes

2 Defining globalization

a Watch the video and note down the main topics mentioned in it. Compare notes with a partner.

b Watch the video for a second time and add information on the topics from **a**.

c Compare your notes in a group and add to them if necessary.

d As a group give a short presentation on globalization with each group member contributing 1–2 sentences on each topic.

► SF 24: Giving a presentation

ANALYSIS ◀

► SF 23: Analysing a film

3 Examining the video

Describe the devices that are employed in the video and explain their function. ► LANGUAGE HELP

LANGUAGE HELP

- explainer video / instructional video
- hand-crafted drawings showing … / scraps of paper
- put sth. on screen / remove sth.
- use audio effects to …

BEYOND THE TEXT ◀

4 YOU CHOOSE ▶ Illustrating globalization

a Comment on the quotation below and find examples that illustrate it further.

OR

b Find a picture that illustrates your personal view on the impact that globalization has on people. If necessary, collect background information about it. Present your findings in class.

B2 The need for a new label *Lucy Siegle*

- What information do the labels on the right give? What information might be missing?

Imagine a label, one that reads: 'An actual, living, breathing human used their own hands to help make this product.' This is just what the (western) world needs, a label affixed to consumer goods. We need this urgent reminder because in those seconds when we decide to purchase another piece of life's apparatus we are strikingly effective at suppressing any ethical doubt over its provenance.

The first thing we do (with varying levels of awareness) is convince ourselves that – from the hottest bits of sleek hi-tech gadgetry to highly embellished fashion garments – these were made by very clever robot arms that can apply toxic chemicals to a touch screen or expertly sew a sequin or bead. But as today's Observer report on Apple products lays bare, our consumer goods still arrive courtesy of the blood, sweat and tears of many human beings. [...] The habitual use of unpaid, enforced overtime is common across many sectors. In the fashion industry, garment workers are effectively set up to fail. When a multinational places an order at the behest of a buyer the workers are set quotas to meet the order. Professor Doug Miller, an expert on the garment supply chain and workers' rights, has identified a discrepancy between the estimated and real time taken for a garment worker to complete an order. So the multinational buyer's calculations are based on standard minute values (SMVs) – virtual minutes based on a factory that operates at near 100% efficiency. However, in countries such as Cambodia (the British high street is heavily reliant on Cambodian production), the efficiency of factories rarely rises above 30%. Garment workers can therefore work flat out without any hope of meeting their targets within their paid working hours. At this point, they are forced to work overtime and sometimes gates may be shut or locked (including the fire escapes). [...] As consumers, we still tend to be most receptive to the voices of brand spokespeople. Time after time, we trust their soothing words: 'We're working on these challenges', 'We've been let down badly by a supplier', 'These are not our values' etc. and placated by their corporate social responsibility reports. Robert Reich warns in his recent book, *Supercapitalism*, corporate social responsibility is 'as meaningful as cotton candy'. But Reich's ultimate position is that we should stop expecting corporations to do the right thing. And I can't see any way of absolving the consumer of responsibility. I used to advocate going through a sort of consumerist catechism before making any consumer purchasing decision. Who made this product? Why did they make it? Why do I need it? I feel as if I urgently need to return to this way of buying. An understanding of the provenance of the product is key.

From: *The Guardian*, 1 May 2011

5 **provenance** ['prɒvənəns] place that sth. has come from
7 **sleek** elegant, shiny
gadgetry collection of modern devices / tools
9 **sequin** ['siːkwɪn] small shiny disc sewn onto clothes as decoration
bead small piece of wood or glass that can be put on a string and worn as jewellery
10 **lay sth. bare** *(fml)* make sth. known that was a secret
courtesy of sb./sth. ['kɜːtəsi] as the result of sb./sth.
11 **overtime** time that you spend at your job after the normal work hours
13 **at the behest of sb.** because sb. has ordered it
14 **quota** amount of sth. that sb. needs to achieve
21 **flat out** *(adv)* completely
26 **supplier** *Lieferant/in*
placate sb. [plə'keɪt] make sb. worry less about something
28 **cotton candy** *Zuckerwatte*
30 **absolve sb.** [æb'zɒlv] state formally that sb. is not responsible for sth.
advocate sth. ['ædvəkeɪt] advise/recommend sth.
31 **catechism** ['kætəkɪzəm] set of questions and answers used to instruct people about Christian beliefs

COMPREHENSION

1 Collecting information
Collect information from the article about the situation in the garment industry, how we consumers deal with it and what we *should* do. Write down 5–9 keywords for each of these topics, then present your results.

ANALYSIS

2 Examining the text
Analyse the tone of the text.

► SF 18: Analysing non-fiction

BEYOND THE TEXT

3 Promoting transparent labelling SUPPORT p. 274
a Design a clothing label that helps buyers make responsible choices.
b Write an article for a magazine in which you promote this new label.

► SF 37: Doing a creative writing task

B3 The Dutch footballer from Japan *Elko Born*

▸ SF 14: Reading strategies

2 **maritime** ['mærɪtaɪm] *(fml)* near the sea
4 **trade route** route that people follow to buy and sell things
kickstart sth. make a process or project start more quickly
10 **recent** in the near past
decade ['dekeɪd] period of ten years
12 **gradual** step by step, slow
diminish sth. reduce sth.
13 **Kettle crisps** brand of crisps
15 **coincide with sth.** [ˌkəʊɪn'saɪd] happen at the same time as sth.
16 **negotiate sth.** [nɪ'gəʊʃieɪt] arrange something by formal discussion
supranational referring to more than one nation
17 **perimeter** [–'– – –] outside edge of an area of land
dub sth. sth. else call sth. sth. else
19 **Pelé** (born 1940) former Brazilian footballer, often considered the best football player of all time
26 **Premier League** ['premɪə liːg] English professional football league
30 **Champions League** annual continental football competition organized by the UEFA, the Union of European Football Associations
31 **deem sth. to be sth. else** consider sth. to be sth. else
prestigious [pre'stɪdʒəs] having a lot of prestige

▪ Skim the text. Within 1–2 minutes find out the gist of the text.

Some scholars argue that the process of 'globalization' (broadly defined as the global integration of various aspects of culture) started in the 16th century, when maritime empires such as Portugal and the Dutch Republic started colonizing parts of Asia and the Americas, setting up trade routes and kickstarting modern capitalism along the way.

Others argue that it wasn't Columbus who 'discovered' the Americas, that the ancient Greeks and the Romans used the so-called 'Silk Route' to trade with China, and that the process of 'globalization' started when humans first started interacting with others of their kind.

Nonetheless, it's fair to state that in recent decades, the process of globalization – whenever it may have started – reached a new phase: the phase of automatization and the gradual diminishing of the relevance of national borders. Just think of the Internet, the EU, and of eating Kettle crisps whilst crossing the border between France and Belgium without showing anyone your passport.

The birth of modern football, of course, largely coincided with this new phase in globalization. During the 1960s, when politicians were negotiating the supranational perimeters of the European Union (dubbed by some as the modern day Habsburg Empire), football produced its first superstars.

The fame of footballers like Pelé reached far beyond Brazil, and across the world, people took time off to sit in front of their black and white television sets to watch the South American legend play. Indeed, when Pelé jokingly put himself ahead of Jesus Christ by telling a reporter that 'there are parts of the world where Jesus Christ is not so well known', he wasn't even being absurd.

In modern day football, we see different manifestations of the ongoing process of globalization. National leagues filled with foreign players provide the obvious example: so far in 2013/2014, only 32.26% of minutes in the Premier League – an 'English' league, but followed intensely by people from all over the world – were completed by English players, with a remarkable 8.1% completed by players from France.

Another obvious example of globalization in football is the Champions League: an international competition, deemed as one of the most important and prestigious in

An early example of globalization: 13th century merchants on the silk route

the world. And it's not just international competitions that make football fans and stadium-goers travel outside the borders of their countries. To name just one example: this season Championship-side Leicester City was pleasantly surprised by a large contingent of R.S.C. Anderlecht fans showing up at the King Power Stadium to sing songs in praise of their former player Marcin Wasilewski – a Polish player – on multiple occasions. Unconstrained international travel and the internet make it all possible. [...]

Back in the early-modern period, trading diasporas functioned as communities of merchants living in foreign lands. They were semi-permanent residents. Not quite Dutch, English or Portuguese, but not quite native either. Often, these diasporas would be linked: with the mother-country, but with other diasporas as well.

Diasporas, and the people living in them, were 'stateless': they lived in the world's twilight-zone, more or less unconfined by regionalism or primitive nationalism. In many ways, football clubs are today's world's trading diasporas, employing footballers as merchants. They travel around, performing their profession.

But while we might be able to typify some of Vitesse's players as 'merchants', we would do well to rid the term of some of its negative connotations. The Arnhemmers' flirt with globalization has manifested itself in wonderful things as well. Take Mike Havenaar, a 6 foot 4 striker who looks Dutch, sounds Dutch, plays in the Dutch league ... but is Japanese.

Mike was born in 1987 in Hiroshima, where his father, the Dutch goalkeeper Dido Havenaar, played for Mazda FC (now called Sanfrecce Hiroshima). Dido had initially planned to only stay in Japan for a short while, but the months became years and the years became a decade, until finally, the family decided to stay forever: 'When I was little, I spoke Dutch with my parents but Japanese with all of my friends. Initially I felt somewhat torn between the two countries but as I got older, my love for the country where I was born grew. When I had to make a decision about my nationality, there was never any doubt', Havenaar told Fifa.com in an interview in 2013.

Havenaar, who conducts his interviews in English rather than Dutch, has a Japanese passport, and as such, he plays for the Japanese national team, making his debut in 2011 and scoring 3 goals in 16 matches.

Besides his name and his appearance, there's little to reveal his Dutch roots. Indeed, when Havenaar first moved to The Netherlands, he felt like a foreigner. 'At first I had trouble acclimatising,' he told Fifa.com, 'but since then the Dutch in me – which I had kind of forgotten – has really come to the fore. Today I feel great, just like at home actually.'

In this regard, the humility he displayed after injuring Stijn Schaars in Vitesse's 6–2 defeat of PSV in December 2013 spoke volumes. Havenaar visibly apologized about ten times, and his whole demeanour contrasted starkly with the reaction of the Dutch on and off the pitch.

Indeed, while merchants travel around and perform their profession, they not only take things, they leave things behind as well. Wonderful things, in the case of Mike Havenaar. The ongoing process of globalization, driving people as well as culture to travel from The Netherlands to Japan and back again, allows for the birth of the hybrid and unique.

Who knows, maybe one day Havenaar will move on to yet another league, and maybe he'll decide to stay there for a long time. Maybe he and his kids will stay there forever.

From: *The False Nine*, 9 January 2014

Mike Havenaar

35 **contingent** [–'– –] group of people who share sth., usually the place they come from
39 **trading diaspora** [daɪ'æspərə] community of merchants who live in a foreign country
40 **semi-permanent** ['pɜːmənənt] living in the same place for most of the time
resident person living in a certain place
41 **native** (here) born in the country you live in
44 **twilight** time between day and night
unconfined by sth. not held back by sth.
47 **Vitesse** football club based in the Dutch city of Arnhem
65 **acclimatize** [ə'klaɪmətaɪz] (here) start feeling at home
66 **come to the fore** start playing an important role
68 **humility** [hjuː'mɪləti] quality of not thinking that you are superior to others
display sth. show sth.
69 **PSV** (= PSV Eindhoven) football club from Eindhoven in the Netherlands
speak volumes ['vɒljuːmz] tell a lot about sb./sth.
70 **demeanour** [dɪ'miːnə] behaviour
stark obvious, easy to see
71 **pitch** football field
75 **hybrid** ['haɪbrɪd] mix of two or more different things

▸ LP 5: Infinitive or gerund after certain verbs

▸ SF 14: Reading strategies

READING **FOCUS ON SKILLS**

Using reading strategies (non-fictional texts)

Reading strategies help you to read more effectively. They can help you to find information quickly, to see if a text is relevant for you or to come to an in-depth understanding of the content.

Before actually reading the text **B3**, *you were asked to skim it to find out what it's about. Now practise your scanning and close-reading techniques.*

1 Scanning

a Scan the text on pp. 134–135 to find the answers to the following questions. For each question decide what keyword, name or number you are going to look out for in the text.

1 What are the characteristics of people living in diasporas?
2 What has Pelé got to do with a globalized world?
3 How does Mike Havenaar feel about his nationality?

b Locate the following ideas in the text and say in which order they appear. What keyword, name or number are you going to look for?

1 Unconstrained international travel and the internet allow fans to visit football matches outside their country.
2 Mike Havenaar felt like a foreigner when he first moved to the Netherlands.
3 Mike Havenaar's father worked as a goalkeeper in Hiroshima.
4 Globalization has reached the phase of automatization.
5 In 2013/2014 less than half of the minutes in the Premier League were completed by English players.

A global sport: football

▸ SF 31: Writing a summary

2 Close reading I: content and structure

a Read the text carefully and make notes on the content of each paragraph.
b Write a summary of the text.
c Read the text again and examine its structure. Add the words below to your notes from **a** where they fit. You can also add your own categories.

background information • cause • conclusion • detail • example • opposite viewpoint • outlook • result quotation • thesis • …

▸ SF 16: Identifying text types (non-fiction)

3 Close reading II: identifying the text type

Explain what type of text this is and analyse its *tone.

English as a global language

C1 Keeping the accent *Aoife Mannix*

- What do you expect after reading the title of the poem?

The barman makes me repeat my order
three times before he finally understands me.
Heads turn and stare, I can feel my hands sweat
and my throat close over the way it did years ago.
Then he tells me my accent is so cute,
he's going to give me one of the drinks for free.
And all the people at the bar smile at me.
And it doesn't make up for the way
they laughed at me at school,
repeating how I said the word potato
over and over like a needle in my ear,
or Alexis Fortgang dropping a worm in my hair
and telling me to fuck off back to the little hole
in the ground I crawled out of.
But still, now that the way I speak is sweet,
I swallow my bitterness
and try not to think about how opening my mouth
used to feel like a betrayal.
The words sounding out of tune,
a fork dropped on a china plate.
Suddenly it's interesting and cool
and everyone wants to go there.
But I still hide behind my pride,
the way I used to long to talk
like everybody else.

From: *The Elephant in the Corner: New & Selected Poems*, 2005

FACT FILE

The term ***third culture kid*** (TCK) is applied to children who spend a considerable time of their childhood or adolescence outside their parents' home country, usually because their parents work abroad. Third culture kids experience the culture they are living in plus the culture from which their parents originated – without really belonging to either of them: they belong to a third culture, which is a mix of the other two cultures.
In the era of modern globalization, the number of third culture kids has increased: global job mobility, proximity to neighbouring countries, international school attendance, multi-ethnic homes and worldwide adoption are on the increase and bring with them not only cultural, but also linguistic opportunities and challenges.

Compile possible advantages and challenges of early cross-cultural education.

Aoife ['ifə]
1 **order** *(n)* request for food or drinks in a pub or restaurant
4 **throat** *Kehle*
close over become very narrow
5 **cute** sweet, nice
8 **make up for sth.** do sth. that corrects a bad situation
19 **out of tune** containing wrong notes and therefore sounding unpleasant
20 **fork** *Gabel*
china ['tʃaɪnə] *Porzellan*

COMPREHENSION ◀

1 Understanding the situation

Describe the speaker's experience in the bar and the memories it provokes.

► LP 18: Writing about texts

LANGUAGE AWARENESS ◀

2 Examining the present participle

a Identify the present participles in ll. 8–14, then reformulate these lines without using participles.

b Compare with the original and explain why the participle constructions are especially helpful in the poem.

► LP 15: Connecting your thoughts (sentence structure)

ANALYSIS ◀

3 Examining the poem

a Subdivide the poem by introducing *stanzas, which may vary in length. Explain the structure you have chosen. Compare it to the original version.

b Examine the *stylistic devices used in this poem to highlight the speaker's attitude towards her accent. Focus on the choice of words and the *imagery used.

► SF 21: Analysing poetry
► SF 17: Analysing stylistic devices

BEYOND THE TEXT

4 YOU CHOOSE **Creative writing** SUPPORT p. 274

a Write a *short story based on the poem.

OR

b Write a dramatic *scene based on the poem.

► SF 37: Doing a creative writing task

C2 English as a global language *David Crystal*

- Try to define the term *global language* and collect reasons why a language might become a global language.

COMPREHENSION

DVD

► SF 22: Listening

► SF 10: Working with closed test formats

1 Understanding the main idea

Listen to David Crystal and decide which statement fits the text best:

1. English-speaking nations are powerful because they speak the global language English best.
2. Throughout the centuries people have had the power to decide which language is the global language.
3. The global language is the language of the people who have the most power globally.

2 Connecting language and power

Listen again and describe the connection between power and language as seen by Crystal.

BEYOND THE TEXT

3 Thinking about global languages of the future

Discuss when and how the four types of power mentioned by David Crystal might one day be dominated by other languages. Which languages might they be? Justify your answer by giving examples.

C3 Linguistic diplomacy: the Eurovision Song Contest *R. L. G.*

- Do you prefer listening to songs in English or in your mother tongue? Explain what difference it makes to you.

Emmelie de Forest, winner of the 2013 Eurovision Song Contest

2 **apple-cheeked** having cheeks *(= Wangen)* the colour of apples
5 **slew** *(infml)* large number
8 **stiff sb. with sth.** (here) reject / mildly insult sb.
nul points [nyl pwɛ̃] *(French)* nil *(= no)* points
11 **ethnicity** [eθ'nɪsəti] fact of belonging to a particular race
12 **Riga** capital of Latvia

Last Saturday saw Denmark win the Eurovision Song Contest, the country's third win in the contest's history. A prototypically apple-cheeked blonde took the trophy for her country, but she did so with the rather un-Danish name of Emmelie de Forest and the equally un-Danish title, 'Only Teardrops'.

The contest has always been about more than music. Every year comes a slew of articles about the political nature of the voting. Countries that share ethnic or political friendships routinely give each other high marks: Greece and Cyprus typically give each other the maximum of 12 points while stiffing Turkey with nul points, for example. Estonia and Latvia this year gave Russia 12 points, no doubt because those countries' large Russian populations voted for their neighbour.

Language, of course, plays a role in this as well. 'Ethnicity' in Europe is often linguistic: an ethnic Russian is not apparent on the streets of Riga until he opens his mouth. Linguistic neighbours will tend to be generous to one another. Finland and Estonia are friendly not only because they are nearby but because their Finno-Ugric languages resemble each other, while being utterly unrelated to their neigbours'. (Hungarian is also Finno-Ugric.) Each country can give 12 points to only one other country, and this year Denmark and Sweden gave their 12's to Norway, Norway its 12 to Sweden, as befits the Scandinavian language continuum.

But the Scandinavians share something else besides apple-cheeked blondes and North Germanic languages: their tendency to sing in English. In that, they are like most countries nowadays. But some interesting variation clouds the picture.

The French, of course, overwhelmingly prefer French. (France has, however, sent two entries in Corsican and one, in 2008, mostly in English.) Spain nearly always opts for Spanish, and Italy for Italian. But it isn't true that big countries sing in their own languages while small ones opt for English. Germany has sung just one German title ('Frauen regieren die Welt', or 'Women Run the World') in the past ten years. And a few small countries opted for linguistic pride over Anglophone Euro-cheer this year. Iceland's EyþórIngi offered up a dreary ballad in Icelandic, the perfect accompaniment to an official video in which he glumly fillets a fish in the rain. The highest-ranking song not sung in English this year was technically Greece's 'Alcohol is Free', an upbeat ska tune in which the verses were in Greek and only the three-word chorus in English. It came in 6th place. The highest-ranking song entirely devoid of English was Italy's 'L'Essenziale' (7th).

Songs mostly in English have won 24 times, while songs in French have won 14. That leaves just about a third of the contests won in any other language. This is despite two periods (1956–1965 and 1977–1999) in which contest rules required countries to sing in their own languages. […]

It is clear that pop is just another area in which English is taking over Europe, alongside business and the politics of the European Union. French is holding a solid second place, as it does elsewhere. The rest of Europe's many language communities divide up what remains. Whether you find this linguistic convergence cheerful as an Abba foot-stomper or depressing as an Icelandic fishing trip will say as much about your politics as it will about your views on language.

From: *The Economist*, 20 May 2013

18 **befit sb.** *(fml)* be suitable for sb.
21 **cloud sth.** make sth. unclear
23 **entry** (here) song that takes part in a competition
24 **opt for sth.** choose sth.
28 **dreary** sad and boring
accompaniment music that is played to support singing
29 **glum** quiet, sad, unhappy
31 **upbeat** *(infml)* cheerful/enthusiastic
ska fast and rhythmic music, related to Reggae
chorus part of a song that is sung after each verse
32 **devoid of sth.** without sth.
41 **convergence** [kən'vɜːdʒəns] process of moving towards each other and meeting at a point
ABBA Swedish pop band that won the ESC in 1973
42 **foot-stomper** lively music that makes you move your feet

COMPREHENSION

1 Understanding the content
Structure the text (introduction, main body, conclusion), then make notes on the content of each part.

► SF 15: Marking up a text / Making and taking notes

2 Mediation (English → German)
You are watching the song contest together with a friend who claims that language does not play any role in the ESC today since almost all songs are sung in English. In German, tell him why he is not quite right using information from the text.

► SF 41: Mediation of written and oral texts

ANALYSIS

3 Examining the tone
a Analyse which elements contribute to the neutral *tone of the text.
b Identify the text type.

► SF 18: Analysing non-fiction
► SF 16: Identifying text types

BEYOND THE TEXT

4 Reacting to a statement
Explain the last sentence and comment on it.

5 Discussion SUPPORT ► p. 275
In groups of five prepare and hold a panel discussion in which you discuss the question of whether each country should be obliged to enter songs in their national language only. One student is the moderator, the others argue either for or against the topic.

► SF 27: Having a discussion

Find a recording tool here:
Webcode context-55

CULTURE SPOT

Keeping our language clean?

CD2 15

1 You're Skyping with an Irish friend of yours and talking about music. She has just come across a song by the a cappella group Wise Guys that she doesn't understand. Listen to the song, then tell her what it's about and what message you think it conveys.

2 Collect other examples of English (or pseudo-English) words often used in German. State for each example whether you accept it and use it or whether you avoid using it.

3 What does this use of English tell you about the role of English in German culture?

4 Radio stations, e.g. in France and Italy, are obliged to play a considerable number of songs in French or Italian, respectively. What do you think of this attempt to promote the native language?

'Slavery? Not today, not in Germany!' Preparing an exhibition

For the project week at your school, you are preparing an exhibition on the topic 'Slavery? Not today, not in Germany!' As a lot of visitors from your foreign partner schools will be attending, posters and presentations will be in English.

Work in groups of five.

1 Planning your work

- **a** Do some research to get a general idea of the topic and to identify suitable subtopics. SUPPORT ▶ p. 275
- **b** Divide the work up among yourselves.

Find some helpful links here: **Webcode** context-24

▶ SF6: Doing project work

2 Preparing your poster

- **a** Research your part. Make sure to use German publications too. Notes, articles, books or worksheets you read at school, including in other subjects like History or Latin, may also be helpful. Make notes.
- **b** Organize your findings and prepare your poster. SUPPORT ▶ p. 275
- **c** In your group, swap posters and check each other's.

▶ SF5: Doing research

▶ SF7: Making visual aids

▶ SF40: Proofreading

3 Preparing and giving your presentation

- **a** In your group, organize and practise your presentation.
- **b** Give your presentation in class.

▶ SF24: Giving a presentation

4 Assessing presentations

Using the assessment sheet your teacher will give you, assess the other groups' posters and presentations. In class, discuss how they might be improved.

Find a tool to help you create your poster here: **Webcode** context-50

7 Science – Enhancing Life?

A

B

Transhumanism
human advancement through technology
Genetic engineering
manipulation or modification of organisms using biotechnology
Energy transition
the path to a sustainable economy, e.g. by using biofuels
Gene pharming
the use of genetically modified organisms to produce pharmaceutical products

C

D

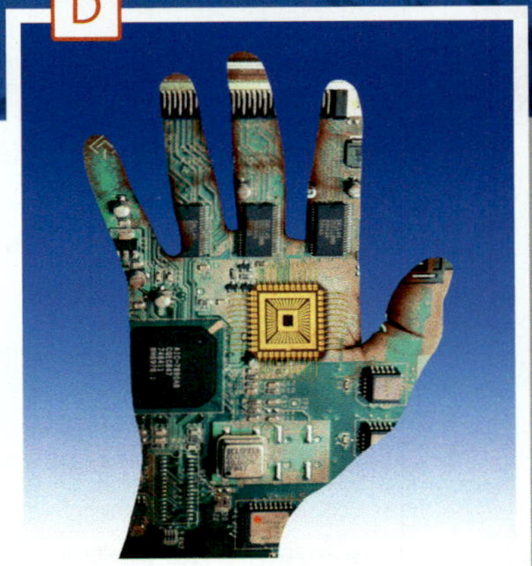

Download a list of chapter vocab here: **Webcode** context-03

1 Identifying current trends in science

a Study the pictures, then match them to one of the topics in the box.

b THINK Pick the photo you find most interesting and speculate about which development in modern science it depicts.

c PAIR Find a partner who chose the same photo. Exchange your ideas, and on the basis of your findings make a chart outlining chances and risks these developments might have for the future.

d SHARE With your chart, move around the classroom. Find a couple who made a chart based on a different picture. Discuss your charts and decide together whether the developments you have discussed will have a positive or negative impact on the future.

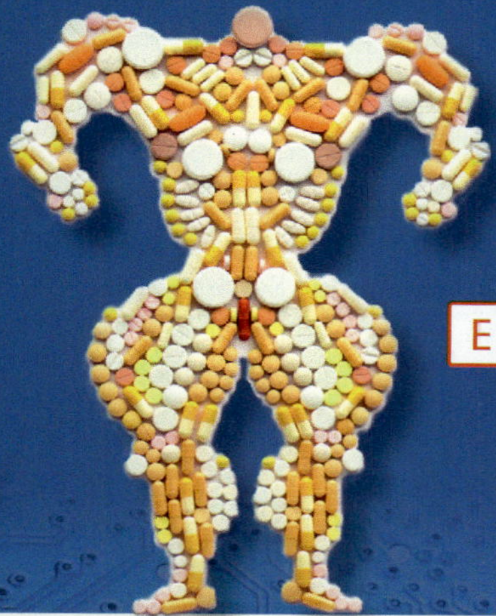

E

F

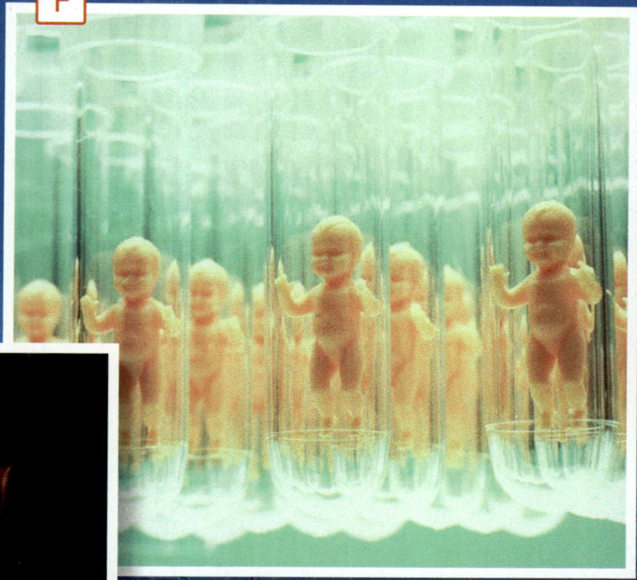

G

H

2 A look into the future

Predicting the future is difficult, if not impossible. Use your imagination and look into the future.

YOU CHOOSE **Examining new technology**

a Choose a modern form of technology (such as Google Glass, 3D printers, driverless cars, etc.) and say why you think it has the capability to transform our society in the future. In small groups present and discuss your ideas.

OR

b Make a ranking of new technologies according to their importance to you. In small groups compare your lists and together choose the three technological inventions that have the biggest potential in the future.

▸ SF24: Giving a presentation

PREVIEW

In this chapter you will learn about attempts to improve human life through genetic engineering and technological advancements. You will also examine the challenges of acquiring energy.

Main topics

Focus on Skills: READING and MEDIATION

CD1 04

Listen to an audio version of the text on the CD or download it here:
Webcode context-04

Science – motor of progress?

Feeding the world, healing deadly diseases and finding renewable sources of energy are some of the challenges we have to meet in the 21st century if we want to continue to live well. It is probably in the fields of science and technology that we will find answers to these problems.

Genetic Engineering

Scientists are now able to map the DNA sequence of the genes of many plants, animals and humans. They hope to use this information to improve the robustness or yield of crops and livestock and to cure human diseases. Genetic engineering (GE) is the process by which the sequence of an organism's DNA is altered by technological means, e.g. by inserting a foreign gene to produce a more desirable result. In order to provide food for an increasingly faster growing world population the commercial use of GE in farming may help increase food production. The first genetically modified (GM) crop was introduced in 1995 – the slow-softening tomato. Others have been made more insect-resistant or disease-resistant. In 2013, GM crops, including maize, cotton and rice, were being grown on more than 175 million hectares in 29 countries. In medicine, genetic engineering may one day be used to repair defective genes. A new widely-debated approach is gene pharming. Pharma crops are genetically modified plants like maize that produce much-needed medicines. The genes for human proteins like insulin could be transferred to animals, which then produce the protein in their milk. However, there are ethical concerns about genetic engineering:

'They used to be called sheep, and they produced wool. Now they're some sort of bioengineered creatures, and they produce antibiotics.'

- **Risk and safety:** Transgenic plants or animals (i.e. containing one or more foreign genes) may in the end prove to be unhealthy or even dangerous.
- **Meddling with reproduction:** In vitro fertilization (IVF) offers the opportunity to preselect an embryo that is free from genetic disorders. Many fear this will lead to custom-made designer babies – children designed to have a particular eye colour or IQ.

These are reasons why GE requires public approval and careful regulation.

Quenching the thirst for energy

With the rise of emerging countries like Brazil and India the global thirst for energy is growing rapidly. Since the Fukushima nuclear disaster of 2011 many nations have agreed on a nuclear power phase-out. Even though renewable sources of energy like solar, wind and hydropower do not seem to be cost-efficient at the moment, experts are researching ways to switch from finite energy sources such as coal, gas and petroleum to sources that are sustainable and more environmentally friendly. This is seen as an important step to reduce humanity's carbon footprint and to stop global warming. Using plants like rapeseed or palm oil to produce biofuels is another way to avoid using fossil fuels. However, environmental and ethical concerns about such technologies are growing.

► SF2: Learning new words

1 Information Stock Exchange

a Choose two of the issues in the text that you feel well-informed about. Write them on green cards.

b Write two terms on red cards that you would like to find out more about.

c Walk around the classroom and find two people with green cards that match your red cards. Ask them to give you the information you want.

d Explain the terms on your green cards to two students.

e On the blackboard arrange your cards in three columns:

- Still lost: red cards with terms that still need clarifying
- Lost and found: green and red matches
- Information pool: green cards that were not talked about

► LP11: Using the right register

2 Formal vs. informal language

Scientific reports strive for accuracy and precision, which is why they rarely use phrasal verbs. Try to substitute the phrasal verbs or informal expressions below with a formal verb from the text.

1 put sth. into sth.
2 move sth. from one place to another
3 make sth. different
4 make sth. less or smaller

► LP10: Using adjectives and adverbs

TROUBLE SPOT

Hyphenated compound adjectives are only used **before** nouns:
It was a well-written report.
↔ *The report was well written.*

3 Compound adjectives

Compound adjectives make texts more formal by condensing information.

a Find examples of compound adjectives such as *custom-made* (l. 33) in the text and categorize them according to their structure:
noun + adjective • noun + participle • adjective + adjective • adjective/adverb + participle

b Make these sentences shorter by forming compound adjectives.

1 Genetic engineering is a business that is growing fast.
2 GE companies hope to make progress at a speed that will break all records.
3 They hope to help farmers keep their fields free from pollution.
4 The development took ten years before GE crops could hit the market.

4 Writing

Describe the picture and discuss it with reference to genetic engineering.

The genetic engineering debate

A1 A saviour sibling *Laura Roberts*

Genetic screening is a new technology that has been helping families with genetically transmitted diseases.

sibling brother or sister
1 **tissue** ['tɪʃuː] *Gewebe*
2 **specifically** intended for a particular purpose
3 **disorder** *Störung*
4 **bone marrow** *Knochenmark*
donor *Spender/in*
7 **conception** *Empfängnis*
15 **suitability** [ˌsuːtə'bɪləti] *Eignung*
16 **umbilical** [ʌm'bɪlɪkl] **cord** *Nabelschnur*
32 **burden** sth. that gives a person a heavy responsibility
35 **bubbly** full of life and energy

Megan Matthews, nine, received tissue donated by her 18-month old brother Max who was created specifically so that he could aid her medical treatment. [...]

Megan, from King's Lynn, Norfolk, was born with a rare blood disorder which can cause bone marrow failure and a worldwide search for a suitable bone marrow donor failed. The condition, Fanconi Anaemia, meant she needed transfusions every few weeks and was unable to fight infections.

Her parents Katie and Andy Matthews wanted another child but natural conception would have provided only a one in four chance that the sibling would be a perfect tissue match. The new child could also have been born with the same life-threatening genetic disorder. To avoid this, Cambridge, Bristol and Nottingham medical teams were involved in a treatment which used donated cells from the specifically created baby and taken to treat Megan's disorder.

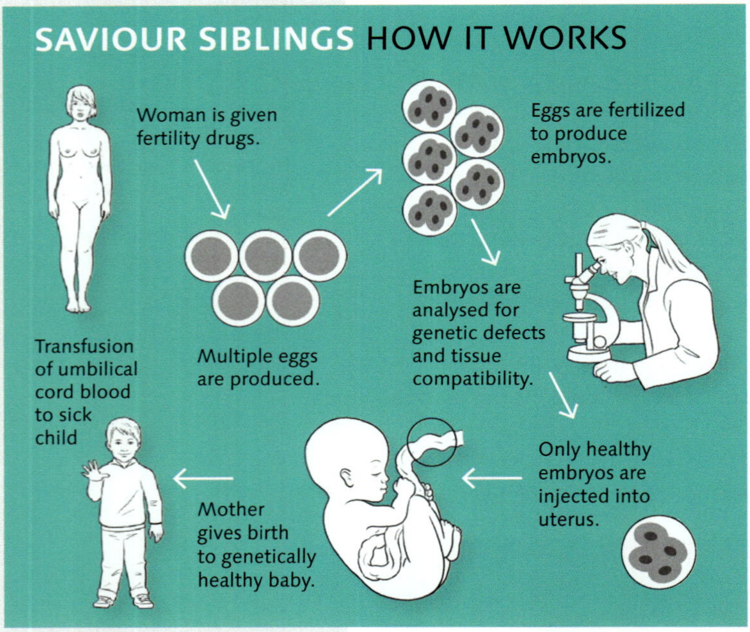

Two embryos were implanted into Mrs Matthews by CARE Fertility in Nottingham after they were checked for transplant suitability. Initially umbilical cord blood was saved and after Max was born an operation was carried out to take bone marrow. The tissue transplant took place in July this year at Bristol Royal Hospital for Sick Children. Compared to her frequent and invasive hospital visits, Megan now only requires a weekly check-up at Addenbrookes hospital in Cambridge.

Simon Fishel, managing director of Care Fertility, said that ethical concerns over creating children with specific genetic material were outweighed by the benefits. He said: 'The ethical issues are in favour of doing this work. We are trying to save the life of a child and achieve a family without the enormous burden of a child with this disorder who would die.' Mrs Matthews also said she had no ethical problems with the treatment her family had received. She said: 'Max is loved for being him and not for what he has done. He has completed our family and now I have a bubbly and healthy girl.'

The use of genetically engineered children for medical treatment has been widely criticised. Josephine Quintavalle, Director of Comment on Reproductive Ethics told the BBC: '[Max] owes his life to his capacity to be of therapeutic use to his sick sister, otherwise he would not have been chosen in the first place. This is the big ethical problem.' Sufferers of Fanconi Anaemia may suffer long-term health problems and Megan may require further treatment.

From: 'First complete "saviour sibling" transplant carried out in the UK', *Daily Telegraph*, 22 December 2010

COMPREHENSION

1 Understanding the concept of saviour siblings
Choose the statement which fits best and give the line that provides evidence for your choice.

- **a** A saviour sibling is a brother or sister …
  1 who has been specifically created for the purpose of curing a sick brother or sister.
  2 whose life was saved by receiving a transplant from a brother or sister.
- **b** Without a transplant Megan would …
  1 have died within a short period of time.
  2 have had to go in and out of hospitals to receive transfusions.
- **c** The use of IVF was necessary to …
  1 produce a healthy embryo.
  2 make sure that the baby would not suffer from Fanconi Anaemia.
- **d** The procedure has been widely criticized as …
  1 human beings seem to have been reduced to commodities.
  2 embryos are killed in the process.

► SF 10: Working with closed test formats

2 Summarizing information
Use the drawing and the information from the text to explain how a saviour sibling is produced.

► SF 31: Writing a summary

ANALYSIS

3 Argumentative structure

- **a** Look at the last sentence of the article and decide whether the writer is in favour of the use of saviour siblings, whether she is against their use or whether he takes a neutral position.
- **b** Analyse the argumentative structure of the article, paying particular attention to the effect of the writer's use of direct and indirect speech.
  SUPPORT ► p. 276

► SF 18: Analysing non-fiction

LANGUAGE AWARENESS

4 Using the passive

- **a** Scientific texts usually contain many passive constructions. Look at the use of the passive voice in ll. 2, 11, 13, 15, 16, 17–18, 28, 34, 36, 39, and analyse its effect. (Hint: it may help to transform one or two into the active voice to see the difference.)
- **b** In German, active sentences with *man* are often used instead of a passive sentence. In which cases do you think *man* might be better than the passive voice if you were to translate the sentences?

► LP 7: The passive

BEYOND THE TEXT

5 PLACEMAT ACTIVITY **Case studies**
Choose one of the cases below and use a placemat to note down the pros and cons for that case. Use the guidelines from the Fact File on p. 148 to consider the ethical dimensions of the topic. Discuss the issue with your group members and prepare a group statement in which you justify your position.

1 Megan's case (cf. text).
2 A pair of deaf parents wants to use genetic screening to ensure that their child is also deaf.
3 Parents who want to use genetic screening to test their foetus for genes that indicate a high risk of their child developing particular conditions, so that they can abort the foetus if they so wish.

► SF 24: Giving a presentation

FACT FILE

Ethics in science

Science is advancing at an ever-accelerating speed. New discoveries and new technologies are affecting all areas of our life. Many new inventions or discoveries have sparked public discussions on whether their use is desirable or should be avoided.

In order to find out which course of action is the moral one, people turn to ethics. Ethics is the branch of philosophy that studies the principles of what is morally right or wrong. When it comes to ethical decision making, the following questions can help you. You can use them to test whether your decision is morally acceptable:

- Are the rights of everyone involved respected?
- Which solution would be the most just, fair or responsible?
- Which solution will probably have the best overall consequences, even if it means that some will not benefit from it?
- Which solution will be most sustainable and help everyone?
- Think of the wisest person you know. What would he or she do in this situation?

Read the Fact File and write down: 3 words or expressions that are new to you and worth adding to your word bank on genetic engineering; 2 ethical principles that are particularly important when it comes to ethical decision making; 1 reason why ethical decision making is important.

The National Theatre's production of Nick Dear's Frankenstein

A2 You are mine to kill *Nick Dear*

The excerpt below is from Nick Dear's 2011 stage adaptation of Mary Shelley's novel Frankenstein *(1818). Considered by many to be one of the first horror stories, Shelley's gothic novel poses many moral and ethical questions about the role of science in a society that was beginning to change due to scientific advances. Victor Frankenstein, a young scientist, has succeeded in creating life. From dead bodies and with the help of newly-discovered electricity he has brought a creature to life. Appalled by its ugliness, he sends it away. After he learns that the creature has killed his brother William, he searches for it in the Arctic ice, where the creature has fled.*

- With a partner, come up with a list of guidelines that a responsible scientist should follow, e.g. whether they should make their findings publicly available.

There is a sound like a great exhalation of breath, as the glacier shudders and shifts. Through the snowstorm the Creature is suddenly visible, standing very still on the ice. He makes a great leap towards Victor.

VICTOR My God! Muscular coordination – hand and eye – excellent tissue – perfect balance! And the sutures have held! I failed to make it handsome, but I gave it strength and grace.

Victor circles the Creature. The Creature swivels to keep an eye on him.

What an achievement! Unsurpassed in scientific endeavour! God, the madness of that night – the heat, the sweat, the infusions, the moment when I saw it crawl towards me, and I – and I –

CREATURE You ran away.

VICTOR What?

CREATURE You abandoned me.

VICTOR *(stunned)* It speaks!

CREATURE Yes, Frankenstein. It speaks.

VICTOR You know my name?

5 **suture** ['suːtʃə] *Naht*
7 **swivel** ['swɪvl] turn round quickly
8 **unsurpassed** better or greater than any other
endeavour *(n)* [ɪn'devə] attempt to do sth. new and difficult
10 **crawl** walk on your hands and knees
13 **abandon sb.** leave sb. with no intention of seeing them again

The Creature hands Victor the tattered journal.

My journal!
CREATURE Why did you abandon me?
VICTOR I was terrified – what had I done?
CREATURE Built a man, and given him life –
VICTOR Well, now I have come to take it away –
CREATURE *(laughs)* Oh, have you?
VICTOR I have come to kill you!
CREATURE To kill me? Why then did you create me?
VICTOR To prove that I could!
CREATURE So you make sport with my life?
VICTOR In the cause of science! You were my greatest experiment – but an experiment that has gone wrong. An experiment that must be curtailed!

Victor runs at him and attacks him with his stick, but the Creature swiftly disarms him and throws him to the ground.

CREATURE Be still, genius! I have a request.
VICTOR Damn you, you can't have requests!
CREATURE Oh, I can! Listen to me. It's your duty.
VICTOR I have no duty to a murderer.

From: *Frankenstein*, 2001

30 **curtail sth.** [–'–] (here) bring sth. to an end
31 **disarm sb.** take a weapon away from sb.

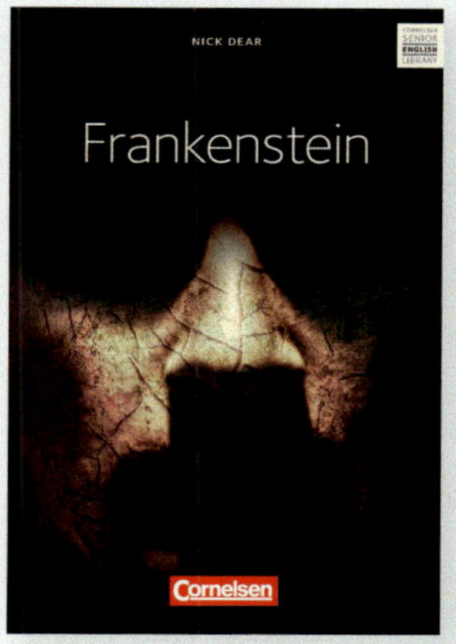

COMPREHENSION

1 Creature and creator
Describe the situation as presented in this scene.

ANALYSIS

2 Responsible or irresponsible scientist?
Examine the attitude of Victor Frankenstein to his creation. Use your list from above to judge whether his attitude shows him to be a responsible or an irresponsible scientist.

BEYOND THE TEXT

3 CHALLENGE **The experiment**
Creature or human? Comment on this question taking into consideration ethical and legal aspects and the character of the Creature. Discuss the consequences this decision will have for the Creature and for possible punishments regarding Williams's death.

'We've created a teenager.'

4 FOUR-CORNERS ACTIVITY **Discussing statements**
Assign each of the four positions below to a corner in your classroom. Then stand next to the statement that comes closest to your own opinion. With the others in your corner discuss the reasons why you each chose that position.

► SF27: Having a discussion

Scientists should have complete freedom in their research and not be controlled by the government.	'Science, in the very act of solving problems, creates more of them.' *Abraham Flexner*	'Whenever science makes a discovery, the devil grabs it while the angels are debating the best way to use it.' *Alan Valentine*	It is not for humans to create life forms and use them for their own purposes.

A3 At the lab

© Guy & Rodd/Distributed by Universal Uclick for UFS via CartoonStock.com

astigmatism optical defect *(Hornhautverkrümmung)*

LANGUAGE HELP

- The ethical/moral question raised by .... is ...
- The most important/The profoundest argument is .../ The least convincing argument
- A valid/sound/serious/ plausible argument
- invalid/arbitrary/implausible argument
- As a consequence, ...
- the result of which would be that ...
- It seems important to me to emphasize/point out ...

COMPREHENSION

1 Describing a cartoon
Describe the cartoon and identify the topic the cartoon addresses.

ANALYSIS

► SF 13: Analysing cartoons

2 Examining a cartoon
Analyse the means the cartoonist employs to make his point.

BEYOND THE CARTOON

3 Comparing texts
Comment on how the topic of the cartoon is similar or different to the dilemma dealt with in *Frankenstein* (cf. **A2**).

4 YOU CHOOSE **Practising speaking**
When doing the following task, use the guidelines from the Fact File (cf. p. 148) to include the ethical dimension of the topic.

a Prepare a monologue on whether designer babies are desirable or not.
SUPPORT p. 276

OR

b Find a partner and discuss in front of the class whether designer babies are desirable or not, with one of you being in favour and one against.

► LANGUAGE HELP

► SF 24: Giving a presentation
► SF 27: Having a discussion

Find a tool for improving your speaking skills here:
Webcode context-51

CULTURE SPOT

The hyperrealistic sculptures by Australian contemporary artist Patricia Piccinini address ethical issues of genetic engineering in an often disturbing or provocative way.

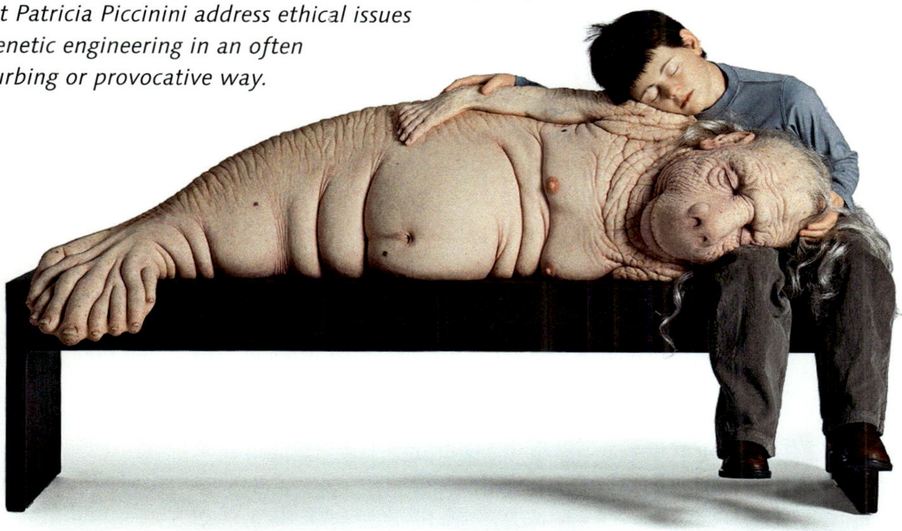

The Long Awaited (2008)

Silicone, fibreglass, human hair, plywood, leather, clothing. 152 x 80 x 92 cm high. Courtesy of the artist and Tolarno and Roslyn Oxley9 Galleries

Patricia Piccinini on *The Long Awaited*:

'Empathy is at the heart of my practice. I don't think that you really can – or indeed should – try to understand the ethics of something without emotions [...]. It is one thing to argue for or against cloning when it is just an intellectual issue. However, things change if you have a mother or son who might need it. I like to think that my work understands that the point at which "good" becomes "bad" does not stand still, which is why it is so difficult to find.'

1 Study the sculpture. Then discuss your reactions to it with a partner. Choose the adjectives from the list below to describe the sculpture and its effect on you.

aesthetic • calming • delightful • disturbing • embarrassing • harmonious • interesting • loving • obnoxious • quaint • shocking • supportive • tasteless • touching • tranquil • understanding • unsettling • warm

2 Analyse the relationship between the boy and the creature on the bench. Explain to what extent the sculpture illustrates Piccinini's comment.

3 Write a formal email to Patricia Piccinini in which you comment on *The Long Awaited* as a statement on genetic engineering.

A4 Animals with bonus features *Bob Holmes*

- FOUR-CORNERS ACTIVITY **Animal rights**
  Read the four statements displayed in four corners of your classroom, then stand next to the one you can identify with most. Explain why.
  1. Through breeding and selection humans have always changed domestic animals. Genetic engineering is basically no different.
  2. The genetic engineering of animals should be forbidden as it violates animal rights and is potentially harmful to the animal.
  3. Using genetically engineered animals to produce drugs is acceptable if it reduces severe human suffering.
  4. Animals with human DNA should be entitled to special rights.

The text below examines the genetic engineering of animals so that they may benefit humans in more ways than they do today.

Unless you live in Europe, your last meal probably contained genetically modified ingredients – 80 per cent of soya grown worldwide is now genetically engineered, for instance. Yet while modified plants are rapidly taking over the planet's farms, the same cannot be said for GM animals. [...]

The main reason is that the genetic engineering of animals – with the exception of mice – has been a slow, tedious process needing a lot of money and not a little luck. Behind the scenes, though, a quiet revolution has been taking place. Thanks to a set of new tricks and tools, modifying animals is becoming a lot easier and more precise. That is not only going to transform research, it could also transform the meat and eggs you eat and the milk you drink. The first transgenic animals were produced by injecting DNA into eggs, implanting the eggs in animals and then waiting weeks or months to see if any offspring had incorporated the extra DNA. Often fewer than 1 in 100 had, making this a long, expensive process. [...]

In mice, geneticists found a way round this problem: producing cells with the desired modification first, before growing entire animals. [...] At the same time, biologists have developed more efficient ways of adding DNA to cells, by hijacking natural genetic engineers such as viruses, and jumping genes capable of 'copying and pasting' themselves. All these advances mean the effort and cost needed to produce GM animals has decreased a hundredfold. [...] The ability to easily and precisely modify animals will undoubtedly lead to huge pay-offs in research and medicine. [...]

Genetically modified farm animals could provide us with more nutritious meat, milk and eggs, while causing fewer pollution problems, and perhaps suffering less too. Pigs whose muscles are enriched with omega-3s have already been created, and researchers are exploring similar options with milk. [...]

Genetic engineering is now a standard technique in the production of many protein-based drugs. Human insulin, for example, has long been produced by cultures of bacteria carrying the human insulin gene. Pharmaceutical companies are eager to turn animals into drug factories, too. That's because animal cells alter many of their proteins by tacking on sugars and other 'decorations', an extra step that bacteria cannot perform. As a result, many proteins – most importantly, antibodies – work much better if they are made in animal cells.

6 **tedious** ['tiːdiəs] taking a long time and requiring a lot of work
18 **jumping gene** gene that can insert copies of itself into other DNA sites in the same cell
25 **omega-3** ['əʊmɪɡə] type of fatty acid
32 **tack sth. on** add sth.
34 **antibody** *Antikörper*

One such animal-produced protein has already been approved for clinical use by the US Food and Drug Administration. An anticoagulant called antithrombin III is purified from the milk of genetically engineered goats created by GTC Biotherapeutics, a biotech company in Framingham, Massachusetts. Many others are under development. [...] Open Monoclonal Technology of Palo Alto, California, has engineered rats to produce human antibodies. Its first product, an anti-cancer antibody for treating lymphoma, should be in clinical trials within two to three years.

From: 'Altered animals: creatures with bonus features', *The New Scientist*, 14 July 2010

36 **anticoagulant** [ˌæntɪkəʊˈægjələnt] *Gerinnungshemmer*
41 **lymphoma** [lɪmˈfəʊmə] *Lymphdrüsenkrebs*

READING **FOCUS ON SKILLS**

Using reading strategies (scientific text)

Scientific texts are challenging both in terms of content and language. The tips below can help you to get a detailed and thorough understanding of such texts.

1 Understanding the gist
Skim text **A4** on the previous page quickly to get a basic understanding of what the text is about. The first sentence of a paragraph is usually the topic sentence that states the main idea of the paragraph. Summarize to a partner what you think the text is about.

► SF 14: Reading strategies

2 Reducing the complexity of the text
Focus on the most relevant pieces of information only. Often it is not necessary to understand a sentence or paragraph word for word.
- **a** Add headlines to the paragraphs to mark what they are about in general.
- **b** The second and the third paragraphs deal with the advancements made in changing the genetic makeup of animals. In order to understand what these are, identify words that describe the development so that you will be able to explain it. (Hint: you can ignore technical details.)

3 Dealing with hard words
- **a** Scientific texts are full of technical terms. Often they are of Latin or Greek origin and are similar to German words, e.g. 'precise' *(präzise)* in l. 8. Find more examples in the text and explain their meaning.
- **b** Scientific texts aim for accuracy. They use *formal instead of *informal style. Use the context to find the equivalent of these words in the text:

change sth. • put sth. into sth. • include sth. • being able • go down • offer sth. / make sth. available • do sth. • accept • make sth. cleaner • create/design sth.

- **c** Often the meaning becomes clear when you look at the word family, e.g. *purify* (v) – *pure* (adj). Now use this strategy to find the meaning of 'engineer' (l. 2), 'nutritious' (l. 22) and 'enrich' (l. 24).

► SF 1: Dealing with unknown words

► LP 11: Using the right register

► LP 20: Word formation

4 Relating information
It is helpful to draw diagrams or flowcharts in order to understand processes. Try to draw a simple diagram or flowchart to illustrate the process of creating a transgenic animal as described in the second paragraph.

► SF 7: Making visual aids

Modifying mankind

DVD

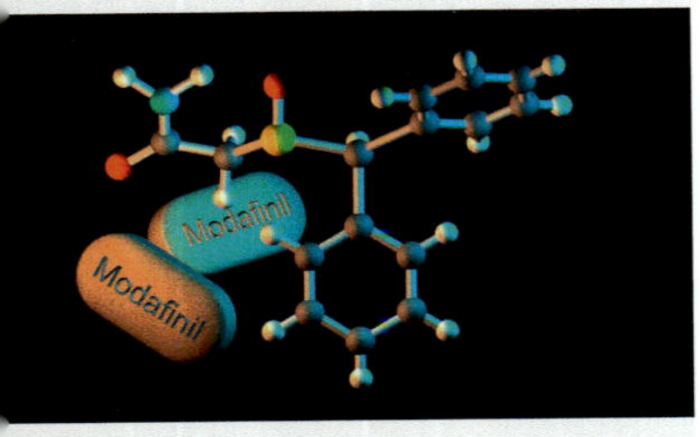

B1 A brain-enhancing pill

*Watch the short *news report on the use of Modafinil.*

COMPREHENSION

1 Understanding the effects of a neuro-enhancing drug
Describe the positive and negative effects of the neuro-enhancing pill as mentioned in the video. Outline why the drug is popular despite the risks that come with it.

2 Mediation (English → German)
A fellow student of yours believes that it's impossible to get such a drug without a prescription. Tell him or her (in German) what you have found out.

► SF41: Mediation of written and oral texts

ANALYSIS

3 Examining the tone
Choose adjectives from the list below to describe the *tone of the report. Provide evidence for your opinion from the news report.

objective • neutral • biased • sensational • critical • exaggerated

► SF23: Analysing a film

BEYOND THE TEXT

4 SILENT-WRITING DISCUSSION **What if there were 'smart pills'?**

a Get together in groups of four (students A–D). Look at the questions below. Write your question at the top of a piece of paper, then answer it. Then pass the paper on to the student to your right. Add your answer to the next question on the paper you receive. Continue until every student has the paper again that he or she started with.

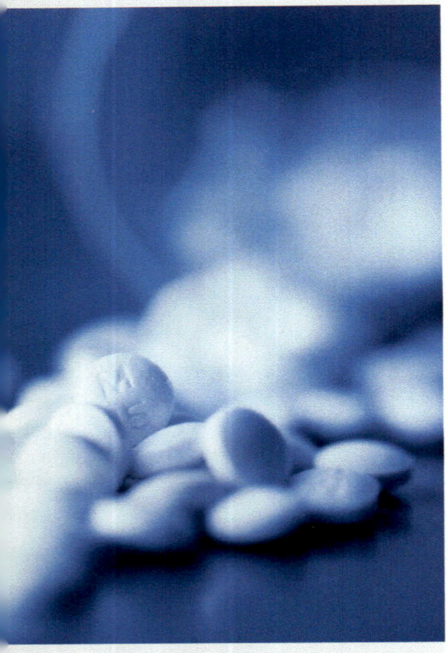

Student A:
Imagine there were pills that could really make people smarter. Should those pills be given to everyone for free?

Student B:
Imagine there were pills that could really make people smarter. If people took such pills before an exam, would you consider it to be cheating?

Student C:
Imagine there were pills that could really make people smarter. Should parents be allowed to give such pills to school-age children?

Student D:
Imagine there were pills that could really make people smarter. Would taking such pills to enhance your brain power be any different from drinking coffee or energy drinks, taking vitamins or going for a run?

b Now read the responses and sum up the comments for your group members.

c Discuss the impact of neuroenhancers on society and recommend how society should deal with them.

B2 Gene doping *Tim Franks*

It seems the fight against doping in sport is an ever-losing battle. The text below points out how genetic engineering may make the fight for a clean sport even harder.

- Before reading the text, speculate about the connection between genetic engineering and doping, then skim the article and check whether your guess was correct.

This could be a battle like no other in sport. The authorities are so concerned, they have been preparing for it for more than 10 years. But it is still unclear whether they have the tools to test for it – or whether anyone has done it successfully. It is gene doping. The idea is simple: to alter our genetic makeup, the very building blocks of who we are, in order to make us stronger or faster. The practicalities are highly complex.

Gene therapists – for example those treating very sick children at London's Great Ormond Street hospital – add a synthetic gene to the patient's genome, and reintroduce it into the bone marrow via a disabled virus. The new gene is expressed by the patient's cells and acts like a medicine, permanently incorporated in the bone marrow. [...]

Dr Philippe Moullier [...] had shown it was possible to produce artificially one particular gene – the erythropoietin gene – and introduce it into the body. And as anyone who had a vague brush with professional cycling in the 90s knows, the hormone erythropoietin, or EPO – which controls the production of red blood cells – was the illicit dope of choice for competitors. It was the wonder drug Lance Armstrong kept in his fridge, to boost his oxygen-carrying red-blood-cell count.

But while injected EPO has been detectable for years, introducing the EPO gene would result in the body producing its own EPO. Could this be an undetectable way of improving oxygen delivery? [...]

And while making a permanent change to the genome may be complex – using a disabled virus to carry the genetic medicine to the cells – Philippe Moullier says there is now a shortcut, which delivers temporary results: injecting the purified gene directly into your muscle. [...]

Even better for the would-be doper, says Moullier, this type of temporary boost may, after a few days, be hard for the authorities to detect. So what is the World Anti-Doping Agency (Wada) doing about it?

Back in 2003, Wada banned gene doping. The agency argues that the practice would not just be unfair, it could be lethal – introducing an extra copy of the EPO gene into your body could lead to too many red blood cells being produced and your blood thickening into sludge. [...]

But there is a deeper question. Even if there were to be or already is a legally and biologically fireproof test for gene doping, what should happen if gene therapy were to become much more widespread, even routine? What if we were all able to buy, over the counter, genetic medicine to slow muscle deterioration? Should we – could we – stop athletes from using the medicine, to prolong their careers or speed a return from injury?

From: 'Gene doping: sport's biggest battle', BBC, 12 January 2014

9 **express** cause (a gene) to manifest its effects in other cells
10 **bone marrow** *Knochenmark*
12 **Philippe Moullier** French doctor who first showed the possibilities of gene therapy
15 **brush** occasion when you have contact with or experience sth.
19 **boost sth.** make sth. more powerful
35 **sludge** thick, soft, wet substance
39 **deterioration** [dɪˈtɪəriəˈreɪʃn] *Verschlechterung*
40 **prolong sth.** make sth. last longer

Part B

The hormone erythropoietin became the illicit dope of choice for competitors in the Tour de France, bringing the competition into disrepute.

COMPREHENSION

▸ SF 31: Writing a summary

1 Getting the facts straight

Use the words below to summarize what the article is about. Include a definition of the term *gene doping*.

authorities • synthetic gene • erythropoietin or EPO • red blood cells • cycling • undetectable • injection • purified gene • lethal • ethical issue • genetic medicine

ANALYSIS

▸ SF 18: Analysing non-fiction

2 Examining the tone

Illustrate how the writer's use of language reveals his attitude to the topic.

SUPPORT ▸ p. 277

LANGUAGE AWARENESS

3 Speculating about effects and consequences

Gene doping is a new technology that is not yet in use but that could become important quite soon. That is why the article contains many speculations about its possible consequences.
Collect examples of modal auxiliaries used in the text to express probability or possibility. Compare their use with the use of the conditional sentences.

BEYOND THE TEXT

4 Discussing doping in sports

a Collect arguments in favour of or against allowing doping in professional sports.

▸ SF 28: Having a debate

b CHALLENGE ▸ Debate the motion 'This house believes the ban on doping should be lifted'. Before debating, search the internet for arguments for your position in the debate. Then meet with your partners and work out a strategy for how to convince the house to adopt your position. Make sure you anticipate your opponent's arguments and be prepared to counter them.

B3 Transhumanism *Zoltan Istvan*

The following text deals with the possibilities of transhumanist technology.

- Before reading, speculate what transhumanist technology means.

As long as they're earthbound, most people shrug off the idea of being anything other than a biological human. Some people are even repulsed or angered by the concept of scientifically tampering with the human body and brain too much. However, the time is coming when radical technology will allow us to expand and significantly improve the abilities of our minds and the forms of our bodies. A transhumanist age is nearly upon the human race – an age where cyborgs, sentient robots, virtual lives based in computers and dramatically altered human beings may become commonplace.

Already, there are hundreds of universities, laboratories and companies around the world where transhumanist projects are underway. A transhumanist is a person who aims to move beyond the human being via science and technology. Some of the most eye-opening projects are military-oriented, such as the 'Iron Man' armor suit being created for American soldiers. Trial runs of the suit are tentatively scheduled for this summer. Another well-known project is at Chalmers University of Technology in Sweden where scientists are connecting robotic limbs to the human nervous system of amputees, essentially creating cyborg-like people. The first arm surgeries are scheduled to occur in less than 12 months. Of course, private companies like Google are also very much involved in the broad field of transhumanism. They are spending many millions of dollars on creating artificial intelligence, which one day may have its own sentience and be thousands of times smarter than humans. [...]

Even though some of these technologies seem frightening to the layperson, they should be here in a matter of years, not decades. One of the most exciting and controversial ideas of transhumanism is the complete integration of the human mind with a machine. Similar to the extraordinary technology featured in the movie *The Matrix*, humans may be able to download themselves into computers and live virtual existences.

From: 'Despite skepticism, many people may embrace radical transhumanist technology in the future', *The Huffington Post*, 18 February 2014

1 **shrug sth. off** treat sth. as if it is not important
2 **repulse sb.** [– ' –] *(fml)* make sb. feel strong disgust
3 **tamper with sth.** make changes to sth. when one should not
5 **sentient** ['sentiənt; 'senʃt] *(fml)* able to feel or see things through the senses
13 **trial run** test of sth. to see how well it performs
tentative ['tentətɪv] not certain or definite
25 **layperson** person who is not an expert in a particular field

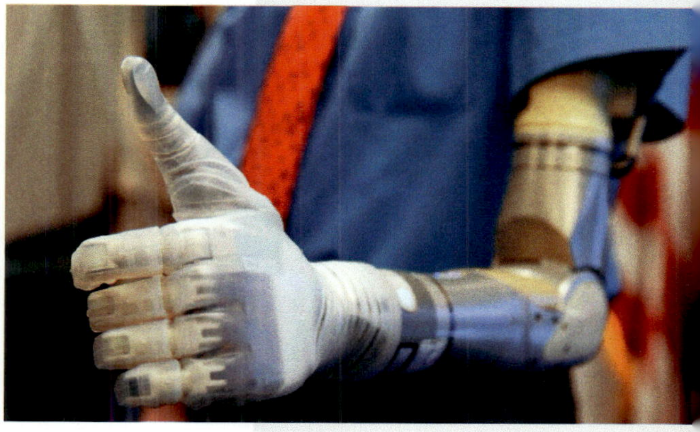

An army veteran gives a thumbs up with a prosthetic arm.

Part B

► SF 10: Working with closed test formats

Find an online dictionary here:
Webcode context-52

COMPREHENSION

1 Transhumanism defined

a Define the term *transhumanism*.

b List examples from the text of transhumanist technology.

c Match them to the categories given in the chart below. (Tip: there are more categories than examples.)

A augmenting	(adding removable attachments that boost capabilities)
B boosting	(enhancing capabilities and improving intelligence)
C embellishing	(changing an external part of a human for decorative purpose)
D replacing	(permanently replacing an organ or limb)
E adding	(integrating something additional into the human form)
F altering	(changing the actual biological structure of a human)
G redefining	(changing a human so much that the person is no longer recognizable as a human)

d CHALLENGE Match the examples below with the categories from **1c**.

modified DNA • *bionic legs* • *a piercing or tattoo* • *plastic surgery* • *consciousness upload* • *a brain chip* • *caffeine or steroids* • *Google Glass*

ANALYSIS

2 YOU CHOOSE New methods or new terms

a Explain how the examples given in the text differ from popular enhancement techniques such as exercising or surgery.

OR

b Innovative new technologies require new words or new combinations of words to label them, e.g. the term *internet* first appeared in 1974. Such newly coined words are called neologisms (from Greek *neo* = new, *logos* = word, speech). Collect examples of neologisms from the text, check their origin and explain their meaning.

BEYOND THE TEXT

3 Using transhuman technologies

a List the transhuman technologies you would embrace, and the ones you would reject. Discuss your views with a partner, explaining your reasons.

b CHALLENGE Use the guidelines from the Fact File (cf. p. 148) to formulate some ethical guidelines for using transhumanist technologies.

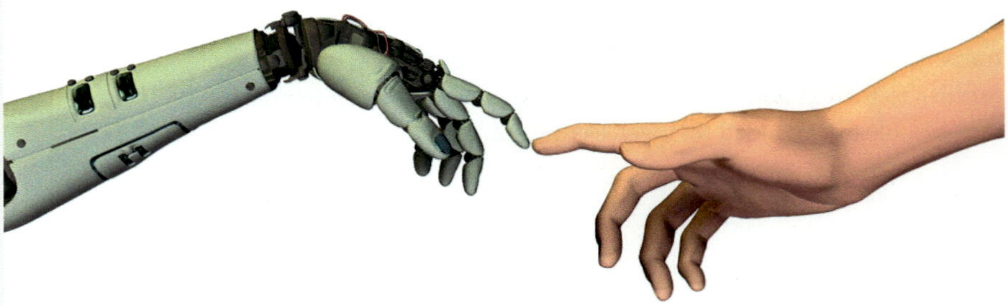

Quenching the thirst for energy

C1 The global demand for energy

With an ever-increasing world population and the economic progress of emerging nations, the global demand for energy poses a challenge that includes environmental, political and technological aspects.

A

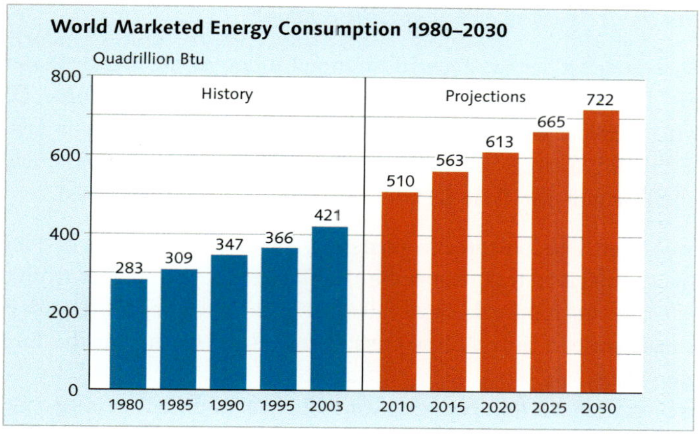

Btu = British thermal unit unit of energy, ca. 1055 joules

B

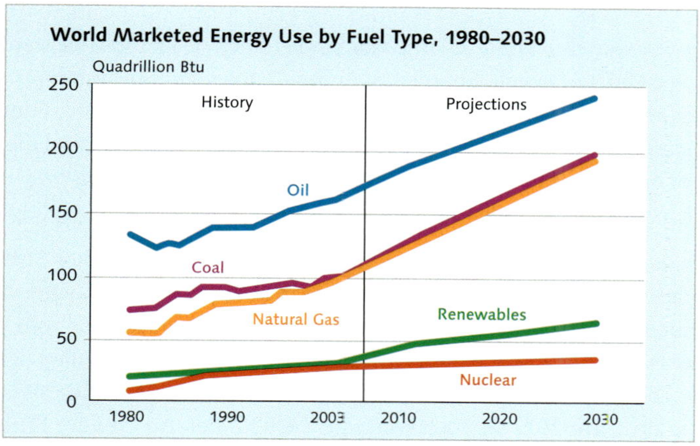

From: US Energy Information Administration, 2006

COMPREHENSION

1 Understanding graphs

Study the graphs and state what information they give about future trends of energy consumption. ▶ LANGUAGE HELP

BEYOND THE TEXT

2 Thinking about future trends

a In small groups discuss the positive or negative consequences these trends might have.

b Suggest ways how to tackle the problematic aspects that these trends could cause.

▶ SF12: Analysing charts and graphs

LANGUAGE HELP

- The bar chart/line graph is about .../deals with ...
- The chart gives/compares/ explains ...
- The size/the number of ...
- The number of ... has increased sharply/ significantly
- Whereas in 2005 ...
- In comparison with .../ Compared to ...

C2 The future of energy in Germany

You are taking part in an international youth conference about how different countries are reacting to environmental awareness. The conference intends to set up a website for young people dedicated to showing recent changes in global energy policies. You are to present the German Energiewende *in a text of about 200 words, explaining the German position and the aims of the* Energiewende. *While searching for information you have come across the following text. Skim the text in order to get the gist of what it is about.*

Die Energiewende ist der Kurzbegriff für eine fundamentale Wende in der Energieversorgung: Das bisherige Energiesystem, das auf Kernenergie, Kohle, Öl und Gas beruht, wird abgelöst von einer neuen Energieversorgung auf Basis Erneuerbarer Energie (EE) – Windkraft, Sonnenenergie, Wasserkraft, Biomasse und Erdwärme. Die wesentlichen Gründe für diese Wende in der Energieversorgung sind:

- Risikovorsorge: Die Risiken der Kernenergie sind prinzipiell nicht beherrschbar. Dies haben die Reaktorkatastrophen in Tschernobyl und Fukushima gezeigt. Zudem ist der hochradioaktive Abfall aus Kernkraftwerken für Hunderttausende von Jahren äußerst giftig, ohne dass bisher eine Lösung für die Endlagerung gefunden wäre.
- Klimaschutz: Bei der Verbrennung von Kohle, Öl und Gas entstehen klimaschädliche Treibhausgasemissionen, die die Hauptverursacher für den Klimawandel sind.
- Knappe Ressourcen: Kohle, Öl und Gas sind endlich. Je knapper sie werden, desto teurer wird ein auf fossile Energieträger basierendes Energiesystem.
- Wertschöpfung vor Ort: Während ein großer Teil der bisherigen Energieträger (insbesondere Öl, Gas, Uran und Steinkohle) importiert wird, sind die Erneuerbaren Energien heimische Energien, die somit die Wertschöpfung vor Ort erhöhen und die Importabhängigkeit reduzieren.

Die Frage der Energieversorgung war lange ein zentraler politischer Streitpunkt – insbesondere die Nutzung der Kernenergie war über Jahrzehnte Gegenstand heftiger Auseinandersetzungen. Seit den Beschlüssen des Bundestages vom Juni 2011 existiert in Deutschland jedoch ein parteiübergreifender Konsens, dass der Weg der Energiewende beschritten werden soll. So sind sowohl der Ausstieg aus der Kernenergie bis zum Jahr 2022 als auch konkrete Ziele für den Ausbau der Erneuerbaren Energien im Strombereich gesetzlich festgeschrieben. [...]

Was sind die zentralen Themen und Herausforderungen?

Stromerzeugung und -verbrauch haben eine besondere Bedeutung für die Energiewende, da die Erneuerbaren Energien hier die riskanten beziehungsweise CO_2-intensiven Energieträger Kernenergie, Braun- und Steinkohle ersetzen müssen. Zudem werden mittelfristig immer größere Anteile des Wärme- und Verkehrsbedarfs durch Strom bereitgestellt werden. Die Energiewende-Ziele im Stromsektor lauten:

- Erneuerbare Energien: mindestens 80 Prozent Anteil Erneuerbarer Energien an der Stromversorgung bis spätestens 2050 mit den Zwischenzielen von 40 Prozent bis 2025 und 55 bis 60 Prozent bis 2035.
- Energieeffizienz: Reduktion des Stromverbrauchs um 10 Prozent bis 2020 und 25 Prozent bis 2050 gegenüber dem Niveau von 2008.

From: agora-energiewende, 2014

MEDIATION **FOCUS ON SKILLS**

Mediating written texts

When mediating a text from one language into another, you always have to take into consideration the following aspects.

1 Content: What information do you want to get across?
Remember that when you are mediating, the final text is always shorter than the original text, as you are only mediating the important or necessary information.
Read the task in the introduction to text **C2** (cf. p. 160) again. What do you have to focus on?
Look at the statements below. Which are correct and which are incorrect?

► SF 41: Mediation of written and oral texts

1 I have to summarize all the information in the text.
2 I need to include the dates by which time goals must be met.
3 I have to explain why the *Energiewende* took place.
4 I can show what the aims are by also explaining what Germany intends to stop doing.
5 I need to discuss why it will be a challenge to meet the aims.
6 I need to discuss the political background.
7 I need to point out the future goals of the German energy policy.

2 Recipient: Who are you mediating for?
Decide who you are mediating for, and in which medium. Are you writing for people who speak English well? Are they experts on the matter?

3 Language: What style of language should you use?

► LP 11: Using the right register

a After deciding who your audience is, consider how this may affect the style and structure of your text. Is the style of the original text formal or informal? Should it be retained in your text? What about the vocabulary?
b In the text there are many words which you don't know in English. Try to translate or explain the following terms in English: *Erdwärme, Biomasse, Treibhausgas, Wasserkraft.* Check your results with a dictionary afterwards. For your audience, how might it be best to mediate theses terms?
c Are there any structural features (e.g. bullet points, boxes, headlines) that you need in your text?

► SF 9: Paraphrasing

Find an online dictionary here:
Webcode context-52

4 Intercultural aspects: Which aspects of the text might be hard to understand for people from a different culture?
Sometimes you have to explain things that are easy for you to understand but hard for other people, because they are specific to your culture.
a Think of the term *Energiewende*. Describe it in a way that would make its meaning clear to somebody with no idea what it is.
b Find other aspects in the text that would have to be adapted, stressed or explained, e.g. when mediating for a Japanese, African or Scottish person.

► CC 1: Cultural awareness

5 Write your text.

6 Peer Assessment
In groups of four evaluate your texts using the assessment sheet your teacher will give you.

CD1 05
► SF 22: Listening
► SF 10: Working with closed test formats

Raymond Kurzweil

FACT FILE

Biofuels are a type of energy derived from renewable plant and animal materials. Approximately 100 billion litres of biofuel are produced each year. Biofuels provide about 3% of the world's fuels for road transport.

DVD
► SF 23: Analysing a film

► SF 5: Doing research
► SF 27: Having a discussion

C3 A possible future

COMPREHENSION

1 Understanding an expert's perspective

Listen to the following interview with Raymond Kurzweil, an expert on technology, and say which of the following statements he made and which he did not.

1. Fossil fuels should be taxed to reflect the true cost they have on the environment.
2. Wind energy will be the most used renewable energy.
3. Within 14 years 100% of our energy needs will come from renewable sources.
4. Governments are unable to aid the change to renewable energies.

BEYOND THE TEXT

2 Examining predictions

a The interview was made in 2008. Discuss to what extent Kurzweil's predictions have come true.
b Discuss how relevant his perspective is today.

C4 Biofuels – the green alternative?

The European Union has committed itself to producing 10% of its energy from renewable sources of energy by 2020. One way of achieving this goal is through the use of biofuels. This concept has been met with both approval and rejection.

COMPREHENSION

1 Arguments for and against

Watch the two video clips about biofuels and note down arguments for and against biofuels.

ANALYSIS

2 Comparing films

a Explain which of the two clips you found more convincing.
b Examine how the use of music, light, cinematic devices and the voiceover contributed to the ideas in the one you found most convincing.

BEYOND THE TEXT

3 Having a discussion

In two groups find arguments in favour of and against biofuels. The motion could be as follows: 'Governments should subsidize biofuels.'

SUPPORT ► p. 277

'No you can't turn your vegetables into bio-fuel.'

Doing a WebQuest

A supermarket in your hometown has announced their decision to stock genetically modified (GM) foods. The public is concerned.

- Do a quick opinion poll to find out what your class thinks about this issue.

In order to decide whether or not to take action, a Committee of Concerned Citizens agrees to consult experts: a scientist, a farmer, an environmentalist, and a nutritionist.

1 Get together in groups of four. Each of you researches the topic from the point of view of one of the experts (cf. the cards below). Make sure to also use German sources.

Find useful links here: **Webcode** context-05

As the **scientist**, you investigate the process of creating GM foods. You need to consider the following questions:
- How are GM foods produced?
- Is there a danger that this process might lead to unsafe products?
- What safeguards should be installed to prevent unsafe products?

As the **environmentalist**, you investigate the environmental aspects of GM foods. You need to consider the following questions:
- What environmental problems might be caused by GM foods?
- What safeguards should be installed to minimize these problems?

- As the **farmer**, you think of the consequences for farmers like yourself. You need to consider the following questions:
- What consequences will GM foods have for farmers (their health, cost of seeds, etc.)?
- What experiences have farmers had with GM foods so far?

As the **nutritionist** you investigate the nutritional aspects of GM foods. You need to consider the following questions:
- Do GM foods have the same nutritional value as natural foods?
- Could there be any nutritional problems or long-term health effects involved in eating GM foods?

2 In your group, exchange the results of your research. Decide whether or not to recommend stocking GM foods.

3 Prepare a presentation for the Committee in which you give a recommendation and justify your opinion (no longer than ten minutes). Make sure your listeners can follow your arguments – they are no experts on the matter!

► SF 24: Giving a presentation

4 Give your presentation.

5 After each group has given their presentation, the Committee (i.e. the class) discusses the recommendations and decides whether to take action.

► SF 27: Having a discussion

6 Repeat the opinion poll you conducted before the WebQuest.

7 Evaluate the presentations with the assessment sheet your teacher will give you.

8 Human dilemmas – from Shakespeare to Today

> My head says, 'Who cares?' But then my heart whispers, 'You do, stupid.'
> *Unknown*

> Our dilemma is that we hate change and love it at the same time; what we really want is for things to remain the same but get better.
> *Sydney J. Harris (1917–1986), US journalist*

> Eternal dilemma: too tired to stay up, yet too awake to fall asleep.
> *Unknown*

> A king realizing his incompetence can either delegate or abdicate his duties. A father can do neither. If only sons could see the paradox they would understand the dilemma.
> *Marlene Dietrich (1901–1992), German-American actress and singer*

Download a chronological word list here: **Webcode** context-65

1 Looking at quotations

- a Work with a partner. Take turns explaining your understanding of the quotations to each other. Use a dictionary if necessary.
- b Choose two of the given examples that you can relate to best. Give reasons for your decision.
- c Together with your partner try to define what a dilemma is for you in your everyday life. Check a dictionary for help to make your definition as precise as possible. Discuss your definitions in class.

2 Describing a situation

Imagine a situation where you encountered or can encounter a dilemma in your everyday life and write a short text of about 100 words about it. Try to describe the situation as clearly as possible.

CAIUS What's to do?
BRUTUS An act that will make sick men whole.
CAIUS But are not some whole that we must make sick?
BRUTUS That we must also.

Julius Caesar, Act 2, Scene 1, ll. 326–329

HAMLET
To be, or not to be – that is the question:
Whether 'tis nobler in the mind to suffer
The slings and arrows of outrageous fortune
Or to take arms against a sea of troubles
And by opposing end them. To die, to sleep –

Hamlet Act 3, Scene 1, ll. 56–60

OTHELLO
Excellent wretch! Perdition catch my soul
But I do love thee! and when I love thee not,
Chaos is come again.

Othello, Act 3, Scene 3, ll. 90–92

3 Thinking about conflicts and dilemmas in drama

a Read the lines from three different plays by William Shakespeare. With a partner decide on the one that appeals to you most.

b Explain what seems to be at stake in each case. Try to identify whether this can be considered as a conflict or a dilemma.

c Share your ideas with other couples who have chosen a different quotation. Compare your different explanations. Assess why at the core of drama there has to be a conflict or even dilemma.

William Shakespeare, 'Cobbe Portrait'

PREVIEW

In this chapter you will gain an insight into how conflicts and dilemmas of the real world are depicted in literature from Shakespeare to modern times.

Main topics

Focus on Skills: READING and VIEWING

Conflicts turned into words

CD4 11
Listen to an audio version of the text on the CD or download it here:
Webcode context-66

► SF 1: Dealing with unknown words

The importance of the spoken word in Shakespeare's time

In Shakespeare's time people went to the theatre to 'hear' a play. The stage was equipped with only the most necessary props. The actors used body language and gestures to express emotions, conflicts etc., while the visual aspect was not so important for the overall dramatic impression. The most important element was the language, the words spoken by the actors performing on stage. Sometimes we even speak of word-scenery, as the characters often describe the scenery for the audience to imagine.

Shakespeare included many scenes in his plays in which a character uses words to persuade other characters to do things they might not want to originally do. Quite a few plays rely on quick verbal exchange, in which characters reply to each other in witty comments. Sometimes the word-fights are playful, sometimes they contain an element of challenge and sometimes they are cynical or evil. All of them demonstrate Shakespeare's mastery of language, as well as his enjoyment at creating these scenes of conflicting ideas.

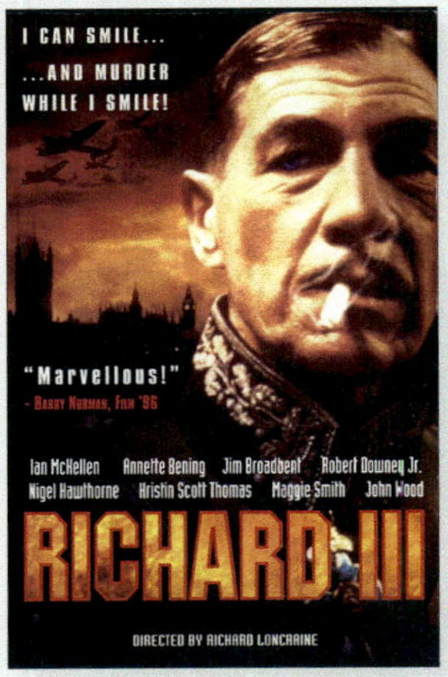

Shakespeare's language and dramatic conflicts in our time

Since Shakespeare's time, the English language has developed considerably, while the themes of his plays have remained relevant up to this day. That is why there is such a wealth of adaptations of the plays both in writing and in films. Sometimes, it is just the main theme that has been adapted, as in the musical *West Side Story* (1957), which is based on Shakespeare's play *Romeo and Juliet*. Here, the language has been changed to fit the setting of New York in the 1950s. Occasionally there are filmed versions of his plays that keep Shakespeare's language but are set in a different location. *William Shakespeare's Romeo and Juliet* (1996) is set in a fictitious modern American city called 'Verona Beach', complete with skyscrapers, large cars, and armed gangs – and yet the characters speak in Shakespeare's verse. The film *Richard III* (1995), for example, is set in a 1930s dictatorship. The popularity of these films shows that is still understandable when accompanied by images that we can relate to. To this day, Shakespeare is not only remembered for his plays, but also for his poetry. His cycle of 154 sonnets deals in different ways with love, the passing of time, and death.

Gender struggles

One topic that has remained popular and caused conflicts throughout the centuries, in reality as well as in fiction, is the relationship between men and women. Poets and writers have always been interested in exploring the feelings, attitudes and experiences of men and women in love and in conflict. Likewise, literature has reflected the social and legal status of men and women, e.g. the struggle for equal rights for women including suffrage (i.e. the right to vote). Thus, literature has forced its audience and readers to form an opinion on issues like these and sometimes to make a stand against them.

1 Performance words

List words from the text that you could use when talking about
a what you can see
b what you can hear
during a performance in a theatre. Add short definitions to each word.

► SF3: Using a dictionary

2 Collocations

a Collocations are words that often 'go together'. Find as many collocations as possible in the boxes below. In some cases you may have to add an article, a pronoun or a preposition.

find	elements
contain	scenery
write	mastery
describe	verse
express	ways
perform	poetry
create	link
demonstrate	feelings

b Use at least four collocations to write a short text about a poem, play or song that you like.

► LP19: Collocations
► LP31: Writing a summary
► LP32: Writing a review

3 Phrasal verbs

A phrasal verb consists of a verb and an adverb or preposition. Fill the gaps with the correct phrasal verbs. Look at the text again for help.

1 While Shakespeare's theatres had little scenery, today's theatres are … up-to-date video and sound projectors.
2 Many of Shakespeare's plays have been … the big screen.
3 Shakespeare is best … his plays and sonnets.
4 The novel, which … a romance between an Englishman and a Lithuanian immigrant, is … a seaside town in England.
5 The reason why Shakespeare is still popular today is because people can still … his ideas and characters.
6 The play, which is … an old legend, has been updated to a modern setting.
7 Bravely, the hero … the oppressor.

4 Word families

a Find the corresponding nouns to these verbs and adjectives. Look at the text for help or use a dictionary.

1 be set in	3 perform sth.	5 popular	7 persuade sb. to do sth.
2 express sth.	4 adapt sth.	6 relevant	8 equip sb./sth. with sth.

b Write a sentence with each of the nouns.

► SF3: Using a dictionary
► LP20: Word formation
Find an online dictionary here:
Webcode context-52

5 Writing

Write an email to a friend telling him or her why you are (not) looking forward to seeing a Shakespeare play with your class. Include as many words and phrases from the text as possible.

Power and love

FACT FILE

William Shakespeare

Ordinary people did not leave behind much documentation in the 16th century, which is why we have few documents that mention Shakespeare. There is a lot of speculation about most of Shakespeare's life. We do know that he was born in Stratford-upon-Avon in 1564 and that he married Anne Hathaway in 1582, with whom he had three children. In 1592 he was working as actor and playwright in London with a company of actors. He also published popular books of poetry. In 1599 he and other members of his company opened The Globe, one of the largest and best theatres in London at that time. He wrote about 38 plays, 154 sonnets and two long poems, which together is often regarded as one of the greatest collections of literature created by one man. He moved back to Stratford shortly before his death in 1616.

William Shakespeare, 'Chandos Portrait'

In Parts A and B there are excerpts from three of Shakespeare's plays. In groups of three, each choose one of the following: Macbeth, Richard III *or* The Taming of the Shrew. *Search the internet for information about your play. Give a *synopsis about it to the others who then formulate two questions about the play. Answer your classmates' questions. Then swap roles.*

A1 Lady Macbeth persuades her husband

In Shakespeare's play Macbeth, *Macbeth has told his wife about prophecies he heard promising him he will become king of Scotland. When the present king, Duncan, honours them with a visit, they plan to murder him so that Macbeth can become his successor. In a *soliloquy immediately before the passage printed below, Macbeth conscience has warned him not to go ahead with the plan. His wife interrupts his thoughts at this point.*

LADY MACBETH He has almost supped: why have you left the chamber?
MACBETH Hath he asked for me?
LADY MACBETH Know you not he has?
MACBETH We will proceed no further in this business:
He hath honoured me of late; and I have bought
Golden opinions from all sorts of people,
Which would be worn now in their newest gloss,
Not cast aside so soon.
LADY MACBETH Was the hope drunk
Wherein you dressed yourself? Hath it slept since?
And wakes it now, to look so green and pale
At what it did so freely? From this time
Such I account thy love. Art thou afeard
To be the same in thine own act and valour
As thou art in desire? Wouldst thou have that
Which thou esteem'st the ornament of life,
And live a coward in thine own esteem,
Letting 'I dare not' wait upon 'I would',
Like the poor cat i' the adage?
MACBETH Prithee, peace:
I dare do all that may become a man;
Who dares do more is none.

1 **supped** finished supper
5 **honoured me of late** showed me respect lately
7 **would be worn** should be enjoyed
8 **cast aside** thrown away
13 **Such I account thy love** I consider your love to be like that
14 **to be the same … as thou art in desire** to be as brave in what you do as in what you are wishing for
16 **esteem'st** *(v)* consider
17 **esteem** *(n)* great respect, admiration
18 **dare** be brave enough to do sth.
wait upon be a servant to
19 **adage** ['ædɪdʒ] proverb, saying; (here) 'A cat likes to eat fish, but doesn't like to get its feet wet.'
20 **Prithee, peace** please be quiet

LADY MACBETH What beast was't, then,
That made you break this enterprise to me?
When you durst do it, then you were a man;
And, to be more than what you were, you would
Be so much more the man. Nor time nor place
Did then adhere, and yet you would make both:
They have made themselves, and that their fitness now
Does unmake you. I have given suck, and know
How tender 'tis to love the babe that milks me:
I would, while it was smiling in my face,
Have plucked my nipple from his boneless gums,
And dashed the brains out, had I so sworn as you
Have done to this.
MACBETH If we should fail?
LADY MACBETH We fail!
But screw your courage to the sticking-place,
And we'll not fail. When Duncan is asleep -
Whereto the rather shall his day's hard journey
Soundly invite him – his two chamberlains
Will I with wine and wassail so convince
That memory, the warder of the brain,
Shall be a fume, and the receipt of reason
A limbeck only: when in swinish sleep
Their drenched natures lie as in a death,
What cannot you and I perform upon
The unguarded Duncan? What not put upon
His spongy officers, who shall bear the guilt
Of our great quell?
MACBETH Bring forth men-children only;
For thy undaunted mettle should compose
Nothing but males.

From: *Macbeth*, Act 1, Scene 7

25 **durst** *(past tense)* dared
27 **Nor time ... adhere** neither the time nor the place were right then
28 **make both** force both to be right
29 **have made themselves** have offered themselves
fitness suitability, being right for sth.
30 **give suck** breastfeed a baby
33 **plucked** pulled away
boneless gums toothless mouth
38 **screw your courage to the sticking-place** get your courage up (image taken from the tuning of a violin: the player tightens each string until it produces the right note and then fixes it)
40 **Whereto ... invite him** to which his long travels will lead him soon
41 **chamberlain** ['tʃeɪmbəlɪn] *Kammerdiener*
42 **wassail** ['wɒseɪl] ale, spiced beer
43 **warder** guard
44 **fume** alcoholic steam
receipt of reason [rɪ'siːt] brain
45 **limbeck** *Destillierkolben*
46 **drenched** drunk
49 **spongy** ['spʌndʒi] like a sponge, soaked with liquid, (here) drunk
bear take, stand
50 **quell** *(n)* killing, murder
52 **undaunted mettle** fearless character

COMPREHENSION

1 Understanding the conflict

a An argument is taking place between Macbeth and Lady Macbeth. Collect keywords that underline the position of each character.

b State what Lady Macbeth is trying to persuade her husband to do.

c Outline what conflicting values and concepts are being addressed. Give proof from the text.

LANGUAGE AWARENESS

2 Analysing ways of addressing

a Study how Macbeth and Lady Macbeth address each other. Read the Fact File on the right and explain what their ways of addressing mean.

b In one part of the dialogue, Lady Macbeth changes the form of address. Identify the change and discuss what may have caused it.

3 Rewriting Shakespeare's questions

Look at how Shakespeare formed questions. Instead of the modern use of the modal verb *do* he used a different form of question. Identify those questions and rewrite them in modern English.

FACT FILE

In **16th-century English** there were two forms of *you*: *thou* (object form: *thee*; possessive form: *thy*, *thine* = your), which was used similarly to German *du*.
The other form was *ye* or *you*. This was used as a term of respect or as the plural form (like the old German use of *Ihr*).

Verbs following *thou* ended in *-st*, e.g. *didst*, *camest*, *hast*. The second-person singular form of *be* was *art*: thou art = you are.

In Shakespeare's time, the third-person singular verb often ended in *-th*, e.g. *doth* (does), *hath* (has), *seemeth* (seems).

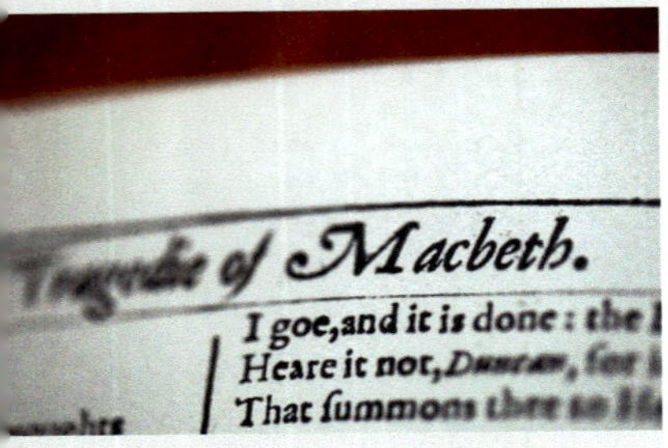

READING **FOCUS ON SKILLS**

Reading for analysis (drama extract)

Look at A1 *again. Now you are going to analyse how the writer has made the content interesting by using the sound of the words, stylistic devices, metaphorical language and forms of characterization.*

1 Reading aloud: The rhythm of the text

a Read the text aloud to get a feeling for its *metre.

b Read the Fact File on the left. Then count the syllables and the metric feet in ll. 1–22 of the extract from *Macbeth*.

c Work with a partner. Read parts of the dialogue out loud again. Pay attention to the speakers completing the blank verse for each other.

► SF 17: Analysing stylistic devices
► SF 20: Analysing drama

2 Understanding *stylistic devices

a Read Lady Macbeth's speeches and identify which form of punctuation appears a lot. Name the stylistic device and explain its purpose here.

b Note down words that are repeated in the text and in which lines they occur. Describe the effect of their repetition.

c Write a statement explaining what both stylistic devices tell you about the argumentation of both Macbeth and Lady Macbeth.

FACT FILE

Blank verse
The type of verse used most often by Shakespeare is called blank verse. It consists of iambic pentameters, which are five iambs. An iamb is an unstressed syllable followed by a stressed syllable, which sounds like 'dah DUM'. Blank verse is considered particularly close to normal English speech rhythm, which was probably what made it so popular in Shakespeare's time.

Note:
Shakespeare's rhythm is varied, lively and never monotonous, because his characters are saying important things. That is why not all lines in the excerpt can be spoken in the 'dah DUM' rhythm.

3 Analysing *images

When reading, you should always try to visualize what the words are telling you and which mental images are created.

a Read ll. 4–6 again. Macbeth speaks about 'buying golden opinions' that he wants to 'wear in their newest gloss': Apparently he sees 'opinions' as new clothes. Explain what that tells you about his character.

b Lady Macbeth responds by using imagery herself. Read ll. 9–12 and explain how she takes up her husband's image and expands it.

c In l. 23 Lady Macbeth mentions a 'beast'. Explain what she is referring to.

4 Understanding *characterization

a Lady Macbeth's passage from ll. 30–35 gives us a good idea of the kind of woman she is. Read the passage out loud. Explain the image she uses and what it tells you about her character.

b Read the extract either aloud or in silence slowly and purposefully. Compare lengths, content and messages of the speakers' passages. Draw conclusions about the characters.

c FREEZE-FRAME Work with a partner. Imagine how the actor and actress would perform the dialogue and create a freeze-frame. Get together with another pair. Present your freeze-frame and let them guess which moment you have chosen.

► SF 35: Writing a character profile

d Write an analysis about the couple Macbeth and Lady Macbeth on the basis of the complete passage. Write at least 150 words.

A2 Richard courts his enemy

In Richard III *Richard, Duke of Gloucester, has killed his enemies King Henry VI and his son Edward Plantagenet. He wants to become king himself, and decides to marry Edward's widow Anne to strengthen his position. In this scene Richard approaches Anne as she accompanies the body of her father-in-law, Henry VI, to his burial place. Read the extract to see how Richard tries to persuade Lady Anne that he is courting her out of love. Try to visualize the scene, imagining how the two characters interact with each other.*

TROUBLE SPOT
court *(n) = Gericht, Hof*
court *(v) = umwerben, den Hof machen*

LADY ANNE Didst thou not kill this king?
GLOUCESTER I grant ye.
LADY ANNE Dost grant me, hedgehog? then, God grant me too
Thou mayst be damned for that wicked deed!
O, he was gentle, mild, and virtuous!
GLOUCESTER The fitter for the King of heaven, that hath him.
LADY ANNE He is in heaven, where thou shalt never come.
GLOUCESTER Let him thank me, that holp to send him thither;
For he was fitter for that place than earth.
LADY ANNE And thou unfit for any place but hell.
GLOUCESTER Yes, one place else, if you will hear me name it.
LADY ANNE Some dungeon.
GLOUCESTER Your bed-chamber.
LADY ANNE Ill rest betide the chamber where thou liest!
GLOUCESTER So will it, madam till I lie with you.
LADY ANNE I hope so.
GLOUCESTER I know so. But, gentle Lady Anne,
To leave this keen encounter of our wits,
And fall somewhat into a slower method,
Is not the causer of the timeless deaths
Of these Plantagenets, Henry and Edward,
As blameful as the executioner?
LADY ANNE Thou art the cause, and most accursed effect.
GLOUCESTER Your beauty was the cause of that effect;
Your beauty: which did haunt me in my sleep
To undertake the death of all the world,
So I might live one hour in your sweet bosom.
LADY ANNE If I thought that, I tell thee, homicide,
These nails should rend that beauty from my cheeks.
GLOUCESTER These eyes could never endure sweet beauty's wreck;
You should not blemish it, if I stood by:
As all the world is cheered by the sun,
So I by that; it is my day, my life.
LADY ANNE Black night o'ershade thy day, and death thy life.
GLOUCESTER Curse not thyself, fair creature; thou art both.
LADY ANNE I would I were, to be revenged on thee.
GLOUCESTER It is a quarrel most unnatural,
To be revenged on him that loveth you.
LADY ANNE It is a quarrel just and reasonable,
To be revenged on him that slew my husband.

2 **grant** admit, allow
6 **the fitter** the better
8 **holp** *(past tense)* helped
thither there
12 **dungeon** ['dʌndʒən] dark underground prison
14 **Ill rest betide the chamber** may there be no peace and quiet to be had in the room
18 **keen encounter of our wits** our fierce argument
20 **timeless** too early
23 **accursed** damned
25 **haunt** follow, chase, stalk
29 **rend** rip, pull
30 **endure** tolerate
31 **blemish** ['blemɪʃ] ruin
40 **slew** *(past tense)* killed

41 **bereft thee of sb.** made you lose sb.
55 **toad** *Kröte*
58 **basilisk** ['bæzɪlɪsk] mythical animal with the power to cause death by looking at a person
62 **shamed … of childish drops** made me feel ashamed as I cried like a child
63 **sued to** [su:d] appealed to, was attractive to
64 **smoothing** ['smu:ðɪŋ] nice, flattering
65 **fee** reward
67 **scorn** ridicule, sarcasm
68 **contempt** hate, disrespect
70 **Lo** Look!
74 **humbly** modest, moderately
77 **nay** no
dispatch go ahead; kill me

GLOUCESTER He that bereft thee, lady, of thy husband,
Did it to help thee to a better husband.
LADY ANNE His better doth not breathe upon the earth.
GLOUCESTER He lives that loves thee better than he could.
LADY ANNE Name him.
GLOUCESTER Plantagenet.
LADY ANNE Why, that was he.
GLOUCESTER The selfsame name, but one of better nature.
LADY ANNE Where is he?
GLOUCESTER Here.

She spitteth at him.

Why dost thou spit at me?
LADY ANNE Would it were mortal poison, for thy sake!
GLOUCESTER Never came poison from so sweet a place.
LADY ANNE Never hung poison on a fouler toad.
Out of my sight! thou dost infect my eyes.
GLOUCESTER Thine eyes, sweet lady, have infected mine.
LADY ANNE Would they were basilisks', to strike thee dead!
GLOUCESTER I would they were, that I might die at once;
For now they kill me with a living death.
Those eyes of thine from mine have drawn salt tears,
Shamed their aspect with store of childish drops: [...]
I never sued to friend nor enemy;
My tongue could never learn sweet smoothing word;
But now thy beauty is proposed my fee,
My proud heart sues, and prompts my tongue to speak.
Teach not thy lips such scorn, for they were made
For kissing, lady, not for such contempt.
If thy revengeful heart cannot forgive,
Lo, here I lend thee this sharp-pointed sword;
Which if thou please to hide in this true bosom.
And let the soul forth that adoreth thee,
I lay it naked to the deadly stroke,
And humbly beg the death upon my knee.
Nay, do not pause; for I did kill King Henry,
But 'twas thy beauty that provoked me.
Nay, now dispatch; 'twas I that stabb'd
young Edward,
But 'twas thy heavenly face that set me on.

Here she lets fall the sword.

Take up the sword again, or take up me.

From: *Richard III*, Act 1, Scene 2

The scene ends with Anne allowing Richard to place his ring on her finger and agreeing to meet him after the burial of Henry VI.

The Tragedy of Richard the Third:
with the Landing of Earle Richmond, and the
Battell at Boſworth Field.

Actus Primus. Scœna Prima.

Enter Richard Duke of Gloſter, ſolus.

Now is the Winter of our Diſcontent,
Made glorious Summer by this Son of Yorke:
And all the clouds that lowr'd vpon our houſe

That waites vpon your Grace?
Cla. His Maieſty tendring my perſons ſafety,
Hath appointed this Conduct, to conuey me to th'Tower
Rich. Vpon what cauſe?
Cla. Becauſe my name is *George.*

The opening of Richard III *in the First Folio of Shakespeare, 1623*

COMPREHENSION

1 Understanding the content

a Outline the gist of the fight between Lady Anne and Gloucester.

b Describe Lady Anne's feelings for her dead husband and for Gloucester.

ANALYSIS

2 A word fight

a Look closely at how one speaker takes up a particular word or concept from the other and changes it according to their own purposes. Make notes.

b Discuss your findings with a partner or in class.

3 Working with imagery

Work with a partner. Identify the *images each speaker uses. Explain them with the help of the annotations and from the context they are used in.

SUPPORT p. 278

4 Persuasive words and actions

a Note down words and phrases that Gloucester uses to change Lady Anne's feelings towards him.

b Examine if her reactions show the desired effect.

c Explain the effect of Gloucester offering Lady Anne his sword to kill him on the spot.

5 Understanding character

On the basis of your analysis, describe the speakers' characters.

SUPPORT p. 278

► SF35: Writing a character profile

LANGUAGE AWARENESS

6 Forms of address

Look at the Fact File on p. 169 again. Analyse the use of *thou* and *you* forms as an indicator of the relationship of the speakers. Interpret their forms of addressing each other.

BEYOND THE TEXT

7 Performing the scene

a Discuss how the characters could be presented on stage.

b In small groups, practise reading the dialogue out loud with appropriate *emphasis and gestures. Then perform your reading in front of the class.

Love: appearance and reality

B1 My future wife

The following extract is taken from William Shakespeare's The Taming of the Shrew. *Petruchio has gone to Padua to find a wealthy wife. On hearing of the shrewish elder daughter of the wealthy Baptista Minola, who so far has driven any potential husband away with her sharp tongue, he decides that she is just the right woman for him. The following extract is from their very first meeting.*

PETRUCHIO Good morrow, Kate; for that's your name, I hear.
KATHARINA Well have you heard, but something hard of hearing:
They call me Katharina that do talk of me.
PETRUCHIO You lie, in faith; for you are called plain Kate,
And bonny Kate and sometimes Kate the curst;
But Kate, the prettiest Kate in Christendom
Kate of Kate Hall, my super-dainty Kate,
For dainties are all Kates, and therefore, Kate,
Take this of me, Kate of my consolation;
Hearing thy mildness praised in every town,
Thy virtues spoke of, and thy beauty sounded,
Yet not so deeply as to thee belongs,
Myself am moved to woo thee for my wife.
KATHARINA Moved! In good time: let him that moved you hither
Remove you hence: I knew you at the first
You were a moveable.
PETRUCHIO Why, what's a moveable?
KATHARINA A joined-stool.
PETRUCHIO Thou hast hit it: come, sit on me.
KATHARINA Asses are made to bear, and so are you.
PETRUCHIO Women are made to bear, and so are you.
KATHARINA No such jade as you, if me you mean.
PETRUCHIO Alas! good Kate, I will not burden thee;
For, knowing thee to be but young and light –
KATHARINA Too light for such a swain as you to catch;
And yet as heavy as my weight should be. [...]
She strikes him.
PETRUCHIO I swear I'll cuff you, if you strike again.
KATHARINA So may you lose your arms:
If you strike me, you are no gentleman;
And if no gentleman, why then no arms. [...]
PETRUCHIO [...] 'Twas told me you were rough and coy and sullen,
And now I find report a very liar;
For thou are pleasant, gamesome, passing courteous,
But slow in speech, yet sweet as spring-time flowers:
Thou canst not frown, thou canst not look askance,
Nor bite the lip, as angry wenches will,
Nor hast thou pleasure to be cross in talk,
But thou with mildness entertain'st thy wooers,
With gentle conference, soft and affable. [...]

shrew *widerspenstige, zänkische Frau*

2 **something hard of hearing** you must be slightly deaf
5 **bonny** beautiful
curst *(participle)* cursed
7 **dainty** sweet
8 **dainties are all Kates** a pun on 'cate', an Elizabethan sweet
9 **consolation** *Trost*
11 **sounded** proclaimed, reported
13 **woo sb.** *jdn. umwerben*
14 **hither** to this place, here
15 **hence** away from here
18 **joined-stool** piece of furniture
20 **ass** donkey
bear *Lasten tragen; gebären*
22 **jade** worthless person
23 **Alas!** [ə'læs] expression of sadness, *Ach!*
25 **swain** lover, wooer (cf. l. 13)
28 **cuff sb.** hit sb.
29 **arms** *Wappen*
32 **coy** shy
sullen unfriendly
34 **gamesome** ['geɪmsəm] playful
passing very, exceedingly
courteous ['kɜːtiəs] polite
36 **frown** [fraʊn] look displeased
askance [ə'skæns] *verächtlich*
37 **wench** girl
40 **conference** conversation
affable ['æfəble] likeable

Thus in plain terms: your father hath consented
That you shall be my wife; your dowry 'greed on;
And, will you, nill you, I will marry you.
Now, Kate, I am a husband for your turn;
For, by this light, whereby I see thy beauty,
Thy beauty, that doth make me like thee well,
Thou must be married to no man but me;
For I am he am born to tame you Kate,
And bring you from a wild Kate to a Kate
Conformable as other household Kates.
Here comes your father: never make denial;
I must and will have Katharina to my wife.

From: *The Taming of the Shrew*, Act 2, Scene 1

42 **dowry** ['daʊri] *Mitgift*
'greed agreed
43 **will you, nill you** if you want or not
44 **for your turn** just right for you
50 **conformable** [kən'fɔːməbl] *angepasst, fügsam*
household Kates wives by the name of Kate
51 **make denial** [dɪ'naɪəl] refuse

COMPREHENSION

1 YOU CHOOSE **Understanding the dialogue**

a Create a cartoon or a comic strip summarizing the scene. Draw 1–2 frames with speech bubbles and captions.

OR

b Write a short modern English version of the dialogue. Practise reading it with a partner, and then present it to the class.

► SF 37: Doing a creative writing task

ANALYSIS

2 Comparing dialogues

Compare the way Petruchio woos Katharina to the way Gloucester woos Anne (**A2**, pp. 171–173). Evaluate what each man reveals about himself and how effectively they each use words to achieve their aims. SUPPORT p. 278

LANGUAGE AWARENESS

3 Playing with words

a Look at ll. 7–31 again. Describe the changes in meaning, grammar or form that occur to certain words.

b Translate those words into German. Explain why in some cases the wordplay does not work and why in others it works the same as in English.

c Think of three more words that have at least two meanings (= homonyms). Write six appropriate sentences.

BEYOND THE TEXT

4 Modernizing the play

a Imagine the scene is going to be adapted for a modern film version. With a partner, discuss a suitable setting and which actors should take the leading roles. Consider in particular which elements from the original scene should be kept and which removed. Share your ideas in class.

► SF 37: Doing a creative writing task

b CHALLENGE Create a storyboard for the scene you are planning.

VIEWING **FOCUS ON SKILLS**

Evaluating a modern Shakespeare adaptation

Kate in a Lift

The film sequence you are about to watch is from a BBC series in which Shakespeare plays were modernized. It represents the same scene from The Taming of the Shrew *that you have studied in* **B1**.

1 Before viewing
Before watching the film excerpt, speculate which aspects might have been modernized. Look at your notes from **B1**, task **3** again.

2 Viewing without sound
You will watch the film extract without sound. Split the class in two groups, with one half doing task **a** and the other doing task **b**.

- **a** Concentrate on the places shown in the scene. While viewing, make notes on them and the atmosphere they create. Explain why the director may have chosen them.
- **b** Examine the body language and facial expressions of the two main characters. While viewing, make notes about what they tell you about their characters.
- **c** Share your findings first with a partner, then report them to the class.

3 Viewing with sound

- **a** Watch the film with sound. With your partner from task **2**, discuss if you get new information from the dialogue. List elements of the dialogue that surprised you.
- **b** View the extract again and concentrate on the music. Describe how it is used, and to what effect.

4 Viewing for the final time
Before viewing the extract for the final time, look at ▸ SF 23 Analysing a film on p. 346. Then, in groups of four, examine the camera work. Two of you concentrate on the part in front of the flat, the other two on the part in the lift. Explain how the camera work affects you as a viewer. Share your findings in your group, then in class.

5 Evaluation
Evaluate how successful the director has been in adapting the material. Name the elements that were changed and the effect the scene has on you.
SUPPORT ▸ p. 279

DVD

quid *(BE sl)* British pound
clap eyes on sb. see sb. for the first time
trout *(infml)* unpleasant woman
chord *Akkord*
take the mick (out of sb.) *(BE infml)* make fun of sb.
certifiable lunatic [ˌsɜːtɪˈfaɪəbl ˈluːnətɪk] crazy person
bugger sth. up *(sl)* ruin sth.
put your cards on the table say what you really want
alluring *(adj)* attractive
arousing *(adj)* sexy
snarl make an angry noise when talking
lewd [luːd] sexually vulgar
obnoxious very annoying
plucky having courage and spirit

▸ SF 23: Analysing a film

'Modernizing Shakespeare'

B2 Responding to a sonnet

APPOINTMENT TASK

- Make an appointment card with the names of three partners.
- With your partners, discuss the statements on the right and make notes on your appointment card.
- Discuss your conclusions in class.

1 *Love for someone does not change, even if the person you love changes.*
2 *Love can be between anyone, no matter what age, gender, race or religion.*
3 *Love is not a physical but a spiritual experience.*

Now read the sonnets. Concentrate on the different images the words create in your mind.

Sonnet 116 *William Shakespeare*

Let me not to the marriage of true minds
Admit impediments. Love is not love
Which alters when it alteration finds,
Or bends with the remover to remove:
O no! It is an ever-fixèd mark
That looks on tempests and is never shaken;
It is the star to every wandering bark,
Whose worth's unknown, although his height be taken.
Love's not Time's fool, though rosy lips and cheeks
Within his bending sickle's compass come:
Love alters not with his brief hours and weeks,
But bears it out even to the edge of doom.
If this be error and upon me proved,
I never writ, nor no man ever loved.

1 **Let me not** May I never
2 **admit** accept
impediment [ɪm'pedɪmənt] *Hindernis*
3 **alter** ['ɔːltə] change
4 **remover** person who goes away
5 **mark** landmark or star that helps a sailor to navigate
6 **tempest** storm
7 **wander** ['wɒndə] travel
bark ship
10 **bending** curved
sickle *Sichel*
compass ['kʌmpəs] *Reichweite*
12 **bear sth. out** endure sth.
edge of doom end of time
13 **upon** against
14 **writ** (have) written

In 1971, Northern Irish poet James Simmons (1933–2001) wrote a series of 'Marital Sonnets'. No. 4 reads like a modern response to Shakespeare's Sonnet 116.

Marital Sonnet 4 *James Simmons*

We murmured passionate language in that trance
when each was famished for the mutual kiss;
but we have altered, and it spoils all chance
of happiness, comparing that with this.
Displays of fireworks were put on by lust,
romantic symphonies, unholy wars:
now contraceptives, unworn, gather dust,
in which we once soared gleaming towards the stars.
In age's Leamington our joys last longer,
the libraries are good, the tea-rooms neat,
good arguments aren't broken off by anger,
new appetites are fed, we are replete.
Let's call this love, that alters when it finds
alteration, the marriage of two minds.

From: *Poems 1956–1986*, 1986

2 **famished** ['fæmɪʃd] very hungry
mutual *gegenseitig*
7 **contraceptive** *Verhütungsmittel*
8 **soar** rise high
gleam *(v)* shine
9 **Leamington** ['lemɪŋtən] a spa town in Warwickshire, England
12 **replete** [rɪ'pliːt] very full

COMPREHENSION

1 Brief summaries
Summarize each poem's message in one sentence.

ANALYSIS

► SF 21: Analysing poetry

Find a tool to make your poster here: **Webcode** context-50

2 GALLERY WALK **Comparing the sonnets**
Compare the two sonnets. Examine structure, development of the idea and style. Present your findings on posters and evaluate the posters in a gallery walk. SUPPORT ► p. 279

BEYOND THE TEXT

► SF 29: Writing a formal letter or email
► SF 34: Argumentative writing
► SF 37: Doing a creative writing task
► SF 38: Writing a well-structured text

3 Creative writing
Write a response to one of the concepts of love you have come across in Part B. Refer to your notes from the pre-reading discussion or to your posters. Your text can take the form of an email or a letter to a friend, or even a short poem.

CULTURE SPOT

Shakespeare for the masses

1. Explain the wordplay on the T-shirt. Consider what wearing this T-shirt would mean to you.
2. What do objects like this tell you about Shakespeare's place in British culture?
3. Design a Shakespeare object. Choose a picture, pun, quote or slogan and present your idea to the class.

► SF 24: Giving a presentation

Gender: still an issue?

C1 All men are created equal – what about women?

In 1848, at a meeting of supporters of women's rights at Seneca Falls, New York, a 'Declaration of Sentiments' was signed, which helped to launch the US campaign for women's right to vote. Here is an excerpt.

When, in the course of human events, it becomes necessary for one portion of the family of man to assume among the people of the earth a position different from that which they have hitherto occupied, but one to which the laws of nature and of nature's God entitle them, a decent respect to the opinions of mankind requires that they should declare the causes that impel them to such a course.

We hold these truths to be self-evident: that all men and women are created equal; that they are endowed by their Creator with certain inalienable rights; that among these are life, liberty, and the pursuit of happiness; that to secure these rights governments are instituted, deriving their just powers from the consent of the governed. […]

The history of mankind is a history of repeated injuries and usurpations on the part of man toward woman, having in direct object the establishment of an absolute tyranny over her. To prove this, let facts be submitted to a candid world.

He has never permitted her to exercise her inalienable right to the elective franchise.

He has compelled her to submit to laws, in the formation of which she had no voice.

He has withheld from her rights which are given to the most ignorant and degraded men – both natives and foreigners.

Having deprived her of this first right of a citizen, the elective franchise, thereby leaving her without representation in the halls of legislation, he has oppressed her on all sides.

He has made her, if married, in the eye of the law, civilly dead.

He has taken from her all right in property, even to the wages she earns. […]

He has so framed the laws of divorce, as to what shall be the proper causes, and in case of separation, to whom the guardianship of the children shall be given, as to be wholly regardless of the happiness of women – the law, in all cases, going upon a false supposition of the supremacy of man, and giving all power into his hands.

After depriving her of all rights as a married woman, if single, and the owner of property, he has taxed her to support a government which recognizes her only when her property can be made profitable to it.

He has monopolized nearly all the profitable employments, and from those she is permitted to follow, she receives but a scanty remuneration. He closes against her all the avenues to wealth and distinction which he considers most honorable to himself. As a teacher of theology, medicine, or law, she is not known.

FACT FILE

Women's suffrage
Both in the UK and in the USA, the 19th century saw growing movements for women's suffrage.

In the **UK**, the right to vote was given in 1918 to women over 30. In 1928, the voting age was lowered to 21.

In the **USA**, the Nineteenth Amendment to the Constitution became the law in 1920. It states that 'The right of citizens of the United States to vote shall not be denied or abridged by the United States or by any State on account of sex.'

Elizabeth Cady Stanton addressing the first women's rights meeting at Seneca Falls, New York, on 20 June 1848

1 **portion** part
3 **hitherto** *(fml)* until now
7 **endow sb. with sth.** [ɪn'daʊ] *jdn. mit etwas ausstatten*
inalienable [ɪn'eɪliənəbl] *(fml)* that cannot be taken away
14 **usurpation** *(fml) widerrechtliche Besitzergreifung*
18 **candid** *(here)* honest, unbiased
22 **elective franchise** *Wahlrecht*
23 **compel sb. to do sth.** ['– –] *(fml)* force sb. to do sth.
25 **withhold sth. from sb.** *(fml) jdm. etwas vorenthalten*
35 **supposition** *(fml)* idea, assumption
supremacy [suː'preməsi] *(fml) Vormachtstellung*
40 **scanty** *karg*
remuneration *(fml)* payment

He has denied her the facilities for obtaining a thorough education, all colleges being closed against her. [...]

He has created a false public sentiment by giving to the world a different code of morals for men and women, by which moral delinquencies which exclude women from society, are not only tolerated, but deemed of little account in man.

He has usurped the prerogative of Jehovah himself, claiming it as his right to assign for her a sphere of action, when that belongs to her conscience and to her God.

He has endeavored, in every way that he could, to destroy her confidence in her own powers, to lessen her self-respect, and to make her willing to lead a dependent and abject life.

Now, in view of this entire disfranchisement of one-half the people of this country, their social and religious degradation – in view of the unjust laws above mentioned, and because women do feel themselves aggrieved, oppressed, and fraudulently deprived of their most sacred rights, we insist that they have immediate admission to all the rights and privileges which belong to them as citizens of the United States.

From: E.C. Stanton, S.B. Anthony, M.J. Gage, eds., *History of Women's Suffrage*, 1 (1887)

47 **delinquency** *(fml) Vergehen*
49 **usurp sth.** *sich etwas widerrechtlich aneignen*
prerogative [prɪˈrɒgətɪv] special right
Jehova *(in the Old Testament)* God
51 **endeavor to do sth.** *(AE)* = *(BE)* **endeavour to do sth.** [ɪnˈdevə] attempt to do sth.
56 **aggrieve sb.** *(usu. adj: aggrieved)* treat sb. unfairly
fraudulent [ˈfrɔːdjələnt] *betrügerisch*

COMPREHENSION

1 The central idea

a Describe the relationship between men and women in US society in 1848 as depicted in this excerpt.

b In your own words, outline the central idea of the text.

ANALYSIS

2 Structure and language

a Identify the four parts the text is divided into. (Careful: They are not necessarily indicated by '[...]'!) Analyse the function of each part.
SUPPORT p. 279

b Explain the terms 'laws of nature' (l. 3), 'created equal' (l. 6), 'inalienable rights' (l. 7) and 'sacred rights' (l. 57).

c Examine the style and language used by the writers to appeal to their audience.

BEYOND THE TEXT

3 Reactions

a Using your findings from task **2**, try to assess how different groups of people (men, women, supporters and opponents of women's right to vote) may have reacted to this declaration.

b CHALLENGE Write a mid-19th century newspaper editorial responding to the Seneca Falls Declaration of Sentiments, either rejecting it or applauding it.

4 Comparing two documents

The Declaration of Sentiments is modelled on the Declaration of Independence (1776). Compare the two documents.

► Excerpts from the Declaration of Independence, p. 415

Find the full text of the Declaration of Independence here:
Webcode context-67

C2 Marco and Kitty argue *Paul Auster*

Set in the late 1960s, the novel Moon Palace *tells the story of Marco Stanley Fogg. Marco, who is also the narrator, is in a relationship with Kitty Wu – a relationship which is put to the test when Kitty becomes pregnant.*

Kitty discovered that she was pregnant in late March, and by the beginning of June I had lost her. Our whole life flew apart in a matter of weeks, and when I finally understood that the damage was beyond repair, I felt as if my heart had been cut out of me. Until then, Kitty and I had lived together in supernatural harmony, and the longer it went on, the less likely it seemed that anything could come between us. [...]

Paul Auster

It was never a question of not loving each other. Even when our battles were at their most intense and tearful, we never recanted, never denied the facts, never pretended that our feelings had changed. It was just that we no longer spoke the same language. As far as Kitty was concerned, love meant the two of us, and that was all. A child had no part in it, and therefore whatever decision we made should depend exclusively on what we wanted for ourselves. Even though Kitty was the one who was pregnant, the baby was no more than an abstraction for her, a hypothetical instance of future life rather than a life that had already come into being. Until it was born, it did not exist. From my point of view, however, the baby had begun to exist the moment Kitty told me she was carrying it inside her. Even if it was no larger than a thumb, it was a person, an inescapable reality. If we went ahead and arranged for an abortion, I felt it would be the same thing as committing murder.

All the reasons were on Kitty's side. I knew that, and yet it hardly seemed to make a difference. I shut myself up in a stubborn irrationality, more and more shocked by my own vehemence, but powerless to do anything about it. She was too young to be a mother, Kitty would say, and while I recognized this as a legitimate statement, I was never willing to concede the point. Our own mothers were no older than you are now, I would answer, obstinately yoking together two situations that had nothing to do with each other, and then we would suddenly be at the crux of the problem. That was fine for our mothers, Kitty would say, but how could she go on dancing if she had a baby to take care of? To which I would answer, smugly pretending that I knew what I was talking about, that I would take care of the baby. Impossible, she would say, you can't deprive an infant of its mother. There's a tremendous responsibility in having a child, and it has to be taken seriously. One day, she said, she very much wanted us to have children, but it wasn't the right moment, she just wasn't ready for it yet. But the moment has come, I would say. Like it or not, we've already made a baby, and now we have to deal with things as they are. At which point, exasperated by my thickheaded arguments, Kitty would inevitably start to cry. [...]

Time was against us. We had only a few weeks in which to make a decision, and each day the pressure grew worse. No other subject existed for us, and we talked about it constantly, arguing back and forth into the middle of the night, watching our happiness dissolve in an ocean of words, in exhausted accusations of betrayal. For all the time we spent at it, neither one of us budged from our original position. [...] When I finally saw that it was hopeless, I told her to go ahead and do what she had to do. [...]

I was nearly broke again, and when I sat by Kitty's bed in the hospital and saw the drained and agonized look on her face, I could not help feeling that everything was

9 **recant (sth.)** *(etwas) öffentlich widerrufen*
21 **abortion** *Abtreibung*
26 **concede sth.** admit that sth. is true
27 **obstinate** ['ɒbstɪnət] stubborn
28 **crux** *(Latin)* most important or difficult part
30 **smug** *selbstgefällig*
36 **exasperated** *(adj)* very annoyed
41 **dissolve** [dɪ'zɒlv] *sich auflösen*
42 **budge** *(v)* move
45 **drained** *(adj)* exhausted
agonized *(adj)* suffering, expressing pain

gone, that my whole life had been taken away from me. [...] We had both managed to convince ourselves that we could forget what had happened, but once we tried to return to our old life, we discovered that it was no longer there. [...]

I told her that I needed to go away for a while to sort things out, but that was only because I did not have the courage to tell her the truth. Kitty understood, however. [...] Then I walked out the door. I was already sobbing by the time I made it down to the street.

From: *Moon Palace*, 1989

COMPREHENSION

1 Marco's and Kitty's arguments
Outline Marco's and Kitty's arguments for and against having a baby.

ANALYSIS

2 Marco
- **a** Examine how the narrator describes his relationship with Kitty.
- **b** Explain to what extent Marco's description of their relationship helps to characterize him.
- **c** Write a character profile of Marco.

► SF 35: Writing a character profile

3 Kitty
Point out what the truth is that Kitty understands in the end (cf. l. 50).

BEYOND THE TEXT

4 YOU CHOOSE **Coping with the conflict**

- **a** Comment on the dilemma Marco and Kitty are in and comment on their ways of dealing with it. Do you think they could have resolved their conflict?

OR

- **b** Imagine that Marco and Kitty meet a year after the break-up. Together with a partner, act out a dialogue between them.

5 Gender issues
Write an essay discussing whether restrictive gender roles are still an issue in relationships.

'I can't wait to see the reviews in the newspaper to find out whether I like the movie or not.'

Writing a review

Reviews are written by critics to inform other people about the positive and negative aspects of a particular book, film, etc. But increasingly ordinary people write reviews on the internet not just about films and books, but also about general products.

For the task at hand, you are going to be the critic of a weekly magazine for young adults. You have been asked to hunt for some 'good stuff' in literature or film and write a review explaining to readers of your own age group why you like the material you have chosen.

When you have finished the task, your teacher will give you an assessment sheet.

1 Get hold of one of your literary favourites. This can be a novel, a short story, a play (that you have either read or watched on stage), a poem or a collection of poems, a song or a film. Take a fresh look at your chosen material and read/view it for analysis.

▸ SF 19: Analysing narrative prose
▸ SF 20: Analysing drama
▸ SF 21: Analysing poetry
▸ SF 23: Analysing a film
▸ Focus on Skills: Reading for analysis (drama extract), p. 170
▸ SF 8: Structuring ideas
▸ SF 32: Writing a review

2 Make an outline for your review and structure your material.

3 Write a catchy beginning for your review.

4 State what the text/film is about and what happens. Don't reveal anything that might ruin the pleasure for someone else (e.g. the ending).

5 Write the main body, which includes the reasons why you have chosen this particular book or film. Include quotes from the text/film that reveal the power of its language.

6 Write a suitable ending in which you recommend your item.

7 a GALLERY WALK When you are satisfied with your review, type a neat copy and present it in a gallery walk.
  b Move around and read all the reviews. Your teacher will give you an assessment sheet. Take a vote on which three should be printed.

▸ SF 40: Proofreading

9 Work and Business – Careers and Perspectives

A

A

B

Download a list of chapter vocab here: **Webcode** context-25

► SF 11: Analysing pictures
► SF 13: Analysing cartoons

1 Talking about pictures

a Choose one of the pictures A–E. Think about the situation it shows and prepare to talk about your response to it. Find other students who have picked the same picture and exchange your thoughts. Select one spokes-person for your group to report back to your class.

b Work with a partner and choose another picture. Think of a question raised by this picture and write it on the board or on a strip of paper that you attach to the board. Take a class vote about the two most interesting questions and start discussing them.

C

D

'I love your business model!'

'I really enjoyed my job. Management found out about it and fired me.'

E

Career decisions: priorities and consequences

FACT FILE

Venn diagrams – named after John Venn (1834–1923), a British logician, philosopher and mathematician – use overlapping circles to illustrate all possible logical relations between a number of sets.

2 Talking about charts and diagrams

With a partner, explain the Venn diagram above with regard to business and entrepreneurs. Try and find an example of a person and a business idea that fits the field in the centre.

► SF 12: Analysing charts and graphs

PREVIEW

In this chapter you will learn about today's challenges and prospects of entering the world of work and business.

Main topics

Focus on Skills: SPEAKING and WRITING

CD3 02

Listen to an audio version of the text on the CD or download it here:

Webcode context-26

The world of work and business

The right to a job – the right job

World economy has two faces. Many countries are recovering from a difficult period of recession. In many countries, average wages have risen so that many people have been lifted out of poverty. Despite minimum wage and unconditional basic income being under discussion, there is a global rise in income inequality – the rich are getting richer, and the poor are getting poorer. The fact that budget cuts have claimed many jobs makes the situation even more tense: people collecting unemployment benefits often have to face tough odds.

Stepping into the world of work

Building a career is not always easy nowadays. In some university courses competition among students is unusually high – for some the job hunt is already on. And once people get into their dream job, more often than not they are expected to move around the world and to adapt to new situations quickly. Furthermore, it is not unusual to change jobs often.

To get your career on track, it is therefore essential to access career advice and gain work experience. Career advisers can do you a huge service, e.g. by telling you which applicants are really needed out there because they are in short supply. Too often there is a massive mismatch between young people's career expectations and the realities of the market. In a paid or unpaid internship you can catch up on missing experience: schools do not, for example, tell you how to deal with difficult customers – this is what you learn best in an internship. Once you know that you have a head for, say, numbers, or that you have a passion for languages, you can narrow down your job sector or employment area.

Applying for a job

Research the companies that have caught your interest and start your application. For example, report on your ability to solve problems and showcase your skills in a professional letter of motivation.

Job interviews

Even though face-to-face interviews are still most popular, you might also be invited for a telephone interview or to an assessment centre. As applicants come from a wide range of backgrounds, it is important that you leave a positive impression on the interviewer. Successful candidates convince employers not only with their interview responses but with professional body language and demeanour too. Don't spoil your chances by asking about the salary package right away!

► SF 2: Learning new words

1 Words and phrases
Complete these phrases (1–6) with the help of the highlighted words from the text and match them with the correct German equivalent (a–f).

1 income …	a Durchschnittsgehalt
2 … package	b Etatkürzungen
3 job…	c Berufsberatung
4 … advice	d Arbeitserfahrung
5 … cuts	e Gesamtgehalt
6 average …	f Einkommensgefälle

2 Prepositions
Test yourself: do you know the right prepositions?

► LP 19: Collocations

- recover … recession
- be lifted … poverty
- a rise … inequality
- be … short supply
- deal … customers
- report … your skills
- a mismatch … expectations and reality

3 Opposites
Find the opposites of these words and expressions:

- have no particular talent for sth.
- employee
- do sb. a disservice
- hide sb./sth.

4 Collocations
Which words usually go together? From the three words offered, choose the correct one.

► LP 19: Collocations

- make/build/form a career
- gain/make/find work experience
- from a big/great/wide range of backgrounds
- the elected/successful/winning candidate

5 The situation in Germany
Using the text as background information, describe the situation for (young) job hunters in Germany. You may draw on the experiences of people you know.

6 Showcase your skills
Think about a talent that you have, or that you have always dreamed of possessing. Talk to your partner about how you can use this talent to start a unique career.

'I see under "special talents" that you always land on your feet. Tell me about that.'

DVD

The right to a job – the right job

A1 The second Bill of Rights *Franklin D. Roosevelt*

In his State of the Union address of 11 January, 1944, US President Franklin D. Roosevelt suggested that an 'economic bill of rights' be adopted to complement the political rights guaranteed by the US Constitution and the Bill of Rights of 1791.

We have come to a clear realization of the fact that true individual freedom cannot exist without economic security and independence. 'Necessitous men are not free men.' People who are hungry and out of a job are the stuff of which dictatorships are made.

In our day these economic truths have become accepted as self-evident. We have accepted, so to speak, a second Bill of Rights under which a new basis of security and prosperity can be established for all – regardless of station, race, or creed.
Among these are:

- The right to a useful and remunerative job in the industries or shops or farms or mines of the nation;
- The right to earn enough to provide adequate food and clothing and recreation;
- The right of every farmer to raise and sell his products at a return which will give him and his family a decent living;
- The right of every businessman, large and small, to trade in an atmosphere of freedom from unfair competition and domination by monopolies at home or abroad;
- The right of every family to a decent home;
- The right to adequate medical care and the opportunity to achieve and enjoy good health;
- The right to adequate protection from the economic fears of old age, sickness, accident, and unemployment;
- The right to a good education.

All of these rights spell security. And after this war is won we must be prepared to move forward, in the implementation of these rights, to new goals of human happiness and well-being.

America's own rightful place in the world depends in large part upon how fully these and similar rights have been carried into practice for all our citizens.

For unless there is security here at home there cannot be lasting peace in the world.

From: the website of the Franklin D. Roosevelt Presidential Library and Museum

FACT FILE

The **State of the Union address** is an annual *speech by the US president delivered to the US Congress in January in which she or he describes the condition of the nation and outlines the administrative policies.

▸ Historical documents: The Bill of Rights (1791), p. 345

2 **necessitous** *(fml)* [nəˈsesɪtəs] poor, needy
5 **self-evident** [ˈevɪdənt] obvious, needing no proof or further explanation
7 **prosperity** success, material or financial well-being
station *(fml)* social position
9 **remunerative** *(fml)* [rɪˈmjuːnərətɪv] well-paid
11 **recreation** [ˌrekriːˈeɪʃn] *Freizeit, Erholung*
13 **decent** [ˈdiːsnt] of a sufficient standard or quality

FACT FILE

F. D. Roosevelt giving his State of the Union address on 11 January 1944

Franklin D. Roosevelt [ˈrəʊzəvelt] (1882–1945), commonly known by his initials FDR, was the 32nd President of the United States (1933–1945). Not to be confused with Theodore Roosevelt (1858–1919), US President of the United States 1901–1908, FDR led the US during times of worldwide economic depression and during World War II. He was a strong supporter of social welfare programmes and work projects, by which the US government created many jobs.

26 **implementation** realization of sth. that has been officially decided
28 **rightful** correct, appropriate, legal

COMPREHENSION

1 Looking at the text

a In your own words, give a brief description of each of the eight rights that Roosevelt wants guaranteed.

b Outline what Roosevelt means by 'People who are hungry and out of a job are the stuff of which dictatorships are made' (ll. 3–4).

LANGUAGE AWARENESS

2 Finding the 'right' constructions

a Collect all the expressions from the text which contain the word 'right' followed by a preposition. Write them down in a table like this:

the right of … to + *verb*	**the right to + *noun (phrase)***
the right of every farmer to raise …	the right to a useful and remunerative job …

b Find a simple rule explaining how you can use the prepositions *of* and *to* in connection with the noun *right*.

► SF 4: Using a grammar book
► LP 19: Collocations

ANALYSIS

3 Examining the text

a Analyse how Roosevelt attempts to convince his audience of his idea of economic fairness. Take the language and the line of argument into account.

b Explain why the realization of the rights listed is essential for Roosevelt.

► SF 17: Analysing stylistic devices
► SF 25: Giving a speech

BEYOND THE TEXT

4 Reacting to the text

Choose the three rights which you consider most important and explain your choice to your partner. After listening to your partner's reasons, work together to decide which in your opinion are the three most important rights.

Find a tool to improve your speaking skills here:
Webcode context-51

5 YOU CHOOSE **Commenting or giving a speech**

'Necessitous men are not free men.' (ll. 2–3)

a Prepare a three-minute speech on the basis of this quote.

OR

b Write a *comment of 200–300 words.

► SF 25: Giving a speech
► SF 34: Argumentative writing
► LP 14: Linking words and phrases

A2 Moving on after recession *Barack Obama*

This is an excerpt from President Barack Obama's State of the Union address, delivered on 28 January, 2014. Obama presents a country that is still struggling but gradually recovering from a difficult period of recession.

Over more than three decades, even before the Great Recession hit, massive shifts in technology and global competition had eliminated a lot of good, middle-class jobs, and weakened the economic foundations that families depend on.

Today, after four years of economic growth, corporate profits and stock prices have rarely been higher, and those at the top have never done better. But average wages have barely budged. Inequality has deepened. Upward mobility has stalled. The cold, hard fact is that even in the midst of recovery, too many Americans are working more than ever just to get by – let alone get ahead. And too many still aren't working at all. [...]

I'm also convinced we can help Americans return to the workforce faster by reforming unemployment insurance so that it's more effective in today's economy. But first, this Congress needs to restore the unemployment insurance you just let expire for 1.6 million people.

Let me tell you why.

Misty DeMars is a mother of two young boys. She'd been steadily employed since she was a teenager. She put herself through college. She'd never collected unemployment benefits, but she'd been paying taxes. In May, she and her husband used their

Job seekers wait to attend a job fair.

4 **corporate** ['kɔ:pərət] of or belonging to a large business company
stock prices *Aktienpreise*
6 **budge** *(v)* move
stall *(v)* stop suddenly

18 **claim sth.** (here) cause the loss of sth.
29 **shake sth. up** change sth., e.g. an organization, to make it more efficient
30 **incentive** [ɪn'sentɪv] *Anreiz*
31 **price sb. out of sth.** prevent sb. from having sth. by making it expensive
32 **cap sth.** *eine Obergrenze für etwas festlegen*
34 **reach out to sb.** show sb. that you are interested in them
35 **corporation** large company or group of companies
38 **Ronald Reagan** ['reɪgən] (1911–2004) US President 1981–1989
39 **Tom Harkin** (born 1939) US Senator (Demokrat, Iowa) 1985–2015
George Miller (born 1945) US Representative (Democrat, California) 1975–2015

Graduation ceremony

life savings to buy their first home. A week later, budget cuts claimed the job she loved. Last month, when their unemployment insurance was cut off, she sat down and wrote me a letter – the kind I get every day. 'We are the face of the unemployment crisis,' she wrote. 'I am not dependent on the government ... Our country depends on people like us who build careers, contribute to society ... care about our neighbors ... I am confident that in time I will find a job ... I will pay my taxes, and we will raise our children in their own home in the community we love. Please give us this chance.' [...]

Of course, it's not enough to train today's workforce. We also have to prepare tomorrow's workforce, by guaranteeing every child access to a world-class education. [...] We're working to redesign high schools and partner them with colleges and employers that offer the real-world education and hands-on training that can lead directly to a job and career. We're shaking up our system of higher education to give parents more information, and colleges more incentives to offer better value, so that no middle-class kid is priced out of a college education. We're offering millions the opportunity to cap their monthly student loan payments to ten percent of their income, and I want to work with Congress to see how we can help even more Americans who feel trapped by student loan debt. And I'm reaching out to some of America's leading foundations and corporations on a new initiative to help more young men of color facing tough odds stay on track and reach their full potential. [...]

Of course, to reach millions more, Congress needs to get on board. Today, the federal minimum wage is worth about twenty percent less than it was when Ronald Reagan first stood here. Tom Harkin and George Miller have a bill to fix that by lifting the minimum wage to $10.10. This will help families. It will give businesses customers with more money to spend. It does not involve any new bureaucratic program. So join the rest of the country. Say yes. Give America a raise.

From: the website of the White House, 28 January 2014

COMPREHENSION

1 Close reading

▸ SF 10: Working with closed test formats

Decide whether the following statements about this text are true, false or whether the information is not given. Give line numbers to support your answer and correct the statement where necessary.

1 The elimination of good jobs began with the Great Recession.
2 On average, wages have fallen despite economic growth.
3 If the current system of unemployment insurance is changed, it will speed up many Americans getting back to work.
4 There is not enough training for today's workforce.
5 School buildings will be redesigned.
6 Misty DeMars and her husband had to sell their home.
7 People who are out of work do not have to pay taxes.
8 Since Ronald Reagan's presidency, wages have fallen by 20%.

ANALYSIS

2 Comparing two State of the Union addresses

Make a list of the issues that Obama wants to tackle. Compare it with the problems mentioned by Roosevelt (cf. A1). Explain similarities and differences in the promises made by the two presidents.

3 Political speeches: convincing the audience

▸ SF 17: Analysing stylistic devices

Look at Obama's style and language and show how he tries to convince his audience of the steps that to his mind need to be taken to come out of recession. SUPPORT ▸ p. 280

BEYOND THE TEXT

4 Reacting to the text

Imagine Misty DeMars is invited to the local TV station for an interview. Choose a partner. One of you is Misty, the other a reporter.

- **a** Before getting together, work on your own:
  Misty prepares herself for the kind of questions she might be asked.
  The reporter thinks of questions the local audience might be interested in.
- **b** With your partner, conduct a trial interview, then decide which questions should be kept.
- **c** Together, practise your interview. Prepare to present it in class.

► SF26: Taking part in an interview

A3 Income inequality and guaranteed income

Felix Oberholzer-Gee

The idea of an unconditional basic income has many supporters in western Europe, but also among US Americans. Felix Oberholzer-Gee, professor at Harvard Business School, seeks an explanation for this.

In Western Europe, there is a lively debate about proposals to guarantee every citizen a basic income. The idea, which has a long history dating back to the 1920s (at least), is increasingly popular in policy circles and the broader population. The German and Spanish parliaments explored it. The Swiss will soon vote on an initiative that would guarantee everyone $2,800 each month — no questions asked, irrespective of whether a person works. Early polls indicate that more than 45 percent of Swiss voters will support the initiative.

The supporters of a guaranteed income are a varied lot. They range from unreconstructed communists to humanists with a strong sense of dignity and the wealthy. One concern that many of them share, however, is the global rise in income inequality. In the past few decades, economic growth lifted hundreds of millions out of poverty. But, at the same time, the distribution of income became increasingly skewed in favor of wealthy individuals.

The current situation is exceptional from a historical point of view. For example, the top 10 percent of earners in the U.S. captured 35 percent of income through the 1950s and 1960s. Today, this share stands at 50 percent. Rising inequality reflects gains at the top in all sources of income: salaries and business income, as well as capital income and capital gains.

There are many reasons why income inequality has risen. One is technology, which tends to benefit the well-educated. Machines increasingly take over routine tasks, leaving low-paid service jobs for unskilled workers. As a result, U.S. employment and wages tend to grow at the very bottom and at the very top of the distribution in skills. The middle is hollowed out.

Import competition from poorer countries is a second reason. Chinese imports, for example, explain about one quarter of the decline in U.S. manufacturing from 1990 to 2007.

Third, globalization produces so-called superstar effects. In a flat world, top talent is handsomely rewarded for its broad appeal. The Brazilian soccer player Pelé, the best ever, earned $1.1 million in 1960 (adjusted for inflation). The Portuguese forward Cristiano Ronaldo made $17 million this past year. Pelé played for 350,000 television sets in Brazil. At the [2010] World Cup, 700 million people watched Ronaldo, as Eduardo Porter writes in *The Price of Everything.*

From: *PBS Newshour*, 7 April 2014

Protesting against income inequality

FACT FILE

In his bestselling book *The World Is Flat: A Brief History of the Twenty-First Century* (2005), Thomas L. Friedman analyses the globalization of markets and the resulting challenges and opportunities both for societies and for individuals. The term **flat world** has become a widely-used catchphrase.

5 **irrespective of sth.** regardless of sth.
9 **unreconstructed** *(adj) (derog) hartnäckig, unverbesserlich*
dignity ['dɪgnəti] sense of your own importance
13 **skewed** *(adj)* not accurate or correct, distorted
23 **hollow sth. out** *(fig)* diminish sth.
27 **flat world** cf. Fact File above

Part A

COMPREHENSION

1 Looking at the text

a Outline the concept of an unconditional basic income.

b Point out what information is given in the text in connection with these countries: Brazil, China, Germany, Portugal, Spain, Switzerland, the USA.

c Using keywords, sum up the three reasons given for the United States' current problem of income inequality.

ANALYSIS

► SF 18: Analysing non-fiction

2 Money and motivation

Analyse how the *article presents the idea of an unconditional basic income. Pay special attention to the writer's line of argumentation and *stylistic devices and use the information in the Venn diagram on p. 185 as a backdrop to your analysis.

BEYOND THE TEXT

► SF 24: Giving a presentation
► SF 41: Mediation of written and oral texts

3 Mediation (English → German)

The topic of income inequality comes up in your Social Studies class. You offer to give a talk in German about the situation in the USA and its causes as presented in this article. Sum it up for a presentation of about three minutes. Make notes and practise the talk.

4 An unconditional basic income for all?

Suppose Germany adopted the concept of an unconditional basic income for all citizens. Think of possible consequences …

a … for employees.

b CHALLENGE … for self-employed people and businesses.

Write an article for your school magazine.

FACT FILE

The concepts of **minimum wage** and an **unconditional basic income** (UBI) are essentially different from each other. While one stipulates a certain level of pay to all employees, the other guarantees an income to all, whether they are currently holding a job or not, in addition to any other income they might receive. In Switzerland, there have been initiatives for both concepts. In May 2014, a majority of voters rejected the proposal for a minimum wage of 22 Swiss francs per hour. Preparations for another, more far-reaching referendum began in September 2013, when activists advocating the introduction of UBI collected around 130,000 signatures from supporters.
As this is the first referendum of its kind anywhere in the world, it requires thorough preparation and is not expected to be held before 2019.

Basic-income activists dumped eight million Swiss coins – one for each citizen – in front of the parliament building in Bern in the autumn of 2013.

Make appointments with two students and exchange your views about the idea of an unconditional basic income.

A4 Teenagers' career aspirations *Sean Coughlan*

In March 2013, a survey listed young Britons' job ambitions according to popularity. Before you read the summary of findings, look at the table below and do task **1** *on page 194. Then read the text and continue with tasks* **2–4**.

Most popular jobs	Percentage 15–16	Least popular jobs	Percentage 15–16
Teacher/Lecturer	4.4%	Locksmith	0.2%
Lawyer (barrister/solicitor)	4.2%	Welder	0.2%
Accountant	4.0%	Surveyor	0.2%
Actor/Actress	3.7%	Speech therapist	0.2%
Police	3.6%	Personnel/HR	0.2%
IT consultant	3.4%	Miner	0.1%
Doctor	3.4%	Call centre	0.1%
Sportsman/woman	3.3%	Audiologist	0.1%
Army/Navy/Airforce/Firefighter	3.2%	Factory worker	0.1%
Psychologist	3.1%	Glazier	0.00%

From: Nothing in Common report, Education and Employers Taskforce, UK Commission for Employment and Skills, B-Live (March 2013)

There is a 'massive mismatch' between young people's career expectations and the reality of the jobs available, a major survey of teenagers suggests. [...]

The study, based on a survey of 11,000 13- to 16-year-olds, is an attempt to map the job ambitions of teenagers against the employment market up to 2020. It shows teenagers have a weak grasp of the availability of jobs – and that large numbers will be aiming for jobs that are in short supply.

For instance, there are 10 times as many people aiming for jobs in the culture, media and sports sector than there are jobs likely to be available. And even though almost a quarter of jobs are in the distribution, hotels and restaurant category, only about one in 40 youngsters are considering careers in these industries. Fewer than one in 30 young people are considering jobs in banking and finance, even though one in five jobs are expected to be in this sector.

This 'misalignment' could mean long-term problems for young people, the report says, because they are making decisions about qualifications and subjects with little awareness of the jobs market ahead of them. And the report warns it can be difficult in later years to catch up with missing qualifications. This lack of informed choices fuels the problem of employers struggling to find suitably skilled staff, even though there are high levels of youth unemployment.

The report also looks at the perceptions of young people about types of employment. Among the 10 least preferred occupations are jobs such as surveyor and speech therapist, even though they are likely to earn above-average pay. The two least preferred jobs, as identified by teenagers, are factory work and glaziers. The most preferred employment areas, from the perspective of teenagers, include teaching, the law, the police, psychology and sport. These might be influenced either by role models such as teachers at school – or else by media images. But the report says it suggests the narrowness of young people's view of the types of work available – and the failure of employers to present a broader picture of opportunities. [...] ·····▸

TROUBLE SPOT

Schauspieler = ***actor***
Schauspielerin = ***actor*** (also: ***actress***)
Gastgeber = ***host***
Gastgeberin = ***host*** (also: ***hostess***)
Kellner/in = ***waiter, waitress, server***
Flugbegleiter/in = ***flight attendant*** (not: ~~stewardess~~)
Polizist/in = ***police officer***
Schriftsteller/in, Autor/in = ****author***
Dichter/in = ****poet***

accountant sb. who keeps or checks financial accounts
welder *Schweißer/in*
surveyor [sə'veɪə] *Landvermesser/in*
glazier ['gleɪziə] sb. who fits glass into the frames of windows, etc.

5 **grasp of sth.** understanding of sth.
6 **in short supply** not available in great numbers, scarce
13 **misalignment** [ˌmɪsə'laɪnmənt] state of not being in the correct position to sth. else
17 **fuel sth.** increase sth.
19 **perception** belief or opinion

Education and Employers Taskforce director Nick Chambers said: 'As a country we are doing our young people a huge disservice if we don't give them enough information to allow them to make proper informed decisions about their futures.' This charity has campaigned to improve the quality of careers education, highlighting the link between social mobility and access to career advice and work experience.

From: the website of the BBC, 19 March 2013

LANGUAGE HELP

If you don't know the English term for a certain job or profession, describe in your words what duties and responsibilities this job involves in order to arrive at a more general job description for the class survey. You can also check in a dictionary.

Find a tool to conduct your own survey here:

Webcode context-56

1 Popular and unpopular job aspirations

a The table on p. 193 shows the ten most popular as well as the ten least popular jobs according to a UK survey among young Britons aged 15–16. Do you find anything surprising? Talk to your partner. ▶ LANGUAGE HELP

b Carry out a class survey: What kind of job(s) do you want to do later? Make a list, ranking jobs according to popularity. Then compare the results with the UK survey, pointing out similarities and differences.

COMPREHENSION ◀

▶ SF 14: Reading strategies

2 The central message

a Spot these percentages in the text and say what they stand for:
'ca. 2.5%' 'less than 3.3%' '20%' 'nearly 25%'

b List the consequences of the 'massive mismatch' (l. 1) as mentioned in the text and say who is most affected by it.

c Sum up the main message of the text in one sentence.

ANALYSIS ◀

▶ SF 15: Marking up a text/ Making and taking notes

3 Examining and reflecting

Find reasons why the jobs at the top of the list are so popular and why the ones further down are unpopular among teenagers. Work on your own and make notes, then compare with your partner.

BEYOND THE TEXT ◀

▶ SF 34: Argumentative writing

▶ LP 15: Connecting your thoughts (sentence structure)

4 Writing

Should you pursue the career of your choice or should you consider only those careers where job demand is fairly certain?

Write an argumentative text in which you consider both sides and state your own view. SUPPORT ▶ p. 280

SPEAKING **FOCUS ON SKILLS**

From informal to formal dialogues

In any form of successful conversation, you should stick to the topic and contribute to a pleasant atmosphere. Moreover, you should adapt your style, vocabulary and your reactions to the situation in general and to the other person's social and professional standing. Sometimes you can be informal and sometimes you have to be more formal, depending on the situation.

▶ CC 5: Making smalltalk

1 An informal conversation

a Imagine you meet somebody your age at a party. You talk to each other about your career aspirations and your dreams about the future.
Before you start, scan **A4** (cf. pp. 193–194) again for phrases and words you might need for this conversation. Then talk to a partner for at least three minutes.

▶ SF 14: Reading strategies

b You probably talked to your partner in a rather colloquial way.
THINK Assess your conversation and make notes on the following aspects:
- style of language
- phrases that you used repeatedly
- sentence structures
- the way you adapted to the given situation
- problems, mistakes, breaks

PAIR Exchange your findings with your partner and add to your notes and your list of phrases.
SHARE Share your most interesting findings with your class. Explain how you could have improved your conversation.

2 A formal conversation

a Imagine you have to have a similar conversation in a more formal context and with somebody older than you and in a different position, e.g. a guidance counsellor at school, an advisor at university or a board member of an organization that awards scholarships, internships or something else you are very interested in. What would you have to change in this form of discourse? Make notes.

► CC1: Cultural awareness
► CC2: Polite behaviour
► CC3: The language of politeness
► CC5: Making smalltalk
► LP11: Using the right register

b Match the following sentences and phrases with the stages of a formal conversation in the box below. Pick out the ones you consider too blunt or even impolite to be used in such a conversation.

Bye. – It's very convenient for me to meet you here. – I absolutely hate that kind of job. – I actually think I am quite good at working in a team as ... – Oh, really, you studied at ABC University! I have heard a lot about it. – I don't think I'm qualified for such a career. – Excuse me for taking up some of your time, but ... – Hi, my name is Tom. – It was very nice talking to you. Thank you for devoting some of your time to me. – I actually always wanted to talk to you in person. – I don't care for other people's experience. – You can't be serious! – It was a pleasure meeting you. Thank you very much for your advice. – Would you mind me asking you a few questions?

- Introducing yourself
- Getting into the conversation
- Showing interest in the other person
- Talking about your qualities, likes and dreams
- Expressing dislikes and rejections politely
- Saying thank you and goodbye

In groups of 3–4, collect more ideas and phrases and add them to your list.

3 Role-play

Talk to a partner about your plans and career aspirations as described in task 2 for at least five minutes.
Partner A: You are a student. You have plans and career aspirations, but you are not sure how to go about them.
Partner B: You are an influential older person and you are willing to give Partner A some help or advice.
After five minutes swap partners and take over the other role.

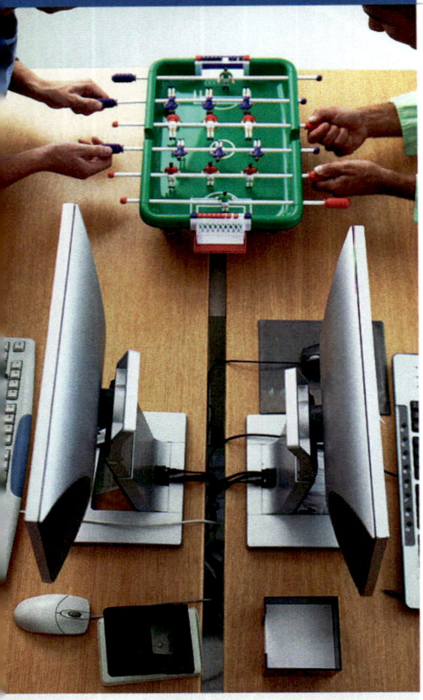

Satisfaction at work – what does it take?

Part A

A5 Do you love your job? *Uwe Jean Heuser*

*In a job interview you may be asked about your ideas of your future workplace and how you can achieve satisfaction at work. The following excerpt from an *article in the German weekly* DIE ZEIT *gives an insight into job satisfaction and its implications.*

Lange gingen Ökonomen davon aus, dass Arbeit reine Last sei: Statt ihre Freizeit zu genießen, litten die Menschen acht oder zehn Stunden am Tag – und für dieses Übel würden sie bezahlt. Eine traurige Theorie war das und gottlob eine falsche. Heute erforschen Wirtschaftswissenschaftler, in welchem Maße der Beruf ihr Lebensglück beeinflusst und wie zufrieden Menschen sind. Und siehe da: Menschen, die sich als hochzufrieden bezeichnen, werden von anderen auch so wahrgenommen. Sie sind offener für positive Einflüsse, nehmen leichter Kontakt auf und blicken optimistischer in die Zukunft. Sogar ihre Immunabwehr ist besser, sie sind selten krank. [...]

Nach einer Umfrage der Beratungsfirma Gallup sind mehr als 90 Prozent der Arbeitnehmer mit ihrem Job zufrieden, aber fast 25 Prozent spüren keine innere Bindung an ihr Unternehmen. Manchmal liegt das an ihnen, oft aber an Firmenkultur und Chefs. Wo Kollegen kooperationswillig sind, wo Führungskräfte schwelende Konflikte rasch lösen und die Mitarbeiter beruflich unterstützen, entsteht Zufriedenheit. Umgekehrt geht es den meisten auf die Nerven, wenn Streitigkeiten ungelöst bleiben, niemand Apathie oder Mobbing entgegentritt. Noch schlimmer ist es nur, wenn Angestellte – zu Recht oder Unrecht – ihren Job permanent für gefährdet halten und keine Möglichkeit für einen Wechsel sehen.

Produktiv ist dieses Gefühl des Ausgeliefertseins nicht, auch wenn umgekehrt ein Wohlgefühl bei den Angestellten noch keine gute Leistung garantiert. Die Wirtschaft braucht eine Atmosphäre, in der sich zufriedene Mitarbeiter über den Dienst nach Vorschrift hinaus engagieren. Und sie schafft umso mehr Wohlstand, je treffsicherer sich die Menschen erst ihren Beruf und später ihre Jobs aussuchen.

Die Bedingungen in der Wirtschaft ändern sich heute rasant, also müssen sich Erwerbstätige öfter fragen, ob die Arbeit ihre Erwartungen erfüllt. Gerade diejenigen, die sich im Job aufzehren, stellen sonst irgendwann fest, dass das übrige Leben leidet. [...] Kein Wunder, dass auch flexible Tätigkeiten und Phasen von Teilzeit das Glück des Einzelnen beflügeln. Und sei es nur, weil er merkt: Ich habe mein Leben selbst in der Hand.

From: *DIE ZEIT*, 23 Oktober 2013

1 Translating or paraphrasing?
Not every word or phrase can be directly rendered in another language; sometimes you have to find a paraphrase.

- ► SF 3: Using a dictionary
- ► LP 16: Avoiding Germanisms

Find an online dictionary here:
Webcode context-52

a Find out whether *luck* or *happiness* are both good equivalents of *Glück* in the context of this article (cf. l. 26). Likewise, check whether *binding* for 'Bindung' (l. 11), and *wellness* for 'Wohlgefühl' (l. 19) are suitable equivalents.

► SF 9: Paraphrasing

b Describe in German what is meant by the following expressions, then paraphrase them in English: 'dieses Gefühl des Ausgeliefertseins' (l. 18), 'Dienst nach Vorschrift' (ll. 20–21), 'sich im Job aufzehren' (l. 25).

2 Mediation (German → English**)**
An English friend of yours thinks that the importance of job satisfaction is overrated. Sum up the main ideas of the article for her in English (ca. 150 words).

► SF 41: Mediation of written and oral texts

3 A tricky question in your job interview

a Some of the aspects of job satisfaction mentioned by Heuser should not be brought up in a job interview. List them, then compare with your partner.
SUPPORT p. 280

b Work with your partner again. One of you acts as the interviewer and asks 'How can you contribute to a healthy working atmosphere?', the other tries to answer this question. Then swap roles and ask or answer the question again.

CULTURE SPOT

Corporate Head (1991)

*The joint work of Terry Allen (sculpture) and Philip Levine (*poem on the plaque next to the sculpture), 'Corporate Head' is located outside the Los Angeles offices of the professional services firm EY (previously Ernst & Young).*

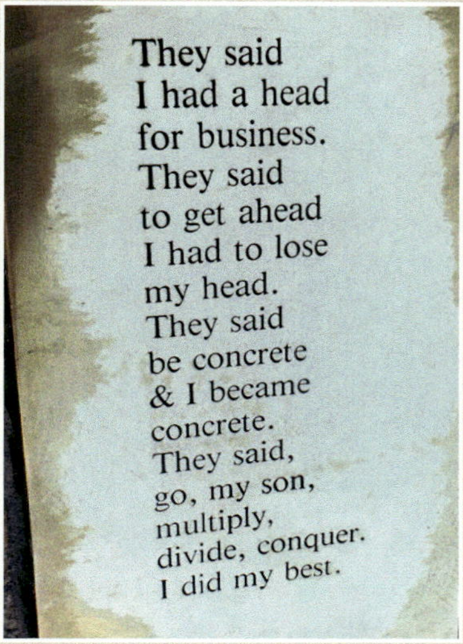

1 Describe 'Corporate Head'.

2 How do the sculpture and the poem relate to the topic of this chapter?

3 Discuss why the company EY may have commissioned 'Corporate Head'.

Stepping into the world of work

B1 Mitch's first glimpses of the world of work

Carl Deuker

In the novel Payback Time *(2010), Mitch True, a not-too-popular high-school student, is a reporter for the school magazine. He has reluctantly accepted the responsibility for the sports section. In the following excerpt, Mitch is on his way to his first interview with the coach of the Lincoln Mustangs – his former PE-teacher McNulty.*

I parked my mom's Ford Focus by the gym, eased out of the front seat, and looked around. When I spotted McNulty loading tackling sleds into a school van, I tensed. To him, I'd always be a fat loser and nothing more. But a reporter has to have the courage to approach people, ask them questions, and get them to talk. 'I'm Mitch True,' I said as I neared him. 'I'm the school sports reporter. I'd like to ask you some questions.'

'I was hoping you'd come around,' he said. 'Step into my office.'

I gaped, dumbfounded. He was hoping I'd come around? When I recovered, I nearly had to run to catch up as he strode across the field and into the coaches' office in the gym. He took a seat behind a neatly organized desk while I squeezed into a wobbly blue plastic chair across from him.

'What's your name again?'

I told him again.

'You were in my gym class last year, right?'

'Two years ago.'

'Well, Mr. True, you are now an important member of the Lincoln Mustang football family.'

I smiled.

'What's funny?' McNulty said, his blue-gray eyes glittering like shiny stones.

Like an idiot, I patted my jiggly belly. 'Me? An important member of the football family. How?'

He leaned forward, pointing his pencil at me. 'You are the person who sends in a game recap to the Seattle Times. You write exciting articles, and the Times will push them to the top of the high school page. That happens, and other newspapers will pick them up, which translates into publicity for the players and for me. It also means a byline for you, some cash, and a summer internship to boot. You remember last year's sports writer, Boyd Harte. He interned at the Bellevue Journal.'

I hadn't thought about the connections I'd be making, but as a sports stringer, I'd be dealing with editors of real newspapers, something that would not have happened if I'd remained the news reporter for the Lincoln Light – unless the big dailies suddenly become interested in the accomplishments of Lincoln High's chess club. 'Sounds great,' I said. 'In fact, it sounds fantastic.'

McNulty leaned back. 'See. We're all part of one big family.'

I cleared my throat. 'How about we get started? I've got some questions. First –'

'No, no, no,' McNulty said, pointing the pencil at me again. 'No questions – not today, not ever. This job takes forever and pays peanuts. Here's how it works. You write down or tape what I tell you. When I'm done, jazz it up whatever you want, but never make me, my coaches, or my players look bad. Understand?'

2 **tackling sled** *„Angriffsschlitten" (schweres Trainingsgerät im American Football)*
7 **gape** *(v)* stare with your mouth open
dumbfounded [dʌm'faʊndɪd] *(adj)* very surprised and unable to speak
19 **pat sth.** touch sth. gently
22 **game recap** summary of a game
24 **translate into sth.** change into sth.
25 **byline** line at the beginning or end of a newspaper article that gives the writer's name
to boot *(adv) (old-fashioned/ humorous) obendrein*
26 **intern** ['– –] *(v)* be on an internship *(Praktikum)*
27 **stringer** ['strɪŋə] freelance journalist
36 **jazz sth. up** *(infml)* make sth. more interesting or attractive

Mr. Dewey had warned us about people like McNulty, but this was my first time dealing with one. 'A reporter who lets himself be pushed around is a traitor to his profession.' That's what Dewey had said.

I could feel myself trying to say: 'Coach, I will ask the questions I want to ask, and I will write what I want to write.'

In the classroom, practicing with bald, bowtied Mr. Dewey, I had spit out similar words like a machine gun spits out bullets. But McNulty's eyes were scary. I squirmed as he stared at me, feeling like a snot-nosed preschooler who'd been caught marking a wall with crayons. 'Understood?' he said again, a threat in his voice, as though he might force me to do cartwheels in front of the football team if I argued.

'Yes, sir!'

From a drawer he took three sheets of paper covered with black type and showed them at me. 'Here's the information for the football preview. Horst Diamond will be the focus, and you'll be leading every game story with his name, too. He's a lock for a D-I scholarship. UW is drooling over him, but he's got a shot at a bigger school – Notre Dame, or even USC. Your job is to get him publicity.'

I scanned the three sheets. 'But what if somebody else has a better game?'

'Nobody's going to have a better game. Run or pass – everything we do goes through Horst. I want a swarm of college coaches around here. They'll see him, and they'll see me and the program I run. I do not intend to spend my life coaching high school.'

McNulty stood. 'Read those pages, prepare a few questions, and before practice tomorrow you can interview Horst. He'll be at the field fifteen minutes early. Have your photographer come along for that.' He paused. 'You've got a photographer, right?'

'A photographer?'

'Every sports story needs pictures. Either you've got to take them yourself, or you've got to get a photographer. Didn't you know that?

From: *Payback Time*, 2010

TROUBLE SPOT

intern ['– –] *(n) = Praktikant/in*
intern [''– –] *(v)* (l. 26) *= ein Praktikum machen*
internship ['– – –] (l. 25) = *Praktikum*
apprentice = *Auszubildende/r, Lehrling*
apprenticeship = *Ausbildung, Lehre*
trainee [–'–] = *Auszubildende/r, Trainee*
hand = *Helfer/in (z.B. in einer Fabrik)*
employee [– –'–] = *Mitarbeiter/in, Angestellte/r*
employer = *Arbeitgeber/in*
superior [suː'pɪəriə] = *Vorgesetzte/r*
boss = *Chef/in, Vorgesetze/r*
chief = *Leiter/in, Chef/in*

43 **bowtied** [ˌbəʊ'taɪd] *(adj)* wearing a bow tie *(Fliege)*
44 **squirm** *sich winden*
46 **crayon** ['kreɪən] *Buntstift*
51 **lock** *(n) (infml)* sure thing, certainty
52 **D-I = Division I** in the USA, highest level of college and university athletics
UW = University of Washington
drool over sb./sth. *für jdn./etwas schwärmen*
53 **USC** = University of Southern California

COMPREHENSION

1 Who said it?

Using the text, point out who says the following and what is being talked about or what is happening at this particular moment: 'I'd like to ask you some questions.' / 'What's funny?' / 'Sounds great.' / 'How about we get started?' / 'Understood?' / 'Nobody's going to have a better game.'

► SF 14: Reading strategies

ANALYSIS

2 Power relations

Work on your own first, then tell each other about your findings.

Partner A: Analyse the meeting between Mitch and McNulty and explain how one of them shows his power and superiority through non-linguistic means (e.g. facial expressions). SUPPORT p. 280

Partner B: Analyse the meeting between Mitch and McNulty and explain how one of them uses language to demonstrate his power and superiority. SUPPORT p. 281

► SF 19: Analysing narrative prose
► SF 35: Writing a character profile

BEYOND THE TEXT

3 Writing about Mitch's experiences

a Outline what Mitch has learned about the world of work. Make notes.

b In an email to a friend Mitch writes about the experience he has gained. Write his email using your notes from **a**.

► SF 15: Marking up a text/Making and taking notes
► SF 37: Doing a creative writing task
► LP 11: Using the right register

B2 Ten things not to say in a job interview *Mark King*

Getting invited to an interview is a big step on the way to getting a job. Now it's important not to spoil one's chances by saying something stupid. The Guardian's *Mark King has some useful advice.*

With the jobs market more competitive than ever it can be hard work just to get an interview, so once you're actually in front of potential employers you don't want to ruin your prospects with an ill-chosen comment.

Sadly, some job hunters still do speak before they think. Corinne Mills, managing director of Personal Career Management, says she can recall many instances of interviewees saying the wrong thing. 'I remember when one man was asked why he wanted the job, he replied, "Because my mum thought it was a good idea",' she says.

She adds that some job hunters have also been known to say they've applied for a job 'because it will pay the rent while I look for a job I really want to do', and a common response to a question about what candidates like to do in their spare time is 'go to the pub'.

Richard Nott, website director at CWJobs.co.uk, says candidates should avoid discussing religion and politics. 'Employers like people who can talk passionately about their own interests as it helps them to get to know you as a person. But we would always advise against sharing your views on these two topics without knowing if the interviewer shares that point of view.'

We asked Nott, Mills and Nik Pratap of Hays Senior Finance for their list of the top things to avoid saying at a job interview:

1. 'Sorry I'm late.' It goes without saying that punctuality is key. Your interviewer doesn't want you to arrive for work 20 minutes late every morning.
2. 'What's your annual leave and sickness policy?' It doesn't look good if, before you've even been hired, you're planning your absence from the company.
3. 'I'll just take this call.' Mills says a large number of candidates think it is OK to take telephone calls, texts etc. during an interview. It isn't.
4. When asked, 'Where do you see yourself in five years?' never say, 'Doing your job.' As much as this might be a genuine answer, Nott says candidates should 'try to build a response around the experience they would like to have gained and the level of responsibility they'd like to have, rather than threatening the interviewer's job.'
5. 'My previous employer sucked.' No matter how mind-numbingly boring those roles might have been, 'speaking badly of a previous employer is not only unprofessional, but also reflects on your character,' Pratap says. Your new employer will contact your former employer for references following an interview, so it's never wise to burn your bridges.
6. 'You make widgets? I thought you made cricket bats.' Failing to research your prospective employer fully is a big faux pas. 'Saying you've looked at their website is only marginally better – employers expect far more research,' Mills explains.
7. 'Bloody hell.' Never swear in your interview. It can happen, especially if your interviewer is themselves prolific with the profanities, but don't let them set the standard of the interview and remain professional at all times.
8. 'I was very good at sorting out PEBs by using ARCs.' Don't fall into the industry jargon of your previous employer or assume the interviewer knows anything about your experience, Pratap advises. Instead, speak clearly about your skills and experience to avoid any confusion or misunderstanding.

TROUBLE SPOT

apply to sb. for sth. (l. 18) = *sich bei jdm. um/für etwas bewerben*
applicant ['– – –] = *Bewerber/in*
applicable [–'– – –] = *anwendbar*
application = *Anwendung*

21 **leave** *(n)* time away from work, holiday
30 **suck** *(v) (sl)* be very bad
mind-numbingly ['nʌmiŋli] **boring** very boring
34 **burn one's bridges** *(idiom)* do sth. that makes it impossible to return to the previous situation
35 **widget** ['wɪdʒɪt] simple software application
36 **faux pas** [ˌfəʊ 'pɑː] (French: 'wrong step') embarrassing action or remark *(Fehler)*
37 **marginally** ['mɑːdʒɪnəli] *(adv)* very slightly
39 **prolific** [prəˈlɪfɪk] producing a lot
profanity [prəˈfænəti] *(usu. pl)* swear word

9. 'Do I really have to wear that uniform?' Any criticism of staff uniform will go down like a lead balloon. Do you think your interviewer enjoyed wearing that flucrescent green ensemble when they performed your role?
10. When asked, 'What do you expect to enjoy most about this role?' never reply with any of the following: the perks, the pay, lunchtimes, my co-workers or the holidays, Nott says.

From: *The Guardian*, 10 May 2012

47 **ensemble** [ɒn'sɒmbl] set of clothes that are worn together
49 **perk** *(usu. pl.)* Vergünstigung

COMPREHENSION

1 Understanding the rules
In groups of three or four, quickly decide which of the mistakes in the list (cf. ll. 19–50) are ones that are easily made and which ones you are sure you would never make.

ANALYSIS

2 The language of the text
a Explain how King tries to amuse the reader. SUPPORT p. 281
b Explain how King makes his advice easy to understand and to remember.

► SF 17: Analysing stylistic devices

BEYOND THE TEXT

3 Your five golden rules
King gives tips for people being interviewed – but what about those asking the questions? In a group, think of five golden rules for interviewers.

► CC 3: The language of politeness
► CC 4: Meeting and greeting

B3 The best job in the world is back! *Emanuel Wetterqvist*

In order to promote the Great Barrier Reef as an international tourist attraction, Australia launched a competition for 'the best job in the world'. The winner of the contest would live on a Queensland island, explore and enjoy the area and write a blog about it.
In 2013, the second round of 'the best job in the world' was announced.

Yes, you read right. As our ex-island caretaker is regretfully handing over the keys to his island hacienda we're looking for someone to take his place.

As our Park Ranger you will be exploring the world's oldest rainforest, watching whales migrate on the Great Barrier Reef, and showcase our five World Heritage areas to the world through blogs and social media.

This is the perfect opportunity for an outdoor lover with a sense of adventure to promote some of the world's most awe-inspiring natural wonders to an international audience. The position is a six-month contract attracting a generous salary package of AUD $100,000 and a free jar of vegemite.

Your responsibilities
- Patrol the beaches – you have 7,400 kilometres of palm and beach-fringed coastline within your jurisdiction, but you only need to show us your favourites.
- Swim, dive and snorkel the world's biggest aquarium. With 600 islands and 1,500 species of fish to hang out with, we're sure the 30 °C water will keep you occupied.
- Feed the fish, and meet and greet with local wildlife, including kangaroos, crocodiles and the short-tempered cassowary.
- Get up close and personal with hatching turtles and migrating whales and share your experience with the world.
- Showcase the best of our 300 national and marine parks and state forests. Like a well-paid Tarzan.

2 **hacienda** [ˌhæsɪ'endə] large farm
4 **showcase sth.** show the best aspects of sth.
7 **awe-inspiring** impressive
8 **attract sth.** (here) be worth sth.
9 **vegemite** ['vedʒɪmaɪt] type of food paste, very popular in Australia
17 **short-tempered** *(adj)* getting angry easily
cassowary ['kæsəwəri] *Kasuar (Laufvogel)*

Part B

TROUBLE SPOT

Conventions for writing currencies (cf. l. 9) vary. Sometimes symbols, sometimes standard abbreviations are used. In English-speaking countries, these are usually placed before, not after, the amount, e.g.
Euros: *€100 / EUR 100 / 100 euros* (~~euro~~)
British pounds: *£200 / GBP 200*
US dollars: *$300 / US$300* (to avoid confusion, e.g. with Canadian dollars) */ USD 300*
Australian dollars: *$400 / A$400 / AUD 400*
Indian rupees: *₹400 / INR 400*

- Report on your adventures through photo blogs, social media channels and media interviews.

Who we're looking for – We will consider applicants from a wide range of backgrounds, but believe you should possess these traits:

- Excellent oral and written English communication skills
- Be adventurous by nature and willing to try new things
- Have a passion for the outdoors and nature
- Good swimming skills and enthusiasm for snorkelling and/or diving

About the job package – The position of Park Ranger attracts a AUD $100,000 salary package (AUD $50,000 salary and AUD $50,000 to cover living expenses) for the six-month contract.
The successful candidate will live amongst the stars with a range of rent-free accommodation. You might spend one night camping on an island and the next in a bunk on a luxury yacht.
You'll receive return airfares from your nearest capital city (in your home country), travel insurance and the cameras and gadgets required to show the world a good time. The six-month contract commences on 1st August 2013.

About your new office – Queensland is regarded as having one of the world's richest natural environments and boasts a rich and diverse array of World Heritage areas including the Great Barrier Reef, Daintree Rainforest and Fraser Island.
The state is home to hundreds of national parks, conservation areas, resource reserves and state forests.

How to apply – The position is open to adventure-hungry outdoor lovers from Australia and overseas. Apply online at http://bestjo.bs/Park_Ranger.

From: *Hello Sunshine*, the official travel blog of Queensland, 5 March 2013

37 **gadget** ['gædʒɪt] small and useful device
38 **commence** [kə'mens] *(v)* start
40 **boast sth.** have sth. you can be proud of
array [-'-] large collection of things

COMPREHENSION

1 Making sense of numbers
Pick three numbers from the text and ask your partner to point out what they refer to. Then swap roles. *Example: '6.' – 'The contract is valid for six months.'*

► SF 14: Reading strategies

ANALYSIS

2 Text type and target group

a Examine characteristic aspects of the text type 'job advertisement' and illustrate them with examples from the text. SUPPORT ► p. 281

b Identify the target group of this text and explain which aspects of the advertisement are likely to appeal to them most.

► SF 16: Identifying text types (non-fiction)

LANGUAGE AWARENESS

3 Language and target group
Show how the *tone and language of the ad aim at its target group. Pay special attention to humorous and colloquial elements.

► LP 11: Using the right register

BEYOND THE TEXT

4 What's your opinion?
THINK Is the above text about proper work or a leisure activity? About a real application process or a casting show? Find evidence to support your argument.
PAIR Exchange your ideas and arguments with your partner. Try to agree on a position.
SHARE Tell your class about your view(s).

WRITING **FOCUS ON SKILLS**

Writing a letter of motivation

When applying for any type of position – an internship, a place at a university, a job – you are usually expected to write a letter of motivation, in which you explain why you are interested and what recommends you for the position. Such letters, which may also be called personal statements, cover letters, statements of purpose or letters of intent, are mostly formal letters.

Imagine you want to apply for the 'best job in the world' (cf. **B3***, pp. 201–202).*

► LP 11: Using the right register
► CC 2: Polite behaviour

1 Thinking about your motivation

a Reread the 'job ad' on pp. 201–202. ► LANGUAGE HELP

b THINK List three reasons that motivate you to apply for this job. If you are not really interested in the job, list the reasons of an invented other person who is.

c PAIR AND SHARE Work with one or two partners and exchange your ideas from **b**. Add convincing ideas to your list.

LANGUAGE HELP

- I have a strong interest in …
- I was particularly impressed by …
- I understand that this position requires …
- I have demonstrated the desired qualities through …
- I would value the opportunity to gain experience in …
- I am very keen to …
- I see that this position offers … In respect to this, one of my key strengths is the ability to … I recently demonstrated this quality through …
- This experience taught me the importance of …
- I have developed skills in …
- My experience in …
- As you can see from the attached CV …
- In addition, my role as …
- My responsibilities included …

2 Presenting your assets

Of course, it is not enough to just write that you have all the requirements as listed in the job ad – you must prove it, either by presenting convincing arguments or by handing in relevant certificates.

a List arguments and certificates proving that you answer the description given in the section 'Who we are looking for'.

b Work with a partner you know well. Exchange your lists and give feedback to each other.

3 Writing your first draft

a Turn your lists from **1** and **2** into a text. Stick to the conventions of formal letters.

b Add typical application phrases to your text.

► SF 29: Writing a formal letter or email
► SF 30: Writing an application

4 Typing your final version

a Reread your first draft after one or two days.

b Type it up on a computer and use your spellchecker to correct it.

► SF 40: Proofreading

5 The winner's application

Watch the application video of Elisa, the young woman who was eventually chosen for the 'best job in the world'. Discuss similarities and differences in content between her video and your letter of motivation.

DVD

take a leap of faith *(idiom)* try one's luck
'roo *(infml)* kangaroo
fervent sincere, dedicated
anthropologist sb. who studies the human race

► SF 23: Analysing a film

Part B

B4 Surviving a telephone interview

► EE4: Making phone calls

Telephone interviews have become increasingly popular in the business world. Easy as they might seem, there are practical dos and don'ts applicants should be aware of, as the audio explains.

► SF22: Listening

CD3 03

sophisticated (here) intelligent, complex
résumé *(AE)* = *(BE)* **CV / curriculum vitae**

COMPREHENSION

1 Expectations
Before listening, arrange the following headings in the order of appearance you expect from the listening text:
Thank your interviewer / Research the company / Practise responses for your phone interview / Keep notes about your work experience / Be friendly during the phone interview
Then listen to the audio and check whether you were right.

ANALYSIS

2 After listening
Explain the functions of the following in the context of a telephone interview: *paper, sticky tape, voice recorder, water, letter.*

BEYOND THE TEXT

► SF26: Taking part in an interview

3 Act out an interview
- **a** Here are some typical questions asked by interviewers. With a partner, add three more questions:
  What is important to you in a job? How would you describe your present workplace? How do you handle stress and pressure? What motivates you? Where do you see yourself in three years' time? In what kind of company do you enjoy working? What does success mean to you?
- **b** Let your partner interview you.

B5 Look them in the eye – the job interview

Though the most frequent type of interview, a face-to-face meeting between an employer and a job seeker has its pitfalls. This video gives helpful advice.

► SF11: Analysing pictures

DVD

non-negotiable (here) obligatory
succinct short and precise
jack of all trades *Alleskönner/in*
unruly disorderly

COMPREHENSION

1 First looks are (not) deceiving
Look at the still on the left and talk to your partner about how this person might come across in a job interview.

2 Do's and don'ts
Watch the video. With your partner, list and rank the given dos and don'ts of job interviews. SUPPORT ► p. 281

BEYOND THE TEXT

► SF26: Taking part in an interview

3 Body language
- **a** Compare Lauren Ferrara's body language to that of the presenter.
- **b** Take your own pictures in which you show good and bad examples of body language in job interviews and/or the oral exams of the *Abitur*. Evaluate the body language and rank the pictures from good to bad.

4 Surprising advice
Which piece of advice given in the video did you find surprising?

Writing your personal statement

'Personal statement' is the term commonly used for a letter of motivation that you send to the university at which you want to study. In this letter you present yourself and explain why the university should offer you a place to study. A standard text type in the English-speaking world, personal statements are becoming increasingly popular with German universities too. They may also be required when applying for an internship, for volunteer work or for a year abroad.

1 Think about yourself

a Imagine you want to apply to a university for a particular course or subject. Alternatively, think of what kind of internship or volunteer work you are interested in.
Then study the table below and make notes on the points in the left column ('What?').

► SF 15: Marking up a text/ Making and taking notes

Your personal statement	
What?	**How?**
• reasons why you are choosing higher education • reasons for your interest in the subject • things you already know about your subject • the subject and its connection to your education, work experience and to your hobbies	• catchy introduction • coherent main part • concise conclusion • max. 600 words • perfect grammar, spelling and punctuation • reader-friendly layout

b Add some notes as to why you think you should be offered a place. Describe your skills, your knowledge and your experience.

c Finally, add any other achievements and attributes that you might mention in your personal statement.

2 Ask for feedback

Work with a partner you know well. Let your partner read your notes and ask if there are any aspects of your personality that you forgot to mention. Then swap roles.

3 Get down to work

Now write out your personal statement for a course of your choice. Make use of your partner's advice, of the tips in the table above ('How?') and of the phrases given on p. 203 (Language help). Your teacher will give you an assessment sheet.

► SF 30: Writing an application

10 Modern Media – Tools or Tyrants?

Download a list of chapter vocab here:
Webcode context-01

retard ['ri:tɑ:d] *(*taboo, sl)* stupid person

▸ SF 13: Analysing cartoons

1 Talking about a cartoon

a THINK Make a few notes on the message of the cartoon above.

b PAIR With a partner, collect examples to illustrate the degree of media literacy that is to be expected of each of the three groups referred to in the cartoon.

c SHARE Present your findings in class. Focusing on your peer group, agree on the three types of media you use most.

I hate television. I hate it as much as peanuts. But I can't stop eating peanuts.
Orson Welles *(1915–1985)*

I fear the day technology will surpass our human interaction. The world will have a generation of idiots.
Albert Einstein *(1879–1955)*

The concept of surveillance is ingrained in our beings. God was the original surveillance camera.
Hasan M. Elahi *(born 1972)*

We're still in the first minutes of the first day of the internet revolution.
Scott Cook *(born 1952)*

surpass sb./sth. [sə'pɑːs] *(fml)* be better or greater than sb./sth. else
surveillance [sə'veɪləns] careful watching of a person or place
ingrained firmly established and therefore difficult to change

2 MARKETPLACE (MILLING-AROUND ACTIVITY) **The digital age**

a Walk around your classroom. As soon as your teacher tells you to stop, turn to the student nearest to you and discuss one of the four quotes above. Say how much you agree or disagree with the statements by Welles, Einstein, Elahi or Cook. Justify your opinion (and take notes).
When your teacher gives a signal, swap partners. Repeat this activity until everyone has discussed all the four quotes.

b Present and evaluate the results of your discussions in class.

PREVIEW

This chapter invites you to explore the impact of modern media on our lives now and in the future.

CD1 02

Listen to an audio version of the text on the CD or download it here:

Webcode context-02

Living interactive lives

Connected

In recent years a great many social networks have been developed to cater for people of different age groups and interests. Not only do they offer an easy way of staying in touch with friends and acquaintances, they also provide a platform to 'meet' like-minded people, exchange ideas and material, seek advice and collaborate on a private and professional level. However, people's 'likes' and 'dislikes' are carefully stored, along with a great number of other details gathered about the users, to be exploited by businesses or political organizations. This pool of information allows for personalized ads as well as effective campaigning, but with it comes the danger of subtle manipulation. Despite warnings as to the potential abuse of data inadvertently revealed, social networks continue to grow in popularity, especially among younger people, who have embraced a virtual lifestyle from an early age on and are therefore used to sharing their everyday lives with an online community.

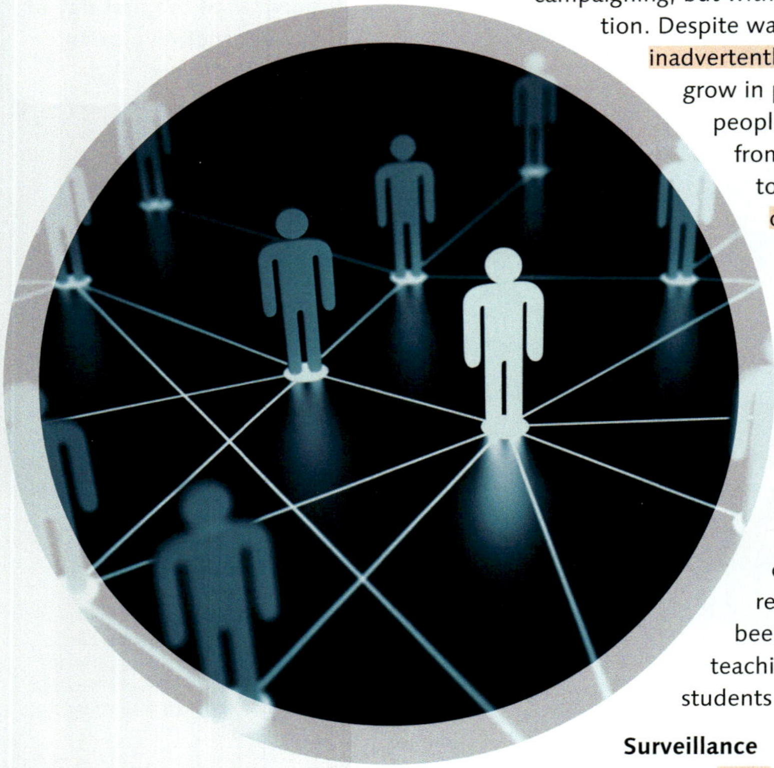

Digital media has also had a major impact on the educational system. Though banned or at least restricted at first, its potential for supporting self-initiated learning has by now been recognized, turning it into a valuable teaching tool for research, cooperative learning and self-study, to name but a few of its numerous uses. With the demand for media literacy increasing in every type of job and schools responding to the requirements of the 21st century, there has been a shift to a more media-based way of teaching, which is more able to integrate students with special needs.

Surveillance

Digital media gives users access to a huge amount of unfiltered information. However, it also reveals details about individual users, be it intentionally or by chance. Hence secret services have benefitted greatly from sophisticated surveillance technology. Moreover, CCTV is starting to be used in schools, both as a security measure and a means of quality control.

> **TROUBLE SPOT**
>
> ***the media*** *(l. 34) + singular verb or plural verb*
> ***Digital media gives/give …***
> ***The media has/have …***

Reality TV

Even though most people show some degree of uneasiness when it comes to video or data surveillance, there seem to be fewer qualms about watching common people's lives exposed on TV for entertainment. The growing popularity of reality TV, which can turn anybody into a celebrity or failure depending on the audience's response, reflects the general trend of people's more interactive approach to the media.

▶ SF 2: Learning new words

1 Words in use
Find the highlighted words or phrases in the text that match these definitions:
1 engage in a way of life that is centred on the internet
2 encourage independent studying
3 make something available
4 feeling uncomfortable with something
5 work and study together
6 friends or contacts you don't know very well
7 show something that is usually hidden
8 unintentionally

2 Improving your style
a Gather phrases from the text that express the idea of 'a lot of'. Go beyond the highlighted words.
b Collect linking words from the text. Classify them in three categories according to their meaning:

▶ LP 15: Connecting your thoughts (sentence structure)

Adding a similar aspect	Introducing a contrast	Drawing a conclusion

c Fill in additional linking words that you know. Compare your results with those of your partner and present them in class.

3 Grammar and style: Participle constructions

▶ SF 4: Using a grammar book
▶ LP 15: Connecting your thoughts (sentence structure)

a Rewrite the underlined clauses using participle constructions.
1 People who use smartphones sometimes seem to become addicted to them.
2 As they are afraid that they might miss out on something, they constantly check their digital device.
3 They often annoy their parents or even friends by the fact that they are glued to their screen while they are having a conversation.
4 Although they realize that they may get into trouble if they use their phone in class, some of them just can't stop playing with their mobile anyway.

b How is the following participle construction different from the others in the text? How would you translate *with* here?
With the demand for media literacy increasing in every type of job and schools responding to the requirements of the 21st century, there has been a shift to a more media-based way of teaching, which is more able to integrate students with special needs. (ll. 26–32)

▶ LP 16: Avoiding Germanisms

c Rewrite this sentence, using *with* followed by a participle construction.
As the rules at school strictly forbid the use of mobile phones in class, teachers are required to take action against mobile phone use in their classrooms.

4 Discussion
Has Facebook changed the concept of 'friendship'? Discuss this question with a partner, using as many of the highlighted words from the text as possible.

Ms Moem

DVD

Dis-connected

A1 Lonely friends *Ms Moem*

Ms Moem is a contemporary English poet, who writes poems, rhymes and verses on all topics. She has her own poetry blog website.

- Watch and listen to Ms Moem's poem 'Connected' – a poem about Facebook, Twitter, YouTube and social media in general.

COMPREHENSION

1 First impressions

a Make notes on the effect of listening to the poem and watching its words unfold in the video clip. Then compare your experiences in class and discuss your first understanding of the content of the poem.

b Sum up the essence of this poem as a Twitter message of no more than 140 characters.

2 Understanding the speaker's attitude towards social media

a List the aspects that are important for the speaker with regard to social networks.

b State how important the speaker considers her own role as a social media user. Give evidence from the text.

3 Mediation (English → German)

► SF41: Mediation of written and oral texts

Your friend is fascinated with social networks and has shared Ms Moem's video clip with you and other friends on a social networking site. He recommended it because he feels it reflects his positive attitude towards social media. Outline to him in German what the poem actually says about social media.

ANALYSIS

4 Poetic devices

► SF21: Analysing poetry

Examine which means the poet uses to draw our attention to the influence of social media on our lives. SUPPORT ► p. 282

5 The message

Interpret what impact the internet has had on human relationships according to Ms Moem's poem.

BEYOND THE TEXT

6 Creating images

In small groups, discuss how you could underline the message of the poem with video sequences or stills instead of showing the words in the video clip. You may also include ideas for background music. Present your ideas to each other.

7 Writing a comment

'Oh why can't we turn the time back.
It was simpler when we could just be friends, and that didn't depend on whether someone had accepted your friend request.'

Write a short comment in which you state why you do or do not agree with this statement from Ms Moem's poem. ► LANGUAGE HELP

LANGUAGE HELP

- win a friend ↔ lose a friend
- make friends with sb. = forge/form/develop/build a friendship with sb.
- cultivate a friendship
- a close/special/intimate ['ɪntɪmət] /trusted/loyal/ true/lifelong/long-time/ long-lost/new-found friend
- a fair-weather friend (= sb. who will let you down when you are in need)
- a casual acquaintance [ə'kweɪntəns] (= a person you don't know very well)

CULTURE SPOT

New media art: ***Viewpoint of Billions with Google Glass*** *(2013)*

- *American artist David Datuna was the first to incorporate internet-connected smartglasses ('wearable computing') into a piece of modern art.*
- *Four interactive cameras have been built into a 12-foot (3.67 m) flag of the United States of America. These will automatically connect with viewers wearing Google Glass.*
- *Photos, newspaper clippings and videos of famous moments in US history have been placed behind thousands of optical lenses. They will be projected to the wearer's 'third eye' when they look at the artwork.*
- *For up to three minutes viewers will have a unique experience, e.g. they can answer questions posed by Glass and have their responses and experiences recorded and uploaded onto the artist's website, YouTube and Tumblr.*

DVD Watch a video on David Datuna's interactive installation 'Viewpoint of Billions with Google Glass'.

1 Describe David Datuna's art installation. How is art created with new media?

2 Explain the title of the installation. Work in pairs and exchange your opinions on this work of art.

3 Discuss in class whether or not you would like to contribute to Datuna's interactive installation.

For another work of art based on the Stars and Stripes, see p. 19.

A2 Online learning in 2044 *Ernest Cline*

*The following text is an extract from a science-fiction *novel. It's the year 2044, and Wade Watts, the teenaged *protagonist, escapes his depressing reality by spending his waking hours immersed in the OASIS, a virtual utopia where you can be anything you want to be on any of ten thousand planets, if you can pay for it.*

I'd attended school in the real world up until the sixth grade. It hadn't been a very pleasant experience. I was a painfully shy, awkward kid, with low self-esteem and almost no social skills – a side effect of spending most of my childhood inside the OASIS. Online, I didn't have a problem talking to people or making friends. But in the real world, interacting with other people – especially kids my own age – made me a nervous wreck. I never knew how to act or what to say, and when I did work up the courage to speak, I always seemed to say the wrong thing.

My appearance was part of the problem. I was overweight, and had been for as long as I could remember. My bankrupt diet of government-subsidized sugar and starch-laden food was a contributing factor, but I was also an OASIS addict, so the only exercise I usually got back then was running away from the bullies before and after school. To make matters worse, my limited wardrobe consisted entirely of ill-fitting clothes from thrift stores and donation bins – the social equivalent of having a bull's-eye painted on my forehead.

Even so, I tried my best to fit in. Year after year, my eyes would scan the lunchroom like a T-1000, searching for a clique that might accept me. But even the other outcasts wanted nothing to do with me. I was too weird, even for the weirdos. And girls? Talking to girls was out of the question. To me, they were like some exotic alien species, both beautiful and terrifying. Whenever I got near one of them I invariably broke out in a cold sweat and lost the ability to speak in complete sentences.

For me, school had been a Darwinian exercise. A daily gauntlet of ridicule, abuse, and isolation. By the time I entered sixth grade, I was beginning to wonder if I'd be able to maintain my sanity until graduation, still six long years away.

Then, one glorious day, our principal announced that any student with a passing grade-point average could apply for a transfer to the new OASIS public school system. The real public school system, the one run by the government, had been an underfunded, overcrowded train wreck for decades. And now the conditions at many schools had gotten so terrible that every kid with half a brain was being encouraged to stay at home and attend school online. I nearly broke my neck sprinting to the school office to submit my application. It was accepted, and I transferred to OASIS Public School #1873 the following semester.

TROUBLE SPOT

attend school (l. 1) = ***go to school*** = *die Schule besuchen, in die Schule gehen*
visit a school = *einen Schulbesuch machen (z. B. als Schulaufsicht zur Kontrolle oder als Besucher/in am Tag der offenen Tür)*

4 **oasis** [əʊˈeɪsɪs] (here) retreat, pleasant place in the middle of sth. unpleasant
13 **thrift store** *(AE)* = *(BE)* **charity shop** shop selling second-hand clothing at low prices
16 **T-1000** fictional robot consisting of liquid metal and therefore capable of changing its shape; evil terminator in the film *Terminator 2*
19 **invariably** [ɪnˈveəriəbli] always
21 **(run a) gauntlet** [ˈɡɔːntlət] deal with a lot of people criticizing or attacking you
23 **sanity** [ˈsænəti] mental health
24 **a passing grade-point average** average of the grades achieved in all of the classes throughout a school year that is sufficient to proceed to the next year

Prior to my transfer, my OASIS avatar had never left Incipio, the planet at the center of Sector One where avatars were spawned at the time of their creation. There wasn't much to do on Incipio except chat with other noobs or shop in one of the giant virtual malls that covered the planet. If you wanted to go somewhere more interesting, you had to pay a teleportation fare to get there, and that cost money, something I didn't have. So my avatar was stranded on Incipio. That is, until my new school e-mailed me a teleportation voucher to cover the cost of my avatar's transport to Ludus, the planet where all of the OASIS public schools were located.

There were hundreds of school campuses here on Ludus, spread out evenly across the planet's surface. The schools were all identical, because the same construction code was copied and pasted into a different location whenever a new school was needed. And since the buildings were just pieces of software, their design wasn't limited by monetary constraints, or even by the laws of physics. So every school was a grand palace of learning with polished marble hallways, cathedral-like classrooms, zero-g gymnasiums, and virtual libraries containing every (school board-approved) book ever written.

On my first day at OPS #1873, I thought I'd died and gone to heaven. Now, instead of running a gauntlet of bullies and drug addicts on my walk to school each morning, I went straight to my hideout and stayed there all day. Best of all, in the OASIS, no one could tell that I was fat, that I had acne, or that I wore the same shabby clothes every week. Bullies couldn't pelt me with spitballs, give me atomic wedgies, or pummel me by the bike rack after school. No one could even touch me. In here, I was safe.

From: *Ready Player One*, 2012

43 **incipio** *(Latin)* I am beginning, I begin
44 **spawn sth.** produce sth.
45 **noob** *(sl)* a person that has just started doing sth. and is very inexperienced in it
49 **ludus** *(Latin)* game, school
55 **monetary constraint** financial restriction
57 **school board-approved** accepted by the institution in charge of local schools
63 **pelt sb. with sth.** attack sb. by throwing things at them
give sb. atomic wedgies *(infml)* pull sb.'s underwear up forcefully as a kind of bullying, usually performed on male victims
64 **pummel sb.** ['pʌml] keep hitting sb.

COMPREHENSION

1 Understanding the situation

a Name Wade's reasons for wanting to attend the new OASIS public school.
b Describe the schools on Ludus.
c Point out what makes OPS #1873 so much better in Wade's opinion.

ANALYSIS

2 Telling names

Refer to the annotations and analyse what the names reveal about the *character and the *setting. SUPPORT p. 282

LANGUAGE AWARENESS

3 Telling images

a Study the following (parts of) sentences in their contexts and paraphrase their meaning.
1 My bankrupt diet of government-subsidized sugar and starch-laden food was a contributing factor … (ll. 9–10)
2 … the social equivalent of having a bull's-eye painted on my forehead. (ll. 13–14)
3 For me, school had been a Darwinian exercise. A daily gauntlet of ridicule, abuse, and isolation. (ll. 21–22)
4 The real public school system, the one run by the government, had been an underfunded, overcrowded train wreck for decades. (ll. 26–30)

b The sentences in **a** all contain *images. Interpret what they tell you about the protagonist.

c CHALLENGE Write an analysis of the telling *images in the text, taking further examples into account.

► SF 9: Paraphrasing

► SF 8: Structuring ideas
► SF 34: Argumentative writing

WRITING FOCUS ON SKILLS

Writing an argumentative text

In argumentative writing, we present arguments for and against a topic in order to convince others of our point of view. Writing an argumentative text is often a requirement in both school-leaving and international language proficiency examinations. You usually have a time limit and must keep within a certain number of words.

A typical assignment could be:
'Discuss whether attending OASIS public school will solve Wade's problems.'

1 Examining the task
Before gathering any arguments, make sure you are familiar with the meaning of the keywords of the task, i.e. *OASIS public school and Wade's problems*. (Refer to your work on text **A2**, p. 213.)

2 Collecting arguments
Divide the class into two groups. One half of the class has to find at least three reasons why OASIS might be considered the perfect school for Wade, the other half has to collect at least three arguments supporting the idea that his problems will remain. Work on your own and make notes.

3 Developing a thesis and an antithesis
Arrange a central meeting point in the classroom, the so-called database. As soon as you have finished collecting your arguments, go to the database and pair up with a student from the other group. Exchange your arguments. Discuss and reach an agreement on how to answer the topic question. The position you support is called the thesis ['θiːsɪz], the one you reject is called the antithesis [æn'tɪθəsɪs].

► SF 38: Writing a well-structured text

4 Composing the argumentative text
1 Introduction
Start your text with an interesting example, quote, definition or statistic related to your topic in order to grab your reader's attention. Then introduce the topic itself with a clear statement or *rhetorical question. Compare and evaluate the following three introductions:

A *Online schooling is a type of distance learning. You take courses without attending an actual school. Students and teachers interact via the internet, rather than meeting face-to-face. Wade sees this aspect as a big improvement on his old school. But will changing schools really solve his problems?*

B *'On my first day at OPS #1873, I thought I'd died and gone to heaven.' This is Wade's first impression of his new online school, after leaving the bullies of his old school behind. But will his opinion change as he gets to know his new school better?*

C *Statistically, one in four students is regularly bullied at school in the USA. So there are lots of real-life Wades looking for a way out of their difficult situation. Wade chooses to attend an online school to escape his problems at school. But will online-education really turn out to be a positive alternative for Wade?*

Either choose one of these introductions for your argumentative text or create your own.

2 Main part
On the basis of your notes from **3** on the opposite page, compose the main part of your argumentative text. Remember to start a new paragraph for every part of your text and avoid using contracted forms like *there's*, *she's*, *he'll*, etc.
Use some of the linking words from **Words in Context** to connect your ideas. Here are some additional phrases to help you structure your text:

► LP 11: Using the right register
► LP 14: Linking words and phrases
► LP 15: Connecting your thoughts (sentence structure)

Presenting various options	*on the one hand – on the other hand* *not only – but also* *either – or*
Giving reasons	*because* *as* *since ('da', 'weil')*
Giving examples	*for example (e.g.)* *for instance* *such as*

Complete the following sentences and add your own reasons and examples illustrating your arguments:

On the one hand, Wade's difficult situation may improve for a while because …
On the other hand, online education is unlikely to completely solve his problems as …

3 Conclusion
The purpose of the conclusion is to round off your argumentative text. For this reason you should not present any new arguments but rather draw a logical conclusion from your line of arguments in order to support your thesis, for example predict what will happen to Wade.

Summing up	*In brief ('kurz gesagt'), …* *To sum up, …* *In conclusion, I would like to say that …* *In the final analysis ('letztendlich', 'alles in allem'), …*

Complete the following conclusion by briefly stating your view and adding your own idea of how Wade might overcome his problem.

To sum up, in my opinion Wade's escape into the virtual world will only create more problems. Instead of trying to avoid all human interaction, he should rather …

Who wrote this essay, Perkins? You or Google?

A3 Digital media at school *Gerhard Witossek*

The following text is from the home page of a German educational institution. It includes information on the kinds of devices and services that are suitable for school, their benefits and potential drawbacks.

Digitale Medien im Lehr- und Lernprozess

Im Wandel

Ist von digitalen Medien im Unterricht die Rede, heißt das in vielen Schulen die Nutzung von Internet, Lernplattformen und Beamern. Diese sind in die Klassenräume eingezogen und sind weitgehend Bestandteil modernen Unterrichts.

In den letzten Jahren hat sich die Veränderungsdynamik deutlich beschleunigt: In der gegenwärtigen Diskussion geht es um die Nutzung von „interaktiven Whiteboards“, „Clouds“, „Tablet-PCs“ und „Smartphones“. Insbesondere die Tablet-PCs, großformatige Smartphones und die Arbeitsmöglichkeiten in der Cloud entwickeln sich rasant weiter.

Dabei stellt sich die Frage, wie diese Medien zielgerichtet im Unterricht eingesetzt werden können. Digitale Medien sollen nicht zum Selbstzweck werden, sondern den Lehr-Lern-Prozess fördern. Darüber hinaus soll den Schülerinnen und Schülern ein sinnvoller und reflektierter Umgang mit den neuen Technologien vermittelt werden. Es gilt also, mediendidaktische, medienerzieherische und mediengestalterische Kompetenzen zu entwickeln und miteinander in Einklang zu bringen.

Im Unterricht

Digitale Medien sicher zu beherrschen, die neuen Entwicklungen zu verfolgen und sinnvoll in den Lehr-Lern-Prozess zu implementieren, stellt für die einzelne Lehrkraft eine große Aufgabe dar. Neben anderen und bewährten Medien und Methoden sollen digitale Medien den Unterricht bereichern: Veranschaulichung, Handlungsorientierung oder die Förderung sozialer Kompetenzen sind nur einige Anforderungen an den Unterricht, die leichter mit digitalen Medien erfüllt werden können.

Die Arbeit mit digitalen Medien ermöglicht auch neue Unterrichtsstrukturen. Die üblichen 45-Minuten-Einheiten können besser verbunden werden. An Kreidetafeln lebte das erarbeitete Ergebnis bislang meist nur in den Heften der Schüler fort. Bedient man sich digitaler Tafeln oder Lernplattformen zur Sicherung der Ergebnisse, können diese wieder gezeigt, verändert und weiterentwickelt werden. Der „rote Faden“ einer Unterrichtssequenz wird dadurch deutlicher und die Entwicklungsschritte im Unterricht greifbarer.

Digitale Medien können Schülerinnen und Schülern auch ein anderes Lernen außerhalb der Schule ermöglichen. Beispielsweise können Unterrichtsmaterialien in die Cloud gestellt, interaktive Übungen im Internet genutzt oder Apps sinnvoll eingesetzt werden. […]

False friends

Beamer = video projector

Handy = mobile phone / cellphone

(Lautsprecher-)Box = (loud)speaker

Die Chancen

Der Einsatz digitaler Medien im Unterricht ist integraler Bestandteil zeitgemäßen pädagogischen Handelns. Schülerinnen und Schüler wachsen mit den neuen Technologien auf, sie gehören zu den Kulturtechniken unserer Gesellschaft. Deshalb liegt es auch in der Verantwortung der Schule, dazu beizutragen, dass Kinder und Jugendliche Medienkompetenz entwickeln können. Es darf auch nicht vergessen werden, dass Jugendliche bereits von sich aus digitale Medien für die Schule nutzen. Beispielsweise recherchieren sie mit Hilfe des mobilen Internets, tauschen sich per Facebook über Unterrichtsinhalte aus oder stellen sich in der Cloud gegenseitig Arbeitsmaterialien bereit. Diese generelle Bereitschaft zum Umgang mit digitalen Medien kann für den Unterricht produktiv genutzt werden.

Digitale Medien können auch die Lehrkraft entlasten. Im Internet finden sich Unterrichtsmaterialien, Freeware, Apps oder Lernplattformen, die schnell verfügbar und benutzerfreundlich sind. Zum Beispiel können der Tafelanschrieb am interaktiven Whiteboard abgespeichert, interaktive Übungen nach Hause mitgegeben oder Arbeitsblätter online zur Verfügung gestellt werden.

Die Nutzung neuer Medien im Unterricht bereitet Jugendliche auf ihr Arbeitsleben vor: In fast allen Berufen ist der Computer das Arbeitsmittel schlechthin. Die hohe Veränderungsdynamik sorgt auch hier für schnelle Entwicklungen, auf die Schülerinnen und Schüler vorbereitet werden müssen.

Die Risiken

Jugendliche werden häufig als „digital natives“ bezeichnet, also als eine Generation, die mit neuen Medien aufwächst und in deren Alltag die Nutzung digitaler Medien ganz normal ist. Dies führt allerdings nicht automatisch zu einem reflektierten und bedachten Umgang mit den Möglichkeiten der digitalen Welt. Beschäftigt man sich im Unterricht näher mit dem Schutz persönlicher Daten in sozialen Netzwerken, so zeigt sich sehr schnell, dass längst nicht alle Schülerinnen und Schüler die Risiken überblicken.

From: *Münchner kommunaler Bildungsserver*, October 2014

Mediation (German → English)

Imagine you are spending a school year as an exchange student at a high school in Oregon, USA. Your exchange school is about to introduce a new media concept. In order to incorporate a wide range of ideas, all of its exchange students are asked to outline the role of digital media at school in their home countries. Use the German article as the basis for your English presentation to the school board. Make some notes.

▸ SF41: Mediation of written and oral texts
▸ SF24: Giving a presentation

Being on display

B1 Should classrooms have video cameras?

- Work in pairs. Partner A deals with text 1 (T1), partner B with text 2 (T2). Read your text and take notes of the arguments you find.

T1 YES

Cameras will protect students and teachers
Video cameras need to be in the classroom in order to protect the safety of both students and teachers. In today's society we have video cameras in lots of public spaces such as libraries, school buses, parks, beaches, public streets, etc. A public school is a public place just like any other public place so people are not entitled to privacy rights.

1. A video recording could be the one thing that saves a teacher's job when there are false accusations.
2. Video recording could protect a student who wants protection from a teacher who is abusing them.
3. A video recording could ensure students are being protected from wrongdoing by other students.

For people who are worried about the security of it, the camera data and controls could be kept in the Principal's office. For people complaining about privacy rights and 'Big Brother': in public property the right to privacy does not exist. If you don't like it, you can either homeschool or pay to go to a private school. Oh by the way, the only eyewitness of the Boston Marathon Bombers? A video camera.

T1
6 **be entitled to (do) sth.** have the right to (do) sth.
8 **false accusations** being charged with sth. one has not done

T2
3 **police sth.** monitor sth. closely, keep control over sth.
interfere with sth. disturb sth., prevent sth. from succeeding
4 **benefit sb.** ['benɪfɪt] be to sb.'s advantage
11 **dehumanize sb.** [ˌdiː'hjuːmənaɪz] make sb. lose their human dignity
train sth. on sb. aim a camera, gun, etc. at sb.
16 **deter sth.** [dɪ'tɜː] prevent sth. from happening
19 **resemble sth.** be similar to sth.
20 **trapped** unable to move or escape

► LP 11: Using the right register

COMPREHENSION

1 Collecting arguments
Share your arguments with your partner and discuss which ones you consider most convincing.

LANGUAGE AWARENESS

2 Using more formal language
Texts T1 and T2 contain some elements of informal language. In an argumentative text, you should aim at using more formal language. Rewrite the underlined parts of these sentences using a more formal *register:

1 A public school is a public place just like any other public place. (T1, l. 5)
2 A video recording could be the one thing that saves a teacher's job. (T1, ll. 7–8)
3 You're treating them like they are already criminals. (T2, l. 12)
4 Think about how you would feel if you had a camera on you. (T2, ll. 20–21)

FACT FILE

CCTV (closed-circuit television) is a system in which television signals are not publicly broadcast but are monitored only by those people who have access to the system's content (**'closed circuit'** ['sɜːkɪt]). The primary purpose of CCTV is to reduce crime and anti-social behaviour, especially in public places and shops. With around 4.2 million CCTV cameras (one for every 14 people), Britain has become the most watched country in the world, a **'surveillance society'**.

What would be your immediate reaction to CCTV cameras in your classroom? Make notes and discuss them with a partner.

NO — T2

The possibility of abuse of power is too great.
I do not believe that cameras in the classroom would be/will be used to prevent bullying and abuse, rather to police and interfere with teaching. It would be too easy to manipulate and use the tapes in a way that benefits the administration and not the teacher. Furthermore, students and teachers should never be observed without their knowing, and I can see that becoming a problem.
You may wonder why teachers have such a problem with the invasion of privacy. It's not about having something to hide, after all, they are frequently observed and, after all, the classroom is full of students. It's dehumanizing to have cameras trained on teachers and students at all times. You're treating them like they are already criminals, and I think students especially have enough to deal with.
Claiming that this will prevent/end teacher or student abuse ignores the real problem. If there is abuse going on, there needs to be actual action taken. It's not enough to think that cameras will deter certain actions, as most people will not think of their actions as bullying, and if they do, they might be talented in hiding it.
I think schools resemble prisons enough as it is. I do not think students need further reason to feel trapped and exposed. Think about how you would feel if you had a camera on you while trying to learn.

From: *Debate.org*

TROUBLE SPOT

the possibility of (doing) sth. (l. 1)
the possibility that sth. may happen
Not: ~~the possibility to do sth.~~

TROUBLE SPOT

actual ['æktʃuəl] (l. 15) = *tatsächlich, wirklich, konkret*
But: *aktuell* = ***topical, current***

► LP 16: Avoiding Germanisms

BEYOND THE TEXT

3 Discussing the pros and cons of surveillance at school

Get together in groups of four and do the following task:
As there have been some cases of bullying and vandalism at your school, the school board wants to introduce CCTV cameras inside and outside the school building (except for the private toilet cubicles) to monitor and protect the students.
As student representatives you are on a committee that will be heard before the school board's final decision.

- **a** Discuss the pros and cons of the proposed idea.
- **b** Develop a concept that you consider acceptable for your school.
- **c** Present your concept to the school board (i.e. the class).

SUPPORT ► p. 282

► SF 27: Having a discussion
► SF 24: Giving a presentation

CD1 03

game changer sth. that changes a situation completely

B2 9/11 – a game changer *Barack Obama*

The following extract is taken from remarks on US intelligence programmes by US President Barack Obama, on 17 January 2014.

- Study the word cloud below, which contains the most frequently used words in Obama's remarks. The size of the letters indicates the frequency of the words. Work with a partner and speculate on the general content of Obama's remarks, using as many words from the cloud as possible.

1 **intelligence** [ɪn'telɪdʒəns] secret information about an enemy
2 **President Truman (Harry S. Truman)** 33rd US President (1945–1953)
4 **avert sth.** [ə'vɜːt] prevent sth.
6 **anchor sth.** ['æŋkə] fix sth. firmly
7 **checks and balances** mutual control

TROUBLE SPOT
ordinary
[*BE:* 'ɔːdnri, *AE:* 'ɔːrdneri] (ll. 7–8) = *gewöhnlich, durchschnittlich*
But: *ordinär* = ***vulgar*** ['vʌlgə]

9 **informer** sb. who gives away secrets, usually for money
13 **revelation** [ˌrevə'leɪʃn] act of disclosing secrets
15 **twilight** (here) final stage of sth. when it becomes weaker or less important than it used to be
18 **emerge** [i'mɜːdʒ] appear, to become known
19 **proliferation** [prəˌlɪfə'reɪʃn] rapid increase

Throughout American history, intelligence has helped secure our country and our freedoms. [...] (I)n the early days of the Cold War, President Truman created the National Security Agency, or NSA, to give us insights into the Soviet bloc, and provide our leaders with information they needed to confront aggression and avert catastrophe.

Throughout this evolution, we benefited from both our Constitution and our traditions of limited government. U.S. intelligence agencies were anchored in a system of checks and balances – with oversight from elected leaders, and protections for ordinary citizens. Meanwhile, totalitarian states like East Germany offered a cautionary tale of what could happen when vast, unchecked surveillance turned citizens into informers, and persecuted people for what they said in the privacy of their own homes.

In fact, even the United States proved not to be immune to the abuse of surveillance. And in the 1960s, government spied on civil rights leaders and critics of the Vietnam War. And partly in response to these revelations, additional laws were established in the 1970s to ensure that our intelligence capabilities could not be misused against our citizens. In the long, twilight struggle against Communism, we had been reminded that the very liberties that we sought to preserve could not be sacrificed at the altar of national security.

If the fall of the Soviet Union left America without a competing superpower, emerging threats from terrorist groups, and the proliferation of weapons of mass destruction placed new and in some ways more complicated demands on our intelligence agencies. Globalization and the Internet made these threats more acute, as technology erased borders and empowered individuals to project great violence, as well as great good. Moreover, these new threats raised new legal and new policy questions.

For while few doubted the legitimacy of spying on hostile states, our framework of laws was not fully adapted to prevent terrorist attacks by individuals acting on their own, or acting in small, ideologically driven groups on behalf of a foreign power.

The horror of September 11th brought all these issues to the fore. Across the political spectrum, Americans recognized that we had to adapt to a world in which a bomb could be built in a basement, and our electric grid could be shut down by operators an ocean away. We were shaken by the signs we had missed leading up to the attacks – how the hijackers had made phone calls to known extremists and traveled to suspicious places. So we demanded that our intelligence community improve its capabilities, and that law enforcement change practices to focus more on preventing attacks before they happen than prosecuting terrorists after an attack.

It is hard to overstate the transformation America's intelligence community had to go through after 9/11. Our agencies suddenly needed to do far more than the traditional mission of monitoring hostile powers and gathering information for policymakers. Instead, they were now asked to identify and target plotters in some of the most remote parts of the world, and to anticipate the actions of networks that, by their very nature, cannot be easily penetrated with spies or informants. [...]

From: the official website of the White House, 17 January 2014

24 **hostile** [*BE:* 'hɒstaɪl, *AE:* 'hɑːstl] belonging to the enemy
26 **on behalf of** as a representative of
27 **bring sth. to the fore** gain public attention for sth.
38 **plotter** sb. making secret plans to harm others

FACT FILE

9/11 refers to September 11th, 2001. On this date four planes were hijacked by terrorists in the USA. One plane crashed in Pennsylvania, one destroyed part of the Pentagon in Virginia, and two flew into the World Trade Center, New York City. About 3,000 people were killed in these attacks which were conducted by the extreme Islamic group Al Qaeda [æl'kaɪdə].

COMPREHENSION

1 The structure of the text

a Divide this extract into parts and give headings to each part.

b Outline Obama's argumentation in your own words.

▸ SF 38: Writing a well-structured text

ANALYSIS

2 Understanding the title

Explain why 9/11 can be considered a 'game changer' with regard to US security policy.

3 Analysing stylistic devices

▸ SF 17: Analysing stylistic devices
▸ Glossary, p. 323

a The phrases in the box on the right are quotes from the text. Explain their meaning.

b Point out what *stylistic device is used in all of these phrases and analyse the effect achieved by employing it.

c Go over the text again and find at least one example of an *antithesis. Describe its effect on the reader.

- 'U.S. intelligence agencies were anchored in a system of checks and balances' (ll. 6–7)
- 'states like East Germany offered a cautionary tale' (ll. 8–9)
- 'the very liberties that we sought to preserve could not be sacrificed at the altar of national security' (ll. 16–17)

BEYOND THE TEXT

4 Evaluating a cartoon

▸ SF 13: Analysing cartoons

a Analyse the cartoon on the right, keeping in mind some of the information presented in Obama's speech.

b CHALLENGE 'It is hard to overstate the transformation America's intelligence community had to go through after 9/11.' (ll. 35–36)
Look for a cartoon on the internet that expresses the idea of the quote, print it and bring it along to class. Tape it to the wall of your classroom and analyse it orally with your classmates as they walk from cartoon to cartoon.
After examining all the cartoons, stand next to the one you prefer in order to select the most popular cartoon. Be prepared to justify your choice.

FACT FILE

Reality TV shows feature ordinary people instead of professional *actors or *actresses. There are basically two types. In one, participants are exposed to TV audiences 24/7 and are required to share an artificial environment with complete strangers for a limited period of time. The second type of show depicts a mixture of carefully selected 'scenes' from participants' real lives and acted-out events in order to create an entertaining and attention-grabbing story for viewers.

2 **require sth.** [rɪ'kwaɪə] need sth.
have the makings of sth. have the necessary qualities for becoming a particular type of person
4 **hopeful** *(n)* sb. who wants to succeed or is likely to win
7 **launch sb. on Mars** [lɔːnʃ] send sb. to Mars
decade ['dekeɪd, dɪ'keɪd] period of ten years
9 **be shortlisted** *(BE)* be selected from a longer list of applicants
10 **undergo sth.** experience sth. challenging or unpleasant
16 **dedicate sth.** ['dedɪkeɪt] give all of one's attention and effort to sth.
pioneering [ˌpaɪə'nɪərɪŋ] *(adj)* first of its kind
18 **expand sth.** make sth. grow larger
21 **from scratch** from the very beginning, with very little preparation
22 **factual** ['fæktʃuəl] based on facts
25 **maintain sth.** [–'–] make sth. continue
38 **approximately** [ə'prɒksɪmətli] nearly; more or less

Reality TV

C1 Big Brother out of this world *Ellie Zolfagharifard*

Creators of a reality TV show plan to broadcast the selection and training of a group of candidates who will be sent on a one-way mission to Mars in 2025. Is Big Brother going to take on the red planet?

It takes a certain type of person to apply for a one-way ticket to Mars. Not only will they require mental and physical strength, but now, they will also need to have the makings of the next reality-TV star. Endemol, the production company behind Big Brother, has announced that it will document the progress of a group of hopefuls as they compete for a 2025 ticket to the red planet.

The reality series will follow the selection process of the privately-funded Mars One mission, which aims to launch 20 humans on Mars within the next decade. During the first selection round, more than 200,000 people signed up to be part of the first human colony on the red planet. The applicants have now been shortlisted to 705 candidates – 418 men and 287 women – who will undergo what is described as 'the world's toughest job interview'.

Darlow Smithson Productions (DSP), an Endemol company, will film the hopefuls as they are 'tested to the extreme as part of an elite training programme'. Candidates do not need to have any scientific qualifications and a Big Brother-style audience vote will be used to make the final choice. Any chosen Mars settlers will then be required to dedicate eight years of their lives preparing for the 300 million-mile pioneering mission. The ticket is one-way and Mars One plans to send additional crews every two years to expand the colony.

DSP said its production will be seen around the world, with the first series likely to be appearing in early 2015. The plan is for the cameras to also follow the first human settlers on the planet as they attempt to build a new society from scratch.

'Our team felt all along that we needed a partner whose strength lies in factual storytelling to an international audience,' Mars One co-founder Bas Lansdorp said in a statement. 'DSP will provide that to Mars One, while allowing our selection committee to maintain control of the applicant selection process.' [...]

The majority of applicants for the one-way trip to Mars came from the US, with India and China coming in second and third place. The second round will include an interview with Mars One committee members, and candidates advancing to the third round will compete against one another. The third round will include a series of challenges to prepare candidates for the potential mission and will be broadcast on television and online.

The group said it aims to have a human settlement on Mars within a decade. Journey time to Mars, which is approximately 40 million miles away depending on its position in orbit, would be around 200 days.

From: *Daily Mail*, 3 June 2014

Bride-to-be Kellie Gerardi (25) says she will leave her fiancé on Earth if she is selected to live on the red planet forever as part of a reality TV show.

COMPREHENSION

1 How the project works

a Outline the basic idea of the project and the stages of the selection process.

b Summarize the role reality TV plays in the project described in the text.

► SF 31: Writing a summary

ANALYSIS

2 What makes the text appealing?

Analyse the methods used to make the text appealing (e.g. heading, *register, *stylistic devices, quotes, bias/neutral position?). SUPPORT ► p. 283

LANGUAGE AWARENESS

3 Word order and emphasis

► LP 13: Placing emphasis on key points

a Look at the beginning of the second sentence of the text again (ll. 1–2). Explain why the auxiliary *will* comes before *they* in the first half of the sentence *(will they require)* but after *they* in the second half *(they will … need)*.

b CHALLENGE ► Write two more sentences about the Mars mission that start with *Not only … (but …)*.

BEYOND THE TEXT

4 Applying for the Mars One astronaut selection programme

a Work out a list of criteria that you consider important when selecting a potential settler on Mars. Try to decide on the three most relevant criteria.

b Write a formal letter of application to the selection committee of Mars One trying to convince them to send you to Mars.

► SF 29: Writing a formal letter or email
► LP 11: Using the right register
► SF 26: Taking part in an interview

5 ROLE-PLAY **The world's toughest job interview**

Act out an interview between the members of the selection committee and four applicants for the Mars One project. The rest of the class then vote on the two applicants to be accepted and give reasons for their choice.

C2 The ultimate reality TV show *DBC Pierre*

Vernon Little is a teenager who has been wrongly convicted of murdering classmates and is now on death row. In his cell he is watching an interview on TV in which Lally (the nickname of Eulalio Ledesma), a journalist, explains his idea of 'the ultimate reality TV show' to the reporter Bob.

be on death row [rəʊ] be a prisoner sentenced to death, waiting for the death penalty to be carried out

'So you're effectively proposing to fund the State's penal system by selling broadcast rights to the prisoners' executions? I mean – isn't a prisoner's last hour a little *personal*?'

'Not at all – don't forget that all executions are witnessed, even today. We're simply expanding the audience to include anyone with an interest in the proper function of law.' Lally puts a hand on his hip. 'Not so long ago, Bob, all executions were public – even held in the town square. Crime went down, public satisfaction went up. Throughout history it's been society's right to punish delinquents by its own hands. It makes plain sense to give that right back to society.'

'Hence the web-vote?'

'Exactly. And we're not just talking executions here – we're talking the ultimate reality TV, where the public can monitor, via cable or internet, prisoners' whole lives on death row. They can live amongst them, so to speak, and make up their own minds about a convict's worthiness for punishment. Then each week, viewers across the globe can cast a vote to decide which prisoner is executed next. It's humanity in action – the next logical step toward true democracy. ''But surely, due process dictates the fate of prisoners?'

1 **fund sth.** provide money for sth.
penal ['pi:nl] connected with lawful punishment
8 **delinquent** [dɪ'lɪŋkwənt] criminal
10 **hence** *(fml)* consequently
12 **monitor sth.** watch and check sth.
16 **due** *(adj)* right and proper

Part C

18 **tamper with sth.** interfere with sth.
appeals process possibility of taking a court case one has lost to a higher court *(Berufungsrecht)*
19 **recourse** [*BE:* -'-, *AE:* '- -] *(fml)* sth. that may provide help in a difficult situation
20 **roster** list
hooshy laugh (here) laughter with loud breathing sounds
21 **momentous** [mə'mentəs] important
25 **breach sth.** violate sth.
26 **forfeit** ['fɔːfɪt] loss of sth. as a punishment
con *(infml)* convict, prisoner
27 **languish** ['læŋgwɪʃ] *(fml)* suffer sth. unpleasant for a long time
29 **expediency** [ɪk'spiːdiənsi] sth. that is useful to achieve a purpose
33 **nod at sb.** move one's head in sb.'s direction
gear up for sth. prepare for sth.
34 **shot at sth.** *(infml)* attempt at sth., effort for sth.

'Absolutely, and we can't tamper with that. But the new fast-track appeals process means prisoners' last recourses at law are spent much sooner, after which I say the public should have a hand in the roster of final events.' Lally lets fly a hooshy laugh at the reporter, and spreads his hands wide. 'In the tradition of momentous progress, it's blindingly simple, Bob: criminals cost money. Popular TV makes money. Criminals are popular on TV. Put them together and, presto – problem solved.'

The reporter pauses as a helicopter settles in the background. Then he asks, 'What do you say to those who claim prisoners' rights will be breached?'

'Oh *please* – prisoners, by definition, live in *forfeit* of their rights. Anyway, cons today can languish in institutions for years without knowing their fate – wouldn't you say *that* was cruel? We're finally giving them what the law has always promised but never delivered – expediency. Not only that, they'll have greater access to spiritual counsel, and musical choices to accompany their final event. We'll even craft a special segment around their final statement, with the background imagery of their choice. Believe me – prisoners will welcome these changes.'

The reporter smiles and nods at Lally. 'And what of reports that you're gearing up for a shot at the senate?'

I switch off the set. I ain't looking forward to cameras in here. We just have an open toilet, see? I guess that's where the money gets made. Internet viewers will be able to choose which cells to watch, and change camera angles and all. On regular TV there'll be edited highlights of the day's action. Then the general public will vote by phone or internet. They'll vote for who should die next. The cuter we act, the more we entertain, the longer we might live. I heard an old con say it'd be just like the life of a real actor.

From: *Vernon God Little*, 2003

COMPREHENSION

1 Lally's ultimate reality TV show
In pairs, briefly sum up the concept of Lally's ultimate reality TV show. With a partner, exchange your opinions of it. Discuss whether you would have asked similar questions if you had been the reporter.

ANALYSIS

2 Lally's mode of argumentation
a Explain Lally's line of argumentation to convince the reporter and the audience of his idea. SUPPORT p. 283
b Identify *stylistic devices that he uses to underline his point of view.

► SF 17: Analysing stylistic devices

3 Vernon's reaction
Examine Vernon's reaction to the interview.

BEYOND THE TEXT

4 Interpreting a cartoon
Compare the criticism of reality shows voiced in the cartoon on the left and the novel extract above.

► SF 13: Analysing cartoons

5 Responding to the interview
Imagine Lally/Eulalio Ledesma invited the viewers to send him some comments on his project. Write him an email.

► SF 29: Writing a formal letter or email

6 Commenting
'Your remote control is the most powerful weapon you have to show the country what you want.' (Quotation from *Hazard County* by Allison Moore)
a Discuss this statement with a partner and make notes.
b CHALLENGE Write a comment on the statement.

► SF 34: Argumentative writing

Discussing the pros and cons of modern media

Write a text on the following topic:

Will the media change our lives for better or worse over the next ten years? Discuss.

Find a tool to make your poster here: **Webcode** context-50

Instructions

1 Create four posters to place along the walls of your classroom. Each poster will have one of the following headings: **the internet – TV – school/work – surveillance**. Divide the posters vertically into two parts for the positive and negative aspects of the headings.

The internet	TV	School/Work	Surveillance
positive	positive	positive	positive
negative	negative	negative	negative

2 Choose one expert per poster.

3 The rest of the class walk from poster to poster, suggesting their ideas for each of the topics to the experts, who are to write down the entries on the posters.

4 Stand next to the poster which you would like to use as the basis for your text.

5 Discuss with your classmates who have chosen the same poster as you which aspects on the poster you consider most important.

6 Check Focus on Skills (pp. 214–215) and write an argumentative text, narrowing down the topic ('Will the media change our lives for better or worse over the next ten years?') to the heading of your chosen poster.

► SF 34: Argumentative writing

7 Having finished this task, exchange your text with a classmate who has chosen the same topic. Your teacher will give you an assessment sheet to fill work. Evaluate each other's work, keeping in mind what you have learnt in this chapter.

► SF 40: Proofreading

11 Visions of the Future – Utopias and Dystopias

Download a list of chapter vocab here: **Webcode** context-08

1 Finding captions for pictures

a Look at the following captions and match them to the images above (there is one more caption than you need).

1 Paradise island
2 Life in a bubble
3 Taking care of you
4 Watch out for the enemy
5 Thought control
6 How I see the world

b Compare your ideas with a partner.

2 Researching topics

Get into groups of five. Within your group, assign a different picture to each member. Make notes on your image, think about what the image could represent and do some research. Present your findings to the others in your group.

► SF 11: Analysing pictures
► SF 5: Doing research

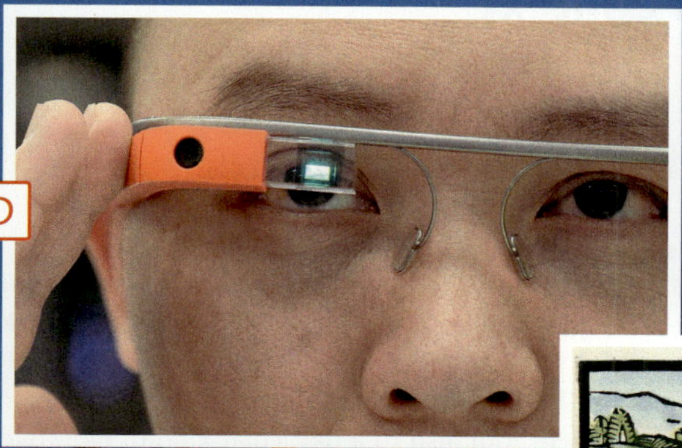
D

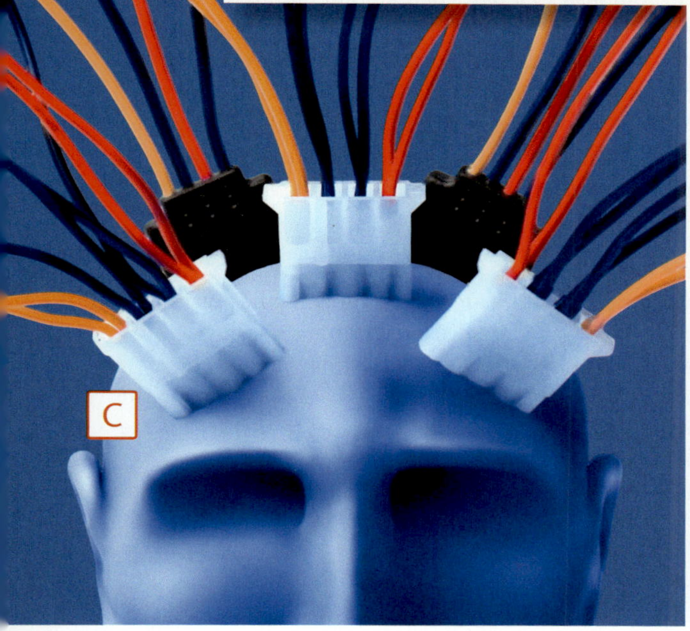
C

E

3 An imaginary journey

a Take another look at the pictures on these pages, then sit back, close your eyes and listen …

CD1 07

b When you have opened your eyes again, picture one or two of the photos that you took when you stepped out of the phone box in the year 2121. Describe your photos to a partner and listen to your partner's descriptions.

c Based on your imaginary journey, write a text about your impressions – were they positive or negative? You can add one or two images of the 'photos' that you took.

PREVIEW

In this chapter you will you will examine works of *fiction in which writers have considered present-day issues and transformed them into imaginary positive and negative depictions of the future.

From utopia to dystopia

CD1 08

Listen to an audio version of the text on the CD or download it here:

Webcode context-09

Exciting worlds

The term 'utopia' comes from Greek and means both 'no-place' and 'good-place'. In 1516 the English lawyer, philosopher and adviser to the king, Thomas More, wrote a work of *fiction describing a society on an island he named *Utopia*. From then on, the term was used to refer to imaginary, paradise-like places, but also to a particular kind of narrative, known as utopian literature.

Today, the word 'utopia' is applied to a wide range of real places: from calm yoga retreats and beautiful holiday destinations to theme parks, shopping malls and other centres of entertainment. Modern day utopias reflect key parts of our society, its lust for self-indulgence and constant excitement.

Peace and safety

In More's day, the imaginary and ideal utopias were often distant, yet to be discovered islands – thus creating the illusion of actually existing. Such utopian societies were governed by strict sets of laws, forcing the individual to repress his unreliable nature and act for the good of society.

Early utopian literature was based on the desire for a better life and a society in which peace was guaranteed. During the Victorian era, political convictions such as socialism and the belief in scientific progress caused utopian literature to flourish. However, as the world had more or less been mapped out, the settings switched from undiscovered territories to familiar places and how the author envisaged them in the future.

Oppressive governments

After two world wars and the horrors of the first half of the 20th century, former utopian ideals seemed absurd. Moreover, totalitarianism often led to the establishment of dictatorships instead of benefitting mankind. As a consequence, the belief of heaven on earth turned into a nightmarish vision: the term 'utopia' was replaced by 'dystopia', meaning 'bad', or 'hard' or – to put it simply – a utopia gone wrong. The main aim of a dystopia is to portray images of the future as realistic and threatening possibilities.

In the 20th century, dystopia became the main form of visionary literature, mirroring society's failures and projecting today's divisive issues (such as capitalism, consumerism, self-indulgence, the power of science and technology and globalization) into the future. If dystopias cause despair, it is because writers want readers to think about the present and see their visions of the future as a serious menace.

However, dystopias that leave no room for hope fail in their intention. Their true purpose is to make us realize that we should be committed to making a better society. For this reason, the distinction between utopian and dystopian literature has become increasingly unclear: dystopian literature often includes utopian elements, and vice versa.

1 Definitions and derivatives

a Copy and complete the chart below. You may not be able to fill all gaps.

Nouns	Verbs	Adjective
narrative	*narrate sth.*	*narratable*
	portray sb./sth.	
		nightmarish
vision		
		divisive
	repress	
		imaginary

b The phrases below are definitions of words used in the text on p. 54. Identify these words, write them in added lines in the table above and complete the table where possible:

- *a strong belief*
- *a type of literature that describes imaginary events and people*
- *a false idea or belief*
- *a threatening person or thing*
- *a system of government in which there is only one political party with complete power*

2 Synonyms

a Match the formal phrases on the left with the corresponding informal phrases on the right. One informal definition is missing, so write your own definition in informal English. Check your solutions with a partner.

► SF 1: Dealing with unknown words

Formal style	Everyday English
1 *undiscovered territories*	a *a certain type of story*
2 *mirror sth.*	b *be willing to work really hard for sth.*
3 *a particular kind of narrative*	c *making people think that*
4 *repress one's emotions*	d *show sth.*
5 *creating the illusion of*	e *places that haven't been found yet*
6 *be committed to sth.*	f *topics which often cause arguments*
7 *divisive issues*	g …

b Fill in the gaps with phrases from the 'formal style' column:

1 Certain social media … privacy, but you never know who is reading your messages!
2 Dystopian literature often … negative aspects of today's society.
3 If we want to keep the earth habitable, we should … sustainability.
4 Science fiction stories are …
5 At present, data privacy and the legalization of cannabis are …

3 Speaking

Explain the development from utopian to dystopian literature in everyday English. Use as many words and expressions from the boxes above as possible.

Part A

Entertain me!

A1 Inside our heads *M.T. Anderson*

Feed is a young adult science fiction novel written by M.T. Anderson. From the viewpoint of an American teenager, it shows the descent of the USA into a culture based mainly on advertising and consumerism.

When I wrote *Feed*, (in 2001) my intention wasn't really to predict future tech – but instead, to think about cultural conditions as they already were then.

All around us ads, TV shows, and movies nudge us with images of the high life, playing on our desire to belong. When I was a teen, this drove me crazy (as it bugs and worries many teens). There's always that subliminal message seducing us and bullying us: *if you just get this, and buy this, and order that, you'll be cool, and you'll be loved. See how much fun these kids are having? If you want to be wanted, then you need to want what other people want. And other people – what they want is this. Buy it. Buy it now.*

This marketing has become even more intense (and not just for teens!) now that most of us are connected all the time through devices of one kind or another. [...]

So I began to conceive a story in which these media connections and social networking connections weren't external, but within us all. What if we no longer needed the devices? What if we had an internet feed within us, so we were never disconnected?

From: *Feed*, 2002

1 **predict sth.** say that sth. will happen
3 **nudge sb.** push sb. gently
4 **play on sth.** take advantage of sth. (e.g. fear or emotions) to get what you want
bug sb. annoy sb.
5 **subliminal** affecting your mind even though you are not aware of it
seduce sb. (here) persuade sb.
12 **conceive sth.** (here) imagine sth., think of sth.

COMPREHENSION

1 The beginnings of a novel
Outline how M.T. Anderson became a writer of dystopian fiction.

BEYOND THE TEXT

2 YOU CHOOSE Giving your own opinion

a Justify why you would like to read the story (or why not).

OR

b Comment on whether you agree with Anderson that 'There's always that subliminal message seducing us and bullying us' (ll. 5–6). Give examples.

A2 Don't let me get bored *M.T. Anderson*

► SF 14: Reading strategies

Feed begins with a journey to the moon. Before reading the extract, make a few notes on what you would expect to find if you went there. Now compare your notes with what Anderson's protagonist finds.

We went to the moon to have fun, but the moon turned out to completely suck.

We went on a Friday, because there was shit-all to do at home. It was the beginning of spring break. Everything at home was boring. Link Arwaker was like, 'I'm so null,' and Marty was all, 'I'm null too, unit', but I mean we were all pretty null, because for the last like hour we'd been playing with three uninsulated wires that were coming out of the wall. We were trying to ride shocks off them. So Marty told us that there was this fun place for lo-grav on the moon. Lo-grav can be kind of stupid, but this was supposed to be good. It was called the Ricochet Lounge. We thought we'd go for a few days with some of the girls and stay at a hotel there and go dancing.

2 **shit-all** *(sl) nichts*
3 **be null** (here) feel nothing
6 **ride shocks off sth.** get electric shocks from sth.
8 **ricochet** ['rɪkəʃeɪ] *abprallen*

We flew up and our feeds were burbling all sorts of things about where to stay and what to eat. It sounded pretty fun, and at first there were lots of pictures of dancing and people with romper-gills and metal wings, and I was like, *This will be big, really big,* but then I guess it wasn't so skip when we were flying over the surface of the moon itself, because the moon was just like it always is, after your first few times there, when you get over being like, *Whoa, unit! The moon! The goddamn moon!* and instead there's just the rockiness and the suckiness, and the craters all being full of old broken shit, like domes nobody's using any more and wrappers and claws.

The thing I hate about space is that you can feel how old and empty it is. Don't know if the others felt like I felt, about space? But I think they did, because they all got louder. They all pointed more and squeezed close to Link's window.

You need the noise of your friends, in space.

I feel really sorry for people who have to travel by themselves. In space, that must suck. When you're going places with other people, with this big group, everyone is leaning toward each other and people are laughing and they're chatting and things are great, and it's just like a commercial for jeans, or something with nougat.

From: *Feed*, 2002

10 **burble** (here) *babbeln*
12 **romper-gills** in the novel, device that allows you to breathe in space (gills = *Kiemen*)
14 **skip** (here) *toll*
19 **dome** *Kuppel*
20 **wrapper** piece of plastic that is wrapped around sth., e.g. food
claw (here) *Greifer*

COMPREHENSION

1 Finding headings for the text

Match the following terms with the appropriate lines in the text (there are more headings than you need):

amusement • belonging • boredom • disappointment • excitement • fascination • loneliness • vandalism

► SF 10: Working with closed test formats

LANGUAGE AWARENESS

2 Using formal English

Look at the narrator's language and put the following phrases from the text into more *formal English:

1 'the moon turned out to completely suck' (l. 1)
2 'there was shit-all to do at home' (l. 2)
3 'lo-grav' (l. 7)
4 'our feeds were burbling all sorts of things' (l. 10)
5 'it wasn't so skip' (l. 14)

ANALYSIS

3 Analysing genre and technique

a Examine what you consider to be utopian and dystopian elements in the text. Compare your findings with a partner.

b Analyse Anderson's narrative technique. SUPPORT p. 284

► SF 36: Writing a text analysis
► SF 19: Analysing narrative prose

BEYOND THE TEXT

4 YOU CHOOSE **Creative writing**

a Re-write the text from the point of view of a third-person *narrator.

OR

b Choose a different futuristic context and write an *interior monologue for a teenager with a feed.

► SF 37: Doing a creative writing task

FACT FILE

Film trailers are designed to capture our attention and to draw us to the cinema. Just like commercials, they are a means of advertising. The idea of the trailer is to summarize the film and to indicate what makes the film different from all the other films on the film circuit.

In contrast to a film clip, which shows a short but complete sequence from a film, in a trailer various scenes from the film are cut and arranged so that the audience is given a good idea of what the film will be about. It can establish the mood, introduce characters and the setting, and reveal the *plot and the main themes.

Typical trailer features

- reveal something of the plot, but not too much,
- are fast-paced – short shots and quick cuts between key scenes,
- do not show events in the correct order,
- use music and sound effects to manipulate emotions,
- build up to a climax, and then finish (cliffhanger), so the final shot leaves a lasting effect on the audience,
- show the title of the film at the end, so that the audience will remember it.

1 *Choose what you consider to be the three most important features of a trailer.*

2 *Together with a partner, compare your ideas and agree on the three most important features.*

A3 The Hunger Games

The trailer you are about to watch is for the 2012 blockbuster film The Hunger Games, *based on the novel by Suzanne Collins and starring Jennifer Lawrence.*

TROUBLE SPOT

star = *die Hauptrolle spielen*
star sb. = *jdn. in einer Hauptrolle zeigen*

DVD

tribute person who fights in the Hunger Games
odds *(pl) Gewinnchancen*
victor winner

COMPREHENSION

1 Identifying key features of a trailer
Watch the trailer. Together with a partner, tick off the features that you noted down after working on the Fact File above. Share your findings with another pair. Were all of the features you listed in the trailer?

▶ SF23: Analysing a film

2 Viewing for detail
Work in groups of three. Copy the viewing log below and decide who is going to be responsible for which topic. Take notes on your topic as you watch.

Characters	Setting(s)	Plot and main themes
Information, behaviour, relationships	When and where is the film set? How is the setting established?	What is the film going to be about?

▶ SF27: Having a discussion

BEYOND THE TEXT

3 Discussing the trailer

a In groups of three, discuss whether or not the trailer is effective.
▶ LANGUAGE HELP

b CHALLENGE ▶ Make notes on the most effective, memorable or impressive parts of the trailer and present them to the class, giving reasons for your choices.

LANGUAGE HELP

- By focussing on … the trailer attracts a target group.
- By showing … the trailer arouses curiosity.
- All in all, the trailer is/isn't effective because …

VIEWING **FOCUS ON SKILLS**

Viewing films

► SF 23: Analysing a film

You will watch three extracts from the film The Hunger Games. *For each extract, you will focus on a different aspect important for film analysis.*

1 Analysing presentation of characters

a In groups of three, watch the first film extract and take notes on the key details regarding how the different characters are shown. Each person in your group should concentrate on one set of characters. Copy the viewing log below, which will help you keep track of what you see:

	Setting	Costumes and makeup	Facial expressions and body language	Camera angles
1 Tributes				
2 Audience				
3 Game makers Sponsors President Snow				

DVD

glimpse *(n)* quick look
overstate sth. exaggerate sth.
goosebumps *Gänsehaut*
have the odds in your favour be lucky

b In your group, discuss how the viewer's impressions of the different groups are influenced.

DVD

TROUBLE SPOT
technique = *Methode*
technology = *Technik*

2 Analysing suspense

a In groups of four, watch the next film extract, concentrating on how the film uses different techniques to create *suspense. Each one of you is responsible for one specific aspect:

1 Feelings: Katniss's emotions and how they are shown	2 Time: How the sense of time is conveyed	3 Sounds: e.g. music, voices, silence	4 Colours: darkness and light

b Discuss how different techniques create suspense in this extract.

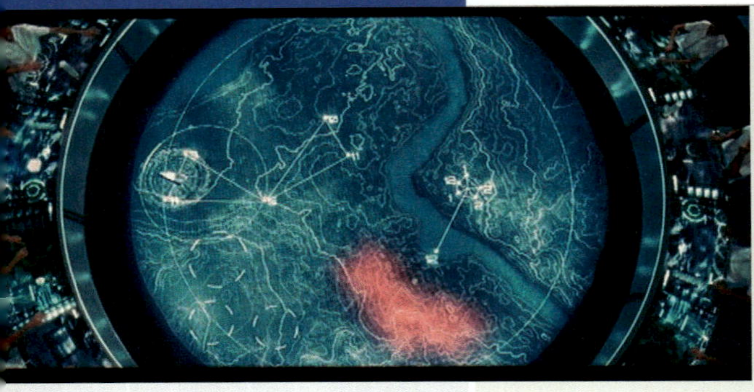

3 The portrayal of themes

a In groups of three, watch the third extract and take notes on the following aspects:

The role of the game-makers	The role of the sponsors	How the tributes cope in the arena

b Examine which contemporary divisive issues are dealt with in *The Hunger Games*.

c Watch all the extracts again and note down utopian and dystopian elements. Compare *The Hunger Games* with reality TV shows you know and note down the similarities and differences.

DVD

starve die because you do not have enough food

A4 Flipping the bird at authority

This article from German media website Spiegel Online *reviews the second film in* The Hunger Games *series:* Catching Fire *(2013).*

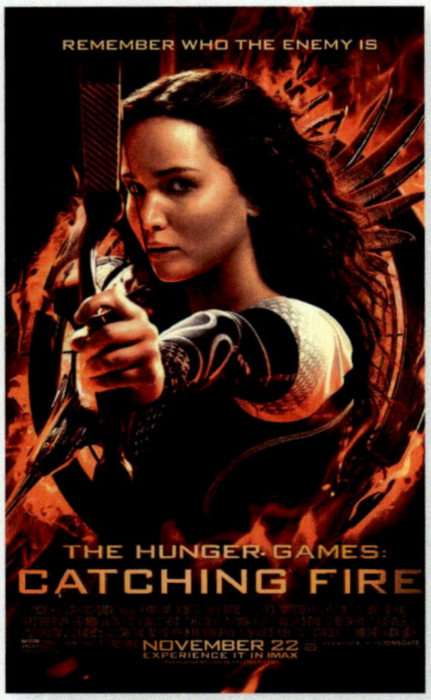

„Die Tribute von Panem – Catching Fire“: Sie zeigt den Mächtigen den Vogel

Die Dystopie von Panem gewinnt sicher keinen Preis für Originalität, zu offensichtlich orientiert sich Collins' Entwurf dafür an vertrauten Vorbildern aus der zivilisations- und autoritätskritischen Science-Fiction. Das ist aber kein Makel, denn die grimmige Welt mit ihrem grausamen Klassensystem erfüllt durchaus ihren Zweck. Simpler, materieller und greifbarer als andere Zukunftsvisionen, ist es der Schauplatz, an dem Katniss, das widerständige „Girl on Fire“, eine neue Art von Teen-Heldin sein kann.

Als unfreiwillige Lichtgestalt des Lumpenproletariats ist sie weit entfernt von den elitären Zauberer- und Vampir-Aristokratien, die Fiktionen wie „Harry Potter“ und „Twilight“ bevölkern und deren Sorgen im Vergleich wie Luxusprobleme wirken. Katniss ist Geschöpf der sozialen, ökonomischen und moralischen Dauerkrise ihrer Welt, und je mehr sie sich von den vermeintlich naturgegebenen Verhältnissen emanzipiert, desto bedrohlicher wird sie für die Herrschenden. Und mag sie auch sehr geschickt (und gefährlich) im Umgang mit Pfeil und Bogen sein, ihre wahren Waffen bleiben Intellekt, Intuition und das Wissen um die Macht von Gesten und Bildern. [...]

Als Impresario der Hunger Games traktiert Heavensbee vom Regiepult aus die Tribute in der megalomanen Arena mit Flutwellen, Giftnebel, Blutregen und

sonstigem telegenen Terror. Die handfeste Survival-Action ist eindrucksvoll bebildert, doch längst nicht so spektakulär wie der Kampf der Symbole, den Katniss mit dem System austrägt. In seinen besten Momenten verbindet „Catching Fire" so großes Melodrama mit offensiver Mediensatire und zeigt das staatstragende Gladiatorenspiel als sadistische Zuspitzung des Casting-Show-Phänomens.
Gegen das Drehbuch der Mächtigen die Deutungshoheit über das eigene Image wiederzuerlangen, ist daher der wirksamste Akt der Rebellion.

So ist Katniss zuallererst die Marianne eines ästhetischen Aufstands, wenn sie in ihren Auftritten das verbotene Bild des „Mockingjay" popularisiert, eines Vogels mit besonderer Bedeutung für die Vergangenheit Panems. Selbiger ist konsequenterweise auch Leitmotiv der millionenschweren Werbekampagne von „Catching Fire", eines Films, der wie sein Vorläufer weitaus besser ist, als er eigentlich sein müsste. Eben weil er sein junges Zielpublikum nicht für dumm hält und unabhängig vom Unterhaltungsdiktat eine Haltung einnimmt, die auch jenseits der Pubertät begeistern kann.

Darum sollte man nach dem abschließenden Cliffhanger auch für die nächste Fortsetzung dranbleiben: The revolution *will* be televised.

From: *Spiegel Online*, 2013

1 Paraphrasing difficult vocabulary

▶ SF 9: Paraphrasing

You want to help a friend who only speaks a bit of German to understand the article. Explain the following words and phrases in English as simply as possible.

1 'Deutungshoheit über das eigene Image' (l. 23)
2 'Drehbuch' (l. 23)
3 'Geschöpf der moralischen Krise' (l. 10)
4 'Klassensystem' (l. 4)
5 'Werbekampagne' (l. 28)
6 'sehr geschickt im Umgang mit Pfeil und Bogen sein' (l. 13)
7 'Zielpublikum' (l. 30)
8 'zivilisationskritisch' (ll. 2–3)
9 'Zuspitzung des Casting-Show-Phänomens' (l. 22)

2 Mediation (German → English)

▶ SF 41: Mediation of written and oral texts

You are spending a year at a US high school. In Media Studies class, each student must present a film. You would like to present *The Hunger Games – Catching Fire*. Although your teacher has never seen the film, she will not allow you to present it as it 'glorifies violence'. Use arguments you found in the article to write her an email to convince her that the film has qualities making it suitable for the class. ▶ LANGUAGE HELP

LANGUAGE HELP
- Taking into account … how about …?
- I would greatly appreciate your permission to …
- I would really appreciate it if …
- I really understand your concern but …
- Although you might not agree, I really feel that …
- Have you considered that …?

3 YOU CHOOSE Writing

a Put yourself in the position of the teacher in **2** and write a response to an email written by someone else in your class.

OR

b Choose a different film with dystopian themes and write a four-minute presentation for the media studies class. Describe the plot, themes and protagonist(s), and explain how the film portrays a dystopia.

Give me stability in the community

B1 Inside the Circle *Dave Eggers*

In his 2013 novel, Dave Eggers depicts the Circle, a fast-growing digital corporation that offers a wide range of community attractions to its employees in the hope of binding them to the company. Mae Holland has just been hired thanks to her best friend Annie, who also works there, and on her first day is given a tour of the campus.

- Quickly list the internet companies you know and say what you have heard about their reputations.
- Discuss with a partner whether you would like to work for such a company, and what you roughly imagine your workday would be like.

Extract 1: A utopian workplace

The rest of the day was a blur of glass rooms and brief, impossibly warm introductions. Everyone she [= Mae] met was busy, just short of overworked, but nevertheless thrilled to meet her, so happy she was there, any friend of Annie's ... There was a tour of the health center, and an introduction to the dreadlocked Dr. Hampton who ran it. There was a tour of the emergency clinic and the Scottish nurse who did the admitting. A tour of the organic gardens, a hundred yards square, where there were two full-time farmers giving a talk to a large group of Circlers while they sampled the latest harvest of carrots and tomatoes and kale. There was a tour of the mini-golf area, the movie theater, the bowling alleys, the grocery store. Finally, deep in what Mae assumed was the corner of the campus – she could see the fence beyond, the rooftops of San Vincenzo hotels where visitors to the Circle stayed – they toured the company dorms. Mae had heard something about them, Annie mentioning that sometimes she crashed on campus and now preferred those rooms to her own home. Walking through the hallways, seeing the tidy rooms, each with a shiny kitchenette, a desk, an overstuffed couch and bed, Mae had to agree that the appeal was visceral.

'There are 180 rooms now, but we're growing quickly,' Josiah said. 'With ten thousand or so people on campus, there's always a percentage of people who work late, or just need a nap during the day. These rooms are always free, always clean – you just have to check online to see which ones are available. Right now they book up fast, but the plan is to have at least a few thousand rooms within the next few years.'

'And after a party like tonight's, these are always full,' Denise said, with what she meant to be a conspiratorial wink.

The tour continued through the afternoon, with stops to sample food at the culinary class, taught that day by a celebrated young chef known for using the whole of any animal. She presented Mae with a dish called toasted pigface, which Mae ate and discovered tasted like a more fatty bacon; she liked it very much. They passed other visitors as they toured the campus, groups of college students, and packs of vendors, and what appeared to be a senator and his handlers. They passed an arcade stocked with vintage pinball machines and an indoor badminton court, where, Annie said, a former world champion was kept on retainer. By the time Josiah and Denise had brought her back around to the center of the campus, the light was dimming, and staffers were installing tiki torches in the grass and lighting them. A few thousand Circlers began to gather in the twilight, and standing among them, Mae knew that she never wanted to work – never wanted to be – anywhere else. Her hometown, and

TROUBLE SPOT

give a talk to sb. on sth. (l. 7) *= speak in front of an audience about sth., give a speech on sth.*
have a talk with sb. *= speak to sb., have a conversation with sb.*

1 **blur** *(n)* series of events that you cannot see or remember clearly
brief quick
2 **thrilled** very happy
8 **kale** *Grünkohl*
11 **San Vincenzo** (here) Italian style of architecture
12 **dorm** building with rooms for people to sleep in
13 **crash** *(v) (sl)* sleep
14 **kitchenette** small kitchen
15 **overstuffed** *prall gepolstert*
visceral ['vɪsərəl] relating to strong emotions
18 **nap** *(n)* short sleep
22 **conspiratorial** suggesting that a secret is being shared
23 **sample sth.** try sth.
24 **culinary** related to cooking and food
28 **vendor** seller
30 **keep sb. on retainer** pay sb. to make sure they will be available to do work when needed
31 **dim** *(v)* fade, get weaker
32 **tiki torch** *Gartenfackel*

the rest of California, the rest of America, seemed like some chaotic mess in the developing world. Outside the walls of the Circle, all was noise and struggle, failure and filth. But here, all had been perfected. The best people had made the best systems and the best systems had reaped funds, unlimited funds, that made possible this, the best place to work. And it was natural that it was so, Mae thought. Who else but utopians could make utopia?

Extract 2: The company's core beliefs

The next day, Mae's team leader Dan explains the philosophy of the company.

'Mae, now that you're aboard, I wanted to get across some of the core beliefs here at the company. And chief among them is that just as important as the work we do here – and that work is very important – we want to make sure that you can be a human being here, too. We want this to be a workplace, sure, but it should also be a *human* place. And that means the fostering of community. In fact, it must be a community. That's one of our slogans, as you probably know: *Community First*. And you've seen the signs that say *Humans Work Here* – I insist on those. That's my pet issue. We're not automatons. This isn't a sweatshop. We're a group of the best minds of our generation. Gener*ations*. And making sure this is a place where our humanity is respected, where our opinions are dignified, where our voices are heard – this is as important as any revenue, any stock price, any endeavor undertaken here. Does that sound corny?'

'No, no,' Mae rushed to say. 'Definitely not. That's why I'm here. I love the "community first" idea. Annie's been telling me about it since she started. At my last job, no one really communicated very well. It was basically the opposite of here in every way.'

Dan turned to look into the hills to the east, covered in mohair and patches of green. 'I hate hearing that kind of thing. With the technology available, communication should never be in doubt. Understanding should never be out of reach or anything but clear. It's what we do here. You might say it's the mission of the company – it's an obsession of mine, anyway. Communication. Understanding. Clarity.'

From: *The Circle*, 2013

37 **filth** dirt
38 **reap funds** make money
41 **be aboard** (here) be a part of a new organization
45 **fostering** *(n)* strengthening
47 **pet issue** topic you feel strongly about
48 **automaton** [–'– – –] robot
sweatshop ['swet-] place where people work for low wages and in poor conditions
51 **revenue** ['revənjuː] money made from business
corny *(sl)* silly and unoriginal
55 **mohair** type of soft wool

COMPREHENSION

1 Mediation (English → German)
You are working on an article for your school blog about young people's first days at new workplaces. In German, outline Mae's experience.

► SF 41: Mediation of written and oral texts

LANGUAGE AWARENESS

2 Compound nouns

a To emphasize a sense of community, Dan creates a new noun to describe the Circle as a '*human*place' – a *workplace* for *humans*. Compound nouns can be one word (e.g. *sunrise*), multiple words (e.g. *washing machine*) or multiple words joined by hyphens (e.g. *daughter-in-law*). Search for further compound nouns in the first extract.

b YOU CHOOSE Creative writing with compounds

1 Write an advertisement or slogan (not more than two sentences) for a utopian company, school or political party using two of the compound nouns you found in **a** plus at least three new ones.

OR

2 Write a short description of a utopian workplace, using two of the compound nouns you found in **a** plus at least three new ones.

► SF 37: Doing a creative writing task

READING FOCUS ON SKILLS

Reading for analysis (novel extract)

The extracts from The Circle *in* **B1** *are from close to the beginning of the novel and form part of the introduction of the reader to the company and to a few key characters.*

1 Looking at the setting and what it means

Location can create mood, develop *characters or function as a *symbol. You can analyse literary *setting by considering how the location influences the characters, the *plot, and your own impression of the novel.

a Make a list of the facilities Mae is introduced to on her tour of the Circle campus (ll. 1–30), adding any additional information we are given about each one. Explain the effect the description of the tour has on you (as a reader).

b The company dorms are given the most space in the text. Discuss the effect of this, and explain what is meant by the sentence 'Mae had to agree that the appeal was visceral' (l. 15).

► SF 17: Analysing stylistic devices

c The tour ends at the beginning of a party (ll. 30–34). Examine the atmosphere at this point by looking at how it is created and the effect it has on Mae.

d Study the last lines of Extract 1, and evaluate their effect on your expectations about the novel.

2 Identifying key themes

The theme of a text is the message the author is trying to get across to the reader.

► SF 39: Quoting a text

a Look at the example in the table below, then find two more important quotations in Extract 1 which represent different themes and complete the table in a similar way:

Quotation	*'Mae knew that she never wanted to work – never wanted to be – anywhere else.' (ll. 33–34)*
Context	*Mae is standing in the twilight, surrounded by happy colleagues after a tour of the Circle campus.*
Themes	*utopia; a perfect workplace; realizing your dreams*

b Discuss your choices with a partner. Do you agree? Why / why not? Together, choose the two most important quotations.

► SF 19: Analysing narrative prose

3 Analysing key themes

a For each of the two quotations you chose in task **2b**, write a sentence explaining how it illustrates a key theme in the text.

b Explain the slogans 'Community First' and 'Humans Work Here' in the context of Mae's tour of the company and Dan's explanations about the company values. ► LANGUAGE HELP

LANGUAGE HELP

- The effect of … on the reader is to emphasize …
- The reader is given the impression that …
- Ultimately, Dan's words serve to …
- … creates an atmosphere of …
- Dan's use of … makes Mae / the reader …

4 Evaluation

Read Dan's final speech again (ll. 56–59). Evaluate the effect this speech has on Mae and is supposed to have on you as the reader.

CULTURE SPOT

A

B

C

D

A tower with its top in the sky *(Genesis 11:1–9)*

1 Match the titles and the captions with the right buildings. **Titles:** *Salisbury Cathedral; the tallest building in the EU; the Tower of Babel; 30 St Mary Axe*
Captions: *the Gherkin; the tallest spire; an artist's impression; the Shard*

2 Bruegel intended his painting of the Tower of Babel to illustrate the story of human pride punished by God and the futility of human endeavour.
 a Together with a partner, list examples of other human attempts 'to reach the sky'.
 b Research the tallest buildings in the world over the centuries and make a list of the most impressive ones.
 c Collect further examples of human endeavours to transgress human limitations.

3 Discuss whether all this inventiveness and activity is more suitable as a subject for dystopias or as a subject for utopias.

B2 Living in the compound *Margaret Atwood*

Margaret Atwood's novel Oryx and Crake *(2003) is set on the North American continent. In this extract, Jimmy looks back on his childhood when his father worked for a company called OrganInc.*

- Imagine that you are the planner or architect of a gated community, i.e. one that is fenced in and guarded. Note down a few ideas or make a sketch of the layout.

When Jimmy was really little they'd lived in a Cape Cod-style frame house in one of the Modules – there were pictures of him, in a carry-cot on the porch, with dates and everything, stuck into a photo album at some time when his mother was still bothering – but now they lived in a large Georgian centre-plan with an indoor swimming pool and a small gym. The furniture in it was called reproduction. Jimmy was quite old before he realized what this word meant – that for each reproduction item, there was supposed to be an original somewhere. Or there had been once. Or something.

The house, the pool, the furniture – all belonged to the OrganInc Compound, where the top people lived. Increasingly, the middle-range execs and the junior scientists lived there too.

Jimmy's father said it was better that way, because nobody had to commute to work from the Modules. Despite the sterile transport corridors and the high-speed bullet trains, there was always a risk when you went through the city.

Jimmy had never been to the city. He'd only seen it on TV – endless billboards and neon signs and stretches of buildings, tall and short; endless dingy-looking streets, countless vehicles of all kinds, some of them with clouds of smoke coming out the back; thousands of people, hurrying, cheering, rioting. There were other cities too, near and far; some had better neighborhoods in them, said his father, almost like the Compounds, with high walls around the houses, but those didn't get on TV much.

Compound people didn't go to the cities unless they had to, and then never alone. They called the cities the pleeblands. Despite the fingerprint identity cards now carried by everyone, public security in the pleeblands was leaky: there were people cruising around in those places who could forge anything and who might be anybody, not to mention the loose change – the addicts, the muggers, the paupers, the crazies. So it was best for everyone at OrganInc Farms to live all in one place, with foolproof procedures.

Outside the OrganInc walls and gates and searchlights, things were unpredictable. Inside, they were the way it used to be when Jimmy's father was a kid, before things got so serious, or that's what Jimmy's father said. Jimmy's mother said it was all artificial, it was just a theme park and you could never bring the old ways back, but

1 **frame house** *Holzhaus*
2 **carry-cot** small bed for a baby
4 **bother** *(v)* care
13 **exec** *(infml)* boss, manager
17 **commute** travel regularly from your home to your workplace
20 **bullet train** very fast train
25 **billboard** large advertisement
27 **dingy** ['dɪndʒi] dark and dirty
34 **leaky** (here) deficient, not very good
35 **cruise around** (here) be somewhere in order to do bad things
36 **loose change** (here) people who don't fit into the social hierarchy
mugger violent thief
pauper ['pɔːpə] *(old use)* very poor person
37 **foolproof** very well designed and unable to fail

Jimmy's father said why knock it? You could walk around without fear, couldn't you? Go for a bike ride, sit at a sidewalk café, buy an ice-cream cone? Jimmy knew his father was right, because he himself had done all of these things. [...]

Long ago, in the days of knights and dragons, the kings and dukes had lived in castles, with high walls and drawbridges and slots on the ramparts so you could pour hot pitch on your enemies, said Jimmy's father, and the Compounds were the same idea. Castles were for keeping you and your buddies nice and safe inside, and for keeping everybody else outside.

'So are we the kings and dukes?' asked Jimmy.

'Oh, absolutely,' said his father, laughing.

From: *Oryx and Crake*, 2003

50 **knight** *Ritter*
51 **duke** *Herzog*
53 **drawbridge** bridge that can be pulled up to stop the enemy from entering a castle
slot long, thin hole
rampart *(usu. pl)* high wall of stone built around a castle
54 **pitch** *Pech*

COMPREHENSION

1 Understanding the situation

a Based on what you know of the text's setting, draw a map. On your map, you should label:

- the OrganInc Compound
- a Module
- bullet trains
- transport corridors
- the pleeblands

b Compare your map with a partner's.

ANALYSIS

2 A story within a story

Read lines 48–61 again. Interpret the message of the short 'history' told by Jimmy's father.

► SF 19: Analysing narrative prose

3 Utopia or dystopia?

Analyse both utopian and dystopian elements in the text.

SUPPORT ► p. 285

BEYOND THE TEXT

4 YOU CHOOSE **Creative writing**

a Write a text of about 200 words, describing the typical working day of a person living in the pleeblands.

OR

b Imagine Jimmy breaks out of the Compound and spends an afternoon in the pleeblands. Write his diary entry for this day.

► SF 37: Doing a creative writing task

Watch over me

C1 Data collection and complacency

You are going to watch a video clip about free web services.

► SF 23: Analysing a film

1 Before viewing

a Discuss with a partner what the title of the clip leads you to expect about its content.

b Make a list of situations in which your data could be collected, and purposes it could be used for.

c Discuss whether this bothers you or not, and whether you would be prepared to do anything about it.

COMPREHENSION

2 While viewing

► SF 10: Working with closed test formats

Decide whether the sentences below are true or false. Correct the sentences that are false.

1 Sending emails via Gmail is a completely private activity.
2 The web service causes ads to be sent to your email address.
3 In 2005 there was a huge protest movement against data collection.
4 There is no real danger with this kind of data collection.

DVD

driving main
party (here) group of people or organizations
complacency feeling of satisfaction with a situation, so that you do not think change is necessary
reassert sth. make other people recognize again your right to do sth.
crucial important
far-fetched *(adj)* hard to believe

3 Watching for detail

a Describe the goals of the 2005 initiative called 'The Attention Trust'.

b Explain why, according to the speaker, it should have been a 'no-brainer', but wasn't.

c Seth Goldstein says it is not right to say that people are 'perfectly happy' with the way our data is traded on the net. Explain his alternatives 'dumb happy' or 'naïve happy'.

ANALYSIS

4 YOU CHOOSE Analysing techniques

a Explain how the video uses images to illustrate what is said by the speaker.

OR

b Near the end of the video the image of sleepwalking is used both visually and *metaphorically. Explain both uses.

BEYOND THE TEXT

5 From data collection to dystopia

► SF 34: Argumentative writing

a In the final section of the video clip, John Batelle mentions the dystopian novel *Nineteen Eighty-Four* in connection with data collection. Discuss how data collection could lead to a dystopian situation.

b Look at the following quotations from the *novel *The Circle* (cf. **B1**, pp. 236–237) and discuss how they can be linked to the video clip. Write a comment.

1 'I have a question, Mae. Do you behave better or worse when you're being watched?'
'Better. Without a doubt.'
'When you're alone, unwatched, unaccountable[1], what happens?'

2 *SECRETS ARE LIES*
SHARING IS CARING
PRIVACY IS THEFT

From: Dave Eggers, *The Circle*, 2013

[1] **unaccountable** not having to explain or give reasons for your actions to anyone

C2 Big Brother is watching you *George Orwell*

Nineteen Eighty-Four *is a dystopian novel George Orwell published in 1949. It is set in Oceania where 'Big Brother', the tyrannical ruler of the state, observes everyone at all times with the help of the telescreen. The protagonist, Winston Smith, secretly hates the government and dreams of rebellion against Big Brother. He has started a secret love affair with his co-worker Julia, who is also against the government, and he is afraid they will be found out.*

He thought for a little while. 'Has it ever occurred to you,' he said, 'that the best thing for us to do would be simply to walk out of here before it's too late, and never see each other again?'

'Yes, dear, it has occurred to me, several times. But I'm not going to do it, all the same.'

'We've been lucky,' he said 'but it can't last much longer. You're young. You look normal and innocent. If you keep clear of people like me, you might stay alive for another fifty years.'

'No. I've thought it all out. What you do, I'm going to do. And don't be too downhearted. I'm rather good at staying alive.'

'We may be together for another six months – a year – there's no knowing. At the end we're certain to be apart. Do you realize how utterly alone we shall be? When once they get hold of us there will be nothing, literally nothing that either of us can do for the other. If I confess, they'll shoot you, and if I refuse to confess, they'll shoot you just the same. Nothing that I can do or say, or stop myself from saying, will put off your death for as much as five minutes. Neither of us will even know whether the other is alive or dead. We shall be utterly without power of any kind. The one thing that matters is that we shouldn't betray one another, although even that can't make the slightest difference.'

'If you mean confessing,' she said, 'we shall do that, right enough. Everybody always confesses. You can't help it. They torture you.'

'I don't mean confessing. Confession is not betrayal. What you say or do doesn't matter: only feelings matter. If they could make me stop loving you – that would be the real betrayal.'

She thought it over. 'They can't do that,' she said finally. 'It's the one thing they can't do. They can make you say anything – ANYTHING – but they can't make you believe it. They can't get inside you.'

'No,' he said a little more hopefully, 'no; that's quite true. They can't get inside you. If you can FEEL that staying human is worth while, even when it can't have any result whatever, you've beaten them.'

He thought of the telescreen with its never-sleeping ear. They could spy upon you night and day, but if you kept your head you could still outwit them. With all their cleverness they had never mastered the secret of finding out what another human being was thinking. Perhaps that was less true when you were actually in their hands. One did not know what happened inside the Ministry of Love, but it was possible to guess: tortures, drugs, delicate instruments that registered your nervous reactions, gradual wearing-down by sleeplessness and solitude and persistent questioning. Facts, at any rate, could not be kept hidden. They could be tracked down by enquiry,

1 **occur to sb.** come into sb.'s mind
9 **keep clear of sb.** stay away from sb.
12 **downhearted** sad
16 **utterly** completely
18 **confess (to sth.)** *(etwas) gestehen*
22 **betray sb.** give information about sb. to an enemy
25 **torture sb.** ['tɔːtʃə] hurt sb. to make them give you information
36 **outwit sb.** beat sb. by being cleverer than them
39 **Ministry of Love** in the novel, government ministry that uses fear to enforce loyalty to Big Brother
41 **gradual** slow
wear sb. down make sb. weaker
solitude state of being alone

43 **object** (here) aim; goal
46 **lay sth. bare** show sth. that was a secret
utmost most extreme
48 **impregnable** impossible to beat or change

they could be squeezed out of you by torture. But if the object was not to stay alive but to stay human, what difference did it ultimately make? They could not alter your feelings: for that matter you could not alter them yourself, even if you wanted to. They could lay bare in the utmost detail everything that you had done or said or thought; but the inner heart, whose workings were mysterious even to yourself, remained impregnable.

From: *Nineteen Eighty-Four*, 1949

COMPREHENSION

1 Understanding the story

a Describe the kind of society that Winston and Julia live in.
b Point out what the two lovers are most worried about.

LANGUAGE AWARENESS

2 Everyday English

Rewrite the following quotes from the text in everyday English.

1 'Yes, dear, it has occurred to me, several times.' (l. 5)
2 'We shall be utterly without power of any kind.' (l. 21)
3 'They could lay bare in the utmost detail everything that you had done or said or thought' (ll. 45–46)

ANALYSIS

► SF 19: Analysing narrative prose

3 Interpreting key aspects

a Interpret Winston's statement 'If you can FEEL that staying human is worth while [...] you've beaten them' (ll. 33–34).
b Analyse the atmosphere of the extract by looking at the content of the dialogue and Winston's thoughts on the one hand, and the fact that this is a dialogue between lovers on the other hand.
SUPPORT p. 285

BEYOND THE TEXT

4 Room for hope?

a 'With all their cleverness they had never mastered the secret of finding out what another human being was thinking' (ll. 36–38). Discuss whether this is true in the 21st century.
b CHALLENGE Think of three steps that people your age can take to avoid a situation like the one in the text becoming reality in the future.

5 Other dystopian worlds

Look at the following quote said by Peeta in *The Hunger Games* (cf. pp. 232–235), then read lines 35–48 in the extract from *Nineteen Eighty Four*. Discuss similarities and differences between the worlds presented in *Nineteen Eighty Four* and *The Hunger Games*.

PEETA I just keep wishing I could think of a way to show them that they don't own me. If I'm gonna die, I wanna still be me.
KATNISS I just can't afford to think like that.

6 Big Brother in popular culture

Big Brother is the name of the fictional tyrannical ruler of Oceania. It is also the name of a famous reality TV show. Discuss why the TV producers might have chosen this name. Do you find the name appropriate? Justify your opinion.

A vision of the future

In this Chapter Task you will consider the texts you have read and tasks you have completed to write your own utopian or dystopian narrative.

1 Preparing your project

a Choose whether you would like to work alone, with a partner or in a small group.

b Decide which divisive issue in our society you are going to focus on. It can be an issue dealt with in the chapter, or something else you feel strongly about.

c Create a mindmap with your chosen issue at the centre. Consider various aspects of the issue, e.g. areas of life that it affects, the opinions different groups of people might have about it, symbols that could be used to represent it, etc.

2 Considering genre and media

a Decide whether your text will be a utopia or a dystopia or a mixture of both. Make notes on which genre would work best for your chosen issue and why.

b Decide on the form of your text. It could be:
- an imaginary journey (p. 53)
- an *interior monologue (pp. 56–57)
- a description of a scene from a film (pp. 59–60) – including the presentation of different characters, film techniques and perhaps even a script
- an extract from a novel (pp. 62–63, 66–67)

► SF 37: Doing a creative writing task

c Depending on which form you choose for your text, go back to the relevant pages in the chapter and look at the material again. Read/view it for analysis. Consider which aspects you could include in your text and what you would like to do differently.

3 Writing your text

a Write an outline of your text. The following table might help you:

► SF 8: Structuring ideas
► SF 38: Writing a well-structured text

Issue	Setting	Characters	Plot

b Write a rough draft. Ask a classmate to proofread your draft and give you feedback.

c Make a neat copy of your text.

4 GALLERY WALK **Presenting and evaluating a text**

Present your finished text to the rest of the class, e.g. in a gallery walk, and evaluate your classmates' products. Take notes on your classmates' work, taking into account their content, which aspects you particularly liked and which aspects you think could be improved. Your teacher will give you an assessment sheet.

12 Living One's Life – Individuals in Society

A

B

C

D

E

F

It is only to the individual that a soul is given.
ALBERT EINSTEIN

You grown ups say you love us, but I challenge you, please make your actions reflect your words.
SEVERN SUZUKI

A hero is an ordinary individual who finds the strength to persevere and endure in spite of overwhelming obstacles.
CHRISTOPHER REEVE

True individual freedom cannot exist without economic security and independence. People who are hungry and out of a job are the stuff of which dictatorships are made.
FRANKLIN D. ROOSEVELT

Don't be afraid to fail. Be afraid not to try.
MICHAEL JORDAN

There is no such thing as society: there are individual men and women, and there are families.
MARGARET THATCHER

Be the change you wish to see in the world.
MAHATMA GANDHI

Remember always that you not only have the right to be an individual, you have an obligation to be one.
ELEANOR ROOSEVELT

Ask not what your country can do for you – ask what you can do for your country.
JOHN F. KENNEDY

1 The individual and society

a Describe one of the pictures and note down what words, phrases and concepts come to mind when you look at it. Make a list or mind map.

b Now read the quotations. Comment on the one that speaks to you most.

c Match one quotation and one illustration. Explain your decision.

Download a list of chapter vocab here: **Webcode** context-06

Find a mindmapping tool here: **Webcode** context-53

► SF 11: Analysing pictures

2 Famous individuals

a Work in groups of four. Each group picks one of the people quoted above. Do some research on their lives and find out what they did for society.

b Present your findings to other groups.

► SF 5: Doing research

PREVIEW

In this chapter you will reflect on your own role in society, consider how people view each other, and discuss ideas for getting involved in society and making a difference.

CD1 06

Listen to an audio version of the text on the CD or download it here:

Webcode context-07

Young people in a multifaceted society

A generation full of hope

Today's young generation has lots of ideas about how to improve our world. Young people are often full of hope and creativity and have an incredible energy. They are not afraid to try something new, to get involved in big issues and to fight for what they want or believe in. They take part in demonstrations against war and discrimination and for equality and education. They use the internet as a means of communication as well as for political purposes. Many young people commit themselves to improving their communities and to making a difference to our world. They volunteer or work for charities, often helping people on the fringes of society like the disabled and homeless or collecting money for victims of natural disasters throughout the world. Today's teens are able to stand up for their beliefs and basic rights, and are smart and strong enough to shape the future of society for the better.

The media and youngsters

Nevertheless, at the same time, the media often paint a grim picture of the younger generation, appealing to stereotypes of young anti-social trouble-makers. They are depicted as individuals who indulge in criminality, or who are obsessed by selfies and their self-image, or they may be depicted as alienated and socially impaired computer nerds with no time for real interaction with others. Age-based prejudice distorts the reality of the generation that will deal with the problems the older generation leaves behind.

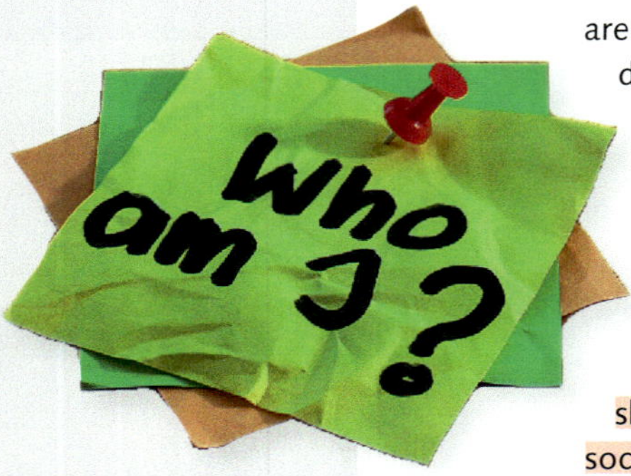

Finding one's identity

Just like other generations, today's teens are not a uniform group. They do not all share a collective identity or share common experiences. Our individual character and our social background influence our identity. Family, education, culture and religion all have an influence on our moral values, attitudes and habits. Our sense of identity accounts for how we perceive ourselves and also how we are perceived and positioned by others. Our identities do not just determine our personal style but affect the opportunities we are given and our access to power, status, education and wealth. Like generations before them, young people must find out who they are and who they want to be in a diverse and ever-changing society. Unlike other generations, young people today have access to an immense variety of individual lifestyles. This opens up new possibilities for them to choose and construct their own identities, but it can also lead to conflicts and divided loyalties.

An unknown future

Living in a 'me-first' society and globalized world, young people are going to face big challenges in the future. Social inequality and unemployment, political instability and terrorism as well as environmental problems are just some of the pressing issues they will have to deal with. At the same time, the world is getting closer. With communication increasing, young people from different countries may be able to find creative solutions together to the most urgent problems.

Young people in a multifaceted society

1 Definitions

Match the definitions below to highlighted words and phrases from the text.

1 engage in
2 way of interacting with other people
3 speak or act in support of
4 constantly changing or developing
5 thinking only of yourself
6 important issues requiring immediate attention or action

2 Word formation and word families

Find the missing word. Use a dictionary if necessary.

verb	noun	adjective
improve		
volunteer		
	value	
	belief	
shape		
	stereotype	
		alienated
		moral
perceive		
	access	

► SF 2: Learning new words

► LP 20: Word formation

Find an online dictionary here:
Webcode context-52

3 Words in use

a Complete each sentence with a verb from the grid.

1 Young people are often … as troublemakers.
2 Our identities are … by the people around us.
3 Young people are concerned about how society … and … them.
4 Many young people … family and friendship over having lots of money.

b CHALLENGE Activate your vocabulary – translate the following sentences. Pay special attention to the underlined expressions, which are highlighted in the text.

► LP 16: Avoiding Germanisms

1 Die großen Herausforderungen unserer vielschichtigen Welt erfordern kreative Lösungen und vor allem engagierte Individuen.
2 Viele junge Leute sind heute bereit, sich einzubringen und sich für die Verbesserung der Lebensbedingungen von Menschen in den unterschiedlichen Teilen der Erde einzusetzen.
3 Unsere Werte, Einstellungen und Gewohnheiten werden maßgeblich von unserer sozialen Herkunft geprägt.
4 Häufig wird die Wahrnehmung anderer Menschen beeinflusst durch Stereotypen, Sichtweisen und Vorurteile, die das soziale Miteinander belasten.

4 Writing

Outline how you see your own generation and what you think are the greatest challenges your generation has to face. Write a short comment.

► SF 38: Writing a well-structured text
► SF 34: Argumentative writing

Future success

A1 What is a role model? *Marilyn Price-Mitchell*

The excerpt below is taken from a web article about a research study on how young people develop into engaged citizens. US teenagers were asked about their role models and the qualities role models have.

- Before reading the excerpt, do a placemat activity based around the question: 'Who is your role model or – if you do not have one – who could be a role model to others, and why?'

Role models come into young people's lives in a variety of ways. They are educators, civic leaders, mothers, fathers, clergy, peers, and ordinary people encountered in everyday life. This study showed that being a role model is not constrained to those with fancy titles or personal wealth. [...]

Role models show passion for their work and have the capacity to infect others with their passion. [...] Role models live their values in the world. Children admire people who act in ways that support their beliefs. It helps them understand how their own values are part of who they are and how they might seek fulfilling roles as adults. [...] Role models are *other-focused* as opposed to *self-focused*. They are usually active in their communities, freely giving of their time and talents to benefit people.

Students admired people who served on local boards, reached out to neighbors in need, voted, and were active members of community organizations. Related to the idea that role models show a commitment to their communities, students also admired people for their selflessness and acceptance of others who were different from them. [...]

As Booker T. Washington once said, 'Success is to be measured not so much by the position that one has reached in life as by the obstacles which one has overcome.' Young people echoed this sentiment, showing how they developed the skills and abilities of initiative when they learned to overcome obstacles.

From: Roots of Action, 2013

4 **fancy** sounding good
16 **Booker T. Washington** (1856–1915) African American campaigner, who was born into slavery and later became adviser of US presidents
17 **obstacle** ['ɒbstəkl] sth. that blocks sb.'s way
18 **echo sth.** ['ekəʊ] (here) share sth.

COMPREHENSION

1 Examining role models

a Describe the qualities of role models that matter to US teens.
b Compare these qualities with your own lists on the placemats and discuss with your group whether you agree with the American teens.

LANGUAGE AWARENESS

2 The language of definition

a Look at ll. 1–10 and examine what methods the writer uses to define the term *role model*.
b Write a similar definition of the word *idol*. Check the difference between *idol* and *role model* in a dictionary first, and illustrate this in the way you use language to define it.

Find an online dictionary here:
Webcode context-52

BEYOND THE TEXT

3 People as models

In groups of four, discuss the following statement by American linguist, philosopher and activist Noam Chomsky: 'I do not feel that we should set up people as "models"; rather actions, thoughts, principles.'

► SF 27: Having a discussion

A2 Successful children *Amy Chua*

- With a partner, discuss what your aims in life are, where these aims come from, who supports you on your way, and what helps you to achieve your aims.

Amy Chua, a professor of law at Yale University, is the child of Chinese immigrants and is herself the mother of two daughters. In her book Battle Hymn of the Tiger Mother *(2011) she describes her strict parenting techniques, which she thinks make children successful.*

A lot of people wonder how Chinese parents raise such stereotypically successful kids. They wonder what these parents do to produce so many math whizzes and music prodigies, what it's like inside the family, and whether they could do it too. Well, I can tell them, because I've done it. Here are some things my daughters, Sophia and Louisa, were never allowed to do:

- attend a sleepover
- have a playdate
- be in a school play
- complain about not being in a school play
- watch TV or play Computer games
- choose their own extracurricular activities
- get any grade less than an A
- not be the #1 student in every subject except gym and drama
- play any instrument other than the piano or violin
- not play the piano or violin.

Amy Chua (centre) and her daughters

I'm using the term 'Chinese mother' loosely. I recently met a supersuccessful white guy from South Dakota (you've seen him on television), and after comparing notes we decided that his working-class father had definitely been a Chinese mother. I know some Korean, Indian, Jamaican, Irish, and Ghanaian parents who qualify too. Conversely, I know some mothers of Chinese heritage, almost always born in the West, who are not Chinese mothers, by choice or otherwise. [...]

What Chinese parents understand is that nothing is fun until you're good at it. To get good at anything you have to work, and children on their own never want to work, which is why it is crucial to override their preferences. This often requires fortitude on the part of the parents because the child will resist; things are always hardest at the beginning, which is where Western parents tend to give up. But if done properly, the Chinese strategy produces a virtuous circle. Tenacious practice, practice, practice is crucial for excellence; rote repetition is underrated in America. Once a child starts to excel at something – whether it's math, piano, pitching, or ballet – he or she gets praise, admiration, and satisfaction. This builds confidence and makes the once not-fun activity turn. This in turn makes it easier for the parent to get the child to work even more. [...]

I think there are three big differences between the Chinese and Western parental mind-sets. ·····▸

4 **whizz** *(infml)* person who is very good at sth.
26 **conversely** [kɒn'vɜːsli] *(adv)* *(fml) umgekehrt*
30 **crucial** extremely important
override sth. reject sth., cancel sth.
fortitude strength of mind
33 **tenacious** [tə'neɪʃəs] not giving up; persistent
34 **rote repetition** method of learning sth. by repeating it continually
35 **pitching** *(in baseball)* throwing the ball at the batter

Part A

43 **notwithstanding** in spite of
44 **mediocre** [ˌmiːdiˈəʊkə] not very good, (only) average
46 **fragility** [frəˈdʒɪləti] weakness
56 **excoriate sb.** *(fml)* criticize sb. severely
65 **foist sth. on sb.** force sth. on sb.

First, I've noticed that Western parents are extremely anxious about their children's self-esteem. They worry about how their children will feel if they fail at something, and they constantly try to reassure their children about how good they are notwithstanding a mediocre performance on a test or at a recital. In other words, Western parents are concerned about their children's psyches. Chinese parents aren't. They assume strength, not fragility, and as a result they behave very differently.

For example, if a child comes home with an A-minus on a test, a Western parent will most likely praise the child. The Chinese mother will gasp in horror and ask what went wrong. If the child comes home with a B on the test, some Western parents will still praise the child. [...] If a Chinese child gets a B – which would never happen – there would first be a screaming, hair-tearing explosion. The devastated Chinese mother would then get dozens, maybe hundreds of practice tests and work through them with her child for as long as it takes to get the grade up to an A. Chinese parents demand perfect grades because they believe that their child can get them. If their child doesn't get them, the Chinese parent assumes it's because the child didn't work hard enough. That's why the solution to substandard performance is always to excoriate, punish, and shame the child. The Chinese parent believes that their child will be strong enough to take the shaming and to improve from it. [...]

Second, Chinese parents believe that their kids owe them everything. [...] Anyway, the understanding is that Chinese children must spend their lives repaying their parents by obeying them and making them proud. By contrast, I don't think most Westerners have the same view of children being permanently indebted to their parents. Jed [Amy Chua's husband] actually has the opposite view. 'Children don't choose their parents,' he once said to me. 'They don't even choose to be born. It's parents who foist life on their kids, so it's the parents' responsibility to provide for them. Kids don't owe their parents anything. Their duty will be to their own kids.' This strikes me as a terrible deal for the Western parent.

Third, Chinese parents believe that they know what is best for their children and therefore override all of their children's own desires and preferences. That's why Chinese daughters can't have boyfriends in high school and why Chinese kids can't go to sleepaway camp. It's also why no Chinese kid would ever dare say to their mother, 'I got a part in the school play! I'm Villager Number Six. I'll have to stay after school for rehearsal every day from 3:00 to 7:00, and I'll also need a ride on weekends.' God help any Chinese kid who tried that one.

Don't get me wrong: It's not that Chinese parents don't care about their children. Just the opposite. They would give up anything for their children. It's just an entirely different parenting model. I think of it as Chinese, but I know a lot of non-Chinese parents – usually from Korea, India, or Pakistan – who have a very similar mind-set, so it may be an immigrant thing. Or maybe it's the combination of being an immigrant and being from certain cultures.

From: *Battle Hymn of the Tiger Mother*, 2011

COMPREHENSION

1 Examining parental styles
Describe the two contrasting parenting styles Chua refers to.

ANALYSIS

2 Examining a book title
Analyse the title of Chua's book and explain what it tells us about her parenting philosophy.

LANGUAGE AWARENESS

3 What if …?

a Read ll. 47–57 and say which type of conditional is being used.
SUPPORT p. 286

► LP 8: Conditional sentences

b Write three conditional sentences, one of each type, based around ideas in the text, for example:

- *If Sophia and Louisa come across this text, they will probably understand their mother better.*
- *If Sophia wanted to play the trumpet, her mother would not let her.*
- *If Amy's parents had not been so strict, she would not have become a successful professor.*

c Find another example of a conditional sentence in the text. Explain what it reveals.

BEYOND THE TEXT

4 YOU CHOOSE Examining statements

a Choose one or more of Amy Chua's statements and comment on them from your own point of view.

OR

b Discuss one of the following statements, referring to Chua:

- Parents can never be friends with their children.
- Strict parents create sneaky kids. (Banksy)
- A child without discipline is, in a way, a lost child. (Ricardo Montalban)

► SF 34: Argumentative writing

5 Giving advice

a Imagine that Chua's daughter, 17-year-old Louisa, is a friend of yours and rebels against her mother's strict parenting style. Discuss with a partner what advice you would give her. Try to see both sides.

b Now write a longer email to Louisa, giving your advice. ► LANGUAGE HELP

LANGUAGE HELP

- If I were you, I'd …
- The best thing to do is …
- I don't think it's advisable to …
- It might be better to …
- You definitely should/ought to …
- If you ask me, I would/wouldn't …

► CC 6: Talking about sensitive issues

6 A mother–daughter argument

a Louisa refuses to obey her mother and they have an argument. Divide the class in two halves. One half prepares Louisa's arguments, the other half Amy's. You may take notes on little cue cards.

b Pair up with another student from the other side and start your argument.

c Tell the others in class about your argument. How did it end? Could you solve the conflict? Why (not)?

► SF 27: Having a discussion

A3 Childhood – the 21st century *Ernestine Northover*

- Before reading, name things that you remember about your childhood, and discuss whether they could have happened to children in earlier generations as well.

The following poem is by a British poet. In it, she considers childhoods of the past and future.

How advanced they are, these children of the future,
Like small adults, within their tiny frames,
They grow up in a fast 'speed driven' culture,
Where 'learning pressures' change their kind of games.
Where is their childhood, in all this hurly burly,
Where is their pure untainted view of things,
Why do they have to grow so old, so early,
And lose the joy that only childhood brings?

Our childhood was filled with thoughts of joy and gladness,
We lived our lives, oblivious to the world
And all the hardships, wars, the grief and sadness,
We stood, waiting for our lives to be unfurled.
We had time to grow, and gain an understanding,
Of each new phase, each change along the way,
As we grew slowly, our senses all expanding,
So with clarity, we slowly changed our play.

We had a framework on which to build and flourish,
Slow and steady, this was no rushed affair,
Taking each step, then step by step to nourish
Our childhood, so finally adulthood we would share.
What will become of these 'New Century' learners?
I doubt if they a dreamy childhood see.
Will they then tell to all those bright discerners
Of their own, how they remembered their childhood to be?

From: PoemHunter, 2005

COMPREHENSION

1 The speaker
Describe the speaker's background.

2 Summarizing
Sum up the main idea expressed in the poem in one or two sentences.

ANALYSIS

► SF 21: Analysing poetry

3 Formal elements
Analyse how the *poem is structured (*stanzas, *rhyme scheme, *rhythm) and what *stylistic devices are used that contribute to the meaning.
SUPPORT ► p. 287

4 Images
Examine the *images used in the poem to refer to children now and in the speaker's past and explain their effect on you.

BEYOND THE TEXT

► SF 27: Having a discussion
► SF 29: Writing a formal letter or email

5 YOU CHOOSE **Another perspective**

a Having grown up in the 21st century, discuss to what extent you agree with the speaker's assessment. Include the results of your analysis of the speaker's own past in your discussion.

OR

b Imagine you are Amy Chua (text **A2**). Write a response to the poem that you might upload on a poetry website.

Them and us

B1 Stereotypes in Los Angeles *Paul Haggis*

The film Crash *(2004) tells the interwoven stories of several individuals in Los Angeles and portrays the racial and social tensions between them.*

- Look at the film stills below and speculate about the characters, their personalities and the relationships between them. How might the lives of the two young men and the couple collide?

Scene 1: Ext. Westwood – Night

Italian restaurant. Anthony flies out the door, Peter just one step behind him. They're in their early twenties, young, hip, well-dressed men, friends since third grade. They button their jackets as they head down the sidewalk.

ANTHONY You see any white people in there waiting an hour and thirty-two minutes for a plate of spaghetti? Huh? And how many cups of coffee did we get?

PETER You don't drink coffee and I didn't want any.

ANTHONY That woman poured cup after cup to every single white person around us. Did she even ask you if you wanted any?

PETER We didn't get any coffee that you didn't want and I didn't order, and this is evidence of racial discrimination? Did you happen to notice our waitress was black?

ANTHONY And black women don't think in stereotypes? When's the last time you met one who didn't think she knew everything about your lazy ass before you even opened your mouth? That waitress sized us up in two seconds. We're black, and 'black people don't tip' so she wasn't gonna waste her time; someone like that, nothing you can do to change their mind.

PETER So how much did you leave her?

ANTHONY You expect me to pay for that kinda service?

Peter laughs; Anthony doesn't.

ANTHONY ... What? What?

PETER Nothing, nothing.

Rick & Jean Cabot, white, early 40s, head for their car. Jean pulls her jacket closed as they walk.

RICK You're seriously jealous of Karen??

1 **Ext.** exterior
Westwood district of Los Angeles
16 **size sb. up** *(infml)* decide quickly what another person is like
17 **tip (sb.)** *(jdm.) Trinkgeld geben*
21 **kinda** *(infml)* kind of

FACT FILE

A **stereotype** is a fixed, over-generalized belief about a particular group of people. One advantage of a stereotype is that it enables us to respond quickly to situations because we may have had a similar experience before. One disadvantage is that it makes us ignore differences between individuals, so that we end up making simplistic generalizations about individuals or groups.

Prejudice is an unjustified or incorrect attitude that is usually negative towards an individual based solely on the individual's membership of a social group. For example, a person may hold prejudiced views towards a certain race or gender, etc.

Discrimination is negative behaviour or action towards an individual or group of people due to their sex/race/social class, etc.

Microaggressions are often unintended racist or sexist comments that make a person feel underestimated on the basis of their colour or gender.

38 **UCLA** *(abbr)* University of California, Los Angeles
43 **trigger-happy** *(infml, disapproving)* willing and quick to use violence, esp. a gun
44 **LAPD** *(abbr)* Los Angeles Police Department
45 **Int.** interior
47 **locksmith** person who repairs locks (= *Schlosser/in*)
52 **pantry** small room next to a kitchen where food is stored
64 **patronize sb.** ['pætrənaɪz] treat sb. like a child

JEAN Hardly. I'd just like to see you get through a meal without calling her, or someone else at your office.

RICK See this? Off. No more calls tonight.

Jean notices Anthony and Peter and takes Rick's arm.

JEAN Ten bucks says she calls on the car phone.

ANTHONY You see what that woman just did?

PETER She's cold.

ANTHONY She got colder as soon as she saw us.

PETER Here it comes.

ANTHONY Look around! You couldn't find a whiter, safer or better-lit part of this city. But this white woman sees two black guys who look like UCLA students strolling down the sidewalk, and her reaction is blind fear. I mean, look at us. Are we dressed like gangbangers? Do we look threatening? No. Fact, if anybody should be scared around here, it's us: the only two black faces surrounded by a sea of over-caffeinated white people patrolled by the trigger-happy LAPD. So, why aren't *we* scared?

Scene 2: Int. Rick & Jean's Home – Night

Jean's feet descend the stairs to the expensive kitchen, where Daniel, the Hispanic locksmith, re-keys the door. He's twentyish, close-cropped hair, baggy pants, tattoos.

JEAN How much longer are you going to be?

DANIEL This is the last door.

JEAN Thanks.

She exits, walking through the pantry into the dining room where several staff members work. She turns into the living room, where Rick and two aides work up strategy.

JEAN *(interrupting)* I need to talk to you for a second.

She exits without waiting for a response. Rick turns to Karen, his top aide (young, black, brilliant).

RICK Just find Flanagan.

Karen dials as Rick exits to the [...] hall off the kitchen where Jean waits, arms crossed so tightly they're squeezing all the air out of her lungs.

JEAN I want the locks changed again in the morning.

RICK Honey, why don't you go to bed? Did you check on James?

JEAN Of course I checked on James. I've checked on him every five minutes since we've been home, don't patronize me! I want the locks changed again in the morning!

RICK Shhh, it's ok. You just need to lie down.

JEAN Didn't I just ask you not to treat me like a child? [...] I want the locks changed again in the morning. And you could mention that we'd appreciate it if next time they didn't send a gang member.

RICK *(lowering his voice)* You're talking about that kid in there?

JEAN Shaved head, pants down around his ass, prison tattoos!

RICK Oh for Christ sakes, those aren't prison tattoos!

JEAN Right, and he isn't going to sell our key to one of his gangbanger friends the moment he's out the door.

RICK Jean, it's been a tough night. Why don't you go upstairs and ...

JEAN ... wait for them to break in? *(in a rage)* I just had a gun pointed in my face.

RICK You lower your voice.

JEAN And it's my fault because I knew it was going to happen. But if a white person sees two black men walking towards them and turns and walks the other way, she's a racist, right? Well, I got scared, and I didn't say anything and ten seconds later I had a gun in my face. Now, I'm telling you that your amigo in there is going to sell our house key to one of his homies! And this time it would be really fucking nice if you acted like you actually cared!!

Jean turns and storms into the kitchen. Rick stares at her as she makes a show of wiping down the counter.

From: *Crash Movie Script Screenplay*, 2005

80 **homie** *(infml)* member of the same gang

COMPREHENSION

1 Knowing what happened

Something happened between these two scenes. What was it?

1 Rick and Jean's house was broken into, and most of the jewellery and computers were stolen.
2 Jean discovered that Rick is having an affair with Karen.
3 Daniel meets Anthony and Peter and they discuss how to rob rich people's houses.
4 Rick and Jean were assaulted by Anthony and Peter, who stole their car, their money and their house keys.

▶ SF 10: Working with closed test formats

2 Understanding disagreements

a Summarize Anthony and Peter's conversation.
b Then write a summary of Jean and Rick's argument at home.

▶ SF 31: Writing a summary

LANGUAGE AWARENESS

3 Spoken language

Find words and phrases in the two scenes which show typical features of conversations. Discuss which of these words and phrases are acceptable in a written document, too, and which should be reformulated.

▶ SF 20: Analysing drama
▶ LP 11: Using the right register

ANALYSIS

4 Examining the characters

a Describe the characters, their different views, their use of language and their behaviour.
b Now view the two film scenes. Analyse the characters' facial expressions, gestures and voices. How do these elements add to their characterization?
c Discuss your personal reaction to the characters with a partner and comment on the characters' views and behaviour.

DVD

▶ SF 23: Analysing a film

5 Examining stereotypes

a Explain what stereotypes are, and give examples from each scene. Use the Fact File (p. 256) for help.
b Analyse the role stereotypes and prejudice play in the dialogues in the text, reflecting on how the characters perceive each other and the influence this has on their relationships.

BEYOND THE TEXT

6 YOU CHOOSE Stereotypes in everyday life

a Describe a situation in which you were or somebody else was confronted with stereotypes. Tell a partner about it and reflect about your experiences.

OR

b Discuss the function of stereotypes in everyday life: how they influence our perception of others and how we deal with them. SUPPORT p. 287

SPEAKING FOCUS ON SKILLS

Resolving a heated argument

When people have opposing points of view or interests, the may start to argue. Everybody – willingly or not – uses different strategies to heat up or cool down a conflict. Usually, people feel offended if somebody orders them around ('Stop this now.'), threatens them ('If you don't ..., I will ...'), blames them ('You are always ...'), evaluates their behaviour ('You're always trying to ...'), or shouts at them. A set of communicative strategies can be helpful to solve a conflict.

1 Strategies to cool down a conflict

Choose five of the strategies below and rank them according to their importance. Exchange your ideas with a partner and try to agree on a list of the five most effective strategies. Present your results to the rest of the class.

1 Respect the other person.
2 Try to find a win–win resolution.
3 Relax. Take a deep breath. Speak slowly and softly.
4 Listen carefully to what the other person is saying.
5 Use 'I' messages. Such as: 'I feel bad when you do that.'
6 Put what the other person said in your own words to make sure you understand. ('I understood ... Is that what you meant?')
7 Watch your language and use words like 'maybe' and 'perhaps'.
8 Ask for a break if you need to collect your thoughts or release stress.

2 Analysing and solving a conflict

► SF 37: Doing a creative writing task

a Go back to p. 256. Describe and analyse the conflict between Rick and Jean. Pay special attention to their language and behaviour.
b Discuss what Rick and Jean might have done to achieve better communication. Which of the strategies could each of them use?
c Rewrite parts of the dialogue between Rick and Jean to make it end in a positive way.

3 Dealing with aggression

► LP 11: Using the right register
► SF 27: Having a discussion

a List a few everyday conflicts between, for example, parents and children, men and women, or friends, in which people become aggressive.
b Together with a partner, role-play a few of these situations. One partner is verbally aggressive, while the other partner tries to calm the other by stating his or her observations, feelings, needs and requests. Here is how it might go:
1 'I noticed you ...' (observation).
2 'When you did that, I felt ...' (feeling).
3 'I need ...' (need)
4 'therefore, I'm hoping you'll ...' (request)
c Change roles so that each of you can try out the observation-feeling-need-request method.
d Report back to the group what you think about this way of reacting to aggression.

CULTURE SPOT

Graffiti

'Imagine a city where graffiti wasn't illegal, a city where everybody could draw whatever they liked. Where every street was awash with a million colours and little phrases. Where standing at a bus stop was never boring. A city that felt like a party where everyone was invited, not just the estate agents and barons of big business. Imagine a city like that and stop leaning against the wall – it's wet.' Banksy

1. Look at the graffiti by the British artist Banksy in the photos. Describe them and say why you think they were made.
2. State which ones you like, and why.
3. Discuss which ones should be saved.
4. Most art can be bought and sold at a price. Discuss who owns street art.
5. Comment on Banksy's statement.

Getting involved

DVD

C1 Volunteering in the wake of the Olympics

Pre-viewing

1 Discuss which of the photos in the Lead-in (p. 246) show people volunteering. SUPPORT ▶ p. 287
2 State whether you have ever volunteered or been engaged in some form of social activism. If yes, tell the others about your experience. If not, explain why not.
3 Explain why people actually volunteer.

While-viewing

▶ SF 23: Analysing a film

4 Watch the news report about volunteering in England after the Olympics and list reasons why young people volunteer.

Post-viewing

5 Explain your reaction to the various reasons given.

C2 Volunteering in Germany *Sophia Seiderer*

A friend of yours from London is involved in 'Team London', a project to help people who want to volunteer. You have been discussing volunteering in England compared to Germany. You come across the following web article about volunteerism in Germany.

Männlich, zwischen 40 und 49 Jahre alt, gebildet, beruflich erfolgreich, Protestant, Familienvater, auf dem Land lebend, Vorstand des lokalen Fußballvereins. So würde er aussehen, der Prototyp eines bürgerschaftlich engagierten Menschen, wenn man den Statistiken folgt. [...]

Mehr als jeder dritte Deutsche ab 14 Jahren ist über die Schule und den Beruf hinaus aktiv an Gruppen, Vereinen oder Organisationen beteiligt, besonders in

The mayor of London, Boris Johnson, at the launch of a Team London volunteer programme

ländlichen Regionen. 36 Prozent haben darüber hinaus langfristig freiwillige und unentgeltliche Aufgaben übernommen. Zudem hat die Bereitschaft der Bürger dazu in den vergangenen zehn Jahren zugenommen. Von 26 Prozent im Jahr 1999 auf 37 Prozent 2009. Besonderes Potenzial liegt in der Altersgruppe der 14- bis 24-Jährigen: 35 Prozent von ihnen engagieren sich bereits, weitere 49 Prozent geben an, dass sie eine Tätigkeit übernehmen würden.

Doch all die Zahlen und Daten können eines nicht zeigen: Wer hinter diesem Engagement steht. Was ist das für ein Mann, der seit 30 Jahren täglich zu einer kleinen Kirche zwischen Müllberg und Autobahn fährt, um „sein" Gotteshaus vor dem Abriss zu bewahren? Was bringt eine Bankerin dazu, jeden Samstag mit ihrem Hund in den Trümmern alter Fabrikhallen zu trainieren, damit sie und das Tier die Rettungshundeausbildung bestehen? Was treibt eine Doktorandin dazu, ihre Zeit in ein Projekt zu investieren, das jungen Studenten aus Nicht-Akademiker-Familien helfen soll, ihr Studium durchzuziehen? Sind das Menschen, die einfach „sozialer" sind als andere? Die so erzogen sind? Die das tun, weil es sich so gehört? […]

„Es handelt sich um Menschen, die über ein bestimmtes Leistungsethos verfügen, also beruflich recht erfolgreich sind. Dieses Ethos setzt sich oft auch außerhalb des Berufs fort", so Joachim Winkler [von der Hochschule Wismar, der über das Ehrenamt promoviert]. Und: „Es muss immer aus ihrer eigenen Motivation herauskommen." Deswegen hält er auch nichts von dem Konzept, Arbeitslose für bürgerschaftliches Engagement zu gewinnen. „Arbeitslose denken an die fehlende Arbeit. Sie suchen Arbeit, haben also keine Motivation, zusätzliche unentgeltliche Arbeit anzunehmen."

Auch in der Politik erfährt das Thema Zivilgesellschaft und bürgerliches Engagement seit mehreren Jahren eine Konjunktur. Aktionen wie die „Initiative Zivilengagement" des Familienministeriums, der Deutsche Engagementpreis oder Internetforen wie Engagiert-in-deutschland.de, auf dem sich die Helfer vernetzen können, sollen die ehrenamtliche Tätigkeit fördern. Nicht zuletzt auch das „Europäische Jahr der Freiwilligentätigkeit", das die EU-Kommission für 2011 ausgerufen hat.

Mit der Förderung des Ehrenamts schwingt immer auch die Gefahr mit, dass der Staat sich aus seinen sozialen Aufgaben zurückzieht und diese immer mehr auf Ehrenamtliche abwälzt. […] Matthias Freise von der Uni Münster sieht eine Verlockung für den Staat: „Er muss sparen, in teuren Bereichen kann er nicht ausbauen. Das Ehrenamt zu fördern, ist kein teures Politikfeld, einfach und sehr medienfreundlich – ein wunderbares Thema für die Politik."

From: 'Ehrenamtliches Engagement für die Gesellschaft', *Die Welt*, 24 March 2010

COMPREHENSION

1 Mediation (German → English)

You and your friend from London have been discussing what kind of people are more or less likely to do volunteer work and who isn't. Write him or her an email, outlining what you have learned from the article. SUPPORT p. 287

▶ SF 41: Mediation of written and oral texts

BEYOND THE TEXT

2 To volunteer or not to volunteer

a With a partner, discuss the question whether the two of you should volunteer or not. One of you wants to, the other does not. You may take notes on little cue cards.

▶ SF 27: Having a discussion

b Tell the class about your discussion and decision.

C3 Young people raising their voices

1 Young people making a difference

a EXPERT GROUPS Get together in groups of four. Each student has a number (1–4). Each group researches one of the three young people featured below. Individually, find information about them, their lives, their stories and their achievements, then compare your results in your group.

Craig Kielburger

'Child labour is an issue of grave importance. It must become a top priority for all governments of the world. How can the world move into the twenty-first century with children still being exploited for their labour and denied their basic right to an education?'

Malala Yousafzai

'Let us pick up our books and our pens. They are our most powerful weapons. One child, one teacher, one book and one pen can change the world.'

Jack Andraka

'If a fifteen-year-old, who didn't even know he had a pancreas at the beginning of this project, could find a new way to detect pancreatic cancer, just imagine what you can do.'

Find a tool to make your poster here: **Webcode** context-50

b JIGSAW GROUPS Form new groups with the students who have the same number as you. As an expert, present 'your' young person to the others. In the end, everyone in your new group should be well informed about each of the three young people.

2 Visions and ideas

a Discuss which of the three young people (including their work and vision) you find most interesting and why.

▸ SF 26: Taking part in an interview

b CHALLENGE HOT SEAT Act the part of one of the young people in question. Answer questions from the rest of the class on your ideas, motives and beliefs.

3 Raising your voice

Apart from children's rights, what do you think are pressing issues that should be discussed and that people should raise their voices for?

Getting your message across

In this section you are going to create a vlog. A vlog is a video blog post or video podcast. Vloggers make videos of themselves or certain events and then upload them to the internet. Vloggers use video to express their thoughts, opinions and interests and to get their messages across. A vlog can be topical, instructional or entertaining.

1 Examine a video campaign or vlog

DVD

Across the world, web video has become a medium to give people a voice concerning political and social issues. The United Nations, for example, created a YouTube channel called 'Raise your voice and change climate change!', where you can find a lot of videos made by people who wanted to speak their minds, among them Desmond Tutu, a South African social rights activist and first black Archbishop of Cape Town, and numerous young people from all over the world.

a Watch Tutu's video. Describe your impressions of the video, and how Tutu tries to convey his message.

b Find other videos from the campaign, and discuss whether such video campaigns can make a difference.

► SF 23: Analysing a film

2 YOU CHOOSE **Create your own vlog**

a Present yourself in a vlog. You may refer to some of the following aspects:
- your aims and ambitions
- voluntary work you do
- your philosophy of life
- a person that impresses you and could be a role model to others
- a thing that is worth fighting for

OR

b Produce a video on an issue that matters to you. If you are uncertain, here are a few subjects you can choose from:
- environment
- education
- children's/women's/men's rights
- freedom and human rights
- homelessness

With a video camera and the internet everyone can become a vlogger.

3 Choose the class's favourite vlog

Get into groups of six and present your vlogs to each other. Choose one to be presented to the entire class. Be prepared to give reasons for your choice. In class, watch the videos you have chosen and discuss them. With the assessment sheet your teacher will give you, evaluate the vlogs and vote for the video you want to win the class contest.

Find a tool to create your video here: **Webcode** context-54

Context Task

This context task gives you the opportunity to consider the topics you have dealt with in class again and to think about their relevance for your future life.

YOU CHOOSE

1 Giving a presentation I

Work on your own or in a group. Choose 3–5 items from the word cloud on the left and prepare a presentation on the topic 'Skills and insights I got from my English course that might be helpful for my future life'. Your presentation should be 5–7 minutes long if you are working on your own or 10–12 if you're in a group. You may want to add examples from your course work to illustrate your statements.

► SF6: Doing project work
► SF24: Giving a presentation

OR

2 Giving a presentation II

Work on your own. Think of 3–5 items that are not in the word cloud and use them as the basis of a presentation as explained in **1**.

► SF24: Giving a presentation

OR

3 Making an advertisement

Work on your own, in pairs or in a group. Make an advertisement for your English class that tells younger students what to expect and/or what to look forward to. Choose a suitable form (e.g. leaflet, poster, electronic presentation, blog ...) and present it in class (and, if possible, on the school website).

► SF37: Doing a creative writing task

Find a tool to design your poster or flyer here:
Webcode context-50

OR

4 Having a debate

Work in a group. Prepare and conduct a debate on the motion 'This house believes that English is the most important subject at school'.

► SF28: Having a debate

OR

5 Writing a quiz

Work in a group.

► SF6: Doing project work

a Choose five chapter topics or items from the word cloud and write a quiz consisting of three questions/tasks for each topic/item, e.g.
Example *lingua franca*:
1 Name three situations in which English is used as a lingua franca.
2 Why is a lingua franca so important in a country like India?
3 Name two possible disadvantages of using a lingua franca.

b Ask fellow students to do your quiz.

Support Pages

Chapter 1 The USA – Still the Promised Land?

A1 ¡Viva América! p. 17

3 Words that convey emotion

b The following text sounds bland because it lacks words that convey feelings. You can give it more emotional impact by adding the words from the box.

anxious • feared • hastily • hoping • nervously • overjoyed • tearfully • thrilled

My father … that his life would change for the worse if Castro came to power in Cuba. He … applied to the US Embassy in Havana, … for an immigration permit for himself and his family. After waiting three … months, he was … to receive a letter saying we could leave for the USA. My parents … packed their belongings and … said goodbye to their friends and relatives in Cuba. On March 11th, 1958, on board a small passenger ship bound for Miami, they were … to have their first glimpse of the US mainland.

When you have finished, compare texts with someone who did not use the Support option. Talk about different ways of modifying sentences to give them more emotional appeal.

B1 The new neighbours p. 23

6 The other side of the coin

Form groups of four. Two of you are Bev and Russ, the other two are the African American couple who have bought the house in Clybourne Street. Imagine that after Karl has left, the black couple come to look at the house. How would Russ and Bev behave? How might the black couple explain their wish to move to an all-white neighbourhood? Discuss the issues at hand, then prepare role cards for your parts.

Step 1: Give the black couple names (e.g. Francine and Albert). Each member of your group chooses one of the characters. Read the list below and decide whether the attitude would better fit the white couple or the black couple:

- a bit embarrassed by the situation
- looking forward to changing neighbourhoods
- want a better life for their children
- feel guilty about their behaviour
- worried about the reaction of the neighbours
- believe in equality and progress
- avoid talking about race and skin colour
- want their share of the American dream

Step 2: Now work together in 'couples' to prepare your role cards. Write down (in keywords) questions your person might ask and statements they might make.

Now practise the scene, then perform it for your class.

D1 Facts and figures p. 32

1 Understanding the figures

a Compare the figures in the table by completing the eight sentences on the opposite page with phrases from the box.

	USA	China	Germany	Brazil	Russia	India
1 GDP	16,244,600	8,277,103	3,428,131	2,252,664	2,014,775	1,841,710
2 Military spending	682,478	166,107	45,785	43,576	90,749	46,125
3 Balance of trade	–784,775	155,142	219,938	19,169	198,760	–154,401

1 The GDP of the USA is almost ... as that of China, the country with the ... largest economy.
2 The Russian GDP is only about ... as China's.
3 China's GDP is ... that of Germany, Russia and Brazil together.
4 Russia's GDP is ... that of Brazil.
5 No country spends ... money on the military as the USA.
6 Germany ranks only ... in terms of GDP, but ... in terms of balance of trade.
7 Russia has a healthy trade surplus, whereas India imports ... it exports.
8 China's trade surplus is almost ... India's trade deficit.

as many • as much • first • fourth • half as big • larger than • (slightly) less than • more than • one quarter as big • second • the same size as • third • twice as big

FACT FILE

GDP (Gross [grəʊs] **Domestic Product)** is defined as the total value of goods and services produced in a country. The **balance of trade** is the difference between the total value of exports from a country and imports into the same country. A negative balance (**deficit** ['defɪsɪt]; opposite: **surplus** ['sɜːpləs]) means the country imports more than it exports.

D3 Better than its reputation p. 34

3 The author's bias

a Point to examples from the text that illustrate the author's bias (selection of facts, word choice, use of *emphasis, *juxtaposition, sentence structure, etc.). Match the words and expressions that have been highlighted to one or more of the categories in the box and describe the effect they have on the reader. ► Glossary, p. 322

*comparison • *juxtaposition / selection of facts • *contrast • word choice (e.g. positive / negative *connotations) • *emphasis • *repetition / *anaphora*

But the American response is already larger – by a factor of hundreds – than that of the largest economy in East Asia. The United States is sending an aircraft carrier to the worst-hit regions and has promised $20 million in emergency aid. Millions more will be raised by U.S. charities. The British are sending a warship and $16 million. Even the Vatican has promised $4 million. And the government of China, the new land of opportunity? $100,000.
(Lines 18–27 of the text on p. 153)

Journalist
Anne Applebaum

Americans, like Europeans, have long believed that strength and wealth entail responsibility. That's why two American ex-presidents voluntarily coordinated the international response to the 2004 tsunami, even though Indonesia was not the site of a U.S. naval base. That's why massive amounts of U.S. aid went to victims of the 2005 earthquake in Kashmir, even though relations between the United States and Pakistan were deteriorating at the time.

That's also why an American president who is actively uninterested in engaging with the Syrian conflict has pledged more than $1 billion in humanitarian aid to Syrian refugees, accounting for nearly 30 percent of all such aid; European contributions as a whole make up a good percentage of the rest. China's contribution, meanwhile, comes to $3 million, less than that of Luxembourg. China plays an enormous political role in Syria – the Chinese veto has helped keep the United Nations firmly sidelined there – but clearly does not feel obligated to help those affected by its decisions.

The Chinese do give development aid, but differently: not in response to tragedies, not to counter disaster, but to facilitate the export of raw materials to China.
(Lines 36–51 of the text on pp. 153–154)

Now go on to **3b** on p. 34; if possible, choose a partner who has not made use of the Support option.

Chapter 2 Americans – Finding Freedom

A1 Defining America p. 41

2 America and Americans

Describe the images of America and 'the Americans' conveyed in each quotation and analyse how these images are created. In the quotations, look for the following stylistic devices and analyse their meaning:

Winthrop:	de Crèvecoeur:	Emerson:
hyperbole/exaggeration • religious allusion • repetition/parallelism • simile	*climax • repetition/ enumeration*	*repetition/enumeration • simile* (2x)

O'Sullivan:	Humphrey:
metaphor/alliteration • religious language	*evaluative/judgmental language • metaphor*

Now summarize the text, then go back to task **3** on p. 41.

B2 The power of ordinary people p. 48

2 The context

Put the issues and events mentioned in the text into the context of US history and of the political system of the USA. If necessary, find more information on the internet.
Consider the following issues and events and, for the context, the keywords given:

- 'same sex couples can now marry in all 50 states' (l. 1): US = secular state, but Christian religion plays a great part in the political discussion; some claim that the Supreme Court is betraying the country's religious roots.
- 'the Confederate flag's hold ... is fraying' (ll. 1–3): Confederate flag = strong symbol of various values – 1. cultural identity of the South, 2. anti-federal sentiments, 3. slavery and racial discrimination.
- 'Obamacare ... is now reaffirmed' (cf. ll. 3–4): American idea of individualism – people are given opportunities, but they are also encouraged to take risks; many Americans think that people should have the right *not* to have any health insurance.

Now summarize the text, then go back to task **3** on p. 48.

D1 A nation of rebels? p. 53

3 Style and register

b Analyse the stylistic devices the writer uses to support his ideas. Look for: allusions to political movements and historical events, enumeration, similes and metaphors, parallelism, rhetorical questions.

Now summarize the text, then go back to task **4** on p. 53.

Chapter 3 The UK – a Kingdom United?

A1 Dangerous books p. 63

A royal footman waits for the Queen to arrive in the royal carriage.

4 Creative writing

b Write the dialogue between the footman and his wife and include the events that probably took place while the Queen was opening the Parliament. The following questions might help you to collect ideas:

- How did the footman experience the incident?
- What is probably the most important aspect for him?
- Imagine the footman's feelings during his encounter with the Queen. Do you think he was embarrassed, frustrated, angry, unhappy, etc.? How could he express this in his conversation with his wife?

Don't forget: You are going to write a dialogue. So the footman and his wife should refer to each other and react to what the other person says.

B2 Between two cultures p. 70

2 Analysing character relationships

Analyse the relationship between Kelly and her father Ibrahim. Reflect on what they talk about and how they speak to each other. Read the following quotes that Kelly and Ibrahim say to each other. How do you imagine the actors are meant to say them? What emotions are being portrayed?

IBRAHIM Would you prefer it if I had been an American? (l. 9)
IBRAHIM I wish we could've met earlier. (l. 23)
IBRAHIM I imagined you might look like Kate Winslet. (l. 32)
IBRAHIM Because you are English. And you don't know any better. (l. 81)

KELLY But I told you I'm not going to go to Iraq, am I? (ll. 12–13)
KELLY This isn't going very well, is it? (l. 34)
KELLY Why are you here? Now, what do you want? (l. 42)
KELLY Yeah, all right then, tell me what I think. (l. 69)

B3 The British and their tea p. 71

2 Analysing style

How does the speaker of the podcast try to hold the audience's attention and entertain his listeners? First make notes on the following aspects of the podcast. What further examples can you find? What effect do they have on you as a listener? Use your points to organize your analysis.

Aspect	Example	Effect
Statistics	By the end of the day, the counter will reach 165 million – that is three cups of tea per person per day.	…
Interesting facts	And it is well-known that the Queen likes a nice cup of tea, as well.	…
Personal facts	Yukk! I cannot stand tea with sugar!	…
Exaggeration	… in the interests of international harmony and understanding I shall now explain …	…

C1 A referendum on the EU p. 74

3 Analysing style

Listen again. Analyse how Cameron tries to convince his listeners of his views. Focus on language and content. Is he successful?

a First fill in the 'Explanation' column of the table. What are the different stylistic devices?

b List examples of the different devices you can hear in the text.

c Describe the effect they have on you as a listener.

d Use your points to organize your analysis of the speaker's style.

Stylistic device	Explanation	Example from the speech	Effect
Alliteration	▪ …	▪ Rules and regulations ▪ …	▪ …
Empathy	▪ …	▪ …	▪ …
Antithesis, contrast	▪ …	▪ Some people say … but the question mark is already there. ▪ They say, but I don't believe	▪ …
Parallelism Repetition Anaphora	▪ The same word / structure is repeated	▪ It will be … ▪ …	▪ …
Rule of three	▪ …	▪ Weeks, years and months ▪ …	▪ …

C3 It's OK to like the Germans p. 76

1 Summarizing

Summarize the writer's main points concerning Britons' relationship to Germany.
In the text, there are several main ideas you need to communicate in your summary.
Choose the seven most important facts from the list below:

- name of the text, author, date and source
- main idea: how British people feel about Germans
- background: the 2014 World Cup final
- quote: 'I can't quite believe it … but I find myself supporting Germany.'
- stereotypes about German people
- the state of Britain's economy
- what Britain cannot copy from Germany
- what Britain can learn from Germany
- German problems
- The chance of a British team winning the World Cup

Now summarize the text, then go back to task 2 on p. 76.

Chapter 4 Countries of the English-speaking World

A1 The making of an Aussie p. 83

3 Examining stylistic devices

Point out stylistic devices that Donnelly uses to persuade his readers and to prove his point. Find examples of each of the following in the text and analyze their effect in the context:

- enumerations,
- positive and negative connotations,
- antithesis (contrast).

Now go back to task 4 on p. 83.

C3 South Africa after Mandela p. 96

3 Imagery

Nkosi frequently uses metaphorical language in his essay, for example in ll. 10–11: 'They feared his departure opened up a door for the angry poor black masses to destroy their comfortable lives.'

a Analyse the *metaphor, explaining why it is appropriate in its context. What does 'opening a door' mean here? Who is inside, who is outside? What were the white South Africans really afraid might happen?

b Point out other examples of metaphorical language in the text and analyse their effect. A good place to look for metaphorical language is the final paragraph of the text (ll. 31–36). Here, Nkosi uses *personification. Find further examples of this device and explain why the writer has chosen it.

Now go back to task 4 on p. 96.

D3 Rich land, poor land p. 100

2 Presenting the candidates

Examine the way Cece Fitzpatrick and her opponent Jim Boucher are presented in the text. Analyze the means the writer uses to influence her readers, especially at the way she presents Fitzpatrick and Boucher. Answering the following questions can help you to do the task:

1. In what context is Cece Fitzpatrick introduced? How does the reader think about her decision to run for chief?
2. How does the writer characterize Jim Boucher and his conduct in office?
3. How does Cece justify her opposition to the oil industry?
4. What effect does the description of the administration building in Fort McKay have on the reader?
5. Why are we given employment information on both candidates?
6. Which of the candidates is given the first and the last word? What effect does this have on you as a reader?

Now go back to task 3 on p. 100.

Chapter 5 India – a Kaleidoscope

A2 Colonizers and colonized p. 107

Comparing a quote and photos

When studying the quote, you could consider the following:

- Who spoke the words?
- What is the speaker's view of colonialism?
- What is the speaker's view of the colonized people?
- What is the main message?

When studying the photographs, you should take the following aspects into account:

- When and where was the photo probably taken?
- Who can you see in the picture?
- What does body language reveal about the relationship of the people in the picture?
- What can you deduce from the picture about India under British rule?

A3 The British Empire from an Indian perspective p. 109

5 The legacy of the Raj

Discuss whether the British Raj was a good thing for India. Consider the following points in **A2**:

- What does Curzon say that he hoped he gave the Indians? Consider whether some of these might have been given to the Indians, and whether the Indians needed what he hoped to give.
- How might the Indians in the photos feel? Has their lives changed much since the Empire?

Also, consider the following points in text **A3**:

- the positive elements listed in ll. 1–2, 6–7, 16–21,
- the failures of the Empire in ll. 2–9, 10–14, 18–19.

B1 Urbanization in India: the big picture p. 113

1 Indian urbanization

When describing a graph, or diagram, start out by mentioning the topic, the type of presentation used (e.g. a bar chart, a line graph, etc.), the span of time it covers and its source and date of publication (if available). Then describe the diagram in detail by turning the graph into words. In the end summarize what you have learned.

Now go back to task **2** on p. 113.

B3 Celebrating Indian culture p. 115

6 Mediation (German → English)

Before writing your email, have a look at the following opening and closing formulas and decide which of them are best used in formal, which ones in informal emails (or letters). Decide on the best for your email.

Dear Dr. Smith, • Dear Madam, • Dear Ms. White, • Dear Prof. Smith, • Dear Sir or Madam, • Dear Mike, • Dear Sir(s), • Dearest • Hello, Mike! • Hey, babe! • Hi, • Tony,	*Best regards • Best wishes • Hugs and kisses • Lots of love • Love • Regards • Sincerely yours • With best wishes • With kind regards • Yours ever • Yours faithfully • Yours sincerely • Yours truly • Yours*

Now choose the most appropriate opening and closing formulas for your email.

C1 The Indian diaspora p. 117

2 Locating the Indian diaspora

a When designing your poster, take the following points into consideration:

- Overall appearance: Does the poster attract your attention? Is it informative? How creative is the work that went into its making?
- Title: Does the poster have a title banner? Is the title clear? Is it eye-catching? Can it be read easily from 3 metres away?
- Layout: Is the text large enough to be read from 2 metres away? Is there sufficient 'resting space for the eye' (i.e. blank space)? Are colours and graphic highlighting used effectively? Are texts and illustrations/photographs integrated in a meaningful way?
- Writing: Is the writing concise? Is the information included in the texts relevant? Can the texts be read easily? Is language used correctly (e.g. vocabulary, grammar, spelling)?

C3 English lessons p. 120

3 The use of tenses

The following passages from 'English Lessons' illustrate the use of the narrative past, narrative present and narrative future tenses in the story:

narrative past:

The police came looking for him. Oh no, not for my protection – no. They were rounding up all Sikh boys between the ages of fifteen and twenty-five for 'questioning'. Tony's parents knew what was in store and they hid him in the servant's quarter, a concrete room on the flat roof of the house. (ll. 75–78)

narrative present:

The phone rings and my heart starts to pound – *dharak, dharak*. Our answering machine message has Valerie's voice, and I follow the words with her accent. (ll. 8–9)

narrative future:

I will tell Tony I will take English lessons, and that she will be my teacher. (ll. 98–99)

Find more examples like this in the story to illustrate each type of narration, then answer the following questions:

- Which type of narration lends the story a sense of immediacy?
- Which type of narration has a distancing effect?
- Which type of narration could be said to add a prophetic tone to the story?

Go back to 'English Lessons' and use your findings to interpret the story: Why are there so many tense switches in 'English Lessons'? What do they reveal about the first-person narrator? And what is their effect on the reader?

Now go back to task 4 on p. 120.

Chapter 6 Beyond the Nation – Europe and a Globalized World

A2 Young, educated – and leaving the country p. 129

4 Creative writing

Form groups of four. Each select one important moment of Melissa Abadía's immigrant experience and write a diary entry. Read out your entries to your group and join your texts to form one coherent diary entry.

1 Look for the description of an important moment in the text.
2 Make notes on what happened and how Melissa Abadía felt at that moment.
3 If necessary add other events and feelings Melissa Abadía may have had.
4 Write your diary entry.

B2 The need for a new label p. 133

3 Promoting transparent labelling

a Design a clothing label that helps buyers make responsible choices.
   1 Make a list of aspects that are important for responsible clothing production.
   2 Choose the most important points and think of a system to evaluate them.
   3 Write the text for a clothing label that contains information about these aspects.

Now go back to task 3b on p. 133.

C1 Keeping the accent p. 138

4 YOU CHOOSE Creative writing

a Write a *short story based on the poem.
   1 Outline the events and emotions you would like to include in your story.
   2 Decide from which character's *point of view to tell the story – the *speaker of the poem, the barman or other people in the bar.
   3 Decide what type of *narrator to use.
   4 Start writing. Do not write an introduction, but start in the middle of the scene, e.g. 'I can feel their looks piercing my back'.
   5 Do not write a clear, conclusive ending, but leave it open, even a bit vague.
   6 Hold writing conferences among four or five students to improve your texts.

OR

b Write a dramatic *scene based on the poem.
   1 Decide on how you are going to convey the *speaker's feelings or memories. You might make her speak a *soliloquy or you might have a second actor who acts as the speaker's 'shadow', articulating her feelings and thoughts.
   2 Write your scene, starting the action right in the middle of the action, e.g. with the barman saying 'Sorry, what was that?'.
   3 Imagine the actors' gestures or movements and write stage directions.

C3 Linguistic diplomacy: the Eurovision Song Contest p. 139

5 Discussion

In groups of five prepare and hold a panel discussion in which you discuss the question of whether each country should be obliged to enter songs in their national language only. One student is the moderator, the others argue either for or against the topic.

Moderator:

- Think of possible arguments and their counter-arguments.
- Collect questions or remarks that might make the participants put these arguments forward.

Discussion participants:

- Think of arguments for your position and collect examples to illustrate your point. Don't just talk about the very obvious topics, but search for arguments and examples the others might not have thought about.
- Collect arguments that your opponents might put forward and think about ways to refute them.

Chapter Task p. 141

1 Planning your work

a Do some research to get a general idea of the topic and to identify suitable subtopics.

Find some helpful links here:
Webcode context-24

1 Don't forget to provide a definition of slavery.
2 Define the areas you want to focus on:
  a You might want to give a short historical survey of slavery. Consider e.g. the situation in Ancient Greece or Rome, the Middle Ages and/or the Americas.
  b You might also want to outline the grievances that have led to slave rebellions throughout history.
  c When considering modern-day slavery, think of e.g. the catering trade or agriculture, the construction industry, private households, the entertainment industry (football) or sexual slavery.
3 Decide whether you want to present a case study or general aspects of slavery.

Now go back to task **1b** on p. 141.

Find a tool to make your poster here:
Webcode context-51

2 Preparing your poster

b Organize your findings and prepare your poster.
1 Structure your text and visual aids in a way that guides the reader of your poster through it: Use symbols, lines, arrows, colours, and fonts in a clear and meaningful way.
2 You may use pictures and/or quotations taken from films and/or literature dealing with slavery.

Now go back to task **2c** on p. 141.

Chapter 7 Science – Enhancing Life?

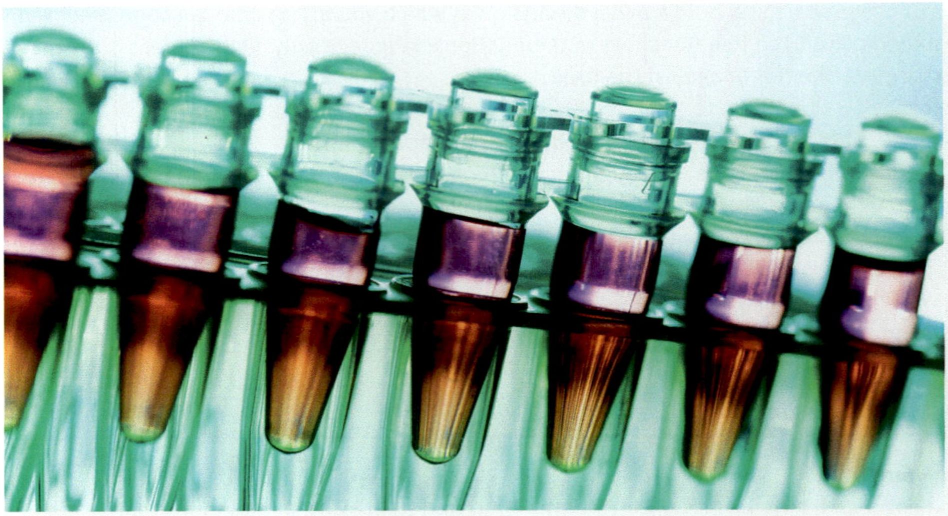

A1 A saviour sibling p. 147

3 Argumentative structure

Analyse the argumentative structure of the text.

1 Structure the text by finding headlines for each paragraph (see example on the right).

2 Examine the direct quotes: Who is quoted and what do they say? Are the quotes in favour or against the procedure?

3 Examine the indirect quotes: Who is quoted and what do they say? Are the indirect and direct quotes from the same person? If so, decide how the direct quotes relate to the indirect quotes.

ll. 1–2	Introduction: sibling was saved
ll. 3–6	Medical history of first sibling
ll. 7–12	Problems facing a second sibling
ll. 13–23	Medical treatment

Now go back to task **4** on p. 147.

A3 At the lab p. 150

4 Practising speaking

a Prepare a monologue on whether designer babies are desirable or not. Think of a catchy introduction to your speech, e.g. start with a provocative statement like 'designer babies are the future' or 'a child has to be smart, intelligent, healthy and cute'.

- State your opinion on the topic clearly: In my opinion …, The point is that …, The way I see it …, My point is …, What I'm trying to say is …
- Make sure you have at least three good arguments in favour of or against the topic:
  Pro: reduced risk of genetic diseases, better opportunities in life, the child can have better genes than his or her parents
  Con: imperfect embryos are killed, no more individuality, only the rich can afford the perfect child, altering a human being is unethical
- Summarize your points at the end of your speech and clearly state your opinion:
  To sum up …, That's why I think …, All things considered …, All in all …

B2 Gene doping p. 156

4 Examining the tone

Identify how the writer's use of language reveals his attitude to the topic. It may be useful to look at these quotes when deciding on the writer's attitude:

- 'a battle like no other in sport' (l. 1)
- 'The authorities are so concerned, they have been preparing for it for more than 10 years.' (ll. 1–2)
- 'as anyone who had a vague brush with professional cycling in the 90s knows' (ll. 14–15)
- 'the illicit dope of choice for competitors' (ll. 17–18)
- 'the wonder drug' (l. 18)
- 'Could this be an undetectable way of improving oxygen delivery?' (ll. 23–24)
- 'even better for the would-be doper' (l. 29)
- 'So what is the World Anti-Doping Agency (Wada) doing about it?' (ll. 30–31)
- 'it could be lethal' (l. 33)
- 'your blood thickening into sludge' (ll. 34–35)

Now go back to task **3** on p. 156.

C4 Biofuels – the green alternative? p. 162

3 Conducting a debate

Find arguments in favour of and against biofuels. The motion could be as follows: 'Governments should subsidize biofuels.'

Discussion boxes for a debate:

Agreeing with and supporting an argument
Exactly!
Definitely!
I couldn't agree more!
That's right!
I agree with …
What … said is (absolutely) right.
I'm of the same opinion (as …)
I would like to support what … said.
You've got a good point there.

Interrupting – Asking for clarification
Sorry to interrupt, but …
I would like to add something here.
What do you think about …?
What is your opinion on …?
Could you explain that again, please?

Disagreeing
I can't agree with you …
I think you're (absolutely) wrong there!
I (completely) disagree with you!
Do you really mean that?
But you just said that now.
I'm sorry, but that can't be right!
But what you've just said is …
I must contradict you …

Chapter 8 Human Dilemmas – from Shakespeare to Today

A2 Richard courts his enemy p. 173

3 Working with imagery

Work with a partner. Identify the images each speaker uses. Explain them with the help of the annotations and from the context they are used in.

It is useful to become aware of your personal mental images when reading any text, and in particular a poetic passage like the one you are dealing with here. Consider

- names that Lady Anne calls Gloucester and whether these are straightforward or evoke certain images,
- personification of abstracts or of body parts,
- *similes,
- *metaphors.

5 Understanding character

On the basis of your analysis, describe the speakers' characters. Gloucester (= Richard) keeps twisting Anne's insults around to make them say something flattering to her in response – which she does not seem to accept, at least verbally. In this context you have analysed her response to Richard's offering her his sword to kill him.

All these things are indicators of what kind of people these two dramatic characters are.

When describing them, consider

- what motivations they have for acting as they do,
- what emotions they display while they are speaking,
- what their actions reveal about them,
- whether their original emotions change and what that tells you about their characters.

B1 My future wife p. 175

2 Comparing dialogues

Compare the way Petruchio woos Katharina to the way Gloucester woos Anne (A2, pp. 171–172). Evaluate what each man reveals about himself and how effectively they each use words to achieve their aims. First look at your answers to A2, tasks 4 and 6 on p. 173. Then use the following questions to help you examine Petruchio.

1 How does Petruchio respond to Kate telling him that her name is Katharina? (ll. 4–8)
2 What does he say he has heard about her from others? (ll. 4–14)
3 How does he respond to her attempts to make fun of him? (ll. 20–24)
4 How does Katharina come across?
5 How does Petruchio describe Katharina? (ll. 34–40 and ll. 49–50)
6 How does he propose to her? (ll. 41–52)

Now consider what sort of person Petruchio is, and whether you think he is successful at wooing Katharina. Then find similarities and differences between Richard and Petruchio, considering the context of each man's wooing and the emotions involved. Finally, decide which of the two men will be more successful.

VIEWING FOCUS ON SKILLS p. 176

5 Evaluation

Evaluate how successful the director has been in adapting the material. Name the elements that were changed and the effect the scene has on you. Use the following categories to create a table in which you contrast the play and the film:
setting *(What is the setting in each genre?)* • **characters** *(How did they come across in the play/film?)* • **relationship** *(What was the characters' relationship like in each genre?)* • **changes** *(What elements were added to/missing in the film?)* • **extras** *(How did the film maker use lighting, music, noise?)*

B2 Responding to a sonnet p. 178

2 GALLERY WALK **Comparing the sonnets**

Compare the two sonnets. Examine structure, development of the idea and style. Present your findings on posters and evaluate them in a gallery walk. These steps may be useful:

1 Look at the structures of the poems by examining the rhyme scheme.
2 State the main idea presented in each poem.
3 Divide each poem up according to the images in it.
4 Examine how the idea of alteration is addressed in each poem.
5 Examine how Simmons uses phrases and ideas from Shakespeare in his own poem.

Find a tool to make your poster here:
Webcode context-50

C1 All men are created equal – what about women? p. 180

2 Structure and language

a Identify the four parts the text is divided into. (Careful: They are not necessarily indicated by '[...]'!) Analyse the function of each part. Look for parts that could be labelled thus:

commonly accepted truths • *conclusion* • *introduction* • *list of complaints*

Then say in more detail what each part is about.

Now go back to task **2b** on p. 180.

Chapter 9 Work and Business – Careers and Perspectives

A2 Moving on after recession p. 190

3 Political speeches: convincing the audience

Look at Obama's style and language and show how he tries to convince his audience. Pay attention, for instance, to how Obama appeals to the audience by

- varying sentence lengths,
- referring to historical events,
- …

Also, observe the effect the story of Misty DeMars has on the audience.

Now go back to task 4 on p. 191.

A4 Teenagers' career aspirations p. 194

4 Writing

Should you pursue the career of your choice or should you consider only those careers where job demand is fairly certain? Write an argumentative text in which you consider both sides and state your own view. For ideas *for* wanting to pursue your preferred career/studies programme, i.e. *against* considering only those careers where job demand is projected, consider

- motivational aspects,
- your talents,
- achieving the goals you set yourself,
- potentially good results in examinations, etc., if you are diligent and hardworking.

For ideas *against* wanting to pursue your preferred career/studies programme, i.e. *for* considering only those careers where job demand is projected,

- look for arguments, facts and figures from the article for support,
- think of the possibility of combining talents and interests with promising career paths.

A5 Do you love your job? p. 197

3 A tricky question in your job interview

a Some of the aspects of job satisfaction mentioned by King should not be brought up in a job interview. List them, then compare with your partner. Remember, for instance: Your future employer is interested in your well-being and job satisfaction, but also wants employees who can work in a team.

Now go back to task 3 on p. 197.

B1 Mitch's first glimpse of the world of work p. 199

2 Power relations

Partner A: Analyse the meeting between Mitch and McNulty and explain how one of them shows his power and superiority through non-linguistic means (e.g. facial expressions). Focus and take notes on

- Mitch and McNulty on their way to the coach's office,
- where and how they are sitting in the office,McNulty's eyes and voice,
- McNulty's pencil.

Partner B: Analyse the meeting between Mitch and McNulty and explain how one of them uses language to demonstrate his power and superiority. Focus and take notes on

- who is asking the important questions,
- who is using imperatives,
- who is trying to be funny,
- who controls the conversation.

Now go back to task 3 on p. 199.

B2 Ten things not to say in a job interview p. 201

2 The language of the text

a Explain how King tries to amuse the reader. Consider the following *stylistic devices used by King: absurd example, exaggeration, metaphor. Find examples of these devices in lines 30, 35 and 46–47.

Now go back to task 2b on p. 201.

B3 The best job in the world is back! p. 202

2 Text type and target group

a Name characteristic aspects of the text type 'job advertisement' and illustrate them with examples from the text. The subheadings of the text give you a first idea about typical elements of job ads. Match the subheadings with their corresponding explanation:

Subheading
Your responsibilities
Who we're looking for
About the job package
About your new office
How to apply

Explanation
financial information
contact information
information about the employer
description of the ideal candidate
description of duties

Now go back to task 2b on p. 202.

B5 Look them in the eye – the job interview p. 204

2 Do's and don'ts

Watch the video. With your partner, list and rank the given dos and don'ts of job interviews. Five of the following aspects are dealt with in the video:

1 conversation openers
2 dress code
3 first impressions
4 hairstyle
5 no-go questions
6 professional documents
7 punctuality
8 selling yourself and your strengths

Now go back to task 3 on p. 204.

Chapter 10 Modern Media – Tools or Tyrants?

A1 Lonely friends p. 210

4 Poetic devices

Examine the means the poet uses to draw our attention to the influence of social media on our lives. Poetic devices are tools used by the poet to emphasize the meaning of a poem. These questions might help you to do the task:

- What effect does the title have on the reader?
- What is striking about the endings of the lines?
- What means does the poet use to make the content appear more vivid and appealing to the reader?
- How does the poet involve the reader in the poem?
- What is the tone of the poem, and what effect does this tone have on the reader?

Now go back to task 5 on p. 210.

A2 Online learning in 2044 p. 213

2 Telling names

Refer to the annotations on pp. 16–17 and analyse what the names reveal about the *character and the *setting.

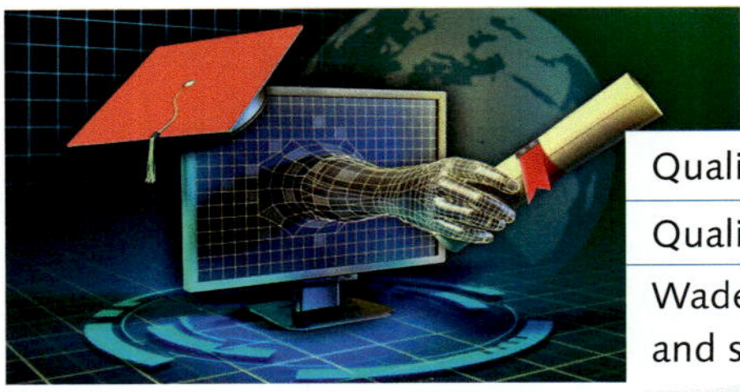

	Public school	OASIS	
		Incipio	Ludus
Quality of the facilities			
Quality of education			
Wade's attitude and status			

Step 1: Gather and structure the relevant information given in the text, using a grid like this one.
Step 2: Relate your findings to the names and explain their significance in the story.

Now go back to task 3 on p. 213.

B1 Should classrooms have video cameras? p. 219

3 Discussing the pros and cons of surveillance at school

c Present your concept to the school board (i.e. the class).

Step 1: Make notes for each of the following steps.

1 Address the members of the school board.
2 State your group's attitude towards surveillance at school.
3 Give reasons for your opinions and provide examples to illustrate your points. Present your concept in a clearly structured way with your most substantial argument at the end.
4 Briefly sum up your main points.
5 Invite the school board to ask questions or comment on your concept.

Step 2: Plan how to present your reasons visually on the board / interactive whiteboard.
Step 3: Use your notes to present your concept.

C1 Big Brother out of this world p. 223

2 What makes the text appealing?
Analyse the methods used to make the text engaging for the reader (e.g. heading, *register, *stylistic devices, quotes, objective / biased?).

Step 1: Copy the table below. Examine the aspects listed and find more examples from the text to illustrate each aspect. Look at all the examples again and try to identify what the author has done to make the text engaging. Add a few notes in the 'Methods' column.

Aspects you should examine	Example from the text	Methods used by the author
Ways of attracting the reader's attention from the very beginning	▪ Big Brother out of this world ▪ Not only will they require mental and physical strength, but now, they will also need to have the makings of the next reality-TV star.	…
Style / Use of words	▪ The ticket is one-way. ▪ 'the world's toughest job interview'	…
Structure	…	▪ The different stages of the project are described chronologically. ▪ …
Way(s) of presenting the content	▪ The applicants have now been shortlisted to 705 candidates – 418 men and 287 women.	…
Author's attitude towards the topic	…	…

Step 2: Use your points to organize your analysis.

Now go back to task **3** on p. 223.

C2 The ultimate reality TV show p. 224

2 Lally's mode of argumentation

a Explain Lally's line of argumentation to convince the reporter and the audience of his idea. Answer the following questions:

1 What historical reason does Lally mention to support his view of broadcasting prisoners' executions? What conclusion does he draw from this argument for society?
2 What political reason does he put forward? What would be a positive effect of his idea?
3 What economic reason does he state? Who might profit from the show?
4 What legal and ethical reasons does he present? In what way would the prisoners benefit from the reality TV show?

Now go back to task **2b** on p. 224.

Chapter 11 Visions of the Future – Utopias and Dystopias

A2 Don't let me get bored p. 231

3 Analysing genre and technique

b Evaluate Anderson's narrative technique.

The extract from *Feed* is told by a *first-person narrator. A first-person narrator is a character in the story who tells us what happened to him or her and how he or she felt about it. The following aspects are often relevant to texts with first-person narrators. Read the list, decide which aspects are most relevant to *Feed*, and use them to structure your analysis.

1 With a first-person narrator it is usually easier for the reader to identify with what is happening, the reader is somehow walking in the character's shoes and may find it easier to understand this character's actions and feelings.
2 In some stories, first-person narrators may refer to information they hear from the other characters, to try to give the reader a larger point of view.
3 If the narrator uses a conversational tone it can feel as if they are telling the reader a story about themselves. This could create more of an air of sympathy because as reader is more likely to relate to a person or feel sympathy for that person if you are in direct contact with them.
4 With direct insight into the narrator's thoughts and motivations, the reader can understand a character that would seem otherwise immoral, boring, stupid or otherwise not relatable.

Now go back to task **4** on p. 231.

B2 Living in the compound p. 241

3 Utopia or dystopia?

Analyse both utopian and dystopian elements in the text. You can use the following hints to help you consider particular points and structure your analysis.

1 Remember that utopias often depict paradise-like places in which people are safe and can lead happy lives. Try to find elements in the text that support this idea. Think of basic categories such as the need to eat, drink, breathe, to live in a clean and supportive environment. Think of a person's need for safety and security, for relationship and education etc.
2 Remember that this better society also needs to deal with individuals who do not conform to the rule. Is this aspect explored in the extract?
3 Remember that a dystopia is often a utopia gone wrong. Which elements in the text support the idea that the society is not perfect in every way?
4 Remember that utopias mirror the failures of society as it is today. Which present-day developments are shown as a future menace?

Now go back to task 4 on p. 241.

C2 Big Brother is watching you p. 244

3 Interpreting key aspects

b Analyse the atmosphere of the extract by looking at the content of the dialogue and Winston's thoughts on the one hand, and the fact that this is a dialogue between lovers on the other hand.

1 Use a table to collect examples of the dialogue's key content and examples of Winston and Julia as lovers. The following quotes should help you.

Dialogue's key content	Winston and Julia as lovers
▪ 'If I confess, they'll shoot you, and if I refuse to confess, they'll shoot you just the same.' (ll. 17–18) ▪ 'If you can FEEL that staying human is worth while, even when it can't have any result whatever, you've beaten them.' (ll. 32–33) ▪ …	▪ 'Yes, dear' (l. 4) ▪ 'If they could make me stop loving you …' (ll. 26–27) ▪ …

2 Think about the feelings that the quotes convey to the reader through the choice of words, Winston and Julia's emotions, the things they mention, etc. First consider the quotes in the left column, then the quotes in the right.
3 Now think about the effect that the quotes have when they are combined together to make one dialogue. Is the atmosphere tenser? Does this combination add new aspects to the atmosphere?
4 Think of a good structure for your analysis and make sure you use quotes from the text to illustrate your points.

Now go back to task 4 on p. 244.

Chapter 12 Living One's Life – Individuals in Society

A2 Successful children p. 253

3 What if …?

a Read ll. 47–57 and say which type of conditional is being used. Here are some hints which will help you with conditional sentences of all three types:

- Conditional sentences type I refer to the future:
  – *If her daughters are not honor students, Amy Chua will …*
  – *If Amy Chua ever has grandchildren, she will …*
- Conditional sentences type II refer to present or future unreal situations. Using type II, Louisa might express her dreams and wishes:
  – *If I had a part in the school play, I would …*
  – *If my mother were not a Chinese mother, I could …*
- Conditional sentences type III refer to the past. Looking back, Amy Chua might think:
  – *If my parents had not been Chinese immigrants, I would not have …*
  – *If I had been less strict with my daughters, they would never have …*

Now go back to task 4 on p. 253.

A3 Childhood – the 21st century p. 254

3 Formal elements

Analyse how the poem is structured and what stylistic devices are used that contribute to the meaning. Do the following tasks and after each decide whether the poet is using traditional style, innovative elements or free rhyme:

1 Count the number of stanzas and lines within the stanzas.
2 Then work out the rhyme scheme.
3 Read it aloud to yourself: how does the rhythm sound?
Decide which of the following stylistic devices the poet uses:
How does the use of the stylistic device(s) affect you?

simile • metaphor • rhetorical question • personification • anaphora

Now go back to task 4 on p. 254.

B1 Stereotypes in Los Angeles p. 257

6 Stereotypes in everyday life

b Consider the following questions. This can also be done as pair or group work.
1 How do stereotypes develop?
2 How do they influence our perception of others, and what are the consequences?
3 Are stereotypes only negative or can stereotypes be positive too?
4 How should we deal with stereotypes?

C1 Volunteering in the wake of the Olympics p. 260

1 Pre-viewing

a Discuss which of the photos on p. 246 show people volunteering. First, write a definition of volunteering in your own words. Then, consider the following phrases and say which are part of volunteering:

giving money to a charity • altruism • helping others • no financial gain • getting life experience • helping sb. secretly • helping raise money for a charity • gaining self-respect • making contacts • helping the community • doing a sponsored run • working full-time for a charity

Now examine each photo in turn, deciding if it shows people volunteering. Some obviously don't, others may.

C2 Volunteering in Germany p. 261

1 Mediation (German → English)

What kind of people are more or less likely to do volunteer work?

- Read the German article, find keywords and note them down in English.
- Write an introductory sentence which tells your friend not only about the author, source and topic of the article at hand, but also about the writer's attitude towards his topic. Is she biased or neutral?
- With the help of your collection of keywords make your first draft. Concentrate on central statements.
- Revise your first draft. Improve its style by using participle constructions and connectives.

You may start your e-mail like this:

Dear …,
We recently talked about the volunteering campaign initiated by the mayor of London, Boris Johnson.
I have just read a thought-provoking article in a German online newspaper and would like to tell you about it.

Language Practice

Focus on Grammar

Focus on Style

Focus on Vocabulary

Download the suggested answers to the tasks here:
Webcode context-29

Focus on Grammar

▶ LP 1 Simple and progressive verb forms

1 BASIC Choose the right form of the verb for each of the sentences below (make sure you choose the correct tense).

1 A man came running out of the bank and (*jump*) into the waiting car.
2 Sorry, I can't talk now – I (*make*) dinner for the family.
3 Smoking (*cause*) over 600,000 deaths in the EU every year.
4 It was a cold evening, and a light drizzle (*fall*). When no one (*come*) to unlock the gates the crowd (*get*) restless.
5 The housing prices in London (*always be*) high, but at present they (*skyrocket*).
6 The last time I talked to her, she (*look*) for a new job.

Most English verbs can be used in all tenses in both the simple and the progressive form:
Jasmin practises the piano three hours a day. She's practising now for her concert on Saturday.

Simple form	Progressive form
▪ For states[1]: Our house *needs* repainting. ▪ For actions that follow a plan or physical law: *Our plane leaves at 8:05 am. Water boils at 100 °C.* ▪ Actions in a series (narration) ▪ Verbs that describe what the author of a text does: *The author criticizes the government's lack of initiative.*	▪ For actions that are taking place at the present moment or were taking place at a certain point in time in the past: *I've been waiting here all morning! When the police arrived, two men were loading boxes into a van.* ▪ For trends and developments: *It's becoming more and more difficult to find a permanent job. It's getting dark – let's go home.* ▪ For descriptions of circumstances (weather, clothing, etc.): *A cold wind was blowing. She was wearing a red woollen sweater over a plaid skirt.*

[1] **state** *Zustand*

Verbs that describe a state (i.e. not an activity) are called **state verbs**. Normally, they can only be used in the simple form:
I heard a voice. Someone needed help. I wanted to help them, but I didn't know how.
A few state verbs can also be used in the progressive form, but with a different meaning. Compare the sentences in the table below and explain the difference in meaning:

Simple form	Progressive form
What do you think of his decision?	What are you thinking about?
You look upset – what's the matter?	Why are you looking at me like that?
For her, success is all that counts.	We're counting on you to help us.
How do you feel about same-sex marriage?	He stayed at home because he wasn't feeling well.
Everybody has a bad day now and then.	We were having lunch when my phone rang.

2 Choose the right form of the verb for each of the sentences below:
1 I (*think*) you should go to her and tell her how you (*feel*) about what happened.
2 Lydia (*love*) going to parties, but she never (*feel*) like organizing one herself.
3 While I (*look*) at the photos on our website I (*have*) a great idea for our next campaign.
4 Everyone (*need*) the feeling that their life (*count*) for something.
5 The last time I (*see*) Bruce and Charlene they (*have*) a big argument about something .
6 When I visited Bob in hospital, I (*think*) he (*look*) awful, but he said that he (*feel*) better.

TROUBLE SPOT
With ***everybody/everyone***, the plural form of the possessive pronoun is commonly used.

Special uses: the progressive form used for emphasis
- Some speakers use the progressive form of state verbs, especially in the present perfect, to underline their message: *'New York? I've been wanting to go there for ages!' / 'I've been meaning to write to you since Christmas!'*
- In some situations, the progressive form of the verb *be* is used to refer to behaviour that is temporary and (perhaps) not genuine: *Why are you being so stubborn? – Ignore him; he's just being a trouble-maker again.*
- The slogan of a US fast-food chain *(I'm loving it!)* belongs to the same category: using the progressive form of the state verb *love* has the effect of underlining the message and makes the slogan more memorable.

▸ LP 2 Present tense or future?

1 BASIC Spot and correct the mistakes in the sentences below:
1 I don't know how he reacts when we tell him the truth.
6 'I need a can opener for this.' – 'No problem, I go look for one.'
3 Is it true that Kai goes abroad next year?
4 The weather forecast says there are scattered showers throughout the afternoon.
5 I'm sure my parents don't let me go to the rock festival.
6 The German students will wait at Stansted until their bus will come to collect them.

Generally speaking, English – like German – uses the **present tense to talk about the present** and the **future to talk about the future**. However, there are a few exceptions to keep in mind:

- In English, when offering to do something, the ***will*-future** is used (whereas the present tense would be used in German): *Hast du Durst? Ich hole uns etwas zu trinken. / Are you thirsty? I'll fetch us something to drink.*
- In German, it is possible to talk about the future in the present tense: *Wir fahren morgen an die See.* You can do this in English too, but only with the **present progressive** when you talk about plans for the future: *We're leaving* for the coast tomorrow. A sentence like *Morgen regnet es wieder* can only be expressed in the *will*-future: *It will rain again tomorrow*.
- **The future is not used** after *if, when, unless, until, as soon as*, etc., even when you are referring to the future: *Phone me as soon as you arrive. – You won't get tickets unless you book in advance.*

2 Use the keywords and phrases to make complete sentences. All verbs are in the present or the future:

1 There's someone at the door. You / please / go / see who it is?
2 The PM says / he / attend to the problem / as soon as / government report / published.
3 In the course of the week / temperatures / drop slightly.
4 By the time / we / arrive at the airport / it / be / too late.
5 The people next door / have / their house repainted / next month.
6 The assistant director says / he / talk to the staff / before / situation / escalate any further.

▶ LP 3 Simple present and present perfect

1 BASIC Decide which of the following sentences are correct. Correct the faulty ones:

1 I have wanted to meet her for as long as I can remember.
2 For the past three years, John is saving his money for a trip to New Zealand.
3 The author and her family live in London since 2006.
4 Four hundred years after his death, Shakespeare has continued to fascinate audiences around the world.
5 We are waiting for this bus for the last half an hour – I don't think it's coming.
6 Leonie has been an avid reader ever since she taught herself to read at the age of five.

The **present perfect** is used in English for actions and states that began in the past, but are still going on or hold true. German uses the present tense in such cases.

German	English
Hunneman leitet die Organisation seit 2008.	*Hunneman has led the organization since 2008.*
Rowling arbeitet seit drei Jahren an einem neuen Roman.	*Rowling has been working on a new novel for three years.*

The **present perfect** is closely connected with the present time. For that reason, English speakers often choose verbs in the present perfect where a German might use a different verb in the present.

German	English
Kennst du den Roman Doktor Faustus*?*	*Have you ever read* Doktor Faustus*?*
Ich kenne Bratislava nicht.	*I've never been to Bratislava.*
Weißt du, ob Justin heute da ist?	*Have you seen Justin this morning?*
Wissen die Praktikanten schon Bescheid?	*Have the interns been informed yet?*

2 Translate the following sentences into idiomatic English. Use the verb in brackets in the present perfect.

1 Kennst du den Film *Casablanca*? (see)
2 Kennst du Paris? (be)
3 Kennt ihr schon das neue türkische Restaurant am Zimmerplatz? (check out)
4 Ich bin noch nie Ski gelaufen. (try)
5 Weißt du über das Treffen heute Nachmittag Bescheid? (hear)
6 Kennst du dich mit 3D-Druckern aus? (use)

▶ LP 4 Present perfect and simple past

1 BASIC Complete the sentences with the correct form of the verb (present perfect or simple past).

1 When … you last … Thomas? (see)
2 The centre … opened in 2004. (be)
3 Until today, no one … a cure for cancer. (discover)
4 Sarah … me the revised version of the text just five minutes ago. (hand)
5 We're still friends, although I … her since we graduated. (not see)
6 I … the book when it first came out, but I … it. (read; not like)
7 Julia and Tobias … at a youth camp in Ireland in 2012. They … in contact ever since. (meet; keep)
8 My brother … to New Zealand yesterday, but we … from him yet. (fly; not hear)

Present perfect (This tense refers to a time that has not yet ended.)	**Simple past** (This tense refers to a time that is over.)
Use this tense ▪ to present results: *Engineers at the Wyss Institute have developed a new kind of biodegradable plastic.* ▪ to talk about states that have existed since some time in the past: *How long have you lived in Germany?* ▪ to talk about actions in the past without saying when they happened: *She's been there before.* ▪ to talk about actions that have happened more than once (or never): *I've seen that film at least five times. I've never been to Denmark.*	Use this tense when talking about events that happened in the past: *When I was a student, I lived in Exeter.*
Examples of signal words and phrases: ▪ *already, ever, never, yet, often* ▪ time phrases with *since* and *for* (*since 2013, for ten years*)	Examples of signal words and phrases: ▪ *before, yesterday* ▪ time phrases of the past (*ten minutes ago, last June, in 2010*) ▪ *When …?*

TROUBLE SPOT
Signal words of the past can **never** be used together with the **present perfect**. Sentences such as ~~*When have you last talked to him?*~~ and ~~*I have seen her just a few minutes ago*~~ are always wrong!

2 Choose the correct form of the verbs in brackets in the following text. You may use the present, the simple past or the present perfect:

Almost everyone (hear) of Stephen King, the best-selling author of dozens of horror stories. King (be) born in 1947 in Maine, USA, where many of his stories (be) also set. After graduating from the University of Maine in 1970, King (find) a teaching position at Hampden Academy. His first novel, Carrie, (be) published by Doubleday in 1973 and (bring) King national attention as well as financial independence. In the summer of 1999, King (be) walking down a road when he (be) hit by a car and badly injured. He (survive), but since his accident, he (write) much less. His son Joseph Hillstrom King, who (use) the pen name Joe Hill, (write) three novels and numerous stories, all of which (belong) to the genre fantasy/horror. Similar to his more famous father, Hill (win) numerous writing awards.

World-famous author, Stephen King

▶ LP 5 Infinitive or gerund after certain verbs

1 BASIC Choose the correct form of the verb complement (infinitive or gerund) in the following sentences:
1 You can leave as soon as you have finished (clean up).
2 Many people dislike (be told) what to do.
3 How long have you wanted (go) there?
4 I don't mind (get) my hands dirty.
5 As she had never intended (take) the job, Sandy was surprised (receive) an offer.
6 She hoped (get) a better offer from a firm in Shanghai.

Infinitive or gerund?	Verbs	Example
verb + **infinitive**	most verbs that can take a complement	*I want to go to Hawaii.* *I wish to speak to your boss.* *I'm planning to study physics.*
verb + **gerund**	*admit, avoid, consider, deny, dislike, enjoy, finish, give up, imagine, include, involve, justify, keep, mention, mind, miss, practise, risk, suggest*	*I dislike waiting for the bus.* *I miss going to school.* TIP To avoid mistakes, try learning these verbs by heart and then use the infinitive with the rest.
verb + **gerund or infinitive** (same meaning)	*love, like, hate, prefer, begin, start, continue*	*I love to play badminton. / I love playing badminton.*

A small number of verbs have **different meanings** when they are used with an infinitive or a gerund. Compare the sentences in the table below. What does the verb mean in each case?

Verb	Used with a gerund	Used with an infinitive
stop	*Stop shouting like that!*	*Let's stop to have a break.*
remember	*I don't remember seeing him at the meeting.*	*Did you remember to lock the door?*
forget	*I'll never forget seeing London for the first time.*	*I forgot to buy a litre of milk – sorry!*
mean	*Sustainability means not using more than we produce.*	*I didn't mean to make her upset.*
try	*If you have the hiccups – try holding your breath.*	*We tried to make him change his mind, but he wouldn't listen.*

2 Decide between a gerund or an infinitive in the following sentences:
1 For Melissa, the job in Los Angeles was a dream come true, but it meant (leave) her family and friends behind.
2 If we don't stop (dump) waste into the world's oceans, it may soon be too late.
3 Suzie mentioned (go) on a date but avoided (tell) us with whom.
4 I tried (reach) you by mobile, but I only got your mailbox.
5 John stopped (read) the newspaper and missed the train.
6 Anthony considered (run) the red light but then imagined (cause) an accident.
7 Students often say that they forgot (do) their homework, but no one really believes them.

► LP6 Infinitive or gerund after certain nouns

1 BASIC Spot the mistakes in the following sentences and correct them. Careful: not all sentences are wrong.
1 I don't know why she entered the competition – she doesn't have a chance of winning.
2 I'm afraid we don't have time of discussing the matter any longer.
3 Mark Zuckerberg wasn't the first person who had the idea to create a social networking site.
4 Our plan of camping in the wild turned out to be completely unrealistic.
5 Rosa Parks was one of the first African Americans who had the courage of speaking out against racism.
6 After their traumatic experience, the victims had the need of talking to someone who could help them.
7 Students often face the problem to find affordable accommodations.
8 The stipend helped Jens of going to New York for a year.

In German, you can add information to any noun using an infinitive phrase: *der Wunsch, reich und berühmt zu sein*.
In English, generally an **infinitive** is used, a **gerund with *of***, or a ***that*-clause**:
the right to state your opinion
the dream of becoming a star
the fact that she could speak five languages.
However, these complements cannot be used interchangeably:

Infinitive or gerund?	Nouns	Example
noun + infinitive	*right, wish, desire, longing, will, courage, strength, decision, time, need, ability*	*the right to bear arms, time to say good-bye, the will to live*
noun + *of* + gerund	most other nouns	*the risk of getting lost, the fear of being left behind*
special cases	▪ *chance, opportunity, plan*: Either the infinitive or *of* + gerund can be used. ▪ *a/any chance*: *of* + gerund is used more often. ▪ *the chance*: The infinitive is used more often.	*This is my chance to earn lots of money. / This is my chance of earning lots of money.* *Any chance of seeing him again?* *The chance to win this game is pretty slim.*

There are a few **more special cases** worth remembering:

- The word *reason* can be used either with an infinitive or with *for* + gerund. When *reason* is followed by *for* + a person, an infinitive must be used: *There's no reason for us to give up without a fight.*
- The word *attempt* can be followed either by an infinitive or by *at* + gerund: *The government's attempt at covering up / to cover up the matter only made things worse.*
- The expression *(to) have trouble / difficulty* is used with a gerund without any preposition: *I had trouble starting the motor. Difficulty* can also be followed by *in* + gerund: *We had difficulty* (not: ~~*difficulties*~~) *in persuading her to come to the meeting.* Careful: In other contexts *difficulty* is treated like a normal noun (*of* + gerund): *the difficulty of living with a permanent disability.*

2 Put the verb in brackets into the correct form; in some cases there is more than one correct solution:

1 All our attempts (reach) an agreement have failed.
2 The dream (find) a better life was reason enough for millions of immigrants (leave) their homeland.
3 The producer had trouble (find) a child star who could both act and dance.
4 Steven spent his first weeks in Kerala learning (cope) with the difficulties (live and work) in India.
5 I would be interested in hearing your reasons (reject) the proposal.
6 You can't imagine the difficulty we had (locate) a garage in Sofia that could repair our car.

► LP 7 The passive

1 BASIC Make complete sentences in the passive using the keywords:

1 Fitzgerald's classic novel, *The Great Gatsby* / first publish / 1925
2 To date[1] / it / adapt for the screen / six times
3 The most recent version / released / 2013
4 It / be / the first screen adaptation / that / film *(v)* / in 3D format
5 The title role / play / Leonardo DiCaprio
6 The film / criticize / some critics / as a costume spectacle
7 Most of the scenes / shoot / in Australia, / where huge sets / build / for the film

Rules for using the passive	Examples
The passive in English is formed using the verb ***(to) be*** and the **past participle**.	*Tchaikovsky's ballet* Swan Lake *was first performed in 1877.*
Generally, the passive is used when the person who does an action is unknown or unimportant.	*Three paintings were stolen from the museum last weekend.*
If the person or force that does something (the 'agent') is named in the sentence, it is introduced using the preposition ***by***.	*The tower was damaged by lightning in 1988.*
Verbs that use a preposition keep the preposition in the passive.	*discriminate against sb.* → *African Americans have often been discriminated against, not only in the past.*
If the so-called **personal passive** can be formed, it is usually first choice.	*We were given our ID cards at the main desk.* (The 'normal' passive would sound awkward here: *Our ID cards were given to us at the main desk.)*
Passive forms of the **infinitive** and the **gerund** can also be formed.	*(to) love* → *(to) be loved* *loving* → *being loved*

[1] **to date** *(adv)* *bisher, bis jetzt*

2 Use an infinitive or a gerund in the passive to rewrite the underlined parts of the following sentences. You may have to change the word order. Avoid using a *by*-agent.

1 After the flood they had to rebuild most of the houses in the village. *(After the flood most of the houses in the village had to …)*
2 Teenagers hate it when adults treat them like children.
3 Even in his darkest moments, Colin never gave up the hope that he would be rescued.
4 It was her fear that people would laugh at her that held her back.
5 She told her doctor that she wanted him to tell her the truth.
6 No one likes the feeling that someone is discriminating against them.

Special uses: the *get*-passive

In colloquial English, many speakers form the passive using ***get*** instead of ***be***. Common phrases are *get hurt, get killed, get lost, get caught*.
The *get*-passive is also used to emphasize the difference between an action and a state:
We soon got lost in a maze of tiny alleyways that all looked the same.
I couldn't spot a single familiar landmark and finally had to admit that I was lost.

▶ LP 8 Conditional sentences

1 BASIC Complete the following sentences with the correct form of the verb in brackets:

1 If I discover a cancer cure, I (become) famous.
2 If I discovered a cancer cure, I (become) famous.
3 If I had discovered a cancer cure ten years ago, I (be) famous.
4 If someone (be) famous, everyone recognizes them on the street.
5 If Romeo (not crash) the Capulets' party, he might never have met Juliet.
6 If the sea level (rise) one meter, hundreds of coastal cities would be in danger.

A variety of conditional sentences are possible in English. Their use depends on the situation.

An imagined condition in the **past** with an imagined consequence in the **past**.	*If Sheila had taken part in the competition, she might have won a prize.*
An imagined condition in the **past** with an imagined consequence in the **present**.	*If you hadn't wasted all your money, you could afford to go with us to Greece.*
An imagined condition in the **present** with an imagined consequence.	*If Sarah worked harder, she would get better marks.*
A possible condition in the **present** with a possible consequence.	*If you have trouble with the new software, Kevin can / will help you.*
A condition that can happen at any time and its consequence.	*If the polar ice caps melt, the sea level rises / will rise.*

2 The text below presents some facts concerning the settlement of North America and its consequences. Draw conclusions from the facts using conditional sentences.
Example: *If European settlers had not come to America, herds of buffalo might still roam the Great Plains.*

When the first European settlers arrived at the shores of the New World, there were about three million Native Americans living in North America. Having no natural immunity to European diseases, thousands of natives fell ill and died. As they moved farther west, the white settlers pushed the natives off their land, at the same time decimating[1] the large herds of buffalo that roamed[2] the Great Plains. The Native Americans, whose way of life depended on the buffalo, could no longer exist. Ancient grasslands disappeared as farms were followed by railroads, towns, highways and factories, further restricting the freedom of movement of the native tribes. An ecological balance between man and nature that had existed for thousands of years was destroyed within a few decades.

► LP 9 Articles, quantifiers and countability

1 BASIC Translate the nouns and noun phrases in brackets, deciding whether you need a singular or a plural and whether or not the definite article is necessary.

1 *(Die menschliche Gesellschaft)* hasn't made *(viele Fortschritte)* in dealing with the forces of *(das Böse)*.
2 We found *(einige interessante Informationen)* on the internet concerning *(die Kunst)* of the Aborigines.
3 *(Die Wissenschaft)* can provide us with *(Erkenntnisse)*, but it can't give us any *(Ratschläge)* on how to use it.
4 Despite all the *(Forschungen)* on cancer, there has been relatively *(wenig Fortschritte)*.
5 Although she grew up in L.A., her *(Kenntnisse)* of *(die Natur)* and *(die Umwelt)* is really impressive.

Find more information on articles, quantifiers and countability here:
Webcode context-30

2 The table below shows which social networking site five young people regularly use:

	Sandy	Carol	Andrew	James	Marvin
Spacebook	X	X	X	X	X
Lightnigram	X		X	X	X
Chatter	X	X	X		
Mumblr			X		X
OurSpace					

1 Make four statements about the group. Example: *A few of them use Mumblr.*
2 Make two statements about Sandy and Carol: what have they got in common?

[1]**decimate sth.** kill large numbers of sth. [2]**roam** walk around with no fixed goal

► LP 10 Using adjectives and adverbs

1 BASIC Put the words in brackets in the right form (adjective or adverb):

1 In science-fiction films, robots (traditional) appear in the role of (soulless) killing machines.
2 The engineers who develop robots for new applications (passionate) believe that they will make our lives (happy and safe).
3 For example, they will free us from (boring) tasks like cleaning the house or mowing the lawn.
4 Most of the (heavy) work in farming is already done (automatic) by machine.
5 (Remarkable) progress has been made in developing robots for a (large) number of everyday uses.
6 Ideas that sounded (impossible) only ten years ago are (rapid) becoming reality.
7 Perhaps someday we will be (complete) dependent on (intelligent) machines for almost everything.

Adjectives

Adjectives are used to modify (i.e. describe) a noun. They can be used directly before the noun (*a short holiday, a famous tourist spot*) or they are used after certain verbs:

Verbs of being, seeming, becoming, etc.	*Why are you sad? She seemed unhappy. Don't get nervous. Injustice always makes me angry.*
Verbs that describe sense impressions	*He looks nervous. That sounds wonderful. The soup smells great and it tastes great too. The stone felt cold to the touch.*

Adverbs

Adverbs of manner are made from adjectives by adding *-ly*. (Exceptions: *fast, hard, early* and *late* are used as both adjectives and adverbs.)
Adverbs modify verbs, adjectives, or other adverbs:

Adverb modifies **verb**.	*She got up quickly and ran to the window.*
Adverb modifies **adjective**.	*The team has been incredibly successful this season.*
Adverb modifies **adverb**.	*The experts worked extremely cautiously to defuse the bomb.*

Certain adverbs can also be used to modify a whole sentence. Such adverbs are known as **sentence adverbs.** They always stand at the beginning of the sentence and are often separated by a comma from the rest of the sentence.

Adverb modifies **sentence**.	*Fortunately, none of the passengers were seriously injured.*

Other common sentence adverbs: *actually, admittedly, apparently, consequently, eventually, evidently, hopefully, incidentally, luckily, obviously, presumably, surprisingly, ultimately, understandably*.

2 Use a sentence adverb instead of the underlined words in each of the sentences below:

1 More and more cars hit the road every year. As a result, the number of traffic jams also increases.
2 A surprising fact is that the interest in car ownership is declining.
3 It seems that many young urbanites regard a car as an unnecessary expense.
4 It is easy to understand that the interest in car ownership is lowest where cheap, reliable public transportation is available.
5 In the course of time cars may disappear altogether from our city streets.
6 I hope that this development will mean cleaner air in cities that presently have a huge smog problem.

Focus on Style

▶ LP 11 Using the right register

1 BASIC In the following excerpt from a student's film summary, the teacher has underlined some expressions in red to indicate that they are inappropriate. Rewrite the text, correcting the stylistic problems.

The film Outsourced is about this guy named Todd Anderson. He works for an American firm that has outsourced its call centre to India to save money. Todd gets sent there to bring the Indian workers up to US standards. When he gets there, he's totally lost, cause he doesn't know the first thing about India. He tries to get the Indians to act like Americans, but it doesn't work out. He only starts getting somewhere when he begins listening to the Indians and taking them seriously.

Like other languages, English has different registers for different situations:

Register	Typical situations	Typical features
Informal	Everyday communication between friends, spoken English	Short or incomplete sentences, short forms (*they've, gotta*), phrasal verbs, colloquial expressions (*make it big, chill out,* etc.)
Neutral	Articles and essays on subjects of general interest	Mix of short and more complex sentences, no short forms, words of the general vocabulary
Formal	Official documents and speeches, business letters	Complex sentences, specialized or technical words

When writing essays for school, use the neutral register. Some teachers allow you to use short forms of negations in your writing (*don't, can't,* etc.); ask if you aren't sure.

2 After finishing school in Germany, you apply to a College of Arts in the United States. One day you receive the following letter:

> On behalf of the Admissions Committee I am pleased to inform you that you have been offered a place in the incoming freshman class. Your application convinced us that you have the talent and motivation required for academic success. Furthermore, after careful review of your family's financial situation, we have decided to award you a full scholarship, comprising all tuition fees as well as room and board for the duration of your studies.
> All our students are guaranteed on-campus accommodation in our newly-renovated dormitories (dual occupancy). Furthermore, the College provides a comprehensive 24/7 meal service. Should you decide to accept our offer, please reply by June 10th.

Look up the words and expressions you don't understand; most of them belong to the vocabulary of formal correspondence. Then write an email to your former host family in the US, telling them about the letter and its contents and asking about points that are unclear to you. Use a *neutral or moderately informal* style.

▶ LP 12 Avoiding German-sounding sentence patterns

1 BASIC Find the mistakes in the following sentences and correct them.

1 If you ask me, Roland paid for his new smartphone far too much.
2 In 2010 was the number of severe storms higher than ever before.
3 Many teenagers use every day the internet to communicate with friends.

4 I download always the latest version of the program.
5 The author writes that the USA ignores all too often the rest of the world.
6 She points out in her latest book the decline of America's influence in the world.
7 This last point illustrates the author with an anecdote.
8 The summer months can be in some parts of Germany quite cool.

You already know that in some ways German and English sentences are formed differently. Here are some points to observe when you are writing English:

German	English
Dependent infinitives and participles are placed at the end of the sentence *(Satzklammer)*: *Er kann hervorragend Klavier spielen.* *Er hat neulich in der Aula ein Konzert gegeben.*	A 'cluster' instead of a 'bracket' is used, i.e. closely connected words (subject, verb, object) stay together: *He can play the piano marvellously.* *Recently he gave a concert in the school hall.*
The subject moves to third position if there is an adverbial phrase at the beginning of the sentence: *Im November 1989 / wurden / die Übergänge zwischen Ost- und West-Berlin / überraschend freigegeben.*	The subject always comes before the verb; in other words, the word order (S–V) stays the same when an adverbial phrase is put at the beginning of the sentence: *In November 1989 / the checkpoints between East and West Berlin / were unexpectedly opened.*
Verb and object are often separated: *Thomas und Harald spielen jeden Mittwoch Tennis.*	Verb and object **must** stay together: *Thomas and Harald play tennis every Wednesday.*

Even if there is no two-part verb, Germans tend to form a 'bracket sentence': *Dies ist in einigen Fällen ein Problem.*
In English the sentence would sound strange: *This is in some cases a problem.*

TIP

Begin your sentences with an adverbial phrase. This helps you to avoid the monotony of sentences that all begin with the subject: *Friedman is an optimist in this respect.* → *In this respect, Friedman is an optimist.*

2 Rearrange sentences in the following text to make it more idiomatic:

Thomas L. Friedman and Michael Mandelbaum collaborated on the book *That Used to Be Us,* which in 2011 was published. The authors point out using numerous examples how the US in global competition has fallen behind. America has lost sight according to the authors of its traditional strengths and values. The authors make in the second half of the book a number of suggestions as to what should be done. Some of these suggestions sounded to a few of the book's critics quite unrealistic. The book was in spite of its gloomy message an instant bestseller.

▶ LP 13 Placing emphasis on key points CD3 07

1 BASIC Listen to three short conversations, then match them to the following techniques:
1 The important words in the sentence are stressed, i.e. spoken louder than the others.
2 The emphatic do-form of the verb is used.
3 The important word is made the subject of the reply.

Listen to the audio file on the CD or download it here:
Webcode context-31

Some of the techniques for emphasis that are used when speaking can also be used in written English; others sound rather formal in spoken English and are mainly used in writing:

Speaking/ Writing	Technique	Example
Speaking	Stressing the important words in the sentence, i.e. speaking them louder than the others	–
Speaking and writing	Using the emphatic *do*-form of the verb	*I do think that's the wrong decision.*
	Making the important word the subject of the reply	*Running is the sport I love most.*
Speaking (esp. in formal contexts) and writing	Special use of *very*	*Very* is used in English to modify words like *first* and *last*: *In the very first scene of the film… • At the very last moment …* It can also be used where in German you would use *gerade* or *genau* to emphasize something: *Gerade die Anonymität des Internets … • The very anonymity of the internet …*
	especially, in particular	Careful: Unlike *besonders*, you hardly ever find them at the beginning of a sentence: *Sitting still for 45 minutes can be a challenge, especially for young children.*
	Other expressions	German compound nouns like *Hauptgrund* or *Hauptfaktor* can be translated with *the main reason, the most important factor,* etc. To emphasize that you are naming the most important item in a list of facts or arguments, use *above all* or *most importantly* to introduce your sentence.

2 Now decide how you could reply emphatically to the following questions using one of the techniques in the table:

1 Do you like Indian cuisine? (You like some dishes, but not the really spicy ones.)
2 What would you like – apple juice or cola? (You choose.)
3 Didn't you read the novel over the weekend? (You didn't finish, but you read the first half.)
4 You're from Hamburg, right? (You went to school there, but you were born in Kiel.)

3 Translate these sentences into English:

1 Die Hauptursache von Hass ist Angst.
2 Besonders in den Entwicklungsländern haben viele Menschen keinen Zugang zu sauberem Wasser.
3 Wir erreichten unser Flugzeug in allerletzter Minute.
4 Vor allem gibt es eine wachsende Kluft *(a widening gap)* zwischen den armen und den reichen Ländern.
5 Schon im ersten Satz macht der Autor seine Meinung deutlich.
6 Die Hauptsache ist wohl die, dass es genug qualifizierte Arbeitskräfte *(workers)* gibt.

In written English, there are ways of structuring a sentence so as to emphasize a certain word or words:

Technique	Example	Comment
Using a subordinate clause that points to the most important idea in the sentence	*Ralph Nader first criticized the US automobile industry. → It was Ralph Nader who first criticized the US automobile industry.* *Society needs people who put the common good above personal gain. → What society needs is people who put the common good above personal gain.*	Pay attention to the forms of *be* used in the examples; why are they both in the singular?
Using a negation (*never, nowhere, not once*, etc.) or *only* + time phrase (e.g. *only later*) at the beginning of the sentence. The verb is put in the question form (inversion).	*Never before have young people had so many opportunities.* *Only then did she realize her mistake.*	This structure is common in political speeches.
Using contrast	*It was greed and arrogance, not simply bad timing, that led to the collapse of the bank.* *Unlike earlier SNS, Facebook appealed to users of all age groups.* *Compared with the US, China lacks a culture of creative entrepreneurship.*	

4 Rewrite the sentences to make them more emphatic, using the techniques from the table above.

1. Shared values hold a society together.
2. China's economy is growing rapidly; that of the EU isn't.
3. It has never before been so easy to communicate with people around the globe.
4. Western countries need a vision that includes the rest of the world.
5. Not lack of ambition, but fear of failure holds most people back.

▸ LP 14 Linking words and phrases

1 BASIC Complete the following text with suitable linking words or phrases from the choices below.

at the same time • for example • for one thing • furthermore • moreover • on the other hand • for instance

Are Americans environmentally friendly? There is no simple answer to this question. In a recent survey, … (1), 65% of American adults agreed that 'preserving the environment is very important.' … (2), 22% of consumers who remodeled their homes in the last 12 months said they had used environmentally friendly products for their renovation. … (3), data from the last five years indicate that consumers are now less willing to pay more or give up convenience for green products. … (4), the percentage of U.S. adults who agreed with the statement 'I am willing to give up convenience in return for a product that is environmentally safe' has declined 16% in the past five years, from 56% in 2007 to 47% in 2011.

… (5), there is definitely a trend among younger Americans toward more environmental awareness. … (6), consumers aged 18–24 are the only adult age group whose willingness to give up convenience or pay more for green products has held steady over the past five years. … (7), 53% of consumers aged 18–24 recycle products and 4% participated in environmental groups or causes in the past 12 months.

Statistics from: Bart King, 'American Environmentally Friendly Buying Habits', 6 April 2012

Linking words and phrases are the signposts of written and spoken communication; they help readers and listeners find their way through texts. Choosing the right phrases also helps you as a writer to think critically about the relationship between your sentences. The table below shows you a selection of useful phrases and their functions.

Use	Linking word or phrase
Stating your opinion	*In my opinion …* • *To my mind …* • *I think/feel/believe that …*
Listing facts, arguments, etc.	*First of all …* • *Firstly …* • *For one thing, …* *Secondly …* • *Furthermore …* • *What is more, …* • *Besides …* • *In addition …* • *Moreover …* *Finally …* • *Above all …* • *Most importantly …*
Giving an example	*for example …* • *for instance …* • *such as …*
Emphasizing	*In fact, …* • *As a matter of fact, …* • *Actually, …*
Contrasting	*On the one hand … On the other hand …* • *However …* • *… though …* • *Nonetheless …* • *Whereas …* • *Although …* • *In spite of …*
Conceding a point	*Of course …* • *Naturally …* • *Admittedly …*
Referring to a point in time or a development	*At the/that time …* • *In those days …* • *Eventually …* • *In the course of …* • *In the long run …* • *Meanwhile …* • *At the same time …* • *As a result …*
Coming to a conclusion	*All in all …* • *In the final analysis …* • *In conclusion …* • *Ultimately …* • *For the reasons mentioned above …* • *To sum up …* • *To conclude …* • *I would like to conclude by saying …*

2 In the following text, linking words and phrases have been left out. Decide where such 'signposts' are missing and choose appropriate ones from the table above. Then write an improved version of the text.

Google wants to change the world – again

Google revolutionized the way we use the Web in the 1990s with a new kind of search engine. Now it wants to change the way we navigate physical space. The California firm has developed a small car that drives itself. The car is equipped with GPS and a host of sensors that collect information about the surroundings as it moves. There is a steering wheel and a brake (for emergencies), but the car is programmed to work without a human driver.

Google is not interested in going into the car business. The real purpose is to change how we think about mobility. Why should you buy a car if you can get one whenever you need or want it? You want to go downtown, you flip open your smartphone and call for an autonomous taxi. The vehicle drops you off at your destination, then goes on to its next job. There would be less need for huge parking lots and parking garages. There would be fewer emissions as people waste less time cruising around looking for a parking space. People who are unable to drive (because of age, disability, or because they are drunk) could still get from one place to another. Self-driving cars would be a new form of public transportation. The way cities are designed would change.

There are still problems to be solved. Who is responsible when an autonomous vehicle is involved in an accident? Will people overcome their fear of losing control over their cars? What about the transition period when human and non-human drivers share the same roads? It is only a question of time until these issues have been settled. The future is coming, and Google wants to get there first.

▸ LP 15 Connecting your thoughts (sentence structure)

1 BASIC Your partner has given you this text to proofread. Rewrite it to improve the style without leaving out any information.

Frank McCourt was born in Brooklyn, New York in 1930, which was the first year of the Great Depression. Both of his parents were immigrants from Ireland. They had come to America like millions of other Irish men and women who were looking for a better life. But they didn't find a better life, they only found poverty and misery. The McCourts, who were disappointed with life in America, decided to move back to Ireland. But their new life in Limerick, which was the hometown of Frank's mother, was no better than their life in Brooklyn. Young Frank had to leave school to support his family. He did odd jobs to earn a few pounds. After he had saved enough money for a ticket to New York, he left Ireland for good and didn't even tell his family.

Texts that contain unnecessary words or that connect ideas too loosely don't read well. A few simple techniques can help you make your sentences more compact and connected:

Loose connection		Stronger connection
Relative clause: *Frank McCourt was born in Brooklyn, New York in 1930, which was the first year of the Great Depression.*	→	**Apposition:** *Frank McCourt was born in Brooklyn, New York in 1930, the first year of the Great Depression.*
Relative clause: *They had come to America like millions of other Irish men and women who were looking for a better life.*	→	**Participle construction:** *They had come to America like millions of other Irish men and women looking for a better life.*
Compound sentence: *But they didn't find a better life, they only found poverty and misery.* *After he had saved enough money for a ticket to New York, he left Ireland for good and didn't even tell his family.*	→	**Gerund construction:** *But instead of finding a better life, they only found poverty and misery.* *After saving enough money for a ticket to New York, he left Ireland for good without even telling his family.*

Participle phrases can also be used instead of adverbial clauses with a variety of meanings:

Example	Function of participle construction
Arriving in New York, he looked for a cheap room.	Time (simultaneous action)
Having served in the Army during the Korean War, Frank was offered the chance to go to college.	Time (antecedent action)
Wanting to improve his status, he got a degree in English from NYU.	Reason
McCourt taught in New York schools for thirty years, never forgetting the bitter poverty he had experienced in Ireland.	Accompanying circumstance

2 Rewrite the final paragraph of the text on Frank McCourt, using participle phrases in suitable places to improve the style.

After he had retired from teaching, McCourt began writing his memoires. They appeared in fictionalized form in 1996 as Angela's Ashes. *The novel was a worldwide success and also won its author a Pulitzer Prize. McCourt looks back on his childhood in Limerick with irony and wit, and he describes how hard life was for poor Irish families in the 1930s and 40s. McCourt was amused at the unexpected success of his book and said that it was the first time in history that a man had become rich by writing about being poor.*

Focus on Vocabulary

▸ LP 16 Avoiding Germanisms

1 BASIC Each of the following sentences contains a 'typically German' mistake in red. Copy the sentences and correct the mistakes:

1 The plot of the film is typical for romantic comedies.
2 Jackie stepped into the corridor to phone with her lawyer.
3 Young people often use the internet to watch videos or hear music.
4 Music critics wondered when the single 'Thrift Shop' by a little-known rapper duo stormed the US charts in 2013.
5 We can meet us later in the city centre.
6 Some schools have introduced programmes to prevent cybermobbing.

German and English have much in common. This is often a help, but sometimes it is a source of confusion. The table below lists some common pitfalls:

	Source of confusion	Examples
a	similar word, different meaning	aktuell ≠ actual; eventuell ≠ eventual; Meinung ≠ meaning; spenden ≠ spend; sich wundern ≠ wonder
b	similar expression, different preposition	married **to** sb. = verheiratet **mit** jdm.; contact **with** sb. = Kontakt **zu** jdm.; example **of** sth. = Beispiel **für** etwas; typical of sb. = typisch **für** jdn.; do sth. **about** sth. = etwas **gegen** etwas tun
c	word-for-word translation of German phrase	~~hold~~/make a speech; ~~with 29 years~~/at the age of 29; on the one ~~side~~/hand; ~~make~~/take a photo; ~~hear~~/listen to music
d	verb used with/without a preposition	phone sb. = mit jdm. telefonieren; surf the internet = im Internet surfen; discuss sth. = über etwas diskutieren; comment on sth: = etwas kommentieren; discriminate against sb. = jdn. diskriminieren
e	Denglish used instead of English	~~beamer~~ (projector); ~~mobbing~~ (bullying); ~~handy~~ (mobile/cellphone); ~~boxes~~ (loudspeakers)
f	reflexive in German, non-reflexive in English	meet = sich treffen; identify with sb. = sich mit jdm. identifizieren; concentrate on sth. = sich auf etwas konzentrieren; feel = sich fühlen

2 For each of the following sentences, decide which word is missing (if any). If you aren't sure, the letter in brackets will tell you where to look in the table.

1 People write letters to the editor when they want to express their … (a)
2 The press secretary refused to comment … the minister's decision. (d)
3 In a speech that he … on March 4, Obama called for a new initiative on gun control. (c)
4 Jared is the only character in the novel that readers could possibly identify … with. (f)
5 Some teens spend far too much time surfing … the internet. (d)
6 The author names three examples … the abuse of power by the present government. (b)
7 It's high time for the town council to do something … this problem. (b)
8 To show the DVD in our classroom, we need a … and a pair of … as well as a laptop. (e)

▶ LP 17 Spelling

1 BASIC Copy the words below, adding the missing letters. Careful: sometimes no letters are missing!

1 int■rested	5 mis■understanding	9 standar■	13 wel■fare
2 nec■essary	6 d■scribe	10 politic■an	14 consc■ous
3 happ■ly	7 public■ly	11 av■rage	15 desp■rate■
4 chara■ter	8 refer■ing	12 assist■nt	16 non-viol■nce

Unfortunately, there are very few rules for English spelling. The best strategy is to keep track of the words that you frequently misspell and practise writing them, for example before exams.

2 The following text is a student's essay on a British novel. There are ten spelling mistakes. Correct them:

Never Let Me Go by Kazuo Ishiguro is one of the best novels I have ever read. The autor tells the story from the point of view of Cathy, a young women, who reflects on her live as a student at a boarding school called Hailsham, and later as a so-called 'carer'. At first the reader thinks this is just an other story about adolesence, but as the novel progresses, we slowly realize that there is something special about the young people at Hailsham: as human as they appear to the reader, they are really clones who must donate their organs to others when they have reached maturity. Although they seem to know this, they don't really understand their situation, and each of them clings to the hope that somehow they will be allowd to live a bit longer then the others. The novel has also been adapted for the screen, and although I usualy avoid films based on books I love, I have to admit that this one is outstanding and succedes brillantly in capturing the spirit of the novel.

▶ LP 18 Writing about texts

There are many special expressions that you need when you write essays in German. The same is true of English. Knowing these phrases makes it easier for you to express yourself clearly.

1 BASIC The table below contains German and English phrases for text analysis. Both lists are in alphabetical order. Copy the table, matching the German phrases and their English equivalents:

German	English
1 angesichts …	a according to …
2 auf den ersten Blick	b as a rule
3 bei näherer Betrachtung	c as for … / as far as … is concerned
4 in Bezug auf …	d at first sight
5 dabei (d.h., während man etwas tut)	e focus on …
6 im Allgemeinen	f in connection with …
7 im Gegensatz zu …	g in contrast to …

German	English
8 im Großen und Ganzen	h in general
9 im Zusammenhang mit …	i in the process
10 in der Regel	j in view of …
11 laut …	k on closer examination
12 seitens …	l on the part of …
13 was … betrifft	m on the whole
13 … auf den Punkt bringen	n put … in a nutshell
15 … in den Mittelpunkt stellen	o with regard to …

2 Translate the following sentences into English with the help of your table:
1 Auf den ersten Blick hält man den Autor für einen Befürworter[1] der amerikanischen Umweltpolitik[2].
2 Bei näherer Betrachtung erkennt der Leser, dass er viele Dinge in den USA kritisch betrachtet.
3 Der Autor stellt die Auswirkungen der globalen Erwärmung in den Mittelpunkt.
4 Der Autor schildert die Folgen des Fracking in den USA. Dabei macht er deutlich, dass er diese Technik ablehnt.
5 Angesichts der Umweltbelastung[3] kann der Leser ihm nur zustimmen.
6 Im Gegensatz zu den Amerikanern, die Fracking im Großen und Ganzen akzeptieren, sind die Deutschen skeptisch eingestellt[4].
7 Im letzten Absatz bringt der Autor das ganze Dilemma auf den Punkt.

► LP 19 Collocations

Verbs and nouns

1 BASIC Choose the right verb for each of the sentences below:
1 Young people today sometimes find it hard to get/make a living in a tight job market.
2 Sam's teachers urged him to give/pay more attention to his school work.
3 The girls apologized to their victim, saying that they hadn't meant to do/make any harm.
4 The journalist calls/attracts attention to the problems in the region.
5 We think our school should make/set a good example by banning plastic tableware from the canteen.
6 The storm made/did considerable damage on its way northward.

In English as well as in German, certain nouns are used together with certain verbs, e.g. you can only *take* (not ~~make~~) a *photo* in English. These 'natural pairs' are called collocations. Knowing the most common ones will help you avoid mistakes. The table below contains a selection of verb-noun collocations:

call attention (to sth.)	do damage	meet expectations	set an example
change your mind	exert influence (on sb.)	pay attention (to sb.)	take measures
commit a crime	make a living	put pressure on sb.	take offence (at sth.)
do justice to sth.	make history	put sth. to a vote	take a photo (of sb./ sth.)
do good/harm	make an impression	reach an agreement	tell the truth/a lie

2 Complete the following sentences with the missing verb. All collocations are from the table above:
1 Did the hotel … your expectations?
2 The only way we'll ever … an agreement is to … the matter to a vote.
3 Yesterday, history was … as government officials and rebel leaders met for direct talks.
4 As a member of the Board of Overseers she still … considerable influence on University policy.
5 It is important to … a good impression when you go for a job interview.
6 To my mind the film doesn't … justice to the novel.
7 The management … pressure on the workers to accept a pay cut.
8 The police agreed that further measures should be … to stop young people from … crimes.

[1] ***Befürworter*** supporter [2] ***Umweltpolitik*** environment policy [3] ***Umweltbelastung*** negative environmental impact
[4] ***skeptisch eingestellt*** sceptical

Adjectives and nouns

3 BASIC The grey boxes on the right contain adjectives and nouns that form collocations. Form matching pairs and use them to complete the sentences:

1 Let's step outside and get some ... ...
2 The firm finally agreed to the protesters' demands to avoid further ... ...
3 The Declaration of Independence names 'life, liberty and the pursuit of happiness' as basic ... ...
4 Listen, everybody! I just had a ... ...
5 The hurricane caused ... ... all along the coast.
6 African Americans have fought a long battle for ... ...
7 I can't believe how ... Tamira's ... are.
8 Don't make jokes about veggie burgers – Katrina has very ... ... about animal rights.
9 This boarding school has very ... ..., and all students are expected to obey them.
10 I wasn't surprised when Steve was chosen for the scholarship – I've always had a ... ... of his character.

bright	*air*
equal	*damage*
fresh	*feelings*
heavy	*idea*
high	*opinion*
human	*parents*
negative	*publicity*
strict (2x)	*rights (2x)*
strong	*rules*

Some adjectives 'belong together' with certain nouns, forming a new 'compound noun': *a human being, fair play, real life*. Others are frequently used together and form a collocation (*hard work, poor health*). Knowing common adjective-noun collocations will help you avoid mistakes and express yourself more idiomatically.

4 What adjective(s) could you use to describe each of the following nouns? Write down your ideas first, then check them with the help of a monolingual dictionary (look at the usage examples):

1 burden
2 conscience
3 example
4 gesture
5 rise
6 treatment
7 topic
8 argument
9 price
10 working conditions

5 Use five of your collocations in sentences that illustrate their meaning, e.g. *In Germany, fracking is a very controversial topic.*

Prepositions

6 BASIC Choose the correct preposition for each of the numbered gaps in the following sentences:

I agree (1) the author that it is high time to do something (2) the problem of toxic waste. We can't just turn our backs (3) the problem or wait (4) industry to take the initiative. Everyone who is worried (5) the future of life (6) this planet should get involved (7) a campaign (8) toxic waste. Photos (9) young children playing on heaps of toxic rubbish in India or other countries can easily be found (10) the internet or (11) newspapers and magazines. No one can look (12) such photos without feeling their own responsibility (13) the present situation.

Many common expressions in English include a preposition. You can't learn them all, but the more you know, the fewer mistakes you will make. If you aren't certain which preposition to use with a certain word, look at the example sentences under the corresponding headword in a monolingual dictionary.

7 Use a dictionary to find out which preposition(s) can be used with each of the following words:

1 a lack ... something
2 a novel written ... someone
3 accuse someone ... something
4 allude ... something
5 an attempt ... something
6 appeal ... something
7 be critical ... something
8 blame someone ... something
9 contribute ... something
10 good ... sth.
11 remind someone ... something
12 struggle ... a goal
13 sympathize ... someone
14 take a look ... something
15 thank someone ... something

▶ LP 20 Word formation

Prefixes

1 BASIC In the table below, match the prefixes to the correct meanings.

Meaning	Prefix(es)
1 against sth.	a multi-
2 for sth., in favour of sth.	b pseudo-
3 having two (sides, aspects, etc.)	c re-
4 having only one	d pre-
5 having or connected with several	e anti- counter-
6 not	neo-
7 no longer	f semi-
8 done badly or wrongly	g ex-
9 one of two	h pro-

Meaning	Prefix(es)
10 new	i non- dis-
11 happening before sth.	j mono-
12 happening after sth.	k co-
13 again, for the second time	l bi-
14 not really	m post-
15 referring to or done by yourself	n ultra-
16 only half, not completely	o mis-
17 extremely	p self-

Adding a prefix to an existing word changes the meaning without influencing the grammatical class: *un + able → unable*. Knowing the meaning of prefixes can help you to understand words you have never seen before.
Some of the prefixes (especially anti-, non-, self-, neo- and pseudo-) are often separated from their root word with a hyphen: anti-aircraft, neo-Colonial, etc.). But as there are no fixed rules for English spelling, it is best to check your dictionary to be sure.

Find an online dictionary here:
Webcode context-52

2 Use a prefix from the list above to create an expression that matches each of the following definitions. Example: strong belief in your own abilities: *self-confidence*

1 a film that presents war in a negative light
2 a measure that produces the opposite of the intended effect
3 a former husband
4 one of the two captains of a team
5 a theory that pretends to be scientific but isn't
6 discover sth. for the second time, e.g. in later life
7 a person who is not a resident of the country they are staying in
8 interpret sth. the wrong way
9 an organization that operates in several countries
10 a worker who has some qualifications but fewer than a skilled worker
11 Germany after the war
12 having two poles

Suffixes

3 BASIC Copy the table below and sort the words on the right into groups. Underline the suffixes.

Nouns	Verbs	Adjectives

apparition • certify • complicity • egalitarian • enactment • furious • hypothesize • identical • laudable • marital • notification • obligatory • supportive

Like German, English can form a new word by adding a suffix to an existing root: *present* + *-able* → *presentable*. Since the suffix determines whether the word is a noun, verb or adjective, recognizing common suffixes can help you figure out the meanings of unfamiliar words. You probably haven't seen any of the words in the box above before, but the suffixes give you information about what they mean.

4 Drawing on your knowledge of English as well as other languages, make an intelligent guess as to the meaning of each word. When you have finished, check your answers using a dictionary.

Find an online dictionary here:
Webcode context-52

Word families

5 BASIC The table below contains words related to each other. Copy the table and fill in the blanks, using a dictionary if necessary. Make sure you know the meanings of all the words:

Verb	Noun	Adjective	Noun
act	(1)	active	activity
create	creation	(2)	creativity
depend (on)	(3)	dependent/dependable	dependability
rely (on)	reliance	reliable	(4)
select	selection	(5)	selectivity
compare	comparison	(6)	comparability
tolerate	(7)	tolerable	tolerability
adapt (to)	adaptation	adaptable	(8)
criticize	(9)	critical	...
destroy	(10)	destructive	destructiveness

6 Use words from the table to rewrite the underlined parts of the following sentences. You may have to change the word order or add words in some cases:

Example: Meteorologists underestimated how destructive Hurricane Ivor would be.
→ *Meteorologists underestimated the destructiveness of Hurricane Ivor.*

1 We've had enough of speech-making; now is the time to act.
2 The author claims that classical music and popular music can't be compared.
3 All children have a natural creativity
4 Gerald quit his job in India because he could not tolerate his working conditions.
5 Our firm expects all employees to be reliable.
6 The fact that our country is dependent on foreign oil and gas is a serious issue.
7 While doing her gap year in Uganda, Shirin demonstrated how well she can adapt.
8 The so-called Ivy League universities in the US are said to select their students very carefully.

Princeton, an Ivy League university

Everyday English

Download the suggested answers to the tasks here:
Webcode context-32

▶ EE 1 Eating in and out

Eating customs often vary from culture to culture and knowing a few basics can come in handy while abroad.

1 In what situation might someone use each of the following expressions?

1 Thanks, I'm fine.
2 Just help yourself.
3 It's delicious, but I'm full.
4 Could you pass the ..., please?
5 This has been a wonderful meal!
6 Could I have some more, please?

2 ROLE-PLAY Use the phrases from part **1** and the role cards to act out a short dialogue.

You can find your role cards here:
Webcode context-33

FACT FILE

Eating out: American style

In sit-down restaurants in the United States where you are served at your table, there are a few customs that you should be aware of that are different from those in Europe:

- 'Please wait to be seated' is posted near the entrance in many restaurants. You are expected to wait to be taken to a table (even if the restaurant is completely empty!). Someone (a host or hostess) will probably ask how many are in your 'party' (e.g.: 'Just the two of you?' or 'How many are in your group?'), and either take you to a table or ask for your name so that they can call you when your table is ready.
- 'Designing your own meal' with your choice of meat and vegetable from the menu is not uncommon in the USA. A typical dish could be, for example, a sirloin steak with a choice of vegetable or side-salad and potatoes cooked in a specific way. Examine the menu and make your selection so that you are ready to order when the server arrives.
- 'Would you like a refill?' is a typical phrase in restaurants in the USA. Most restaurants offer free refills of at least coffee and soft drinks. The server exchanges your empty glass for a full one or refills your glass at your table. Tap water (usually with ice cubes) is provided for free.
- A 'service charge' is usually not included on the bill. Servers are not well paid in most regions of the USA and a tip of 15–20% is expected. You can either leave a cash tip on the table or, if paying with a credit card, there will be a place on the bill where you can add a tip to the total.

In groups of 4–5, write and act out a short theatrical scene that takes place in a US restaurant. Use the information above and the vocabulary below to help you.

TIP

Soft drinks are called different things in different parts of the USA. As a general rule:
On the East and West Coasts: ***soda***
In the Midwest: ***pop***
In the South: ***coke***
(even for soft drinks that are not cola)

Some useful terms			
main dish entrée ['ɒntreɪ] (AE)	*Hauptgericht*	menu ['menjuː]	*Speisekarte*
starter (BE) appetizer (AE)	*Vorspeise*	four-course dinner / meal	*Vier-Gang-Menü*
side dish, side order	*Beilage*	tip	*Trinkgeld*
dessert [dɪ'zɜːt] sweet (BE), pudding ['pʊdɪŋ] (BE) afters (BE, *infml*)	*Nachspeise*	VAT (BE) sales tax (AE)	*Mehrwertsteuer*
bill; check (AE)	*Rechnung*	tap water	*Leitungswasser*

TROUBLE SPOT

Ger. *Menü* ≠ Eng. ***menu***

TROUBLE SPOT

entrée (BE) ≠ ***entrée*** (AE)

▸ EE 2 Planning a trip using the internet

The internet is a handy tool for making travel plans. You can book travel arrangements and hotel accommodation, find out information about museums and other places of interest, order food and make restaurant reservations, as well as even reserve concert, theatre or movie tickets.
Imagine your class is planning a week-long trip to London. You will be in the city from Monday to Friday. Form three groups (A, B, C). Each group has its own planning task.

Group A: Getting around in London
Explore the options for public transport during your stay. London offers a variety of tickets with different prices and conditions. It might be helpful to know how many students there are in your class and their ages.

- Split your group into 3–4 smaller groups. Each of the mini-groups explores one option and presents it to the rest of the class.
- Consult relevant websites to find out what options are available, what conditions are attached to their use, and how much they would cost. Calculate the total cost for the group.

Find links to helpful websites here:
Webcode context-34

Group B: A day trip to Greenwich
While in London, your class wants to take a day trip to Greenwich. How will you get there? The closest station to your hotel is Bayswater Tube Station.

- Divide your group into 3 mini-groups. Each mini-group researches a different way of getting to Greenwich.
  Mini-group 1: Docklands Light Railway
  Mini-group 2: Thames Riverboat
  Mini-group 3: Greenwich Foot Tunnel
  Take into account what interesting sights different travel options might offer along the way.
- What is the total price for the group (not including the cost of any Tube travel)?

Find links to websites of interest here:
Webcode context-35

Group C: The Royal Museums Greenwich
The Royal Museums Greenwich (RMG) is a complex of buildings and sites of historical, architectural and scientific interest.

- What does the RMG consist of? Use the internet to explore the various possibilities.
- Divide your group into 3 mini-groups. Each mini-group puts together a different suggestion for a visit to the RMG.
- What can you see and do? When and where? How much does it cost for your group?
- Are there adequate food options available there for a group of your size?

Find links to help start your search here:
Webcode context-36

Some useful terms			
peak (hours, etc.)	*Spitzenzeiten*	fare	*Fahrpreis*
entry (to a building, etc.)	*Zutritt*	swipe card	*Magnetstreifenkarte*
opening hours	*Öffnungszeiten*	vending machine	*(Verkaufs-)Automat*
admission (fee)	*Eintritt(spreis)*	destination	*(Reise-)Ziel*
exhibition	*Ausstellung*	venue	*(Veranstaltungs-)Ort*
surcharge	*Aufschlag*	closing time	*Schließzeit*
concession/discount	*Ermäßigung*	pay-as-you-go credit	*Prepaid-Guthaben*

FACT FILE

Greenwich [ˈɡrenɪtʃ], a district of South East London, is on 0° Longitude *(Prime or Greenwich Meridian)* and sets the global time standard *(Greenwich Mean Time)*.

▸ EE 3 Dealing with medical emergencies CD3 08

A medical emergency can happen anywhere. The cause can be an accident or a sudden illness. Before you go abroad, make sure you have health insurance coverage[1] for your country of destination. Travel medical insurance[2] is inexpensive and covers all medical expenses during a brief foreign stay.

FACT FILE

Getting medical assistance
In the event of an emergency, call 999 (UK), 911 (USA) or 000 (Australia). From mobile phones, the number 112 will also connect you with the emergency services in many countries.
Hospital: If you or someone else needs medical help, consult a physician/doctor or go to the outpatient clinic[3] of the nearest hospital, where you can be treated without being admitted to the hospital[4].
Pharmacy: In the UK and the US, shops that sell medicine are called pharmacies, drugstores (US) or chemist's (UK). They offer a wider range of products than a German *Apotheke*, including cosmetics, health and beauty products, and sometimes travel essentials.
Prescriptions: Medicine that has been prescribed by a doctor is dispensed at the pharmacy counter within the shop. In the US, you are given the exact dosage prescribed by the doctor. If, for example, your prescription says three capsules daily for five days, you will be given 15 capsules in a small bottle, not the original package.

TROUBLE SPOT
ärztliches Rezept = ***prescription***
Kochrezept = ***recipe*** ['resəpi]

A group of students in the eighth class at your school are about to go on their first exchange to the UK. Prepare an informative and funny two-minute talk for them in English on medical assistance abroad.

1 In the event that you need medical help, it is important that you understand the doctor's questions and can give precise answers. Test your knowledge by matching the English words to their German equivalents.

1	abdomen	11	have a temperature
2	allergic	12	headache
3	bowel movement	13	nausea ['nɔːziə]
4	bruise [bruːz]	14	numb
5	congested	15	scrape
6	constipated	16	shiver
7	cough [kɒf]	17	sore throat
8	cut	18	stomach ache [eɪk]
9	diarrhoea [daɪərɪə]	19	vaccination
10	dizziness	20	vomit

a	allergisch	k	Schnittwunde
b	Bauch, Unterleib	l	Schürfwunde
c	Durchfall	m	Schwindel
d	Fieber haben	n	sich übergeben
e	Halsschmerzen	o	Stuhlgang
f	Husten	p	taub
g	Impfung	q	Übelkeit
h	Kopfschmerzen	r	verschnupft
i	Magenschmerzen	s	verstopft
j	Prellung	t	zittern

2 Sabine is staying with her host family in the USA. She isn't feeling well and her host parents take her to the doctor. Listen to the dialogue and answer the questions.
1 How does Sabine describe her symptoms?
2 What information does Dr Felter want from her?
3 What does Dr Felter give her?

Listen to the audio file on the CD or download it here:
Webcode context-37

3 ROLE-PLAY **Partner A** is cycling near Bristol with his or her British host-brother, Toby. All of a sudden, Toby hits a hole in the road and falls off his bike. He is badly hurt. Phone for help! **Partner B** will be the person taking calls for emergency services in the Bristol area. Use the role cards.

You can find your role cards here:
Webcode context-38

[1]**health insurance coverage** *Krankenversicherungsschutz* [2]**travel medical insurance** *Auslandskrankenversicherung*
[3]**outpatient clinic** *Ambulanz* [4]**admit sb. to the hospital** *jdn. stationär aufnehmen*

▸ EE 4 Making phone calls

Talking on the telephone has become less common in the age of text messages, but there are still situations in which it is unavoidable. The box below lists example phrases that can be used when talking on the phone.

1 Match the phrases from the box below to the following typical situations:

1 You phone a number and say who you are.
2 You explain why you are calling.
3 You answer the phone.
4 You are not the intended recipient of the call.
5 You ask for clarification.
6 You want to end the conversation and hang up.

a Hello. My name is Lisa Weber. I'm calling from Cologne in Germany.
b The reason I'm calling is …
c I'm sorry, I didn't catch that. Could you repeat your name please?
d May I ask why you are calling?
e Can I take a message?
f It was nice talking with you.
g Good morning. This is Max Kunze in Dresden, Germany.
h I'm afraid she isn't here. Would you like her to call you back?
i I'd like to speak to …
j May I ask who's calling, please?
k I think you've dialed the wrong number.
l I'm calling about the advert you posted …
m Thank you for returning my call / Thanks for getting back to me. *(infml)*
n Good afternoon. Caroline Schlegel speaking.
o Could you spell that, please?
p I have a problem, could you connect me with Customer Services, please?
q Robert Peters here. What can I do for you?
r Sorry, the line is busy. Would you like to speak to someone else?
s Mr Adams tried to reach me while I was out. I'm returning his call.
t Thank you for your call.

2 ROLE-PLAY Working together with a partner, use the information on the role cards to carry out a conversation on the phone.

You can find your role cards here:
Webcode context-39

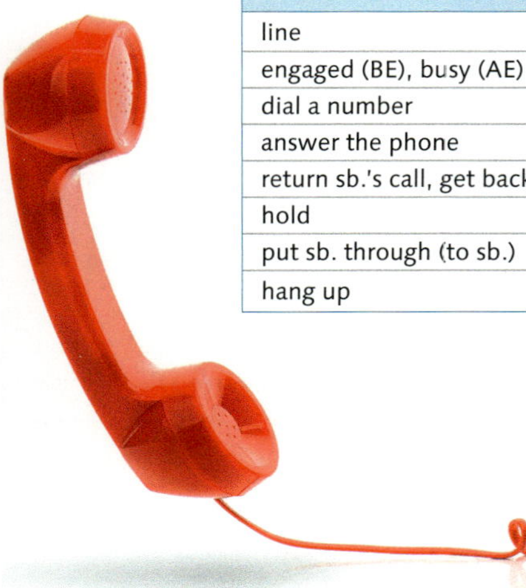

Some useful terms	
line	*Leitung*
engaged (BE), busy (AE)	*besetzt*
dial a number	*eine Nummer wählen*
answer the phone	*einen Anruf entgegennehmen*
return sb.'s call, get back to sb.	*jdn. zurückrufen*
hold	*in der Leitung bleiben*
put sb. through (to sb.)	*jdn. (zu jdm.) durchstellen*
hang up	*auflegen*

► EE 5 Watch your valuables!

When staying abroad, whether on holiday or as part of an exchange programme, you will need money. There are different ways of taking money abroad.

1 Match the lettered boxes to their corresponding method of taking or accessing money abroad.

Money Management Methods:
1 a bank card / debit card (AE)
2 a credit card
3 traveller's cheques
4 cash

A
- must be exchanged for local currency
- no way of preventing a thief from using it

B
- equivalent to the German 'ec-Karte' or Girocard
- can be used to withdraw cash at an ATM[1] (more commonly called a cash machine or 'hole in the wall' in the UK) or to pay for goods and services in many countries

C
- can be used to pay bills in many hotels and restaurants without a PIN
- can sometimes be used with the PIN to withdraw cash from an ATM
- can be cancelled if lost or stolen

D
- must be bought before you leave home
- can be cashed in any bank during opening hours

Plastic money is very practical, but use caution:
- Before you travel, check whether your bank at home has a partnership with a bank where you're staying abroad. It might be cheaper for you to use that bank to withdraw cash.
- In many countries, ATMs are not inside banks, but on the walls outside. For safety reasons, try to use an ATM in a well-lit area or inside the bank building.
- Make sure nobody can see the number keys while you are entering your PIN.
- Be aware that there will probably be a fee every time you withdraw cash from a foreign ATM.

If your card is lost or stolen, take immediate action:
- Make sure you know how to reach your bank and/or credit card company in case you need to block or cancel your card. (The phone number can change depending on where you are travelling.)
- Phone and have the card blocked as soon as you realize your card is lost or stolen.
- Report the theft to the local police.

2 ROLE-PLAY Oh, no! You have been robbed! Report the theft to the local police. Use role cards and the vocabulary in the box below for your dialogue.

You can find your role cards here:
Webcode context-40

Some useful terms			
valuables	*Wertsachen*	bank card, debit card	*ec-Karte; Girocard*
purse / wallet	*Geldbörse, Portemonnaie*	have your card blocked / cancelled	*deine Karte sperren lassen*
cash	*Bargeld*	suspicious [sə'spɪʃəs] behaviour	*auffälliges Verhalten*
pickpocket	*Taschendieb/in*	report a crime, etc. (to the police)	*eine Straftat usw. anzeigen*

TROUBLE SPOT
rob sb. = *steal sth. from sb.*

[1] **ATM** *Geldautomat*

Communicating across Cultures

Download the suggested answers to the tasks here:
Webcode context-41

▸ CC 1 Cultural awareness

Like a fish out of water: A fish doesn't know what water is – until the water suddenly isn't there anymore. Likewise, we often take the culture we grow up with for granted – customs, body language, how people interact in everyday situations – and don't really notice it while it surrounds us. As a result, experiencing different cultures can open our eyes to aspects of our own culture and also give us insight into ways other people behave.

1 Put yourself in each of the following situations and choose the reaction that comes the closest to your own.

1 A crowded cafeteria at lunchtime. You have been waiting patiently for the last ten minutes. Someone comes into the room, spots a gap near the front of the queue and jumps in.
  a You look away and say nothing.
  b You grumble to your neighbour, 'So selfish!'
  c You shout out loud, 'Hey you! Go to the back of the queue!'

2 While waiting at the bus stop, you see an exchange student who is in one of your courses. He comes over to chat and stops about thirty centimetres in front of you (try it out with a partner, using a ruler to measure the distance between the tips of your noses).
  a You take a step backward.
  b You turn a bit to the side to avoid facing the other student directly.
  c You stand your ground and look the other person directly in the eye.

3 You get a note from a guidance counselor asking you to come to her office after school. When you arrive, the door is half open; the counselor is working at her desk.
  a You walk in, say hello and sit down opposite her.
  b You stand in the doorway and say, 'You wanted to see me.'
  c You knock lightly on the door and say, 'Excuse me, may I interrupt you?'

2 In groups of not more than three, compare your reactions to the situations in exercise **1** and your reasons for choosing them. Discuss the following points:

- How do you feel about (not) playing by the rules?
- How close is too close – when do you feel that someone is invading your personal space?
- What does eye contact signify?
- What does an open (or closed) door mean?

Compare your views and decide which forms of behaviour you think are typical in your society.

▶ CC 2 The language of politeness

1 People don't always say what they really mean; sometimes they even say the opposite:

To a certain degree, understatement and exaggeration are part of national culture. Americans tend to be highly enthusiastic ('Fantastic!' – 'I'd love to!' – 'I'm dying to meet him!'), whereas the British are more reserved in their way of expressing themselves ('I'm afraid we've got a bit of a problem.'). These are, of course, just generalizations, as each person has their own style.
In conversations, always try to be friendly and polite, but remember that polite phrases cannot always be taken literally. The list on the left in the table below shows some polite phrases you might hear, especially in the UK. First, decide what you think they mean, then choose the 'translation' from the list on the right.

1 There's room for improvement.	a I'm just being polite.
2 I wouldn't mind.	b I'm very annoyed.
3 Very original work.	c I expect you to read it.
4 You must come over for dinner.	d I'd love to.
5 I was a bit disappointed that …	e That's really good.
6 You might want to have a look at it.	f I expect you to apologize.
7 I'm sure it was my mistake.	g Hopeless stuff.

2 The table below contains polite phrases that can be used in everyday situations. Match them, then use one or two of the matching pairs to write a short dialogue (with a partner, if you prefer):

1 Would you mind if I borrowed one of these? I can't find mine.	a Great idea! I'd love to!
2 Sorry, I didn't know …	b Sure, come in and have a seat.
3 Thanks a lot!	c Certainly. Here you are.
4 Is it all right with you if I …?	d I'll have to think about that.
5 Could I bother you for a minute?	e Sure, help yourself.
6 Would it be possible for me to …?	f That's all right. Don't worry about it.
7 We were wondering if you would be interested in …	g You're very welcome.
8 Could I get a …, please?	h Of course. Feel free.

► CC3 Polite behaviour

Leon is an exchange student in the USA. Read the following descriptions of everyday situations and decide whether he breaks any rules of polite behaviour. Then discuss your reactions in a group. Have you experienced similar situations? Why do you feel that certain behaviour is polite or impolite?

Compare your views with additional comments here:
Webcode context-42

1 Leon meets his host parents and host brother, Matt, for the first time. He offers them his hand in greeting.
2 Leon calls his host parents 'Frank' and 'Brenda'.
3 At his American home, Leon always keeps his bedroom door shut.
4 Leon and Matt are watching TV when Matt's grandparents enter the room. Leon stays seated.
5 It's dinner time and Leon is very hungry. He starts eating as soon as he has something on his plate.
6 Leon can't follow the conversation at the dinner table, so he starts playing games on his smartphone.

► CC4 Meeting and greeting

1 The phrases below can be used in different social situations: when you meet someone for the first time, when you meet a friend on the street, or when you want to end a conversation. Copy the table below and put the phrases from the list in the correct column (some can be used more than once).

1 Fine thanks. And you?
2 Hi, how's it going? (infml)
3 Hi, nice to meet you. (infml)
4 How are things going? (infml)
5 How do you do? (fml)
6 Sorry, I've got to run. (infml)
7 I'd like you to meet XY.
8 It's been wonderful talking to you.
9 Not too bad. What about you? (infml)
10 (I'm very) Pleased to meet you.
11 Thanks, and the same to you!
12 See you later. (infml)
13 Bye now. Take care! (infml)
14 Have a good time!

Meeting someone for the first time	Meeting someone you know	Saying goodbye

2 Select an appropriate response from your table for each of the following situations:
1 You work for an organization that employs mostly young people. Your supervisor brings a new colleague over to meet you and says: 'Hi Rebecca, this is James, our new trainee.' You say:
2 You see a co-worker in the hallway. She says: 'Hi, how are things going?' You say:
3 Going back to your office, you see your supervisor talking to an older woman. He calls you over and says: 'Rebecca, I'd like you to meet our regional coordinator, Deirdre O'Connor.' You say:
4 After Ms O'Connor has asked you a couple of questions about your job, you want to end the conversation and go back to work. You say:
5 You drive a friend to the train station. As he gets out of the car, he says: 'See you later!' You say:
6 You're a bit late for work when you run into an old friend. When she starts telling you all about her new boyfriend, you make it clear that you're in a hurry and say:
7 On the last day of work before the holidays, a co-worker waves to you as you are leaving and calls out: 'Have a good break!' You say:

TIP
- 'How do you do?' isn't really a question; it is just a very formal way of saying 'Nice to meet you'.
- When someone asks 'How are you?', they usually don't want a medical update. Just say 'Fine, thanks' or 'Not too bad, thanks'.

▸ CC5 Making small talk CD3 09

Small talk is an art. That means that some people are, by nature, better at it than others. However, everybody can work on their skills and practise developing them.

Listen to the audio file on the CD or download it here: **Webcode** context-43

1 Listen to two short conversations and describe the differences between them. Why is one more successful than the other?

2 The list below contains tips for making small talk. In each tip, one or more phrases is missing. Complete the tips with phrases from the box below right.

1 Stand roughly at arm's length from your partner and … while you are talking.
2 Choose a topic that involves something you and your partner … (e.g. social or regional background, personal experiences, present situation, the weather, etc.).
3 Don't ask any questions that you wouldn't …
4 Avoid … ('Do you like sport?'); use … instead ('What's your favourite sport?').
5 Give your partner the opportunity to talk about him- or herself before you make a comment or …
6 Encourage your partner to … by interjecting remarks such as 'That's really interesting!' or 'Wow! That must have been awesome!'.
7 Pay attention to the silences; they may be a sign that your conversation is …
8 Phrases like 'It's been great talking to you' or 'We'll have to continue this conversation some other time' can help you to … elegantly.

a change the subject
b keep talking
c have in common
d end the conversation
e coming to a natural end
f open questions
g look them in the eye
h want to answer
i 'yes-or-no' questions

3 ROLE-PLAY You meet someone new at a youth hostel in Germany. Use the role cards to guide your conversation with a partner.

You can find your role cards here: **Webcode** context-44

4 Choose a new partner and practise making small talk without the help of role cards. Try to keep your conversation going for at least two minutes.

▸ CC6 Talking about sensitive issues CD3 10

Which topics are considered sensitive and which are absolutely taboo varies from culture to culture. A good indicator is humour: which topics do people make jokes about? Which do they seem to avoid? (Watching comedy shows on TV can tell you a lot about social norms.)

1 Imagine you are going to the USA for a year. Rank the ten topics below on a scale from 1 (harmless) to 10 (taboo) as discussion topics. Compare lists with your partner or in a group and discuss your reasons.

food preferences • sports • patriotism • gun control • religion and church-going • parents' jobs • politics • race relations • career goals • the United States' role in the world

2 Emma, a German exchange student in Ohio, is asked by her American social studies teacher about her impressions of life in the USA. Listen to two different versions of the story and make notes on the differences. How is the tone of the conversation affected by the way Emma responds?

Listen to the audio file on the CD or download it here: **Webcode** context-45

FACT FILE

Political correctness

In the mid-20th century in the USA, political correctness became an important topic when minority groups criticized how people spoke about them as a form of discrimination. Other groups soon followed suit.

Racial minorities: During the Civil Rights Movement, African Americans rejected names such as 'negro' or 'colored' that identified them on the basis of skin colour. They preferred the term 'African American', which was similar to traditional terms such as 'Irish American' or 'Italian American'. (Note: Today, it is also acceptable to use the adjective 'black'.) American Indians often want to be called 'Native Americans' or 'First Nations Peoples', and the indigenous peoples of Canada and Alaska prefer to be called 'Inuit' or 'Alaska Natives' instead of 'Eskimos'.

Gender: There are various job titles in English that refer only to the male (or, less often, to the female) gender: postman (*AE:* mailman), salesman, actress, stewardess, etc. Such terms have generally been replaced by gender-neutral ones: 'the chair' (instead of 'chairman/chairwoman'), postal carrier (*AE:* mail carrier), salesperson, flight attendant, etc.

Health: Certain terms used to refer to health issues are sometimes regarded as discriminatory, as they can suggest that there is something inherently wrong with people. People who are physically handicapped should be referred to as 'physically disabled' and mentally challenged people have 'special needs', 'learning disabilities' or are 'intellectually impaired'.

Other politically correct terms would be, for example, 'vision impaired' for the blind or 'hearing impaired' for the deaf.

Think of other politically correct terms that are used in German. Can you find the English equivalents?

► CC 7 Making polite complaints CD3 11, 12 and 13

Travelling abroad is always complicated, and mix-ups and misunderstandings can easily happen. The important thing is to stay calm and, if necessary, get competent help as quickly as possible.

1 Michaela Börner from Düsseldorf is spending a year abroad in North Carolina. When she arrives at the airport in Charlotte, her host family is waiting for her. Listen to the dialogue. What phrases do they use to greet each other? What questions have to be resolved before they can communicate easily?

Listen to the audio files on the CD or download the audio files that correspond to exercises **1**, **2** *and* **3** *here:* **Webcode** context-46

2 At the baggage claim, Michaela and her host family wait for Michaela's suitcase. Listen to the sound file and identify the English words for the following terms:

1 Förderband 2 Gepäckstück 3 Haupthalle 4 Schalter 5 zurückbekommen

3 Michaela and her host family go to the baggage services office. Listen to the sound file. Write down the English equivalents of the following expressions:

1 Kann ich Ihnen behilflich sein?
2 Darf ich bitte …?
3 Ist das so richtig?
4 Ihr Ärger ist verständlich.
5 Sie dürfen sich jederzeit an uns wenden.
6 Wäre es vielleicht möglich, dass unser Gast …
7 Sie waren sehr hilfreich.
8 Gern geschehen.

4 When you encounter a situation for the first time, you may be confronted with vocabulary you haven't heard before. Here is a short list of words that Michaela had trouble understanding. Just as Amanda would have tried to help Michaela, try explaining in English what the following terms mean.

1 baggage receipt 2 written confirmation 3 toll-free number 4 reimbursement

5 ROLE-PLAY Waiting at the airport baggage claim, you see your suitcase coming down the belt. Read the role card and act out the scene with your partner.

You can find your role cards here: **Webcode** context-47

Skills File

P A task allows you to practise the skill.

Download the suggested answers to the Skills File PRACTICE tasks here:
Webcode context-48

Language and study skills

► SF 1 Dealing with unknown words

READING, LISTENING AND MEDIATING ENGLISH INTO GERMAN

When you read or listen to texts, you usually won't understand every single word. Luckily, in many cases, you won't need to because you can understand texts without knowing each individual word. However, if the meaning of a word is essential, there are some techniques that can help you work it out.

Look at the highlighted words in the text on the left and, on the right, read what strategies to use to work out their meaning.

> In order to remain competitive, the industrial nations have to raise their productivity, encourage innovation and lower their production costs.
>
> To reduce costs and to maximize profits, multinational companies often relocate facilities to other countries (= outsourcing) to profit from lower wages they pay their workers and from less restrictive laws. The problem is that it diminishes work prospects for workers here.

- *competitive:* think of words from the same word family *(competition / (to) compete / competitor)*
- *encourage:* identify parts of the word that you know *(courage → give someone courage)*
- *maximize:* think of similar words in other languages (German *maximieren*) but watch out for false friends *(prospects = Aussichten*, not: *Prospekte)*
- *multinational:* identify suffixes or prefixes *(multi = many → multinational = belonging to many nations)*
- *wages:* use the context of the word ('pay their workers')

PRACTICE

Using different strategies, try to infer the meaning of the underlined words:

> One of the Queen's recurrent royal responsibilities was to open Parliament, an obligation she had never previously found particularly burdensome and actually rather enjoyed: to be driven down the Mall on a bright autumn morning even after fifty years was something of a treat. But not any more.

From: Alan Bennet, *The Uncommon Reader*, 2008 (cf. *Context* p. 62)

SPEAKING, WRITING AND MEDIATING GERMAN INTO ENGLISH

When you want to express a certain concept in English when talking, writing or mediating and you don't know the word, you can paraphrase it. (► SF 9: Paraphrasing)

► SF 2 Learning new words

Learning vocabulary is a lifelong activity – even in your own language you never stop learning new words. There are different methods for expanding your vocabulary. Try out a variety of methods until you find the one that works best for you.

Step 1: Identify words that could be useful to you. These might be:
- words that are related to the topic you are dealing with (e.g. Shakespeare's dramas)
- words that help you talk or write about texts or topics in class
- words that go together with other words (collocations) or that belong to a word family that you already know
- words that belong to a neutral *register (words that are either very formal or very informal can only be used in limited situations).

Step 2: Arrange your words in a suitable form. This could be a mind map or a list – or you might want to use index cards. Indicate the meaning of your words by:
- giving synonyms (e.g. dogma = *belief / principle*)
- giving antonyms (e.g. upheaval ≠ *stability*)
- making sketches/drawings
- giving examples (e.g. the arts = *art, music, literature, etc.*)
- giving the German equivalent (e.g. achievement = *Errungenschaft*).

If possible, write down words in contexts or collocations; this will help you to use them in a sentence (e.g. *be torn between, remember sb. for sth.*).

> The Elizabethan Age is often remembered as a Golden Age for its many achievements in the arts. However, England was struggling for peace and stability at home – religious, social, political and economic developments challenged society.
> People were torn between a traditional world view and a more modern one; they generally accepted the Earth as the centre of the cosmos and the Church as the centre of life on Earth, but were keen to discover new truths beyond the old dogmas. Shakespeare's drama reflects this upheaval.

Find a mindmapping tool here: **Webcode** context-53

Find an online thesaurus here: **Webcode** context-52

Step 3: Use your new vocabulary as soon and as often as possible, e.g. include it in a short text, prepare a one-minute speech, study your index cards, etc.

Step 4: Revise your vocabulary regularly; first in short intervals, then in longer ones.

TIP

Be active when learning new words: do not just write them down, say them out loud as well. Sometimes movements, e.g. walking around while learning or giving them a rhythm or tune, can also be helpful.

▸ SF 3 Using a dictionary

There are both mono- and bilingual dictionaries. Both serve different purposes and they complement each other. They can be digital or print.

USING A BILINGUAL DICTIONARY

Here you can look up translations of words. For example if you do not know the English word for *Ruf* you can look it up in the German-English section or type it into your digital dictionary.

- The running heads at the top of each page help you find the right page quickly (top left-hand corner: first entry on page, top right-hand corner: last entry at bottom of page).
- In the example on the right, *Ruf* is the headword: the different translations are listed, numbers or letters in boxes indicate the different meanings.
- The notes in *italics* help you to find the particular meaning you are looking for.
- Examples and collocations are found below the headword.

Ruf
1 *auch übertragen* call /kɔːl/; *lauter* shout /ʃaʊt/: ***der Ruf nach schärferen Gesetzen*** the **call for** tougher laws
2 ≈ *Ansehen* reputation /ˌrepjuˈteɪʃn/

From: *Schulwörterbuch English G 21*

TIP

- To find the pronunciation of an English word, check the English-German section of your dictionary or listen to the soundfile in a digital dictionary.
- In the English-German section you will also find references to irregular verb forms, irregular plural forms, etc.
- Always read the additional information next to your headword (above: in *italics*). This will prevent you from using the wrong translation.

USING A MONOLINGUAL DICTIONARY

Sometimes a monolingual dictionary can prove more helpful than a bilingual dictionary because it doesn't only give equivalents of words in another language, but definitions and example sentences. In this way, an English-English dictionary will help you to find the words that fit best to express exactly what you want to say. If you don't understand an English word of Latin or Greek origin, a monolingual dictionary will usually be more helpful than a bilingual one because the bilingual one will often give you a translation that is similar to the English word, e.g. *cosmopolitan* = *Kosmopolit*.

- In order to choose the right meaning from those given, always read the whole entry.
- The information on usage and style helps you to avoid using the wrong *register.
- Looking at the examples of common collocations and idioms can help you avoid false friends.
- Many dictionaries provide more specific information on typical error areas.

grim /ɡrɪm/ *adj.* (**grim·mer**, **grim·mest**) **1** looking or sounding very serious: a ***grim face/look/smile*** ◊ *She looked grim.* ◊ *with a look of* ***grim determination*** *on his face* ◊ ***grim-faced*** *policemen* **2** unpleasant and depressing: *grim news* ◊ *We face the grim prospect of still higher unemployment.* ◊ *The outlook is pretty grim.* ◊ *Things are* ***looking grim*** *for workers in the building industry.* **3** (of a place or building) not attractive; depressing: *The house looked grim and dreary in the rain.* ◊ *the grim walls of the prison* **4** [not before noun] *(BrE, informal)* ill/sick: *I feel grim this morning.* **5** [not usually before noun] *(BrE, informal)* of very low quality: *Their performance was fairly grim, I'm afraid!* ▸ **grim·ly** *adv.*: *'It won't be easy,' he said grimly.* ◊ *grimly determined* **grim·ness** *noun* [U]

From: *Oxford Advanced Learner's Dictionary*

PRACTICE

Translate the following sentences:

1. *Genetisch veränderte Lebensmittel haben in vielen europäischen Ländern einen eher schlechten Ruf.*
2. *Es gibt auch noch den Ruf nach mehr Beschränkungen für den freien Markt.*
3. *Sein Rufen schien niemand zu bemerken.*

Find an online dictionary here:
Webcode context-52

▸ SF 4 Using a grammar book

A grammar book is useful for correcting mistakes and improving your grammar. You should consult it when you come across a grammar problem while writing a text (e.g. if you are not sure whether or not to use a gerund) or when you realize that you keep making mistakes in certain fields of grammar. To identify these areas, analyse the feedback you receive from your teacher on your tests or homework.

Step 1: Find your grammatical problem area (e.g. word order or tenses) in the contents page or in the index pages at the back of the book. Read the relevant entry (both rules and examples).

Step 2: In order to avoid mistakes in the future, use your grammar book in different ways, e.g.:

- Copy problematic grammar rules onto index cards and use them to revise your grammar points. (Use the same colours for similar aspects or leave space on the cards for examples you add later, etc.)
- Create a poster with your own typical grammar traps.
- Look for the grammar point in question in texts you are working with or in your own texts.
- Do some exercises on the topic.
- Say the rule and some example sentences out loud, perhaps using your grammar card.

Find a tool to make your poster here:
Webcode context-50

PRACTICE

In your latest test the sentences below have been marked as wrong. Say what grammar topic you will look up in your grammar book, then correct the mistakes.

1 *They never went to England before.*
2 *They have known each other since six years.*
3 *If they would be older, they would do it.*
4 *Alicia feels not comfortable.*
5 *She asked me if I am happy.*
6 *They were all the time there.*

▸ SF 5 Doing research

For projects, presentations or other school work you usually have to research individual aspects and find specific information. For this you can use the internet, but also other sources of information. Here are some ways to make your research more effective.

THE PREPARATION STAGE

Step 1: Clarify what your topic is, then brainstorm it. Decide what information you need so that you can structure your research accordingly.

Step 2: Plan your research:

- Decide which sources are helpful for your research: the internet, textbooks, encyclopaedias, newspapers or magazines, experts or contemporary witnesses?
- Concentrate on English language sources. Using German information and translating it into English will take a long time and often leads to unidiomatic English.
- Make a list of keywords that you want to check.

THE RESEARCH STAGE

Step 1: Check your sources: Older publications may contain outdated information; information published by individuals, interest groups or companies may be biased (i.e. have a tendency to be in favour of this group or company). Check for cross-references and do not just rely on one source.

Step 2: Make notes on the information you find. (▸ SF 15: Marking up a text / Making and taking notes)

- Using index cards might make it easier to organize the information later.
- Copy the exact wording and note down the source (▸ SF 39: Quoting a text), as it normally needs to be given in a bibliography (an alphabetical list of sources used) at the end of your presentation or project work.

····▸

TIP

When doing research on the internet, the following tips may help you to find useful information:

How can you determine whether a website provides reliable information?	Domain names ending with *.gov* or *.edu* indicate that the information is likely to be accurate, as it is usually an official website. Sites of scientific institutions are also usually reliable. Personal blogs or homepages often just give statements by individuals – they tend to be biased.
How can you limit the number of hits so that you will find useful information more quickly?	Brainstorm which keywords would most likely appear in the perfect article to answer your search question. Combine them to get the most exact results. Typing in 5–7 keywords is better than just two or three. The more specific the word(s), the better.
How can you find the original source of a quote?	Enter the full quote or parts of it, using quotation marks. This way you will only find websites with that exact quote. From these, you will normally be able to find the original source of a quote.

PRACTICE

'German vs. British political system – similarities and differences'. Use the internet and/or printed works to find out about the German political system and compare it to your findings from Chapter 3, p. 64.

► SF 6 Doing project work

A project is a complex task usually done in a group, involving several hours of work and often resulting in a written or oral product, e.g. a wall display or a presentation. Project work typically proceeds along the following stages:

Step 1: Plan your work:
- Agree on a topic or look closely at the topic assigned to you.
- Decide what has to be done and how to present your results (e.g. a display, a presentation, a web page, a class magazine).
- Discuss how everybody can contribute best to the project and assign the tasks accordingly.
- Agree on a schedule, including regular group meetings at which all group members give status reports, present their results so far and discuss problems.

Step 2: Research your topic. (► SF 5: Doing research)

Step 3: Organize your findings (► SF 8: Structuring ideas) and start preparing your final result, i.e. your presentation (► SF 24: Giving a presentation) and/or any kind of written material (e.g. a wall display, a written text to be handed in, your web page, etc. (► SF 7: Making visual aids). Bear in mind any specifications you were given by your teacher (e.g. length of presentation or text, etc.).

Step 4: Check your written and visual material. Is it well organized and clear? Is the English correct? (► SF 40: Proofreading) Give your product to someone else in your group to check it again.

Step 5: Present your results. (► SF 24: Giving a presentation)

Step 6: After your presentation, assess your work. With your group, discuss what went well and what you could do better next time or ask your audience or teacher for feedback.

► SF 7 Making visual aids

Visual aids can have three purposes:

- *to help you get a clearer picture of the content of a text*
- *to structure information before writing a text (► SF 8: Structuring ideas)*
- *to present information to accompany a presentation (► SF 24: Giving a presentation).*

Some typical examples of visual aids are

- *timelines: order of events, dates*
- *flow charts: cause and effect*
- *pie charts: percentages, amounts (► SF 12: Analysing charts and graphs)*
- *clusters/mind maps: structured ideas.*

The following instructions explain how to make a flow chart after reading a text:

Step 1: Read the text and highlight the most important information. (► SF 15: Marking up a text / Making and taking notes)

The reduction of oxygen-giving forests, especially the tropical rainforests, is one component of the climate change that scientists have been observing over the past few decades. This global warming appears to be causing the polar ice caps to melt, which could lead to the flooding of many coastal regions. At the same time as we rob the earth of its natural resources, we pollute the air and water with the waste products of those resources. Some of the emissions our technology produces are to blame for the greenhouse effect, which further contributes to the global warming phenomenon.

Step 2: Work out how the different aspects are connected.

- *reduction of forests: leads to climate change / global warming*
- *climate change / global warming: leads to melting of the polar ice caps*
- *melting of the polar ice caps: can cause floods*
- *pollution of air and water through waste: emissions cause greenhouse effect*

Step 3: Show the connection with arrows or other symbols.

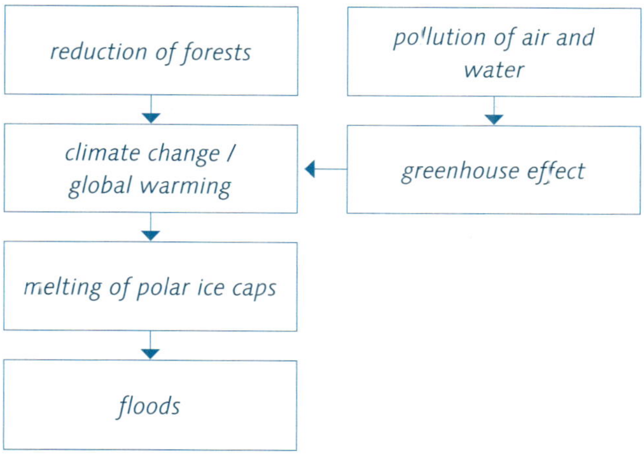

TIP

Use single terms or short phrases if possible; otherwise your chart will look too full and be visually confusing.

PRACTICE

Read ll. 22–34 of the Fact File on p. 67. Make a visual aid that presents the information on the Commonwealth in a suitable way.

► SF 8 Structuring ideas

Structuring ideas is an important step after collecting information and before preparing a text (which may be written or spoken). Arranging your arguments in a logical order is a prerequisite to an effective text. (► SF 38: Writing a well-structured text)

Step 1: When you have collected your ideas, decide on an order in which to present them:
Most texts you produce will follow the general structure **1. Introduction** → **2. Main part / Body** → **3. Conclusion**. Decide on the order in which to present your ideas in the main part. Often the text-type you are being asked to produce will demand a specific structure (► SF 16: Identifying text types).
For example, if you are asked to discuss a statement you will probably divide up your ideas into pro- and con-arguments (► SF 34: Argumentative writing). Other possibilities are a chronological order or *problem* → *cause* → *solution*. It may be helpful to use a flow-chart (► SF 7: Making visual aids) at this stage.

Step 2: Make an **outline** of your text (cf. the box on the right).
All 'main ideas' are of equal importance, as are the 'important facts', etc.

Step 3: Add the ideas you have collected to your outline. Use keywords.

Step 4: Before you start producing the final text or notes, review your outline. Make sure you have found the most appropriate place for each piece of information. (► SF 38: Writing a well-structured text)

OUTLINE
1. Introduction
2. Main part / Body
I. Main idea 1
A. Important fact
1. Supporting fact
2. Supporting fact
a. Example or detail
b. Example or detail
B. Important fact
...
II. Main idea 2
...
3. Conclusion

► SF 9 Paraphrasing

Paraphrasing is useful when you don't know the exact word or phrase in a conversation, when writing a text or mediating into English. There are different techniques for paraphrasing:

Paraphrasing technique	Example
Antonym Antonyms denote the opposite of the original word.	*Reichtum:* 'the opposite of poverty'
Comparison Comparisons help you illustrate what you mean by creating images.	*Handschuh:* 'It's like a sock for your hand.'
Definition or explanation (often using relative clauses) With definitions or explanations, relative clauses help you add detail to general terms (e.g. 'a person', 'a machine').	*Freiwillige/r:* 'a person who offers to do something but doesn't ask for money in return' *Navigationsgerät:* 'a machine that tells you how to get to your destination; often in a car'

PRACTICE

Paraphrase the German words and phrases using the strategies in brackets:

Krankenschwester (definition/explanation)	*Dach* (comparison)
unangenehm (antonym)	*langweilig* (antonym)
Herbergsvater (definition/explanation)	*Garage* (comparison)

► SF 10 Working with closed test formats

In both lessons and written examinations you will come across test formats that don't ask you to write complete texts or answers to questions:

- *In **half-open formats** you write keywords only, e.g. when taking notes, completing tables or finishing sentences.*
- *In **closed test formats**, you don't write at all, but just indicate which of the given solutions is correct or which items go together. The most common forms are multiple-choice tasks, true/false statements, matching tasks and gapped texts (see below).*

Before an exam, ask your teacher which closed test formats you might expect.

The following strategies will help you deal with closed test formats.

Step 1: Preparing for the test

- Read the **instructions** carefully and work out what information you have to look for. It might help to underline keywords in the task.
- Try to **imagine** the situation of the text and anticipate what you might read or hear.

Step 2: Doing the test

- Focus on the **information that is necessary** to complete your task. Take notes. (► SF 15: Marking up a text / Making and taking notes)
- In **listening tasks**, complete as much as possible during the first listening. Use the second listening to add the missing information or to correct what you have done before. (► SF 22: Listening)
- Keep an eye on the time while working on **reading tasks**. Tasks that require you to read for gist only allow you a short time to skim the texts (► SF 14: Reading strategies). First work on the questions you are sure about, then go back to those you're struggling with.
- Never leave an **item unanswered**. If you do not know the answer, make a sensible guess – your chances of getting the credit for it are 25% in a multiple-choice task with four options!

Here are some specific tips for the different types of closed test formats:

Multiple-choice task (i.e. choosing the correct answer from multiple given options; cf. p. 162 above, task 1)

- Read the given options carefully – they may contain traps: They may use keywords from the text, but e.g. say the exact opposite of what is said in the text!
- If you are unsure which of the options is correct, go through them one by one and ask yourself why they might be incorrect.

True/false statements (i.e. classifying each given statement as 'true' or 'false'; cf. p. 123, task 2)

- In the case of false statements, you will typically find the opposite information in the text.
- In a half-open version of this format, you may be asked to give evidence for why you think an answer is right or wrong or to correct it.

Matching task (i.e. matching items from two lists, e.g. paragraphs with headings; cf. p. 46, task 1d)

- Don't match items just because they contain words or phrases that are similar. Instead, paraphrase the items and match those with a similar meaning.

Gapped text (i.e. identifying passages that have been left out of a text; cf. p. 108, task 1)

- Watch out for words that link sentences/ideas such as connectors (e.g. *therefore, moreover*), pronouns (e.g. *she, there, this*) or connected vocabulary (e.g. *bird – eagle, sparrow*) and pay attention to the sequence of time in the text. They may provide useful hints.
- After completing the text make sure that the grammar fits and the line of thought works (e.g. *cause and effect*).

Text skills

▶ SF 11 Analysing pictures

There are different types of pictures: photos, posters, paintings, drawings, or sketches. Often they are combined with written text, either as a title or a caption.

John Gast, *American Progress*, 1872

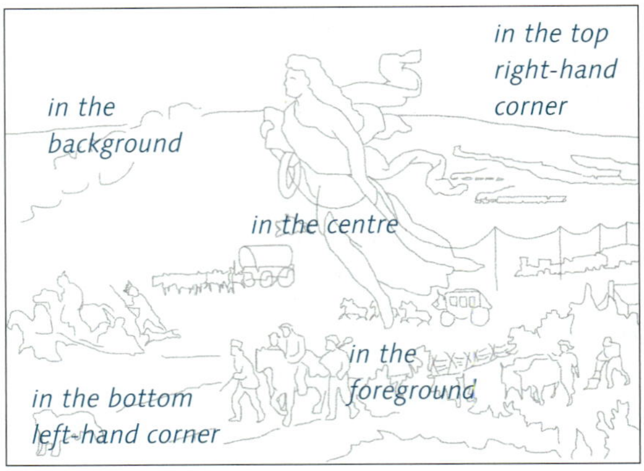

Step 1: Basic information

- State your first impression of the picture.
- Read the title or caption and identify the general topic.
- Check when (and where) the picture was created or published.

- *title: 'American Progress'*
- *general topic: American settlers moving west / conquering the continent*
- *artist, date: John Gast, 1872*

LANGUAGE HELP

- This picture/painting/photo/poster/drawing/sketch … shows / provides proof of / gives information on / introduces the topic of / conveys the impression that / depicts / portrays/ illustrates / is about/ …
- In the picture, … can be seen.

Step 2: Description

Choose one of these approaches:

- Start with the main subject, i.e. a dominant object, describe it in detail, then describe the background (useful for a picture with one dominant image).

  OR
- Start at the left of the picture and work across to the right or vice versa (useful for pictures with a lot of activity).

  OR
- Start at the top of the picture and work down to the bottom or vice versa (useful for pictures where the interest tails off towards the top or bottom).

- *dominant figure in the middle of the painting: woman, made to appear like a goddess or angel, holding a book in her left hand, moving towards the left of the picture, …*
- *painting shows landscape with a lot of detail*
- *right-hand side: bright, especially at the top; background: ships and railway lines*
- *in the bottom right-hand corner: farmers and a horse-drawn coach*
- *left-hand side: considerably darker / more threatening: clouds, ragged mountains, wild landscape*
- *bottom-left corner: Native Americans*
- *…*

Step 3: Analysis and interpretation

Draw conclusions about what the picture is meant to convey, whether it does this effectively and how it achieves its effect. You can look at …

- the technique, colours
- the effect on the viewer
- who is addressed and why
- the artist's/photographer's intention/ message.

- *right half of the painting (i.e. east) represents the American east (where the first settlers landed and lived); left half of the painting represents the 'wild west'*
- *colours and light: the east appears warm/bright; the west seems to be threatening and dark ('wild' west)*
- *all objects/people (trains, coaches, dominant figure) move from right to left → westward movement of American settlers → picture illustrates the idea of 'Manifest Destiny', which was …*
- *dominant figure. could represent culture, learning and progress (cf. the title); her angelic impression underlines the importance and positive connotation the artist places on those aspects*

LANGUAGE HELP

- The artist's/photographer's use of … creates … / conveys the impression of …
- By … the picture effectively illustrates …
- The dominance of … / The way the light/shadow … directs the viewer's attention to …
- As the foreground/ background is …, the impression given is that …
- … is a symbol of … / … helps to create an atmosphere of / which …
- This has the effect that …

Step 4: Evaluation

Evaluate the picture by describing its effect on you and by analysing how or how well it achieves an effect.

- *painting clearly/effectively illustrates the idea that American people were chosen by God to conquer the American continent*

PRACTICE

Analyse one of the pictures on p. 104.

▸ SF 12 Analysing charts and graphs

Charts and graphs present complex information visually. There are different types, e.g. pie charts, bar charts, line graphs or tables.

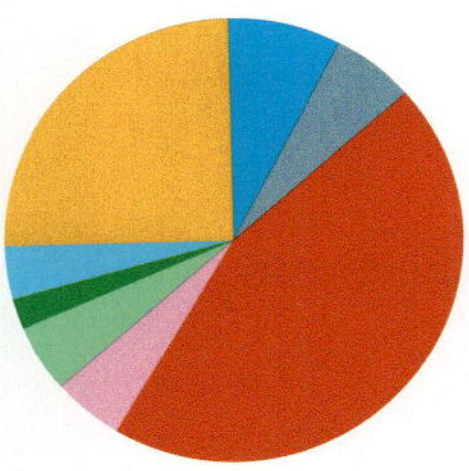

pie chart ('Tortendiagramm', 'Kreisdiagramm')

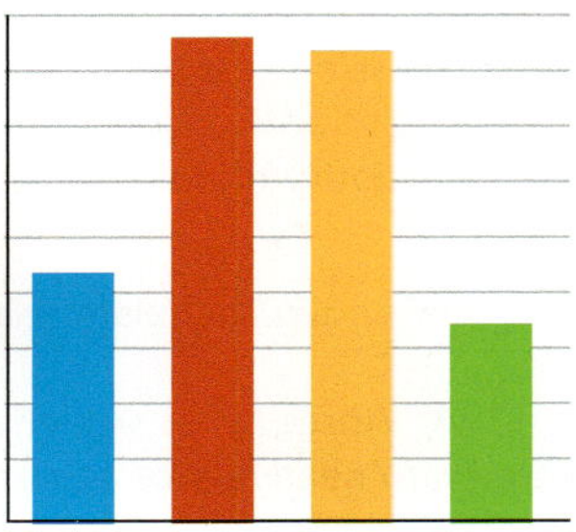

bar chart ('Säulendiagramm')

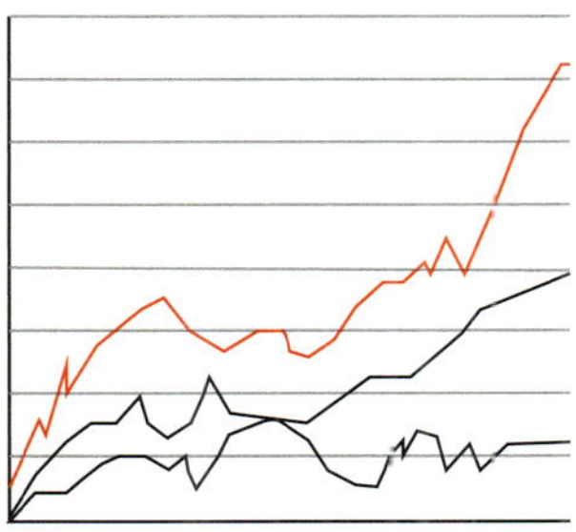

line graph ('Kurvendiagramm')

table ('Tabelle')

·····▸

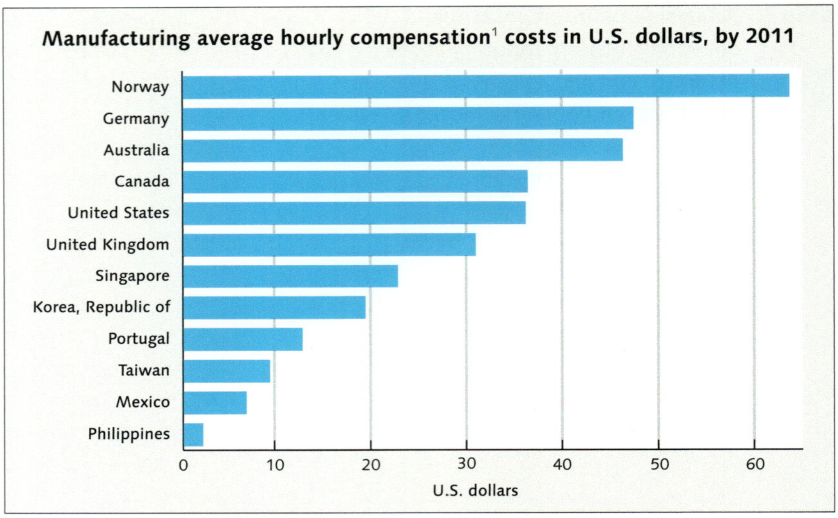

From: the website of the U.S. Department of Labor

When analysing charts and graphs like the one on the right, follow these three steps:

Step 1: Identify the type of chart or graph you are dealing with. Analyse the source:
- Is the source reliable?
- Is the data up to date?

- *bar chart*
- *source: U.S. Dept. of Labor: reliable*
- *data from 2011: not exactly up to date*

Step 2: Describe the graph/chart:
- What is it about and what information does it give?
- Does it show a development or does it compare different items at one point in time?
- Does it use absolute figures or percentages?

- *shows the differences in the hourly wage of workers in manufacturing in different countries in 2011*
- *gives the hourly compensation in $ (absolute numbers)*
- *compares data from 2011*
- *at the top of the ranking: countries with the highest hourly compensation (Norway: first, Philippines: last)*
- *countries at the bottom: hourly compensation is less than a sixth of the countries at the top*

LANGUAGE HELP

- The bar chart / pie chart / line graph / table … shows the different / compares the size/number of … / deals with / is about … / contrasts … with …
- It shows … in contrast to…
- It is taken from / It contains data from … / It was published in …

Bar chart:
- The bars are arranged horizontally/vertically.
- There are big/vast/surprising differences between …
- At the top/bottom of the ranking comes…
- … is first/last in rank
- … has the largest / second largest …

Pie chart:
- The chart is divided into … segments, which show/ represent …
- The smallest/biggest segment / The segments representing … and … constitute the majority … / A huge majority/minority is …

Line graph:
- The graph shows the relationship between … and …
- … is twice/three times as high as … / … There are more than / nearly twice as many … as there are …
- increase/decrease / reach a high point / rise/fall/ drop/ grow steadily

[1] **compensation** *wage*

Step 3: Draw conclusions from the chart/graph.

- *vast differences in the hourly wage → huge differences in the production costs of the goods → outsourcing of time-consuming jobs to countries with a lower hourly wage*

PRACTICE

Look at the table on the right and decide whether the figures would best be shown in a pie chart, a bar chart or a line graph and why. Use a computer to design the chart.

The world's most livable cities		
Rank	**City**	**Score (out of 100)**
1	Melbourne/Australia	97,5
2	Vienna/Austria	97,4
3	Vancouver/Canada	97,3
4	Toronto/Canada	97,2
5/6	Calgary/Canada Adelaide/Australia	96,6
7	Sydney/Australia	96,1
8	Helsinki/Finland	96,0
9	Perth/Australia	95,9
10	Auckland/New Zealand	95,7

From: *The Telegraph*, 6 August 2014

Find a tool to create infographics here:
Webcode context-57

► SF 13 Analysing cartoons

The following steps will help you to describe and analyse a cartoon systematically.

Step 1: Basic information

- What is your first impression of the cartoon?
  first impression: humorous, eye-catching, cartoon exaggerates a common school situation to illustrate a serious topic
- What is the cartoon about?
- What is its topic?
  topic: genetic engineering and its uncontrollable consequences
- (Where/when was it published?)

'Okay – is there anybody ELSE whose homework ate their dog?'

Step 2: Description

- Describe the cartoon systematically.
  - *classroom with students who all have brought colourful fantasy animals / monsters with them*
  - *in the background: blackboard with writing 'Genetic Engineering 101' (= name of the class); in front of the class: teacher looking angry*
  - *one student: putting up his hand, looking at his dinosaur-like animal*
  - *caption: the teacher's words*
- What people, events or trends does the cartoon refer to? Mention any labels, speech bubbles or captions. (► SF 11: Analysing pictures)

LANGUAGE HELP

- In the centre/foreground/background / At the top/bottom of …
- On the left/right side of the cartoon …
- Underneath there is … The caption reads …

Step 3: Analysis

The following questions may help you when analysing a cartoon:

- Are the figures or issues presented in a positive or negative light? How is this impression achieved?
- Does the cartoon make use of *symbols or *irony? Explain their use.
- Does the cartoon depict well-known persons? Who are they and what is their role in connection with the topic of the cartoon?
- What point is the cartoonist trying to make? What means are used to get the message across?
  - *cartoonist reverses a common classroom cliché: a common excuse for students who don't have their homework is that their dog ate their homework; here, the homework (i.e. the genetically engineered animal) has eaten the dog*
  - *illustrations of the fantasy animals: exaggerated, eye-catching, funny shapes and colours*
  - *cartoon = criticism of uncontrollability of genetic engineering; even experts (here: the teacher) are unable to control the risks*

LANGUAGE HELP

- The cartoon may be meant to show … / It is very eye-catching because of its use of … / It speaks to the observer directly by …
- The layout / use of colour / … is criticizing / making fun of …
- The cartoon conveys its message through … / brings its message across by …

Step 4: Evaluation

Is the cartoon effective or not? Give reasons, using your background knowledge about the topic.

*The cartoon criticizes the dangers of scientific research and genetic engineering effectively. To get its message across, it uses a funny twist by turning a well-known *cliché upside-down. By choosing a seemingly harmless setting to illustrate the devastating consequences of genetic engineering, the cartoonist criticizes it in a forceful way.*

'I'd like to change my major from electrical engineering to English or something.'

PRACTICE

Describe and analyse the cartoon on the left.

▸ SF 14 Reading strategies

When working with longer texts, there are different ways of reading. Which strategy you need to apply depends on what you want to do with your text: look for the main ideas or specific information, read for pleasure or analyse it. You also need to have a strategy to deal with unknown words (▸ SF 1: Dealing with unknown words).

SKIMMING

Skimming (or reading for gist) means going through a text quickly to identify its main ideas. This technique is helpful when there is lots of material to be taken in and only a limited amount of time, e.g. when you are doing research on a certain subject and you have to find out which texts could be relevant for your topic.

Step 1: Look at illustrations, pictures, keywords, headings or subheadings to get an idea of the content of the given text.

Step 2: Don't read every sentence. Let your eyes run over the whole text and look for words or phrases that contain useful information.

Step 3: Read the first and the last sentence of each paragraph – one of them usually states the main idea of that paragraph and the very last sentence of the text often contains a summary.

Step 4: Summarize the text. If you are able to do this without a problem, your skimming was probably successful.

SCANNING

Scanning means looking out for for specific information. You can use this technique when you want to find answers to a particular question or to compare particular aspects in different texts.

Step 1: Think of keywords or phrases that might be useful to search for when looking for the information you need.

Step 2: Move your eyes quickly down the page. Stop when you find a keyword or phrase and read the part where you found it. Then continue scanning the text.

EXTENSIVE READING

Extensive reading means reading for pleasure, e.g. when reading a novel. You read at your own speed and concentrate on what's happening (the events of the plot) without looking up unknown words.

CLOSE READING

Close reading is necessary when analysing a text (▸ SF 17–21). You will need to understand not only *what* is being said in the text, but also *how* it is being said. To do that, you will have to read the text more than once and make sure you understand every word.

PRACTICE

1 Skim the text 'Young, educated – and leaving the country' (p. 128) and note down what the text is about in a few words.
2 Scan the third paragraph of 'India then and now' (p. 104) for facts and figures showing which challenges India has to face.

▸ SF 15 Marking up a text / Making and taking notes

When working with photocopied texts or printouts, you can mark up important information so that you can find it more easily when you are working with the text again, e.g. when you are writing about it or preparing for a test.

> **TIP**
> When working with a borrowed book, put a transparency on the page and mark important information on it.

MARKING UP A TEXT

Step 1: As you read the text, bear in mind what information you are looking for. You may want to read the task/question again.

Step 2: When you find the relevant information in your text, mark it by underlining, highlighting or circling the relevant words or passages. Only mark key-words.

> **TIP**
> 1. Use different colours for different tasks.
> 2. Also mark words which show that a different opinion or a contrast is being introduced to help you understand the logical structure of the text.

Step 3: Finally, add headings or keywords in the margin or summarize passages with short phrases or sentences.

Tasks:
a Point out what recruiters do and how they work.
b Collect tips on how to write a CV to arouse a recruiter's interest.

How to please recruiters
Clare Whitmell

A recruiter can be your short cut into a new job. With a good understanding of industry trends – and insider knowledge of that particular employer's preferences and needs – a recruiter will be briefed to find exactly the right candidate with a specific set of skills, experience and qualities. To even be considered for the role, you need to make sure that your CV hits the right notes with them.

recruiters' knowledge
recruiters' tasks

Recruiters can be generalists working in a number of sectors or headhunters specialising in one, but there are a few pet hates they all share. Avoid these and you'll be giving yourself a better chance of getting into the yes pile each time. […]

recruiters' areas of work

Zena Everett, director and career coach at Second Careers and career guru at Mumsnet, has researched how headhunters, recruiters, employers and HR professionals screen CVs. She found that they all – without exception – looked first at the most recent work experience and job title. These must be relevant for the CV to get a second look in a competitive job market.

Show that your most recent work experience is relevant for the job.

For recruiters to put you forward to an employer, they need to see that your background matches the role. A simple way to ensure that you're giving your CV the best possible chance is to search the job description for key criteria, then make sure you include relevant details on your CV that show you're a good match.

Show that you fulfil the most important criteria for the new job.

From: *The Guardian*, 8 April 2014

MAKING AND TAKING NOTES

In cases where you cannot mark up a text (either because you are not working with your own book or because you are listening to an audio file), you can first *take notes* (i.e. extract important information from the text), then *make notes* (i.e. organize your ideas). Making notes will also help you structure your own ideas, e.g. after brainstorming or when preparing for a speaking task (▸ SF 8: Structuring ideas; ▸ SF 24–28).

► SF 16 Identifying text types (non-fiction)

In class you often have to analyse texts. The first step of the analysis is to identify the text type you are dealing with.

Texts can be classified into two main categories:

Fictional texts (i.e. literary texts, *Dichtung*, ► SF 19–21)	**Non-fictional texts** (i.e. *Sachtexte*, ► SF 18)
▪ The text describes a world that was created in the mind of its *author. ▪ Its *setting, *characters and events may or may not seem realistic.	▪ The text talks about the real world. ▪ It was written to convey information, convince the reader or criticize something.

Knowing what type of non-fictional text you're dealing with and what characteristic features this text type has will help you to anticipate what kind of information might be given and how it might be presented. Follow these steps:

Step 1: Skim the text (► SF 14: Reading strategies) and try to get a general idea of its content:
- Sum up in one or two sentences what the text is about.
- If possible, find out when and where it was published (newspaper, book, journal, website).

Step 2: Examine the text more closely. Look at:
- its content and purpose: Is the text meant to inform, persuade, entertain, …?
- its *style and *tone: Is the language formal or informal, simple or complex?

Step 3: Identify the text type. The following table will help you.

Non-fictional texts	
Text type and examples	**Contents and purpose**
Expository texts: *feature story, *news story, summary, etc.	▪ contain comprehensive and detailed information ▪ are intended to be objective and factual ▪ give no personal opinion ▪ describe a situation, scientific findings, historic occurrences
Descriptive texts: travel book, biography, etc.	▪ describe actual places, objects, events or people based on the writer's observations and impressions ▪ are intended to create a vivid picture in the reader's mind ▪ tend to give a lot of detail
Argumentative texts: *editorial, *column, *letter to the editor, *review, *speech, *comment, etc.	▪ discuss problems and controversial ideas ▪ evaluate a topic by giving reasons and stating the pros and cons of an issue ▪ show a clear line of argument ▪ tend to use expert opinions, statistics, quotations and technical/scientific language ▪ aim to convince the reader
Persuasive texts: *speech, advertisement, etc.	▪ use stylistic devices ▪ often use imperatives as an appeal to do something specific ▪ try to persuade or convince the reader/listener
Instructive texts: manual, brochure, etc.	▪ are intended to instruct the readers, tell them what to do or how to do it ▪ use imperatives and passive constructions (► LP 7: The passive)

► SF 17 Analysing stylistic devices

*When you listen to or read texts, you will normally notice that they have some kind of effect on you – you might strongly agree or disagree or you might feel amused, entertained, informed or perhaps irritated. This effect is created through the way the text is written, and especially by the *stylistic devices used. So when analysing texts, you should try to find out how certain effects are created. Stylistic devices may relate to sound (e.g. *alliteration), structure (e.g. *repetition, *parallelism) or meaning (e.g. *imagery).*

Step 1: When reading the text pay attention to the effects that certain passages have on you.

Step 2: Study the passages in question to find the stylistic devices that create these effects. In the table below there are some examples.

Step 3: Consider why these effects may have been intended in this context. (► SF 36: Writing a text analysis)

TIP

If you cannot pinpoint any specific effects while listening or reading, you can try it the other way round: Study the text for the most common stylistic devices (cf. the table below) and see if you can find a reason why the author may have used them.

Example	Effect	Stylistic device
'The most restless, the most adventurous, the most innovative, the most industrious of people […].' From: William J. Clinton, 'The changing face of America', 13 June 1998; cf. *Context* p. 24, ll. 14ff.	▪ reader/listener may feel overwhelmed, impressed by positive qualities	▪ *enumeration of superlatives
'What do the changes mean? They can either strengthen and unite us, or they can weaken and divide us.' From: William J. Clinton, 'The changing face of America', 13 June 1998; cf. *Context* p. 24, ll. 27ff.	▪ reader/listener may feel drawn into the argumentation by being asked a direct question ▪ reader/listener feels a little under pressure, even manipulated to answer the question in a specific way	▪ *rhetorical question ▪ *contrast of two possible answers: one with strongly positive, the other with strongly negative *connotations
'With a growing UK Muslim population currently standing at 2.7 million (Census 2011) with a £20.5 billion a year spending power and expected to rise to 5.5 million people by 2030 (Pew Report, *The Future of the Global Muslim Population* 2011) access to delicious halal food in the UK is becoming increasingly important.' From: the website of HalalFocus; cf. *Context* p. 72, ll. 15ff.	▪ reader may feel convinced by factual information / objective numbers	▪ statistical data ▪ reliable sources (Pew Report)
'Many Indians despair over the divisiveness[1] of caste and would prefer to wish it away. However, the hold of the Indian way of life is also a bulwark[2] against the onslaught[3] of the global culture.' From: Gurcharan Das, *India Unbound*, 2001; cf. *Context* p. 106, ll. 14ff.	▪ reader may have difficulty understanding individual words, may find this irritating	▪ *register, sophisticated/academic choice of words ('divisiveness', 'hold', 'bulwark', 'onslaught')

[1] **divisiveness** force that splits people into different groups [2] **bulwark** *(fml)* thing that protects sth. [3] **onslaught** strong attack

From the beginning of a job advert for a park ranger: 'Yes, you read right. As our ex-island caretaker is regretfully handing over the keys to his island hacienda[4] we're looking for someone to take his place.' From: the website of the Queensland tourism board, 5 March 2013; cf. *Context* p. 200, ll. 1ff.	▪ reader may feel directly addressed and involved, connected to the writer	▪ direct address of reader without introduction ▪ imitation of spoken language, of personal interaction ▪ use of personal pronouns ('we', 'you')
'For me, school had been a Darwinian exercise. A daily gauntlet[5] of ridicule, abuse, and isolation.' From: Ernest Cline, *Ready Player One*, 2012; cf. *Context* p. 212, ll. 21ff.	▪ reader will be able to picture the situation very clearly	▪ *images/*metaphors ('Darwinian exercise', 'gauntlet of ridicule') ▪ incomplete sentence
'War is as old as Europe. Our continent bears the scars of spears and swords, canons and guns, trenches[6] and tanks[7], and more.' From: Herman Van Rompuy, 'From war to peace', 10 December 2012; cf. *Context* p. 127	▪ reader gets a lively idea of the wounds inflicted on Europe through war ▪ list of nouns draws reader's attention to the numerous weapons which caused the injuries	▪ *personification of an object ('continent bears the scars') ▪ alliterations ('spears and swords', 'trenches and tanks')
'I fear the day technology will surpass our human interaction. The world will have a generation of idiots.' (Albert Einstein)	▪ reader may be taken aback by this provocative statement ▪ the reader's interest will be aroused	▪ *exaggeration (to stress a point)
'... we're talking the ultimate reality TV, where the public can monitor [...] prisoners' whole lives on death row[8]. They can [...] make up their own minds about a convict's worthiness for punishment. Then each week, viewers across the globe can cast a vote to decide which prisoner is executed next. It's humanity in action – the next logical step toward true democracy.' From: DBC Pierre, *Vernon God Little*, 2003; cf. *Context* p. 223, ll. 9ff.	▪ reader will be irritated/ shocked by the description of the game show as 'humanity in action' ▪ text evokes indignation	▪ *irony: author uses the term 'humanity in action' to denote the exact opposite: a truly inhumane TV show

When analysing the effects created by a text, make sure you also pay attention to its *tone (i.e. the way a writer treats his/her topic). The tone may be formal, intimate, playful, ironic, humorous, etc.)

LANGUAGE HELP

The author	uses employs makes use of	a metaphor a simile enumeration irony personification	to illustrate ... to show ... to emphasize ... to underline ... to draw the reader's attention to ...

[4]**hacienda** large farm [5]**gauntlet** fight with a lot of people attacking you [6]**trench** *Schützengraben*
[7]**tank** *Panzer* [8]**death row** cells for prisoners who are waiting to be executed

▸ SF 18 Analysing non-fiction

*When analysing a non-fictional text you have to say more than just what it is about. You have to find out what type of text it is, for example a *feature story, an *editorial or a *comment (▸ SF 16: Identifying text types). By looking at how its content, its structure and its language interact you can find out what its function and its message might be.*

Here is an excerpt from a newspaper article written by a young British woman. Analyse the way she presents her own experiences as a non-white woman in Great Britain.

Step 1: Read the text and decide what type of text it is. Collect extracts that help you analyse the text, e.g. its line of argument, *stylistic devices, choice of words, etc. (cf. the highlighted passages). (▸ SF 17: Analysing stylistic devices)

> ... It's not that I'm embarrassed about my ethnic background. I don't think about it much, though it's good for jokes ('I'm half Iranian, half American – so basically, I hate myself'). But some people seem to want me to think about it. 'Why don't you visit Bombay?' they enthuse. 'You'd love it.' They may be right, but have yet to explain to me why I'd love it more than Tokyo, or Guatemala, or any of the other places I haven't yet been. It's an odd misconception that you should somehow feel connected to a far-flung country because your ancestors lived there centuries ago, even if your entire life has been spent morris dancing[1] in Loughborough.

From: Ariane Sherine, 'It may not be racist, but ...', *The Guardian*, 3 March 2010

Step 2: Organize your findings. Make sure all examples e.g. for stylistic devices go together.

- *line of argument: does not think much about her background (l. 1), people seem to think she ought to care about it (ll. 3–4), she thinks her parents' country of origin is just as relevant for her as any other country (ll. 5–7)*
- **humour: joke (ll. 2–3), compares her parents' country of origin with other countries she does not know (ll. 5–7)*
- *choice of words: 'odd misconception' (l. 7), 'far-flung country' (l. 8), 'ancestors' (l. 9), 'morris dancing' (l. 10): humorous*
- **stylistic devices: *exaggeration 'centuries ago' (l. 9), quotations (ll. 4–5)*

Step 3: Analyse the effect that is created by the stylistic devices that you have identified.

- **humour, choice of words: give the text a light-hearted tone*
- *quotations: help the reader imagine the specific situation, make the text more lively*
- **exaggeration: shows how absurd she finds other people's ideas*
- *light-hearted tone: she's not seriously offended*

Step 4: Examine the connection between the effect identified in **Step 3** and the author's line of argument.

- *readers ought to realize how ridiculous it is to keep identifying the descendants of immigrants with their parents' country of origin, to not accept them as fellow-citizens*
- *no acid criticism, no fierce accusation of racism, but a fairly lighthearted account of people's everyday misconceptions*

[1] **morris dance** *(v)* do a traditional English dance

TIP

When working on **Step 1** do not only follow the chronology of the text and wait until something catches your eye. Make sure you examine the text systematically by checking its use of stylistic devices, its choice of words, etc.

LANGUAGE HELP

- The author uses vivid/colloquial/objective/emotive … language.
- The sentences are long-winded/paratactical/simple/complex/ …
- The author's tone is friendly/humorous/critical/optimistic/sarcastic …
- His/her choice of words underlines …
- The stylistic devices used support/emphasize/underline …
- The reader can easily picture the situation / follow her/his train of thought / line of argument …

► SF 19 Analysing narrative prose

*When you have to analyse a *short story, a *novel or any other narrative text you are usually asked to pay attention to one or two specific aspects. The most common aspects for a text analysis are:*

Aspect	Example
Character constellations or relationships (► SF 35: Writing a character profile) ▪ Who is in the story? ▪ What relationships do the *characters have to each other? Are they dependent on each other/equals, etc.? ▪ Do they belong to similar/different groups (social/ethnic, etc.)? ▪ Do they serve as foils for each other, i.e. do they contrast with another character to highlight particular qualities of the other character? ▪ How does the author characterize them, *directly or *indirectly? ▪ Are the characters *round or *flat?	High-school student Mitch is a reporter for the school magazine and on his way to his first interview with his former PE-teacher McNulty: I parked my mom's Ford Focus by the gym, eased out of the front seat, and looked around. When I spotted McNulty loading tackling sleds[1] into a school van, I tensed. To him, I'd always be a fat loser and nothing more. But a reporter has to have the courage to approach people, ask them questions [...]. From: Carl Deuker, *Payback Time*, 2010; cf. *Context* p. 198, ll. 1ff. ▪ *reporter and coach share a history* ▪ *reporter feels inferior; tries to overcome his fear* ▪ …
The narrator or the narrative perspective ▪ Who is telling the story and to whom? Is it a *first-person or a *third-person narrator? ▪ How much does the narrator know or not know? What are the limiting factors? Does the narrator have a *limited or an *unlimited point of view (cf. *omniscient narrator)?	Some nights I lie next to Tony, here in America where I live like a worm avoiding the sunlight, and I wonder if he knows. And is it only because it was his brother that he does not sense that another man's body has come between us. From: Shauna Singh Baldwin, *English Lessons*, 1996; cf. *Context* p. 118, ll. 46ff. ▪ *first person narrator (*protagonist), probably female, might be an immigrant* ▪ *tells the reader a secret that apparently the husband does not know; but since the narrator cannot know the husband's thoughts, neither he/she nor the reader know for sure* ▪ …

[1] **tackling sled** *Angriffsschlitten (schweres Trainingsgerät im American Football)*

The *plot

- How are the events connected by cause and effect to form a plot?
- How does the author attract or keep the reader's attention by creating *tension or *suspense?
- Is there a *climax and/or a *turning point?
- Does the story have an ending or a conclusion? Or is there an *open ending / a *denouement?

Dan, a high-school student whose parents have recently lost their jobs, is approached by another student, who tries to recruit him for a protest march:

> I felt myself tense. All my friends, plus a couple of kids at the sign-up table, were watching and listening. 'Why do you ask?' 'Seems like a good time,' he said. Had he heard that we'd lost our home? Did he think that would make me more sympathetic to his cause? 'Why's that?' I gave him a hard look.

From: Todd Strasser, *No Place*, 2014; cf. *Context* p. 30, ll. 4ff.

- **tension between characters is building up*
- **suspense: reader does not know if the secret is going to be discovered*
- ...

The *setting and the *atmosphere

- Where and when does the action take place?
- Are there any people? How do they react to the setting?
- How does the setting influence the atmosphere? (E.g. sunny spring days usually create an optimistic atmosphere, a crowded place may create a tense or exciting atmosphere, etc.)
- Are you told directly or do you have to draw your own conclusions?

Her Majesty the Queen is on her way to open Parliament:

> One of the Queen's recurrent royal responsibilities was to open Parliament, an obligation she had never previously found particularly burdensome[1] and actually rather enjoyed: to be driven down the Mall[2] on a bright autumn morning even after fifty years was something of a treat.

From: Alan Bennett, *The Uncommon Reader*, 2008; cf. *Context* p. 62, ll. 1ff.

- *autumn, sunny*
- *the Queen: about to do a job she enjoys*
- *positive atmosphere (to be concluded from the setting)*
- ...

LANGUAGE HELP

- The relationship between the characters is strongly influenced by ... Their power struggle reveals itself when ... Their lack of communication shows ...
- X's behaviour when ... reveals that ...
- The description underlines/emphasizes ... / conveys the impression that ...
- The image suggests ...
- By using words like ... the author stresses ...
- The overall effect is ... It can be portrayed as ...
- The perspective is biased/one-sided ...
- As the first-person narrator has a limited perspective, the reader must ... The author chose an omniscient narrator because ...
- The story has an open ending, so ...
- In the end the conflict is solved when ...

[1] **burdensome** implying hard work [2] **the Mall** road leading to Buckingham Palace

▸ SF 20 Analysing drama

*A *drama or *play is a script in which a *playwright presents what *characters say and what they do. A drama is written to be performed on stage, so when you read a play, you will enjoy it more if you imagine what it would look and sound like on stage.*

When analysing drama, typical aspects to look at are:

Aspect	Examples and explanations
Structure ▪ Is the play divided up into ***acts** and ***scenes** or is there a different structure? ▪ What function do these divisions have in the play? ▪ Do they correspond to action, time, place or a combination of these?	▪ Shakespeare's plays used to be performed without intermissions – *rhyming couplets would indicate the end of one scene. Nowadays his plays are conventionally edited to have four or five acts and scene divisions, which usually mark a change in the set of characters on stage. ▪ Most modern plays have two or three acts. Some (e.g. *Artefacts*, cf. pp. 68f.) have no act division at all and are meant to be performed without a break. Still, *Artefacts* is divided into three parts, which are set in the two different countries. *Clybourne Park* (cf. pp. 21f.) has two acts, separated by a time gap of 50 years.
The construction of action ▪ Does the script contain ***stage directions**? If so, what information do they provide? ▪ How does the **action** unfold through the **dialogue**? ▪ Are there ***monologues**? What function do they have? ▪ What kind of **language** is used?	▪ In *Clybourne Park* (cf. pp. 21f.) there are some stage directions. They describe how actors should speak certain lines or move (e.g. 'chuckles with amazement, shakes his head', p. 22, ll. 109f.), but there are very few descriptions of settings or actions except at the beginnings of each of the two acts. ▪ Dramatic dialogue has to be very carefully constructed (and yet sound realistic) so that it never gets boring and gives enough clues about what is actually happening. ▪ Monologues usually serve to show a character's thoughts to the audience, but not to the other characters, i.e. they are not part of the interaction. Shakespeare often made use of them to give the audience more insight into a character's mind. ▪ In the extract from *Macbeth* (cf. pp. 168f.) Lady Macbeth uses aggressive language, calling her husband a coward when he hesitates to commit the murder as planned. His question 'If we should fail?' shows his hesitation, whereas her answer 'We fail!' shows her determination to succeed (cf. p. 168, ll. 36f.). This interchange actually drives the action forward because it serves to persuade Macbeth to act as planned. ▪ In *Artefacts*, Kelly's informal language (cf. pp. 68f.) serves to characterize her as a modern British teenager and makes the dialogue more realistic, e.g. 'Yeah, all right then, tell me what I think.' (ll. 69)

·····▸

Characters (► SF 35: Writing a character profile) ▪ Who are the *characters? ▪ What information do we get about them and what issues do they have to deal with in the play?	▪ Normally it's not the playwright who tells us directly about the characters, but as in real life we get an idea of them through the way they act or talk about themselves, their lives or about others. *Monologues in particular can give the audience an insight into a character's motivations, feelings or problems.
▪ Do they develop over the course of the play?	▪ Macbeth (cf. pp. 76f.) develops from a man reluctant to kill into a ruthless murderer. In *Artefacts* (cf. pp. 68f.) Kelly first refuses to go to Iraq, but later we see that she has actually gone there.
▪ Do they stand for a particular idea or are they part of the play's message?	▪ In *Clybourne Park* (cf. pp. 21f.), the members of the white community who oppose black neighbours represent racist ideas. Lady Macbeth (cf. pp. 76f.) represents ruthless ambition as she is even willing to commit murder to achieve the ultimate success she wants.
Audience ▪ What does the audience know or see that the characters don't know or see?	▪ In Shakespeare's *Romeo and Juliet*, Romeo has heard that Juliet is dead and kills himself. The audience however knows that she only looks dead – an example of *dramatic irony.
▪ What is left to the audience's imagination?	▪ Sometimes characters speak of actions that do not actually happen on stage, even though they are important for the plot.

LANGUAGE HELP

- The play is divided into … acts and … scenes / The development of the action corresponds with the play's division into acts/scenes …
- The overall theme of the play is …
- In the play the conflicts develop between …
- The audience is drawn into the plot by … / The action is supposed to please/shock/enrage/fascinate the audience …
- The … act ends in a cliffhanger / In the end the conflict is solved …
- The stage directions draw a concise picture of the scenery / There are almost no stage directions, so … / The play works with almost no props / a bare stage …
- Even though X appears as a friendly character at first, he later shows … / … stands for / represents …
- The social differences between the characters can be seen in the language they use … / The characters speak in blank verse …

The Globe Theatre, London

TIP

**play* = Theaterstück
**drama* = Drama (i.e. text form), e.g. *modern drama or Elizabethan drama* (i.e. the plays produced during the time when Queen Elizabeth I reigned)
**playwright, dramatist* = Stückeschreiber/in, Dramatiker/in
**character* = Figur
**actor, actress* = Schauspieler/in

► SF 21 Analysing poetry

*When you are asked to analyse a poem, you should not only look at its poetic features such as its form, its *rhythm or its language, you must also look at its content and link this to the poem's form. Only then will you be able to fully understand what the poem conveys.*

Here is a poem by Gavin Ewart, followed by a step-by-step guide.

Ending *Gavin Ewart*

The love we thought would never stop
now cools like a congealing[1] chop[2].
The kisses that were hot as curry
are bird-pecks[3] taken in a hurry.
The hands that held electric charges
now lie inert[4] as four moored barges[5].
The feet that ran to meet a date
are running slow and running late.
The eyes that shone and seldom shut
are victims of a power cut.
The parts that then transmitted joy
are now reserved and cold and coy[6].
Romance, expected once to stay,
has left a note saying gone away.

From: Poetry Archive

Step 1: Read the poem two or three times, then summarize it in one or two sentences. Consider
- the poem's title, *setting and *theme
- the *speaker and the addressee
- the link between the title and the poem's content.

- two people in a relationship that has lasted for some time
- title: ending of a relationship
- couple: one person is speaker, one is addressee
- contrast: what the relationship was like before and what it is like now

Step 2: Look at the poem's structure (*stanzas, *rhythm, *rhyme scheme, *metre). (It may help to read the poem out loud to get a feeling for the way it sounds.)
- Is it built regularly or are there interruptions in the rhythm or rhyme scheme?
- Is there a *refrain?
- Is it a *sonnet?

*- seven *couplets*
- each couplet rhymes (aa, bb, cc, etc.) → regular pattern, conventional
- regular metre, regular rhyme scheme

·····►

[1] **congeal** (here) become unpleasantly dry [2] **chop** thick slice of meat with a bone attached to it [3] **peck** quick kiss/bird's bite [4] **inert** unable to move [5] **moored barge** *(here)* small boat that has been fixed to land [6] **coy** not willing to give away much about yourself

Step 3: Examine the poem's language more closely. Look for
- *imagery, e.g. *simile, *metaphor, *analogy, *personification
- sound effects, e.g. *alliteration, *assonance, *onomatopoeia
- *contrasts, *repetitions and specific sentence structures (simple/complex sentence, *enjambement)
- mythological/literary/social/historical references
- *symbols.

- *contrast between past and present, e.g. 'love that never ends' (l. 1) ↔ 'congealing chop' (l. 2)*
- *changes are conveyed through descriptions of body parts: hand (l. 5), feet (l. 7), eyes (l. 9), parts (l. 11)*
- *vivid images for love in the past, e.g. 'hot curry' (l. 3), 'electric charges' (l. 5)*
- *images of disconnectedness/cold/passiveness of love today, e.g. 'lie inert as four moored barges' (l. 6), 'power cut' (l. 10)*
- *personification: 'romance' (l. 13)*
- *short and simple sentences*
- *down-to-earth metaphors*

Step 4: Describe the poem's effect and analyse how it is achieved by connecting your findings on its form to its content.

- *clear and regular structure → monotony, conventionality*
- *clear and precise images → easy to understand, common problem*
- …

→ lack of drama

LANGUAGE HELP

- The poem by … deals with/is about … In the poem … describes/reflects on … The poet addresses the topic of …
- The title reminds the reader of …/refers to …
- The poem is made up of …/consists of … verses/stanzas.
- The rhyme scheme is …/There is no consistent rhyme scheme. The word … rhymes with … The use of … creates a certain rhythm.
- Line … runs into line …, which emphasizes …
- The poet employs specific images, such as metaphors or similes, in order to …
- The diction/register is simple/colloquial/formal, which intensifies the feeling of …
- The most prominent stylistic device used in the poem is …, which serves to …
- All in all, … The overall effect is … The poem aims to show/illustrate/convey/express the idea that … The overall message of the poem is …

Listening and viewing skills

▶ SF 22 Listening

When you have to deal with a listening task at school, you are normally first given time to read the questions you will have to answer. These questions may be closed such as multiple choice (▶ SF 10: Working with closed test formats) but they can also be more open. After reading the tasks you are usually allowed to listen to the audio file twice.

> **TIP**
>
> In contrast to listening at school, you will not normally have the opportunity to listen to something twice in real life situations, e.g. to a train announcement. You then need to be able to identify relevant information right away – or you may ask people for clarification who have listened to the same thing. In a conversation, you may ask the speaker to repeat what they have said.

LISTENING FOR GIST

Listening for gist is what you do to find out what the main topic of a spoken text is, e.g. when you want to see if an audio file is relevant for you.

Step 1: Before listening for gist, collect information on the following if possible:
- the text type (e.g. newscast, lecture, panel discussion, interview) and its addressee
- the situation and *setting
- the number of speakers and their role in the audio file. For example, will there be conflicting points of view?
- the topic dealt with in the audio file and what points of view or concepts you are likely to encounter.

Step 2: When listening for gist,
- do not try to understand every detail that is said
- watch out for 'signpost expressions' that show somebody's train of thought, e.g. *the biggest issue is …, the most important argument is, on the one hand …*
- listen carefully to a speaker's intonation; it may help you identify their attitudes or intentions.

Step 3: Summarize the text so as to prove that you can identify its topic.

LISTENING FOR DETAIL

You listen for detail if you need specific information, e.g. tips given for a specific problem.

Step 1: Before listening for detail,
- remember what you know about the text (its speaker, addressee, situation, setting and/or topic) and try to anticipate what might be said in the text
- collect keywords that are relevant to your question, e.g. names, dates or numbers
- prepare your notepad so that you can take notes quickly. (▶ SF 15: Marking up a text / Making and taking notes)

Step 2: When listening for detail,
- watch out for the keywords you collected
- take notes, using abbreviations and symbols.

▸ SF 23 Analysing a film

*Watching a film can make you laugh or cry, feel angry or scared. Those reactions are not only caused by the story the film tells but also by the way it tells its story. Just like written texts can provoke a reaction in their readers through the choice of words and *stylistic devices, films can achieve a certain response in the viewer through, for example, their camera work, editing and sound.*

BEFORE VIEWING

Step 1: Find out what kind of film you are going to watch and try to get an idea of what to expect by looking at available information on the film (e.g. film posters, reviews, DVD covers, magazine information). What genre does it belong to (feature film, documentary, video clip, commercial, etc.)?

WHILE VIEWING

Step 1: Watch one or more scenes and make notes on how the characters act, what the *setting is like or what information is presented. You may also add some observations on cinematic devices such as camera angle, sound and light. A **viewing log** can help you structure your notes. Here is one example for the first scene of *Never Let Me Go* (you may choose other categories to serve your own purposes):

Scene	What?	Where?	Who?	Camera	Sound	Light	Effect
1	*a patient (Tommy) is being prepared for a surgery*	*hospital: operating room*	*carer (Kathy) and patient*	*close-up of Kathy, over-the-shoulder shot towards Tommy → Kathy's point of view*	*only voice-over of Kathy, no other sound*	*operating room is illuminated, no additional light*	*very emotional*
...	...	...	...	...	...	...	...

Step 2: Watch the specific scenes once more and have a closer look at the cinematic devices used and the effect they achieve. Add your observations to your viewing log. The table below may help you.

Camera angle/movement or sound	Example	Possible effect
The camera seems to be looking through the eyes of the character or is looking directly over his or her shoulder (**over-the-shoulder shot**). One character's face is shown in **close-up** (cf. the picture on the right), while the other characters are presented through **long** or **medium shots**.		Close-up: the character's emotions are revealed and you identify with that character.
A character is shown through a **low-angle shot**.		The character appears bigger. He or she seems to be dominant, i.e. to have power over the other characters in this scene.

A character is shown through a **high-angle shot**.		The character appears smaller. He or she seems to be inferior, i.e. to have less power than the other characters in this scene.
Two or more characters are shown through **eye-level shots**.		The characters appear to be on the same level.
The scene is rather dark. People and objects cannot be clearly distinguished. The **soundtrack** is eerie or moves towards a *climax.		The viewer may feel tense or scared.
There are short **shots** and lots of **cuts**. ***Flashbacks** (showing past events) or **flash-forwards** (showing future events) are used.		The *action is fast-paced and exciting.
The camera takes a steady position.		The action appears slower.
The music is uplifting, pleasant or catchy.		The viewer feels relaxed and in a good mood.

LANGUAGE HELP

- The film is about … / shows … / tells the story of …
- The music intensifies/fades as … / creates/builds tension/suspense/joy/…
- The actor's body language and facial expressions add to the feeling of …
- In this scene the music and lyrics / the props support the plot / underline the feeling of …
- The soundtrack/lighting/editing establishes/reinforces the mood of the scene.
- The camera movement creates a feeling of …
- The camerawork/soundtrack helps to … / underlines/emphasizes …
- The close-ups reveal his/her emotional state.
- The props characterize her as a … person.

DVD **PRACTICE**

You are going to watch an extract from *The Hunger Games*, a 2012 science fiction film. It depicts a dystopian state in which every year a group of teenagers, the 'tributes', are forced to take part in a televised event and fight each other to the death until only the victor remains alive. In the extract you are going to watch the protagonist Katniss is being chased by other tributes.

1 Watch the extract and use a viewing log to structure your observations. Work with a partner to complete your notes.

2 The extract is full of contrasts: the wild forest vs. the television headquarters, Katniss on her own vs. the group of other tributes, the wild chase vs. a moment of rest when the other tributes let Katniss be for some time. Choose one of the contrasts, watch the extract again and examine the cinematic devices used to create this contrast.

Speaking skills (monologues and dialogues)

▸ SF 24 Giving a presentation

Informing an audience about a topic is an important skill to master and one that will be useful not only in school (classroom presentations, etc.) but also in later life (university, work, etc.). To give a successful presentation the following steps may be a helpful guide.

PLANNING A PRESENTATION

Step 1: Find out about the general framework for your talk, e.g.
- its topic
- the time limit for your presentation
- your audience and their background knowledge of the topic
- the kind of equipment available (smartboard, blackboard, flip chart, digital/video projector, laptop).

Step 2: Research your subject and make notes in English. (▸ SF 15: Marking up a text / Making and taking notes; ▸ SF 5: Doing research)
- If you are working in a team, decide who is going to work on which aspect.
- Use different sources so that you cover all relevant aspects and your information is reliable.

PREPARING A PRESENTATION

Step 1: Decide what information you need and work out a structure for it. (▸ SF 8: Structuring ideas)

Step 2: Think of ways to make your talk interesting and easy to understand for your audience:
- Plan the beginning of your presentation carefully: refer to interesting facts or give anecdotes which lead to the topic of your presentation.
- Remember the KISS-rule: **K**eep **i**t **s**hort and **s**imple!
- Keep your audience's attention by naming interesting or funny details or examples.
- Check whether there are words or phrases that need to be explained to the audience so that they can follow your presentation.
- If suitable, prepare charts, visuals, diagrams, etc. to present facts and figures visually. (▸ SF 7: Making visual aids)

Step 3: Prepare a handout or poster or use a presentation programme to accompany your presentation:
- Design them in a way that helps your audience to follow your presentation (cf. the tips on the right).
- Proofread your material. (▸ SF 40: Proofreading)
- Before the actual presentation, make sure that any electronic media you want to use are working and that you can handle them.

Find a tool to make your poster here:
Webcode context-50

TIP

When preparing a **poster** or **wall display**:
- Give it a clear structure or line of thought that guides the reader through the various sections of the poster.
- Make it visually attractive and informative.
- Present complex information visually, e.g. through diagrams.
- Keep a good balance between visuals and written information.
- Make sure that the writing can be read from the back of the room.
- Use bullet-points, short sentences or key-words and try to avoid any redundancies.
- Indicate the sources you used.

When preparing a **handout**:
- Decide if you want to distribute it before the presentation so that it helps your audience to follow your talk (in that case it might make sense to leave room for notes) or if you want to hand it out after the presentation to remind your audience of the main points (in that case tell them that a handout will be distributed at the end).
- Give it a clear structure.
- Present the most important information, key quotations, diagrams and/or charts on it.
- Use bullet-points, short sentences or key-words and try to avoid any redundancies.
- Indicate the sources you used.

Step 4: If you are giving your presentation in a team
- decide who is going to present which parts
- check that the different parts add up to a coherent presentation
- make sure that everybody takes part in the presentation.

Step 5: Prepare notes that will guide you through your presentation and help you to speak freely without reading from the page. (► SF 15: Marking up a text / Making and taking notes)

> **TIP**
> Write keywords or notes on index cards, number the cards and use only them during your presentation.

Step 6: Practise your presentation:
- Look up the pronunciation of difficult words in a dictionary.
- Practise your presentation in front of friends or a mirror or record it, e.g. using a smartphone. If you are doing a team presentation, practise as a team.
- Make sure you don't exceed your time limit.

Find an online dictionary here: **Webcode** context-52

Find a recording tool here: **Webcode** context-55

DOING A PRESENTATION

Step 1: Give your presentation:
- Wait until the audience are quiet, then greet them and give an overview of your presentation.

> **LANGUAGE HELP**
> 'Hello everybody. My talk today is going to be on … First I will give you a general idea of … After that I will tell you more about … At the end of the talk I will explain why … and give you some examples.'

- Speak clearly, loudly and not too fast. Make suitable pauses.
- Speak freely and don't read out complete sentences.
- Avoid extremely long sentences and too many figures or new words. Remember that your audience can only listen to your presentation once.
- Refer to your poster, wall display or handout if appropriate, but don't read it out word for word.
- Try to maintain eye-contact with your classmates.
- If you use new or difficult words, help your audience by writing them on the board and explaining them.

> **TROUBLE SPOT**
> ***word by word*** = *one word at a time, one word after the other*
> ***word for word*** = *in exactly the same words*

Step 2: Round off your presentation by
- summarizing the most important aspects
- thanking your audience for their attention
- asking them if they have any questions.

> **LANGUAGE HELP**
> 'So, as I have pointed out, … It is important to keep in mind that … That was my presentation on … Thank you for listening. I hope you enjoyed my/our presentation. Do you have any questions?'

► SF 25 Giving a speech

*When you give a speech you want to reach your audience and persuade them of your point of view on a topic. In order to achieve this goal, you need two things: firstly, a well-structured text with carefully chosen words and *stylistic devices and secondly, an effective way of delivering it.*

PLANNING A SPEECH

Step 1: Find out about the general framework for your speech, e.g.

- its topic
- the time available
- the purpose of your speech: do you want it to inspire people / lead to a specific action / …?
- your audience and their background knowledge / attitudes.

- *task: convince your student body council that your school should become more environmentally friendly*
- *purpose: lead to action*
- *audience: some students have talked about it in class; some might be tackling the issue already*

Step 2: Brainstorm and/or research your topic: collect any ideas, stories or arguments that fit your topic and form your own opinion on it. Make notes (► SF 15: Marking up a text / Making and taking notes).

- *things you can do every day, e.g. separate rubbish, turn off lights, don't use paper cups for your coffee, …*
- *may be inconvenient at first, but will become normal*

PREPARING A SPEECH

Step 1: From your ideas choose essential points that are relevant to your topic and the message you wish to get across to your audience. Make notes and organize them

- by structuring them into introduction/body/conclusion (► SF 8: Structuring ideas)
- by choosing the best two to five ideas for the body of your speech and putting them in a suitable order (► SF 8: Structuring ideas).

- *introduction: watching* The Day after Tomorrow *made me depressed – how can I make a change?*
- *body: little things done by normal people can make a change; it's no use blaming politicians for not acting; …*
- *conclusion: be the change!*

Step 2: Unless you are a highly experienced speaker, write out your complete speech:

- Choose the correct *register for your specific audience, e.g. scientific, colloquial, … (► LP 11: Using the right register).
- Refer to your own experience.
- Use clear and short sentences. Make logical connections clear by using linking words (► SF 38: Writing a well-structured text).

- *register: colloquial, e.g. 'Look at this school. We are a huge number of people. Think about the mountain of rubbish we produce every day. Is it really necessary?'*
- *personal experience: 'We throw away a lot of different things at school: paper, Kleenex, sweet wrappers, broken pens.'*
- *short sentences: 'So, take a stand. Ask the school for separate bins for paper, plastic and other rubbish.'*

- Be persuasive: use *stylistic devices to convince your audience, e.g. *contrasts, *rhetorical questions, *enumerations, *alliterations, direct address of audience …

- *contrast: 'A small act – like closing the window before you leave – can have a big effect.'*

Step 3: Write introduction and conclusion:
- Write a conclusion: sum up the main points, give a final effective example supporting your message, further food for thought or an appeal for action.
- When you have prepared most of your speech, think of a good introduction, e.g. a true story, a quotation, a rhetorical question, an interesting statistic, a joke.

- *conclusion: 'You could argue that some students might not be interested in environmentally friendly behaviour and I have to agree. That is why I need your support. Set an example. Do the right thing. Help our school become active in our fight for a healthier planet.'*
- *introduction: 'Last Saturday I watched the film* The Day after Tomorrow *and felt really depressed. I don't want my world to be flooded or frozen over. I want to be able to live in a beautiful, clean world. So if I want that, what can I do to make a change?'*

Step 4: Prepare the presentation of your speech:
- Print out your speech in a format that is easy to read out from (fonts and margins not too small). If you know your speech by heart write keywords or notes on index cards.
- Mark passages and words that you want to emphasize.

Step 5: Practise your speech by reading or saying it out loud (check the pronunciation of difficult words if necessary). Even if you read it, try to make it sound as if you were delivering it freely. Practise it in front of friends or a mirror or record it, e.g. using a smartphone. Make sure you don't exceed your time limit.

Find a recording tool here:
Webcode context-55

TIP

Write keywords or notes on index cards, number the cards and use only them during your presentation.

GIVING A SPEECH

Giving a speech is not like reading something out (even if you have written it down). Try to speak as freely as possible and maintain the attention of your audience.

- Wait until the audience are quiet, then greet them and state your topic.
- Speak clearly, loudly and not too fast. Pause in suitable places.
- Use facial expressions and gestures to emphasize important points.
- Try to maintain eye-contact with your listeners.
- Thank your audience for their attention.

Find a tool for improving your speaking skills here:
Webcode context-51

PRACTICE

Your school is planning to introduce bilingual classes for History and Biology. The lessons are to be held in English from Year 8 on. Decide on your position, then write and practise a speech. Present it to your classmates.

▸ SF 26 Taking part in an interview

In lesson situations but also when applying for a job you may be asked to take part in interviews, either asking or answering questions. It is essential to prepare for an interview and to follow some general guidelines.

PREPARING FOR AN INTERVIEW

- On the basis of your role card or the task given prepare questions you are going to ask (as interviewer) or think of possible answers to questions you might be asked (as interviewee).
- For **job interviews,** you need to be prepared to say why you might be suitable for the offered position. Do research on the company you are applying to and prepare some questions you might want to ask. It might be useful to rehearse a job interview with a friend or parent.

MASTERING THE INTERVIEW

- Speak loud enough and clearly. Be aware of your non-verbal communication: Try to maintain eye-contact with the interviewer/interviewee and smile when saying hello at the beginning or thanking your interviewer/interviewee at the end. (▸ CC 4: Meeting and greeting)
- As an **interviewer**: Start off by using your prepared questions, but be flexible – phrase new questions if some interesting aspect is touched on or rephrase a question if you feel that it was not answered fully.
- As an **interviewee**: Take your time to think about your answers rather than blurting out a reply that does not show you in a good light. Do not simply answer questions with *yes* or *no*, but use your answers to show your qualifications or to express your thoughts. If you have not understood a question fully, ask the interviewer to clarify it.

LANGUAGE HELP

Interviewer

- Nice to meet you. / Thank you for coming.
- To start off, would you like to say something about …? / First, let me ask you … / My next question would be … / If you think so, then why didn't you … / Let's get back to my original question …
- You just said …, how does that relate to …?
- Thank you very much for taking part in this interview.

Interviewee

- Nice to meet you too. / Thank you for inviting me today. / I am fine, thank you.
- I am not sure I have understood your question correctly. / Sorry, could you rephrase that?/ I'm glad you asked that question because … / … is very important to me, as … / A good example of the aspect you mention is … / Let me explain that in some more detail.
- Thank you for the chance to speak to you.

PRACTICE

You want to find out your fellow students' priorities for their future lives – earning a lot of money or following their dreams? Choose someone from your class and prepare and conduct an interview with them.

▸ SF 27 Having a discussion

In a (classroom) discussion you exchange ideas and opinions with others. Discussions may be spontaneous or they may be more formal, e.g. in panel discussions or debates (▸ SF 28: Having a debate). If possible, you should prepare for the discussion so that you have your arguments and useful words and phrases ready.

THE PREPARATION STAGE

Step 1: Research the topic and make notes (▸ SF 5: Doing research, ▸ SF 15: Marking up a text / Making and taking notes). Form an opinion on it and note down arguments. Think of counter-arguments and of ways to reject them. In a role-play you may have to take a position which is not really your own, so make sure that your arguments are in line with *your role*.

Step 2: Structure your notes (► SF 8: Structuring ideas) and arrange them in a way that helps you to have the relevant facts ready during the discussion.

Step 3: Prepare an initial statement on the topic; this will ease your way into the discussion. If you are assigned a specific role, be prepared to introduce yourself.

THE DISCUSSION STAGE

Step 1: State your point of view on the topic, e.g. give your prepared statement.

Step 2: Listen to what others say and refer back to their statements, e.g. by saying which of their arguments do not convince you and why. You might also counter an argument by asking a provocative question. Remember to bring in the facts you collected to support your view.

LANGUAGE HELP

Stating your opinion

- In my opinion/view …
- As far as I'm concerned …
- Well, I'd say …
- It's a fact that …
- The way I see it, …
- Personally, I think …
- If you ask me …
- It seems to me that …
- I think/feel/reckon/believe …
- First of all … / To start with I'd like to point out that …
- There can be no doubt that …
- Nobody will deny that …
- I'm absolutely convinced that …

Asking for clarification

- I'm sorry, but I don't understand/know what you mean by …
- Could you give an example/ explain that, please?
- Can you prove that?/I would be very interested in some data/ examples that prove your statement.

Agreeing

- I quite agree.
- I couldn't agree with you more.
- Quite!/Exactly!/Precisely!
- Certainly!/Definitely!
- You're quite right.
- I agree entirely/completely.
- That's just how I see it/feel about it.
- You've got a good point there.
- That's exactly how I see it.
- Yes, indeed.

Signalling that you would like to say something

- May I interrupt?/Excuse me, I would like to add to that.
- An important aspect is missing here, namely …
- That illustrates perfectly what …
- Can I just say/explain that …?
- I would just like to jump in here, to clarify that …
- I hope you don't mind me interrupting, but it is important to stress …

Disagreeing

Polite disagreement:

- I'm afraid I don't quite agree there.
- I'm not so sure, really.
- Do you really think so?
- Well, that's one way of looking at it, but …
- I'm not convinced that …
- Well, I have my doubts about that.

Strong disagreement:

- I doubt that very much.
- That doesn't convince me at all.
- I don't agree with you at all.
- I disagree entirely.
- It's not as simple as that.

Adding a point

- Another thing is …
- What's more, …
- On top of that, …
- We must also consider …
- I would like to add to that …
- Have you ever considered/ thought about …

Buying time

- Well, that is an interesting point. / I see what you mean.
- I think the question we were discussing was …
- You have given your opinion, however …
- Why don't we see what X has to say about that?

Step 3: At the end of the discussion, summarize your point of view or your main arguments.

LANGUAGE HELP

- I have shown that … / It has become clear that …
- Let me just state again that it is vital to … / The most important argument is … / At the end of the day you can't deny that …
- If we don't … then… / In spite of everything we have heard from the other side …

Step 4 *(optional)*: If a chairperson has moderated the discussion, he/she may summarize the main line of the discussion and round it off.

LANGUAGE HELP

- We have seen/heard that … / The majority on the panel / in the audience thinks that … / Some are in favour of …, others against it, but in general you can say that …
- The general trend seems to be … / On the one hand, … On the other hand, …
- All in all this discussion has shown …

▸ SF 28 Having a debate

A debate is a formal discussion of a 'motion' (proposal) that ends in a vote. Similar to a discussion, the aim of a debate is to present arguments as convincingly as possible, so participants need well-prepared arguments as well as rhetorical skills. There is often a particular set of rules for the debate, which participants have to agree on before holding the debate. The following steps outline how you could go about holding a formal debate.

Step 1: Organizing a debate

The 'motion' (i.e. a controversial topic) is the starting point for a debate. Often it is provided by the teacher, but in other cases, your class may be asked to suggest a number of motions and then agree on one of them. The motion is then phrased in a formalized way:

- 'This house proposes that *(… students should be allowed to use smart phones during lessons)*.'
- 'This house would *(… abolish the death penalty world-wide)*.'
- 'This house believes that *(… minimum wages are a threat to the German economy)*.'

The class is then divided into two groups, one for and one against the motion.
Usually a chairperson and a timekeeper are chosen and a time-limit for each speaker is specified (often 3–6 minutes per speaker).

Step 2: Preparing the debate

- In your group (either for or against the motion) research the topic, collect and note down arguments for your side. Your personal opinion on the motion is not relevant here – you must argue for your team. List and rank the arguments that you have for your team in order of importance.
- Write your arguments on index-cards so that you have them ready during the debate.
- Think of arguments for the opposing view and ways to reject them.
- Choose speakers for your side. The other students are the audience, called the 'floor'.

Step 3: Holding the debate

A debate follows a clear structure. The 'chair' will make sure that the rules are followed and that time-limits are respected.

A debate in the House of Commons

Team in favour of the motion

FIRST PROPOSAL: The first speaker proposes the motion (= argues in favour of the motion) and gives some main arguments.

LANGUAGE HELP
- This house firmly believes that …
- Not only is … but also …

Team opposing the motion

FIRST OPPOSITION: The first speaker of this team opposes the motion (= argues against the motion).

LANGUAGE HELP
- We strongly advise against following the proposed motion because …
- The most obvious reason for this is that …

SECOND PROPOSAL: The second speaker of the affirmative team presents further arguments in favour of the motion. He/she also responds to the aspects mentioned by the first speaker of the opposing team, outlining where the positions conflict.

LANGUAGE HELP
- The opposing team has tried to create the impression that …
- However, we can prove that …
- It is therefore evident that …

SECOND OPPOSITION: The second speaker of the opposing team presents further arguments against the motion and/or restates the position of his/her team. The main task here is to defeat the arguments presented by the team in favour of the motion.

LANGUAGE HELP
- Again it needs to be stated that by following the arguments, …
- … would lead to/cause …

A short recess may be taken here to prepare for the following 'rebuttals'.

FIRST REBUTTAL: The team against the motion defends their arguments and tries to rebut the arguments of the affirmative team.

SECOND REBUTTAL: The affirmative team supports their point of view and tries to rebut the arguments of the opposing team.

THIRD REBUTTAL: The opposing team gives their closing statements.

FOURTH REBUTTAL: The affirmative team gives their closing statements.

Rules for the debate:
- Speakers may not interrupt each other at any point.
- Speakers must wait their turn.
- The time-limits as given by the chair must be respected.
- Speakers must remain polite and respectful of the other team.
- Statements must be backed up by giving examples or proof, by referring to research, experience, etc.

Step 4: Concluding the debate
- The 'floor' (i.e. the audience) may ask questions and/or present their ideas on the topic.
- The 'house' (i.e. everyone present) may take a vote on the motion by a show of hands, not based on what they personally agree or disagree with, but on who made the better case by presenting the best arguments and speaking most convincingly.
- Members of the two debating teams may get some feedback from their classmates.

Writing skills

▸ SF 29 Writing a formal letter or email

When you apply for a place at university or ask for information from a company or organization, etc., your email or letter should follow certain formal rules.

Buechelstrasse 52
53157 Bonn
Germany

Ref. Nr.: 315/14
Joanne Sutton
14 Springfield Place
Chelmsford
CM2 7ZA
United Kingdom

3 February 2015

Application for an internship

Dear Mrs Sutton

I am writing to apply for an internship at the National Gallery. I will be finishing school in July 2014, with A-levels in English, Art, History and Maths. As I have always had a particular interest in art and history, I would like to get a deeper insight into work in this field before I start my university course in art history at the University of Cologne in October 2014. As your website specifies that short-term internships are possible, I would be delighted to be given a chance to work at the National Gallery.

I enclose a copy of my CV, which shows that I have some experience of running educational classes and as a tour guide at our local museum in Bonn. I have also had the opportunity to take part in several art classes. As I speak English and German, I would also be able to deal with international visitors.

I would welcome the opportunity of enhancing my experience. As I am reliable, willing to learn and enthusiastic, I would certainly be a helpful addition to the team at the National Gallery.

Thank you for considering my application for the internship. I look forward to hearing from you soon.

Yours sincerely,

Lea Sindern

Lea Sindern

Write your address (without your name) in the top right corner of your **letter**. Don't use typical German letters like *ä, ö, ü* or *ß*.

Write the address of the person or company you are writing to on the left. If you have a reference number, write it above the recipient's address.

Write the date on the right.

Show what the letter is about in a heading.

Start your letter with *Dear Madam or Sir* if you don't know the recipient's name, otherwise write *Dear Mr/Mrs/Ms …* In BE, there is usually no comma after the greeting; in AE a colon after the greeting is used in formal letters.

Always start with a capital letter (e.g. *With great interest, I read …*).

State the reason you are writing in the opening paragraph.

Add more detailed information in the following paragraphs (reasons for applying, qualifications, why you are the right person for the position etc.).

Use long forms (*I am / We are/I would*) rather than short forms (*I'm / We're/I'd*) and abbreviations.

If you are asking for information or a favour, thank the recipient in advance.

Finish your letter with *Yours faithfully* if you don't know the recipient's name, otherwise write *Yours sincerely* (AE: *Sincerely, Sincerely yours* or *Yours truly*).

Type your name at the end of the letter, leaving space for a handwritten signature.

When writing a **formal email**

- you don't need to include the recipient's address or the date in the body of your email, as they appear automatically in the header
- open and close your email the same way you would when writing a formal letter
- do not use emoticons, smileys, etc.
- type your name and contact details at the bottom.

A **letter to the editor** follows most of the conventions of a formal letter or e-mail. Note the following, however:

- Nowadays, letters to the editor are very often sent by email. Watch out for contact information on the magazine's or paper's website.
- Your letter should be brief.
- Start like this: *Sir or Madam* (i. e. leave out *Dear*).
- Omit the closing remarks (*Yours faithfully/sincerely*).
- Don't forget to give your name, address and phone number.

▸ SF 30 Writing an application

If you want to apply for a holiday job or a position in a company (e. g. an internship), you should send them a cover letter and a CV (curriculum vitae).

THE COVER LETTER

The cover letter for an application (cf. p. 356) follows the rules of a formal letter (▸ SF 29). Since you are presenting yourself, it is important to avoid mistakes and to use formal language (▸ LP 11: Using the right register). State in what ways you are suited for the position you are applying for. Show that you have collected information about the company you are writing to and that you have a real interest in the position advertised. Mention what documents you are enclosing. At the end of the letter, express hope for a reply or an invitation to an interview.

THE CV (*AE*: résumé ['rezəmeɪ])

Your CV (cf. p. 358) gives information about you, about your education, qualifications, etc. to the person you are applying to. A CV should be clear and effective – remember the KISS rule ('Keep it short and simple'). Use a clear and easy-to-read font, highlight particularly relevant information, and don't forget to check your CV for spelling mistakes.

CURRICULUM VITAE
Lukas Meister

Rheinuferstrasse 2, 53158 Bonn, Germany
Telephone: +49(0)201 000 8177 Mobile: +49 178 000 4235
Email: Lukasmeister@mail.de

← Give your personal details: name, contact details, nationality, etc.

Personal statement ← Add a personal statement explaining why you are suitable for the specific place or job.

I have always enjoyed working with visual media, i. e. films, photographs, etc. and with computers. Being creative, I enjoy developing ideas to solve problems.
English is my favourite subject at school and I expect to improve my language skills further and to become a more independent person by spending time in the UK.

Education ← Show the stages of your education so far (schools, exams, etc.).

2008–date	Secondary School: Alfred-Krupp-Schule, Essen
2004–2008	Primary/Elementary School Gartenstrasse, Essen

Qualifications/skills ← List your qualifications and present your key skills, especially those the employer is looking for.

IT skills	Excellent knowledge of MS Word, PowerPoint, Excel, web design, Photoshop
Language skills	German native speaker; good written and spoken English, basic French
Technology	Winner of the gold medal 2014 for 'school inventors' in the 'Junior Ingenieur Akademie' (school engineering course)

Work experience ← Give information on any work experience.

May 2014	Placement: two weeks at local IT company, organized by my school

Hobbies and interests ← Write something about your hobbies or interests.

Member of school drama club, member of school computer club, member of after-school basketball club. I enjoy listening to and playing music and making films.

References ← Note down that references are available on request.

Available on request

PRACTICE

Read the job advert on the right. Then write an application, consisting of a cover letter and your curriculum vitae, for the position of management assistant. (You may also make up a person applying for the job.)

SELLIT

International advertising company based in Nottingham, UK, is looking for a Management Assistant (entry level) for office-based work.
Requirements:
- degree in International Management
- good IT-skills
- fluent English (spoken and written)
- long-term availability.

CONTACT:
Sellit
Peter Miller
pmiller@sellit.co.uk
12 Springfield Road
Nottingham
NG1 5ZA
Great Britain

▶ SF 31 Writing a summary

When you work with written or spoken texts, you are often asked to summarize the text or certain aspects of it. To do this, you need a proper overview of the text, its content and its message. Then you have to decide what to include in your summary and what to leave out. The following steps and rules can guide you.

PLANNING YOUR SUMMARY

Step 1: Listen to or read the text carefully. Either make notes or mark the most important words and phrases (▶ SF 15: Marking up a text / Making and taking notes). Find out which text type you are dealing with (▶ SF 16: Identifying text types).

Step 2: Listen to or read the text again and try to answer the '5 Ws' (*Who? What? Where? When? Why?* Perhaps also *What is the consequence?*). To get a better understanding of the text, you may also want to use the reading strategies explained in ▶ SF 14: Reading strategies.

Step 3: Decide which passages of the text (marked green in the example below, cf. *Context* pp. 138ff.) contain essential information that needs to be part of your summary and which passages can be left out. Take your time to check which parts of the text contain examples, numbers, comparisons, quotes, *imagery, direct speech, etc. – these parts do not belong in a summary.

Linguistic diplomacy: the Eurovision Song Contest *R.L.G.*

Where?/What? Last Saturday saw Denmark win the Eurovision Song Contest, the country's third win in the contest's history. A prototypically apple-cheeked[1] blonde took the trophy for her country, but she did so *Who? What?* with the rather un-Danish name of Emmelie de Forest and the equally un-Danish title, 'Only Teardrops'.

The contest has always been about more than music. Every year comes a slew[2] of articles *What/Why? (Examples)* about the political nature of the voting. Countries that share ethnic or political friendships routinely give each other high marks: Greece and Cyprus typically give each other the maximum of 12 points while stiffing[3] Turkey with *nul points*[4], for example. Estonia and Latvia this year gave Russia 12 points, no doubt because those countries' large Russian populations voted for their neighbour.

What? Language, of course, plays a role in this as well. 'Ethnicity'[5] in Europe is often linguistic: an ethnic Russian is not apparent on the streets of Riga until he opens his mouth. *Why? (Examples/ numbers)* Linguistic neighbours will tend to be generous to one another. Finland and Estonia are friendly not only because they are nearby but because their Finno-Ugric languages resemble each other, while being utterly unrelated to their neigbours'. (Hungarian is also Finno-Ugric.) Each country can give 12 points to only one other country, and this year Denmark and Sweden gave their 12's to Norway, Norway its 12 to Sweden, as befits[6] the Scandinavian language continuum.

But the Scandinavians share something else besides apple-cheeked blondes and North *What?* Germanic languages: their tendency to sing in English. In that, they are like most countries nowadays. But some interesting variation clouds the picture.

From: *The Economist*, 20 May 2013

[1] **apple-cheeked** having cheeks *(= Wangen)* the colour of apples
[2] **slew** *(ifml)* large number
[3] **stiff sb. with sth.** *(here)* reject/ mildly insult sb.
[4] **nul points** [nyl pwɛ] *(French)* nil (= no) points
[5] **ethnicity** fact of belonging to a particular race
[6] **befit sb.** *(fml)* be suitable for sb.

WRITING YOUR SUMMARY

Step 1: Write your summary in your own words.

1 Write an introductory phrase, mentioning the essential aspects, such as the title, *author, topic, main message and source of the text. (▸ LP 18: Writing about texts)

The article 'Linguistic diplomacy: the Eurovision Song Contest', written by an author abbreviated as R.L.G. and published in The Economist *on 20 May 2013, investigates the languages of songs entered for the Eurovision Song Contest and points out that English has had a leading role over the years.*

LANGUAGE HELP

- The story/text is about …
- The text deals with …
- In the text the reader gets to know …
- The topic of the text is …
- The article shows …

2 Use the present tense (▸ LP 3: Simple present and present perfect). Don't copy the original text – use your own words. Use linking words to connect your ideas (▸ SF 38: Writing a well-structured text).

In the article, the author takes Denmark's win of the last ESC as a starting point to look into different influencing factors of the voting.
After mentioning political reasons, i.e. neighbouring or politically close countries, the writer moves on to the main topic: the chosen languages of the songs being entered. Countries seem to give more points to songs from countries sharing the same language.
Using the starting point of Denmark's win again, the writer focuses on the dominance of English …

3 Round off your text by restating the main message or *action.

All in all, the text focuses on … and invites the reader to make up their mind whether …

Step 2: Check your summary. Does it contain the most important facts and ideas from the original text? Have you left out examples, unnecessary details, etc.? Have you checked the spelling, punctuation, tenses, etc.? (▸ SF 40: Proofreading, ▸ LP 12: Spelling)

PRACTICE

Summarize the extract from Alan Bennet's *The Uncommon Reader* (pp. 62f.) in no more than 200 words.

▸ SF 32 Writing a review

When writing a review, you provide information on a book, play or film you have read or watched, as well as expressing your opinion about it. Reviews are meant to either recommend the work in question or to discourage people from reading or seeing it.

PREPARING YOUR REVIEW

Step 1: Read the book or watch the film/play you want to write about, making notes of interesting, very good or very bad aspects. It may be useful to consider typical elements of the text type in question (▸ SF 16: Identifying text types).

Step 2: Add to your notes, writing down important information about the book or the film. Structure your ideas (▸ SF 8). The grid on the next page will help you to identify the relevant aspects, but you could also use a mind map to structure your ideas.

Find a mindmapping tool here:
Webcode context-53

Scenes from the film 2012

Header Title Running time Your rating Year Director's name	 *2012* *157 minutes* **** (out of five) (= okay)* *2009* *Roland Emmerich*
Introduction Basic information: type of movie/book, characters	▪ *disaster film / science fiction action film* ▪ *science fiction writer Jackson Curtis tries to rescue his two children and his ex-wife from a geological and meteorological super-disaster*
Main part Short summary of the plot (Be careful: perhaps your readers don't want to be told the ending before they have read the book or watched the film themselves.) Cast/characters	▪ *2009: scientist discovers that the temperature of the Earth is rising unexpectedly; international leaders plan to save a certain number of people on arks* ▪ *2012: Jackson Curtis (John Cusack), a divorced writer of science fiction, takes children Noah (Liam James) and Lily (Morgan Lily) camping in Yellowstone National Park, hears fears about the end of the world by Charlie Frost (Woody Harrelson)* ▪ *they return home; earthquakes are everywhere; Jackson rents plane for his children and ex-wife; they leave LA before California is destroyed* ▪ *family tries to get to the arks; the President of the US dies in a tsunami* ▪ *Jackson and his family reach the arks and manage to get on board*
Comments Your opinion, e.g. on *plot, *actors, *characters, *dialogues, special effects, the 'message', etc.	▪ *great special effects in the depiction of the catastrophe, impressive when famous buildings collapse* ▪ *dramatic music/great sound* ▪ *the film is fun to watch if you like action films* ▪ *John Cusack convincing as Jackson Curtis: not the typical action hero, but likeable and a bit quirky – good contrast to the action scenes* *BUT:* ▪ *parts of the film are not logical, i.e. characters use mobile phones while the earth is exploding around them* ▪ *film has some quite scary parts* ▪ *film is far too long* ▪ *all in all, film seems to be a bit far-fetched*
Conclusion Summary of your opinion, recommendation/target group	▪ *quite good science fiction disaster film with great action scenes* ▪ *too long and partly exaggerated* ▪ *only suitable for lovers of action/disaster movies – don't expect too much!*

WRITING YOUR REVIEW

▪ Start with a catchy title and a **header** which contains basic facts. ▪ Use the present tense. ▪ Avoid imprecise words like *good, really bad,* etc. ▪ Start with an **introductory paragraph** with basic information.	***A film review: 2012: not quite the perfect disaster*** *2009 running time: 157 minutes rating: *** (okay)* *The science fiction disaster film 2012, directed by Roland Emmerich, is an action-packed and generally enjoyable film, which has some riveting images and lots of gripping scenes, but which is also rather far-fetched in many places …*
▪ In the **main part** first give a short summary of the plot without giving away the end of the film/book.	*After a scientist …* *After having obtained a map from Charlie, who dies while reporting about the events, the family tries to get to the arks, …*
▪ Then **comment** on the positive or negative aspects of the book/film/play.	*The special effects in 2012 are definitely worth seeing: images of the earth being destroyed are powerful and often scary. The special effects are sometimes truly breath-taking …* *… all this is underlined by a dramatic score. So for all lovers of action films, 2012 definitely is fun to watch. It even has some good acting: John Cusack shines in his role as …*
▪ Finish your review by **summarizing** the main aspects and by giving a **recommendation** whether the book/film is worth reading/watching. ▪ Use linking words to connect your ideas. (► SF 38: Writing a well-structured text; ► LP 12: Linking words and phrases; ► LP 15: Connecting your thoughts)	*But is the film a real masterpiece? Unfortunately not. It is irritating for the viewers that …* *… And last but not least, the film might be considered just a bit too scary for the faint-hearted!* *All in all, it might have been a good idea to tone the film down a little.* *So here is my final verdict. Is 2012 a perfect film or is it a disaster? It is neither one nor the other but it is a perfect disaster film, and lovers of action films and disaster are going to get their money's worth – and perhaps even more than they bargained for. However, if you are looking for a scientifically correct, logical plot and deeper insights into life, I recommend finding a different film for your Saturday night.*
▪ Proofread your text. (► SF 40: Proofreading; ► LP 17: Spelling)	

PRACTICE

Choose a film that you enjoyed watching in the past six months. Write a short review, focusing on the film's strengths and – if you found any – weaknesses and recommending it to your classmates.

▶ SF 33 Writing a report

Reports offer factual information about a recent event. The information is given in a chronological order and the language used is objective and formal.

The following instructions will guide you through the steps of writing a report. Your task is to write a report on a family dispute that caused extreme reactions on the father's side.

Steps	Example
Step 1: Gather as much information about the event as possible. Try to answer the '5 Ws' (who? where? what? when? why? and if possible: what are the consequences?). If your report is based on a fictitious event (e.g. from a novel or play) you might need to add missing details such as last names, place names or dates.	(The story deals with the experiences of second-generation Indian immigrants in London. The narrator, Karim, is visiting his cousin, Jamila. Jamila and her father, Anwar, are fighting.) 'What's going on here?' I asked her. 'Look at him, Karim, he hasn't eaten or drunk anything for eight days! He'll die, Karim, if he doesn't eat anything won't he!' 'Yes, you'll cop it[1], boss, if you don't eat your grub[2] like everyone else.' 'I won't eat. I will die. If Gandhi could shove out the English from India by not eating, I can get my family to obey me by exactly the same.' 'What do you want her to do?' 'To marry the boy I have selected with my brother.' 'But it's old-fashioned, Uncle, out of date,' I explained. 'No one does that kind of thing now. They just marry the person they're into, if they bother to get married at all.' This homily[3] on contemporary morals didn't exactly blow his mind[4]. 'That is not our way, boy. Our way is firm. She must do what I say or I will die. She will kill me.' From: Hanif Kureishi, *The Buddha of Suburbia*, 1990
Step 2: Put the information in chronological order. If necessary, add further details.	▪ *London* ▪ *family of Indian origin* ▪ *domestic dispute* ▪ *daughter's refusal to agree to arranged marriage* ▪ *day eight of father's hunger strike* ▪ *...*

Step 3: Write your report:

- Use the simple past. (▶ LP 4: Present perfect and simple past)
- Start off with a summarizing sentence.
- If you write a longer report, divide it into paragraphs. (▶ SF 38: Writing a well-structured text)
- Use linking words to connect your ideas. (▶ SF 38: Writing a well-structured text)
- Make your report sound formal and matter-of-fact by using objective language and the passive voice where possible. (▶ LP 7: The passive; ▶ LP 11: Using the right register)
- Don't state personal thoughts, feelings or opinions. Try to focus on the facts, even if you use quotes from witnesses.

Step 4: Proofread yout text. (▶ SF 40; ▶ LP 17: Spelling)

[1] **cop it** *(BE, infml)* die [2] **grub** *(infml)* food [3] **homily** *(fml)* talk that gives advice on how to live
[4] **blow sb.'s mind** *(infml)* produce a strong feeling in sb.

LANGUAGE HELP

- On … an incident/occurrence of … was reported to …
- … domestic disputes such as … / another case of …
- It is believed/assumed that …
- … confirmed/claimed/revealed that …
- People are concerned about … / that …
- … took it to extremes when … / The intervention by … has not been successful …
- neighbours / a relative

PRACTICE

Look at the examples given for **Step 2**. Add further details from the text or invent them. Then put them in a suitable order and write your report. You may start like this: *Last night a middle-aged man of Indian origin was brought to St George's Hospital after having nearly starved himself in a hunger strike.*

▶ SF 34 Argumentative writing

When writing an argumentative text, you have to structure your text clearly and argue in a logical manner.

THE PLANNING STAGE

The starting point for an argumentative text can be a statement, a text you have read or a thesis you have been given, for example:
'For learners of English at German schools, Shakespeare's plays are incomprehensible, outdated and simply irrelevant. Therefore, his plays ought to be deleted from the curriculum of English classes.'
Discuss.

In a written **discussion** (*Operator: discuss*) you give arguments for and against something and come to a justified conclusion. In a **comment** (*Operator: comment on / write a comment*) you want to convince the reader of your own opinion on an issue. You have to give arguments to support it and may even introduce counter-arguments which you refute to make your own arguments even stronger.

Step 1: Brainstorm your topic and make notes.

Step 2: Collect pro and con arguments.

***Pro:** Shakespeare's plays ought to be deleted from the curriculum of English classes.*

- *Students struggle with the language and ideas of the Elizabethan Age and therefore don't enjoy studying Shakespeare's works.*
- *Students would benefit more from reading about events, characters and stories that are relevant to their own daily lives.*
- *…*

***Con:** Shakespeare's plays should not be deleted from the curriculum of English classes.*

- *Shakespeare's works are a vital part of English culture – learning about him and his works is part of general knowledge.*
- *The topics and conflicts dealt with in Shakespeare's works are universal and can easily be transferred to a modern world (cf. the numerous modern versions of his plays).*
- *…*

Step 3: Arrange your arguments in a logical way, following either of these two patterns:

Pattern A
Present the arguments for and against in separate paragraphs:
1. Introduction
2. Arguments pro
3. Arguments con
4. Conclusion

Pattern B
Answer each argument immediately with its counter-argument:
1. Introduction
2. Argument 1 ► counter-argument 1
3. Argument 2 ► counter-argument 2
4. Argument 3 ► counter-argument 3
5. Conclusion

It is usually a good idea to finish with the argument that supports your position most strongly because this is the one the reader will remember most. Sometimes, however, it may be helpful not to postpone your strongest argument until the very end because you want to catch the reader's attention.

- ***my position: con***, *i.e. Shakespeare's works should not be deleted from the curriculum*
- ***line of argument***: *pattern B (argument → counter-argument)*
- ***argument 1***: *Most students find Shakespeare's texts difficult to read.*
  → ***counter-argument 1***: *Shakespeare's texts are a vital part of English culture and are often referred to in everyday speech, so understanding them will eventually help students in everyday situations.*
- ***argument 2***: *Shakespeare's texts are set in a remote past, so students can't profit from them in their everyday lives.* → ***counter-argument 2***: *Once students have understood a text from Shakespeare's plays, they will realize that the themes dealt with depict universal conflicts which can easily be transferred to modern life.*
- …

THE WRITING STAGE

Step 1: Write your introduction. Refer to the topic. In a comment, you can give your point of view here.

Young people today are confronted with a world that is becoming more and more complex and which offers new technology, new information and new forms of literature. Classic literature, notably the plays by William Shakespeare, no longer seem to be relevant to some people today. So they claim that Shakespeare's plays ought to be taken off the curriculum for English classes.

Step 2: Present your line of argument, following either pattern A or B (see above). Use linking words (► SF 38: Writing a well-structured text; ► LP 14: Using linking words and phrases; ► LP 15: Connecting your thoughts)

Many students claim that reading Shakespeare's plays is a challenge and not worth the effort: they argue that not only his language but also the ideas from his times are incomprehensible to young people in the 21st century.
However, Shakespeare's plays are a vital part of English culture – quotations from his plays have found their way into everyday English, into sayings and proverbs. Knowing about Shakespeare's works provides an important background for understanding the heritage of modern language and modern texts.
When I was first made to read Romeo and Juliet *in school, I also struggled with Shakespeare's language and ideas and initially only saw the story in its historic context. But once I had fully understood …*

TIP

Your arguments will appear more convincing if you
1. quote authorities, experts or statistics; present facts
2. refer to your personal experience whenever possible

…►

Step 3: Write a conclusion. Round off your text by stating your thesis once again, but do not give new information and do not use the same phrases that you used in the introduction.
In conclusion, it seems clear that taking Shakespeare's plays off the curriculum for English classes would mean that students would be denied the chance of getting to know …
Those precious works of English literature should therefore remain a compulsory part of the curriculum for English classes.

Step 4: Proofread yout text. (► SF 40)

► SF 35 Writing a character profile

**Characters in fictional texts are presented through descriptions by the *narrator or other characters (*direct characterization) and through their appearance, language, attitude, behaviour, relationships to other characters and their thoughts and actions (*indirect characterization).*

TIP

When writing a character profile, do not describe *what* the character does, but explain *why* he/she says or does what he/she does.

Read the excerpt from the *novel *Payback Time* on pp. 198f. and describe Coach McNulty's character.

Step 1: Collect relevant passages in the text and make notes on

- general information we get about the character (outward appearance, social background, etc.)
  - 'He took a seat behind a neatly organized desk.' (l. 9)
- what the narrator or other characters say about the character you are dealing with
  - (Mitch:) 'To him I'd always be a big fat loser and nothing more.' (l. 3)
  - 'But McNulty's eyes were scary. I squirmed[1] as he stared at me, feeling like a snot-nosed preschooler who'd been caught marking a wall with crayons[2].' (l. 44)
- what the character says about him-/herself
  - 'I do not intend to spend my life coaching high school.' (l. 57)
- what the character says and does.
  - ' "What's funny?" McNulty said, his blue-gray eyes glittering like shiny stones.' (l. 18)
  - ' "No, no, no," McNulty said, pointing the pencil at me again. 'No questions – not today, not ever.' (l. 34)
  - 'You write down or tape what I tell you. When I'm done, jazz it up[3] whatever you want, but never make me, my coaches, or my players look bad. Understand?' (l. 35)
  - ' "Understood?" he said again, a threat in his voice.' (l. 46)
  - 'Every sports story needs pictures. Either you've got to take them yourself, or you've got to get a photographer. Didn't you know that?' (l. 63)

[1] **squirm** *sich winden* [2] **crayon** *Buntstift* [3] **jazz sth. up** *(infml)* make sth.more interesting or attractive

Step 2: From your notes draw conclusions about the character.
Always note down examples from the text to give evidence on what you have concluded.

- *according to Mitch: judges people by their outward appearance and athletic ability, not their character → superficial, biased*
- *neatly organized desk → disciplined, conscientious*
- *controls what is being done and said → hungry for power superior, patronizing*
- *uses intimidation to achieve his aims → ruthless, cold*
- *makes others feel stupid → patronizing, condescending*

LANGUAGE HELP

- X appears to be … is portrayed as … This behaviour shows/indicates … Evidence for this can be found in lines … The way she/he talks implies that …
- Her/his dress sense shows … This proves that … X is a person who can be considered courageous/optimistic/trustworthy/unreliable/disloyal/…

Step 3: Write up your text.

- Structure your text (► SF 8) into
  - introduction (should include names, general information, the role the character plays in the story, etc.)
    - *Coach McNulty is a PE teacher and high school football coach who considers himself destined for greater things and therefore openly displays his superiority and power.*
    - *…*
  - main part (should include details about the character, e.g. character traits, ambitions, aims, problems, inner conflicts, etc.)
    - *McNulty is very ambitious and does not 'intend to spend [his] life coaching high school football' (l. 57).*
    - *To make sure he can achieve that goal he is willing to use threats ('Understood?', l. 46)*
    - *He is very condescending towards the reporter.*
    - *…*
  - conclusion (should summarize why the character acts/reacts the way he/she does).
    - *In summary, one can say that Coach McNulty's ruthless ambition, his condescension and his patronizing manner reveal him to be an unfeeling, cold-hearted character and not a stereotypical friendly high school coach and teacher.*
- Use the present tense. (► LP 3: Simple present and present perfect)
- Use linking words to connect your ideas. (► SF 38: Writing a well-structured text; ► LP 14: Linking words and phrases)
- Support your findings using quotes from the text. (► SF 39: Quoting a text)

Step 4: Proofread yout text. (► SF 40; ► LP 17: Spelling)

▸ SF 36 Writing a text analysis

*Text analyses can be done with different types of texts, *fictional or *non-fictional texts. The aspects you analyse may differ from text type to text type (see the entries in the Skills File to find out which information is relevant for each text type, ▸ SF 18–21), but the process of analysing texts is usually the same for all of them.*

PREPARING YOUR TEXT ANALYSIS

Step 1: Read the task carefully to make sure you know exactly what you are asked to do (cf. 'Verbs for tasks', pp. 410f.). Sometimes you will be given a specific aspect to analyse, sometimes you will be free to select aspects yourself. The following are some suggestions for questions you might ask yourself:

- Which *stylistic devices are used? To what effect? (▸ SF 17: Analysing stylistic devices)
- Which noteworthy words and phrases are used? To what effect?
- How does the structure of the text add to its general meaning / line of argument?
- How is the reader influenced by the text? To what effect?
- What information is being withheld? Why / To what effect?
- In what way does this text differ from other texts of the same type? (▸ SF 16: Identifying text types)
- ...

Step 2: Read the text carefully and make sure you understand it properly. Use a dictionary where necessary (▸ SF 3). Make notes on features or aspects of the text that strike you as relevant to your analysis (▸ SF 15: Marking up a text / Making and taking notes). Remember to note down references from the text that support your analysis (▸ SF 39: Quoting a text).

Find an online dictionary here:
Webcode context-52

Step 3: Structure your ideas (▸ SF 8). Do not follow the text chronologically, but structure your ideas according to the different aspects you are analysing.

WRITING YOUR TEXT ANALYSIS

Step 1: Write an introductory sentence in which you give the source and author of the text, the topic and a first general idea to answer your question. Write only one short paragraph, e.g.
In his speech given at Portland State University on 13 June 1998, President Bill Clinton focuses his speech around the topic of ethnic diversity in the US and stresses its positive aspects and the opportunities it offers, using various stylistic devices to bring his message home. (Cf. pp. 24f.)
Use the present tense. (▸ LP 18: Writing about texts)

Step 2: Write the main part of your text:

- Present your findings to support the central idea you stated in the introduction.
- Use different paragraphs for different ideas and introduce these paragraphs with topic sentences to guide the reader. Use linking words. (▸ SF 38: Writing a well-structured text)
- Remember to provide evidence from the text, i.e. to use quotations. (▸ SF 39: Quoting a text)

Step 3: Write a short conclusion:

- Refer to your introduction and write a concluding sentence in which you restate your first general idea or your main findings.
- Do NOT add new aspects at this point!
- Do NOT give your personal opinion or an evaluation!

Step 4: Proofread yout text. (▸ SF 40; ▸ LP 17: Spelling)

PRACTICE

Read the text 'Linguistic diplomacy: the Eurovision Song Contest' (pp. 138f.). Write an outline (▸ SF 8) for the following task: 'Analyse the different means the author of this article uses to get the reader's attention.'

► SF 37 Doing a creative writing task

Most creative writing tasks ask you to create a text using an existing piece of writing as a starting point.

NON-FICTIONAL TEXTS

Your creative task may take a *non-fictional text (such as a *speech or newspaper *article) as a starting point. In this case you usually have to assume a certain perspective and evaluate a situation through the eyes of a (fictitious) *character. You might, for example, be asked to read an article on a climate conference and then write an article from the perspective of a reporter who attended the conference. (► SF 18: Analysing non-fiction, ► SF 34: Argumentative writing).

FICTIONAL TEXTS

When dealing with *fictional texts a common creative task might be to write an ending to a story or to rewrite the story from a *character's point of view, i.e. to change perspective.

Continuation of a story

Step 1: Brainstorm ideas. Look at the *setting, events, dates, characters and their relationships in the original text and watch out for hints as to how the story might continue.

Step 2: Compare your ideas to the original text to make sure they don't contradict the reality depicted in the story.

Step 3: Identify the narrative perspective of the original text (e.g. *first-person or *third-person narrator) and consider what limitations that specific perspective might have or not have.

Step 4: Write your continuation. Try to imitate the style and language used in the original.

Change of perspective

A change of perspective means that you take over the role of one of the characters in the story from whose perspective the story is *not* told. You retell its events from this character's point of view e.g. in a diary entry, a letter or an interior monologue.

Step 1: Brainstorm ideas. Pay attention to the relationships your character is involved in and to specific features such as his/her social status, age or special character traits.

Step 2: Ask yourself what your character might think and feel in a specific situation and also what your character knows and doesn't know.

Step 3: Write your text in a way that is appropriate to your character. Age, social status and other features usually determine how you speak or write.

Step 4: Pay attention to the *text type you're using. For example if you write a letter, you must address the addressee and sign the letter; if you write a dialogue, you should use typical elements of spoken language; if you write a diary entry you should focus on thoughts and feelings.

TIP

- Do not stray too far from the original text because your text may become illogical or far-fetched.
- Do not invent things that contradict the events of the original story.

····►

► SF 38 Writing a well-structured text

A well-structured text makes it easy for your reader to follow your line of thought and to understand your text. The structure you use will depend on the kind of text you are writing. For instance, if you are telling a story or writing a report (► SF 33: Writing a report), you might want to relate the events in a chronological order. However, there are some rules which apply to all kinds of texts.

Step 1: Collect ideas. Make an outline for your text and structure your ideas accordingly. (► SF 8: Structuring ideas)

Step 2: Write your text:
- Begin a new paragraph for each new event, point, argument or idea.
- Structure your text visually, for example by leaving spaces between your paragraphs.
- Make the first sentence in each paragraph a **topic sentence**, i.e. a sentence that states what the paragraph will be about.
- Use **linking words** to make the connections between individual ideas clear (► LP 14: Linking words and phrases; ► LP 15: Connecting your thoughts).

Step 3: Proofread your text. (► SF 40: Proofreading; ► LP 17: Spelling)

LANGUAGE HELP

Linking words

Enumeration/ Structure	first, second, third; firstly, secondly, ...; to begin/start with ..., in the first place ...; next, then; finally, last (but not least), lastly, to conclude
Addition	furthermore, moreover, in addition (to that), above all, what is more ...
Comparison	equally, likewise, similarly, in the same way ...
Summary/Conclusion	then, all in all, to conclude, to sum up, in summary/conclusion ...
Exemplification	namely, for instance/for example (e.g.), that is to say ...
Reasoning	that is why ... because ..., one reason for this is that ...
Result	consequently, as a consequence, therefore, thus, after all, as a result, this leads to/ results in ...
Reformulation	or rather, to put it another way, in other words ...
Alternatively	on the one hand ... on the other hand ..., either ... or, neither ... nor ...
Contrast	on the contrary, in contrast to, opposite to, unlike ...
Concession	however, nevertheless, still, though, in spite of that, despite that, ...

▸ SF 39 Quoting a text

*Quoting is used when you want to support your own statements (e.g. in an analysis) by giving evidence from other texts or the text you are working on. You can either paraphrase/**quote indirectly** (i.e. use your own words to express ideas from a text,* ▸ *SF 9**) or you can use a **direct quote** (i.e. use the exact words of the text).*

Here are some rules for quoting properly:

- With a direct quote, repeat exactly what the author wrote – this also refers to spelling, punctuation, etc.
- Use quotation marks to show where the direct quote begins and ends: A direct quote must be clearly indicated as someone else's thoughts to avoid giving the impression of plagiarism. Remember that in English, quotation marks start and end above the line ('…').
- Always give the exact **source** of your quotation: line or verse numbers and – when dealing with longer texts – page numbers. If you are quoting from more than one text, indicate the author and year of publication. Remember these **abbreviations**: *p./l.* is used for one page/line (e.g. 'p. 4'); *pp./ll.* for more than one page/line (e.g. 'pp. 207–210'); *f./ff.* after the number of a page/line means 'and the following page(s)/line(s)'.
- Especially when working on projects, you may have to quote from more than one text. In this case you need to indicate in a **bibliography** which texts you have used. For each text, provide the author, title, place and date of publication, publisher or URL.

Strategy	Example
Indirect quotes If you use an indirect quote (i.e. you paraphrase or summarize ideas from a text in your own words) you do not use quotation marks, but indicate that you are referring to somebody else's ideas by using *cf.* (= German *vgl.*) and the page number and/or line.	*Franklin D. Roosevelt suggests in his speech that people who are threatened by poverty are easy prey for dictators (cf. p. 188, ll. 2f.).*
Direct quotes: complete sentences When quoting complete sentences make sure that you explain them, refer to or comment on them, so as to avoid disconnected quotations. Using quotes without further comment may give the impression that you have no ideas of your own! Use a colon (:) to separate the quotation from your introductory phrase or sentence.	*Americans and Europeans feel that their wealth and power oblige them to get involved: 'Americans, like Europeans, have long believed that strength and wealth entail responsibility' (p. 33, ll. 35–36).*
Direct quotes: words or phrases If you want to refer to individual words from the text (e.g. in an analysis), you can incorporate words/phrases into your own sentence. Be careful: Work the quotations into your sentences as smoothly as possible so that they fit syntactically.	• *In the prologue to* Romeo and Juliet, *the unhappy ending of the play is already foreshadowed by the phrase 'starcrossed lovers' (Prologue, v. 6).* • *In her text 'Better than its reputation' Applebaum claims 'that the American dream is looking rather tarnished' (p. 33, l. 8), especially when compared to East Asia, which she describes as 'the new land of opportunity' (p. 33, l. 11).*
Direct quotes: poems or plays in verse With texts written in verse, indicate the end of lines with a slash (/). When quoting from plays, provide the act, scene and verse, i.e. II/2/6 = act II, scene 2, verse 6.	*In Aoife Mannix's poem 'Keeping the accent' the speaker experiences that her accent is seen as something positive: 'Then he tells me my accent is so cute, / he is going to give me one of the drinks for free' (p. 137, ll. 5f.).*

……▸

Deleting from or adding to a direct quote If you want to leave out part of a quote indicate this by using square brackets [...]. If you need to add to a quote, for example to make it fit into your sentence syntactically or logically, indicate this by adding words in square brackets, too. Make sure that you don't change the meaning of the quote and that it is still syntactically correct.	▪ *'But these differing responses [...] also signify a different set of attitudes to power [...]: Americans, like Europeans, have long believed that strength and wealth entail responsibility'. (p. 33, ll. 34f.)* ▪ *At some point the speaker realizes that 'No words can help [her] now'. (p. 89, l. 20)*
Direct quotes: texts containing quotation mark When quoting a passage that includes quotation marks (e.g. in direct speech), use two different kinds of quotation marks, i.e. '...' and "...".	*In Genesis, the first book of the Bible, it says: 'And God said, "Let there be light" and there was light' (Genesis 1.6).*

TIP

Check your assignment before using quotes – when answering comprehension questions, you are often asked to express ideas from the text in your own words and are therefore not supposed to quote.

PRACTICE

In the following extract from an essay on why people emigrated to the US, certain passages have been underlined. Quote them to complete the sentences given below the text. Add line references.

Political and Economic Freedom *Milton and Rose Friedman*

Ever since the first settlement of Europeans in the New World – at Jamestown in 1607 and at Plymouth in 1620 – America has been a magnet for people <u>seeking adventure, fleeing from a tyranny, or simply trying to make a better life for themselves and their children</u>.

<u>An initial trickle</u>[1] swelled after the American Revolution and the establishment of the United States of America and became <u>a flood</u> in the nineteenth century, when millions of people streamed across the Atlantic, and a smaller number across the Pacific, driven by misery and tyranny, and attracted by the promise of freedom and affluence[2].

When they arrived, they did not find streets paved with gold; they did not find an easy life. <u>They did find freedom and an opportunity to make the most of their talents</u>. Through hard work, ingenuity[3], thrift[4], and luck, most of them succeeded in realizing enough of their hopes and dreams to encourage friends and relatives to join them.

From: *Free to Choose*, New York 1980

1 The text states that the people who came to the US did this for a variety of reasons, as there were people ...
2 The text describes the rising number of immigrants as ... after the American Revolution and as ... during the nineteenth century.
3 Even though the immigrants couldn't expect to become rich without effort, they did get the chance to fulfil their dreams if they were willing and able to work hard: ...

[1] **trickle** *Rinnsal* [2] **affluence** wealth [3] **ingenuity** ability to find solutions to problems [4] **thrift** careful spending of money

▸ SF 40 Proofreading

Whenever you write a text, it is important to check the correctness and the style of the English you have used. Ideally ask someone else to read it through. Others will often see more because they are not as involved with the text as you are. If possible, read your text out loud. This will help you spot if you have accidently left out any words.

Step 1: Checking structure

- Check that you have included an introduction and a conclusion. (▸ SF 8: Structuring ideas)
- Check that you have followed all the rules for a sensible text structure, e.g. topic sentences, paragraphs, etc. (▸ SF 38: Writing a well-structured text)
- Make sure that your paragraphs include more than one sentence but still focus on one basic thought, argument or idea.

Step 2: Checking style

- Look at your sentences. If your text consists of lots of unconnected main clauses only, then add linking words to express logical connections between your ideas and thus make your text more readable. (▸ SF 38: Writing a well-structured text)
- Make sure you used the right collocations. (▸ LP 19: Collocations) If in doubt, look them up in a dictionary. (▸ SF 3: Using a dictionary)
- Check for repetitions. Substitute words you have used repeatedly with synonyms.

Find an online dictionary and a thesaurus here:
Webcode context-52

- *He is a very conscientious person. He goes to work even when he feels sick. People know that if he is not at work, something serious must have happened. →*
  He is a very conscientious person who goes to work even when he feels sick. That is why people know if when he is not at work, something serious must have happened.
- *Social networks can hurt people's privacy. →*
  Social networks can violate people's privacy.
- *Not everybody can achieve the American Dream but there are some people who work hard and achieve it in the end. →*
  Not everybody can achieve the American Dream but there are some people who work hard and reach it in the end.

Step 3: Checking correctness

- Keep a checklist of mistakes you have regularly made in the past, e.g. correct tenses in the *if*-clause, the use of adverbs, etc. Look specifically for these mistakes when reading your text.
- Check spelling and punctuation. (▸ LP 17: Spelling) If possible take advantage of your computer's spell-checker, but always double-check its suggestions rather than accepting them blindly.

- **She is terrible upset about her husband's death. →*
  She is terribly upset about her husband's death.

TIP

Try to think in English when you write because otherwise phrases or sentence patterns sometimes sound more German than English.

PRACTICE

The following is the beginning of a student's text analysis. It includes nine mistakes (both grammatical and stylistic errors). Find all the mistakes and correct them.

In the short story 'No speak English' from Sandra Cisnero the main character which is called Mamacita, is a beautiful woman. Actually she never leave her apartment, instead the narrator basically speculates about why she behaves in this way. He only knows that she is married and has one kid and he only knows that she speaks only eight words of English. The narrator thinks that she doesn't like English. She always listens to the Spanish radio shows. The husband wants that she integrates into US-American society but she misses her real home, Mexico, too much.

Mediation skills

▸ SF 41 Mediation of written and oral texts

Not everybody speaks and understands both German and English. So you may sometimes find yourself in a situation where you have to help people understand each other – where you have to mediate between speakers of German and English or where you have to explain what is written in texts in the other language.
A mediation is not *a translation, i.e. you do* not *translate a text word for word.*

Your English-speaking e-pal is leaving school next year but is finding it difficult to decide on his career plans. You have just read the article below and want to send him an email giving some advice on how to proceed.

Hilfen bei der Berufswahl

Wenn die Berufswahl für Jugendliche ansteht, dann tun sich viele häufig schwer. Sie wissen nicht so recht, ob sie lieber studieren sollen oder erst einmal einen Beruf erlernen möchten. Weiter lernen oder gleich Geld verdienen? Ein Studium nach der Ausbildung beginnen und damit weiter auf Unterstützung angewiesen sein? Oder in einem handwerklichen Beruf Karriere machen? Alles scheint offen und alles möglich. [...]

Was soll man nun aber tun, wenn man als Jugendlicher eine Ausbildung finden möchte? Erst einmal sollte für die Berufswahl des Jugendlichen klar sein, welche Interessen er hat. Dafür gibt es im Internet oder auch bei der Bundesagentur für Arbeit verschiedene Tests. Soll lieber mit Menschen oder Tieren, mit Maschinen und Geräten gearbeitet werden? Sind die eigenen Fähigkeiten eher theoretischer Natur oder besteht eine Veranlagung zum praktischen Basteln? Gibt es aus der Schule Neigungen, die sich beruflich nutzen lassen? [...] Wichtig ist, dass mit der Suche nach einem Ausbildungsplatz für den Jugendlichen zeitig begonnen wird, denn häufig endet die Einstellung der neuen Azubis schon im Jahr vor dem Abschluss in der Schule. Auch für einen Studienplatz sollte sich der Schüler rechtzeitig bewerben, vor allem wenn es sich um einen Studienplatz handelt, der an einen Numerus Clausus gebunden ist, oder um einen, für den es nur eine begrenzte Zahl an freien Plätzen gibt.

From: www.deine-staerken.org

How to proceed		Example
Step 1:	Select the relevant information from the text, bearing in mind what specific information your partner needs. Remember: the mediated text will usually be much shorter than the original because you select only the information you need.	▪ *first find out what you enjoy doing* ▪ *get some help from online-tests or the 'Bundesagentur für Arbeit'* ▪ *start early*
Step 2:	Analyse the communicative situation:	▪ *Your friend needs to know the basic steps he can take to decide on his career.*
	▪ Who are you talking or writing to? What is the appropriate *style and *register? (► LP 11: Using the right register)	▪ *a friend → informal language* (If you were e.g. giving a speech at a symposium on young people's career choices you would use a formal style.)
	▪ What text type are you expected to produce (an informal letter or email, an article for a school magazine? (► SF 29: Writing a formal letter or email; ► SF 33: Writing a report)	▪ *an email*
	▪ Will you be speaking or writing? (Speaking allows you to use gestures and other non-verbal means of communication.)	▪ *written text*
Step 3:	Structure the relevant information, then phrase it in the target language. (► LP 12: Avoiding German-sounding sentence-patterns) Watch out for aspects that are specific to one culture and explain them in more detail. (► LP 12: Avoiding Germanisms) If you don't know words in the other language, paraphrase them. (► SF 9: Paraphrasing)	*The article I have read gives you some advice:* ▪ *The first step is to find out what you enjoy and what you are good at. You can use online-tests or you can get help at the Job Centre.* ▪ *It's important to start early – here in Germany you have to apply well before for trainee programmes or places at university.* ▪ *'Bundesagentur für Arbeit': Job Centre / a state institution that helps people find jobs*

Find a tool to improve your speaking skills here:
Webcode context-51

PRACTICE

A 'career's night' is being held at your school for your entire year group. You are asked to give a short talk in German about what careers young people tend to choose and why. Using the text 'Teenagers' career aspirations' (p. 193), prepare a script for your speech (► S25 Giving a speech).

Exam Practice

P A task allows you to practise this skill.

Download the suggested answers to the PRACTICE tasks here:
Webcode context-49

▸ EP 1 How to do exams in general

You are likely to come across many different tests and exams for English at school, for your *Abitur* or after school. Before sitting an exam, you should therefore familiarize yourself with its specific format. However, there are certain general tips that might help you to be successful. In this *Exam Practice* you will find guidance for both written and oral test formats.

BEFORE THE EXAM

Start early and organize your work.

Collecting information

- Make sure you know how to use aids that are allowed in the exam, e.g. dictionaries. (▸ SF 3: Using a dictionary; ▸ SF 4: Using a grammar book)
- Find out details of the exam situation. Who will be present? Where will it take place? How long will you have? (Especially for oral exams:) Will you be given preparation time? (▸ EP 5)
- Try to get hold of old test papers to see what they require.
- Make sure you understand what the different tasks require from you (cf. 'Verbs for tasks', pp. 410–411).
- Learn about the evaluation criteria of the exam – this will help you to focus on the relevant aspects.

Practising

- Go over old tests or homework tasks to identify your problem areas and learn from your mistakes.
- Don't practise what you already know but focus on your weak areas. (▸ LP 1–20)
- Practise the specific type of exam you will be sitting. If you have to pass an oral exam, practise with a partner. If you have to write a comment, write comments or different parts of a comment.

IN THE EXAM

- Be on time for the exam.
- Read the instructions of the test carefully, they provide crucial information. Make sure you understand what you are supposed to do – it may help to highlight the instructions.
- If you are allowed to choose between different tasks, read all alternatives before deciding which one you want to do.
- If you notice that you are becoming nervous, take a quick break before continuing.
- Use your time efficiently, e.g. leave enough time for checking your work.

PRACTICE

A teacher has added this comment to a student's text:

The argumentation of your comment is convincing. You might put forward some more arguments though and back up all your findings with passages from the text. The overall structure of your text is well-chosen, but try to connect the paragraphs more effectively. Linking words and special phrases may help you to do so. Your style of writing is your strength: you write fluently and right to the point. You have expanded your vocabulary successfully and most passages are idiomatic. There are hardly any mistakes, but you should revise conditional sentences.

1 Look at the following list of criteria and say whether the student's text fulfilled them very well or just satisfactorily or whether it needs improvement in that area.

Criteria		
▪ Content: quality	▪ Content: quantity	▪ Structure
▪ Use of quotes	▪ Linking words	▪ Useful phrases for interpretation
▪ Vocabulary: general flexibility	▪ Ability of expression	▪ Grammar

2 Look at the sections Skills File (pp. 320–375) and Language Practice (pp. 288–309) and identify relevant sections that could help the student to improve his/her weak areas.

3 Now collect your own 3–5 weak areas and identify the relevant sections in Skills File and/or Language Practice. Develop an action plan to work on your weak areas.

▶ EP 2 Working with texts

In most of your exams you will be faced with one or more texts, which you have to respond to (▶ SF 11–13, ▶ SF 16–21). These may include:

- *fictional texts (e.g. *short stories, *poems; extracts from *novels, *dramas or *film scripts)
- *non-fictional texts (e.g. articles, *speeches)
- visuals (e.g. *cartoons, pictures, films, advertisements, leaflets).

You may be given a single written text or a written text combined with another text or a visual. You will be expected to work on different tasks. For instance, you may be asked to analyse a short story or to mediate a newspaper article. In order to be successful you will need to apply different skills, e.g.:

- skimming, scanning (▶ SF 14: Reading strategies)
- underlining or highlighting important sections (▶ SF 15: Marking up a text / Making and taking notes)
- making notes in the margin (▶ SF 15: Marking up a text / Making and taking notes)
- making notes on a separate piece of paper, e.g. mind maps, outlines, drawings (▶ SF 7: Making visual aids; ▶ SF 8: Structuring ideas)
- writing a well-structured text (▶ SF 38).

Find a mindmapping tool here:
Webcode context-53

In general, when dealing with a text you will be asked to consider the following three aspects:

Anforderungsbereich I	*Anforderungsbereich II*	*Anforderungsbereich III*
comprehension (focus on content) ▶ EP 2.1	analysis/interpretation (focus on form and function) ▶ EP 2.2	composition (focus on evaluation and re-creation) ▶ EP 2.3

In an exam, you may be given tasks that clearly relate to one of these three aspects, or there might be complex tasks that combine two or all three of them.

▸ EP 2.1 *Anforderungsbereich I*: comprehension

This type of task focuses on the content of a text and is intended to check whether you have understood the information. Comprehension tasks can be quite open, i.e. they require you to write a free text, as in summary writing (▸ SF 31) or answering comprehension questions. They can also occur in the form of closed test formats, e.g. multiple choice or true/false exercises (▸ SF 10: Working with closed test formats; ▸ EP 6).

TYPICAL INSTRUCTIONS FOR *ANFORDERUNGSBEREICH I* (OPEN TASKS)

Here are some instructions that are frequently used for *Anforderungsbereich I*. To see the complete list of instructions, have a look at pp. 410–411 ('Verbs for tasks').

Instruction	Example	What you are expected to do	Tips
outline ['– –] *umreißen, skizzieren*	**Outline** the writer's views on …	*Give the main features, structure or general principles of a topic, omitting minor details.*	Structure your answer using main and subordinate points.
state *darlegen*	**State** the author's opinion on the main character's decision.	*Specify something clearly.*	Be precise and brief.
summarize (*also:* **give/write a summary of; sum up**) *zusammenfassen*	**Summarize** the incident in the church in no more than four sentences.	*Give a concise account of the main points of something.*	Be concise; leave out details and examples.

To practise *Anforderungsbereich I*, have a look at **Practice I** (p. 382) or **Practice II** (p. 383).

▸ EP 2.2 *Anforderungsbereich II*: analysis/interpretation

In this part of the exam, you 'read between the lines' of a text. You might examine why an author gives the text a certain form, why he/she characterizes the figures in a drama in a certain way, etc. To do exactly what you are asked to do, make sure you understand the instructions (cf. 'Verbs for tasks', pp. 410–411). Also, provide a suitable structure for your findings (▸ SF 8: Structuring ideas).

TYPICAL INSTRUCTIONS FOR *ANFORDERUNGSBEREICH II*

Here are some instructions that are frequently used for *Anforderungsbereich II*. To see the complete list of instructions, have a look at pp. 410–411 ('Verbs for tasks').

Instruction	Example	What you are expected to do	Tips
analyse *(BE)*, **analyze** *(AE)* ['ænəlaɪz]/ **examine** [ɪg'zæmɪn] *analysieren, untersuchen*	**Analyse** the main elements of the poster. **Examine** the writer's attitude towards the protagonist.	*Describe and explain certain aspects and/or features of the text in detail.*	Do not just list e.g. stylistic devices the author uses, but always connect them to the effect they are used to create.
explain *erklären*	**Explain** the main character's reaction to her mother in the first scene.	*Describe and define in detail.*	Do not just describe something, but give reasons why it is the way it is.

Authors always write their texts to achieve an effect – they may want to persuade or inform the readers, they may try to arouse compassion or contempt for a character in their story, etc. When analysing a text, you need to examine which means the author has used to create a specific effect (▸ SF 17: Analysing stylistic devices; ▸ SF 18: Analysing non-fiction; ▸ SF 19–21: Analysing fiction). The table below gives some examples.

Category	Some typical means	Possible effects
techniques of persuasion	quote from or use of statistics from reliable sources and experts	creates credibility
	example from everyday life	makes an argument more comprehensible and concrete
	direct address of reader	makes the reader sympathize with a concept or adopt the writer's view
use of language	use of *images (e.g. *metaphor, *symbol, *simile, *personification)	helps to evoke a graphic, vivid picture in the reader's mind
	use of *stylistic devices such as *anaphora, *alliteration or *repetition	stresses a certain aspect
	use of *irony, *sarcasm	creates humour, emphazises a point or message
	use of technical jargon	creates credibility, makes the writer appear more expert
narrative techniques	use of a *first-person narrator	helps the reader to identify with the narrator, to understand his or her attitude

To practise *Anforderungsbereich II*, have a look at **Practice I** (p. 382) or **Practice II** (p. 383).

▸ EP 2.3 *Anforderungsbereich III*: beyond the text

Part III of the exam requires you to produce a text. It may be based on a text or on visuals (e.g. cartoons or photos) or it may take just a topic as a starting point. It may be called *comment, composition, creative writing* or *writing.*

In some exams you will be asked to write a certain type of text. The task may also give you aspects that need to be (or may be) taken into consideration. The following table gives you an idea about the most common text types, their purpose, content/structure and specific language.

Text type	Purpose	Content/Structure	Language
***feature story/ article**	▪ inform sb. ▪ entertain sb. ▪ provide background information	▪ catchy headline ▪ first paragraph must arouse reader's interest (example, anecdote) ▪ use of anecdotes, examples, quotes ▪ personal angle	▪ less formal language, some slang may be used
report (▸ SF 33: Writing a report)	▪ inform sb. ▪ provide background information ▪ influence sb.	▪ catchy headline ▪ clear paragraphs ▪ from general aspects to detail	▪ less formal language, some slang may be used

·····▸

***comment** (► SF 34: Argumentative writing)	▪ pass judgment on an issue ▪ express and support your opinion	▪ introduction: outline of topic and attitude ▪ body: arguments for personal position, refutation of counter-arguments ▪ conclusion: summary of personal position ▪ use of examples to illustrate arguments	▪ formal/neutral language
argumentative essay/ discussion (► SF 34: Argumentative writing)	▪ weigh up both sides of an issue remaining fairly neutral	▪ introduction: outline of topic ▪ body: pros and cons of the issue ▪ conclusion: summary of arguments, statement of personal opinion ▪ use of examples to illustrate arguments	▪ formal/neutral language
(written) **interview** (► SF 37: Doing a creative writing task; ► SF 26: Taking part in an interview)	▪ present a topic/a person's views ▪ portray a celebrity	▪ introduction: basic facts on interviewee ▪ official welcome of interviewee ▪ body: interviewee's answers to questions (which should be polite, may be provocative) ▪ concluding statement or question; words of goodbye and expression of gratitude	▪ imitation of spoken language ▪ polite language
***letter** (e.g. letter to the editor, cover letter for an application, personal letter) **email** (► SF 34: Writing a formal letter or email)	▪ various, e.g. apply for a job, tell reader about a topic, express your opinion	▪ content varies according to addressee and purpose ▪ structural elements: letterhead, greeting, body, signature	▪ varies according to addressee and purpose
review (► SF 32: Writing a review)	▪ describe something you have read or experienced (book, film, etc.) and express your opinion on it ▪ make recommendations	▪ introduction – body (brief summary, evaluation) – conclusion	▪ varies according to type of magazine or newspaper ▪ use of words that describe the film, book, etc. and your opinion in a differentiated way (adjectives, adverbs; words with positive or negative connotations)

***speech script** (► SF 25: Giving a speech)	▪ various, e.g. move/ convince/inform/ entertain sb	▪ introduction: welcome audience; outline topic and intention of speech ▪ body: well-structured arguments backed up with evidence/examples ▪ conclusion: summary, appeal to listeners, expression of gratitude	▪ varies according to context, i.e. audience, speaker, occasion ▪ stylistic devices

Your task may also be creative writing (► SF 37: Doing a creative writing task), i.e. you may be asked to add something to an already existing text (mostly fictional) or to change it. You might change the *point of view of a text, add an ending to a story (or write a different one), add a part to the text or fill a gap in it (e.g. an *interior monologue). Remember that your writing must match the language style of the original.
You may also come across 'free' creative writing tasks. They are not based on or linked to a certain text but require you to apply your knowledge and skills – as for example when writing a poem on a given topic.

TYPICAL INSTRUCTIONS FOR *ANFORDERUNGSBEREICH III*

If you are not given a certain text type to write, you may find one of the tasks listed in the table below. See pp. 340–341 for a complete list of instructions ('Verbs for tasks').

Instruction	Example	What you are expected to do	Tips
comment on ['kɒment] *kommentieren, Stellung nehmen zu*	**Comment on** the speaker's belief that …	*State clearly your opinions on the topic in question and support your views with evidence.*	Say exactly what you think and why.
discuss *diskutieren, erörtern*	**Discuss** how education influences attitudes towards immigration.	*Investigate or examine by argument; give reasons for and against.*	Structure your ideas clearly. Weigh up both sides of an issue and support your final position with arguments.
justify *begründen, rechtfertigen*	**Justify** your answer.	*Show adequate grounds for decisions or conclusions.*	If possible and suitable, use statistics or research results as support.

In all your writing tasks make sure to apply general writing skills such as structuring a text or linking ideas (► SF 8: Structuring ideas; ► SF 38: Writing a well-structured text).
To practise *Anforderungsbereich III*, have a look at **Practice I** (p. 382) or **Practice II** (p. 383).

Working with a non-fictional text: *Anforderungsbereich I, II* and *III*

PRACTICE I

A great honour *Ewen MacAskill*

NSA whistleblower Edward Snowden said he was humbled and honoured after Glasgow University students voted overwhelmingly for him to serve as their rector for the next three years. In a statement to the Guardian, Snowden described it as bold and historic decision in support of academic freedom. 'In a world where so many of our developing thoughts and queries and plans must be entrusted to the open internet, mass surveillance is not simply a matter of privacy, but of academic freedom and human liberty,' Snowden said. The vote is purely symbolic as Snowden is unlikely to be in a position to become a working rector, able to represent students at meetings of the university's administrators. He is wanted by the US for leaking tens of thousands of documents to journalists and has been granted temporary asylum in Russia. The result of the online election was announced to candidates and their supporters shortly after polls closed at 5pm on Tuesday. Snowden was nominated by a group of students at the university who said they had received his approval through his lawyer. He defeated the former champion cyclist Graeme Obree, the author Alan Bissett and the Rev Kelvin Holdsworth, who also stood for the post. Chris Cassells, Snowden's spokesman for the rectorial election campaign, said: 'We are delighted to see Edward Snowden elected as the new rector of the University of Glasgow. We have a proud and virtuous tradition of making significant statements through our rectors and today we have once more championed this idea by proving to the world that we are not apathetic to important issues such as democratic rights.' […] Charles Kennedy, the outgoing rector and former Lib Dem leader, said: 'It has been a pleasure and a privilege to serve the students of the University of Glasgow for the past six years. The post of rector is an important one, and I would like to wish my successor all the very best for his term of office.'

Snowden, in his statement, said: 'I am humbled by and grateful to the students of Glasgow University for this historic statement in defence of our shared values. We are reminded by this bold decision that the foundation of all learning is daring: the courage to investigate, to experiment, to inquire.' He added: 'If we do not contest the violation of the fundamental right of free people to be left unmolested in their thoughts, associations, and communications – to be free from suspicion without cause – we will have lost the foundation of our thinking society. The defence of this fundamental freedom is the challenge of our generation, a work that requires constructing new controls and protections to limit the extraordinary powers of states over the domain of human communication. This election shows that the students of Glasgow University intend to lead the way, and it is my great honour to serve as their rector.'

From: *The Guardian*, 18 February 2014

1 **whistleblower** *Enthüller*
2 **rector** *(BE)* head of a university or college
3 **bold** (here) brave
8 **leak sth.** (here) reveal sth.
13 **Rev Kelvin Holdsworth** clergyman of the Scottish Episcopal Church in Glasgow
17 **Lib Dem** (= The Liberal Democrats) a socially liberal political party in the United Kingdom
21 **humble sb.** *jdn. mit Demut erfüllen*
23 **daring** ready to do dangerous or unusual things, brave
24 **unmolested** not disturbed by anybody

1 Possible task for *Anforderungsbereich I*
Summarize what the article tells you about Snowden's election and his personal reaction to it. (► SF 31: Writing a summary)

2 Possible task for *Anforderungsbereich II*
Examine how MacAskill expresses his indirect support for Snowden's actions. Consider his line of argument, his techniques of persuasion and his use of language. (► SF 18: Analysing non-fiction)

TIP
Reread EE 2.2, then collect ideas and structure them before starting to write. (► SF 8: Structuring ideas)

3 Possible tasks for *Anforderungsbereich III*

Before working on the tasks you might want to do some research on the controversy around Edward Snowden.

a Some people have called Snowden a traitor because he leaked confidential information from the NSA. Discuss this view. ▶ LANGUAGE HELP (▶ SF 34: Argumentative writing)

b Write an interview with an American politician who considers Snowden a hero who opened the world's eyes to mass surveillance. ▶ LANGUAGE HELP (▶ SF 37: Doing a creative writing task)

c Imagine you are a student at Glasgow University before Snowden's election as rector. You have been asked to give a speech in front of undecided fellow students convincing them (not) to vote for him. Write a speech.
▶ LANGUAGE HELP (▶ SF 25: Giving a speech)

LANGUAGE HELP

- endanger national security
- destabilize international relationships
- commit a crime
- cause unpredictable political turmoil
- be on an ego-trip
- brave hero
- support freedom of speech
- fundamental democratic right
- trigger a much needed debate
- defense of democratic values
- principles of the American Dream
- international peacekeeping

Working with a fictional text: *Anforderungsbereich I, II and III*

PRACTICE II

In the novel *The Uncommon Reader* Queen Elizabeth II discovers a travelling library outside of Buckingham Palace. She starts to borrow books regularly and slowly, her character begins to change. In this excerpt she is talking to her equerry after performing a ceremony.

The monarch's truly human side *Alan Bennett*

'Less spontaneous this morning, ma'am,' one of the bolder equerries ventured to say.

'Was I?' said the Queen, who would once have been most put out at even this mildest of criticisms, though these days it scarcely impinged. 'I think I know why it is. You see, Gerald, as they kneel one looks down on the tops of people's heads a good deal and from that perspective even the most unsympathetic personality seems touching: the beginnings of a bald patch, the hair growing over the collar. One's feelings are almost maternal.'

The equerry, with whom she'd never shared such confidences before and who ought to have been flattered, simply felt awkward and embarrassed. This was a truly human side to the monarch of which he'd never been previously aware and which (unlike its counterfeit versions) he did not altogether welcome. And whereas the Queen herself thought that such feelings probably arose out of her reading books, the young man felt it might be that she was beginning to show her age. Thus it was that the dawn of sensibility was mistaken for the onset of senility.

Immune to embarrassment herself, as she was to any that she might cause, the Queen would once not have noticed the young man's confusion. But observing it now she resolved in the future to share her thoughts less promiscuously, which was a pity in a way as it was what many in the nation longed for. Instead she determined to restrict her confidences to her notebooks, where they could do no harm.

The Queen had never been demonstrative; it was not in her upbringing; but more and more these days, particularly in the period following Princess Diana's death, she was being required to go public about feelings she would have preferred to keep to herself. At that time, though, she had not yet begun to read, and it was only now that she understood that her predicament was not unique and that she shared it, among others, with Cordelia. She wrote in her notebook: 'Though I do not always understand Shakespeare, Cordelia's "I cannot heave my heart into my mouth" is a sentiment I can readily endorse. Her predicament is mine.'

From: *The Uncommon Reader*, 2007

2 **equerry** [–'– –] male officer who acts as an assistant to the royal family
venture to do sth. *etwas zu tun wagen*
4 **scarcely** almost not
impinge have a noticeable effect
6 **bald patch** area on top of the head without hair
collar *Kragen*
7 **maternal** *mütterlich*
8 **be flattered** *sich geschmeichelt fühlen*
9 **awkward** uncomfortable
10 **counterfeit** fake
11 **arise out of sth.** happen as a result of sth.
12 **dawn of sensibility** *Anflug von Empfindsamkeit*
onset beginning
16 **promiscuously** *(here)* with lots of people
17 **harm** damage, injury
18 **be demonstrative** show your feelings in public
upbringing education
19 **Princess Diana** (1961–1997) first wife of the Queen's son Charles
21 **predicament** situation where it is hard to know what to do
22 **Cordelia** character from William Shakespeare's drama *King Lear*
23 **endorse sth.** say publicly that you support sth.

1 Possible task for *Anforderungsbereich I*
Briefly describe the situation as well as the monarch's and Gerald's attitudes and feelings.

2 Possible task for *Anforderungsbereich II*
Examine how the author employs narrative perspective to show the differences between the behaviour and views of the Queen and the equerry. (▸ SF 19: Analysing narrative prose)

Step 1: Put a transparency over the text and mark relevant passages revealing information on
1 the Queen's behaviour and how she explains it
2 the equerry's observations and how he explains them.

Step 2: Determine the narrative perspective and examine how it influences the reader's perception of both characters. What effect does it have on the presentation of both characters' behaviour and views?

Step 3: Add your observations to the structure below to create an outline. (▸ SF 8: Structuring ideas) Don't forget to use quotes and to indicate the lines. (▸ SF 39: Quoting a text)

Paragraph 1: *narrative perspective*
…

Paragraph 2: the Queen's behaviour and her self-image
2.1. Her behaviour … | *2.2. How she explains it* …

Paragraph 3: the equerry's view
3.1. The equerry's observations … | *3.2. How he explains them* …

Step 4: Add suitable notes for introduction and conclusion, then write a coherent text. (▸ SF 38: Writing a well-structured text)

Introduction
- *an 'uncommon' picture of the British monarch*
- *Queen's new hobby → effect on her behaviour → effect on her subjects / the equerry*

Conclusion
- *omniscient third-person-narrator → two perspectives (Queen, equerry)*

…

3 Possible tasks for *Anforderungsbereich III*
a Discuss whether the British monarch is supposed to 'go public about feelings' (l. 19) considering his/her duties and function. (▸ SF 34: Argumentative writing)
b The Queen takes Cordelia's utterance as a starting point for her notebook entry (l. 22f.). Finish her entry reflecting on her latest experience and self-image. (▸ SF 37: Doing a creative writing task)

▶ EP 3 Mediation

Mediating basically means to summarize information (from a written or oral text) in another language. (▶ SF 41: Mediation of written and oral texts). Note that a mediation is *not* a translation; i.e. you do *not* translate a text word for word.
Your task is normally embedded in some kind of context, so you have to consider the situation and your relationship to the addressee to find out what information to select from the original text and in what form to put it. *Form* here can refer to a specific *text type but also to a suitable *register.
To get the maximum number of points in your exam, it is helpful to know which criteria your teacher will apply when assessing your exam:

- **content:** selection of relevant aspects for the situation given (answers given to all the addressee's questions, but no superfluous information)
- **form:** choice of suitable text type and ability to apply its rules
- **appropriateness** of *style and *register for the given situation
- **powers of expression:** ability to deal with unknown words/technical terms or culture-specific concepts; lexical and syntactical flexibility, etc.
- **grammar:** amount and types of mistakes.

TIP

Be aware of (cultural) misunderstandings, German idioms and false friends. (▶ CC 1–7) Do not translate word for word because cultural peculiarities often do not have a translation. Paraphrase. (▶ SF 9: Paraphrasing)

PRACTICE

Your British friend is coming to visit you. She has heard that a new Primark shop has just opened in your town and cannot wait to go there during her stay with you. You come across the article below.

Erschütternder Hilferuf in Kleid von Primark eingenäht

In westlichen Kleiderläden verführen bunte, billige Klamotten zum Kauf. Die Arbeitsbedingungen der Näherinnen in den indischen Textilfabriken sind dabei meist ganz weit weg. Nicht so für eine britische Primark-Kundin: Denn jemand hatte eine Botschaft in ihr Kleid genäht. Die britische Primark-Kundin Rebecca Gallagher hat überraschend erfahren, unter welchen Bedingungen ihr Kleid offenbar hergestellt wurde, berichtet die „South Wales Evening Post online". Sie habe in ihrem zwölf Euro teuren Sommerkleid von Primark ein Etikett mit einer Nachricht gefunden. „Forced to work for exhausting hours", zu Deutsch etwa „gezwungen, stundenlang bis zur Erschöpfung zu arbeiten", sei handschriftlich auf dem Etikett gestanden, das jemand mit der Hand zwischen die anderen genäht hatte. Es sei ihr aufgefallen, als sie nach der Waschanleitung geschaut habe, erzählte die 25-Jährige der Zeitung. Daraufhin habe sie gelobt, das Kleid nie wieder anzuziehen. Sie fühle sich schuldig und habe Angst, dass eine übermüdete Arbeiterin sich dafür in einem Sweatshop irgendwo in einem fernen Land quälen musste. „Um ehrlich zu sein, habe ich noch nie darüber nachgedacht, wie die Kleider hergestellt werden", sagte sie. „Aber das hat mich jetzt zum Nachdenken darüber gebracht, woher wir unsere billigen Klamotten bekommen." Ein Primark-Sprecher sagte der Zeitung, ihm seien keine weiteren Vorfälle dieser Art bekannt. Trotzdem bat er um Rückgabe: „Wir wären der Kundin dankbar, wenn sie das Kleid an uns übergeben würde, damit wir untersuchen können, wie das Schildchen an das Kleid gelangte und ob dieser Sache weiter nachgegangen werden muss."

Vor mehr als einem Jahr stürzte das Rana Plaza in Bangladesch ein. Beim schwersten Unglück in der Textilindustrie starben mehr als 1130 Menschen, mehr als 2500 wurden teils schwer verletzt.

·····▸

Die Arbeitsbedingungen der Näherinnen, die dort zu Dumpinglöhnen Hosen, T-Shirts und Kleider für westliche Kunden herstellen, gerieten in die Kritik. Zu den Unternehmen, die in einer der Fabriken in dem Gebäude produzieren ließen, gehörte auch das irische Unternehmen Primark.

From: *Focus*, 25 June 2014

Possible mediation task

After reading the article, you are concerned about buying new clothes. Write an email to your friend (in English) in which you tell her what you have found out about working conditions in Asian textile factories.

Step 1: Look at the following pieces of information from the text and say whether you would include them in your email or not.

1 A British customer found a message sewn into her Primark dress saying 'forced to work for exhausting hours'.
2 The customer is 25-year-old Rebecca Gallagher.
3 She found the message when looking for the washing instructions.
4 The shopper feels guilty because of the exploitation of workers in clothes factories.
5 Primark asked the young woman to return the dress to find out how the label got there.
6 In 2013, more than 1130 people were killed when a factory which produced clothes for western companies collapsed in Bangladesh.

Step 2: Collect more information from the text that you consider relevant for your email, then structure your ideas. (► SF 8: Structuring ideas)

Step 3: Read the following model answer, which is not at all perfect. Say what might be improved.

> *Hi there,*
>
> *I have a serious problem. Primark forces children to produce cheap clothes. I read that in an article in some newspaper. A woman discovered a label sewn in her Primark dress saying 'forced to work for exhausting hours'. She only paid €12 for the dress. There was also an accident in one of those sweatshops abroad. It's horrible, isn't it? I suggest we don't go there.*
>
> *Hope to hear from you soon!*

Step 4: Write your email, bearing in mind the following points:

- form: email (fairly informal)
- addressee: a friend from the UK you do not know that well (→ don't be too informal!)
- situation: your friend wants to go to the new Primark shop, but you have found out about sweatshops and want to dissuade her.
  - Don't get right to the point: make polite small talk first, maybe tell her how happy you are about the visit.
  - Try to voice your doubts about the idea without offending your friend. You might suggest some kind of compromise.

▸ EP 4 Listening and viewing

Your exam task may be based on a short audio (e.g. an interview, a speech) or video (e.g. an interview, a documentary, an extract from a film) of about four minutes.

To prepare for this exam, use every opportunity you get to listen to spoken English. For instance, listen to BBC radio or watch your favourite British or American TV show on DVD or online in English. Start with English subtitles and switch them off when you feel ready. If possible, listen to a wide variety of speakers (different accents, different speeds, various topics).

In listening tasks, you will often only be asked to answer questions on *Anforderungsbereich I*, i.e. text comprehension (▸ EE 2.1), and they are often closed test formats such as multiple choice (▸ SF 10: Working with closed test formats; ▸ SF 22: Listening). Viewing tasks, but also some listening tasks, go beyond simple understanding and require you to analyse the film clip or audio, so make sure you are familiar with aspects to examine. (▸ SF 23: Analysing a film)

There is usually a standard exam procedure when it comes to listening or viewing:

Step 1: You get some time to read the instructions and further information and vocabulary, if provided. The questions will normally come in the same order as the information in the recording.

Step 2: First listening/viewing: you are allowed to write while listening/viewing, so start working on your tasks right away. Try to complete as much as possible.

Step 3: Time to work on the tasks: fill in missing information and/or read through the tasks again. Mark things you are not sure about and any gaps that are still there.

Step 4: Second listening/viewing: try to fill any gaps that might be left and check the answers you've already noted down.

Step 5: Time to complete your tasks and check your answers.

In a viewing activity your teacher might show you the video a third time.

TIP

Before listening/viewing:
- Read the instructions carefully and make sure you know what you have to focus on.
- Try to make predictions about the audio/video and the answers to the questions.

While listening/viewing:
- Read all answers, even if you are sure that you have found the correct one. The differences between the right and the wrong answers are often subtle or tricky.
- If you need to take notes, only jot down keywords or short phrases.
- If your task requires you to write a text, try to note down particular phrases from the audio/video and use them as quotes in your text.

After viewing/listening:
- Don't leave an item unanswered. If you don't know the answer, make an educated guess – you still stand a good chance of getting the credit for it (e.g. 25% in a multiple choice item with four options!)
- If you are asked to write a text, …
  - don't forget to use all the background information from the instructions.
  - back up your findings with concrete evidence, i.e. refer to relevant phrases or expressions used by a speaker/actor or describe special (cinematic) moments.

·····▸

Listening (► SF 22: Listening)

PRACTICE

Former First Lady Hillary Rodham Clinton was US Secretary of State from 2008 to 2012. You are going to listen to an extract from an interview with her broadcast in 2014, in which she speaks about the challenges as a female Secretary of State and women's issues in general.

CD3 14

perseverance *Beharrlichkeit*
hostility *Feindseligkeit*
private capacity private life
inconsequential unimportant
break through the highest glass ceiling *die letzte Hürde nehmen*
renowned famous
assertive *durchsetzungsfähig*

1 Choose the correct answers. Sometimes more than one answer is correct.

a On women as US Secretary of State:
1 When Clinton came to office, three women had done the job of US Secretary of State before.
2 Having a female Secretary of State has changed the way people perceive women considerably.
3 In countries like the UK, a female US Secretary of State is nothing special.
4 Hillary Clinton never got used to being the only woman in the room on meetings in some foreign countries.

b To Clinton, making women and girls an important element of US foreign states policy is …
1 a necessity
2 a luxury
3 both a luxury and a necessity
4 neither a luxury nor a necessity.

c During her fight for women's rights she was often faced with …
1 hostility
2 interest
3 people rolling their eyes at her
4 people who considered this topic an unimportant hobby horse of hers.

2 List three brutal actions that girls are confronted with in a lot of countries according to Clinton.
3 List two fields of life in which women still face challenges in Western civilization.
4 List two ways in which women break the law in Saudi Arabia.
5 How does Clinton decide if and how to speak out in cases where women are treated badly?

Viewing (► SF 23: Analysing a film)

PRACTICE

Margaret Thatcher was the first and only female British Prime Minister (1979–1990). Her nickname 'the Iron Lady' was coined because of her tough opposition towards the Soviet Union and socialism as such in the Cold War era. The scene from the film *The Iron Lady* (2011) that you are going to watch shows her with the members of her Cabinet discussing a new tax.

DVD

council estate (here) *(oft sehr armer) Wohnort*
resent sth. (strongly) dislike sth.
slacker *(infml) Faulenzer/in*
sovereignty *Souveränität*
concession *Zugeständnis*
beret type of French hat

1 **Possible task for *Anforderungsbereich I***
Briefly sum up the content of the scene.

2 **Possible tasks for *Anforderungsbereich II***
a Examine Margaret Thatcher's character as presented in this scene. Focus on her attitudes and her behaviour towards the members of the Cabinet present. (► SF 35: Writing a character profile)
b Analyse the cinematic devices employed to create this picture of Thatcher. (► SF 23: Analysing a film)

3 **Possible tasks for *Anforderungsbereich III***
a Assess Margaret Thatcher's leadership qualities as shown in this scene.
b After the meeting, two Cabinet members talk about the incident, commenting on Thatcher's leadership qualities. Write their dialogue. (► SF 23: Doing a creative writing task)

▸ EP 5 Speaking

Many exams nowadays are exclusively communication exams or they may include a part in which you have to prove your communicative capacity. Preparing for and successfully passing a speaking exam is different from a written exam because you need to use different skills and strategies. (▸ SF 24–SF 28)

Usually, oral exams consist of two parts which are thematically linked, a monologue and a dialogue:

Monologue	Dialogue
In this part, you are asked to give a presentation based on e.g. a diagram, statistics, picture, cartoon, quote or short text.	In the second part, you are asked to interact with a partner or a group of students in a role-play or a discussion. It may be based on the material you have worked on for the monologue. Your fellow students have probably dealt with similar material.

To prepare for your exam, ask your teacher about the specific conditions of your exam, e.g.

- What kind of prompts can you expect (i.e. cartoons, pictures, quotes, etc.)?
- Will you be given time to prepare only the monologue or both parts?
- If there is preparation time for the dialogue, will it be at the very beginning or shortly before the dialogue?
- How long will the preparation time be?
- How long will both parts of the exam be?
- How many people will take part in the dialogue?
- Will the participants in the dialogue be other students or teachers?

To get the maximum number of points in your exam, it is helpful to know which criteria you teacher will apply when assessing your exam:

- **communicative strategies** (structure, eye contact, interaction with partners, etc.)
- **pronunciation** (clarity, fluency, intonation, accuracy)
- **powers of expression** (choice of words, ability to deal with unknown words/technical terms, flexibility, etc.)
- **grammar:** amount and types of mistakes
- **content:** quality and meaningfulness of statements/arguments, etc.

TIP

Before the exam:

- Practise monologues by describing a picture to a fellow student. (▸ SF 24: Giving a presentation)
- Learn phrases which you can use during presentations, speeches or discussions (cf. the table on p. 320).
- Study your classroom material and look for controversial issues which could be discussed, then collect arguments for and against them.
- Watch (current) political debates online to get an idea of the culture of reflection and debate.

In the exam:

- If there is a preparation time, use it to arrange your material so that you can use it effectively. Structure your ideas clearly. Use clear handwriting. Use abbreviations, keywords, etc. (▸ SF 7: Making visual aids)
- You may have to adopt a role or defend a position which you don't like. Try to disregard your personal opinion, stick to the facts and give evidence if possible.
- In the dialogue part, take your time to react but do not hesitate too long. (▸ SF 27: Having a discussion)
- Ask for clarification of crucial points. Be provocative and polite at the same time; avoid attacks or insults.
- Don't be too emotional.
- Use appropriate body language and facial expressions.
- Choose the right moment to sum up your points and introduce a new aspect.

.....▸

Stages of conversation

Every communicative situation consists of different stages. If you know about these stages and useful expressions to use, you can keep a conversation going and make it successful:

Stage of conversation	Explanation	Phrases
starting a conversation	You either introduce the situation or explain the topic.	Well, our topic seems to be very controversial … Why don't we … first? Recently, I heard that somebody …
expressing one's opinion	You elaborate the arguments concerning the topic.	I'm convinced that … It seems to me that … To me …
involving a partner	You invite a partner who so far hasn't contributed much to the conversation.	What do you think about …? Is there anything you'd like to add? How about you? Would you agree with that?
contradicting	You politely express that you have an opposing opinion.	That's not the way I see it. That is true to a certain extent but …
interrupting	You try to find your way into the conversation without cutting the other person short.	Sorry to interrupt you but … May I interrupt you for a moment, please?
asking for clarification	You are not sure that you have understood your partner correctly.	Excuse me, I didn't quite catch your point about … Do you mean …? Sorry, could you say that again, please?
gaining time to think	You need time to think or work on your own argumentation.	Well, that's a good point, but I think … Well, now, let me see … It's difficult to say exactly, but … If I understood the question correctly, … I don't know whether this is what you meant, but …
summing up	You bring the conversation to an end, e.g. by mentioning the most important aspects or giving a view into the future or establishing a compromise.	So, to sum up … In brief … To cut a long story short …

····▸

PRACTICE

1 Monologue: preparing and giving a presentation (► SF 24: Giving a presentation)

a Work with a partner. Each of you choose one of the cartoons below, then prepare a presentation in which you comment on it.

b First partner A presents his/her cartoon, then Partner B.

A

B

'Congratulations, it's a Versace!'

2 Dialogue: discussing a topic (► SF 27: Having a discussion)

You are going to have a discussion on the benefits and dangers of scientific progress.

a Work with a partner. Read the role cards below, then decide who is going to take which role.

Partner A	Partner B
Your little brother had leukemia and the doctors were able to treat it with a bone marrow transplant[1]. You are glad about scientific progress and the possibility that it might one day help to prevent leukemia.	You suffer from strong allergic reactions to certain foods and you suspect it's because you might have eaten genetically modified soy[2]. You are afraid of fast progress in science because you fear that its side effects cause more harm than good.

b Collect arguments for your position. Also collect counter-arguments and think of possible ways to refute them. You might tackle the following issues: pre-implantation genetic diagnosis, designer babies, genetically modified food, genetic engineering in health care, stem cell research, etc.

c Discuss the topic for about 10–15 minutes. Begin by introducing yourself and your general standpoint. You can take your cartoon as a starting point for the debate.

[1] **bone marrow transplant** *Rückenmarksspende* [2] **soy** *Soja*

► EP 6 Closed test formats

In many exams in and after school there are special forms of tests that are called 'closed test formats' (► SF 10: Working with closed test formats). In closed test formats, you don't write at all, but just indicate which of the given solutions is correct or which items go together.

Closed test **formats** include:
- multiple choice tests with one or more correct answer/s
- true/false statements
- matching: matching questions, statements or headings to different texts or sections of a text
- gapped text: locating and replacing missing segments of a text

Before an exam, ask your teacher which closed test formats you might expect.

Closed test formats tend to occur mostly in listening and reading comprehension tasks (► EP 2.1, EP 4). In language tests such as TOEFL, Cambridge Certificate and TELC they may also be used for grammar or vocabulary.

To be successful in a closed test format, the following **skills** may be helpful:
- strategies of dealing with unknown words (► SF 1: Dealing with unknown words)
- the ability to identify different *text types and to know what to expect from them. For example, if you follow a discussion, you can expect the speakers to have different opinions on a topic.
- knowledge about typical text structures and the use of linking words, which may indicate e.g. a contrast, an addition, a conclusion (► SF 8: Structuring ideas; ► SF 38: Writing a well-structured text).

If you are taking part in a test for a language certificate such as TOEFL, you should try to get information from this organization. Look for sample questions to get a better idea of what to expect in the exam. Since some of these tests are computer-based, you should get some computer practice in how to handle them.

TIP

- Read the instructions carefully and make sure you know what you have to focus on.
- Try to make predictions about the listening/reading text and about the answers to the questions.
- Read all answers, even if you are sure that you have found the correct one. The differences between the right and the wrong answers are often subtle or tricky.
- Fill in answers to questions that you are sure about straight away. If you are unsure, leave the item aside and come back to it later.
- Don't skip questions you cannot answer. Make educated guesses – you still stand a good chance of getting the credit for a question (e.g. 25% in a multiple choice item with four options!).

Glossary

When looking for a term in the Glossary, go to the alphabetical list of terms on p. 339 to find its exact page. An asterisk (*) before a term indicates that it is explained in the Glossary.

Literary texts

▶ Fiction

A fictional text is an imaginative work in which an author ['ɔːθə] creates his or her own world and/or presents an invented story. The reader is expected to accept this world or story as existing or true (this is called suspension of disbelief). Fiction can take different forms. The main types are *narrative prose (e.g. *novels, *short stories) and *drama.

Fiction usually comprises a variety of elements, such as *characters, *action and plot, *setting and *atmosphere. The *mode [məʊd] of presentation (scenic or panoramic) and the *point of view adopted (first-person or third-person, limited or unlimited, *reliable or *unreliable *narrator) play a central role in how the reader reacts to the story.

A literary text is often structured and held together by a specific theme [θiːm] or a so-called motif [məʊ'tiːf], which may be a recurring image or a specific phrase or sentence.

▶ Narrative prose

A narrative ['nærətɪv] prose text is a *fictional text which is told by a *narrator and is written in prose [prəʊz], i.e. writing that is formed by sentences in a continuous flow and is broken up only by paragraphs (cf. verse [vɜːs], which is used in poetry and refers to a single line of a poem, or a *stanza). Typical examples of narrative prose are *novels and *short stories. Fiction can further be subdivided by aspects of content (e.g. *coming-of-age stories or *fables).

novel ['nɒvl] *Roman* TROUBLE SPOT ***novel*** = *Roman* Not: ~~*Novelle*~~	A novel is a long and complex fictional narrative text often divided into chapters. The storyline and structure of a novel are normally more complicated than those of shorter fictional works and, accordingly, there may be greater variety and a more detailed development of *characters and *setting (i.e. the time and the place). In every novel the author must decide from which *point of view the story will be told. In some cases there is more than one *narrator. No other art form can recreate life on the same scale as the novel with its almost unlimited possibilities.
short story [ˌʃɔːt'stɔːri] *Kurzgeschichte*	There is no generally accepted definition of the short story that clearly separates it from other narrative texts like the *novel. However, there are some elements that can be regarded as characteristic. Most short stories can be read at one sitting and concentrate on one *character, situation, dilemma or problem. In a short story the characters, the situation, etc. are not fully developed (unlike in a novel); the focus is on one single aspect which undergoes a change in the course of the story. There are different types of short stories, e.g. the *coming-of-age story or the slice of life story (which shows just one particular aspect of everyday life).
microfiction, flash fiction *Kürzestgeschichte*	Microfiction (or flash fiction) is an extremely short fictional text. It refers to a new literary genre [ʒɒ̃rə, 'ʒɒnrə] that originates from the *short story. Although there is no general agreement regarding its length, microfiction is much shorter than a short story and usually does not exceed one thousand words.

fable *Fabel*	A fable is a short narrative text in which animals represent human types or act like human beings. Fables are usually didactic since they intend to teach a moral lesson, make a satirical comment or illustrate some general truth. A moral may be understood from the text or there may be a moral (epilogue ['epɪlɒg]) at the end, which in modern fables is often *ironic.
coming-of-age story *Entwicklungsroman, Initiationsgeschichte*	A coming-of-age story is a *short story or *novel in which the process of growing up is portrayed. Usually the *protagonist is a child/an adolescent undergoing an experience which changes his/her outlook on life and marks an important stage in his/her development towards adulthood. It is also called story of initiation.
frame story *Rahmenhandlung*	A frame story is a *novel or *short story which contains one or more quite independent stories within it. The main story provides the frame for the other stories. Often the main story consists of a *character in one *setting recounting another story in another setting.

► Poetry

A poem is a piece of creative writing structured by lines and rhythm ['rɪðəm] (i.e. the arrangement of stressed and unstressed syllables in a line). The lines of a poem are often arranged into groups called stanzas ['stænzəs]. Phrases or lines repeated at intervals throughout a poem form the refrain [rɪ'freɪn]. To emphasize the structure and to create certain effects, traditional poets frequently make use of *rhyme. Modern poetry often uses free verse [ˌfriː 'vɜːs], which makes little use of rhyme. The poetry comes from *repetition, *imagery and the arrangement of words and stresses in the poem. Poems are often lyrical ['lɪrɪkl] (i.e. they express personal thoughts and feelings), but they can also be narrative (i.e. they tell a story). The speaker is the voice in which a poem is spoken, especially when the personal pronoun *I* is used. This speaker is not always identical with the voice of the poet.

sonnet ['sɒnɪt] *Sonett*	A sonnet is a special form of a poem that consists of 14 lines. Sonnets became popular in England in the 17th century and were mostly used for love poetry, but later they came to embrace a wide number of themes. There are various types of sonnets with different structures and forms. Shakespeare's sonnets comprised three quatrains ['kwɒtreɪns] (i.e. four lines with a shared rhyme scheme) and a couplet ['kʌplət] (i.e. two successive lines which rhyme). The couplet has a rhyme scheme that differs from the rest of the sonnet and it is used to sum up the theme or thought. The couplet is usually accompanied by the volta ['vɒltə], i.e. the turning point in a sonnet, which can be identified by words like *but*, *yet* or *and yet*. *Example:* William Shakespeare, 'Sonnet 116'; cf. *Context* p. 177
shape poem, concrete poem ['kɒŋkriːt] *konkrete Poesie*	A shape poem (also called a concrete poem) is a poem in which the printed words form a shape or picture. The shape usually reflects the theme or contents of the poem.
rhyme [raɪm] *Reim*	Rhyme is the similarity of sounds between certain words (especially stressed syllables), usually at the end of lines. When identifying the rhyme scheme ['raɪm skiːm] (i.e. which words at the end of the lines rhyme), it is usual to use small letters to indicate that words share a rhyme. If e.g. the words *abide, thee, wide* and *see* occur respectively at the end of four successive lines, the rhyme scheme is written as **a b a b** (this pattern is called alternate rhyme [ɔːl'tɜːnət]). If *abide, wide, thee,* and *see* occur respectively at the end of four successive lines, the rhyme scheme is written **a a b b** (this pattern is called rhyming couplets). Other letters are then used for other rhymes.

metre ['miːtə] *Metrum, Versmaß*	Metre is the regular rhythm of the words in a poem. Traditionally, this is achieved by the arrangement of stressed and unstressed syllables in the line of a poem. The most common metre in English is the iambic pentameter [aɪ'æmbɪk pen'tæmɪtə], which consists of a line of five feet (each foot consists of an unstressed syllable followed by a stressed syllable).	*Example:* O ***no***! It ***is*** an ***ev***-er *fix*-ed ***mark*** From: William Shakespeare, 'Sonnet 116'; cf. *Context* p. 85 The syllables **in bold** are stressed.

► Drama

A drama or play is written to be performed by actors or actresses in a theatre, in a film, on TV or on the radio. The author of a play is called a playwright ['pleɪraɪt] or dramatist ['dræmətɪst] while a scriptwriter creates scripts for films and television. Plays are usually divided into several acts (in classical drama, there were usually five acts, but modern plays normally consist of three and sometimes of only one act). An act may be subdivided into scenes.
A scene [siːn] is a smaller unit of action in which there is no change of place or break in time. The actors take on roles of *characters, perform the *action and express themselves in the form of dialogues, monologues or soliloquies. While a dialogue ['daɪəlɒg] involves at least two actors engaged in a conversation, the monologue ['mɒnəlɒg] is a lengthy speech by just one character in the company of others. The soliloquy [sə'lɪləkwi] differs from the monologue as it is spoken by one person who is alone on stage. It can give the audience more knowledge of events or individuals than the other characters and actions can take on different meanings for the audience than for the other characters of the play (this literary device is called dramatic irony). The actors' way of speaking, their appearance and their movements, as well as the *setting, the arrangement of props (i.e. all kinds of objects used by actors on stage or in a film), the sound and lighting, etc. are often given in the stage directions – this helps an acting company perform a play.

tragedy ['trædʒədi] *Tragödie, Trauerspiel*	A tragedy is a type of *drama in which the *protagonist passes through a series of misfortunes towards his or her downfall. Usually the downfall is brought about partly by the protagonist's own fault, e.g. through too much pride, weakness, uncertainty, etc. *Example:* William Shakespeare, *Macbeth*; cf. *Context* pp. 168f.
comedy ['kɒmədi] *Komödie, Lustspiel*	A comedy is a type of *drama which deals with a light topic or a more serious one in an amusing way. A comedy always has a happy ending. *Example:* William Shakespeare, *The Taming of the Shrew*; cf. *Context* pp. 174f.
feature film ['fiːtʃə] *Spielfilm*	A feature film is a full-length film that has a story and *characters, who are played by actors. A feature film is based on a film script, which the director then turns into a film. Important elements in a film are the dialogue, the use of camera techniques and the acting.
TV/radio series ['sɪəriːz] *Fernseh-/Radioserie*	A series is a regular programme on TV or radio about the lives and problems of a *character or, more usually, a group of characters. A series may centre on a couple or family life or a leading character's career, and some involve magic and/or fantasy. Each programme is self-contained, i.e. it deals with a particular issue or storyline which is concluded at the end of the programme. The lives of the characters evolve slowly over the course of a series. *Example: Downton Abbey*; cf. *Context* p. 77

sitcom *Sitcom*	A sitcom *(= situation comedy)* is a comic TV/radio *series which usually centres around a *character or group of characters. They are often stereotypes as they do not evolve over the series. It may be filmed in front of a live audience or have canned laughter added to make the audience aware of or to reinforce the funny lines.
soap (opera) *'Seifenoper'*	A soap *(= soap opera)* is a regular TV or radio programme about the everyday lives of a group of people. The storyline of a soap, unlike that of a normal TV/radio *series, develops from programme to programme and may often end with a cliff-hanger ['klɪfhæŋə] (i.e. an exciting situation that makes you want to know what will happen next) to encourage the audience to tune in to the next episode.

▶ Narrator

The narrator [nə'reɪtə] is the voice or *character who tells the story and is part of the fictional world created by the author. There are three types of narrator:

first-person narrator *Ich-Erzähler*	The narrator is a *character in the story and refers to him- or herself as *I*. The reader must take care when reading the text, as only one person's point of view is given. *Example:* I'd attended school in the real world up until the sixth grade. It hadn't been a very pleasant experience. From: Ernest Cline, *Ready Player One*, 2012; cf. *Context* p. 212, ll. 1–2
third-person narrator *personaler/auktorialer Erzähler*	The narrator is not a *character in the story and refers to the characters as *he*, *she* or *they* or by their names. *Example:* It was with some relief that she got back into the coach and reached behind the cushion for her book. It was not there. Steadfastly waving as they rumbled along, she surreptitiously felt behind the other cushions. From: Alan Bennett, *The Uncommon Reader*, 2008; cf. *Context* p. 62, ll. 34–36 In this example, the narrator is a third-person narrator as he or she is not part of the fictional world and refers to the *protagonist by using the personal pronoun *she (= the Queen)*. This excerpt is, however, told from the Queen's point of view (i.e. there is a *limited point of view) as the readers experience the story from her perspective. They are informed about her feelings and are also puzzled about the disappearance of her book.
omniscient narrator [ɒm'nɪsɪənt] *allwissender Erzähler*	The narrator has an *unlimited point of view, i.e. he or she can move freely in place and time and enter the minds of the *characters at will.

▶ Point of view

The point of view is the perspective from which *characters, events, etc. are presented in a *fictional story. This has an important effect on the reader: for example, we tend to respond more sympathetically to a character whose mind we enter, as we experience for ourselves what he or she goes through. A fictional work can have several points of view (depending on the *narrator):

limited point of view	A *first-person narrator can have a limited point of view: a *character in fictional work does not know everything that occurs, therefore he or she imposes his or her understanding and interpretation on the action.
	A *third-person narrator can have a limited point of view: the *narrator looks at the events and characters from the perspective of one of the *characters or from the outside (as an observer narrator) and so does not have access to the thoughts and feelings of all the characters.
unlimited point of view	A third-person narrator can have an unlimited point of view: the narrator can move freely in place and time and enter the minds of the *characters at will (here we speak of an omniscient narrator [ɒm'nɪsɪənt]).

Often, the point of view changes to make for more interesting reading. A reader must ask him- or herself how reliable a narrator is. Often one cannot take everything in a fictional work at face value:

reliable narrator [rɪ'laɪəbl]	The reader may take everything the *narrator tells at face value.
unreliable narrator [ˌʌnrɪ'laɪəbl]	The reader must find out just how much of what the *narrator says can be accepted. *First-person narrators are usually unreliable as they give only one perspective on the action and the *characters.

▶ Mode of presentation

The way a writer narrates events is known as mode of presentation. There are two modes of presentation, and usually a combination of both is used in a narrative text:

scenic presentation

If the author shows an event in detail as it occurs, using dialogue, depicting thoughts and emotions, describing a scene, etc., he or she uses scenic presentation (also known as showing).

Example:

> When they arrived at the palace she had a word with Grant, the young footman in charge, who said that while ma'am had been in the Lords the sniffer dogs had been round and security had confiscated[1] the book. He thought it had probably been exploded.
>
> 'Exploded?' said the Queen. 'But it was Anita Brookner.'[2]
>
> The young man, who seemed remarkably undeferential[3], said security may have thought it was a device.
>
> The Queen said: 'Yes. That is exactly what it is. A book is a device to ignite[4] the imagination.'
>
> [1] **confiscate sth.** take sth. away [2] **Anita Brookner** (born 1928) British novelist and art historian [3] **undeferential** showing no respect [4] **ignite sth.** *etwas entzünden*

From: Alan Bennett, *The Uncommon Reader*, 2008; cf. *Context* p. 63, ll. 42–50

interior monologue [ɪn'tɪəriə 'mɒnəlɒg] *innerer Monolog*	This is a particular kind of *scenic presentation in which the author depicts the thoughts and feelings passing through a *character's mind. Often an interior monologue does not follow a chronological [ˌkrɒnə'lɒdʒɪkl] order, since when people think, their thoughts jump from one subject to another. Interior monologues are normally narrated in the present tense. However, it is more common to find reported thought, in which the thoughts are presented as reported speech (i.e. in the past tense).

·····▶

panoramic presentation	If the author tells the story as a condensed series of events, summarizing in a few sentences what happens over a longer period of time (e.g. an hour, a week, months), he or she uses panoramic presentation (also known as 'telling'). *Example:* For me, school had been a Darwinian exercise. A daily gauntlet[1] of ridicule, abuse, and isolation. By the time I entered sixth grade, I was beginning to wonder if I'd be able to maintain my sanity[2] until graduation, still six long years away. [1] **(run a) gauntlet** ['gɔːntlət] deal with a lot of people criticizing or attacking you [2] **sanity** ['sænəti] mental health From: Ernest Cline, *Ready Player One*, 2012; cf. *Context* p. 212, ll. 21–23

▸ Characters

Characters ['kærəktəz] are the people in a fictional text. They are usually presented through their actions, speech and thoughts as well as by description. The main character in a story is called the protagonist [prə'tæɡənɪst]. There are generally speaking two types of characters in *fictional works:

round character	A round character may be similar to real individuals and have several traits and behave in a way that is life-like. A round character usually changes in the course of a story. The main character in a story, the protagonist, is almost always a round character.
flat character	A flat character has only a limited number of traits or represents only a single quality. A crude representation of a character which is meant to be laughed at is called a caricature.

TROUBLE SPOT

When talking about the characters in a fictional text, do not use the words *people* or *person*.

▸ Characterization

Characterization [ˌkærəktəraɪ'zeɪʃn] is the way in which the author presents his or her characters. We usually distinguish between two kinds of characterization, which are often combined by authors in their presentation of the characters.

direct [də'rekt, dɪ'-, daɪ'-] or **explicit characterization**	The reader is told about a character's personality directly by a) the *narrator, b) another character or c) the character him- or herself.	*Example:* 'But McNulty's eyes were scary.' From: Carl Deuker, *Payback Time*, 2010; cf. p. 199, l. 44
indirect [ˌɪndə'rekt, ˌɪndaɪ'rekt] or **implicit characterization**	The reader is expected to draw conclusions about a character by studying his or her behaviour, opinions, choice of words and/or way of talking. *Example:* I cleared my throat. 'How about we get started? I've got some questions. First –' 'No, no, no,' McNulty said, pointing the pencil at me again. 'No questions – not today, not ever. This job	

> takes forever and pays peanuts. Here's how it works. You write down or tape what I tell you. When I'm done, jazz[1] it up whatever you want, but never make me, my coaches, or my players look bad. Understand?'
>
> [1] **Jazz sth. up** *(infml)* make sth. more interesting or attractive

From: Carl Deuker, *Payback Time*, 2010; cf. p. 198, ll. 33–37

TROUBLE SPOT

An author *characterizes* somebody, i.e. invents the traits of a character. A reader *describes the character* of somebody when talking about his or her traits.

LANGUAGE HELP

- main/central/major character/figure
- minor/secondary character/figure
- hero/heroine

▶ Action

Action ['ækʃn] is everything that happens in a *fictional story. Action may be on two levels:

external action [ɪk'stɜːnl]

The author describes what the *characters do and the events that take place.

Example:

> [...] she got back into the coach and reached behind the cushion for her book. It was not there. Steadfastly waving as they rumbled along, she surreptitiously[1] felt behind the other cushions.
>
> [1] **surreptitious** subtle

From: Alan Bennett, *The Uncommon Reader*, 2008; cf. *Context* p. 62, ll. 34–36.

internal action

The author describes what is going on in the minds of the *characters, i.e. the reader is shown the thoughts of the characters.

Example:

> She was dreading the two hours the whole thing was due to take, though fortunately they were in the coach, not the open carriage, so she could take along her book.

From: Alan Bennett, *The Uncommon Reader*, 2008; cf. *Context* p. 63, ll. 6–7.

▶ Plot

Plot [plɒt] refers to the structure of events in a *fictional story. The story is usually told through cause and effect. The English novelist E.M. Forster described plot in these terms: '"The king died and then the queen died" is a story. "The king died and then the queen died of grief", is a plot.' (*Aspects of the Novel*, 1927).
The plot usually develops in a number of stages:

1. **exposition** [ˌekspə'zɪʃn]	The *characters, theme, *setting, etc. are introduced.
2. **rising action**	A conflict ['kɒnflɪkt] is developed (i.e. the struggle or opposition between different forces, characters, etc.).
3. **climax** ['klaɪmæks]	The conflict reaches its highest point.
4. **turning point**	There is a change in the conflict or *suspense.
5. **falling action**	The *suspense is reduced.

·····▶

6. **denouement** [deɪ'nuːmɒ̃] (also known as the **solution** [sə'luːʃn])	Some resolution of the conflict is achieved.
which may also be: **surprise ending**	The reader's expectations concerning the course of the story are not fulfilled but instead an unexpected solution of the conflict is presented.
or instead: **open ending**	The conflict is not fully resolved and the reader is left wondering what might happen next.

A plot will have some element of *suspense and *tension. In order to create suspense or to make a story more exciting, authors also make use of flashbacks and foreshadowing:

suspense [sə'spens] *Spannung*	Suspense is created when the reader does not know the outcome of a conflict or of the action.
tension ['tenʃn] *(An)spannung*	Tension is the feeling evoked in the reader when a story/drama is full of *suspense, i.e. the reader is curious about what will happen.
flashback ['flæʃbæk] *Rückblende*	Authors do not always tell their stories strictly chronologically [ˌkrɒnə'lɒdʒɪkli]. In some stories the authors make use of flashbacks, i.e. the *narrator goes back into the past to describe a scene that has relevance to the plot.
foreshadowing [fɔː'ʃædəʊɪŋ] *Vorwegnahme*	Foreshadowing (also called anticipation) is the technique of hinting at later events in a *fictional text so that the reader is prepared for them or can anticipate them. *Example:* In William Shakespeare's *Macbeth*, the three witches allow the audience to believe that Macbeth will become king.

TROUBLE SPOT

happy ending
Not = ~~*happy end*~~

LANGUAGE HELP

- open/surprise/unexpected/happy/sad/tragic ending
- centre around sth.
- a conflict between ... and ...

► Atmosphere

Atmosphere ['ætməsfɪə] is the feeling or mood created by an author in his or her work. The *setting, use of language and *characterization all contribute to the atmosphere of a work.	*Example:* One of the Queen's recurrent royal responsibilities was to open Parliament, an obligation she had never previously found particularly burdensome[1] and actually rather enjoyed: to be driven down the Mall[2] on a bright autumn morning even after fifty years was something of a treat. [1] **burdensome** implying hard work [2] **the Mall** road leading to Buckingham Palace From: Alan Bennett, *The Uncommon Reader*, 2008; cf. *Context* p. 62, ll. 1–4 Here the description of the Queen's drive down the Mall together with the bright autumn morning creates a positive atmosphere.

▶ Setting

Setting is the time and place in which a literary work takes place. The setting can have symbolic overtones; it may serve to reveal something about the characters and also contribute to the *atmosphere of the story.
Example: The extract quoted above from the novel *The Uncommon Reader* by Alan Bennett (cf. *Context* p. 62, ll. 1–4) is set in contemporary Britain on a sunny autumn morning. The season contributes to the positive and light-hearted atmosphere of the story.

Non-fictional texts

▶ Non-fiction

A non-fictional [ˌnɒn 'fɪkʃənl] text (e.g. *news story, *advertisement, *speech, *letter, etc.) normally refers to the real world whereas a *literary text creates its own fictional world. Non-fictional texts may serve a variety of practical purposes, e.g. to inform, persuade, express personal opinions, criticize, etc. There is a variety of non-fictional text types:

news story *Zeitungs-bericht*	The terms *news story*, *news item* and *news report* can be used interchangeably to refer to reports of recent events of general interest that appear in newspapers, on television or on the radio. News items can be of any length. In theory, they are meant to be objective and unbiased presentations of the facts, providing answers to the five w's, i.e. the questions *who?*, *what?*, *when?*, *where?* and *why?*. In practice, totally impartial reporting is impossible. The choice of words, the *style and *tone, the choice of detail and examples, the emphasis ['emfəsɪs] given to certain aspects of the story, the position of the article in the paper and on the page, the headline and layout all contribute to influence the reader. There are two common formulas used in news stories: a) The pyramid, in which the most important item or element in the story is reported first and then the rest of the information is offered in descending order of importance. b) The Wall Street Journal formula, in which the news story starts with a particular (usually personal) example to attract the reader's attention before the topic is discussed. It differs from a *feature story in that the latter puts more emphasis on the personal account in order to illustrate a topic, while the former uses the personal account merely to attract the attention of the reader.
biography [baɪ'ɒgrəfi] *Biografie*	A biography is a book or text written by one person about the life of another person. If the person writes his or her own life story, this is referred to as an autobiography [ˌɔːtəbaɪ'ɒgrəfi]. Usually the biography belongs to the genre of *non-fiction as it portrays the life of a person that really exists/existed. However, there are also *fictional biographies, where the author invents a *character and his life story (e.g. *Robinson Crusoe*).
feature story ['fiːtʃə] *Zeitungsre-portage*	A feature story deals with a topic by concentrating on a particular person or on particular people. It often takes an individual case as its starting point to discuss the different aspects of the topic on a personal level and leaves the reader to draw more general conclusions from this individual case. The writer of a feature story makes use of direct quotes from the people involved in the story and relies on first-hand reporting, i.e. the journalist writes mostly about things and people he or she has actually encountered. A feature story often opens with the description of an event or a person in order to attract the reader's attention. *Example:* 'Eastern Europeans in the UK'; cf. *Context* p. 73

editorial [ˌedɪ'tɔːriəl] *Leitartikel*	An editorial (in British English also known as a *leading article* or *leader*) is an article that expresses the opinion of the newspaper's editor or editorial team about an item of news or a political or social issue, etc. In American usage an editorial can also be a comment ['kɒment] on radio or television that expresses the opinion of the station or network. Unlike *columns, editorials are not supposed to be personal and do not appear with a byline, i.e. with a line that gives the writer's name.
column ['kɒləm] *Kolumne*	a) *Column* is the term used for any of the vertical sections into which the printed page of a newspaper is divided. b) *Column* is the term used for a regular item in a newspaper or magazine which either deals with a particular subject (e.g. gardening, gossip, financial, agony column) or is written by a particular writer (called a columnist). Columnists often write highly personal essays on topics of their choosing. Unlike *editorials, columns appear with a byline, i.e. with a line that gives the writer's name.
speech *Rede, Ansprache*	A speech is an address delivered to an audience. A speaker may try to establish contact with his or her listeners in various ways: by flattering them, addressing them directly (direct address) or using the first person plural (e.g. *we*, *our*) to involve them in what he or she is saying. A speaker may appeal to shared experiences and values, e.g. by quoting from or alluding to sources such as the Bible or history. A speaker often uses *stylistic devices to heighten the impact of what he or she is saying. Contrast ['kɒntrɑːst] may be used to highlight differences between the speaker and his or her opponents. *Repetition and *alliteration often help the audience follow the speech and remember key ideas and phrases. *Example:* '9/11 – A game changer'; cf. *Context* pp. 220f.
essay *Essay*	An essay is a text form in which the writer expresses his or her personal views on some topic. Essays can vary widely in length, subject matter and *tone, some being serious and others light-hearted and entertaining.
letter *Brief*	There are many types of letters. They can be personal or business-oriented, depending on the relationship between the sender and receiver, the occasion and the purpose of the letter. Letters are a very flexible text form and comprise thank-you notes, emails, covering letters (in American English, *cover letters*), letters of complaint, *letters to the editor, etc. The beginnings and endings of letters follow certain conventions. Usually, letters consist of the following parts: **1** the address of the sender (and in the case of a business letter, the address of the recipient), **2** the date, **3** the salutation (e.g. *Dear Mark*), **4** the body of the letter, i.e. the information the sender wants to convey, **5** a conventional phrase to close the letter (e.g. *Yours faithfully*, *Yours sincerely*, *Love*) and **6** the signature. *Example:* the letter from Chetan Bhagat to Gandhi; cf. *Context* pp. 109f.
letter to the editor *Leserbrief*	A letter to the editor is a letter in which a reader expresses his or her opinion concerning an article in a newspaper/magazine or a problem which is of public interest. The letter may criticize or support an article, or state a personal opinion concerning a topic which is being discussed in public or attract the attention of other readers to a topic that has been ignored or is worthy of attention.
blurb [blɜːb] *Umschlagtext, Klappentext*	A blurb is the short promotional text on the back cover of a book or a DVD case.
advertisement [əd'vɜːtɪsmənt] *Werbung, Anzeige, Annonce*	An advertisement (informally also called an *advert* or *ad*) is a text which attempts to persuade people to do something (e.g. buy a particular product or contribute money to a cause). It normally consists of pictures and text (called *copy*) and is designed to catch the attention of the reader through its layout.

	Common elements of advertisements are *wordplay in the title or headings and *humour to win the sympathy of the reader. Advertisers often use the AIDA formula (**A**ttention, **I**nterest, **D**esire, **A**ction) in their advertisements. Newspaper or magazine advertisements dealing with job offers, buying, selling or renting something, etc. are called *small* or *classified ads.* Advertisements on the radio or on television are known as *commercials*. *Example:* 'The best job in the world is back!', cf. *Context* p. 201
blog [blɒg] *Blog*	A blog is a regularly updated website created by an individual or a small group. Usually, the chosen language is colloquial and informal.
cartoon *Karikatur, Cartoon*	A cartoon is an amusing drawing in a newspaper or magazine that deals with human nature or a current political or social issue. Complex issues are reduced to memorable pictures. Cartoons often include captions or speech bubbles. Techniques employed by cartoonists include caricature ['kærɪkətʃʊə], *exaggeration, *wordplay and the use of *symbols. Cartoons usually presuppose that the reader has background knowledge of the political, social and cultural issues being dealt with, which often makes them difficult for the non-native reader to understand. *Example:* 'Being five. A boy and his blog'; cf. *Context* p. 206

Style and Language

▸ Style

Style [staɪl] is the way in which a text is written. In order to examine the style of a text it is necessary to examine aspects such as the *register, the *diction and the *tone of the text as well as the grammar and the sentence structures used in the text.

tone [təʊn] *Ton(fall)*	Tone is the way in which a writer treats his or her topic, thereby reflecting his or her emotional attitude towards that topic and also towards the reader. The tone can be formal, intimate, solemn, playful, serious, ironic (cf. *irony), humorous (cf. *humour), angry, etc.
humour ['hju:mə] *Humor*	Humour is based on the human ability to see and laugh at the strangeness of a *character, an action or comment, etc. because it is unexpected or unsuitable in a particular situation. At one end of the spectrum, humour is gentle, understanding and tolerant and makes the reader smile at human weaknesses; at the other end, it is divisive, bitter or sarcastic, evoking contempt and moral indignation at human vices and corruption. Not all forms of humour will be appreciated by every segment of society since humour relies on shared cultural values. *Example:* [The Queen] got quite good at reading and waving, the trick being to keep the book below the level of the window and to keep focused on it and not on the crowds. From: Alan Bennett, *The Uncommon Reader*, 2008; cf. *Context* p. 62, ll. 7–9 Here the Queen's well-known behaviour of waving at the crowd is ridiculed by the fact that she is reading a book at the same time.

diction
Diktion, Ausdruck, Wortwahl

Diction is the words a writer chooses for his or her text. Diction is very important as words influence the reader or listener. In many argumentative texts, for example, the writer will use words that have a positive connotation [ˌkɒnə'teɪʃn] (i.e. the associations a word has beyond its literal or dictionary meaning) to support his or her arguments, or words with negative connotations to attack those he or she opposes. The choice of words often reveals the writer's attitudes. A writer can also use emotive language (i.e. words and expressions with particular connotations that appeal to the reader's or listener's emotions) and so influence him or her to react in a particular way. When the writer makes use of the literal and limited meaning of a word, regardless of the ideas and emotions it might connote, this is called denotation [ˌdiːnəʊ'teɪʃn].

register
['redʒɪstə]
Sprachebene, Stilebene

Register is the level of language (the choice of words, grammar, etc.) used in a particular situation. The register in a text may be formal, neutral or informal.

Formal style consists of difficult vocabulary, often of Latin origin, and complex sentence structure; it is usually only used for serious purposes, e.g. essays or academic publications, or in official situations, and would not be appropriate in normal everyday conversation.
Example:

> A new widely-debated approach is gene pharming. Pharma crops are genetically modified plants like maize that produce much-needed medicines.

From: 'Science – motor of progress?', cf. *Context*, p. 144, ll. 22–24

The writer uses difficult words and grammar so that the reader must examine the sentence closely to understand what the writer is saying.

Neutral style falls between *formal and *informal style and is the style generally used by educated people; it is used in *feature stories, *news stories, etc.
Example:

> [P]eople's 'likes' and 'dislikes' are carefully stored, along with a great number of other details gathered about the users, to be exploited by businesses or political organizations.

From: 'Living interactive lives', cf. *Context*, p. 208, ll. 6–9

The writer uses straightforward sentences and words that are neither formal nor informal.

Informal style is characterized by fairly simple, often incomplete sentences, short forms (e.g. *can't, you'll*), phrasal verbs and colloquial words, often of Germanic origin; it is used between friends or in a relaxed or informal situation.
Example:

> That waitress sized us up in two seconds. We're black, and 'black people don't tip' so she wasn't gonna waste her time; someone like that, nothing you can do to change their mind.

From: Paul Haggis, *Crash*, 2004

The short forms like 'we're', 'wasn't' or gonna, the use of simple words like 'do', 'go' and phrases like *to* 'size sb'. *up* indicate that the characters are using informal style.
Informal style may include the use of slang and/or taboo words: Slang is very informal language, mainly used in dialogue between people of the same age or from a similar background, etc.
Taboo words [tə'buː] are generally considered obscene, vulgar or shocking and are used only if the writer is trying to make a particular point or shock his or her reader.

layout *Layout, Aufbau*	The way elements are arranged on a printed page is known as the layout. The layout includes elements such as the type and size of letters, the use of **bold** or *italic* typeface, underlining, headings and sub-headings, bullets (i.e. dots or other symbols used at the beginning of a text passage), the size and number of *columns, the length of paragraphs, the colour and the placement of illustrations. The layout determines whether a text attracts the attention of the reader and is pleasant to read, and it helps writers to structure their texts and to emphasize certain words, phrases or passages. The layout is particularly important when considering newspaper articles, *advertisements and brochures.
thesis ['θiːsɪs] *These*	An idea or a view that an author of an argumentative text presents and discusses in a formal way.
antithesis [æn'tɪθəsɪs] *Antithese*	An antithesis is an idea that is the opposite of an idea (thesis) already put forward by a writer. Often the writer will put forward the antithesis in order to stress his own thesis.

▸ Stylistic devices

Stylistic devices [staɪ'lɪstɪk dɪ'vaɪsɪs] (also called *rhetorical devices* [rɪ'tɒrɪkl dɪ'vaɪsɪs]) are methods and techniques used to produce a particular effect. Stylistic devices may e.g. relate to sound (e.g. *alliteration), structure (e.g. *repetition, *parallelism) or *imagery.

LANGUAGE HELP

The author uses alliteration/contrast/exaggeration/repetition ... (uncountable nouns)
In line 5 there is a metaphor/allusion/symbol/rhetorical question/pun (countable nouns)

Imagery

metaphor ['metəfə, 'metəfɔː] *Metapher*	A metaphor is a comparison between two things which are basically quite unlike one another without using the words *as* or *like* (cf. *simile).	*Example:* There's daggers in men's smiles. From: William Shakespeare, *Macbeth*
personification [pəˌsɒnɪfɪ'keɪʃn] *Personifikation*	Personification is the technique of representing animals or objects as if they were human beings or possessed human qualities. *Example:* Love's not Time's fool, though rosy lips and cheeks / Within his bending[1] sickle's[2] compass[3] come: / Love alters not with his brief hours and weeks, / But bears[4] it out even to the edge[5] of doom. — [1] **bending** curved [2] **sickle** *Sichel* [3] **compass** *Reichweite* [4] **bear out sth.** endure sth. [5] **edge of doom** end of time — From: William Shakespeare, 'Sonnet 116', cf. *Context*, p. 85. Here, both love and time are personified. Love in particular is described as a person with the appearance of 'rosy lips and cheeks'.	
simile ['sɪməli] *Vergleich*	Like a *metaphor, a simile is a type of comparison. But while metaphors say that something *is* something else, a simile says that something *is like* something else and uses the words *like* or *as* to draw the comparison.	*Example:* My mistress eyes are nothing like the sun. From: William Shakespeare, 'Sonnet 18'

symbol ['sɪmbl] *Symbol*	A symbol is a thing, word or phrase signifying something concrete that stands not only for itself but also for a certain abstract idea. As in the case of a *metaphor or a *simile the meaning of a symbol goes beyond the literal. *Example:* A red rose is often a symbol of love.

TROUBLE SPOT
symbol of sth.
Not: ~~*symbol for sth.*~~

Sound

alliteration [əˌlɪtə'reɪʃn] *Alliteration*	Alliteration is the repetition of a sound, normally a consonant, at the beginning of neighbouring words or of stressed syllables within such words, to produce a usually rhythmic, but sometimes also comic effect. *Example:* Around the rugged rock the ragged rascal ran.	
assonance ['æsənəns] *Assonanz*	Assonance is the repetition of the same or similar vowel sounds within stressed syllables of neighbouring words.	*Example:* Beside the lake, beneath the trees, Fluttering and dancing in the breeze. From: William Wordsworth, 'I wandered lonely as a cloud'
onomatopoeia [ˌɒnəˌmætə'piːə] *Lautmalerei*	Omatopoeia is the use of a word which imitates the sounds it refers to, e.g. *buzz* or *hum*. In a group of words or a phrase it may evoke a particular feeling, mood, sound or movement.	*Example:* Only the stuttering rifles' rapid rattle. From: Wilfred Owen, 'Anthem for doomed youth' The repetition of 't's and 'r's sounds like the shooting of rifles, which the words describe.

Structure

accumulation [əˌkjuːmjə'leɪʃn] *Akkumulation, Ansammlung*	Accumulation is a listing of words and expressions with similar meaning. Thus, the words are emphasized or become more descriptive. *Example:* Then shall our names / Familiar in his mouth as household words / Harry the King, Bedford and Exeter / Warwick and Talbot, Salisbury and Gloucester, / Be in their flowing cups freshly remembered. From: William Shakespeare, *Henry V* This excerpt displays an accumulation of several addresses for 'King Harry'.
analogy [ə'nælədʒi] *Analogie*	Analogy is the comparison of two things which are similar in several aspects. By comparing an object, situation or person to something familiar, the explanation becomes easier to understand. *Example:* What's in a name? That which we call a rose. / By any other word would smell as sweet. / So Romeo would, were he not Romeo called. From: William Shakespeare, *Romeo and Juliet* Juliet states that just like a rose that will always keep its sweet smell whichever name it is called, Romeo will stay the same even if he changes his name.

anaphora [ə'næfərə] Anapher	Anaphora is a form of *parallelism which repeats the same word or group of words at the beginning of successive clauses.	*Example:* Come in, I say. Come in and eat with us. From: Imtiaz Dharker, 'The right word', *The Terrorist on My Table* (2006)
enjambement [ɪn'dʒæmbmənt] *Enjambement*	Enjambement describes incomplete syntax at the end of the line where the meaning runs over to the next line without any punctuation at the end. An enjambement is also called *run-on line.*	*Example:* The child steps in And carefully, at my door, Takes off his shoes. From: Imtiaz Dharker, 'The right word', *The Terrorist on My Table* (2006)
enumeration *Aufzählung*	Enumeration is the listing of words, phrases or ideas. In instructive or argumentative texts the list of enumerated elements can be given numbers or bullet points so the reader can see each new element clearly.	*Example:* [...] go, my son, multiply, divide, conquer. From: Philip Levine, 'Corporate Head'; cf. *Context* p. 197
parallelism ['pærəlelɪzəm] *Parallelismus*	Parallelism is the deliberate repetition of similar or identical words, phrases, sentence constructions, etc. in the same or neighbouring sentences. Parallelism draws the attention of the reader to certain ideas that the writer may consider important. It may be used to show that the elements are of similar importance, or it may be used in a climactic sequence, with the most important element listed at the end.	*Example:* [...] Which alters[1] when it alteration finds, Or bends with the remover to remove[2]. [1] **alter** change [2] **remover** person who goes away From: William Shakespeare, 'Sonnet 116', cf. *Context* p. 177, ll. 3–4
repetition *Wiederholung*	Repetition is the deliberate use of a word or phrase more than once in a sentence or a text to create a sense of pattern or form, or to emphasize certain elements for the reader or listener.	

Miscellaneous

allusion [ə'lu:ʒn] *Allusion, Anspielung*	Allusion is the direct or indirect reference to something or somebody the reader or listener is supposed to recognize and respond to. An allusion may be to a work of literature, a historical event, a religious text like the Bible, etc. *Example:* 'This place is like the garden of Eden'. This allusion refers to the 'garden of God', i.e. paradise, which appears in the Bible.
cliché ['kli:ʃeɪ]	A cliché denotes the fact that an expression has been overused to the extent that the original meaning has been lost. It may also refer to predictable events or actions.

·····▸

exaggeration [ɪɡˌzædʒəˈreɪʃn] *Übertreibung*	Exaggeration is the use of a strong overstatement. It may be used to create either a serious or comic effect. A single phrase containing an exaggeration is called hyperbole [hʌɪˈpɜːbəli]. (cf. also *understatement)	*Example:* I fear the day technology will surpass our human interaction. The world will have a generation of idiots. *Albert Einstein*
irony [ˈaɪrəni] *Ironie*	Irony is the term used when a person makes fun of somebody or something without openly doing so. A person using irony may use certain words and actually mean the opposite of what those words normally mean. Also, a person may appear to support someone or something while at the same time making it clear (e.g. by his or her tone of voice) that he or she is actually criticizing or revealing the contradictions in the other person's behaviour. A text which uses irony to ridicule or make fun of an institution, person, set of beliefs, etc. is called a satire [ˈsætaɪə].	
juxtaposition [ˌdʒʌkstəpəˈzɪʃn] *Gegenüberstellung*	Juxtaposition is a very strong contrast [ˈkɒntrɑːst] of opposing ideas, arguments, views, mostly introduced by words like *but*, *however* or *nevertheless*.	
rhetorical question *rhetorische Frage*	A rhetorical question is a question to which the answer seems obvious and is therefore not necessary. Such questions push the reader or listener to a certain conclusion. As such they are popular in political *speeches, etc. when a person is trying to influence others.	*Example:* What do the changes mean? They can either strengthen and unite us, or they can weaken and divide us. From: William J. Clinton, 'The changing face of America'; cf. *Context* p. 24, ll. 27–28 Here the rhetorical question is used to draw the reader/listener into the argument by posing a direct question. The reader/listener might feel a little under pressure, even manipulated to answer the question in a specific way.
understatement *Untertreibung*	Understatement is a statement in which the true magnitude of an idea, event or fact is minimized, so that something is deliberately presented as being much less important, valuable, etc. than it really is. Understatement is often used for *ironic effect, e.g. saying 'It is a bit cold today', when the temperature is 10 degrees below freezing. (cf. also *exaggeration)	
wordplay or **pun** [pʌn] *Wortspiel*	Wordplay (also called pun) is the use of a word which may be understood in two different ways or which may be put into a different context to alter the meaning. *Example:* The magician got so mad that he pulled his hair out. Here, the word *hair* alludes to *hare* (= *Hase*), an animal commonly associated with magicians.	

Alphabetical list of words in the Glossary

Words in **bold** print have their own entries in the Glossary; words in blue print do not have their own entry and appear as part of another entry.

Verbs for Tasks ('Operatoren')

Context uses the same special vocabulary ('Operatoren') for tasks that is used in standard tests, including the 'Abitur'. Be sure you understand what's required of you when you come across one of the verbs below.

'Anforderungsbereich I' COMPREHENSION
refers to text comprehension and definition.

'Anforderungsbereich II' ANALYSIS
focuses on text analysis and comparison, and stylistic devices.

'Anforderungsbereich III' BEYOND THE TEXT
concentrates on discussion, comment, evaluation and text production.

Find a further list of verbs for tasks, this one ordered by skills (writing, mediation, listening, speaking), here:
Webcode context-58

The instructions say	Example	What you are expected to do
	'Anforderungsbereich I' COMPREHENSION	
outline *präsentieren, vorstellen, nennen*	**Outline** the author's views on love, marriage and divorce.	*Give the main features, structure or general principles of a topic, omitting minor details.*
delineate *skizzieren*	**Delineate** the concept of integration.	*Give the main features of something.*
describe *beschreiben*	**Describe** the living conditions of the family.	*Give an account in words, present a picture with words.*
summarize (also: **sum up**) *zusammenfassen*	**Summarize** the main points of the German newspaper article.	*Give a concise account of the main points or ideas of a text, issue or topic.*
	'Anforderungsbereich II' ANALYSIS	
point out / depict *darstellen*	**Point out** the author's main ideas on ... / **Depict** the meaning of the cartoon.	*Present the main aspects of sth. briefly and clearly.*
put into the context of *einordnen, zuordnen, in einen Zusammenhang bringen mit*	**Put** this speech **in the context of** the Hispanic experience in the USA.	*Link an incident/statement to relevant historical or topical knowledge.*
analyse (BE), **analyze** (AE) ['ænəlaɪz] *analysieren*	**Analyse** the narrative perspective in the given excerpt.	*Describe and explain certain aspects and/or features of the text in detail.*
examine [ɪɡ'zæmɪn] *untersuchen*	**Examine** the author's use of language.	*Name and explain the meaning of specific aspects and/or features of the text and their effects on the reader/audience.*

The instructions say	Example	What you are expected to do
explain *erklären*	**Explain** the protagonist's obsession with money.	*Make clear and plain; give the reason or cause.*
relate (to) *in Beziehung setzen*	**Relate** the protagonist's principles **to** a text read in class.	*Show the relationship between two or more concepts.*
compare / contrast [kən'trɑːst] *vergleichen, kontrastieren, gegenüberstellen*	**Compare** X's and Y's views on education. / **Contrast** the author's concept of multiculturalism with concepts you have encountered in class	*Tell how things are alike and/or different, use concrete examples.*
write a characterization of [ˌkærəktəraɪ'zeɪʃn] *charakterisieren, detailliert beschreiben und erklären*	**Write a characterization of** the heroine.	*Describe somebody's character and provide suitable examples.*

'Anforderungsbereich III' BEYOND THE TEXT

discuss *diskutieren, erörtern*	**Discuss** advantages and disadvantages of introducing fullbody scanners at airports.	*Consider all sides of an issue by providing relevant arguments and concrete examples.*
assess [ə'ses] *auswerten, beurteilen, bewerten, einschätzen*	**Assess** whether the statement applies to the short story as well.	*Give a carefully considered opinion, include all the important aspects of a question.*
evaluate [ɪ'væljueɪt] / **comment on** ['kɒment] *kommentieren, Stellung nehmen zu, darlegen*	**Evaluate** the chances of the protagonist's plan to succeed in life. / **Comment on** the future of multiculturalism in the USA.	*Give your opinion, back it up with all the relevant points.*
interpret [ɪn'tɜːprɪt] *interpretieren, deuten, auswerten*	**Interpret** the message the author wants to convey.	*Explain the meaning or purpose of something.*
write a ... *gestalten, entwerfen, verfassen*	**Write** the girl's diary entry.	*Compose a text in line with the conventions of the required genre.*

Charts

The British System of Government

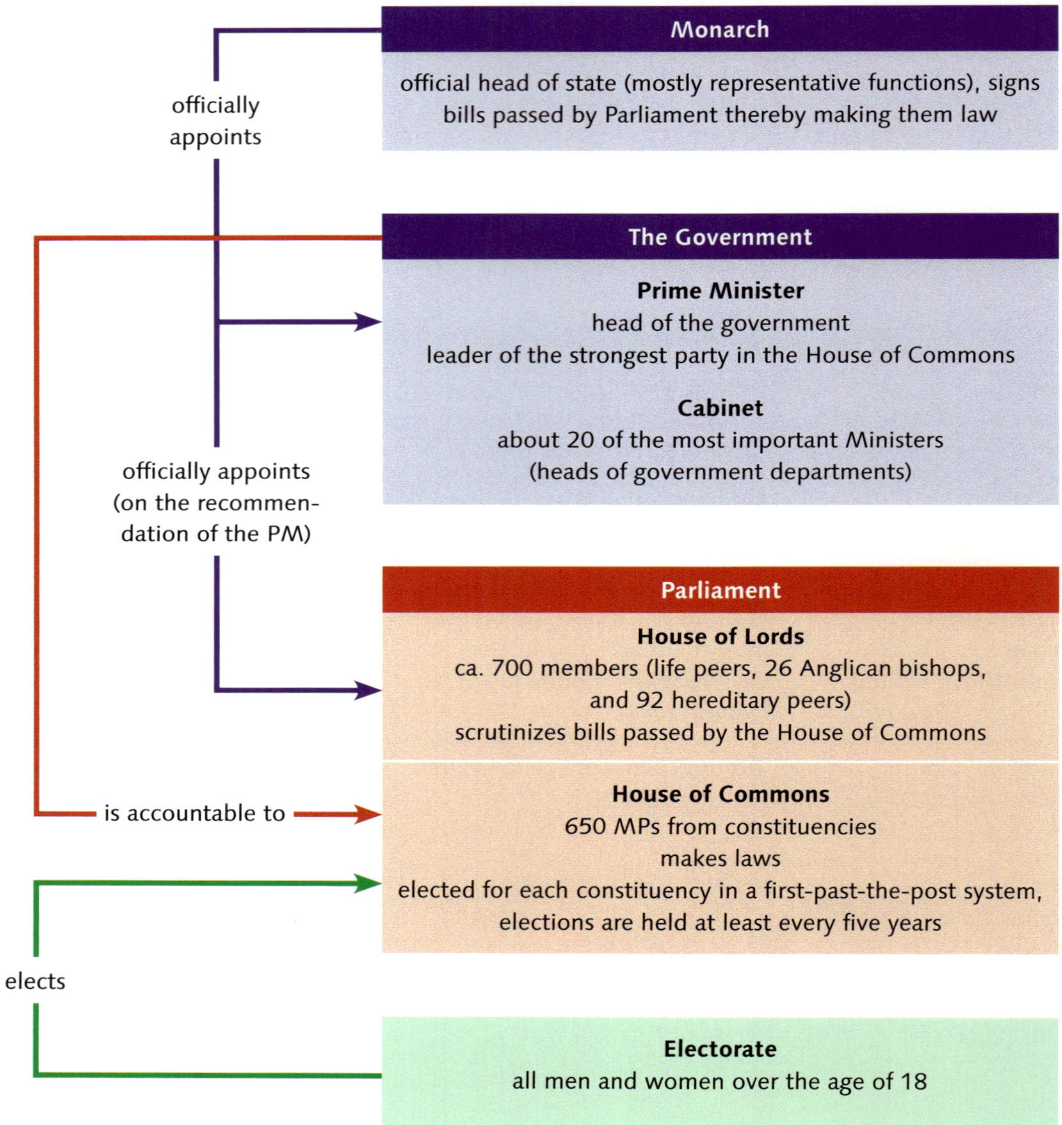

The US System of Government

System of Checks and Balances

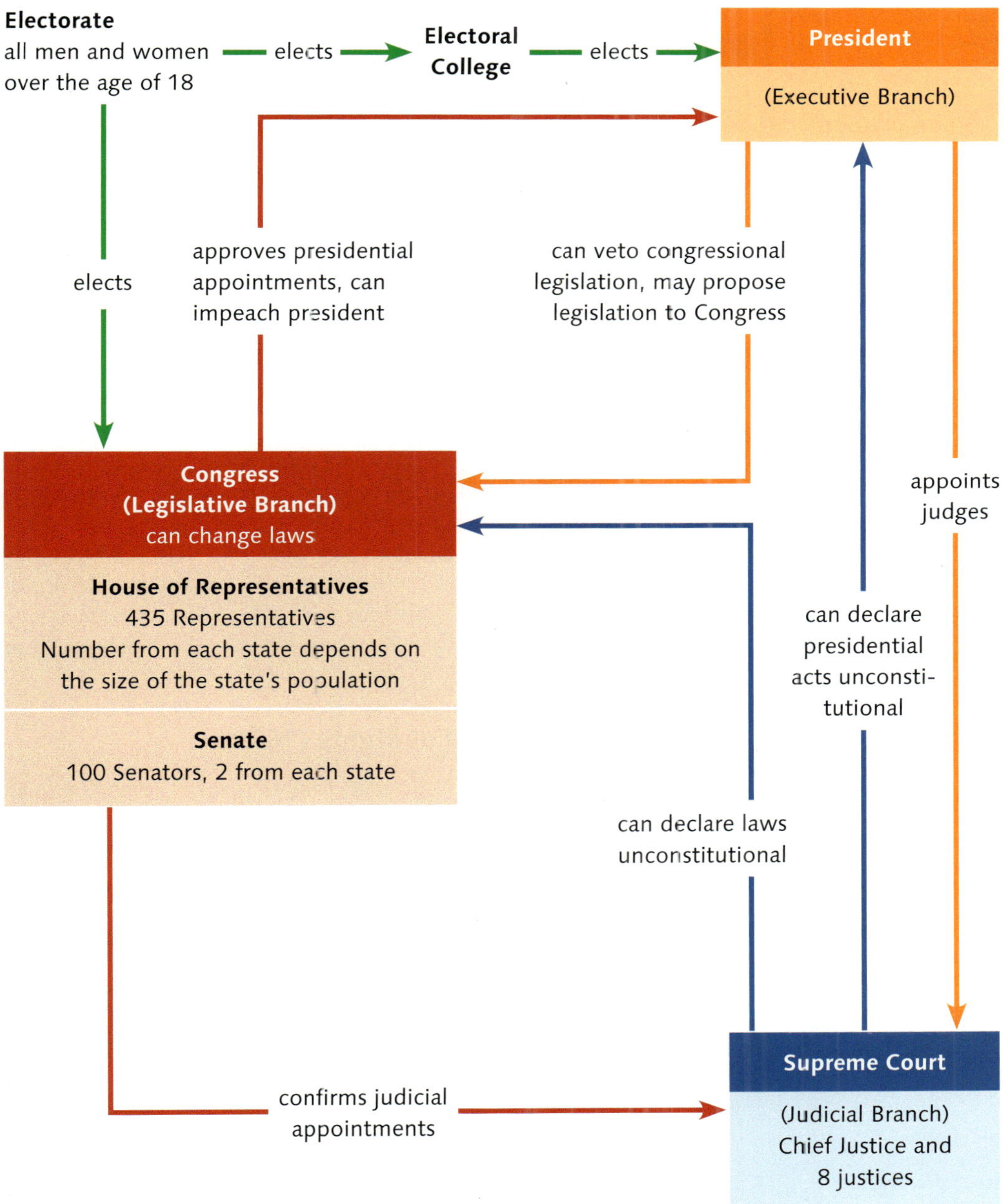

Historical Documents

Excerpts from the Magna Carta (1215)

Until King John (king from 1199–1216) was forced by his barons to sign a document called the Magna Carta ('great charter'), the will of the king had been law. The Magna Carta was the first step on the long road which led to the constitutional principle that the 'Law is King'. Six of its 63 articles are printed here.

1 **scutage** ['skju:tɪdʒ] (in feudal times) money paid by a knight instead of doing military service, or by a landowner instead of personal service
6 **aforesaid** [– '– –] mentioned before
7 **summon sb.** *(fml)* order sb. to come to you
9 **freeman** ['– –] (in feudal times) a citizen
amerce sb. [ə'mɜ:s] make sb. pay a fine
in accordance with sb./sth. *in Übereinstimmung mit jdm./etwas*
11 **imperil sth.** [– '– –] endanger sth.
12 **stock-in-trade** goods kept on sale by a merchant
villain ['vɪlən] (hier) Leibeigene/r
13 **wainage** *(old use)* profit or produce from the cultivation of land
if their liability is to us if the offence they committed was against us
14 **sworn evidence** *Aussage unter Eid*
16 **official** *(n)* person in a position of authority
18 **freehold** ['– –] ownership of land

(12) No scutage or aid shall be imposed in our kingdom, unless by the general council of our kingdom; except for ransoming our person,making our eldest son a knight and once for marrying our eldest daughter; and for these there shall be paid no more than a reasonable aid. [...]
(14) And for holding the general council of the kingdom concerning the assessment of aids, except in the three cases aforesaid, and for the assessing of scutage, we shall cause to be summoned the archbishops, bishops, abbots, earls, and greater barons of the realm, separately by our letters. [...]
(20) A freeman shall not be amerced for a small offence, except in accordance with the degree of the offence and for a grave offence he shall be amerced according to its gravity, without imperilling his status; and a merchant similarly without imperilling his stock-in-trade; and similarly a villain shall be amerced always without loss of wainage – if their liability is to us. And none of the aforesaid amercements shall be imposed except by the sworn evidence of worthy men of the neighbourhood.
(38) In future no official shall put anyone to trial merely on his own testimony, without reliable witness produced for this purpose.
(39) No freeman shall be taken or imprisoned, or deprived of his freehold, or outlawed, or banished, or in any way destroyed, nor will we take or order action against him, unless by the lawful judgment of his peers, or by the law of the land.
(40) We will sell to no man,we will not deny to any man, either justice or right.

Excerpts from the Bill of Rights (1689)

When James II (king from 1685–1688) tried to restore Catholicism to Britain, he met with resistance from all sides. Parliament forced James into exile in the 'Glorious Revolution' of 1688. Prince William of Orange and his wife, Princess Mary, were offered the throne on the condition that they accepted the 'Bill of Rights'. Thus Britain's constitutional monarchy was established. From then on, the British monarch ruled not by the grace of God, but by the grace of Parliament.

1 **said** *(adj; fml)* mentioned before
Lords Spiritual archbishops and bishops
Lords Temporal ['tempərəl] lords who are concerned with worldly affairs, rather than with spiritual things; together with the Lords Spiritual they constitute the House of Lords
Commons House of Commons consisting of representatives of counties and towns
5 **of late** in recent times
6 **by pretence of prerogative** ['prɪ'tens, prɪrɒgətɪv] by claiming that the king has the right to do sth.

The said Lords Spiritual and Temporal, and Commons [...] do declare:
(1) That the pretended power of suspending of laws, or the execution of laws, by regal authority, without consent of Parliament, is illegal.
(2) That the pretended power of dispensing with laws or the execution by laws by regal authority as it has been assumed and exercised of late is illegal.
(4) That levying money for or to the use of the Crown by pretence of prerogative, without grant of Parliament, for longer time or in other manner than the same is or shall be granted, is illegal.

(5) That it is the right of the subject to petition the King, and all commitments and prosecutions for such petitioning are illegal.
(6) That the raising or keeping a standing army within the kingdom in time of peace, unless it be with the consent of Parliament, is against law.
(8) That elections of members of Parliament ought to be free.
(9) That the freedom of speech, and debates and proceedings in Parliament, ought not to be impeached or questioned in any court or place out of Parliament.
(10) That excessive bail ought not to be required nor excessive fines imposed; nor cruel and unusual punishment inflicted.
(13) And that for redress of all grievances, and for the amending, strengthening, and preserving of the laws, Parliament ought to be held frequently.

9 **commitment** *(old use)* = **committal** act of sending sb. to prison
15 **impeach sth.** (here) prevent sth.
16 **bail** *Kaution*
impose a fine demand money as punishment
18 **redress of grievances** *(fml)* correction of sth. considered unfair

Excerpts from the Declaration of Independence (1776)

Unhappiness with British rule had been on the rise in the American colonies during the 1760s. In 1775, open fighting broke out between British troops and American colonists – the beginning of the Revolutionary War. When Congress adopted the Declaration of Independence on 4 July, 1776, this ended more than a century and a half of colonial dependency, even though the war was to go on until 1783.

Find the full text of the Declaration of Independence here:
Webcode context-67

When in the Course of human events, it becomes necessary for one people to dissolve the political bands which have connected them with another, and to assume among the powers of the earth, the separate and equal station to which the Laws of Nature and of Nature's God entitle them, a decent respect to the opinions of mankind requires that they should declare the causes which impel them to the separation.

We hold these truths to be self-evident, that all men are created equal, that they are endowed by their Creator with certain unalienable Rights, that among these are Life, Liberty and the pursuit of Happiness. That to secure these rights, Governments are instituted among Men, deriving their just powers from the consent of the governed. That whenever any Form of Government becomes destructive of these ends, it is the Right of the People to alter or to abolish it, and to institute new Government, laying its foundation on such principles and organizing its powers in such form, as to them shall seem most likely to effect their Safety and Happiness.

3 **assume sth.** *etwas übernehmen*
station *(old-fashioned or fml)* status
5 **impel sb. to sth.** [–'–] force sb. to do sth.
8 **endow sb. with sth.** [ɪn'daʊ] *(fml)* give sb. sth.
unalienable *(old use)* **= inalienable** [ɪn'eɪliənəbl] *(fml)* that cannot be taken away
9 **pursuit of sth.** *(fml)* act of trying to achieve sth.
10 **consent** [–'–] *(n)* agreement

The Bill of Rights (1791)

At the time the Constitution of the USA was discussed and ratified, critics felt it did not sufficiently protect individuals against abuse of their civil liberties and rights by the federal government. Therefore, ten amendments to the Constitution known as the Bill of Rights were proposed by Congress and passed in 1791.

First Amendment Congress shall make no law respecting an establishment of religion, or prohibiting the free exercise thereof; or abridging the freedom of speech, or of the press; or the right of the people peaceably to assemble, and to petition the government for a redress of grievances.

1 **respecting** concerning
2 **the free exercise thereof** *deren freie Ausübung*
abridge sth. limit sth.
4 **redress of grievances** *(fml)* correction of sth. considered unfair

6 **infringe sth.** *(fml) etwas verletzen*
8 **but** except
11 **effects** *(pl; fml)* personal property
seizure ['si:ʒə] *Beschlagnahme*
12 **warrant** *Durchsuchungs- oder Haftbefehl*
13 **affirmation** [ˌæfə'meɪʃn] *eidesstattliche Erklärung*
15 **hold sb. to answer for sth.** accuse sb. of sth. (in a court of law)
16 **infamous** ['ɪnfəməs] evil, shameful
presentment [– '– –] *formelle Anschuldigung*
indictment [ɪn'daɪtmənt] *Anklage*
grand jury *(AE)* panel of 12 or 23 citizens who investigate accusations and officially charge criminals to be tried before a jury if there is sufficient evidence
19 **in jeopardy of life and limb** ['dʒepədi] *in Gefahr für Leib und Leben*
21 **due process of law** proper legal procedures
26 **ascertain sth.** [ˌæsə'teɪn] *(fml)* determine sth.
28 **obtain sb.** (hier) *jdn. vorladen*
counsel lawyer giving legal advice
30 **common law** unwritten law based on custom, usage and former decisions of courts of law
31 **trial by jury** *Verfahren vor Geschworenen*
32 **try sth.** examine and decide sth. in a court of law
34 **bail** *Kaution*
37 **construe sth.** [– '–] interpret sth.
disparage a right [dɪs'pærɪdʒ] *ein Recht schmälern*

Second Amendment A well-regulated militia, being necessary to the security of a free state, the right of the people to keep and bear arms shall not be infringed.

Third Amendment No soldier shall, in time of peace be quartered in any house, without the consent of the owner, nor in time of war, but in a manner to be prescribed by law.

Fourth Amendment The right of the people to be secure in their persons, houses, papers, and effects, against unreasonable searches and seizures, shall not be violated, and no warrants shall issue, but upon probable cause, supported by oath or affirmation, and particularly describing the place to be searched, and the persons or things to be seized.

Fifth Amendment No person shall be held to answer for a capital, or otherwise infamous crime, unless on a presentment or indictment of a grand jury, except in cases arising in the land or naval forces, or in the militia, when in actual service in time of war or public danger; nor shall any person be subject for the same offense to be twice put in jeopardy of life or limb; nor shall be compelled in any criminal case to be a witness against himself, nor be deprived of life, liberty, or property, without due process of law; nor shall private property be taken for public use, without just compensation.

Sixth Amendment In all criminal prosecutions, the accused shall enjoy the right to a speedy and public trial, by an impartial jury of the state and district wherein the crime shall have been committed, which district shall have been previously ascertained by law, and to be informed of the nature and cause of the accusation; to be confronted with the witnesses against him; to have compulsory process for obtaining witnesses in his favor, and to have the assistance of counsel for his defence.

Seventh Amendment In suits at common law, where the value in controversy shall exceed twenty dollars, the right of trial by jury shall be preserved, and no fact tried by a jury, shall be otherwise re-examined in any court of the United States, than according to the rules of the common law.

Eighth Amendment Excessive bail shall not be required, nor excessive fines imposed, nor cruel and unusual punishments inflicted.

Ninth Amendment The enumeration in the Constitution, of certain rights, shall not be construed to deny or disparage others retained by the people.

Tenth Amendment The powers not delegated to the United States by the Constitution, nor prohibited by it to the states, are reserved to the states respectively, or to the people.

Preamble to the Charter of the United Nations (1945)

Drafted immediately after the Second World War, the Charter of the United Nations set out to formulate the aims of this new organization.

2 **scourge** [skɜ:dʒ] *(fig)* person or thing that causes suffering
4 **reaffirm sth.** *etwas erneut bekräftigen*

WE, THE PEOPLES OF THE UNITED NATIONS, DETERMINED,

to save succeeding generations from the scourge of war, which twice in our lifetime has brought untold sorrow to mankind, and

to reaffirm faith in fundamental human rights, in the dignity and worth of the human person, in the equal rights of men and women and of nations large and small, and to establish conditions under which justice and respect for the obligations arising from treaties and other sources of international law can be maintained, and

to promote social progress and better standards of life in larger freedom,

AND FOR THESE ENDS

to practise tolerance and live together in peace with one another as good neighbours, and

to unite our strength to maintain international peace and security, and

to ensure, by the acceptance of principles and the institution of methods, that armed force shall not be used, save in the common interest, and

to employ international machinery for the promotion of the economic and social advancement of all peoples,

HAVE RESOLVED TO COMBINE OUR EFFORTS TO ACCOMPLISH THIS AIM.

7 **obligation** *Verpflichtung*
10 **end** aim, purpose
14 **ensure sth.** *(BE)* = *(AE)* **insure sth.** guarantee sth.
18 **resolve** [rɪ'zɒlv] decide firmly

Preamble to the Universal Declaration of Human Rights (1948)

The Universal Declaration of Human Rights, which was adopted by the General Assembly of the United Nations on 10 December, 1948, outlines a basic view of human rights, but it is not a legally binding document.

Whereas recognition of the inherent dignity and of the equal and inalienable rights of all members of the human family is the foundation of freedom, justice and peace in the world,

Whereas disregard and contempt for human rights have resulted in barbarous acts which have outraged the conscience of mankind, and the advent of a world in which human beings shall enjoy freedom of speech and belief and freedom from fear and want has been proclaimed as the highest aspiration of the common people,

Whereas it is essential, if man is not to be compelled to have recourse, as a last resort, to rebellion against tyranny and oppression, that human rights should be protected by the rule of law,

Whereas it is essential to promote the development of friendly relations between nations,

Whereas the peoples of the United Nations have in the Charter reaffirmed their faith in fundamental human rights, in the dignity and worth of the human person and in the equal rights of men and women and have determined to promote social progress and better standards of life in larger freedom,

Whereas Member States have pledged themselves to achieve, in co-operation with the United Nations, the promotion of universal respect for and observance of human rights and fundamental freedoms,

Whereas a common understanding of these rights and freedoms is of the greatest importance for the full realization of this pledge,

Now, therefore, the GENERAL ASSEMBLY proclaims this UNIVERSAL DECLARATION OF HUMAN RIGHTS as a common standard of achievement for all peoples and all nations, to the end that every individual and every organ of society, keeping this Declaration constantly in mind, shall strive by teaching and education to promote respect for these rights and freedoms and by progressive measures, national and international, to secure their universal and effective recognition

1 **whereas** because of the fact that
inalienable [in'eɪliənəbl] *(fml)* that cannot be taken away from you
4 **disregard** *(n)* *Missachtung*
contempt feeling that sb./sth. is without value and deserves no respect
5 **outrage sb.** make sb. very shocked and angry
advent of sth./sb. ['– –] coming of sth./sb. (an important event, person, technology, etc.)
9 **compel sb. to do sth.** [– '–] *(fml)* force sb. to do sth.
have recourse to sth. *Zuflucht zu etwas nehmen*
as a last resort [rɪ'zɔ:t] *als letzten Ausweg*
14 **reaffirm sth.** *etwas erneut bekräftigen*
18 **pledge yourself to sth.** formally promise to do sth.

30 **jurisdiction** *Zuständigkeit, Gerichtsbarkeit*

and observance, both among the peoples of Member States themselves and among the peoples of territories under their jurisdiction.

Preamble to the Treaty of Rome (1957)

The European Economic Community (EEC), the precursor to today's much larger European Union, was established on 27 March, 1957, when the six founding members – France, West Germany, Italy, Belgium, the Netherlands and Luxembourg – signed the Treaty of Rome, which is also called the Treaty Establishing the European Community.

5 **determined** [dɪ'tɜːmɪnd] *(adj)* having made a firm decision to do sth.
7 **resolved** [rɪ'zɒlvd] *(adj) (fml)* having made a firm decision to do sth.
11 **concerted** [– '– –] *(adj) gemeinsam, gemeinschaftlich*
13 **anxious to do sth.** ['æŋkʃəs] wanting to do sth. very much
15 **backwardness** state of having made less progress than normal
17 **abolition** [ˌæbə'lɪʃn] *Abschaffung*
21 **pool sth.** collect sth. (money, information, etc.) from different people or groups so that it can be used by all of them
resource supply of sth. that a country, an organization or a person has and can use, esp. to increase their wealth

His Majesty the King of the Belgians, The President of the Federal Republic of Germany, The President of the French Republic, The President of the Italian Republic, Her Royal Highness the Grand Duchess of Luxembourg, Her Majesty the Queen of the Netherlands,

DETERMINED to lay the foundations of an ever closer union among the peoples of Europe,

RESOLVED to ensure the economic and social progress of their countries by common action to eliminate the barriers which divide Europe,

AFFIRMING as the essential objective of their efforts the constant improvements of the living and working conditions of their peoples,

RECOGNIZING that the removal of existing obstacles calls for concerted action in order to guarantee steady expansion, balanced trade and fair competition,

ANXIOUS to strengthen the unity of their economies and to ensure their harmonious development by reducing the differences existing between the various regions and the backwardness of the less favoured regions,

DESIRING to contribute, by means of a common commercial policy, to the progressive abolition of restrictions on international trade,

INTENDING to confirm the solidarity which binds Europe and the overseas countries and desiring to ensure the development of their prosperity, in accordance with the principles of the Charter of the United Nations,

RESOLVED by thus pooling their resources to preserve and strengthen peace and liberty, and calling upon the other peoples of Europe who share their ideal to join in their efforts,

HAVE DECIDED to create a EUROPEAN COMMUNITY ...

Texts

p. 16: Liz Balmaseda, Carnegie Foundation, http://greatimmigrants.carnegie.org/your-stories/, used by permission; **pp. 17–18:** June Sochen, used by permission; **pp. 21–22:** Bruce Norris, used by permission; **pp. 24–25:** William J. Clinton Commencement Address at Portland State University in Portland, Oregon; **pp. 30–31:** Todd Strasser, used by permission; **pp. 33–34:** Anne Applebaum, used by permission; **pp. 41–42:** From The New York Times, © 2015 Matthew Hutson, The New York Times. All rights reserved. Used by permission and protection by the Copyright Laws of the United States. The printing, copying, redistribution or retransmission of this Content without express written permission is prohibited; **pp. 44–45:** © 2011 The Atlantic Media Co., as first published in The Atlantic Magazine. All rights reserved. Distributed by Tribune Content Agency; **p. 47:** © 2015 Stephen Collinson. Reproduced with permission of CNN. All rights reserved; **p. 49:** Sabrina Fritz, used by permission; **p. 50:** Excerpt from BETWEEN THE WORLD AND ME by Ta-Nehisi Coates, copyright © 2015 by Ta-Nehisi Coates. Used by permission of Spiegel & Grau, an imprint of Random House, a division of Penguin Random House LLC. All rights reserved
pp. 52–53: © 2010 Claude Fischer. All rights reserved; **pp. 54–55:** Grover Norquist, used by permission; **pp. 62–63:** Alan Bennett, used by permission; **pp. 68–70:** Mike Bartlett, used by permission; **p. 72:** Halal Events Ltd, London, used by permission; **p. 73:** Amelia Gentleman, used by permission; **pp. 74–75:** phw, used by permission;
p. 76: Stewart Wood, used by permission;
pp. 82–83: © 2013 Kevin Donnelly. All rights reserved; **pp. 86–87:** Waiariki by Patricia Grace, Penguin NZ, 1975; **p. 88:** © 2011 Kanza Azeemi. Reproduced with permission of The Express Tribune. All rights reserved.; **pp. 91–92:** From Forbes, © 2015 Daniel Runde, Forbes LLC. All rights reserved. Used by permission and protection by the Copyright Laws of the United States. The printing, copying, redistribution or retransmission of this Content without express written permission is forbidden; **p. 93:** Thuso Khumalo, Deutsche Welle, 22.04.2014; **pp. 95–96:** "Nelson's Mandela's Death – South Africa one year on" Milton Nkosi – BBC Africa 2014; **p. 97:** © 2013 Murtaza Hussein. All rights reserved; **p. 99:** "The Canadian town that sold itself to tar sands" Suzanne Goldenberg © Guardian News & Media Ltd 2015;
pp. 107–108: Gurcharan Das, India Unbound, used by permission of Janklow & Nesbit, USA;
pp. 109–111: Chetan Bhagat, used by permission;
p. 116: Carolin Roder, Sandra Kurz, Maxim Derenko, Hochschule Heilbronn, Campus Künzelsau, Reinhold-Würth-Hochschule, Daimlerstr. 35, 74653 Künzelsau;
p. 117: Michelle Warwicker, used by permission;
pp. 118–120: "English Lessons" was originally published in *English Lessons and Other Stories* copyright © 1996 by Shauna Singh Baldwin. Reprinted by permission of Goose Lane Editions; **pp. 128–129:** Liz Alderman, used by permission; **p. 130:** Sascha Schmierer, used by permission;
p. 133: Lucy Siegle, used by permission;
pp. 134–135: Elko Born, used by permission;
p. 137: Aoife Mannix, www.tall-lighthouse. co.uk, used by permission; **pp. 138–139 and 359:** R.L.G., used by permission; **p. 146:** Laura Roberts, used by permission; **pp. 148–149:** Nick Dear, used by permission; **pp. 152–153:** Bob Holmes, used by permission; **p. 155:** Tim Franks, used by permission;
p. 157: Zoltan Istvan, used by permission;
p. 160: Agora-Energiewende mit freundlicher Genehmigung; **p. 177:** James Simmons, Poems 1956–1986 (Bloodaxe Books, 1986);
pp. 181–182: "Moon Palace" © 1989 by Paul Auster;
p. 188: Franklin D. Roosevelt, State of the Union Message to Congress, January 11, 1944. http://www.fdrlibrary.marist.edu/archives/address_text.html;
pp. 189–190: President Barack Obama's State of the Union Address, January 28, 2014;
p. 191: Felix Oberholzer-Gee, used by permission;
pp. 193–194: Sean Coughlan, used by permission;
p. 196: Uwe Jean Heuser, mit freundlicher Genehmigung; **pp. 198–199:** Carl Deuker, Graphia/Houghton Mufflin Harcourt, used by permission;
pp. 200–201: Mark King used by permission;
pp. 201–202: Emanuel Wetterqvist, used by permission; **pp. 212–213:** Excerpts from READY PLAYER ONE by Ernest Cline, © 2011 by Dark All Day, Inc. Used by permission of Crown Books, an imprint of the Crown Publishing Group, a division of Random House LLC. All rights reserved.;
pp. 216–217: Gerhard Witossek von www.muc.kobis.de, mit freundlicher Genehmigung;
pp. 218–219: Adapted from www.debate org 2014;

pp. 220–221: Adapted from www.whitehouse.gov 2014; **p. 222:** Ellie Zolfagharifard, used by permission; **pp. 223–224:** Excerpts from Vernon God Little by DBC Pierre, Faber and Faber Limited, 2003.; **pp. 230–231:** © 2002 M.T. Anderson. From FEED by M.T. Anderson. Reproduced by permission of Walker Books Ltd., London SE111 5HJ www.walker.co.uk; **pp. 234–235:** David Kleingers, mit freundlicher Genehmigung; **pp. 236–237:** Excerpts from THE CIRCLE by Dave Eggers, ©2013 by Dave Eggers. Used by permission of Alfred A. Knopf, an imprint of the Knopf Double-day Publishing Group, a division of Random House LLC. All rights reserved; **pp. 240–241:** © Margaret Atwood, 2004, Oryx and Crake, Bloomsbury Publishing Plc.; **pp. 243–244:** George Orwell, used by permission; **p. 250:** © Marilyn Price-Mitchell, 2014; **pp. 251–252:** From BATTLE HYMN OF THE TIGER MOTHER by Amy Chua, © 2011 by Amy Chua. Used by permission of The Penguin Press, a division of Penguin Group (USA), LLC.; **p. 254:** Ernestine Northover, used by permission; **pp. 255–257:** Screenplay by Paul Haggis and Bobby Moresco, story by Paul Haggis. Mit freundlicher Genehmigung der ApolloMedia Gmbh; **pp. 260–261:** Sophie Seiderer, used by permission; **p. 334:** Clare Whitmell, used by permission; **p. 338:** Ariane Sherine, used by permission; **p. 343:** Gavin Ewart, used by permission; **p. 363:** Hanif Kureishi, used by permission; **p. 372:** Milton and Rose Friedman, Houghton Mifflin Harcourt, used by permission; **p. 374:** Jonas Huticker, used by permission; **p. 382:** Ewan MacAskill, used by permission; **pp. 383–384:** Alan Bennett, used by permission **p. 385:** Anna Schmid, used by permission

Illustrations / Graphics

Roland Beier, Berlin (p. 226 B; p. 240; p. 242; p. 346; p. 347); **Andreas Fischer**, Köln (p. 146); **Petra Eberhard (designcollective)**, Berlin (p. 11 bottom; p. 159; p. 175 storyboard; p. 177; p. 220; p. 250; p. 264; p. 328; p. 330); **Yvonne Thron (designcollective)**, Berlin (p. 74; p. 79; pp. 102/103 caleidoscope; p. 113 top; p. 132 bottom)

Photos

A1PIX – YOUR PHOTO TODAY, Taufkirchen (p. 208: SPL_SciencePhotoLibraryRF; p. 239 bottom left: Karl_Thomas); **action press**, Hamburg (p. 29 bottom: EXTRAPRESS; p. 62 bottom: SOLO SYNDICATION; p. 77: Collection Christophel; p. 111: ZUMA PRESS INC.; p. 113: Everett Collection; p. 115: ZUMA PRESSS, INC.; p. 140 top and bottom: GEORG NOWOTNY; p. 156: Bas Czrwinski / ANP Photo; p. 166 top: Everett Collection, bottom: Rex Features; p. 176 left and right: TSW / Rex Features; p. 201: QKD / Rex Features; p. 222: Exclusivepix; p. 232: Collection Christophel; p. 246 B: London News Pictures / Zuma Press; p. 259 top: SWSNS.com / Adam Gray; p. 262 centre: Lucy Young); **akg-images**, Berlin (p. 12 A: Joseph Martin; p. 20 top (and bottom) © VG Bild-Kunst, Bonn 2015; p. 104 bottom: Album; p. 134; p. 227 E; p. 239 bottom right: Wien, Kunsthistorisches Museum; p. 328: IAM); **Alamy Images**, Abingdon (p. 247 Einstein: Everett Collection Historical, Thatcher: Mary Evans Picture Library, Roosevelt: nsf); **ALL STAR Picture Library**, Frankfurt/Main (p. 54: Allstar/Columbia); **Andertoons.com** (p. 185 D: Mark Anderson; p. 187: Mark Anderson); **ApolloMedia Film** (p. 255 left and right); **BBC** (p. 204 bottom); **beingfivecomics** (p. 206 bottom: George Sfarnas); **bpk-images**, Berlin (p. 40 Ralph Waldo Emerson: adoc-photos; p. 53; p. 112 bottom: Jürgen Schadeberg); **Bush Theatre / nabokov** (p. 69: with kind permission from Nabokov and the Bush Theatre); **Cagle Cartoons**, Santa Barbara (p. 19: Cameron Cardow; p. 221: Nate Beeler); **CartoonStock**, Bath (p. 14: Peter Steiner; p. 42: Simon Bond; p. 45: Alfredo Martirena; p. 124: Karsten Schley; p. 144: S. Harris; p. 149 bottom: Grizelda; p. 150: Universal Uclick; p. 162 bottom: Grizelda; p. 183: Delgado, Roy; p. 185 E: Abbot, Bill; p. 215: John Martin; p. 225: 2012 Jeff Stahler, dist. by Universal Uclick; p. 312: Rex May Baloo; p. 318: Royston Robertson; p. 332: Baloo Rex May; p. 391 A: Jackson Graham, B: Clive Goddard); **ClipDealer** (p. 239 top left: AdstockRF; p. 315: Sergej Khackimullin; p. 334: Markus Gann); **Colourbox.com** (p. 91; p. 121 flag: Ruskpp; p. 289 top: Pressmaster); **Corbis**, Düsseldorf (p. 12 B: GraphicaArtis, C: Bettmann; p. 16 top: Brett Hufziger / Retna Ltd; p. 27: Leon Harris / cultura; p. 29 top: Ariel Skelley; p. 35: Sigrid Olsson / Photo-Alto; p. 38: BRIAN SNYDER / Reuters; p. 41: Wally McNamee; p. 43 top: (c) Clarence Holmes / Demotix, bottom: Corbis / Paul Colangelo; p. 47 top: BRIAN

SNYDER/Reuters, centre: ZUMA Wire; p. 49 top: TAMI CHAPPELL/Reuters, bottom: Amy N Harris; p. 51: Seth Kushner/Retna Ltd.; p. 52: Julie Dermansk © 2010; p. 61 top: Gail Orenstein/NurPhoto; p. 62 top glasses (M): Vladimir Godnik/moodboard; p. 64 bottom: POOL/Reuters; p. 72 top: Sabiha Mahmoud; p. 75: Paul Davey; p. 89: HUANG ZONGZHI/Xinhua Press; UANG ZONGZHI/Xinhua Press; p. 94: Peter Andrews/Reuters; p. 103 E: Lindsay Hebberd; p. 110: Dinodia; p. 116 bottom right: Purcell-Holmes; p. 121 dancers: Juls Ibanez/Demotix; p. 135: Jose Breton/Cordon Press; p. 138: Korolyova Kristina/ITAR-TASS Photo; p. 142 D: Science Photo Library; p. 143 F: Jason Horowitz; p. 148: Robbie Jack; p. 157 top: Science Photo Library; p. 158 bottom: Science Photo Library; p. 163 left: Sergei Karoukhin/Reuters; p. 165 Shakespeare; p. 227 D: Imaginechina; p. 251: Corbis Outline/Gail Albert Halaban; p. 262 left: C.J. Lafrance; p. 316 E: Jose Luis Pelaez, F: Nancy Siesel/Demotix; p. 188: Bettmann; p. 343: 2/Ocean; p. 354: POOL/Reuters); **culture-images**, Köln (p. 21: Lebrecht Music & Arts); **ddp/360°**, Hamburg (p. 36 B: © NASA/eyevine; p. 55 top: INTERTOPICS; p. 95: ddp images/ZUMA; p. 100: Xinhua/ddp images); **dpa Picture Alliance**, Frankfurt/Main (p. 13 E: Everett Collection; p. 56: AP Photo; p. 86: Maja Moritz; p. 112 top: AP Photo; p. 116 centre: Robert Harding Imagery; p. 127 A: Zentralbild, B: dpa, C: ASSOCIATED PR, D: ASSOCIATED PR, E: dpa/dpaweb, F: ASSOCIATED PR; p. 155: Andreas Frank; p. 192: dpa; p. 247 Kennedy: ASSOCIATED PR); **explainity®** (p. 132); **F1 online digitale Bildagentur**, Frankfurt/Main (p. 200 bottom: Flirt); **Fotofinder**, Berlin (p. 163 right: Stillpictures/images.de; p. 171: The Art Archive/images.de; p. 185 C: CHAPLIN/UNITED ARTISTS/Kobal Collection/Max Munn Autrey/images.de); p. 234 bottom: COLOR FORCE/Kobal Collection/images.de; **Fotolia** (p. 44: Fotolia365; p. 64 top: Beboy; p. 65 bottom: rabbit75_fot; p. 71 top: determined; p. 72 bottom: photollurg; p. 78 South Africa: mozZz, Canada: md3d, New Zealand: Stillfx; p. 79 Australia: Andrey Kuzmin, Pakistan: Ilyes Laszlo; p. 101 top: Christian Schwier, bottom left: sveta, bottom right: Voyagerix; p. 117: paul_brighton; p. 118: Andrew Lever; p. 119: 9photos; pp. 122–123: niroworld; p. 123 C: Lance Bellers, D: william87; p. 125: koya979; p. 130: Kzenon; p. 133 Made in Bangladesh label (and 274): Jörg Lantelme; pp. 142–143 background computer electronic circuit board: joephotostudio; p. 142 B: Africa Studio, C: Sergey Nivens; p. 152: freshidea; p. 160 top, centre and bottom: luigi Giordano; p. 165 abstract starburst light background: striZh; p. 182: Frédéric Prochasson; p. 205 bottom: peshkova; p. 223 (and 283): kiono; p. 229: Andre B.; p. 230: snapgalleria; p. 231: style67; p. 243: Uolir; p. 258: higyou; p. 263 top: Tim, bottom: Paylessimages; p. 276: science photo; p. 277: Sophia Winters; p. 282 Andrea Danti; p. 290: Claudio Divizia; p. 296: visceralimage; p. 297: digitalstock; p. 299: sgursozlu; p. 306 fottoo; p. 309: Natalia Bratslavsky; p. 311 top: Bikeworld-travel, centre: Darren Green, bottom: dbrnjhrj; p. 313 top: Andrei Nekrassov, bottom left: Brian Jackson; p. 333: rasstock; p. 349: Syda Productions); **Gannet-USA Today** (p. 211 From USA Today 2015 @ Gannett-USA Today. All rights reserved. Used by permission and protected by the Copyright Laws of the United States. The printing, copying, redistribution, or retransmission of this Content without express written permission is prohibited); **Ben Goode** (p. 284); **Glow Images**, München (p. 57 top: Cultura; p. 66; p. 73: imagebroker.com; p. 142 A: Image Source; p. 193: StockbrokerXtra; p. 246 D: Hill Street Studios/Eric Raptosh LLC; p. 293: Image Source); **Shawn Gruver**, Hermosa Beach (p. 197 left); **Houghton Mifflin Harcourt Publishing** (p. 198: 2010 by Carl Deuker. Reprinted by permission of Houghton Mifflin Harcourt Publishing Company); **imago Sportfotodienst**, Berlin (p. 50: ZUMA Press; p. 247 Christopher Reeve: imago); **INTERFOTO**, München (p. 13 F: Danita Delimont/David R. Frazier; p. 40 John Winthrop u. J. Hector St. John de Crèvecoeur: Granger, NYC; p. 104 top: Mary Evans/Ronald Grant Archive; p. 107 right: Mary Evans/Nigel Sorrell Collections; p. 173: Sammlung Rauch; p. 179: The Granger Collection, New York; p. 247 Gandhi: Sammlung Rauch; p. 361 top, centre and bottom: NG Collection); **Nick Kim**, Wellington, New Zealand (p. 331); **LAIF**, Köln (p. 28: Polaris; p. 30: Willie Davis 2008/Redux; p. 37 D: Copyright Brendan Hoffman/Polaris; p. 71 bottom: 2014 Nils Jorgensen/i-Images/Polaris; p. 82: Gavin Hellier/robertharding; p. 121 bottom right: Luke Duggleby 2010/Redux;

p. 181: Timothy Fadek/Polaris; p. 189: Polaris; p. 261 right: Lucy Young/REX); **Lions Gate Entertainment Inc.** (p. 233 top, bottom left and right: The Hunger Games © 2012 Lions Gate Entertainment Inc.; p. 234 left and right: The Hunger Games © 2012 Lions Gate Entertainment Inc.); **LOOK Die Bildagentur der Fotografen**, München (p. 154 bottom: Glasshouse Images); **mauritius images**, Mittenwald (p. 13: Alamy/Archive Pics; p. 16 bottom: Alamy/RosalreneBetancourt 2; p. 40 John L. O'Sullivan: Universal Images Group Limited/Alamy; p. 47 bottom: Planetpix/Alamy; p. 55 bottom: BLM Photo/Alamy; p. 60 bottom: Alamy/Justin Kase z12z; p. 61 bottom: Alamy/Peter Alvey; p. 67 bottom: Alamy/Classic Image; p. 68: United Archives; p. 71 centre: Alamy/Adrian P. Chinery/Nelson's Ship in a Bottle by Yinka Shonibare © VG Bild-Kunst, Bonn 2015; p. 80: Bill Bachman/Alamy; p. 93: Greg Balfour Evans/Alamy; p. 98: nature picture library; p. 99: Ashley Cooper/Alamy; p. 105: imagebroker/Olaf Krüger; p. 107 left: United Archives; p. 133 Made in India label (and 274): Alamy/Carolyn Jenkins, Made in U.S.A. label (and 274): Alamy/Independent Picture Service; p. 141 right (and 275): Alamy/brianafrica; p. 168 top: United Archives; p. 170: Alamy/brenton west; p. 186: Alamy/Roger Bamber; p. 191: Alamy/Eric Anthony Johnson; p. 197 right: Alamy/Robert Landau; 205 top: Alamy/Mick Sinclair; p. 212: Alamy/Carol and Mike Werner; p. 219 top: Alamy/Gary Lucken, bottom: Raimund Linke; p. 236: Alamy/ Massimo Petranzan; p. 259 centre: Alamy/Bruce McGowan, bottom: Alamy/Steven May;. p. 267: Alamy/D Legakis; p. 269: Alamy/MICHAEL DUNLEA; p. 313: Alamy/The Protected Art Archive); **Amy Mohammed** (p. 210 top); **Nobelmedia** (p. 126); **PantherMedia**, München (p. 57 bottom: Nadja Blume); **Patricia Piccinini and Tolarno and Roslyn Oxley9 Galleries** (p. 151: Courtesy of the artist and Tolarno and Roslyn Oxley9 Galleries); **Photoshot** (p. 25: RICHARD B. LEVINE; p. 109: Xinhua; p. 116 left: World Illustrated/Bill Coster; p. 154 top: BSIP; p. 254: Digital Light Source; p. 260: David Wimsett; p. 314: Imagebroker/Ingeborg Knol); **Reuters** (p. 33: US Marines/Handout; p. 102 A: X80002; p. 122 A: Johannes Eisele; p. 123 E: Pawel Kopczynski; p. 157 Kevin Lamarque; p. 162 top: Fred Prouser);

Royal Shakespeare Company (p. 168 bottom: Stewart Hemley; p. 172 (and 278): Stewart Hemley); Sheila Burnett (p. 174 (and 278)); **Shutterstock** (p. 13 Statue of Liberty: Marcio Jose Bastos Silva; p. 18: 1970s; pp. 58/59 flag (M): Rsinha; p. 60 top: jorgen mcleman; p. 65 like/unlike: Alhovik, crown: Sashkin; p. 67 top: Maran Garai; p. 70: Frank L Junior; p. 76: AGIF; p. 103 C: Jeremy Richards, D: gnomeandi; p. 106 India: Tupungato, Qutb Minar: Chris Pole, mountain railways: Attila JANDI, Sanchi: saiko3p, Taj Mahal: RuthChoi, Ellora Caves: JeremyRichards, Chola Temples: msankar4; p. 121 camera (M): photka, map in camera (M): Katsiaryna Pleshakova, food: Joe Gough, p. 122 B: Cyril Hou; p. 128: michaeljung; p. 133 Cotton label (and 274): STILLFX; p. 136: phoenixman; p. 139: Reeed; p. 143 E: Fisher Photostudio, G: Shevs, H: Vuk Varuna; p. 145: Vuk Varuna; p. 149 top: Igor Kovalchuk; p. 158 top: Ase; p. 175: Peshkova; p. 178 T-shirt (M): Syda Productions, Shakespeare portrait (M): Stefanina Hill; p. 184 A: Lurin, B: AVAVA; p. 195: Robert Kneschke; p. 200 top: takayuki; p. 204 top: Goodluz; p. 206 top: Christopher Titze; p. 207: Rawpixel; p. 210 bottom: Photographee.eu; p. 216 left icons (M): Palsur, whiteboard: Nerthuz; light bulb icon (M): Alvaro Cabrera Jimenez; p. 217 top: tmcphotos; p. 218 classroom (M): Monkey Business Images, camera (M): Vasin Lee; p. 226 A: ktynzq; p. 227 C: MaleWitch; p. 237: Valerio Pardi; p. 239 top right: olavs; p. 241: Unholy Vault Designs; p. 245: Xeron; p. 246 A: Photographee.eu; C: Zurjeta; p. 248: marekuliasz; p. 249: littlesam; p. 253: Lorelyn Medina; p. 261: mangostock; p. 286: everything possible; p. 270: ruskpp; p. 289 bottom: tassel78; p. 292: Featureflash; p. 295: emin kuliyev; p. 304: Stokkete; p. 305: Barbara Delgado (M); p. 316: Syda Productions; p. 341: bikeriderlondon; p. 342: Ron Ellis; p. 344: Ed Samuel; p. 345: alexwhite; p. 351: hxdbzxy; p. 357: Andrey_Popov); **SZ Photo** (p. 36 A: KPA Archival Collection/Süddeutsche Zeitung Photo) **toondoo.com** (p. 217 bottom: Hanoverscience); **toonpool.com** (p. 224: © Claudia Reinhardt – all rights reserved); **TOPICMedia Service**, Putzbrunn (p. 216 bottom right tablet (M) (and 164): Simon Belcher; p. 250 bottom: imagebroker.net); **Visum Foto**, Hamburg (p. 24 top: Panos Pictures, bottom: Andrew Lichtenstein/The Image; p. 37 C: The Image Works; p. 92: Chris Stowers/PANOS; p. 102 B: Philippe Lissac/Godong/Panos Pictures; p. 108: Mark Henley; p. 141 left (and 275): Panos Pictures)

Cover

Corbis, Düsseldorf (skyscrapers: Pawel Libera)

Abitur kompakt

ABI to go … das Abi in der Tasche

Alles aus einer Hand – passend zu *Context*

Die Reihe *ABI to go* gibt einen Überblick über die im Abitur vorausgesetzten Kompetenzen, festigt den Themenwortschatz und wiederholt die wichtigsten grammatischen Strukturen.

- **Für die Abiturvorbereitung:** Konzentration aufs Wesentliche
- **Für die Tasche:** praktisches Format für unterwegs
- **Viele Extras:** unterstützende Angebote zum Lernen, Üben und zur Selbsteinschätzung

Weitere Informationen zur Reihe *ABI to go* sowie zum Workbook und zur Vokabeltrainer-App zu *Context* gibt es im Buchhandel oder auf unserer Website *www.cornelsen.de/context*.

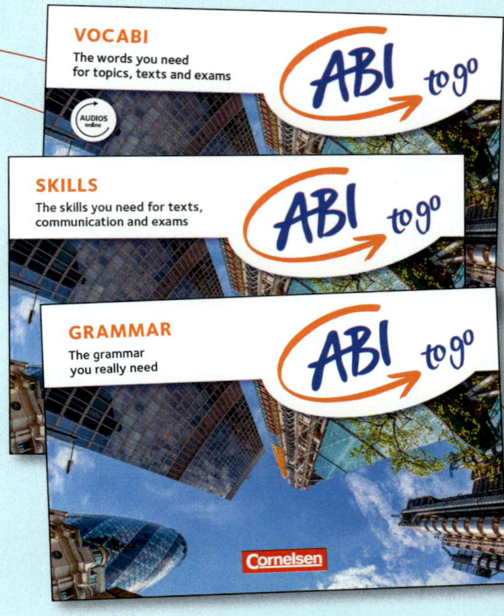

ABI to go – VOCABI
Vokabeltaschenbuch und Lernwortschatz, kartoniert
978-3-06-033490-2

ABI to go – SKILLS
kartoniert
978-3-06- 33858-0

ABI to go – GRAMMAR
(3. Quartal 2016) kartoniert
978-3-06-034842-8

***Context* – Workbook**
Kompetenz- und Prüfungstrainer
978-3-06-031667-0

Vokabeltrainer-App
Mit Wortschatz zu *Context*
Erhältlich im App-Store

Cornelsen Verlag • 14328 Berlin • www.cornelsen.de

Willkommen in der Welt des Lernens

Cornelsen